In the past several decades there has been a significant increase in our knowledge of the economic history of the United States. This has come about in part because of the development of economic history, most particularly with the emergence of the statistical and analytical contributions of the "new economic history," and in part because of related developments in social, labor, and political history that have important implications for the understanding of economic change. *The Cambridge Economic History of the United States* has been designed to take full account of new knowledge in the subject, while at the same time offering a comprehensive survey of the history of economic activity and economic change in the United States, and in those regions whose economies have at certain times been closely allied to that of the United States, Canada and the Caribbean.

Volume I surveys the economic history of British North America, including Canada and the Caribbean, and of the early United States, from early settlement by Europeans to the end of the eighteenth century. The volume includes chapters on the economic history of Native Americans (to 1860), and also on the European and African backgrounds to colonization. Subsequent chapters cover the settlement and growth of the colonies, including special surveys of the northern colonies, the southern colonies, and the West Indies (to 1850). Other chapters discuss British mercantilist policies and the American colonies, and the American Revolution, the constitution, and economic developments through 1800.

Volumes II and III will cover, respectively, the economic history of the nineteenth century and the twentieth century.

THE CAMBRIDGE ECONOMIC HISTORY
OF THE UNITED STATES

VOLUME I

The Colonial Era

THE CAMBRIDGE
ECONOMIC HISTORY
OF THE UNITED STATES

VOLUME I

The Colonial Era

Edited by

STANLEY L. ENGERMAN
University of Rochester

ROBERT E. GALLMAN
University of North Carolina, Chapel Hill

CAMBRIDGE
UNIVERSITY PRESS

Published by the Press Syndicate of the University of Cambridge
The Pitt Building, Trumpington Street, Cambridge CB2 1RP
40 West 20th Street, New York, NY 10011-4211, USA
10 Stamford Road, Oakleigh, Melbourne 3166, Australia

First published 1996

Printed in the United States of America

Library of Congress Cataloging-in-Publication Data
The Cambridge economic history of the United States / edited by
JK   Stanley L. Engerman, Robert E. Gallman.
p.   cm.
Includes index.
Contents: v. I. The Colonial era
ISBN 0-521-39442-2 (hc)
1. United States – Economic conditions.   I. Engerman, Stanley L.
II. Gallman, Robert E.
HC103.C26   1996
330.973 – dc20   95-860
                                                                 CIP

A catalog record for this book is available from the British Library.

ISBN 0-521-39442-2 Hardback

CONTENTS

MAPS

PREFACE TO VOLUME I OF
THE CAMBRIDGE ECONOMIC HISTORY
OF THE UNITED STATES

Prefaces to sets of essays, such as this one, are often devoted to explaining why publication was delayed or why certain planned essays are missing from the completed book. This Preface is an exception. All of the authors met their deadlines – or near to – and they produced a very close approximation to the volume that the editors had imagined when they laid out their original plans. These plans did not imply, however, that all authors would agree on the interpretation of specific events and patterns of change. Rather, aware of the present state of historical knowledge and the disagreements among scholars, we expected that some differences across chapters would appear, and, in that expectation, we were not disappointed.

Two moderately unusual ideas informed our original plans for the series. While the volumes were to be concerned chiefly with the United States, we decided that the American story could not be properly told unless some attention were given to other parts of British North America. Specifically, we thought that the volumes must contain essays on Canada and the British West Indies, the latter at least down to the time of emancipation. Second, we thought that the first volume should begin by treating the prior economic histories of the societies that came together during the colonial period – the societies of Native Americans present in North America before Columbus, of Africans who were involved in trade with Europeans, including the slave trade, and of Europeans.

These ideas were carried out. Three of the nine chapters are concerned with the origins of the populations that mingled in America during the colonial period; a fourth treats the West Indies. The remaining chapters are organized around the subject of economic change. One treats the overall population change and economic development of the mainland colonies; a second is concerned with the southern regions; a third is on the North, including parts of what was to become Canada; a fourth takes up British economic policy toward the colonies; and the last is devoted to the Revolutionary war, the Articles of Confederation, and the Constitution. Volume II covers the long nineteenth century, from 1790 to 1914, and Volume III, World War I and the years following it, down to the present.

These volumes, like all Cambridge histories, consist of essays that are intended to be syntheses of the existing state of knowledge, analysis, and debate. By their nature, they cannot be fully comprehensive. Their purpose is to introduce the reader to the subject and to provide her or him with a bibliographical essay that identifies directions for additional study. The audience sought is not an audience of deeply experienced specialists, but of undergraduates, graduate students, and the general reader with an interest in pursuing the subjects of the essays.

The title of Peter Mathias's inaugural lecture (November 24, 1970) when he took the chair in economic history at Oxford was "Living with the Neighbors." The neighbors alluded to are economists and historians. In the United States, economic history is not a separate discipline as it is in England; economic historians find places in departments of economics and history – most often, economics, these days. The problem of living with the neighbors nonetheless exists since economic historians, whatever their academic affiliations, must live the intellectual life together, and since historians and economists come at things from somewhat different directions. Another way to look at the matter is to regard living with the neighbors not as a problem but as a grand opportunity, since economists and historians have much to teach one another. Nonetheless, there is a persisting intellectual tension in the field between the interests of history and economics. The authors of the essays in these volumes are well aware of this tension and take it into account. The editors, in selecting authors, have tried to make room for the work of both disciplines.

We thank the authors for their good and timely work, Rosalie Herion Freese for her fine work as copy editor, Glorieux Dougherty for her useful index, Eric Newman for his excellent editorial assistance, and Frank Smith of Cambridge University Press for his continued support and friendship.

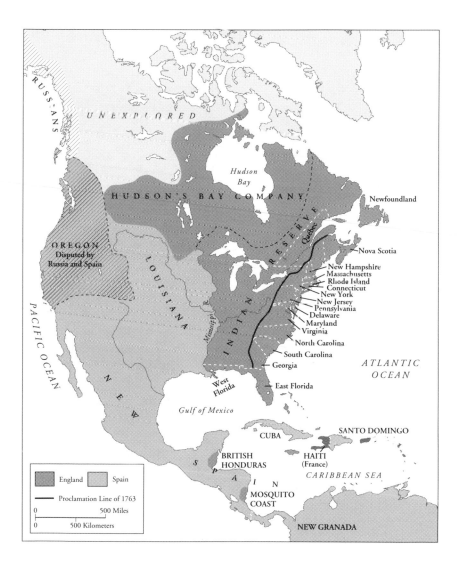

North America in 1763

1

THE HISTORY OF NATIVE AMERICANS FROM BEFORE THE ARRIVAL OF THE EUROPEANS AND AFRICANS UNTIL THE AMERICAN CIVIL WAR

NEAL SALISBURY

The economic history of North America began thousands of years before the arrival of Europeans, as the ancestors of modern Indians dispersed over the continent to nearly every kind of environmental setting and then, over time, elaborated and modified their various ways of life. Although generalizations about this diversity of peoples and their long history are hazardous, certain basic themes run throughout it and into the period of European encounters that followed. One theme is that because Indian communities represented collections of kin groups, both biological and fictional, rather than of individual subjects or citizens, the norms, roles, and obligations attending kinship underscored economic, social, and political life. A second theme is that economic life consisted largely of activities relating to subsistence and to the exchange of gifts. A third theme is that religious beliefs and rituals generally underscored these economic activities.

The arrival of Europeans after A.D. 1500 brought a people whose norms and customs presented a sharp contrast to those of Native Americans. While most Europeans likewise owed allegiance to families and communities, these were frequently superseded by loyalties to more abstract nation-states and institutionalized religions. Moreover, Europeans were elaborating practices of capital accumulation and market production that were utterly foreign to Native Americans. Finally, there was a biological discrepancy between the two peoples. By their exposure to a wide range of

This chapter was written while the author was a fellow at the National Humanities Center in 1991–2. He wishes to thank Sheila R. Johansson, the members of the Triangle Economic History Workshop for their comments and suggestions, and Colleen Hershberger for her assistance in preparing the map.

Areas of Non-Indian Settlement and Locations of Selected Indian Groups, ca. 1763

Eastern Hemisphere pathogens, Europeans had transformed smallpox and numerous other epidemic disorders into childhood diseases. Native Americans, on the other hand, utterly lacked previous exposure to such diseases and were thus far less effective in resisting them.

Despite the vast differences between them, Indians and non-Indians interacted in a variety of ways and settings in the centuries after Columbus's first landfall in 1492. After outlining pre-Columbian history, this chapter will explore those interactions through the first two-thirds of the nineteenth century.

INDIGENOUS NORTH AMERICA

PEOPLING OF NORTH AMERICA

The human history of North America originated when bands of Upper Paleolithic hunters began crossing the Bering land bridge to Alaska sometime during the period of Wisconsin glaciation (ca. 75,000–12,000 B.C.), as an extension of a larger dispersal from central Asia into the northern tundras of Siberia. These continuous movements were probably stimulated by population increases resulting from the hunters' success in pursuing mammoths, bison, reindeer, and other herd mammals. Although some peoples may have moved south of the North American Arctic at an earlier date, most remained in the far north until ca. 10,000 B.C., when the melting of the massive Cordilleran and Laurentide ice sheets facilitated movement onto the northern Plains and, from there, to points throughout the Western Hemisphere.

PALEO-INDIANS, 10,000–8000 B.C.

While still in the Arctic, the *Paleo-Indians*, as the earliest North Americans are called, developed a distinctive *fluted* projectile point, so termed for the way it was shaped to attach to a spear. Armed with these weapons, they spread rapidly throughout the continent, preying on mastodons, mammoths, and other large game animals that lacked experience as prey. The massive environmental consequences of deglaciation and climatic warming, of which the advent of human beings was but one, led to the extinction of several species of large game by ca. 9000 B.C.

Paleo-Indians lived in bands of fifteen to fifty people that moved annually through informally defined, roughly circular territories averaging 200 miles in diameter. Band members resided together during spring and summer and in smaller groups for the fall and winter. Many bands traveled beyond their territories to favored quarries, where they interacted socially and ritually with other groups.

ARCHAIC NORTH AMERICANS, 8000 – 1500 B.C.

The atmospheric warming associated with deglaciation continued until about 4000 B.C. Below the glacial shields, northward-moving boreal and coniferous forests were replaced by deciduous forests in the east, grassland prairies in the center, and desert scrub and shrub steppes in much of the west. The inhabitants turned to exploiting the widening range of smaller mammals, marine life, and wild plants in their new environments. As they grew more knowledgeable about local sources of food and materials, these *Archaic* peoples, as archaeologists term them, fine-tuned their annual rounds, opting for more sedentary settlement patterns and increasing their band sizes, often doubling their populations. Still, settlement patterns varied widely, from permanent villages covering one or two acres in areas of the Eastern Woodlands to hunting-gathering bands in the Great Basin and Southwest, whose size and mobility were unchanged from those of the Paleo-Indians.

In parts of the continent, particularly the Eastern Woodlands, the stabilization of the environment, by ca. 4000 B.C., was followed by social, political, and ideological change of great magnitude. As bands became more sedentary and their technology more sophisticated, labor became more specialized. The most basic division of labor determined subsistence activities on the basis of gender: men hunted and fished while women gathered wild plant products and shellfish, besides preparing all the food. Technological sophistication also led bands to increase their production and consumption of materials and objects, both utilitarian and nonutilitarian, for exchange. The most highly valued materials, especially obsidian, copper, and marine shells, appear at sites hundreds and even thousands of miles from their points of origin. The presence of grave goods fashioned from these materials suggests that these networks and their attendant rituals underlay the spread of shared assumptions about the relationship between life and death. Certain Archaic centers, such as Indian Knoll in Kentucky, amassed unusually large concentrations of exotic materials, implying that they enjoyed preeminence within a large network. In the burials at these centers, goods from such materials were reserved for a small minority of, presumably, elite individuals.

SOCIAL AND CULTURAL DIVERGENCE,
1500 B.C. — A.D. 1500

After ca. 1500 B.C., the divergences from Archaic patterns of subsistence, settlement, and political organization became even more pronounced. While hunting remained central for Arctic, Subarctic, and most Plains peoples, others turned to gathering, fishing, and farming as primary means of obtaining food. But regardless of the magnitude, all peoples were changing. And in spite of the radical divergences among native North Americans, they continued to share in certain common developments, such as the spread of ceramic pottery and the advent of the bow and arrow, until the beginning of contact with Europeans.

In the Arctic, the ancestors of modern Eskimo peoples had spread across northern Alaska and Canada to eastern Greenland between 2000 and 1500 B.C., replacing Indian groups moving southward toward warmer climates. Though environmental constraints militated against the more radical innovations undertaken by natives to the south, it is noteworthy that – long before Columbus – some Eskimos were using iron, obtained via Siberia from Russia at the onset of the Christian era and in Greenland via the Norse after A.D. 986. But the quantities of the metal were insufficient for inducing major cultural changes.

In much of the west, bands focused on gathering and fishing to supplement, in some cases nearly to supplant, hunting. In the Great Basin, women refined seed-milling through a series of technological innovations after A.D. 1000, enabling the ancestors of the modern Utes, Shoshones, and other groups to lessen their mobility and their dependence on hunting. Indians in most of California turned increasingly to acorns, along with fish, in around A.D. 1, while those on the Northwest Coast concentrated on salmon and other spawning fish. Food processing became more labor-intensive but, because the food was both readily available and storable, the people could reside in permanent locations. Populations grew, so that villages generally numbered in the hundreds by the time Europeans arrived. The resulting pressure on resources led to exclusive definitions of territoriality, increased warfare, and elaborate social ranking. In California, groups divided into several small communities presided over by chiefs in central villages. In the Northwest Coast, leaders of more prominent clans regularly confirmed their power at *potlatches*, during which they gave away or destroyed much of the material wealth they had accumulated.

Elsewhere in North America, Mesoamerican influences, combined with local practices, opened the way to plant domestication. By about 5000 B.C., the peoples of Tehuacán Valley in southern Mexico were cultivating small quantities of maize, beans, squash, and other plants. From this beginning, agriculture and related influences moved north via two distinct streams, one overland to the southwest, the other across the Gulf of Mexico to the southeast. The earliest evidence of domesticated plants north of Mexico is maize and squash at Bat Cave, New Mexico, from ca. 3500 B.C. But for another 3,000 years, the new plants remained marginal to the subsistence of southwestern peoples.

Around 400 B.C., a new, drought-resistant strain of maize enabled southwestern cultivators to spread from highland sites to drier lowlands. Increased yields and the development of storage pits led to larger, permanent villages that in turn became centers for the production of finished goods and of long-distance exchange. The earliest irrigation systems were developed in the villages of the Hohokam culture, in the Gila River valley, after 300 B.C. The coordination of labor required by these systems led to social ranking and hierarchical political structures. In the larger villages, platform mounds and ball courts, modeled on those in Mesoamerica, served as social and religious centers. In the Mogollon and Anasazi cultures, which emerged over a wide area after the third century A.D., surface structures supplemented the pit-houses, and specialized storage rooms and *kivas* (religious centers) appeared. Turkeys and cotton were domesticated, with the latter being woven on looms.

The period from the tenth to mid-twelfth centuries, a period of unusually abundant rainfall in the southwest, marked the height of Anasazi expansion and centralization. At Chaco Canyon in northwestern New Mexico, 15,000 people inhabited twelve villages, or *pueblos*. Each pueblo consisted of dozens or hundreds of contiguous rooms for dwelling, storage, and religious services, built around a central plaza with a large kiva. Despite such intricate organization of such dense populations, there is no evidence of social ranking or political hierarchy at Chaco. At least seven other pueblos, at distances of up to 100 miles in all directions, were linked to the canyon by a system of roads. Chaco Canyon's power appears to have been based on its role as a major source of turquoise production and as a principal center for exchange of turquoise, marine shells from California, and macaw feathers and copper bells from Mexico.

In the mid-twelfth century, Chaco Canyon abruptly declined, and its population dispersed. Whether the rise at that time of Casas Grandes, about 400 miles south, as a new center for trade in turquoise, marine shells, and macaw feathers, was a cause or an effect of Chaco's decline is not clear. Some argue that Chaco collapsed because the smaller towns in the canyon, resenting the control over water distribution exercised by the largest pueblo, revolted. Others maintain that decreasing rainfall was responsible. Drought was definitely responsible for far larger migrations from Mesa Verde and other population centers in the Southwest in the late thirteenth century.

Dispersing Anasazi peoples settled in the various pueblos, stretching from the Rio Grande Valley west to Hopi country, where the Spanish found them in the sixteenth and seventeenth centuries. While spurning the elements of confederation that characterized Chaco Canyon, the post-Anasazi pueblos retained the basic structure of the old religion, centered in the kivas. Most of them now supplemented it with special attention to the *kachinas*, spirits considered capable of encouraging rainfall. The pueblos also continued their roles as centers of exchange, both local and long-distance, importing and redistributing such items as buffalo hides and meat from the Plains, marine shells from California, and bird feathers from Mexico, while exporting turquoise, cotton cloth, maize, and a range of other materials and products. Among those with whom they exchanged most actively were the Athapaskan-speaking Apaches and Navajos who arrived in the region in about A.D. 1400 after a series of migrations from the Mackenzie Basin in Canada.

As in the Southwest, plant cultivation in the Eastern Woodlands began modestly. The earliest evidence consists of some Mexican squash and gourds grown, along with several local species, at two separate sites in the Mississippi Valley in ca. 2500 B.C. Even after maize appeared in the fourth century B.C., agriculture continued for several more centuries as a minor component of a subsistence system oriented primarily toward hunting, fishing, and gathering. Unlike in the Southwest, where complex, centralized redistribution systems appeared only after farming became the primary means of subsistence, such systems in the east long predated agriculture.

At Poverty Point, Louisiana, work on two large mounds and a set of concentric embankments was probably begun before 1200 B.C. The labor entailed in the construction of these earthworks (an estimated 3 million person-hours for the embankments alone) indicates a level of political coordination found nowhere else in North America at the time. Poverty Point is also distinguished by the variety and quantity of exotic materials deposited there – galena, quartz, copper, grizzly bear claws, obsidian, crystal, and other materials – originating in a range of locales from the Appalachians to the Rockies and north to the Great Lakes. Poverty Point was the center of a network of communities, distributing goods to surrounding tributary communities while drawing labor from them.

In the central Ohio Valley, a system of mound-centered communities of the Adena culture emerged in the fifth century B.C. Most of its 300 sites feature mounds built atop burials and within circular or square enclosures. Grave goods included objects manufactured from North Carolina mica, Lake Superior copper, and Gulf Coast marine shells. The labor involved in building the mounds and manufacturing the grave goods and other artifacts suggests a highly centralized system of authority, presumably wielded by those adult males who received the most lavish burials. The distribution of Adena grave goods over much of the Northeast indicates an organized movement based on shared beliefs and rituals connected with death.

By the first century B.C., Adena culture was developing into the more complex Hopewell, distinguished from the former by even more elaborate mounds and burials and by the greater geographic extent of its influence. Hopewell villages of 100 to 500 people usually stood on river banks below bluffs at intervals of about 12 miles. Mounds averaged 100 feet in diameter, 30 feet in height, 500,000 cubic feet in volume, and 200,000 person-hours of labor. The most elaborate burials included as grave goods thousands of freshwater pearls plus ornaments, figurines, and tools of copper, mica, tortoise shell, silver, obsidian, galena, and other materials that were brought to Hopewell centers and manufactured by specialized artisans. A grouping of Hopewell centers emerged in the Illinois Valley, and Hopewell mounds and copper burial effigies were spread widely in the Mississippi Valley.

The Hopewell centers in the Ohio and Illinois valleys were abandoned in the fifth century A.D. Some archaeologists note that this decline coincided with the advent of the bow and arrow and with evidence of increased warfare in and around Hopewell communities, suggesting that the system was destroyed by violence from within or without. Others point to changing subsistence factors that might have undermined Hopewell hegemony, particularly to climatic cooling or to evidence of increased maize cultivation by Ohio and Illinois peoples, although agricultural products were clearly not yet dietary mainstays. In the Southeast, on the other hand, Hopewell communities continued to develop, influencing the rise of agriculturally based Mississippian culture, beginning in the eighth century.

Flourishing throughout the Mississippi Valley and the southeast, Mississippian culture represented a qualitative transformation among native North Americans. Mississippian peoples cultivated a new strain of maize, adapted to the short growing season of the northern Mississippi Valley, along with beans and squash; practiced a religion based on the sun as a source of fertility; and fortified their villages while developing more lethal arrow points. Political power was centralized in the hands of a hereditary chief who coordinated the collection and distribution of food surpluses and of materials and goods obtained through exchange. These *chiefdoms,* as anthropologists term them, typically centered on large villages built around open plazas featuring platform burial mounds topped by temples and elaborate residences for leading families. From the eleventh century onward, most of these chiefdoms were grouped with anywhere from three or four to several dozen others into *complex* or *paramount* chiefdoms.

The largest, most complex Mississippian center was Cahokia, located at the confluence of the Mississippi and Missouri rivers, near modern East St. Louis. Cahokia was first settled in the seventh century by farming peoples attracted to its rich floodplains. Three centuries later, its population was 20,000, and it featured over 120 mounds within a 5-square-mile area. Social stratification and ritual sacrifice lay at the center of Cahokia's religious beliefs as well as its distribution of power. Laborers worked in Cahokia's ongoing construction projects; artisans fashioned products from shell, copper, clay, and a variety of other materials both local and exotic; a managerial class coordinated the productive and commercial life of the city; and hereditary rulers were accorded religious veneration, expressed in tributary payments of agricultural produce and manufactured goods. This stratification is reflected in the range of human burials found at Cahokia, from mass graves outside the city walls to the graves of rulers, who were encased in extraordinary amounts of exotic materials and accompanied by dozens of individuals who were sacrificed so they could accompany their master in the afterlife.

By the thirteenth century, Cahokia had developed beyond other paramount chiefdoms into an incipient city-state. It was surrounded by nine smaller mound centers and several dozen villages that produced its food and managed its waterborne commerce with other urban centers in the Midwest and Southeast. But the thirteenth century represented Cahokia's peak. The city's demand for food and wood outstripped local supply while allied centers in the Midwest and Southeast broke away as they surpassed Cahokia in size and military power. By the end of the fourteenth century, Cahokia was abandoned, and by the time Europeans arrived in the upper Mississippi Valley, the region was characterized by small, dispersed agricultural villages linked only by ties of reciprocal exchange.

Although Mississippian culture came to an end in and around Cahokia, it continued to flourish in the Southeast until the arrival of Europeans. The southeastern centers were inhabited by forerunners of the Cherokees, Creeks, Natchez, and other peoples known to the later colonists of the region. To be sure, fluctuations and inequities in agricultural production, the accumulation of tribute, and military conflict resulted in frequent power shifts whereby the location of a paramount chiefdom shifted from one community to another within a regional alliance. But this very instability prevented a concentration of regional power like Cahokia's, ensuring the survival of Mississippian culture and the system of paramount chiefdoms.

Natives elsewhere in the East did not directly encounter Mississippian culture but were nevertheless affected by its proximity, above all in their adoption of agriculture as a primary mode of subsistence. Wherever a growing season of 100 frost-free days could be counted on, Indians incorporated farming into their hunting-fishing-gathering economies.

The configuration of Indian peoples and cultures that Europeans encountered after 1500 was the product of a complex array of historical forces. Some groups were descended from peoples who had inhabited the same locale for thousands of years; others had arrived only within the preceding century or two. Similarly, some institutions and practices such as autonomous communities and hunting-gathering-fishing economies were deeply rooted, while others, such as agriculture and political confederations, had arisen only recently. The combination of ancient traditions and continuous adaptations and innovations, along with the ecological diversity of the continent, helps to account for the social and cultural diversity of North American Indians at the outset of the sixteenth century. A paucity of firm evidence renders demographic descriptions of Native Americans imprecise and general at best. Physical anthropologists estimate life expectancy at birth to have averaged in the low to mid-twenties, comparable to worldwide rates for groups with similar subsistence economies and technologies. Probably numbering somewhere between five and ten million in 1500, Native Americans were developing in directions about which we can only speculate.

THE SIXTEENTH CENTURY

Many of the challenges posed to Indian communities by European expansion during the sixteenth century were analogous to those that some had faced earlier, especially in relation to Anasazi and Mississippian centralization. Others were unprecedented in the North American experience because of Europeans' technology, modes of organization, beliefs, and, above all, disease pathogens.

BEGINNINGS OF EUROPEAN ACTIVITY, 1480 – 1550

Sustained European contact with North America was initiated when Bristol fishermen began frequenting the Grand Banks off Newfoundland during the 1490s or, possibly, the 1480s – before Columbus' first voyage. After the English-sponsored expeditions of John Cabot (1497–8), fishermen, whalers, and explorers from Iberia and France were a regular presence from Newfoundland to the Gulf of Maine. By the mid-1520s, Beothuks, Micmacs, and other Indians in the region regularly encountered Europeans, some of whom traded metal goods for furs and others of whom captured natives for sale into slavery. In the meantime, Spanish slave-raiding expeditions, followed by two efforts to establish colonies (1521, 1526–8), were alienating groups of Indians on the South Atlantic coast. And Giovanni da Verrazzano's voyage for France (1524) made contact with Indians at several points along the coast from Carolina to New England.

Indian-European encounters spread beyond the Atlantic coast with the remarkable travels of Alvar Nuñez Cabeza de Vaca and three companions, including an African slave, Estevanico (1528–36). They were part of a colonizing expedition to the Gulf Coast of Florida that fought with the Apalachees and other Indians. After the expedition was scattered and they were shipwrecked on the coast of Texas, the four walked through the southwest to Mexico, where their reports of interactions with natives provided a direct impetus for more substantial Spanish efforts, led by Hernando de Soto in the Southeast (1539–43) and Francisco Vásquez de

Coronado (1540–2) in the Southwest. Both these expeditions were heavily manned and financed, wandered over vast expanses of territory in search of gold, alienated Indians by their demands for tribute and their militaristic bearing, and spread deadly epidemic diseases among the natives before finally withdrawing.

Meanwhile, three French expeditions to the St. Lawrence River led by Jacques Cartier and Jean-François de la Rocque de Roberval (1534–43) likewise alienated numerous Indian groups and ended in futility. During the same period, fishermen and whalers from Spain, Portugal, France, and England frequented the Northeast in growing numbers. Although the evidence of their contacts with the natives is sketchy, it is clear that coastal Indians had become accustomed to trading furs to European visitors.

Recent scholarship on Indians' motives in this earliest stage of trade indicates that they sought glass beads and other "trinkets" for religious reasons, regarding them as the equivalents of the quartz, mica, shell, and other sacred substances that they had exchanged among themselves for millennia. And many of the metal utilitarian goods initially traded to Indians, such as copper pots and iron axes, were transformed into objects that were worn as means of displaying one's access to such supernatural power.

Although relatively few Indians had directly encountered Europeans by the middle of the sixteenth century, many more had felt the latter's presence. One source of such indirect contact was European material goods. As early as 1524, Verrazzano found Indians with European objects in New England, and de Soto found items of Spanish manufacture deep in the southeastern interior in 1540. Natives also obtained European goods via indigenous exchange networks and from European shipwrecks. And they learned from other Indians about the strange people who came over the water in large boats. Depending on the experiences of their informants, they might have regarded the Europeans as mythological figures (an impression that was typically short-lived), as friendly allies, or as dangerous enemies. The most potent form of indirect contact was through disease pathogens, which traveled via indigenous exchange routes beyond the range of the Europeans themselves. De Soto, for example, found native communities already ravaged by smallpox spread by earlier expeditions.

NEW APPROACHES, 1550–1600

European approaches to North America and its natives changed somewhat after the middle of the sixteenth century as would-be colonizers came to realize the impracticality of massive conquest expeditions. Moreover, growing challenges by France and England to Spain's position in the Americas meant that each country's efforts were undertaken with its rivals, as well as the natives and the resources of the land, in mind.

After suppressing a French Huguenot settlement on the Carolina coast in 1565, Spain established a permanent base at St. Augustine that soon anchored a chain of forts and religious missions along the Atlantic coast as far north as Chesapeake Bay. Although some Indians were initially receptive, the Spanish ultimately failed to establish their legitimacy as political and religious authorities. Forced tributes of food, a devastating smallpox epidemic, the alien religious teachings and discipline imposed by Jesuit and Franciscan missionaries, and atrocities committed by Spanish soldiers led the depopulated Guales to move their villages inland. Armed uprisings by the Powhatans in the Chesapeake (1571) and the Guales (1576–81, 1597–1601) temporarily ended the Spanish presence everywhere north of St. Augustine.

In the meantime, an English group attempted to colonize Roanoke Island, on the North Carolina coast, in 1585. Although native-settler relations were initially amicable, the colony's insistence that the local Algonquian-speaking Indians provide it with corn led to hostilities. When its English backers failed to supply provisions, Roanoke was doomed. By the end of the century, a succession of epidemics and violent encounters with Spanish and English colonizers, plus a desire for European trade, had led Indians on the lower Chesapeake to coalesce around a *werowance* (chief) known as Powhatan.

As with St. Augustine, Spanish expeditions into the southeastern interior led by Tristan de Luna (1559–61) and Juan Pardo (1566–8) hoped to strengthen Spain vis-à-vis its European rivals. Instead of attempting all-out conquest of the natives, these expeditions allied with Mississippian centers, which had been reduced in size and power in the aftermath of de Soto's expedition, and helped them collect tribute from recalcitrant neighbors and wage war against rival centers. In so doing, they further spread European diseases and material goods.

In contrast to the Southeast, no European power established a territorial base in the Northeast in the latter half of the sixteenth century. While fishermen, whalers, explorers, colonizers, and traders from Spain, Portugal, and England frequented the region from the Hudson River to Newfoundland, it was the French who predominated. By the 1580s, Indian–French contacts were focused on the beaver trade and had expanded inland.

French traders made annual voyages to Tadoussac on the St. Lawrence and, on a few occasions, as far upriver as modern Montreal. Indian hunters and traders brought them furs from as far west as the Ottawa Valley in return for iron axes, copper pots, glass beads, and other manufactured objects. The trade helped France to solidify its position in North America while the pelts fed a growing demand for beaver hats among the middle and upper classes in Europe.

The effects of these contacts on northeastern Indians were numerous. As they turned from hunting solely for subsistence in order to meet the demands of European traders, Indians altered their customary subsistence cycles. Where women farmed, the transition posed no great difficulty. But nonfarming groups now spent less time fishing, shellfishing, gathering wild plants, and preserving food. They compensated for the resulting deficits by intensifying their exchanges of meat for maize with nearby farming Indians, by raiding farming Indians, or by receiving food from the French as part of their payment for pelts. A second effect was depopulation from disease. Although not easily documented in this period, diseases had clearly reduced the population of the Micmacs and, possibly, other Indians of the Maritimes region. A third effect was the warfare that erupted as Indians fought to control access to French trade goods. The Iroquoian-speaking communities contacted earlier in the century by Cartier were apparently attacked and dispersed by Mohawks and other Iroquois who resented being denied direct access to French goods. The refugees from these communities joined the Hurons and other Ontario Iroquoian-speakers.

European trade also had important political effects for some Indians. The Iroquois' efforts to break into the St. Lawrence trade appear to have strengthened their recently formed confederacy. The latter half of the sixteenth century also witnessed the coalescence of the Huron Confederacy into its seventeenth-century form. By geographically consolidating, the Hurons were better positioned to obtain French goods as well as to produce surplus maize for their northern neighbors.

The late sixteenth century also saw the resumption of Spanish activity in the Southwest, forty years after Coronado's failure. Although the Royal Ordinances of 1573 outlawed conquest and mandated benevolence in Spanish dealings with the natives, the actual outcome for Indians was unchanged. After two expeditions (1581, 1591) met violent receptions among the Rio Grande Pueblos, Juan de Oñate in 1598 led 400 settlers in founding a missionary colony in the same area. Before the year was out, the forcible seizure of corn provoked rebellions at three pueblos, which the Spanish managed to crush.

The period also saw less sustained contacts with natives by the English in the Canadian Arctic, where Martin Frobisher aroused the antagonism of Inuits in 1576, and in California, where Francis Drake established brief but amicable ties with the Miwoks in 1579.

Despite their failure to establish permanent colonies during the sixteenth century, Europeans substantially affected portions of North America. Nevertheless, Indian life continued along familiar lines at the end of the sixteenth century. Most of the continent remained unaffected by the newcomers, while the absence of colonial activity in the southeastern interior enabled populations there to recover from the epidemics. Only along the Atlantic coast and in portions of the northeastern interior and Southwest did Europeans follow up immediately on their sixteenth-century beginnings, and even in these areas, Indian cultures and communities showed a remarkable adaptability and persistence in the face of enormous challenges.

NATIVE AMERICANS AND THE ADVENT OF EUROPEAN COLONIZATION, 1600–60

The beginning of the seventeenth century marked the turn toward large-scale, permanent colonization of North America by western Europeans. The weakness of Spain and the rise of England, France, and a newly independent Dutch Republic led to influxes of settlers, traders, missionaries, and imperial officials in certain areas of the continent. During the first sixty years of the new century, these newcomers extended and consolidated their presence through their interactions with Indian groups.

COLONIAL BEGINNINGS IN THE NORTHEAST

The most far-reaching effects of colonization on Indian societies occurred in the Northeast, where the French, Dutch, and English converged in the early years of the seventeenth century. The French built on their trade ties with the Montagnais and Micmacs to establish posts at Quebec (1608) and Port Royal (1613), respectively. On the St. Lawrence, they used guns to help the Montagnais, Algonquins, and Hurons prevail in counter-raids against the Mohawk Iroquois. After 1615 they shifted their trade interests primarily to the Hurons, who annually supplied them with 12,000 to 22,000 pelts from the Great Lakes and Ottawa Valley during the 1620s. For a generation, the French-Huron alliance was the centerpiece of the two peoples' economies and societies. French ties with the Micmacs also flourished after 1600. Overcoming food shortages and depopulation, possibly by as much as 75 percent during the preceding century, the Micmacs acquired food and prestige by using French guns and shallops to raid Indians from Cape Cod to Newfoundland.

Beginning in 1610, Dutch traders flocked to the Hudson Valley and began a flourishing trade with Algonquian- and Iroquoian-speaking Indians there, including the Mohawks, who were frustrated by their chronic exclusion from the St. Lawrence. By 1620, the Dutch had extended their trade to coastal Indians between Narragansett Bay and the lower Delaware Valley.

On the New England coast north of Cape Cod, successive English colonizing expeditions from 1602 to 1614 repeatedly coerced, assaulted, or kidnapped Abenakis, Massachusetts, and Wampanoags, while French traders were establishing successful ties. But from 1616 to 1618, an epidemic, probably of French origin, swept through the very groups allied to the French, causing a population decline from ca. 70,000 to ca. 7,000. Soon afterward, the *Mayflower* arrived at Plymouth in November 1620 and established a new English colony among the devastated Wampanoags.

Thereafter, each of the three colonized regions was affected by developments in the others. In 1622, a Dutch trader discovered the many values to Indians of *wampum* – marine shell beads that were gathered, drilled, and strung by Algonquian-speaking Indians from Long Island Sound to Narragansett Bay, where the shells were found in greatest abundance. Indians throughout the Northeast valued wampum as sacred material and used it in rituals and exchanges to convey messages of peace and condolence as well as in belts to record their histories. The Dutch began trading cloth and metal goods to coastal Indians for wampum and then using the wampum, in addition to their own wares, to obtain furs from inland natives. During the mid-1620s, the Dutch temporarily lured some Montagnais and Algonquins away from the French with wampum. In 1627, they began selling wampum to Plymouth's traders after the latter agreed to confine their trading to the coast north of Cape Cod. By then the wampum trade was transforming Indian life in lower New England and Long Island. The Dutch introduced metal drills to increase production, and Indian men and women spent winters crafting the beads. Two groups, the Narragansetts and Pequots, emerged to dominate exchanges between native producers and Dutch traders.

The advent of wampum also transformed relations among Indians around the Dutch trade center at Fort Orange, on the site of modern Albany. Although located on land occupied by the Algonquian-speaking Mahicans, Fort Orange was initially open to all Indians. But when Montagnais and Algonquins began trading there in 1624, the Mohawks feared that these Indians would cut them off from direct European trade on the Hudson as they formerly had on the St. Lawrence. To ensure their access, they launched a war against the Mahicans in 1624 and, despite Dutch support of the Mahicans, defeated them and secured control of the land around the fort by 1630. Thereafter the Mohawks were the major trade partners of the Dutch, controlling the exchange of beaver pelts for vast quantities of wampum and European goods between New Netherland and the Five Nations Iroquois Confederacy.

The wampum trade in southern New England was altered, but not disrupted, by the "Great Migration" of some 20,000 English settlers between 1629 and 1642. Initially, the newcomers overran the lands of the coastal Massachusetts Indians, who had been reduced to about 200 people in a few tiny communities. But a smallpox epidemic that spread to Indians throughout the Northeast in 1633–4 drew the attention of many colonists to the rich floodplains of the Connecticut River Valley. The epidemic coincided with growing resentment among both Connecticut River Indians and coastal wampum producers against the Pequots for monopolizing trade with the Dutch. In 1637 the Narragansetts and Mohegans aided Massachusetts and Connecticut troops in a war of near-extermination against the Pequots. As a result, Connecticut was opened to English settlement, and English traders acquired direct access to producers of wampum.

During the mid-seventeenth century, Indians in southern New England retained varying degrees of economic and political autonomy. With the defeat of the Pequots, the Narragansetts dominated wampum production in eastern Long Island and on the mainland coast. They maintained their independence from the mainstream Puritan colonies by allying with dissenting Rhode Island, by retaining their ties with Dutch traders, and by conveying wampum directly to the Mohawk Iroquois. Indians in the Connecticut and Merrimack valleys not only produced furs and consumed trade goods themselves but oversaw the movement of these materials between the English and interior Indians. Groups directly allied to colonies, particularly the Pokanoket Wampanoags with Plymouth and the Mohegans with Connecticut, sought to satisfy English desires for land and allies without endangering their subsistence autonomy and cultural identity. The Indians with the least maneuverability in southern New England were those with the largest losses from disease, who were now engulfed by settlers and isolated from exchange ties with other Indians. These were the Massachusetts, plus Wampanoag communities on Cape Cod and Martha's Vineyard, who turned to Christianity in large numbers in the 1640s and 1650s.

Munsee and related Indians on Long Island and the lower Hudson experienced similar effects from Dutch settlement but lacked missionaries to mediate between them and the colonists. These Indians had initially supplied New Netherland with pelts and maize, but Dutch expansion not only threatened their land holdings and other resources but also threatened to subject them to the colony's authority. At the same time, overhunting had depleted the supply of beaver skins, isolating the natives from the elaborate network of Indian–European trade in New Netherland. In three brief but decisive wars (1643–5, 1655, 1663–4), Dutch troops, with Mahican and Mohawk support, killed or drove out most of the Munsee and other Indians below Fort Orange. The refugees moved north to live among the Mahicans or west to the Delawares.

THE RISE OF THE IROQUOIS

By the 1630s, two major fur-trading alliances had arisen in the Northeast that dwarfed all others in scale and political significance – the French–Huron and the Dutch–Iroquois. Each was the major prop for a colonial economy, and each reinforced the position of a powerful native confederacy. Moreover, commercial beaver hunting had exhausted each group's supply of beaver pelts, and epidemics were striking both their populations. Their responses to these crises put the two alliances on a collision course and revealed important differences between them.

As they sought new sources of furs during the 1630s, the Hurons built on established ties in which they exchanged corn for meat, copper, and other materials with the Nipissings, Ottawas, and other peoples to the north and west. The Five Nations Iroquois, with their more southerly location, lacked the Hurons' access to the thicker, more valued northern pelts as well as the latter's extensive trade links. The Iroquois Confederacy had been formed by deflecting internal hostilities outward against common enemies, and this militant tendency had been reinforced by half a century of battling to overcome exclusion from direct trade ties with Europeans. Beginning in the 1630s, Iroquois raiders attacked parties of Hurons and other French allies carrying pelts to Quebec and returning with French goods.

The discrepancies between the two alliances were heightened by the degree of control each European power exercised over its Indian partner. In 1633, the French insisted that the Hurons accept Jesuit missionaries as a price for maintaining the alliance. The arrival of the Jesuits coincided with the smallpox outbreak of 1663–4 and a subsequent series of other epidemics that resulted in a population decline of 50 percent, to about 10,000 by 1640. While the epidemics raged, most Hurons blamed Jesuit witchcraft for the mortality. But as the Hurons grew more dependent on the French for trade and for protection against the Iroquois, the French offered incentives to converts in the form of higher prices and guns. Although only a minority of Hurons responded, their avoidance of communal rituals and most other contacts with "pagans" undermined the consensus on which Huron society depended for its coherence.

While French efforts to control their native allies increased, the Dutch West India Company in 1639 relinquished its monopoly on the Indian trade in New Netherland. The volume of trade in New Netherland rose markedly thereafter, and with it the flow of previously outlawed guns and ammunition to the Iroquois. From the early 1630s, the Iroquois were responding to a depopulation rate almost identical to that of the Hurons by raiding their rivals for captives, in addition to furs and European goods. Although some captives were tortured, most were adopted into families as replacements for Iroquois who had died. With more guns at their disposal, the Iroquois turned in the 1640s to all-out warfare in an attempt to eliminate rival political entities and absorb their populations and trade connections. In 1648–9, they dispersed the Hurons and then moved west to inflict similar treatment on the Petuns, Neutrals, and Eries. As the Iroquois took over their hunting lands, the refugees were absorbed into Iroquois ranks or fled to more remote Indian communities. Some Christian Hurons were given refuge in Quebec. The Iroquois then advanced against the Algonquian-speakers of the Great Lakes and Ohio Valley, where French trade links now extended, scattering Shawnees, Ottawas, Potawatomis, and others. Only a determined stand by a large body of refugees at Green Bay in 1653 finally stalled the Iroquois advance.

NATIVES AND COLONISTS IN CHESAPEAKE AND
DELAWARE BAYS

English colonists also settled in Chesapeake Bay, beginning in 1607 at Jamestown, Virginia. After initially exchanging metal goods for corn, the Virginians alienated the Powhatan Indians by insisting on tributary payments of grain. The English were nearly starved out until reinforcements in 1611 gave them an upper hand, enabling them to subject the Powhatans to a humiliating peace in 1614.

After the beginnings of commercial tobacco production in 1618, a massive influx of planters and laborers brought new tensions as the English pressured the Powhatans to cede additional land. The Indians mounted a surprise attack in 1622, killing 350 (nearly one-third) of the settlers. The colony recovered and launched a war of near-extermination. By 1634, it had driven the Powhatans from the lower James and York valleys, gaining 300,000 additional acres of tobacco-growing land. With Virginia's population having risen to 8,000, the Powhatans launched a second surprise attack in 1644. Again the colony recovered and retaliated. In 1646, the Powhatan Confederacy was dissolved and its people confined to tiny, scattered reservations, where they continued to be harassed by hostile colonists.

In the upper Chesapeake, the Iroquoian-speaking Susquehannocks struggled to maintain a dominance achieved during the late sixteenth century through the control of exchanges between Indians and visiting Europeans. With permanent colonies established on the Hudson and the James, the Susquehannocks were no longer a major conduit for such trade. A Virginia trader, William Claiborne, gave them a European connection in 1631, but the new colony of Maryland expelled Claiborne three years later, with the aid of Piscataway Indians eager to bypass the Susquehannocks' monopoly. After the founding of New Sweden (1638) provided them with a source of arms, the Susquehannocks soundly defeated Maryland troops in 1643 and then inflicted a similarly decisive defeat on the hitherto invincible Mohawks in 1651. But New Sweden's demise at the hands of the Dutch in 1655 forced the Susquehannocks to turn to less friendly Maryland and New Netherland in order to maintain European trade ties.

FLORIDA

Although the Guales had nearly destroyed Spanish Florida by the end of the sixteenth century, the colony soon recovered. In 1601, Spanish soldiers, aided by interior Indians, suppressed the Guale revolt. Four years later, Franciscan missionaries resumed their order's work among the Guales and eastern Timucuans and built several new missions among the western Timucuans. Mission Indians grew corn for the Spanish in return for European cloth and glass, some of which they circulated to interior Indians. While claiming far-reaching successes, the missionaries despaired over the persistence of polygamous marriages and other "pagan" customs among their converts. During the 1610s, a new round of epidemics cost the lives of about half of the 16,000 mission Indians. The Guales were urged to settle at new locations on offshore islands, but many fled to the interior.

In 1633 the Franciscans extended their missionary efforts westward to the Apalachees. Although the Spanish were careful to separate the "republic of Spaniards" from the "republic of Indians," with Indian *caciques* and other leaders holding official positions in the latter, abuses by soldiers and missionaries continued to alienate many Indians. This alienation was reflected in major rebellions by Apalachees (1647) and by Apalachees and Timucuas (1655). Continued depopulation from epidemics added to Indian demoralization. Nevertheless, the Franciscans claimed 26,000 converts in 1655.

THE SOUTHWEST

As the seventeenth century opened in New Mexico, the proprietary governor, Juan de Oñate, maintained oppressive levies of corn on the Pueblos. Besides leaving the Indians without adequate food, the levies deprived the Pueblos of their principal item of trade with the nonfarming Apaches and Navajos of the region. Apaches and Navajos began raiding Pueblos for corn, European livestock, and metal goods. After Oñate resigned in 1607, the Spanish ended the levies and offered substantive military support to the Pueblos, with the result that conversions to Catholicism rose from 400 to 7,000 in a single year and to 34,000 by 1625. Spanish traders sold Apache and Navajo captives seized in the counteroffensive as slaves in Mexico. After 1617, periodic intervals of peace were marked by Spanish–Apache trade at Pecos, long the center of exchange between peoples of the upper Rio Grande and southern Plains, respectively.

Despite intervals of peace and stability, the patterns of the first years continued to characterize relations between Spanish, Pueblos, and non-Pueblo Indians. Episodes of drought and epidemic disease, along with Spanish exactions of tribute (*encomienda*) and labor (*repartimiento*), lessened

the Pueblos' agricultural productivity, leaving them with inadequate food
and vulnerable to raids by Apaches, Navajos, Utes, and Jumanos. These
factors also led to population decline and the consolidation of seventy
pueblos into thirty-five by 1650. These troubles and the conduct of Franciscan missionaries, who exacted labor as well as inflicting corporal punishment and outlawing traditional rituals, contributed to demoralization and
resentment among the Pueblos. By mid-century, the Indians in at least
five pueblos had unsuccessfully attempted to get rid of their missionaries
through violence or by petitioning the authorities.

Over a period of sixty years, the presence of Europeans had markedly
affected native life in several areas of North America. Along portions of
the eastern seaboard – between the Merrimack and the Hudson and on the
lower Chesapeake – the relatively few remaining Indians were minorities
in their own homelands, surrounded as they were by Europeans who had
replaced them as the principal cultivators. Natives of the lower Great
Lakes and the Ohio Valley had fled their homelands in the face of aggression not by Europeans but by Iroquois who were responding to the European presence. The Iroquois themselves used their relationship with New
Netherland to become a major power in the Northeast, threatening the
very future of New France. At the edges of European settlement in the
Northeast, Indians were being drawn into ever closer links with their still-
expanding European neighbors. Although Indians in New France, Florida, and New Mexico remained a majority and were not threatened with
the loss of land, they were nevertheless subjected to frequent outbreaks of
disease, to pressures (coercive in the Spanish colonies) to produce for a
market economy or for tributary levies, and to missionaries who sought to
invalidate crucial aspects of their cultural identities. Beyond the areas of
direct European contact – in the interior of the Eastern Woodlands, in the
eastern Subarctic, and in the northern and southern Plains – Indians were
encountering increased quantities of European goods and (in the Eastern
Woodlands) native refugees from areas torn by upheaval.

IMPERIAL-COLONIAL EXPANSION AND NATIVE AMERICAN STRATEGIES, 1660–1715

In the half century after 1660, the competition among European nations
for control of North America and its resources sharpened. Native Ameri-

cans responded to these developments in a number of ways. Some, facing encroachments by settlers, political authorities, or missionaries, sought to restore autonomy and cultural integrity by mounting armed uprisings, threatening the existences of several colonies in the process. Elsewhere, Indians allied with one or another European power as the best means of ensuring communal survival and, in some cases, enhancing their power, in a period of rapid flux.

NORTHEAST: TRANSFORMATION OF THE IROQUOIS

The 1660s marked a halt in the remarkable rise of the Iroquois. Their Dutch ally was expelled from North America while their Indian neighbors along with the French took steps to counter Iroquois attacks. To the south, the Maryland-armed Susquehannocks beat back 800 Iroquois who assaulted their main village in 1663. In New England, Jesuit and Puritan missionaries encouraged Indians to close ranks with their fellow Algonquian-speakers in Canada against the Mohawks. The Mahicans, humiliated by the Mohawks forty years earlier, joined the new movement and decisively repulsed a Mohawk attack on one of their villages in 1664. In the upper Great Lakes and Illinois Valley, the victory of refugee Indians over the Iroquois at Green Bay in 1653 and the emergence of interethnic villages contributed to the subordination of tribal loyalties to a larger Algonquian and, implicitly, anti-Iroquois identity. At the same time, French trade posts and missions drew this new force closer to New France.

To the north, New France took direct action to halt the destructive attacks that the Iroquois had extended during the 1650s to French communities themselves. In 1665, France dispatched 1,000 troops to Canada. Their mere presence, along with the coalition of Indians now arrayed against them, led the four westerly Iroquois nations (Senecas, Cayugas, Onondagas, Oneidas) to make peace with New France. The troops launched two attacks against the recalcitrant Mohawks in 1666. While inflicting few casualties, they burned villages and food supplies with such impunity that the Mohawks joined the new accord in 1667. The French quickly established two trade posts near Iroquois country and dispatched Jesuit missionaries to work in Iroquois villages. Although the minority of Iroquois converts moved in 1673 to the village of Caughnawaga (now Kahnawaké), near Montreal, they maintained close ties to their homeland, enabling all Iroquois to trade and communicate with both New France and New York.

While making peace with New France, the Iroquois also consolidated their relationship with the English in New York. As a result, the Indians of the New England colonies who had retained some measure of autonomy found themselves diplomatically isolated after the mid-1660s, just as their fur sources were being depleted and expanding settler societies were pressuring them for land. Such pressures led to "King Philip's War" (1675–6), between several Indian groups and the southern New England colonies. Although the Indians enjoyed considerable success at the outset, hunger and disease in their ranks, along with the participation of the Mohawks and some local Indians on the English side, enabled the colonists to prevail. Thousands of Indians fled the region, were killed, or were sold into slavery. Those remaining in the colonies, whether friendly or hostile during the war, were subjected to laws restricting their movements, occupations, and autonomy. Tensions between settlers and Eastern Abenakis in coastal Maine led to the war's spreading there, but the Abenakis held their own, and the treaty ending the war in 1677 represented no significant gain for either side.

Similar tensions gripped the Chesapeake. Maryland allied with the Five Nations in 1674, isolating the Susquehannocks and pressuring them to abandon their land for a site on the Potomac. After relocating, the Susquehannocks were attacked by Virginia and Maryland militia in 1675 as the beginning of a broader campaign to remove by force Indians who occupied potential tobacco-growing lands. In Virginia this campaign led to the civil war known as Bacon's Rebellion (1675–7), when the royal governor, William Berkeley, attempted to restrain settlers from attacking Indians friendly to the colony. As in southern New England, the Indians in both colonies were defeated and the remaining survivors confined to tiny reservations.

In 1677 New York's Governor Edmund Andros convened two treaty conferences in which the Iroquois met with government representatives from the southern New England and Chesapeake colonies, respectively. The conferees agreed on the disposition of New England Indian refugees to villages near Albany and of Susquehannock refugees to lands near Iroquois country. They also declared that Indians remaining in the colonies would be tributaries of the Iroquois as well as colonial subjects. These were the first two of the Covenant Chain treaties by which the Iroquois took an active role in British Indian policy and colonial expansion. The protocol of Covenant Chain conferences was an elaborate synthesis of Indian and

European diplomatic forms, some of which had precedents in earlier Iroquois—Dutch conferences.

Although the Iroquois now enjoyed stability on their eastern and southern frontiers, the last quarter of the seventeenth century was marked by tumultuous upheavals to the north and west. English efforts to break the French trade monopoly in Canada and the Ohio Valley led to fierce competition in which guns became a prominent commodity on both sides. During the 1670s the newly chartered Hudson's Bay Company established several posts on the Hudson and James bays from which they dealt with Crees and other Indians as far west as Lake of the Woods. At the same time, the English at Albany were urging the Iroquois to divert some of the Great Lakes trade their way. With well-armed Indians impinging on one another's hunting territories in quest of additional furs, tensions ran high. Then in 1679 a smallpox epidemic killed 10 percent of the Iroquois population, leading the Five Nations to launch a new round of devastating assaults on the Illinois, Miamis, and other western allies of the French in order to obtain captives. To deter French support, they also renewed their attacks on French settlements in Canada. In response, the French deliberately increased their volume of trade with Indian allies from Maine to Lake Superior, as a matter of policy rather than in response to market demands, and dispatched a new body of troops to Canada.

The French–Iroquois conflict eventually merged with King William's War (1689–97), between England and France. Political upheavals associated with Leisler's Rebellion (1689) and its aftermath produced a series of New York governments that were ineffective in mounting a military effort against the French and in supporting the Iroquois. In the face of this vulnerability, French troops invaded Iroquois country and destroyed several villages while their Indian allies likewise attacked with great effectiveness. By 1698 the Iroquois had lost about 25 percent (500) of their fighting force, about 1,600 of their total population of 8,600, and the Canadian hunting territories seized from the Hurons and other Indians half a century earlier.

In the meantime, Iroquois influence to the south waned with the establishment of Pennsylvania (1681). William Penn carefully purchased land from the Delawares and established trade agreements with them, ignoring Iroquois claims, based on the Covenant Chain, to oversee Delaware affairs. The new colony also welcomed refugee Susquehannocks and other Indians seeking to escape Iroquois control.

By the end of the century, the Iroquois were deeply divided into pro-English, pro-French, and neutralist factions. But defeat at the hands of the French and the inability of the English to offer substantive military support had strengthened the arguments of those Iroquois who sought new means to achieve peace and trade. The result was the Grand Settlement of 1701, in which the Five Nations reached new agreements with each of the major powers. The Iroquois agreed with France to make peace with that nation's western allies and to remain neutral in future Anglo–French wars. In return the Iroquois would be allowed to hunt and trade as far west as Detroit. A new Covenant Chain treaty with the English pointedly excluded military support from the Iroquois' obligations but opened the way for Protestant missionaries to work among the Five Nations.

In making peace with the Iroquois, both England and France expected to garner the bulk of the Great Lakes fur trade. To consolidate its grip on the trade, the French built a fortified post at Detroit. However, the Iroquois persuaded many of the Indians there to take their pelts to Albany for the better prices offered by the English. French efforts to halt this trade led some Iroquois to join renewed English military efforts against the French during Queen Anne s War (1700–13). As during King William's War, English military ineptitude reminded the Iroquois of the dangers of allying too closely with Britain and prompted the confederacy to resume its neutrality.

SOUTHEAST: INDIANS AND THE SLAVE TRADE

The last third of the seventeenth century marked the end of Spain's monopoly on trade with Indians in the Southeast. The suppression of the Powhatan Confederacy in 1646 enabled Virginia traders to make direct contact with Cherokees, Westos, Tuscaroras, and Catawbas to the west and south. By the mid-1660s the Virginians were arming the Westos – refugees from Iroquois attacks on Lake Erie – who returned with deerskins and with captives, mostly Guales seized from Spanish missions, whom the Virginians sold as slaves. English-inspired raids on Spanish–Guale missions increased rapidly after the new colony of Carolina allied with the Westos in the early 1670s. The Carolinians sold most of their slaves in the West Indies, although some went to New England. In 1683, a group of independent traders defied the proprietary monopoly and allied with the Savannah Shawnees, refugees from Iroquois attacks on the Ohio River, to attack and enslave the Westos themselves. These traders assumed control of Indian trading and policy in South Carolina. After 1685 they attracted many Guale refugees to the colony, where they became known as Yamasees, and extended their activities to interior Muskogean-speakers, then coalescing as the Creek Confederacy, and to the Chickasaws on the east side of the Mississippi River. These allies brought them deerskins and Timucuan, Apalachee, Cherokee, and Choctaw captives.

Responding to English expansion in both the North and South, and to Spanish weakness on the Gulf Coast, France in 1699 established a colony at Louisiana and rooted it in an alliance with the Choctaws, who were eager for means of defending themselves against slave raiders. The advantages held by the English and their Indian allies were magnified with the outbreak of Queen Anne's War in the Southeast in 1702. English and Creek forces destroyed the remaining Florida missions and reduced the Spanish presence to St. Augustine and Pensacola, while English and Chickasaws devastated the French at Mobile and the Choctaws in their villages.

Even as it won these victories, Carolina's hold on its allies was being undermined by its own colonists. Trader abuses and squatting by settlers led the Savannah Shawnees to raid some English settlements in 1707. Carolina enlisted the aid of the Catawbas while the Shawnees turned to the Iroquois, now at peace with all their neighbors in the North. The Shawnees returned to their Ohio Valley homes under Iroquois protection, while the Iroquois and Catawbas began a rivalry that would persist in the form of raids and counter-raids for most of the century. Massive settler immigration in North Carolina similarly undermined English relations with their Tuscarora allies. The attempt of some Tuscaroras to drive the settlers from their land was defeated in 1712 when the English summoned the aid of Yamasees and Cherokees. In the same year the Creeks, the most powerful Indian force in the Southeast, negotiated their own peace with France and Spain because of repeated abuses by English traders. Then in 1715, the loyal Yamasees mounted the most serious challenge yet. Resenting the abusive actions of both traders and settlers, they staged coordinated attacks on several trading houses and settlements, while Creeks and Catawbas assassinated English traders in their villages. Only the support of the Cherokees, who considered joining the uprising but declined because of deep-seated resentments against the Creeks, enabled the English to prevail. Defeated Yamasees fled inland to Creek villages or back to now-revived Guale missions, while the Creeks pursued a policy of neutrality vis-à-vis Europeans. In the meantime, the Indian slave trade came to an end, as it became clear that Native Americans were utterly unable to survive the disease environment of the West Indies.

SOUTHWEST AND SOUTHERN PLAINS: NATIVE REVOLTS AND NEW LIFEWAYS

Although far removed from the Atlantic and the forces sweeping across it between Europe and the Americas, the Southwest and its native peoples were likewise transformed in substantive ways in the late seventeenth and early eighteenth centuries. Pueblo resentment against Spanish rule hardened after 1660 as conditions worsened. A long cycle of drought (1666–71) brought starvation not only to Pueblos but to Apaches and Navajos, who renewed their raids. An epidemic in 1672 only added to Pueblo miseries. Along with continued resentment against both secular and religious officials, these factors prompted a resurgence of Pueblo traditionalism. Missionary charges of idolatry and witchcraft led the governor, Juan Francisco Treviño, in 1675 to order the destruction of religious kivas and objects and the arrest of forty-seven prominent natives. When a large contingent of normally peaceful Pueblos appeared at his palace and demanded the prisoners' release, Treviño assented, hoping to retain Pueblo support against the Apaches and Navajos.

Treviño's concession accomplished little because Pueblo resentment had passed the breaking point. One of the imprisoned leaders, a San Juan shaman named Popé, became the focal point of a movement to expel the Spanish altogether and restore the traditions that prevailed before 1598. After five years of preaching and organizing, and even gaining some support from non-Pueblo raiders, the Pueblos united to drive the Spanish from the province and defeated an attempted reconquest in 1681–2. A new governor, Diego de Vargas, returned in 1692 with a formidable force, but did not complete the restoration of Spanish control until 1700. Even then, the Hopis remained independent.

During the twenty years of conflict, the Pueblo population in New Mexico declined from 17,000 to 14,000, due to warfare, starvation, enslavement for labor in Mexican mines, and voluntary emigration to the Hopis, Navajos, and Apaches. Many villages were abandoned, and most others were relocated. Many communities were divided both by these moves and by differences in attitudes toward the Spanish. But the Spanish reconquest was a partial one. The authorities did not reintroduce *enco-*

mienda (although they retained *repartimiento*) and they enjoined the Franciscans to moderation and toleration in their evangelizing.

In their hasty departure from New Mexico in 1680, the Spanish left behind thousands of animals. This windfall accelerated the adoption of domestic animals by Indians in the Southwest. For the Navajos, horses and sheep became the basis for a more sedentary way of life than either the hunting and gathering of the pre-Spanish past or the raiding of the seventeenth century. The Apaches combined horses with guns, some stolen from the Spanish, others introduced to the southern Plains by Carolina-armed Chickasaws or by French traders based in Illinois and Louisiana. In coming years, this combination of horses and guns would transform native life on the Plains.

By 1715, the escalating scale and intensity of warfare was leading many Indians to search for new strategies for maximizing the benefits of European trade while minimizing their subordination to imperial interests. In much of the East, this meant "playing off" the European powers in a policy of active neutrality. Elsewhere in the East, and also in the Southeast, it meant a cautious approach in dealing with the sole European power in the region. On the Plains, where Europeans had yet to establish a direct presence, Indians embraced European material culture as part of their adaptations to new circumstances triggered by European presences elsewhere.

NATIVE AMERICANS AND THE EUROPEAN CONFLICT FOR EMPIRE, 1715–63

Although the conclusion of Queen Anne's War in 1713 marked the beginning of three decades of peace among Europeans, that peace did not diminish imperial competition for supremacy in North America. In the absence of overt war, each of the European powers sought to extend and strengthen its ties to various native groups, not only for profits but – where two or more of them competed – as means of securing diplomatic (and potential military) allies. Indians with access to two or more sources of European goods could use their positions to play these sources off one another and avoid becoming dependent on any one. Other native groups fought among themselves to control access to such goods or to advance the interests of their European ally. Even many Plains Indians were drawn into such rivalries. The outbreak of a new Anglo–French war in 1744, along with the expansion of British settlement, began the unraveling of the system of alliances and play-offs in the Eastern Woodlands, a process that ended with the defeat of France and its withdrawal from North America in 1763.

NEUTRALITY AND DEPENDENCE IN
THE EAST, 1715 – 44

In the Northeast, the Iroquois remained formally at peace with both European powers, but their success at diverting western Indians' furs to Albany led the French to establish a post at Niagara (1721), which the English countered by building Fort Oswego (1727). Together, the two posts enabled Great Lakes Indians to bypass the Iroquois and trade directly with the British and French. As a result, the Iroquois increasingly looked southward for allies, tribute, and additions to their ranks. In 1722 they incorporated the Tuscaroras as the sixth member of their confederacy. In the same year, they met with New York, Pennsylvania, and Virginia officials to revive the Covenant Chain and agree upon the disposition of Indians within the later two colonies. In return for being granted trade privileges in Pennsylvania, the Iroquois agreed that Shawnee refugees from South Carolina, along with some indigenous Delawares, would be moved from Pennsylvania to the Ohio Valley. The new treaty also enabled Iroquois parties to travel freely in their raids for captives, now centered on the Cherokees and Catawbas. In 1737 the Iroquois cooperated with Pennsylvania in imposing the fraudulent Walking Purchase on most of the Delawares remaining in the colony, obliging them to move to the southern periphery of Iroquois country and west of lands sought by Pennsylvania for settlers.

The arrival of refugees in the Ohio Valley in the second quarter of the eighteenth century marked the reoccupation of a region emptied by Iroquois raids a century earlier. Besides the Delawares and Shawnees from Pennsylvania, the region was settled by "Mingos" – Iroquois who moved west in search of less congested hunting areas – and some Algonquian-speaking allies of the French. As French and English traders vied for their business, these Indians sought to avoid dependence on, and deference to, the French, English, and Iroquois, a tendency that led the French to label them "republican."

North of the Great Lakes, Anglo–French competition extended commercial fur trading west to the Rocky Mountains. Although Indians sought wherever possible to trade with both powers, the French arming of the Sioux in the 1720s led Crees, Ojibwas, and Assiniboins to rely more heavily on the Hudson's Bay Company. After 1730, the French established new posts among the latter three groups, leading the Sioux to turn against the French. The Ojibwas used French arms to mount an all-out war on the Sioux, inaugurating the westward movement that would lead many Sioux to the Plains and a radically new way of life. Meanwhile, in 1736, the French quashed a twenty-five-year effort by several Indian groups, led by the Foxes, to drive French traders from the area west of Lake Michigan.

In upper New England and the Maritimes, on the other hand, Abenakis, Malecites, and Micmacs displayed their decided preference for the French to the encroaching presence of the British. The awarding of Nova Scotia to Britain in the Treaty of Utrecht (1713) and English recovery from King Philip's War (1675 6) led to tensions between English traders and settlers, on one hand, and Indians supported by French missionaries on the other. After full-scale war erupted in 1722, the English introduced troops whose ranks included subject Indians from the southern New England colonies. Although enjoying limited success against the Micmacs in Nova Scotia, the English destroyed the Abenaki village that was the center of hostility in Maine and killed its resident missionary. In treaties signed in 1725 and 1727, the Indians and English agreed to live in peace and recognize each other's legitimacy, but tensions continued and occasionally erupted in violence.

In the Southeast, the Creek Confederacy developed the diplomatic "play-off" system to perfection in the generation after 1715. In the manner of the Iroquois, they drew on internal factions to establish ties with the British in Carolina, French in Louisiana, and Spanish in Florida. Under the *mico*, or "emperor," Brims, the Creeks granted limited trade concessions to each of the three powers while declining to favor any one over the others. Above all, they sought to maximize their profits from the deerskin trade and minimize European control of that trade. To that end they fought both the French-allied Choctaws and the Carolina-allied Cherokees, but joined with the powerful, Carolina-allied Chickasaws who so successfully harassed the French on the Mississippi River. They supported the refugee Yamasees in attacks against Carolina traders and settlers, and the Iroquois in their raids on Cherokees and Catawbas.

The Creeks' success depended in part on their geographic position, as the Cherokee experience during the same period illustrates. Although the Cherokees had intervened on the side of Carolina at a critical moment in the Yamasee War, that colony continued to favor the Creeks over the Cherokees by paying the Creeks higher prices for deerskins and by providing them with guns and ammunition. For the Carolinians, such a policy was needed to prevent the Creeks from shifting their trade entirely to the French and Spanish. Because the Cherokees lacked ready access to French and Spanish traders, the Carolinians could charge them higher prices and deny them guns with impunity. The lack of adequate weapons left the Cherokees vulnerable to attacks by Chickasaws, Choctaws, Iroquois, and the Creeks.

Over time, the growing strength of the British in the Southeast, relative to that of the Spanish and even the French, altered these patterns. The inability of the latter two nations to produce adequate supplies of guns and other goods on a consistent basis, the inability of the Spanish to prevent the English from destroying Yamasee villages in Florida in 1728, and the death of Brims in the early 1730s combined to weaken the Creeks' play-off system. In this context, Creeks welcomed James Oglethorpe's proposal in 1733 to establish an English settlement on Creek land as a means of balancing South Carolina's growing dominance. Desperate for solid ties with other Europeans, the Cherokees turned briefly in the 1730s to two successive European eccentrics — Sir Alexander Cuming, who promised salvation through a direct treaty with the English crown, and Christian Priber, a German mystic who urged the Cherokees toward a policy of neutrality. Although the two men's presences were only fleeting, they did heighten the demoralized Cherokees' sense of national identity. Even more vulnerable were the Piedmont Catawbas, beset by a declining deer population, Iroquois raids, and encroaching settlers. As a result, they became more dependent on close ties with the South Carolina government, allying with it against common Indian enemies and seizing runaway slaves.

Britain's strength in the Southeast was evident as far west as the Mississippi River. Although the French, with Choctaw aid, cursed the Natchez in 1729 and seized their lands, the English-armed Chickasaws regularly raided the French-allied Illinois for captives and frequently disrupted French traffic on the Mississippi. After 1730 the uncertainties of French supplies and the aggressive trade tactics of the Carolinians split the previously loyal Choctaws, setting off a civil war that lasted two decades.

Meanwhile, small enclaves of Indians, surrounded by settlers, struggled to survive and maintain their cultural identities in the heavily populated areas of the British seaboard colonies. In the face of poverty, discrimination, and restrictions imposed by legislation and white overseers, many served as soldiers, seamen, indentured servants, or casual laborers. Besides poverty, the effects of alcohol and disease reduced their already small numbers still further. With military and maritime occupations taking a higher toll of males, many native women married outsiders, particularly free blacks who were similarly marginalized in colonial society. For the most part, Indians in the colonies were ignored by whites except when their military services were desired or when significant numbers were attracted to evangelical Christianity as preached in the Great Awakening revivals of the 1740s.

EASTERN INDIANS AND THE FALL OF FRANCE, 1744–63

The outbreak of war between England and France in 1744 further exposed French weakness and the vulnerability of the Indians' play-off system. British naval supremacy prevented the French from importing many of the trade goods needed to shore up their alliances with Indians. Neutral and even many pro-French Indians in the Ohio and Mississippi valleys perceived the shortages and the resultant high prices as insulting. On the Mississippi, dissident Choctaws openly allied with the hated Chickasaws and South Carolina in 1745, widening the bloody civil war between pro- and anti-French factions. Two years later, Mingos, Shawnees, Miamis, and others launched attacks on French posts in Ohio and began dealing with Pennsylvania traders.

Recognizing that their empire itself was at stake, the French resorted to decisive military action. French troops helped sympathetic Choctaws to suppress the pro-English faction once and for all and moved to reassert French power in the Great Lakes and Ohio Valley. At Pickawillany on the Ohio, they led an attack that resulted in the death of the Miami leader, Memeskia, a key figure in the anti-French movement. In so reasserting themselves, the French were aided by the conduct of the English in each region. The abuses that South Carolina's traders were regularly accused of by other Indians became a point of resentment among the Choctaws. At a treaty conference at Logstown, Pennsylvania, in 1752, Pennsylvania, Virginia, and the Iroquois pressured Ohio Indians into confirming Virginia's claim to land south of the Ohio and accepting construction of an English post at the junction of the Monongahela and Allegheny rivers. With the English now perceived as a more direct threat to their lands, most Ohio Indians returned to pro-French or neutral positions. French troops then drove all English traders from the region and began the construction of a series of forts, including Fort Dusquesne, where the Virginians had begun theirs.

When Anglo–French war broke out in 1754, Indian support enabled the French to defeat efforts by George Washington at Fort Necessity (1754) and James Braddock's British regulars (1755) to capture Fort Duquesne. Shawnees and Delawares then launched attacks on frontier settlements in Pennsylvania in a concerted effort to drive back settlers impinging on their lands. The Iroquois–English Covenant Chain was essentially a dead letter as even many Iroquois joined the French in a stunning series of victories in 1756–7.

Although the rise to power in England of William Pitt was a principal factor in the reversal of military fortunes in the Seven Years' War, the effort of Indians to maintain balance between the two powers was equally decisive in North America. By 1758, most Iroquois and even Shawnees and Delawares had come to fear that the French would prevail. At a treaty conference at Easton, Pennsylvania, in October 1758, the Ohio Indians agreed to abandon their support for the French, who thereupon withdrew from Fort Dusquesne. With Indians now aiding them, the English seized Fort Dusquesne and Fort Niagara in the summer of 1759. In September 1760, New France surrendered to the English.

Even before the war's end, some Indians were uneasy about their inability to contain the ascendant British. Afterward, these suspicions were borne out when Britain's commander, General Jeffrey Amherst, ordered large garrisons to remain in the occupied French posts, halted the giving of all presents, including food, to allied Indians, and demanded the return of all British captives held by the allies, even those who had been adopted and wished to remain with their captors. He also seized some Seneca land for his officers at the same time that some Connecticut settlers massacred Delawares in the Wyoming Valley of Pennsylvania and took over their land. In the South, the Cherokees had entered the war on the English side. But their ill treatment by soldiers and traders while Virginians and South Carolinians squatted on their land led them in 1759 to join the weakened French cause. Although the Cherokees initially drove back the frontier of settlement, a contingent of British troops in 1761 moved through their lands, burning homes and crops. Shortly thereafter, the Cherokees submitted to South Carolina. With the British having defeated the French, the resentment of Native Americans against the British was greater than ever.

HORSES AND GUNS: THE PLAINS AND
SOUTHWEST TRANSFORMED

Well before Europeans set foot on the Plains in significant numbers, Native Americans were transforming their lives and the region with objects of European origin, principally horses and guns. Although there was more than one source of each, most Plains horses originated among those left behind or seized during the Pueblo Revolt in New Mexico (1680–1700). From there they were diffused northward by the Utes to their fellow Numic-speakers, the Shoshones, some of whom subsequently acquired distinct identities as Bannocks and Comanches. First used for meat or transporting goods, horses were being ridden to hunt and raid in the 1730s and, soon after, became an object of prestige in many societies, to be accumulated and given away.

Guns, on the other hand, originated in the deliberate actions of French traders seeking to extend that nation's influence west of the Mississippi. In 1718–9, Charles Claude du Tisné established alliances with the Osages, Wichitas, and Pawnees, designating these groups as middlemen in the French trade and giving them guns to reinforce their roles. French-armed Pawnees and Kansas defeated a Spanish–Pueblo expedition seeking to establish trade on the southern Plains in 1720. By the mid-1720s, all the Indian nations on the lower Missouri River had been brought into the French fold. After 1738, French contacts extended to the upper Missouri as well.

By the mid-eighteenth century, horse-mounted Indians from the periphery of the Plains had evolved new lifestyles as equestrian nomads and moved onto the grasslands to follow bison herds. Among the most notable of these were the Lakota Sioux, Cheyennes, Arapahos, and Comanches. In addition, village-dwelling natives of the region, such as the Pawnees, Arikaras, Mandans, and Hidatsas, incorporated horses into their village-based agricultural societies for hunting and transportation. Such peoples were highly vulnerable to surprise raids by the equestrians, as were the eastern Apaches, who, despite having horses and a few captured guns, were no match for the French-armed Comanches. As a result, the Apaches made peace with the Spanish during the late 1710s.

Similarly in the Southwest, the Spanish and Pueblos grew ever more interdependent as raids by mounted Comanches and Utes threatened both. The Pueblos were increasingly integrated into the colonial economy and polity, though never at the expense of their autonomy. The Navajos like-

wise modified their ways in response to Ute raids and other new conditions. They shifted to a pastoral economy based on the sheep herds created
after the Spanish departure in 1680 and, under the influence of Pueblo
refugees accepted during the Spanish reconquest, adopted some Pueblo
religious ideas and European materials.

Albeit in very different ways, native lives over much of the continent were
significantly transformed during the first two-thirds of the eighteenth
century. (During the last years of this period, a third theater of Native
American–European interaction was opened by the arrival of Russian fur
traders in southwestern Alaska, a topic discussed in the next section.)
Except for subject Indians in the British and Spanish colonies, the French
presence had affected directly or indirectly the material lives of virtually
all Indians east of the Rockies. The elimination of France as a territorial
power in 1763, then, marked the end of an era and the opening of a large
power vacuum.

NATIVE AMERICANS AND THE RISE OF THE UNITED STATES, 1763–1815

The half century after France's defeat in the Seven Years' War marked a
profound shift in the balance of power among Europeans. After emerging
as an independent nation in 1776, the United States asserted itself as a
major power and quickly came to dominate most of the old British Empire
in North America, as well as France's Louisiana territory, while Britain
consolidated its hold over the previously French stronghold of Canada.
The opening of European colonial activity in the Pacific was initiated by
Spain in California and by Russia in Alaska, but Britain and the United
States soon took over the lucrative trade in the Northwest Coast. In very
different ways, each of these developments had profound consequences for
Native Americans.

INDIANS AND THE AMERICAN REVOLUTION, 1763–83

The signing of the Treaty of Paris in January 1763, confirming France's
expulsion from North America, only heightened the concerns of Great
Lakes and Ohio Indians over British policies and settler incursions. Many
natives placed hope in rumors that, despite the treaty, the French would

return while others were drawn to the preachings of Neolin, the "Delaware Prophet," who called on Native Americans to reject all European goods and alliances in order to restore their former abundance, autonomy, and cultural integrity. Pontiac, an Ottawa Indian, and other leaders drew on these widespread resentments and hopes to mount coordinated assaults on the British-occupied posts formerly owned by the French. Although several forts were seized or besieged, shortages of food, divisions among the natives, and a smallpox epidemic – deliberately instigated by the English when they distributed infected blankets at Fort Pitt – combined to end the offensives by 1765.

In the meantime, the British government moved to allay Indian fears through a royal proclamation of October 1763, asserting direct imperial control, as opposed to that of colonial governments, over Indian–white relations west of the Appalachian crest. Although Britain would exercise ultimate sovereignty beyond this "Proclamation Line," Indians would retain title to all lands not previously ceded by treaty. Indian superintendents, appointed for northern and southern districts, would approve all future sales of such land as well as regulate trade and enforce imperial law.

The crown's utter inability to enforce this new policy was soon apparent. Squatters, speculators, traders, hunters, and outlaws crossed the Proclamation Line at will, while revenue shortages prevented the crown from adequately staffing its garrisons and the superintendencies, and from furnishing gifts to the Indians. In 1768, Britain returned control of Indian trade to the colonial governments. In the same year, the northern superintendent and the Iroquois agreed in the Treaty of Fort Stanwix to cede thousands of acres of Shawnee, Delaware, and Cherokee land on the Ohio River, opening it to speculation and settlement. Other coerced cessions during the same period created tensions all along the colonial frontier as whites encroached on Indian land while Indians resisted. All-out war erupted in Virginia in 1774 after some colonists massacred eight friendly Mingos, and Mingos and Shawnees retaliated. After its troops defeated the Indians, Virginia forced the Shawnees to cede all their lands south of the Ohio River.

With the outbreak of war between Britain and its colonies, most Indians were pressured by each side to support its cause or at least remain neutral. The Cherokees used the opportunity to mount a series of highly effective attacks on encroaching settlers. But the southern colonies retaliated with expeditions that burned most Cherokee towns and forced the nation to cede more than 50,000 square miles of territory to Virginia and the Carolinas in 1777. Although the Oneidas and Tuscaroras, under the influence of Congregationalist missionary Samuel Kirkland, joined the colonists, most other Iroquois supported the British. Shawnees mounted raids on settlements throughout the recently ceded lands of Kentucky. Kickapoos, Miamis, and other Ohio and Great Lakes Algonquian-speakers assisted in the British capture of Vincennes in 1778. Meanwhile, the British invasion of the South in the same year was supported by all the major Indian groups there. Besides the Oneidas and Tuscaroras, the colonists were supported by Indian minorities in the seaboard colonies and by steadfastly pro-French groups in upper New England, eastern Canada, and the upper Mississippi Valley.

Pro-British Indians paid dearly for their allegiance when the Americans launched a series of retaliatory expeditions in 1779. Iroquois, Shawnees, Delawares, Cherokees (many of whom had reentered the war in 1778), Foxes, and others had homes and villages burned. More than 5,000 Iroquois fled to Canada as a result of raids that destroyed over forty of their villages, and many Ohio Indians moved farther west. After the devastation of the war, all Indians discovered to their consternation that the Treaty of Paris (1783) between Britain and the United States left them to deal with the latter on their own.

FEDERAL POLICY AND ANGLO–INDIAN RESISTANCE, 1783–1815

The new Confederation government attempted to assert its authority on the frontier by dictating, between 1784 and 1786, a series of treaties of cession with Indian groups in both North and South. The rationale for the treaties was that Indians should compensate the new republic for expenses incurred in prosecuting the war. But the government lacked the means for raising a military force capable of enforcing the treaties in the face of resentful natives on one hand and expansion-minded settlers on the other, so that some of the treaties were ineffectual.

Under the leadership of Henry Knox, Secretary of War for both the Confederation and the early Washington administration, United States policy was directed toward facilitating white expansion and "civilizing" Native Americans, which meant assimilating them into European–American society and culture. The United States henceforth would acquire western lands only through treaties of purchase, in which Indians fully and freely consented. A series of Trade and Intercourse acts, passed during the

1790s, sought to regulate and control relations between Indians and non-Indians along lines similar to those of Britain's Proclamation of 1763. In 1796, Congress went further by establishing a system of trading factories at which Indians could expect fair prices and treatment. Both the treaties and factories served the "civilization" policy by dispensing agricultural tools, domestic animals, and other goods expected to hasten the Indians' acculturation.

Despite the altruism of these intentions, many Indians recognized that the underlying goals of expansion and assimilation were fundamentally threatening to their ways of life. Most natives north of the Ohio River, as well as large numbers of Cherokees and Creeks in the South, resented pressures to cede their lands and move away. These resentments were actively encouraged by the Spanish in the South and the British in the North. From 1789 to 1794, warfare between the Indians and the United States raged over much of the frontier. After much bloodshed, the United States succeeded in obtaining treaties that ceded most of southern and western Ohio and additional portions of Cherokee country, and confirmed earlier cessions of Creek lands.

Although Jefferson continued the twin goals of expansion and assimilation after 1800, the realities of European-American demography, economy, and politics almost inevitably pushed expansion to the forefront. To be sure, significant numbers of Cherokees, Creeks, Choctaws, and Chickasaws in the South responded to efforts by the federal government to foster farming among native men and domesticity among women. But such responses were limited to a small minority, mostly mixed-blood children of British traders or Loyalists and Indian women. Most Indians were far more directly affected by United States efforts to open up additional land for settlers. By applying relentless pressure on Indian leaders, federal agents during Jefferson's administration obtained cessions to additional portions of Ohio, Tennessee, and Georgia as well as parts of Indiana, Illinois, Michigan, and Wisconsin.

Organized resistance to these pressures soon emerged in the Northwest, led by the "Shawnee Prophet," Tenskwatawa, who urged a complete repudiation of European–American ways, and among a group of Creeks known as "Red Sticks." Influential in both areas was Tenskwatawa's brother, Tecumseh, who argued that Indians should unite to counter United States expansionism and that the generally coerced treaties signed by individual tribes were invalid. These tensions escalated to violence in the Northwest in 1810 and thereafter merged into the War of 1812, during which

virtually all the northwestern Indians, along with the Red Sticks, allied
with the British against the United States. The decisive crushing of Indian
resistance came in attacks led by William Henry Harrison in the North
and Andrew Jackson in the South. Virtually all of the Northwest was
thereafter open for white settlement while, in the South, the Creeks lost
over half their remaining lands.

EXPANDED TRADE IN THE NORTH
AMERICAN HEARTLAND

The defeat of France in the Seven Years' War, and subsequent expansion by
Britain and the United States, served to increase the presence of Europeans
and Euro-Americans from the Mississippi River and Lake Superior to the
Rocky Mountains and Columbia Plateau. Although Spain assumed formal
sovereignty in Louisiana under the Treaty of Paris (1763), its characteristic
inability to dispatch human, financial, and material resources to North
America limited its control of this burgeoning activity. To be sure, the
new town of St. Louis, founded in 1764, emerged as the single most
important center in the Missouri–upper Mississippi region. Here and in
New Orleans, elite Spanish families intermarried with their French counterparts and with leading families among Indian middlemen to strengthen
the positions of Creoles and mixed-bloods as brokers in the trade. But in
most of Louisiana, trade continued to be carried out by French and Métis
(French–Indian) *coureurs de bois* (fur traders).

Britons and Americans proved to be far more influential newcomers
than the Spanish in central North America. Following the British takeover
of Canada, the North West Company was chartered to assume control of
the former French trading network. Until 1821, the new company engaged in furious competition with the Hudson's Bay Company for control
of Indian trade in the upper Plains and central Subarctic. Instead of
relying on Indians to bring them pelts, the two companies built networks
of posts in the Canadian interior and dispatched specialized crews of
Europeans, mixed-bloods, and eastern Indians to man them. By the end of
the eighteenth century, these networks extended west to the Peace River
valley, north to the Mackenzie River, and south to the Missouri. Between
Lake Superior and the Peace River, where competition was most intense,
traders went directly to Indian camps to secure furs, and engaged natives
in supplying meat and other provisions to the posts. As a result of this
increased demand, the populations of beaver, deer, and moose were se-

verely depleted in much of the region, and Indians were often forced to turn to the traders for imported food, thereby compounding their dependence. British and French traders frequently took Indian wives.

The influx of Europeans brought a new round of devastating "virgin soil" epidemics to western North America. As much as one-third of the previously unexposed populations in the Plains, the Southwest, and other regions during the 1780s were struck down by smallpox, supplemented by localized outbreaks of influenza and other diseases.

The epidemics, along with the advent of the Americans after the Louisiana Purchase, marked a major turning point in Indian relations with Euro-Americans in the Plains (from the Missouri Valley southward) and Columbia regions. Several expeditions, beginning with that of Lewis and Clark (1804–6), reported in great detail on the land, resources, and peoples of the Missouri and Columbia drainages, encouraging entrepreneurs to take advantage of American sovereignty in this fur-rich region. Thereafter, trading parties took pack trains of goods directly to Indian villages, instead of waiting for middlemen to bring pelts to company posts. In some areas, American-employed trappers of many backgrounds including whites, Métis, eastern Indians (principally Iroquois, Delawares, and Shawnees), and even native Hawaiians procured their own pelts rather than trading with the local natives. Traders also dispensed guns for their clients to use in the growing competition for hunting territories. The spread of trade and warfare heightened Indian demand for horses for the mobility they provided in raids. On the Missouri, these developments favored the nomadic Sioux over the village-dwelling Mandans, Arikaras, and Hidatsas. The latter's large, settled populations were more vulnerable to epidemic mortality and raids by equestrian nomads, and their middleman positions were undermined by the nomads' mobility. The Americans established amicable relations with Indians as far up the Missouri as the Yellowstone River during this period; the Blackfeet and other groups farther upriver remained hostile.

The epidemics of the 1780s were equally devastating in the southern Plains and in the Southwest, leading the Comanches, Utes, Navajos, and Jicarilla Apaches to make peace with Spain during that decade. Thereafter, western Apaches were the principal raiders of Spanish and Pueblo communities. Although ravaged by drought as well as smallpox, the Hopis continued to resist Spanish authority. Spain's deteriorating position in the Americas generally, the growing influx of American and British interlopers in the southern Plains, the devastating epidemics, and the advent of the Americans on the Plains and of the British, Russians, and Americans in the North Pacific all contributed to the weakening grip of Spain in western North America.

NATIVES, SEA OTTERS, AND THE CHINA TRADE: THE NORTH PACIFIC COAST

European expansion from a different direction began when Russian traders and hunters seeking sea otter pelts moved from Siberia to the Aleutian Islands of Alaska during the 1740s. Over the ensuing decades, private companies expanded their activities eastward, often brutally subjugating the Aleuts and Eskimos on whose labor they depended and extracting heavy *yasak* (tribute) from them. Epidemic diseases undermined native resistance efforts, as did the activities of Russian Orthodox missionaries. By the end of the century, the highly profitable Russian trade had largely depleted sea otters from the Aleutians to Sitka Sound.

Meanwhile, other nations were being drawn to the region. Spanish expeditions patrolled the Northwest Coast after 1774, engaging in some trade, but primarily guarding against incursions by other Europeans. Despite Spanish vigilance, British and American traders were soon active along the coast between Alaska and California. The market for sea otter skins was China, but whereas Russian access to this market was limited to an inland border crossing in Mongolia, the British and Americans traded pelts in Canton for silks, tea, and other Chinese goods sought by growing numbers of west Europeans and North Americans. British activity remained limited by the monopolies of the British East India and South Sea companies, but Boston-based Americans made at least 127 voyages from the Northwest Coast to China between 1788 and 1826.

Concerns over foreign competition, destruction of fur sources, and exploitation of the natives led the imperial government to grant a monopoly to the Russian–American Company in 1799. Under the company's charter, all able-bodied native males were to serve as wage-earning hunters, although no more than half would do so in a single season. The company also pledged to respect native property rights. In keeping with Russian practice at home, the Orthodox Church was subordinated to secular authority, effectively stifling missionary criticisms of company employees' exploitation of native workers and sexual abuse of native women.

The Russian–American Company's efforts to expand south of Sitka after

1800 were significantly limited by the Tlingits, whose resistance was aided by American arms, and by its inability to match the quality and prices of British and American goods. Although some Tlingits and other Northwest Coast natives later traded with, and occasionally worked for, the Russians, they were never enticed into the dependency of the Aleuts. Using Aleut labor, the Russians established a post as far south as Fort Ross, California, in 1812.

HISPANOS AND NATIVES IN ALTA CALIFORNIA

Spanish expansion into California began in 1769, prompted by fears that Russia and Britain would establish themselves on the Pacific and encroach on Mexico. Spain quickly asserted its territorial sovereignty and its authority over coastal natives with the construction of twenty one Franciscan missions, extending from San Diego to Sonoma, and four military presidios. Although their intentions were ostensibly religious, the missions served as instruments for Spanish economic development and for social control of the native population. Devastated by diseases from the outset, Indians were drawn into missions where, as neophytes, they were required to work in vineyards, herd cattle, and perform other laboring and servile tasks. Missionaries administered corporal punishment frequently and harshly in order to replace native authority and cultural values with their own. Natives were similarly treated at the presidios. At the presidios and even in the missions, Indian women were sexually exploited.

Indian resistance to Spanish authority took many forms, including armed uprisings, individual acts of violence, escape, suicide, abortion and infanticide by native women, and the persistence of traditional religious practices. Escaping Indians often took horses and guns, introducing them to inland Indians and urging their use against the Spanish. After 1800, when most coastal natives had converted, escaped, or died, the missionaries turned inland. Although many inland Indians also converted and died from diseases, they were more successful than coastal Indians in minimizing the effects of Spanish colonization.

Mortality among Indians in Alta California was among the highest anywhere in North America. The devastating epidemics were followed by life in the missions and presidios with their poor diets, unsanitary crowding, corporal punishment, sexual abuse, native demoralization, and various efforts at resistance. As a result, the native population in the missionized area of California was reduced from approximately 72,000

Indians in 1770 to about 18,000 in 1830. As many as 10,000 more from inland areas also died.

The rise of the United States and the expansion of Euro-American trade and colonization meant that by 1815 most Indians in North America were engaged in economic relations with Europeans, with varying demographic and cultural consequences. The War of 1812 ended military resistance, and British support of such resistance, as viable options for Indians confronting the spread of Anglo–American settlement in the Eastern Woodlands. The Louisiana Purchase opened the way for the spread of American traders over much of the trans-Mississippi west. On the Pacific coast, Russian, Spanish, British, and American activity was transforming the lives of Native Americans. In each of these areas, Indians were developing new strategies for interacting with Euro-Americans that they would continue to pursue in the coming decades.

NATIVE AMERICANS AND U.S. EXPANSION, 1815–65

The half century from the end of the War of 1812 to the end of the Civil War was marked by upheavals that reverberated throughout the North American continent. Above all, these resulted from a cluster of developments in the United States – the beginnings of the market, industrial, and transportation revolutions, and a demographic growth in which the non-Indian population increased by more than 30 percent every ten years from 1800 to 1860. By the end of this period, the United States had expanded to the Pacific coast while waging a civil war that vanquished slavery and the pretensions to sovereignty of individual states. The consequences of these developments for Native Americans were enormous. Through death and dispossession, Indians east of the Mississippi River and in much of California were reduced to tiny, scattered remnants, while those elsewhere faced a republic determined to finish the process of acquiring Indian lands and extinguishing Indian sovereignty.

U.S. POLICY IN THE EAST: FROM "CIVILIZATION" TO REMOVAL

As in previous North American wars involving nation-states, the Treaty of Ghent (1814), ending the war of 1812, made no reference to Indian nations, leaving the natives to deal with the victors on their own. During the ensuing decade, native groups ceded most remaining land north of the Ohio and east of the Mississippi and agreed to emigrate westward. The only overt protests came from the Winnebagos in Wisconsin in 1827 and from a group of Sauks and Foxes who, led by Black Hawk, attempted to reoccupy land in Illinois in 1831. Federal troops defeated this effort in a brief war the following year.

Violence in the Southeast centered in Florida, where Georgia and Tennessee militia units had pursued runaway slaves during the war and come into conflict with the Seminoles, former Creeks who harbored the runaways. In the First Seminole War (1817–8), Andrew Jackson led federal and Creek troops in a concerted campaign that led not only to the Seminoles' defeat but to Spain's decision to sell Florida to the United States.

Except for the Red Stick Creeks, other natives in the Southeast had not joined the anti–United States movement instigated by Tecumseh, and they retained far more land after the War of 1812 than did the defeated nations to the north. Moreover, the Cherokees, Creeks, Choctaws, and Chickasaws had, to one degree or another, come under the influence of Anglo-Indian mixed-bloods and other elites who were educated in both Indian and white societies. Small but significant numbers of these bicultural elites were adopting Euro-American modes of farming and domesticity, literacy in English, and Christianity. A few of them even owned black slaves or operated businesses. According to the proponents of "civilization," such developments should have led Indians to abandon their traditional identities and claims to sovereignty, and to cede most remaining lands to whites. But such was not the case. The adoption of "civilization" by an elite minority actually reinforced the traditionalist orientation of most members, and even the elites sought to retain tribal land bases and strengthen claims to Indian sovereignty out of a combination of self-interest and patriotism.

In the face of such obstacles, expansionist interests in the United States pressed the government to replace the goal of "civilization" with that of removing all eastern Indians, providing them with lands west of the Mississippi in exchange for those left behind. Jefferson had raised the possibility of such exchanges after the Louisiana Purchase, and some southeastern groups had moved west voluntarily. Monroe proposed a removal bill to Congress in 1825, and in 1830, after Andrew Jackson's election to the presidency, the Indian Removal Act was passed. During the 1830s, treaties were imposed on the "Five Civilized Tribes" of the Southeast.

Although protests by the Chickasaws and Choctaws were relatively muted, a brief Creek War (1836), a far more bloody Second Seminole War (1835–42), and an extraordinary Cherokee campaign consisting of congressional lobbying, judicial appeals, and a public relations effort among white Northerners revealed the depths of Indian attachments to their homelands and opposition to forced removal. The forced removal of the southeastern Indians left only a small minority who remained as individual citizens of states or who had hidden out to evade removal.

AMERICAN CONQUEST OF THE TRANS-MISSISSIPPI WEST

The first half of the nineteenth century marked two political revolutions in the Southwest – the Mexican overthrow of Spanish rule, completed in 1821, and the American conquest, completed in 1848. In New Mexico, the first revolution brought a wave of new settlers northward from Mexico, many of whom violated Pueblo land and water rights and others of whom revived the practice of raiding the Navajos for slaves. At the same time, the Mexican government failed to maintain the peace achieved by Spain with the Navajos, Comanches, Utes, and Apaches in the late eighteenth century. As a result, some of these Indians resumed their raids on Hispano and Pueblo communities. Hispanos and Pueblos cooperated in an unsuccessful popular revolt in 1837–8 against political corruption and federal policies, and a second one ten years later against the imposition of American military rule.

Despite the latter revolt, the new American authorities in New Mexico identified the Pueblos as village-dwelling, landholding Indians whom, unlike the eastern Indians, they could not remove. With settler encroachments increasing dramatically, the territorial government in 1854 confirmed Spain's land grants to the Pueblos. However, Congress, in organizing a territorial government for New Mexico, refused to maintain the Pueblo voting rights granted by Mexico.

The United States also assumed responsibility for defending the Hispanos and Pueblos, as well as its own citizens, against non-Pueblo Indians. Tensions arose after 1848 because of Anglo and Mexican incursions on Indian land and because of several incidents involving soldiers and Indians. In 1862 the United States dispatched a new commander, General James Carleton, and additional troops to New Mexico to suppress the Apaches and Navajos. Carleton determined to move the Indians to Fort Sumner in eastern New Mexico as a means of neutralizing and "civilizing" them. Employing deception and terror, Carleton's troops rounded up and forcibly moved more than 9,000 Navajos and 500 Mescalero Apaches to the new location. Shortages of food, water, and wood, along with disease, raids by other Indians, and general demoralization, plagued the imprisoned natives. By 1865, most of the Mescaleros had escaped. In 1868, the United States concluded a new treaty with the Navajos, allowing them to return to their homeland. However, their new reservation of 3.5 million acres was just one-tenth of their former territory.

As in New Mexico, Mexican rule in California brought increased settlement and, despite a theoretical recognition of Indian citizenship, little change in the actual status of Native Americans. Military campaigns continued to coerce Indians into the missions until 1834, when the federal government instituted a policy of secularization. Although mission property was to be divided between the Indians and the clergy, the land and most of its improvements actually went to colonial officials and their relatives. The 15,000 neophyte laborers scattered, some to the new haciendas as peons, others to Mexican pueblos as domestics and other menial laborers, and still others to the interior regions. As the ranching economy expanded, conflicts between Mexicans and interior Indians became more or less ongoing until the outbreak of the Mexican War.

The American takeover was followed immediately by the gold rush that brought an onslaught of unmarried white males to California, most in search of quick fortune and entertaining no regard for nonwhites. Outright extermination became deliberate policy as private military expeditions, funded by the state and federal governments, hunted down Indians in northern and mountainous areas. By 1860, more than 4,000 natives, representing 12 percent of the population, had died in these wars. The invasion had ecological consequences as well. Gold and silver mining disrupted salmon runs, while farming and fencing restricted hunting and gathering. The breakup of the Mexican ranchos meant that even more Indians flocked to the pueblos in search of work, just as the end of the gold boom was putting many Anglos on the same road. An act of 1850 provided that any Indian could be charged with vagrancy on the word of any white. The convicted vagrant would be auctioned off to the highest bidder, who would employ him for up to four months. Indian children and young girls were kidnapped for service as laborers and prostitutes. Not surprisingly, disease, alcoholism, and poverty were the lot of many Indians, and diseases – primarily tuberculosis, smallpox, pneumonia, measles, and venereal diseases – were the major cause of mortality, accounting for two-thirds of Indian deaths between 1848 and 1860.

After the overthrow of Spanish rule in Texas, the new Mexican government encouraged immigration by Americans as a way of strengthening the thinly populated province. But the immigrants quickly overwhelmed the Mexicans and seceded to form an independent republic in 1836. Despite the pacific policies of the first president, Sam Houston, settler aggressions against Indians drove out all but the equestrian Kiowas and Comanches before Texas was annexed by the United States in 1845.

The decades from the 1820s through the 1850s marked the zenith of the fur trade west of the Mississippi. During this period, virtually every Indian group in the Plains, Rocky Mountains, and Columbia Plateau was immersed in an American-dominated trade in buffalo robes, beaver skins, and the pelts of smaller mammals, as well as meat and other animal byproducts. Whereas European trade was formerly a means of acquiring relatively small quantities of guns, glass beads, and cloth for incorporation into societies that remained subsistence-oriented, market priorities now affected Indian life in more fundamental ways. Instead of accompanying their husbands on the hunt, women remained in the camps to process hides. Because hunters procured animals faster than their wives processed them, the demand for female labor increased. This demand was satisfied by increased raiding for female captives who became additional wives of the productive hunters. Some Indian women married white and Métis traders and trappers who resided with the natives for at least part of each year. The children of these marriages grew up in the native villages, often becoming traders themselves and later serving as cultural brokers with the white world. Goods of cloth, metal, and glass were incorporated into native material, social, and aesthetic life, along with – in the case of some tribes – alcohol. These goods were obtained at American trading posts, which were now within reach of most Indians. European diseases were more destructive than ever during the 1830s, particularly a smallpox outbreak in 1837 that killed half the population of the Plains and virtually destroyed the village societies of the upper Missouri.

The annexation of Mexican territory by the United States in 1848 heightened American traffic west of the Mississippi, initiating a change in relations between the federal government and Indians in the region. Conflicts between emigrants and natives led the federal government to seek new treaties with the western nations and to extend the American military presence, along with that of the Bureau of Indian Affairs, among the western tribes. In treaties signed during the 1850s and early 1860s, various Indian groups accepted the formal bounding of their land and the right of the United States to build forts and roads in the vicinity. Some were obliged to give up their homelands altogether and move to lands designated Indian Territory. To one degree or another, Indians were restricted to reservations where, unable to pursue their full subsistence rounds, many became dependent on annuities – annual allocations provided for in the treaties and administered by the Bureau of Indian Affairs. Indians often did not understand or accept the terms of these treaties, leading on a few occasions to armed conflicts with settlers or federal troops. The most serious such incident was the Santee Sioux uprising in Minnesota (1862). Indian violence was the pretext for the slaughter by Colorado volunteers of peaceful Cheyennes at Sand Creek (1864). These outbreaks helped set the stage for the intensified military conflict that followed the Civil War.

The removal across the Mississippi of the "Five Civilized Tribes" from the Southeast also occasioned the extension of United States power westward. The Osages and other natives who hunted in Indian Territory resented the newcomers' presence while squatters attempted to settle on Indian lands. The government built several forts and dispatched troops to protect the removed Indians from both these threats. Other manifestations of an American presence were the traders who attempted to profit from the cash annuities received by the Indians under terms of the removal treaties, and missionary schools that attempted to extend the benefits of Euro-American material and spiritual life. To one degree or another, each of the tribes was split between a small faction, including elites, favoring assimilation to the dominant culture, and a larger, tradition-oriented group. While the former, whose ranks included most Indian slaveholders, favored the Confederacy, many of the latter favored the Union, and some volunteered their military services. Nevertheless, the United States used the tribes' pro-rebel positions to justify reducing their landholdings so as to make room for other Indians being forcibly removed from elsewhere in the West.

BEYOND THE AMERICAN SPHERE: CANADA AND THE FAR NORTH

The period after the War of 1812 saw British Canada develop a policy of "civilization" similar to that adopted earlier in the United States. Begin-

ning with American and British missionaries, the goal of urging Indians
in Upper Canada to settle in permanent villages and adopt Euro-American
modes of farming became official colonial policy in 1830. Reserves,
sought by Indians in earlier treaty negotiations so they could pursue
traditional subsistence practices, were now to foster acculturation. The
new reserves were resented by many natives while attracting squatters and
traders who sold alcohol or put Indians in their debt. But while enacting
legislation in 1850 to protect Indians from such outside influences, the
government simultaneously sought to relocate some reserves in white-
settled areas and to encourage whites to settle near others, on the grounds
that such contacts would encourage "civilization." An act of 1857 provided for the "enfranchisement" of individual Indians – that is, the granting of full rights of citizenship to adult Indian males who met criteria of
literacy, financial solvency, and "good moral character." Despite minimal
results, these policies were continued after Canada achieved dominion
status in 1867.

Beyond Upper Canada, the Hudson's Bay Company reigned supreme.
Its absorption of the North West Company in 1821 put many Métis and
British mixed-bloods out of work as the new monopoly sought to stream-
line and professionalize its work force. Many of these men settled in Red
River Colony, where they hunted for bison on their own or set up as free
traders with the Indians. In lower Hudson Bay and James Bay, meanwhile, the decline of beaver led the company to increase its employment of
Crees in jobs other than hunting and trapping – principally warehousing
and the building and repairing of ships. In this way, the already close
social and economic connections between Indian communities and the
Company's factories were made still closer. In the far North, from the
Churchill to Mackenzie drainages, the Company extended its network of
trading posts so that most Indians were drawn into at least casual trade ties
by the beginning of the Dominion period.

The Hudson's Bay Company also took over the sea otter trade with
natives on the Northwest Coast. During the 1830s, it outbid and supplanted American traders there, and extended its range by leasing the
Alaska panhandle from the Russian–American Company. Because the
traders were seasonal visitors rather than permanent residents, the Indians
controlled its most direct effects on themselves and their culture. The
principal commodities they sought during the nineteenth century were
cloth and guns, which enhanced the power of chiefs in potlatches and
wars, respectively. These and other goods supplemented rather than sup-

planted their functional equivalents in the native material culture. The upsurge in trading actually enhanced ceremonialism and the production of totem poles and other objects associated with trade and expressions of power. At the same time, the longer-range effects of contact were more destructive. By the mid-nineteenth century, the sea otter population was significantly depleted throughout the region; European epidemics had drastically reduced the native population everywhere; alcohol had become a staple of the trade; and warfare and slavery among natives was more widespread.

The Russian–American Company's abandonment of the Northwest Coast, which also included the sale in 1741 of its post at Fort Ross, California, was part of a shift in the focus of its trading activities to western Alaska. A series of explorations from 1819 to 1844 brought the Inuits and Athapaskans of the Nushagak, Kuskowim, and Yukon drainages into the company's trading orbit. Because these contacts were limited to the exchange of selected material objects for beaver skins, the impact of Russian culture on the natives remained minimal during the nineteenth century.

European exploration of the Arctic coast was initiated after 1819 by a series of Russian expeditions in northwestern Alaska and British expeditions in the Canadian Arctic. The expeditions established contacts, both friendly and hostile, with various Eskimo bands. A few of these contacts were regularized after 1840, when British whaling ships began frequenting sites at Baffin Island and in northern Hudson Bay. Much of the Arctic interior remained entirely unknown to Europeans until the end of the nineteenth century.

As of 1865, the Indian population north of Mexico probably numbered no more than 350,000 — a steep decline from the estimated five to ten million of four centuries earlier. The self-sufficient communities, linked by extensive exchange networks, found throughout the continent in 1500 were to be found only in some Arctic and Subarctic areas. Elsewhere, surviving Indians were being forced into positions of economic dependency, the most glaring form of which was the barren reservation with its annuities, government agents, and missionaries holding out the promise of "civilization." In the face of such conditions, the most remarkable feature of native life in 1865 was the extent to which even the most deprived and demoralized communities survived and continued to reflect, if only in attenuated form, identities and traditions that predated the upheavals of recent centuries. At the same time, a survey of the continent and the immense wealth it had generated by 1865 would have to acknowledge the process by which Indians were separated from the land and other resources as fundamental to American economic history.

2

THE AFRICAN BACKGROUND
TO AMERICAN COLONIZATION

JOHN K. THORNTON

GEOGRAPHICAL BACKGROUND

The vast majority of the Africans who came to populate the English colonies of North America and the Caribbean came from a region we can designate as Atlantic Africa. It stretched from the Senegal River in northern Africa to the Angolan port city of Benguela in the south. A few African Americans did come from outside this region – inventories and shipping records reveal some people from Madagascar, the areas around the Zambezi basin and perhaps from the east coast of modern-day South Africa – but they were not numerous and came relatively late in the trade.

This region was defined first and foremost by the Atlantic Ocean, because the ease of access to the African coast was dictated not only by the presence of water transport routes but also by the fact that once mastered, the wind and current regime of the south Atlantic made fairly easy linkage for sailing ships between African and American destinations. It was also defined on the north and south by desert regions. North of the Senegal, the Sahara desert and its barren coast made for little trade or navigation; to the south, the Namib desert formed a similar barrier. Even though the Portuguese had a colony in Angola since the late sixteenth century, they had barely explored the region south of Benguela by the 1780s.

Visitors to Atlantic Africa from the sixteenth to the eighteenth centuries divided this vast stretch of land into "coasts," each characterized by its own demographic composition, climatic conditions, transportation network, and economy. The names varied from language to language and time period to time period, but the general geography was sufficiently consistent for a clear pattern to develop. In all, there were five coasts –

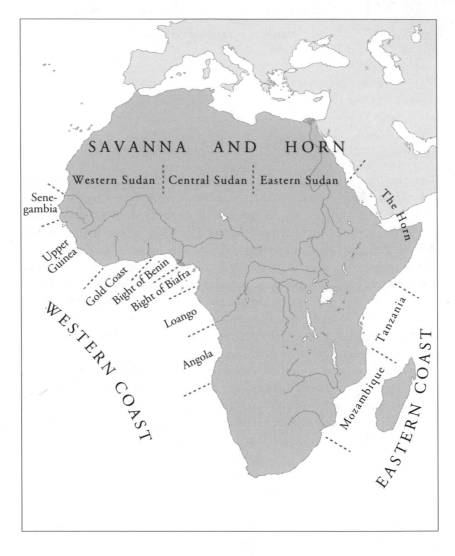

SAVANNA AND HORN

Western Sudan | Central Sudan | Eastern Sudan

Sene-
gambia

The Horn

Upper
Guinea

Gold Coast
Bight of Benin
Bight of Biafra

Loango

Tanzania

WESTERN COAST

Angola

EASTERN COAST

Mozambique

Slave origins

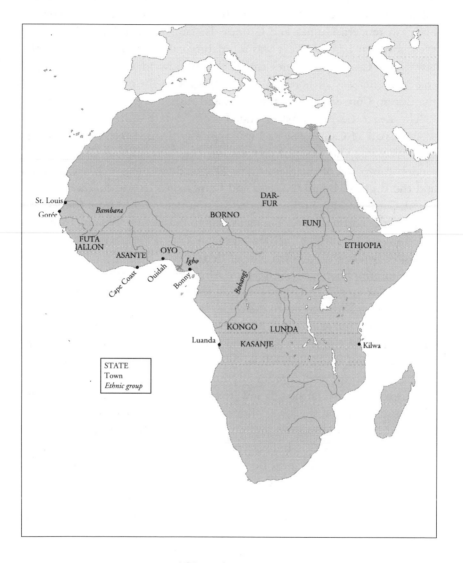

St. Louis
Gorée
Bambara
FUTA
JALLON
ASANTE
OYO
Igbo
Cape Coast
Ouidah
Bonny
Bobangi
BORNO
DAR-
FUR
FUNJ
ETHIOPIA
KONGO
LUNDA
Luanda
KASANJE
Kilwa

STATE
Town
Ethnic group

African slavery, 1750

Upper Guinea Coast, Ivory Coast, Lower Guinea Coast, Gabon Coast, Angola Coast – with some subdivisions.

Starting in the north was the *Upper Guinea Coast*, defined by the system of communication delineated by the Senegal and Gambia rivers; it is probably appropriate to add to this region the area that the Portuguese called "Guiné do Capo Verde," which the French called the "Rivières du Sud," in modern Guinea and Guinea–Bissau, down to Sierra Leone and even northern Liberia. Next was a territory called the *Ivory Coast*, or the Kwa Kwa Coast, sometimes called the Windward Coast. The wooded coastal region was anchored in central Liberia on the north and west, and the eastern Côte d'Ivoire on the south and east.

The *Lower Guinea Coast* extended from eastern Côte d'Ivoire to the western part of Cameroons and was typically divided into two parts: the Gold Coast on the west, mostly eastern Côte d'Ivoire and Ghana, and a section composed of the Slave Coast (Togo, Bénin, and western Nigeria) and the Bight of Benin (Nigeria and Cameroons). It was followed by the *Gabon Coast*, another highly wooded section that reached from Cameroons down to the northern part of modern Congo Brazzaville. Finally, there was the *Angola Coast*, which included most of Congo Brazzaville, Zaire, and Angola down to the Angolan port of Benguela.

The interior boundaries of Atlantic Africa were defined in large measure by transport access. In Upper Guinea, where rivers coming from deep in the interior provided access to the coast, the Atlantic zone extended inland to the great "interior delta" of the Niger river, from 1,000 to 1,500 kilometers from the sea – a reach which by a European scale equals that of the Danube but which still fell short of the greatest American rivers such as the Mississippi and Amazon. Other rivers also gave interior people access to the coast, although few rivers united such disparate regions. Navigation based on the lower Niger and coming to the Gulf of Guinea in modern Nigeria allowed regular and inexpensive communication between people living 400 to 600 kilometers inland and the coastal people (on the scale of a Rhine or Rhone in Europe or the Hudson and Susquehanna in America), but none of the other river systems in west Africa were as helpful. In central Africa, the Zaire river connected people as far as 600 kilometers from the coast with the Atlantic, and the Kwanza gave similar deep access.

Where river routes did not allow deep access, Atlantic Africa was really a coastal region. The Ivory and Kwa Kwa coasts were virtually unknown to Europeans even in the early nineteenth centuries, largely because their business there was restricted to the people along the immediate coastline. Another such stretch lay along the Gabon Coast, where contact with the Atlantic was restricted to coastal people.

Where rivers connected the coastal regions with the interior, the coastal rivers, lakes, and lagoons often allowed considerable lengthwise navigation and communication along the coast, in many ways equivalent to the great inland waterway of North America's East Coast. One such system stretched along the west African coast from the Gambia south to Liberia. Although there were interruptions (mostly falls and rapids), it made for nearly 600 kilometers of navigable waterways that gave the Upper Guinea Coast its unity, at least on the coast. A second system made possible coastal navigation between the eastern Gold Coast and the mouth of the Niger, although here, too, there were interruptions over this 1,000-kilometer section of coast that unified the Lower Guinea Coast. Finally, a less useful system of coastal navigation connected the Kwanza with the Ogowe rivers, again with some interruptions but covering some 1,000 kilometers of the Angola Coast.

Climatic and vegetation zones had little role in defining Atlantic Africa, although they shaped the economies and societies of the people who lived in the various zones. Broadly speaking, Atlantic Africa was divided into three climatic and vegetation zones: a northern zone lying south of the Sahara where the scrubland of the Sahel gradually turned to open savanna, then wooded savanna, and the lush tropical rain forest on the south. The different vegetation results from rainfall patterns: annual rainfall increased steadily from north to south. A line passing about 100 to 200 kilometers inland from the south coast of west Africa demarcated the northern border of the great equatorial tropical rain forest, with its very high rainfall. With one exception, the so-called "Benin Gap" in modern Bénin, the entire south coast of west Africa was originally thickly forested, as was the central African region extending south toward the mouth of the Zaire river. Below the Zaire, and stretching south to the Namib desert, is another zone of wooded savanna, savanna, and scrubland that mirrors the pattern in the north of west Africa. It is delineated by a similar rainfall gradient, anchored in the forest on the north and the desert to the south.

The division of climatic and vegetation zones did not exercise a decisive effect either on settlement patterns or on the pattern of interaction with the Atlantic. Thus the open country of west Africa north of modern Guinea Bissau was moderately well populated and deeply involved with the Atlantic, as was the similar country to the south of the rain forest. On

the other hand, the two regions least involved with the Atlantic, the Ivory
and Gabon coasts, lay in the forest. But this was not a decisive climatic
determinant – the Gold Coast (modern Ghana) and the coast of modern
Nigeria also lay in the rain forest but were among the most deeply involved regions in Africa.

Neither did the climatic and vegetation zones shape the demography of
Africa decisively. While population was quite sparse in the central African
rain forest, the highest population densities of Atlantic Africa – over
thirty people per square kilometer in 1700 – were found in the forested
regions of southern Nigeria and Ghana along the lower Guinea Coast. The
open plains and wooded savannas of Upper Guinea had lower population
densities, averaging perhaps ten people per square kilometer in 1700,
with higher concentrations along the rivers and lower levels in the spaces
between them. The southern savannas of Angola, however, south of the
equatorial rain forest, were very sparsely populated. Overall densities
rarely exceeded five people per square kilometer in the eighteenth century,
and in many areas, densities below five people per square kilometer were
common.

The uneven distribution of the population, as was the case with differ-
ing climatic zones, was not particularly important in determining the
propensity of Atlantic Africans to participate in trade with other Atlantic
countries in Europe and America. The sparsely populated Angolan Coast,
for example, was one of the most vigorously participating regions and
supplied nearly half of all the slaves that Africa sent to the Americas. On
the other hand, the Ivory and Kwa Kwa coasts, which had population
densities at least double those of Angola, scarcely participated in the
Atlantic economy at all and sent only a handful of slaves. Still, the great
demographic heartland of Atlantic Africa, the Lower Guinea Coast, was
also a major participant in the slave trade, matching Angola in raw
numbers of slaves exported, even if its per capita participation was much
lower.

POLITICAL AND SOCIAL DIVISIONS

Clearly, the decisions to participate in Atlantic trade and the slave trade
were the outcome of human choices, and these choices defined the historical, cultural, and political contours of Atlantic Africa. The divisions and

variations of the Atlantic Africans were critical to understanding the nature of African participation in the Atlantic economy; they also provide an essential background to understanding the role of African people in the Americas.

Atlantic Africans were divided in two ways – by states (political units) and nations (cultural units). These two divisions almost never completely overlapped, and the belief in African *tribes* – combining a common language and custom with a political structure – that had dominated anthropological study of Africa early in this century is now seen to be mistaken. Rather, states and nations made very different claims on their members, were variously defined, and shaped daily life in different ways.

Nations in Africa, as in preindustrial Europe and elsewhere, were ethnolinguistic units, where common language, customs, and religious practices prevailed. Nations commanded no loyalty on their own, and the membership in a nation was either ill defined or changed according to circumstances. Nations were not strictly linguistic divisions. Sometimes common customs, commercial interactions, and exchanges helped to reduce the cultural distance that a strictly linguistic analysis might emphasize.

Recent studies of African religions, art, and archaeology suggest that the distribution of cultural items is not necessarily perfectly correlated with language. Language boundaries, drawn according to mutual intelligibility, can be quite flexible when neighboring languages are closely related, and language ceases to be a useful defining characteristic when there is widespread multilingualism. Similarly, customs, aesthetic norms, religious practices, and other cultural indicators were often exchanged between groups. Inventories of African slaves in French and Iberian colonies recognized about forty different language-based nations among Africans, probably based as much on African perceptions as European or American ones, but modern linguists would recognize as many as 150 languages in the area from which these slaves were drawn.

Religion also helped to define nationality, although like many other customs, it was not as clearly differentiated between nations as language could be. Most African religions were based on continuous revelation rather than scriptural or traditional revelations – that is, religious practice focused on direct and immediate contact between people in This World and the Other World, typically through augury, divination, prophecy, or spirit mediumship. The human priests who facilitated spiritual contact often did not create a religious orthodoxy, since this year's revelations might not be acceptable next year. In only a few cases, such as the Ifà divination of the Yoruba-speaking people and their neighbors, did a widely recognized body of texts create something of a standard system.

Virtually all African religions focused some attention on the recently dead ancestors of living people. These ancestors typically devoted their attention to the affairs of their immediate descendants and were thus family focused. As such, they did little to define nations, and most families accepted that the ancestors of other families were real and valid but of little help to anyone save family members.

On the other hand, most African religions recognized other supernatural beings as well. These might be the ancestors of the ruling group, of the first people to settle an area, deities responsible for particular sections of territory, or eternal deities with power over natural phenomena. Such deities were far more likely to be specific to a nation – or, more commonly, a state – and might regulate the affairs of a large community.

Thus national religions might be defined by such a group of royal ancestors or deities but would not deny the existence or legitimacy of the religious traditions of other nations. Often gods from one tradition might be revealed in another one as contacts between two nations intensified, and the borrowing of deities from one tradition to another was quite common – specifically noted for Allada, Dahomey, and Oyo, who had come to share many of their originally specific deities with each other by the end of the eighteenth century.

This feature was also applied to Christianity and Islam, in that acceptance of these two religious traditions often helped to define an African nation (specifically noted in the Christian Kongo or Muslim states of west Africa). They rarely suppressed the cult of ancestors and often did not replace territorial deities. Africans often had revelations that identified national deities with saints, *jinn*, or angels in Christianity and Islam.

While language, culture, religion, or nationality might make for sentimental attachments between peoples, it was the state that demanded loyalty and service. For most Africans who looked beyond the purely parochial concerns of family or village, it was the state that claimed their loyalty and from which they derived their identity. Ethnonyms of seventeenth- and eighteenth-century Africa were usually state rather than nation names. This was true even in such large states as Asante (which was multinational), or in areas such as the Yoruba-speaking region, where the nation was larger than each state. It was only among African slaves in the Americas that cultural and linguistic identities, rather than state citizenship, determined membership in the "nations" or "countries" into which they divided, and many of the American national names had no corresponding unit in Africa.

African states varied widely in size, composition, and structure. Some were quite large, such as the empire of Mali, or its latter-day successors in the western Sudan: the empire of the Great Fulo, Kaarta, or Segu; or the great central African empire of Lunda. Others were of more modest proportions, such as the Oyo Empire, Benin, Asante, Dahomey, Kongo, Ndongo, or the larger Ovimbundu kingdoms such as Viye or Mbailundu in Angola.

But what is perhaps most striking is the very large number of small, even tiny, states that could be found in Africa. Although it is not possible to map the boundaries of every state in Atlantic Africa before the mid-nineteenth century (or sometimes after), there were surely several hundred states found in that region alone. Most were small, perhaps the size of a county in the United States, a comfortable day's walk across. Such small states — one might call them ministates or even microstates — were completely independent, possessed a capital town of perhaps a few thousand people, and had a dozen or so villages under their immediate control. These would describe the small states along the seventeenth-century Gold Coast and in the region along the Gambia river and Sierra Leone. Olaudah Equiano described his eighteenth-century childhood in one such state in the Igbo-speaking area of modern southeastern Nigeria as "little more than a single large and somewhat dispersed village." In the seventeenth century, as many as 70 percent of the people in Atlantic Africa lived in states whose total population was under 10,000; in the eighteenth century, fewer probably did, for several large states, such as Asante and Dahomey, absorbed many of the smaller states of their region.

The economic impact of such parceled sovereignty varied. On the one hand, as the Upper Guinea region clearly reveals, these small states might form a constant nuisance to trade, charging transit taxes every few miles to travelers engaged in long-distance business. Some were predatory on commerce and their neighbors; others were too small and weak to be able to impose order or enforce law. Because they lacked control over alternate routes, they were also unable to restrict trade very much, and the great merchant groups were able to come to understandings concerning transit taxes, enforcement of laws, and other essentials by threatening to change trade routes to areas that were more amenable. Trade and specialization do not seem to have been adversely affected by the parceled sovereignty: the

internal and international commerce of areas like Sierra Leone and the
Gambia, where there were many small states, was just as vigorous and
efficient as that of the larger states, such as Asante.

ECONOMIC ORGANIZATION

One of the most important roles that African states played was in the
redistribution of wealth. All African states, even the smallest ones, levied
taxes on their inhabitants, sometimes by demanding monetary payments,
often by making demands of a share of production to be delivered in kind,
frequently by demanding labor service. The African wealthy classes, in
turn, derived at least a portion of their own wealth by taking a share of
this revenue, distributed according to office. In this way, officeholding,
whether it was hereditary or appointed, was an important means of achieving income, and the concentrations of wealth generated by kings, territorial rulers, bureaucrats, council members, and other state officials created
a single and primary means of inequality.

This inequality, in turn, helped to shape the economy. Some rulers
demanded that each of the territorial nobles receive labor services to
cultivate fields on behalf of the state, with the revenues from those fields
being a salary for the officeholders. This was done, among other places, in
the seventeenth-century kingdom of Loango. The officeholder might consume the product of the field himself, or with his clients and family
members, or he might sell the product on the market. The market economy would clearly be shaped by decisions that the state official made with
regard to what was planted in the fields, where it was sold, and even how
it was sold.

There were also private channels for state officials to obtain wealth.
Unlike the rich and powerful of Europe and Asia, those of Africa were not
landowners; rather, the people who are called nobles and landowners in
European accounts of Africa were typically state officials who derived their
income from taxes rather than rents. The politically powerful landowner,
whose income was derived from rent and was thus wholly or partially
independent of the state, was not possible in Africa.

African law did not recognize the right to own land as property, although cultivators could have rights to usufruct to any land they had
cleared or used recently, and villages or other units of local life might
distribute land for farming. But such rights did not include the right to

sell land or, more importantly, to let land out to tenants in exchange for rent. Thus, one owned land only as long as one cultivated it or used it as part of a fallowing system.

Private wealth derived instead from rights over dependents. Such dependents might be clients, pawns (people who were contractually dependent for a period of time, often to pay debts), wives, or slaves. Such people might be given land to cultivate by their masters and be required to share their harvest with them, but such land donations did not amount to tenancy. The relationship that drew income from the dependent was a personal one rather than one mediated through ownership of a factor of production.

Clients and pawns were people who had voluntarily attached themselves to the service of a wealthy or powerful person. In exchange for his protection, payment of debts, or perhaps opportunities, the client or pawn would perform labor and other services on behalf of his patron, either for a fixed period or for the duration of the perception of mutual benefits.

In polygamous households, wives might also perform substantial labor on behalf of their husbands. As men became wealthier, they could pay bride price for many wives, whose labor might in turn generate further income. The most visible examples of female labor being used in this way come from the palace economies of Lower Guinea, where households that sometimes had wives numbering in the thousands produced specialty goods (typically textiles) for palace, local, and international consumption.

By far the most important form of dependent labor was slavery. It was common for travelers to find whole villages of slaves producing for a master along major trade routes. Most merchants employed their slaves not only in production but also as porters of goods, as local agents in long-distance business, and even as assistants; slaves also performed personal service of one sort or another.

The great advantage of slaves was they and their production were the personal property of the master. One did not have to hold state office to obtain slaves, although in some societies, such as the seventeenth-century Gold Coast, a person had to pay a fee and perform an expensive ceremony before obtaining the right to own slaves. In this respect, slaves and other dependents performed the function that private landholding did in Europe or Asia. In some cases, private wealth in slaves was more important than state-generated wealth: in seventeenth-century Kongo, for example, the real wealth of the nobility was said to be in their slaves rather than in the incomes of the provinces to which they were assigned.

Private wealth could also have political implications. Detailed records for the coastal region of the Gold Coast, for example, show that men who acquired private wealth and invested it in slaves might ultimately use the wealth, the people they controlled, and weapons to make themselves independent or even masters of the rulers of the state. John Cabes, a merchant who eventually became ruler of a quasi-independent state composed of his slaves and subjects in the late seventeenth century, provides a model of what private wealth could do when invested in politics.

AFRICAN POLITICS: THE DYNAMICS OF STATES

Much of the domestic politics of African states was shaped by this dynamic of wealth as well as by constitutional principles that were buried more deeply in their history. The actual form of African states varied almost as widely as they did in size. One late-seventeenth-century observer, the Dutch merchant Willem Bosman, classed the states of the Gold Coast into two sorts: republics and monarchies. The republics were governed by councils, one called the *caboceiros* (chiefs) and the other the *mancebos* (young men), while the monarchies were under the absolute rule of a single executive authority. Much of the history of Atlantic Africa in the sixteenth to eighteenth centuries involved the dynamic between these two extremes of state form.

With modifications, Bosman's analysis could work for many parts of Africa. In the Senegal valley, the early explorers found the Jolof Empire dominating the regions. While Jolof controlled a large area, power within it was diffuse – the king had no powers to tax, and his government was checked by territorial nobles who controlled local areas. This loose organization was challenged in an extended civil war in the early sixteenth century, from which smaller but more autocratic states, such as Kajoor and Waalo, emerged. In these states, royal slaves (later called, disparagingly, *ceddo*) acted as dependent agents of the rulers, thus allowing more centralized control. In the eighteenth century, the *ceddo*, acting as a corporate group, often organized informal but effective collective government. Efforts at centralization in this region were often resisted by collectively organized bodies (often called *republics* in European sources) of religious leaders (*marabouts*), who occasionally led revolts (as did Nasir al-Din in 1673–7) or even seized power (as did Malik Sy in Bondu in 1690, and Abd al-Kadir in Futa Tooro in 1776).

In the south of Upper Guinea and in the interior of the Senegambian region, the states of the period descended from the powerful medieval empire of Mali. In the valley of the Senegal, the empire of Great Fulo succeeded Mali in the seventeenth century, although it disappeared as a regional power by the early eighteenth century. Along the south coast, Mali rule had never interfered with local polities, beyond taking tribute, and even this stopped in the early seventeenth century. Reports from the period after 1580 mention many local systems of government. Some involved councils (often composed of members from specific families) who ruled in place of a king, or through a figurehead king. Others involved much more autocratic forms. In Sierra Leone, in particular, kings appear to have been strong; they selected the members of their councils as well as the territorial rulers, who served at royal pleasure.

Lower Guinea was often characterized by the rise of new, large, and powerful centralized states, especially after 1650. In the sixteenth century, the Gold Coast was composed of dozens of small, independent states whose wars sometimes disrupted the trade of the area. In the late seventeenth century, however, much more powerful and unitary states emerged in the interior and began to exercise an incomplete authority over the coast. The first of these, Denkyira and Akwamu, arose in the 1680s. They yielded to the Asante kingdom, which by the middle of the eighteenth century had come to dominate the interior, although never quite swallowing up the coast, where a Kingdom of Fante prevailed. Asante rulers were not absolute; its original constitution had been a federation bound together by oaths of loyalty, and leaders of the original state exercised a substantial check on the ruler. As a bureaucracy under royal control emerged in the mid-eighteenth century, checks were still placed on royal power. Even the rulers of conquered territories still had some leeway for operation. In the eighteenth century, Asante was disrupted by major revolts, such as those in the 1720s and again in the 1750s, in which conquered rulers disrupted either Asante's rights over them or the members of the federation challenged royal authority.

The rise of Dahomey in the interior of the so-called "Slave Coast" in the late seventeenth century was similar to the rise of Asante. Dahomey's predecessors, Allada and Whydah, both had quite autocratic systems of government, founded in part on slaves and royal wives as dependent rulers and administrators, a system which was perfected as Dahomey took over the coast in 1724–7. By the mid-eighteenth century, Dahomey had become the epitome, for foreigners at least, of African despotism. Older states of Lower Guinea, such as the Oyo Empire and Benin, were governed by hereditary rulers whose power was checked by councils of various compositions. The rulers often sought to create dependent positions, but the political dynamic included considerable resistance by council members to royal absolutism. A civil war that pitted councils against the king, and each other, tore Benin apart in the late seventeenth century, and it was a much more decentralized balance between king and council that replaced it after about 1720. Oyo, like Benin, was governed by a combination of king and councils and suffered through a long and devastating civil war when the two components of government fought each other after the 1780s, a war that lasted intermittently into the nineteenth century.

As the western end of Lower Guinea saw the emergence of more centralized states, the eastern end, especially the Niger Delta and surrounding areas, became a realm of tiny states governed by republican types of government. Olaudah Equiano's home state of Essaka, in the Igbo-speaking part of the Niger delta, was in an area of very small states. Essaka was ruled entirely by members of an association of titleholders, most of whom had obtained their titles by purchase or co-optation, whom Equiano called (by a Classical analogy) "judges and Senators." They acquired their titles by wealth, could not necessarily pass the titles on to their children, and governed the state collectively.

Central Africa, called the Angola Coast by European visitors, was dominated by three states in the sixteenth and early seventeenth centuries. In the north, the kingdom of Loango held sway, while south of the Zaire River lay the kingdoms of Kongo and Ndongo. There were also smaller states, in the highlands between Kongo and Ndongo, and in the great central Angolan plateau south of Ndongo. In the seventeenth century, Kongo was a highly autocratic society, mostly because Kongo kings succeeded in concentrating large dependent populations around their capital of Mbanza Kongo (São Salvador after 1596). However, a succession dispute and civil war after 1665 resulted in the destruction and abandonment of the capital and the partitioning of the kingdom among several factions of the royal family. This situation both decentralized the country and promoted frequent civil wars. Although less well documented, Loango seems to have undergone a similar, though much less violent, transformation. The central state of seventeenth-century descriptions was not nearly as authoritarian in the mid- to late eighteenth century, when regional-based powers challenged the monarch by disrupting succession of kings.

Ndongo, on the other hand, was in the process of becoming much more centralized in the sixteenth century, as royal slaves under the king's control provided military strength and staffed a bureaucracy. But a civil war that involved the claims of territorial rulers, a succession dispute, and Portuguese interference from their coastal colony of Angola, disrupted Ndongo throughout most of the seventeenth century. Queen Njinga (1582–1663) eventually reconstituted a highly centralized kingdom in eastern Ndongo and Matamba toward the end of her life. Njinga's combined kingdom and Kasanje, another state founded out of the same turmoil, dominated the middle reaches of the Kwango. Both these states, however, were torn apart by tensions between central power and wealthy private slaveholders in the late eighteenth and nineteenth centuries.

Beyond the Kwango in the interior, the rise of a powerful and centralized Lunda empire in the late seventeenth century was the most important state process; while south of Ndongo in the central highlands, in the seventeenth century, a little-known state called Bembe was replaced by two important larger states, Viye and Mbailundu. Viye was less centralized – some of the local nobility had substantial powers – while Mbailundu was much more autocratic and also more capable of expanding rapidly.

The dynamics of state interactions had important impacts on the economy. In the more centralized states, for example, royal interests played an important role in economic decisions, private wealth tended to be limited, and trade was centralized. In the less centralized polities, on the other hand, commercial decisions were made by a diffuse group of merchants, and private wealth was more extensive. Furthermore, the connections between wealth and political power, especially in promoting the interests of private wealthy citizens, played an important role in creating stability or instability.

THE PRODUCTIVE ECONOMY

Atlantic Africa, this diverse area of many states and nations, was also a region of considerable economic diversity. It is difficult to generalize about the economy of Atlantic Africa, just as it is difficult to delineate its geographical, political, and ethnic boundaries.

As in all preindustrial economies, African economies were essentially agricultural in the sense that the majority of the time that people spent in productive activities was to tend crops or raise livestock. Contemporary descriptions allow the delineation of several distinct agricultural regimes. In coastal west Africa, from modern Liberia north to Senegambia, rice was the main staple, grown in a complex agronomic system that produced high yields but required considerable labor. Rice growing along the coast and in marshy areas, as well as along river basins farther inland, was supplemented by other crops in less well watered areas. Millet and sorghum were particularly important. They were later supplemented by exotic crops such as American maize and cassava.

Where ecological conditions permitted it, stock was raised, and cattle were plentiful in the drier inland areas. Other parts of the region were less favorable to cattle raising, and small stock, such as chickens and pigs, provided much of the dietary protein. Fish were consumed fresh along the entire African coast and near fish-bearing rivers and were preserved by salting or drying for areas without substantial fishing areas.

Africans produced beer and, in most areas, made wine from a variety of palm oils. Tree crops and peanuts were especially important for edible oils, and arboriculture was an important activity in all regions.

Lower Guinea had a different regime of crops from Upper Guinea, making much more extensive use of yams and, later, exotic root crops, such as cassava. Rice was fairly rare in this region, though millet and sorghum and, later, American maize provided the basic grain crops. Most of the region was not favorable for cattle; small stock provided protein, along with fish. Palm wine was especially important as a beverage, while palm oil figured prominently in cooking.

The Angola region also had less rice cultivation, though some was grown along the lower course of the Zaire River in Kongo. Millet and sorghum were gradually replaced by American maize and then often by cassava in the seventeenth and eighteenth centuries. Stock raising was variable; some highlands regions, such as Ndongo, were major cattle-raising areas, while other regions, such as the majority of the kingdom of Kongo, produced few cattle. As in other parts of Africa, fish — caught fresh along rivers and the coast, or dried and salted elsewhere — were critical in the diet. Angolans, like Africans in other regions, drank palm wine and various brewed grain drinks and used palm oils extensively in cooking.

Although the exact mode of food preparation varied widely, some generalizations are appropriate for Atlantic Africa. Grain crops were mostly eaten in the form of stiff gruels or porridge. Typically, in the case of American maize, millet, and sorghum, the grain was pounded into fine powder and then boiled to the desired consistency. Rice was boiled without much preparation, while cassava was made into flour and then boiled. The gruel was then eaten with stews made of an oil (usually palm or peanut) base, using whatever meat or fish was available, beans, spices, and vegetables. Often the gruel was rolled in balls and dipped in stews, though sometimes the stew was put on the gruel. Fresh fruit, leaves, and green vegetables were sometimes cooked separately as side dishes.

By modern standards, African agriculture of the period was not very productive, but by the standards of the seventeenth or eighteenth century, Africa was a fairly advanced region. Although Africans used quite simple tools (no group in Atlantic Africa used the plow, for example) and practiced various forms of what is called *shifting cultivation*, crop yields were high. European visitors, who presumably had the performance of their home economies as a base, typically described African agriculture as very productive. They usually believed that Africans did not work very hard, but they thought that the yields they obtained were very high by the standards of the time. Levels of productivity achieved by modern farmers using similar tools and techniques in Africa point to high yields relative to those achieved by sixteenth- or eighteenth-century European farmers. In the more recent past, crop yields were much higher than those of seventeenth-century Europe, though low by the standards of modern scientific agriculture.

One measure of the efficiency of agriculture is vital rates, since they reflect at least indirectly on the capacity of the society to provide itself with adequate food and shelter. It is possible to discuss vital rates in this period only for the region of Angola, where Christian baptismal records from Kongo and the Portuguese colony of Angola provide data. Birth rates were quite high during this period, as high as forty-five to fifty per thousand – somewhat higher therefore than the birth rates for western Europe, though equaled and even exceeded in many parts of America, such as French Canada. These high birth rates were probably accomplished by a fairly low age of first conception, since data on the spacing of children suggest intervals equal to or even longer than those experienced in Europe at the same time. Perhaps the spacing reflected low rates of fertility of the polygamous households.

Infant and child mortality kept the high birth rates from causing explosive population growth. Infant mortality in seventeenth-century Kongo was probably around 250 to 300 per thousand in normal (nonfamine) years, which compares favorably with infant mortality rates in western Europe and America. Somewhat higher rates of child mortality in Africa, however, gave societies in Europe and Africa general parity in survival rates to age 18: roughly half of all children born survived to this age.

As in other parts of the world, population growth was checked by periodic catastrophic episodes of mortality occasioned by drought and famine, which affected rates of infant and child mortality and tended to kill off the elderly. Warfare and enslavement, which affected otherwise healthy people in the adult age brackets, also killed or removed many. These phenomena produced an overall low growth rate, in central Africa tending toward two per thousand, but this figure is not well supported by data and must be considered a rough guess.

The level of productivity in basic food production necessarily required that the majority of the population work in agriculture and hence live near the lands that they farmed. As elsewhere in the world, Africa was a land of rural villages with relatively small towns. African villages varied widely in size and form, often according to ecological conditions. In some areas, such as the Senegal valley, where the river was essential for irrigation, settlements spread out along the river valley without clear nucleation, although, based on social conditions, one can speak of villages. In central Africa, on the other hand, villages were fairly compact and frequently stockaded, as the low population density encouraged wild animals. These villages were quite small, however, according to travelers and Portuguese administrative reports, averaging about 200 people each. But in Lower Guinea, much larger settlements were the norm, often exceeding 1,000 people, though many were not highly nucleated. Such concentrated numbers were made possible by reliance on high-yielding root crops, although the fields were often located some distance from the village. In the Yoruba-speaking regions, settlement was more often in small towns than in villages, with populations in excess of 1,000, but this distribution frequently meant that people had to walk fairly long distances to reach their fields.

African residential construction, especially in areas with small villages, adopted a strategy of building fairly small and uncomplicated structures that required little investment in skill and labor and that were abandoned and rebuilt often. In a tropical climate, where severe cold was rarely a problem, this strategy met the shelter requirements of the population and allowed more sanitary conditions than building more complex and permanent structures might. Thus, the tendency for buildings in tropical climates to become rotten and infested with insects, rodents, and reptiles was offset by frequent destruction and rebuilding. This construction strategy made

African villages very mobile, moving every few years. It fit in, on the one hand, with the absence of private landed property, which gave villagers little stake in particular locations, and on the other hand, with shifting, long-fallow cultivation, which favored movement of the population.

This construction strategy was not universal, however. Larger and more permanent constructions were built to meet the needs of religious and political elites for prestige construction, or for strategic and defense considerations. Large cities, such as Oyo and Benin on the Guinea Coast, and Jenne and Timbuktu on the Niger River, and São Salvador in Kongo, can be documented in the same location for centuries, and their buildings were more permanent. Such cities typically emerged as capitals or political centers, and the most elaborate buildings were temples, mosques, churches, and palaces. In some cases, such as the Yoruba cities and Benin, the move toward more permanent and elaborate residential structures accompanied the growth of such cities. In other cases, such as central Africa, the residential population continued to be quite mobile, and cities were more population concentrations than nucleated settlements. The capitals of the Lunda Empire moved frequently within a fairly small densely settled zone, for example, while São Salvador's population was spread out over more than 100 square kilometers. Sometimes construction of elite buildings conformed to the rural pattern, as in the case of the Njinga's palace, which was large but constructed impermanently. Njinga's display of wealth came not so much from the architecture as from the elaborate and expensive mats that made up the walls of her palace.

In addition to its agriculture and construction industry, Africa possessed a manufacturing sector that supplied the population's needs for tools and clothing as well as luxury goods. As with agriculture, African manufacturing was done with fairly simple tools and techniques, yet the quality of output was as high as that from any other part of the world. Recent archaeological and anthropological research has revealed, for example, that Africans had discovered a process to make high-quality steel using a furnace design that was fairly simple and required little concentration of labor. This created a mobile smelting industry that was characterized by fairly small enterprises, since furnaces were often only used a few times before being abandoned. The mobile smelters, in turn, could better exploit fuel sources with their small, technically simple production processes.

African textiles have also been reevaluated in recent years, and their quality is now generally regarded as good, even if the looms on which they were produced were simple. In general, Africans relied in textile production on a large and highly skilled work force rather than on machines. Africans were particularly interested in textiles; in addition to textile use in clothing, textiles were used as wall coverings – a use that may have accounted for as much textile production as clothing. Woven mats, used as floor covering or for sleeping, were also employed widely.

In many parts of Africa, production was integrated into village life rather than being undertaken by specialists in urban centers, as was true in much of seventeenth-century Europe. In central Africa, the major textile-producing centers were located in rural areas, and industrial towns were unknown, though some of the villages, especially those located close to sources of supply of raw materials, did focus special attention on textile production. Most textile workers were not specialists, since they were also engaged in agricultural production, but the level of skill was high, as was the quality and quantity of their output. Trade statistics gathered in Luanda in the early seventeenth century, where many of the textiles produced in eastern Kongo were sold, suggest that hundreds of thousands of meters of textiles were produced and sold annually. Such a level of production places Kongo among the major textile-producing centers of the world, though the production was done in rural areas using very simple tools.

But decentralized industrial production with thousands of part time but highly skilled rural workers was not necessarily the only way in which manufacturing was organized. In Lower Guinea, there was concentrated textile production, often of high-quality products for sale on regional markets, which coexisted with rural village industry geared to local needs. Seventeenth-century reports, for example, mention a palace industry in the coastal city of Whydah employing king's wives (who sometimes numbered in the thousands) to produce textiles for local consumption and sale on local, regional, and even world markets. A similar palace industry was found in Warri, in southern Nigeria, at about the same time, and was no doubt found in other towns and palaces of the area. Later travelers' accounts of the Oyo Empire, which, like Kongo, was a major textile-producing area, speak of an urban-based industry which might include as many as 1,000 weaving establishments in a single city. But this weaving always coexisted with the local production of cloth. The Igbo ex-slave, Olaudah Equiano, recalling life in his home village in eastern Nigeria in the mid-eighteenth century, noted both the home production of cloth by local people as well as the importation of cloth made elsewhere in the same region, and perhaps abroad.

In many parts of Upper Guinea, there were specialists in textile production, forming what some have called *artisan castes*. Although the industry was not concentrated in towns, and the making of thread was done in every village, weaving was done by migrant specialists. This finished cloth, like that from other parts of Africa, often entered regional markets, frequently being transported along the rivers by both African and European merchants.

The production of metals tended to be more concentrated than that of textiles, simply because the geography of metals required some concentration. Typically, industrial centers or districts were concentrated in areas where abundant local deposits of iron could be found, near wooded areas that could supply fuel, especially (in Upper and Lower Guinea) along the margin between the rain forest and the wooded savanna. However, within such industrial regions, the actual production sites were quite mobile and small and, as in textile production, often employed many part-time workers assisting a core of skilled masters.

A recent archaeological study of the industry in Bassar (modern Togo in Lower Guinea) shows that as the industry grew, there was a concentration of people, though never in industrial towns. Since African metal production relied on wood to fire the furnaces, smelters and smiths had to move frequently as forests were cut for fuel. This discouraged concentration of the industry, as can be seen by the long-range ecological degradation of the Sankarani river in the heartland of the old empire of Mali, when the presence of the city forced the concentration of smelteries. This led to the eventual abandonment of the area and of the industry in the seventeenth century.

The result of these environmental and organizational factors was that steel was produced in great industrial regions where furnaces were scattered throughout the area. Bassar in Lower Guinea was one such district, while in central Africa, one can still see considerable slag heaps formed by the steel industry of Kongo, which was concentrated along the Inkisi valley in the eastern part of the country and along the banks of the Zaire River. In the Portuguese colony of Angola, eighteenth-century officials complained that the relative decentralization of steel production made taxation difficult. They sought to concentrate it at Nova Oeiras and to endow it with some European technology, though without long-term success.

The mining and smelting of metal coexisted with a blacksmithing industry that had branches in a great many villages. Raw metal was shaped or reshaped to meet the specific needs of villagers or to sell on local markets. Occasionally, such final production was centralized. The city of Benin in Lower Guinea was the center of a concentration of smiths, mostly working on copper or other precious metals. A whole quarter of the city was given over to metalworkers, and they had dozens, if not hundreds, of shops in the quarter, according to visitors of the seventeenth century.

THE COMMERCIAL ECONOMY

The African productive economy gave rise to extensive trade and commerce. Regional specialization and fairly long-range trade were supported wherever transportation axes made them possible. Rivers and inland waterways were especially important in the development of substantial trade networks. For example, the coastal system of rivers, creeks, and lagoons in Upper Guinea allowed for waterborne transport and, as a result, made it possible for agricultural specialization to develop. Thus, there were regions that specialized in the production of rice, others that produced yams, and yet others that produced grain crops such as millet. Surpluses were shipped to large regional markets by small, shallow draft watercraft. The maze of waterways that made up the delta of the Niger River and its surrounding waterways was a similarly integrated region of highly specialized production, as was the great inland waterway that stretched westward, with interruptions, as far as the Gold Coast. Seventeenth- and eighteenth-century reports note a vigorous trade in grain, fish, salt, and other goods along these waterways, as well as villages and even whole districts that specialized in the production of bulk agricultural goods for the market.

Even in areas that were not as blessed with transportation networks, local markets were still quite active, even if the villages tended more toward self-sufficiency in foodstuffs and bulk goods. But salt, iron, other metals, some types of foodstuffs (for example, dried fish), and some types of textiles could still be profitably transported considerable distances to allow markets.

With this level of market activity, African economies needed currencies, and there was a variety in use. In Africa, as elsewhere, it was common for frequently demanded or precious commodities to perform a monetary role, as seen by the iron bar or copper wire currencies of west and central

Africa. Peasants might often make transactions using cloth, chickens, or other domestic animals as a standard of value.

In west Africa, gold and cowrie shells formed the major monetary substances. Sources dating from the twelfth century onward provide information on the conversion rates between gold and cowries. Accounting (even if done without writing) and credit or long-distance monetary exchanges were often done using cowries as monies of account. In central Africa, the shells known as *nzimbu* were clearly such a monetary unit, used to calculate debt and taxes and to settle debts even when actual specie did not change hands or when the real exchange was made in goods rather than money. By early in the seventeenth century, the shells had been joined by cloth of a special length and quality, typically the high-quality cloth of eastern Kongo or Loango, called *libongo*.

Most goods that came to local markets were carried there by their makers, as far as the limited documentation permits us to know. Africa also had professional merchants, specialists in trade, although they tended to concentrate their energies on the kinds of goods that could travel long distances profitably. Such products were typically goods with high value to weight (precious metals, finished quality manufactures, salt, or dried meat and fish), and were often consumed by the upper classes and wealthier people.

Professional merchants could be found in every part of Atlantic Africa. They often formed communities that settled in towns under their own government and linked in networks that Philip Curtin has dubbed a "trading diaspora." A good example of such a trading diaspora is the Mandinka-speaking Juula and Jakhanke of the Upper Guinea. According to Jakhanke histories, these traders began in the city of Jakha (on the Bafing River, a tributary of the Senegal) and, following their business, fanned out to other locations. Jakhanke towns were founded, under the auspices of local rulers in the areas where they settled, and were permitted the right to govern themselves. Sixteenth-century Europeans met Jakhanke at coastal points as far afield as Gambia and the Gold Coast; hence, they imagined that the city called "Jaga" (Jakha) was some great metropolis that controlled the trade of all west Africa. The Jakhanke and other trading groups like the Juula did indeed dominate the commerce of Upper Guinea, becoming involved not just in moving goods but also in the production of goods on plantations worked by their slaves or in ships where artisans employed or enslaved by them made cloth or tanned leather or produced metal goods.

Although they were not quite as concentrated a group as the sixteenth-century Europeans imagined, they did manage to operate in concert and shared commercial information to permit switching the direction of trade from one port or one town to another as market conditions warranted. This was not through political control but simply through information sharing and informal meeting among the most important leaders, whose combined business gave them the capacity to influence the market.

Both the Jakhanke and the Juula were also professional Islamic religious scholars (*'ulama* or marabouts), and their business as traders and their profession as scholars and judges were intertwined. Indeed, this connection between trade and religion was so intimate that both contemporary witnesses and modern scholars have debated whether they were principally religious scholars who took up commerce as a sideline, or traders first who, upon conversion to Islam, became devoted to scholarship. Whatever the historical relationship or the self-perception of the merchants, however, they were the dominant professional trading group in Upper Guinea.

A similar network, made up of people from the Hausa states in what is now northern Nigeria and Niger, bordered on the Mandinka-speaking trading networks along the Niger River. Hausa-speaking merchants, like their Mandinka-speaking counterparts farther west, developed a complex trade diaspora connecting the Hausa cities of the interior with coastal locations, especially in what is today Nigeria, and communities of them were to be found in the courts of Oyo and Benin in the eighteenth century, as well as farther afield in the northern districts and courts of Asante and Dahomey (where one could also find Mandinka-speakers).

In addition to these large networks based in the interior cities of west Africa, there were smaller ones in other parts of the coast. For example, traders from the Balanta region in Upper Guinea operated a complex trading network along the coastal waterways of modern Guinea–Bissau, while Akani traders in the seventeenth-century Gold Coast posted "trade captains" in most of the major trading ports to look after the interests of the major inland towns of the Akan federation (later to become the kingdom of Asante).

When European merchants set up operations on the various coasts of Africa, their local employees, both European and African, took to private trading in the immediate area of the coastal forts, posts, or offshore islands where European commerce was based. These local employees often broke the official bonds of loyalty to their country and shipping concerns (such as the great slave-trading houses or government-sponsored companies) and joined local elite families or merchants, creating a group of culturally and racially mixed people. They in turn developed a trading diaspora that stretched into the interior, especially along the Senegal and Gambia rivers but also along the coast in Upper Guinea.

One group, who spoke a form of Creole Portuguese as their trade language, was originally based on the Portuguese offshore island colony of Cape Verde, with branches on the mainland and offshoots in the interior. This section was joined in the seventeenth century by French Creole-speaking groups based on the French post on the island of Gorée in Senegal that focused on the trade of that river, and by English Creole-speaking groups on the Gambia and along the coast of Sierra Leone. A second group was based originally at the Portuguese posts of Mina (on the Gold Coast) and on the offshore island of São Tomé. Their trade was focused on the Gold Coast and Lower Guinea in general. In the seventeenth century, this group was joined by merchants with Dutch, Danish, German, French, and English connections focused on various Gold Coast forts or the trading port of Whydah.

All these commercial groups were proud of being Christian (though unlike their Muslim counterparts, and sometime rivals, they were not priests), spoke Creole versions of English, French, or Portuguese, and dressed in modified European fashion. Although their origin was rooted in European commerce, by the late sixteenth or early seventeenth century, they had become essentially an African commercial group whose relations with the European-based trading concerns were not always cordial.

The Angola region possessed its own trading diaspora. By the seventeenth century, one of the most important of these diasporas was the Vili network, based on the ports of the kingdom of Loango in modern-day Congo–Brazzaville and Gabon and on the ports Malemba in Kakongo and Kabinda in Ngoyo. Vili traders controlled a network of towns and settlements across the Kingdom of Kongo into the interior as far as the Maleba Pool and Kwango River and south to the Portuguese colony of Angola and its eastern neighbors along the Kwango River. Although these settlements did not answer to the government of their home countries, each one did have a "captain" who was strictly obeyed by others in the settlement. A second network, based on the Kongo province of Zombo in the Inkisi valley, was interlocked with the Vili merchants but reached into the interior beyond the Kwango to the Lunda Empire, which came to prominence in the late seventeenth century.

The Angolan region had an even more extensive and developed Afro-European trading network than did west Africa, surely because the Portuguese colony of Angola (founded 1576) was both larger and more extensive than any holding by any other European power in west Africa. The *pombeiors*, originally slaves employed by Portuguese merchants based in Luanda to travel to markets in Kongo and Maleba Pool (known in the sixteenth century as Mpombo), had become much more independent of the European interests during the seventeenth century. There were two great interior diasporas. One was based in eastern Angola at Mbaka (Ambaca) and stretched into the interior as far as Lunda by the late eighteenth century. The second one was based on the port of Benguela and the interior Portuguese presidio of Caconda (founded 1769) and mingled with the first diaspora in the Ovimbundu kingdoms of the central highlands of Angola.

European trade, and with it the slave trade, fit into this larger dynamic of African politics and economy. Europeans were unable to accomplish much in the way of conquest in Africa. Early attempts at raiding the African coast, by the earliest Portuguese sailors to reach west African waters (after 1444), were largely unsuccessful and ultimately resulted in several Portuguese defeats. By 1462, Portuguese emissaries to various African rulers had established diplomatic and commercial relations with them, a situation that was to prevail over the remaining period of the slave trade, being taken up in turn by Dutch, French, and English traders who followed Portuguese merchants to African waters. Outside of Angola, European posts in Africa from the fifteenth to the nineteenth centuries were essentially trading posts that remained there under the sufferance of African rulers, often being required to pay rent or tribute.

EUROPEAN TRADE WITH AFRICA

European trade with Africa was of two sorts: shipboard trade or factory trade. Shipboard trade took place in areas where Europeans were either unwilling or unable to establish posts on shore. Such trade prevailed, for example, along the Ivory and Kwa Kwa coasts and on the Gabon Coast, where there was relatively little trade and where African authorities were sometimes hostile to any shore-based participation. Trade in these areas was always problematic, with considerable bad faith and trickery on both sides.

Factory trade of one sort or another was far more common. Factories were established by formal arrangements between African political authorities and European merchants or governments. They often originated in gold-exporting regions like the Gold Coast or the Senegambian area because of the security needs created by high-value trading items. The formality of the arrangements allowed for (1) debts to be collected, (2) those who violated market rules to be punished, and (3) general security for goods and slaves to be provided. Portuguese communities dotted the entire coast of Upper Guinea by the end of the sixteenth century, although the Portuguese government sometimes discouraged actual settlement. When Dutch, French, and English merchants began to take over the seaborne trade, some of these communities were occupied by the new powers, and other posts were established under their own control, such as Gorée Island (French) and James Island (English).

Factories were more elaborate on the coast of Lower Guinea, especially in the Gold Coast area. Formal Portuguese presence began with the establishment of the post of São Jorge da Mina (later known as Elmina) in 1482, with outstations established at other points along the coast in the following century. When merchants from northern Europe entered this trade in the late sixteenth and seventeenth centuries, they established more posts. Many of these were fortified and came to be almost independent of the African rulers on whose hospitality they relied, but for the most part, they kept making tribute payments to Africans for the right to maintain their forts.

The Slave Coast, which included the area between the Volta and Niger rivers, was less well established, a variety of posts being established for greater or lesser amounts of time. The Portuguese, French, English, and Dutch posts at Whydah were unfortified and coexisted within the same town under the sovereignty of the ruler of Whydah, and subsequently the king of Dahomey when Whydah came under Dahomey's control in 1727.

The Niger Delta and Benin region (sometimes called the Bight of Benin) were areas where commerce was less well established in posts. An early Portuguese post at Ughoton, Benin's port, was abandoned in favor of shipboard trade early in the sixteenth century, and no post was reestablished until the Dutch reopened the factory from 1716 to the 1740s, only to abandon it later. The French attempted a similar post in the 1780s, although the Niger River area nearby never had any formal factory.

Trade in central Africa was somewhat different from west Africa. The Portuguese founded a factory at the Kongo port of Mpinda in the early sixteenth century and had another at the Kongo capital far in the interior, both of which were so firmly under Kongo sovereignty that they might not be considered as really being European posts. When the Portuguese established the colony of Angola after 1575, the city of Luanda, which was fully under Portuguese sovereignty, became the center for their commerce, and indeed, even interior posts, such as Massangano, Cambambe, and Ambaca, were commercial centers under Portuguese sovereignty. To describe a colony with hundreds of thousands of subjects and a substantial surface area as simply a factory, by analogy to west Africa, is obviously false.

Other European powers established a similar presence. The Dutch established a post at Mpinda in Kongo in the 1620s; like the earlier Portuguese post, it was under Portuguese sovereignty. Kongo's King Garcia II closed it down in 1642, because Calvinist Dutch preachers were not allowed in Catholic Kongo. At the same time that they were experiencing trouble in Kongo, the Dutch sought to seize control of the Portuguese colony of Angola. They succeeded in taking Luanda in 1641 but were never able to extend their control over the interior posts and were finally driven out of the area in 1648. Subsequently, the Dutch, and the English and French who followed, based their operations in central Africa on the Kingdom of Loango or its neighbors north of Kongo, especially at the town of Kabinda. There merchants fanned out along the coast of Kongo, and sometimes even along the Angola Coast south of the Kwanza, to deal with Africans through shipboard trade.

These essentially peaceful commercial relations were, however, occasionally disrupted in a variety of ways. Sometimes private traders sought to improve their position by raiding, kidnapping African merchants who came aboard their vessels, or landing armed bodies to raid coastal people. Generally, these operations were limited and often were immediately punished by African authorities, who closed ports, seized European goods, and set embargoes. These actions were sufficiently successful that on more than one occasion, European or colonial American governments sought to locate the offenders and restore the lost people or property, as Massachusetts did when a Boston-based captain seized some people off Sierra Leone in 1645.

A slightly different type of relationship involved European armed forces fighting in African wars at the behest of African rulers. Portuguese soldiers became mercenaries in African armies in Kongo, Benin, and Sierra Leone in the sixteenth century, while English marines served in a similar capacity in Sierra Leone toward the end of that century. When the Portuguese established their fort at São Jorge da Mina on the Gold Coast in the late fifteenth century, the post became a center for Portuguese involvement in African politics in the sixteenth century. Portuguese soldiers, or rather Portuguese and African soldiers under Portuguese command, attempted to extend Portuguese influence, mostly to block trade connections by other European powers.

When the Dutch, Danish, Prussian, and English commercial companies took up fortified trading posts along the Gold Coast during the seventeenth century, they also brought small bodies of soldiers to defend their forts and occasionally to raid the forts of their commercial rivals. Sometimes these bodies also served as mercenaries in African wars. Complicated conflicts, such as the Komenda war of the late seventeenth century, involved several African armies, bodies of mercenaries under command of Dutch and English merchants, and other mercenaries under African command developed.

European-led mercenaries also played a role on the coast of Allada and Whydah in the early eighteenth century, but both in this area and on the Gold Coast, Europeans lost much of their room to maneuver as the large inland polities, Asante and Dahomey, came to dominate coastal politics after the 1720s. As long as coastal politics were dominated by the rival concerns of tiny independent states, commanders of small mercenary armies or even private African and European traders could operate freely and with effect. Once larger military forces loyal to the interior states came into play, however, the possibility of a European military presence evaporated.

The largest military operation by a European power in Africa was culminated by the Portuguese invasion of Angola in 1575. As with the situation on the Gold Coast and at Allada and Whydah, it began through European involvement as mercenaries, first with Kongo (after 1491) and then with Ndongo (in the 1520s). The Portuguese invasion of 1575 began in cooperation with Kongo and was aimed at the coastal provinces of Ndongo. Once some success had been achieved, however, Kongo changed sides, and Portuguese advance was halted after their defeat at the battle of the Lukala in 1590.

Further Portuguese advance was achieved largely by their organization of an African army (called *guerra preta*) under Portuguese command and then by employing Imbangala mercenaries. This combination allowed the Portuguese to raise sizable armies in Angola and to fight in the war of the Ndongo succession (1624–56) and to make successful attacks against Kongo (1665) and Pungo Andongo, one of their former allies (1671–2). Portugal also suffered defeats in these wars. The crushing defeat at the battle of Kitombo (against Kongo in 1670) was probably crucial in the much lower level of Portuguese ambition for conquest in the last years of the seventeenth, the eighteenth, and the early nineteenth centuries.

Europeans bought and sold a variety of goods in Africa through these trading arrangements. The most important early export from Africa was gold; Africa also exported a wide variety of other items, including exotic goods of the tropical environment, such as wild animals and their skins, ivory, perfumes, and wild products, such as gum. Africa also exported copper in varying quantities and textiles of all qualities for both the European and the American markets.

THE SLAVE TRADE

From the American and European perspective, however, Africa's most important export was slaves. Slaves were among the first exports in the mid-fifteenth century and had come to dominate the value of exports in the seventeenth century, reaching their peak numbers in the last decades of the eighteenth and early nineteenth centuries.

Although some of the earliest slaves were captured directly by European ships, this pattern quickly ceased. Direct capture was quite rare after that, with the notable exception of Portuguese operations in Angola. Most slaves were delivered to European buyers by African merchants or state officials and exchanged peacefully in markets controlled by African state officials. This type and scale of exchange could only have developed because the institutions of slavery and slave marketing were widespread in Africa at the time of earliest contact. Thus, African law recognized the status of slavery and the right of the owners of slaves to alienate them freely. We have already noted the significance of slaves in the development of private wealth in African society, and one could add that rulers increased their power by using slave soldiers, officials, and servants. However, the great majority of the slaves who were sold to Europeans during the period of the slave trade were not drawn from an existing stock of slaves in Africa but were usually recent captives in wars or the victims of recent banditry and judicial proceedings.

This legal and commercial background explains how it came to be that Africa generated such substantial exports of slaves in a short period after contact with Europe generally through peaceful commercial transactions. In west Africa, of course, a preexisting trans-Saharan slave trade, oriented

Table 2.1. *Average annual exports of slaves from Africa, 1500–1700*

Coast	1500	1501–50	1551–1600	1601–50	1651–1700
Western	2,000	2,000	2,500	2,500	5,500
Gulf Guinea	1,000	2,000	2,500	3,300	19,500
West Central	2,000	4,000	4,500	8,000	11,000

Source: Thornton, *Africa and Africans*, Table 4.1.

Table 2.2. *Slave exports in the eighteenth century, by decade (thousands)*

Decade	Senegambia	Sierra Leone	Gold Coast	Bight of Benin	Bight of Biafra	Angola
1700–9	22	35	32	139	23	110
1710–19	36	6	38	139	51	133
1720–9	53	9	65	150	60	180
1730–9	57	29	74	135	62	241
1740–9	35	43	84	98	77	214
1750–9	30	84	53	87	106	222
1760–9	28	178	70	98	143	267
1770–9	24	132	54	112	160	235
1780–9	15	74	58	121	225	300
1790–9	18	71	74	75	182	340
1800–9	18	64	44	76	123	281

Source: Richardson, "Slave Exports," Table 7, p. 17, rounded to nearest thousand.

to north African and Mediterranean markets, had existed since perhaps the sixth or seventh century, and many of the early exports came from the diversion of this trade to Atlantic ports by African merchants such as the Jakhanke and Juula. But even central Africa, where there had been no contact with slave-using societies outside the region, was already exporting half of Africa's total slaves in 1520.

The accompanying tables show the regional distribution of the slave trade by coasts by annual average export for each 50-year period prior to 1700 (Table 2.1), and then by decades for the eighteenth century (Table 2.2), the best-documented period and the one when the overwhelming bulk of slaves was imported into North America and the Caribbean. The maps on pages 54 and 55 indicate the locations of these areas. The number of people exported had grown steadily from 1500 to 1620 or so, then expanded rapidly in the mid to late seventeenth century, reaching its peak in the last decades of the eighteenth century. It fell off rapidly as the various abolition campaigns began to take effect in the early nineteenth century, rapidly declining after 1820. Much of the growth of the trade in the seventeenth and eighteenth centuries took place due to the involvement of Lower Guinea in the trade, particularly with the rapid growth of the area as a slaving center in the eighteenth century. By contrast, Upper Guinea exports remained fairly stable, although growth did take place in the eighteenth century, especially in Sierra Leone in the 1750s and 1760s. Angola showed a higher rate of growth than did Upper Guinea, although never the explosive expansion shown by Lower Guinea in the eighteenth century. Still, Angola accounted for roughly one-half of Africa's export of slaves throughout the entire period of the trade, even though it was the least densely populated area.

The majority of people who eventually were transported to the Americas were enslaved by Africans in Africa. The devices by which enslavement took place included: judicial enslavement, kidnapping, private raiding, and military enslavement.

Judicial enslavement, the first of these mechanisms, was a result of the sentence of transportation ("passing salt water" as it was called in Angola) as punishment for a crime. Such crimes might include unpaid debt, violation of religious sanctions, certain types of adultery, as well as theft, destruction of property, or assaults. The punishment often extended beyond the guilty party to include kinspeople and even allies. The courts that handed out such sentences and the law that they applied varied widely, as would be expected from a region with over 100 legally sovereign entities. Witnesses in Africa and interviews with slaves in America point out that in some areas at least (Angola and Upper Guinea are well known in this regard), there was a tendency to extend enslavement as a punishment for more and more crimes, and a greater willingness to include relatives who were not immediately guilty among the enslaved. Walter Rodney suggested that this legal corruption was a product of the demands of the slave trade, as it may well have been. There are, indeed, many accounts of fairly trivial pretexts for enslavement in the literature of the seventeenth and especially the eighteenth century.

It is difficult to make statistical measure of the percentage of people enslaved through different means. The only quantitative source that has been extensively studied is a series of life histories, collected by linguist S. W. Koelle, of a large number of people rescued from slave ships by the

British Navy in nineteenth-century Sierra Leone. These life histories do not constitute a statistically random sample, and they were collected very late in the history of the slave trade. They show that less than one person in five was enslaved through judicial means. Other sources, typically based on interviews with slaves in America or with slave sellers in Africa, generally confirm the relatively low numbers.

Those who fell afoul of the law were not always the most desirable slaves, because some were real criminals, while others, such as those convicted of witchcraft or religious crimes, made troublesome slaves for other reasons. The judicial process was also not well attuned (even in areas where it was quite corrupt, such as Upper Guinea) to produce slaves who were salable or desirable for prospective buyers from Europe or America. Sentences of enslavement were passed against family groups and often resulted in the enslavement of the old and infirm as well as the healthy people capable of the work that American slavery demanded.

By far the most common form of enslavement was one or another form of forcible capture – through either kidnapping or private raiding – or war. Koelle's life histories support this conclusion: 34 percent of the people whose histories he recorded had been captured in war, and 30 percent had been kidnapped or seized in other violent ways. These figures are again broadly supported by other sources, mostly based on testimony of slaves in America or slave dealers on the African coast, although these sources place more weight on war as a source than kidnapping or private raiding.

Kidnapping typically took place through the operations of small bodies of armed men, sometimes with government approval, often without it. Throughout Upper Guinea, especially in the Senegal valley and the Mandinka-speaking world of the interior, there was a long tradition of informal operations conducted by off-duty soldiers of the various royal cavalries against civilian populations. Such raids, typically involving a few dozen horsemen using their mounts to achieve surprise, were illegal in the context of their own country's laws – but the *ceddo* of the Senegambia and the *sofas* of the Mandinka kingdoms of Kaarta and Segu were able to conduct such raids anyway and with virtual impunity. Juula and Jakhanke merchants played a crucial role in these small-scale operations by arranging to buy the captives (sometimes in advance) and using their wide-ranging commercial contacts to smuggle the slaves out of the area.

In coastal Upper Guinea, there was considerable piracy conducted by people who used the rivers and creeks of the area to move about small bodies of armed men quickly and silently. Such pirates were not necessarily a part of the military or naval establishments of the states of the area, as were the horsemen of Senegambia or Segu; rather, they were private bandits or outlaws. They preyed on people who necessarily had to leave their homes and strongly defended villages to fish, wash clothes, travel to market, or tend to their complex rice cultivation.

Such private kidnapping, especially along rivers and creeks, is also documented in Lower Guinea, especially in the Niger Delta area, where it was widespread. Olaudah Equiano's description of his own enslavement and that of many of his countrymen describes the manner in which such pirates operated. These pirates were not only slave raiders; they also engaged in peaceful trade or struck at other economic targets.

Banditry which resulted in the enslavement of people was quite common in the seventeenth-century Gold Coast, where it was known locally as *panyarring*. People and goods were often seized in the course of commercial disputes, and not all such captives were sold abroad, although many times they were. With the rise of the larger states of Asante and Dahomey, however, this sort of disorder was greatly curbed.

Informal kidnapping and raids also occurred throughout Angola. Soldiers of the Portuguese garrisons in Angola often seized people in their off-duty time, in operations analogous to those of off-duty soldiers in Upper Guinea. No doubt, other armies did the same, although the records are less complete for other areas. Mid-seventeenth century travelers in Kongo occasionally noted the arbitrary seizure of people and goods by the elite of the country, which sometimes resulted in considerable destruction and, of course, the sale of many of the victims. In the confusion of Kongo's lengthy civil wars of the late seventeenth and eighteenth centuries, this situation was exacerbated. During the civil wars, groups of raiders attacked travelers on the road and occasionally in villages. There was a strong tradition of selling such people to slave traders, particularly to the Vili traders, who had many settlements throughout Kongo that served as collecting points and in-transit holding areas.

Kidnapping and informal raiding had their limitations, however, even though abolitionist writers tended to focus attention on them – to the point that it is often seen in popular treatments as the usual means of enslavement. Small groups of soldiers or private raiders were necessarily limited in the amount of damage they could inflict; by fortifying their homes or villages and posting scouts and lookouts, villagers could make such raiding less effective.

Most seventeenth- and eighteenth-century writers believed that the most important source of enslavement was war. In this case, enslavement resulted from the fact that the armies of African states conducted military operations against their neighbors. It may be that African states waged war to acquire slaves, and there is some evidence that at least some wars were conducted for that purpose alone. Some of the warfare in the Senegambian region involved raids that appear to have been more concerned with obtaining loot (including slaves) than with other objectives. The cycle of wars between Kaarta and Segu in the interior of the Upper Guinea region in the late eighteenth century might thus be seen as a series of extended slave raids rather than as wars for aggrandizement, strategic position, or commercial advantage.

Warfare was more or less endemic in the world of this period, and to reduce all African wars to simple slave raids would be incorrect. Many wars were waged concomitant to the rise of larger states. The history of the early slave trade from central Africa, for example, shows that many slaves were taken from wars linked to expansion of the kingdom of Kongo and its southern neighbor, Ndongo. The kingdom of Benin was also in the process of expansion in the first half of the sixteenth century when it exported slaves. The emergence of Oyo, Dahomey, and Asante, and their territorial expansion in the late seventeenth and early to mid-eighteenth century, also resulted in wars in which people were captured and exported. The emergence of the central African kingdoms of Viye, Mbailundu, and Lunda in the mid- to late eighteenth century similarly resulted in lengthy wars.

In all of these cases, however, the process of expansion was part of a larger, complex, and multifaceted political environment, and in no case were the wars simply the triumphant march of an overwhelming army. The emergence of Kongo, for example, involved the knitting together of several allied provinces, war against their neighbors, occasional defense against neighboring state incursions, and suppression of rebellion in other regions. Even much of the warfare in the development of the Portuguese colony in Angola was conducted to take strategic areas, suppress rebellions, or engage in the politics of succession, as much as to take slaves.

Both Asante and Dahomey emerged in complex multistate politics through warfare that was both offensive and defensive as they contended with their neighbors and rivals. In Asante, these rivals were Akwamu, Denkyira, and the Fante Confederation; for Dahomey, they included Allada, Whydah, Popo, then Oyo, and the Nago and Mahi states. The politics of state building involved setbacks and defeats as well as victories.

This pattern of war and its resulting enslavement is best demonstrated by the situation of Dahomey, which many contemporary observers argued was a state dedicated to slave raiding. A detailed survey of Dahomey's late eighteenth-century wars – conducted by Lionel Absom, an English factor (merchant representing a company) resident at Whydah and married to a local woman – augmented by recent research shows that Dahomey's military record was a checkered one. Only about one-third of its military operations were unqualified successes, which resulted in the capture of thousands of slaves. Another third were bloody draws in which Dahomey took few of its objectives and captured few, if any, slaves. In the other third, Dahomey suffered defeat and sometimes heavy loss, in which the erstwhile victim of a Dahomian slave raid/war was able to sell Dahomian captives to European factors. Clearly, Dahomey was not a pariah state that lived by continuously successful slave raiding against weaker neighbors. Rather, one must understand Dahomey's wars in terms of its larger state aims, especially a long-standing attempt to extend its control to the northern areas, and the successful resistance of those whom it tried to take over.

In other cases, civil wars within states were the cause of military action that involved the enslavement of people. The Kongo civil wars, which went on sporadically from the end of the seventeenth century to the early nineteenth century, had their causes rooted in deep-seated political rivalries between factions of the royal family, and they resulted in considerable enslavement. The Benin civil wars of the late seventeenth and early eighteenth century were also rooted in the domestic politics of the state but resulted in a rash of enslavement.

Civil wars not only caused substantial enslavement through the operations of armies connected with rivals for state power; they also resulted in a decrease in internal order, which loosed bands of raiders and increased the ability of criminal elements to undertake raids against small villages and travelers. This was clearly the result of the civil war in eighteenth-century Kongo, where political rivalry, raiding, and crime were inextricably intertwined.

Whatever the causes, however, the slave trade had a considerable demographic impact on Africa. Various scholars have attempted to match the increasingly detailed and accurate information on the number, age, and sex of slaves shipped to the Americas on European craft against estimated African populations. While methodological assumptions vary, and we are still some distance from having all the relevant demographic data for

Africa analyzed, the first results show that African population size and structure was affected by the loss of people through the slave trade.

IMPACT OF THE SLAVE TRADE

The most successful attempts to estimate African population loss examine, as closely as possible, the number of slaves shipped out from a number of carefully defined regions. It is obvious from the preliminary results that the demographic impact varied considerably, both in time and space. Upper Guinea probably suffered the least, since it had a fairly dense population and a relatively small export of slaves. Lower Guinea shipped many more slaves, but its very dense population kept the overall demographic impact from being too great. Angola and central Africa, on the other hand, exported very large numbers of people from the least densely populated region of Atlantic Africa and suffered, as a result, the greatest demographic damage.

The nature of the demographic change involved, first, an absolute loss of population, although most often the regional impact was a lowering of the rate of population increase rather than an absolute decline. Nevertheless, short-term declines were noted in some regions for periods as long as 40 or 50 years, especially in the late eighteenth century when slave exports reached their peak.

A second impact was the change in the age and sex structure of the population. Export slaves were drawn from quite specific age and sex groups: adults of the age group 18–35 were overwhelmingly favored, and, in general, male slaves outnumbered females by roughly two to one in the trade as a whole. While the age structure of the export slaves was stable over most of the period, the sex ratios varied widely (but rarely did females actually outnumber males).

The results of such long-term losses are well illustrated by late-eighteenth-century Angola, probably the worst effected by the slave trade (as well as being the best-documented area). Other regions of Africa probably suffered similar changes, although it is unlikely that they were as pronounced as in central Africa. In Angola, Portuguese censuses reported that the adult population was substantially smaller in proportion to the population of children than one would expect from underlying birth and mortality schedules. This resulted in an adverse dependency ratio, which meant that the needs of attending to a dependent (generally juvenile) population lowered the amount of production available for investment.

In addition to the adverse dependency ratio, there was an imbalance in the sex ratio among adults. Angolan data suggest that women outnumbered men in the adult age group by more than two to one. One probable result of these imbalances was the development of widespread polygamy, but it may have had other, as yet undetected, impacts on family structure as well as the sexual division of labor.

Moreover, the effects of the population change took place over a long period of time, so it is quite likely that slaves who departed Africa in the eighteenth century came from societies that were quite different demographically from those in existence a century earlier. Insofar as other elements of the culture were affected by demographic structure, these changes may even have had an impact on the way in which the American community of Africans developed and altered their own cultural institutions.

The demographic changes described above were generated by a model using rather simple assumptions about the nature of the slave trade and initial African population – buttressed, for later periods, by actual demographic data. But the peculiar demography of precolonial Africa probably cannot be explained solely in terms of the Atlantic slave trade. Along with the movement of slaves to the Atlantic coast, there was considerable movement of people as slaves within Africa and military losses resulting from warfare that had only a partial (if any) connection with the slave trade overseas, as well as other population movements. The fact that the Angolan census reports almost equal imbalances among the free population as among the slaves suggests that this region (specifically the deep hinterland of Luanda) was losing male population relative to females due to military losses and other causes, not only because of slave selling. The sex ratio may also have been affected by the import of females from further inland.

Thus, in central Africa, population in some areas grew rapidly, as it did in the central highlands in the late eighteenth and early nineteenth centuries, while other areas were largely depopulated, as were the regions east of the Kwango in the nineteenth century. The transfer of women in childbearing ages from one area and one society to another within Africa could have had dramatic impacts on population sizes and structures.

Such transfers of population in conjunction with the demands of local African slave markets, and following the development of the African domestic economy, can be seen in Upper Guinea (especially Senegambia) as well as in Angola. Thus, if imbalanced sex ratios were caused by gains of women (imported as slaves in the Angolan central highlands in this period) rather than losses of men (shipped overseas), the overall impact might be rapid population growth even with unbalanced sex ratios and adverse dependency ratios. The central highlands experienced considerable economic growth in this period. Thus, it is difficult to generalize about the overall effects of the slave trade, even at a regional level, and even more so at the more local level.

The impact of the export of slaves may also have affected African development in ways other than the strictly demographic. Some historians, following the lead of Walter Rodney, speak of the transformation of slavery, and indeed of African society, as a result of supplying such a large number of slaves to external buyers. For example, the tendency to alter law and custom in order to create more crimes punishable by enslavement, and then to use corrupt methods to entrap people in the legal process, may well have altered relations between social groups and especially between people and the legal system. Likewise, the number of people enslaved in Africa may have grown as a result of the larger number of people captured and transported through the demands of the export market. Finally, the level of exploitation of lower classes in general and slaves in particular may have increased.

These suggestions are difficult to evaluate. In many cases, we do not know enough about African society before the export slave trade to be able to speak authoritatively about such matters. For example, it is difficult to determine what proportion of the African population was enslaved at any point prior to the nineteenth century and, thus, to judge the impact of exporting slaves on the number of slaves held in Africa. Finally, the discipline of African history is just beginning to unravel the complexities of African social, diplomatic, and constitutional history, but it is unlikely that all the changes in these fields can be traced back to the impact of the slave trade.

It is important to keep in mind, however, that African political leaders and merchants played the most important role in determining the level of the slave trade. Europeans rarely could exert direct influence on them, although their willingness to buy thousands of people was a powerful indirect influence. Virtually all European positions in Africa were held at the discretion of African rulers; African political authorities determined where and when exchanges would take place and even played a major part in determining prices.

FROM AFRICA TO AMERICA

The thousands of slaves who left African shores for American destinations followed complex shipping routes to various American ports. Each American region received a different mixture of people from the various exporting regions of Africa; thus, the cultural and social experience of Africans varied in different parts of the American world at different times. Portuguese shipping, which supplied Brazil, for example, drew an overwhelming number of slaves from central Africa and a relatively restricted region of Lower Guinea in the eighteenth century, while in the seventeenth century, Angolan sources were even more pronounced and complemented by limited numbers of slaves from Upper Guinea. French captains drew relatively little on the Gold Coast but focused much more attention on the Slave Coast (around Whydah especially) and Angola, with Senegambia as a relatively small component.

English shippers, on the other hand, drew their slaves from all parts of Africa, although after 1750, they focused their attention on the Bight of Biafra especially (including Whydah). Angola, however, always attracted English attention. Generally, around one-quarter and sometimes more of the people that the English purchased as slaves came from this region. Table 2.3 shows the major African sources of slaves imported into the British West Indies and North America during the eighteenth century. It is a good indicator of the regional origins of the African component of the population of English-speaking America.

These different patterns were the product of commercial organizations in Europe, the specifics of relations with various African suppliers, and the competition among Europeans for access to various ports. The regional origins of the American slave population were not just a product of the trading patterns of the metropolitan suppliers – some colonies changed hands often and were thus variously supplied by official shipments. Moreover, both legal and clandestine slave traders of various nations introduced slaves into the colonies of other American colonizers. Thus, New York was originally supplied by Dutch slavers, then English. Louisiana had Spanish, French, and American suppliers. The English companies sent thousands of slaves to Spanish America but smuggled many slaves into the French Caribbean colonies as well. Dutch captains, though never commanding the bulk of the slave trade, often supplied countries other than their own colony of Surinam.

As can be seen from Table 2.3, sometimes these conditions resulted in

Table 2.3. *Regional origins of slaves in English-speaking America, 1700–1800*

	As Percentage of Imports			
	Whole	Jamaica	South Carolina	Virginia
	ca. 1700			
Senegambia	12.1	10.5	8.1	4.0
Sierra Leone	22.6	16.1	0.0	1.0
Gold Coast	18.4	34.8	9.5	20.0
Bight of Benin	11.7	30.5	0.0	0.0
Bight of Biafra	12.9	1.6	4.8	60.0
Angola	22.4	7.5	77.4	5.0
	ca. 1750			
Senegambia	6.6	6.7	32.0	15.4
Sierra Leone	18.8	16.5	8.4	0.0
Gold Coast	11.1	39.0	37.9	28.6
Bight of Benin	7.3	13.8	13.8	0.0
Bight of Biafra	41.4	25.1	0.7	39.4
Angola	14.4	5.1	18.0	16.7
	ca. 1800			
Senegambia	0.8	2.7	1.9	
Sierra Leone	15.3	6.0	5.1	
Gold Coast	10.7	8.1	31.2	
Bight of Benin	0.8	0.0	0.0	
Bight of Biafra	43.8	48.6	3.4	
Angola	28.6	34.6	56.7	

Sources and notes: British trade as a whole based on Richardson, "Slave Exports," Table 5, p. 13; Jamaica based on Curtin, *Atlantic Slave Trade*, Table 46, p. 160; South Carolina based on William Pollitzer, "A Reconsideration of the Sources of the Slave Trade to Charleston, S.C.," as Table 4 in Holloway, *Africanisms*, p.7; and Virginia based on Kulikoff, *Tobacco and Slaves*, Table 34, p. 322. There is considerable fluidity in coastal designation in all these categories, especially the Windward Coast, which is probably the Gold Coast in most accounts (and has been so merged in compiling these tables) – see Jones and Johnson, "Slaves from the Windward Coast" – but is also sometimes in Sierra Leone. Likewise, many lists and documents do not distinguish clearly between Bight of Benin and Bight of Biafra.

widely varying mixes of slaves reaching different colonies at the same time. While the data on the North American slaves leave much to be desired, even if they are only generally accurate, they show wide disparities. Note, for example, the extreme predominance of Angola slaves in early South Carolina, and their relative absence in Virginia; while Bight of Biafra slaves were noticeable in Virginia, they were scarcely imported into South Carolina.

This vast migration of people – the largest intercontinental migration in history up to its time – helped to shape the demography and culture of the Americas. It also linked the two hemispheres through the constant economic interaction necessary to continue the commerce and, with it, cultural contacts as well. Europe influenced Africa as its merchants came to African ports and its diplomats established relations with African rulers, and Africa influenced America through the steady stream of population to American shores. African history has been important in the development of the history of the Atlantic basin for this reason. Since Africans controlled their end of this trade, it was influenced by events in Africa's development. Insofar as history shaped the culture of African people, it also shaped the culture of Americans, both those from Africa and those from other continents.

3

THE EUROPEAN BACKGROUND

E. L. JONES

IN WHAT SENSE DID EUROPEAN ORIGINS MATTER?

Originally the colonial American economy was constructed from European materials. It cannot be questioned that the predominant influence among the European traits was British, or more accurately English, and that until the War of Independence this became ever more firmly established. The admixture of other Europeans does not gainsay this fact, even though their role has been played down in a literature of early Americana that is inordinately concerned with the Pilgrim Fathers. The other major influences on what became a Euro-American way of life were the distant location of the colonies, together with their lavish resource endowment, and the slowly fading aboriginal culture.

The Native Americans had been present since prehistory, and the uses they had made of the land created capital improvements subsequently taken over by the immigrants from across the ocean. These "capital works" included cleared openings in the forest cover; burning to produce browse for their prey, the deer, thus encouraging sprout hardwoods, reducing fire-sensitive species (especially the understory); introducing from farther south crop plants like maize; and pioneering tracks and pathways. There were hundreds of semipermanent Indian villages in the northeast of the future United States, some with up to 150 acres cleared for crops and larger areas ecologically modified for hunting.

This was no longer a land of dense, unbroken forest. The benefit to small, struggling settlements was undoubtedly great. It has been suggested that it would have taken a generation to produce the clearings that the Puritans found ready-made. Competition for existing openings was often what brought whites and Indians into conflict, despite both being such low-density populations. The voluntary immigrants of recent centuries, their equipment and capital, tools, techniques, institutions, and "invisible baggage," the back-home market for their exports, were each and every one of them European. Only their slaves were not. Yet appearances may blind us to the deeper processes which decided the nature of the American economic system. Although observation tells us that colonial settlement was Anglo-American, or at any rate Euro-American, and that a cousinhood has persisted to the present, the American colonies held up a distorted mirror to the old country – or old countries.

Observation does not tell us why certain features rather than others crossed the Atlantic, why some began to fade almost as soon as they got there, why others survived, or why they combined in novel ways. If we confine ourselves to tracing origins – that is, to a genetic approach – we miss the underlying dynamic or structural forces that help to explain why at any given time things were as they were. No one will overlook the extent to which a new geography and different factor proportions (relative quantities of land, labor, and capital) changed economic relationships, but it is possible to neglect the fact that more subtle forces altered the mix. These forces are vital to an understanding of why some elements in the economic system were path-dependent when others, and the mix as a whole, were original to America.

While the case for examining the English, British, and European background is undoubted, we also need to recognize that colonial Americans were faced with opportunities to select from more than one social tool-kit and to create new approaches of their own. It can scarcely be overemphasized how easily that fact is obscured by the continued presence of so many European features, mostly English ones, some of them truly ancient in their essence. The translocation of these elements remains, of course, the place to start.

The initial settlement of New England may even be conceived as a renewal of far earlier efforts by Europeans to expand the area under their control. For instance, it is sometimes said that the trans-Atlantic migration was a continuation or fresh episode of a land-hungry movement that included the Crusades. This depends on playing down the religious motives of the Crusaders. Economic historians are liable to give the impression of treating any and every activity as motivated by material concerns. Unwary ones do indeed write as if other motives were disguises for the profit motive. In reality, most are merely paying the attention their profession demands to the large material component and enormous material consequences of territorial gains, without intending to deny that other motivations exist.

An economic element was certainly present in the rather direct carry-over of Spanish arms to Mexico after the "Reconquista." Islamic power had been ousted from the Iberian peninsula, but both Spain and Portugal realized that they could not hope to conquer Moorish North Africa. Their shift in focus to Central America was a deflection of reconquest energies. Economic motives were present even in the settlement of Massachusetts: preference falsification cannot be ruled out among the inhabitants of a theocracy and may indeed be implied by moral backsliding; many settlers were Anglicans rather than Puritans; besides which the London merchant backers were certainly interested in the repayment of their loans. In any case, whatever the inspiration, the material consequences were enormous.

It is not too fanciful to accept that what we are seeing with respect to North America was, in long perspective, a resumption of the westward Germanic movement that had dissolved the Roman empire and brought the Saxons to England. That migration had created the kingdoms within England, where the Saxons paused for one thousand years and more until they leapt across the Atlantic in the early seventeenth century. The technical level of production of seventeenth-century Europeans was probably not very much more developed than in Saxon times, although, compared with the Native Americans, the successful adoption of arable farming as the universal basis of life greatly raised the productivity of the land and the population it could support. Ironically enough, this was achieved partly through incorporating a local crop, maize. The practical result was a rapid growth of the white settler population, proof against Indian assault despite a serious threat during King Philip's war. The trans-Atlantic migrants were often farmers; those who were not had to turn to farming – they did so gladly enough where land was plentiful. For a long time, the sectoral division of labor was much less marked than in the metropolitan country.

Admittedly, there were differences from earlier movements within Europe. Whereas in Viking times ships and navigation were already adequate for skirting along the shores of the north Atlantic, weapons technology was scarcely up to maintaining a foothold. The Iron-Age Vikings in Vinland had been unable to hold out against the native "Skraelings" with their Stone-Age weapons. By the time of the Pilgrim Fathers, guns had been adopted. Whether or not the native Indians were mainly defeated by European diseases which, somehow, the Vikings had not brought, powder and shot gave the Puritans an enormous additional advantage.

The Puritans and other immigrant groups were impelled by a religious ideology scarcely conceivable to the modern agnostic mind and absent during either the Viking excursion or the original Saxon invasion of Britain. A strong ideological sense of purpose was a great support. But the Puritans dominate the literature more than they dominated historical reality; other English migrants, especially the second or younger sons of the landed gentry who because of primogeniture would not inherit their fathers' estates, had more prosaic motives for their move. Thus the Salopian Col. Richard Lee, ancestor of Robert E. Lee, who emigrated in 1640, proudly claimed descent from a Saxon family rather than from some upstart supporter of the Conqueror. Political discontent at home and the magnet of land were push and pull.

During the centuries since the Saxon invasion, the rustic English had considerably increased their involvement in the market and refined their institutions for regulating it. In England they had become accustomed to a less wooded environment than in continental Europe. They had cleared the oak forest for farms, as they would do again and again in America. In general they had avoided the Romano–British settlements in England, making clearings of their own, although adopting some of the originally prehistoric routeways. This reluctance to usurp existing "capital-in-land" was rare among invaders and may have been because Celtic populations were much denser than those later met in America (smallpox dealt the Indians a savage blow).

Despite some differences, the discovery, exploration, and settlement of North America can thus be interpreted as a giant step in the old land-hungry game of probing at the edges of the Saxon world. The populations of Europe had long been checked in the north by ice, in the south and east by other peoples. Even on the western fringes the compressed remnants of the Celtic cultures still held sway at the end of the Middle Ages. Repeated attempts to expand finally exploded in the least likely direction, across the broad, open ocean. Once the great divide of the Atlantic had been robbed of its worst terrors, the impetus to acquire more land took on new life. Puritan ideology merely reduced some of the psychic costs, while powder and shot cut some of the real ones. More rhetorically, Chamberlain's formulation of imperial federation in 1897 referred to "the all-Saxon home." Although by then the United States had long since defected, there had been a genuine as well as a spurious Saxon cast to England's overseas expansion.

Some of the original West Country Puritan migrants of 1630 soon moved on from Massachusetts to Connecticut, then dispersed again within a very few years. In later times, their descendants took part in the westward movement across the United States. Among them was the Maverick family, which came from the line of the rector of Beaworthy in Devon; it was a descendant who reached Texas in the nineteenth century and gave the family name the modern connotation. The Southern frontier of the Scotch-Irish may be seen as continuing the violent expansion that had taken place in Britain, renewed in the Western Isles and Ulster under Elizabeth I, as well as under James VI of Scotland and the same king when he became James I of England. The carry-over to New England and Virginia was very direct, even to the involvement of some of the main personalities on both sides of the Atlantic.

We could speculate about other pasts – non-European options – for North America. Had that continent been settled by others, say the Islamic Moors of the western Mediterranean, the resultant economy would have looked different. They would have brought other living entourages and modes of economic organization. They would have brought different forms of political organization, with their own implications for levels of productivity and the distribution of income. In any event, it is "to England that we owe this elevated rank we possess," said de Crèvecoeur, "these noble appellations of freeman, freeholders, citizens; yes, it is to that wise people we owe our freedom. Had we been planted by some great monarchy, we should have been mean slaves of some distant monarch."

Many world cultures were expansionary: although we shall not pursue it more explicitly, a thought-experiment on the likely behavior of other colonists is what is needed as a control against which to assess the actual behavior of the English and Europeans in the New World. We certainly need to take a broad approach where what we are discussing is the establishment in uncharted territory of an entire economic system, wrapped round with its own sociopolitical system, where nothing so elaborate had ever existed before. The immigrants did not merely bring their tools and methods, their institutions and laws – that is, everything on the supply side – they brought their own tastes, too, and thus a demand side which introduced and was likely to perpetuate Europeanness.

Even had the French or Spaniards prevailed over the British in North America, the structure of the economy would surely have been different. It would have been encased in a more rigid polity, with weaker supply bases and less eager markets across the ocean to back it up. The factor proportions of the American continent would have distorted the European nature of the settler economy, as they did British settlement, but they would not have obliterated all the Absolutist tendencies of mainland European governments. They did not in Canada.

The foregoing statement represents a limited measure of agreement that history matters, that what happened in America was path-dependent. The view expresses disbelief that the environment of the New World could transform any settlement into something unheard of among human societies or disguise its particular origins. New attributes emerged, to be sure, perhaps different ratios of the old personality types – "who is this new man, the American?" – but the *factual* importance of starting English is demonstrable. As in biological evolution, there was a Founder Effect. History ran controlled experiments to show what difference this made, most pointedly the Iberian colonization of Central and South America. Such experiments do not replicate the exact environment of North America, but they come close enough to be persuasive.

However, beginning English was not quite a sufficient determinant of what America would become. The classification fails in at least three ways. First, Englishness is too general. Regions within England (let alone Britain or Europe) differed from one another ecologically and in economic organization. A large literature attempts to trace transplanted regional complexes of social life and farming system.

Second, the English economy was not the same seed-bed at successive periods. Over the seventeenth and eighteenth centuries, it changed to an unprecedented extent. Although it has sometimes been suggested that what America offered was space to persist in the old ways, unthreatened by later changes in the metropolitan world – in other words, to reproduce an idealized version of the life where one came from – anything that later waves of immigrants brought, the fashions they spoke of, could still be adopted. Contact with the host culture never completely stopped. The backwoods was not a time capsule. The incipient Balkanization projected by "Franklinia" and one or two other jurisdictions conceived after the Revolution across the Appalachians in the "Caintuck" was defeated by the transportation improvements of the canal age, imported from industrializing Britain. The Erie Canal soon tied the interior to the East and hence to Europe. America, even western America, could never cut itself off completely from the permanent normality of change in the whole Atlantic economic system.

Third, the colonies as they progressed from wilderness to civilization themselves changed even faster in some respects than the originating society. After all, they started from an undeveloped base.

Nothing so far said grapples closely enough with the ultimate question about the English, British, and European background: in what sense did it really matter? The surface record – the factual history – is unequivocal. England, Britain, and Europe were the "onlie (direct) begetters" of the economic apparatus transplanted; they were the sine qua non of the developing economy in America. Their legacy, continually supplemented with borrowings, persisted into the life of the independent United States and to some extent continues, although the signal is weaker and there is more noise today.

Early in the nineteenth century, Chancellor James Kent of New York observed wryly that the Acts of Congress which regulated shipping trades and fisheries in 1792 and 1793 corresponded with the British statutes as they had been applied under George III. Despite constant grumbling about the English admiralty and prize courts in the years leading up to the War of 1812, the law as practiced in those courts was rapidly and completely adopted by the U.S. Supreme Court.

The direct heritage of regulation, productive method, and European taste has been demonstrated in detail by several authors. Despite a general forgetfulness in America about the English past and reverence for the fresh start apparently implied when a written constitution was adopted in 1789, such scholars proclaim that antiquity need not mean irrelevance. It has even been proposed that the successful ethnic groups among the colonists were ones whose farming systems were "preadapted" by the similarity of the ecology of their homelands to the districts they settled. The supporting evidence seems rather to be of some settlements that did fail in a seemingly incongruent landscape; whether the reasons were ecological is a matter of opinion.

The preadaptation argument is an extreme statement of the significance of the European background: move to an ecologically strange locality and fail. It implies no melting pot and no cultural malleability, points that are at once contradicted by the fact that, having failed, migrants could and did switch to the methods of groups from other homelands. Ethnic communities seldom died out in the wilderness, although surprisingly many settlements were physically abandoned. However, success and continuity are much more evident, most strikingly in the persisting folkways and splendidly tidy horse husbandry of the Amish people in Lancaster County, Pennsylvania. Theirs is the polar case, an antiquated society scarcely matched in modern Europe itself.

The case for a path-dependent economic history of colonial America seems unassailable. The importance of the European background seems certain. In particular, English, or at any rate British, people had re-created what was to almost all intents and purposes a new set of British-like localities overseas, trading with the home regions; corresponding with home about business, religion, science, and government, slower at receiving the mails but often eager to hear about metropolitan fashions; somewhat insulated by higher transport costs but never cut off.

The dominating Englishness, or more broadly Europeanness, of colonial America can surely have no explanation other than the power of its origins. However, on reflection, this is reminiscent of the "blind watchmaker" fallacy, in which the intricacy of nature, from spiders through penguins to giraffes, was assumed to require the explanation of a grand design, until the advent of Charles Darwin's theory of evolution. A Darwinian-style explanation can be introduced in the present case. What it says is not that America remained English because England is where it began, but that Englishness survived only as long as adverse selective pressures were not strong enough to alter it. The fact that the colonists did not seek to incur the costs of change if no benefits were apparent does not mean that they could and would not change their ways when this was necessary or profitable. Meanwhile, the known ways were comfortable, and there was cultural reinforcement through links with the homeland.

Rules were set up that seemed to Anglicize the economic organization of America from the start. The market connection and continued stream of immigrants protected the links. But what was done may best be seen as the choice of a least-cost solution, not an adamantine necessity. Part of the choice meant differences rather than similarity. Within one generation, the English village had become the New England village, with new materials and new layout, despite some remaining similarities.

The process was adaptation, not mimicry, but then the immigrants were never a representative sample of the English, and they no longer lived in an English setting. Voluntary immigrants were a self-selected group, and involuntary ones were hardly a cross-section of the population either. The former were often extruded by economic distress, political disturbance, and lack of religious freedom. Migrants were never those who had been wholly satisfied with England, nor those who had succeeded best there or knuckled under soonest. The cavaliers were remounted in Virginia after they had been dismounted in England. The North Carolina Highlanders, who had left after the 'Forty-five Rebellion, were most decidedly those whose faces did not fit. Men like that were so atypical of society in Britain that it is almost surprising how British America was to remain amidst all its novel variety.

In New England, especially, there was no truck with manorialism or the establishment of an hereditary landed aristocracy. Although a number of common fields survived for a long time in Massachusetts, they were sometimes cleared and tilled for the first year only. By and large, individual landownership was the rule from the outset. Even with communalism, each holding's home paddock was usually sizable, much bigger than in England, big enough for subsistence. Where common fields appear in the landscape of eighteenth-century Massachusetts they were sometimes recreations, emphasizing the aspect of choice from a menu of institutions rather than an automatic transfer. In the South, great wealth immediately established itself on plantations – but not personal titles. By the time of Independence, a greater equality of wealth and income than in the old country demonstrated the benefits of a few generations spent accumulating capital in the colonies more than it reflected titular advantage.

England could not maintain full control over distant colonies occupied by men who sometimes thought themselves truer Englishmen, reverting to older ways or deliberately concerned with planting the New Jerusalem, the City on a Hill. Even in Virginia, the laws were versions of English law adapted to new circumstances, which included a scarcity of men with legal training. Law and order were seen as necessary to the conduct of business and essential if further immigrants with skill and capital were to be attracted, but this did not mean and could not mean unchanged law or an exact replica of the English legal apparatus.

Learned, then, from handbooks and faced with unexpected difficulties like Indian attack, the law began to alter. Its English origin is obvious, but the change of form is obvious, too: Latin and French vanished from the courtroom. Elements of substance changed as well. Americans were not "born free," but they did manage to discard some ancient English exactions. Massachusetts soon abolished heriots, reliefs, and escheats. Whereas the poor in England had been disarmed and no one worth less than £100 per annum could possess a gun, the Indian threat in Virginia meant that adult males were soon required by law to own gun, powder, and ammunition. There, what in England would have been quite minor courts took on wide powers. Increasingly, legislative initiatives flowed up from the burgesses.

The West Country Pilgrims ran their colonies through what were in effect Dorset and Somersetshire J.P.s sitting in Quarter Sessions. Enforcement lay in the hands of officers who were, like the town officers of Dorchester, Beaminister, or Crewkerne, clerks of weights and measures, leather sealers, way wardens. The stuff of economic regulation was certainly English but collapsed into simpler forms with more authority at local levels.

The borrowings continued through time, and not merely via new immigration. Personal connections and pen friends remained. As an instance, members of the Wolcott family, clothiers from Wellington in Somerset, revisited England for decades. The colonies and the home country, whatever the frictions, operated with substantially the same information pool. Understandably, more ideas flowed westward than eastward across the Atlantic, from the more populous home country to the little colonies. Yet the American resource endowment – meaning, above all, more abundant land – besides the distance from government in London, fear of the Indians, and the presence of other European nationals, meant new problems and possibilities. Americans borrowed, but they also substituted and invented.

From England came everything up to and including the jointed wooden dolls clad in the Season's Parisian dress fashion, which in the eighteenth century reached as far away as Boston. The flow eventually included even virtual industrial spies, such as the renegade Samuel Slater, bursting with desire to tell the Browns of Providence, R.I., how to make a water-powered Arkwright's cotton-spinning machine like his employer's in Derbyshire.

Much that America borrowed or retained from its English past was trivial. There were other ways of living than English ones, but in the absence of compulsion or enticing alternatives, they would be the ones to prevail and persist. Why should other Europeans not adopt the English language and ways unless they happened to settle in distinct localities of their own? Even then they would at last find overwhelming advantages in speaking English. Despite this, some of the seemingly English solutions mutated beneath their reassuringly familiar names and labels. As with the law, colonial ways were sometimes fresh responses to new problems, including those induced by different factor proportions. Still others were old

solutions to old problems, invented anew. Colonial life, including economic life, emerged from a swirl of possibilities in which the large English
component only seems assured because there was usually no special reason
for it not to be.

Nothing seems culturally more tenacious than dietary preference, yet
the Puritans swiftly adopted maize and started to experiment with squash
and pumpkins. Later, the theocratic authority of the preachers themselves
was eroded when their real incomes fell in a great inflation and they turned
to supplement their pay and dilute their energies with other occupations.
Social relationships in New England were not so fixed as to index the
earnings of clerics.

The idea that the culture of the Scotch-Irish was transferred unchanged
to the colonies is part of the case that the folkways of Britain were
replicated. Preadaptationism seems improbably fortunate if the same practices that gave the Scotch-Irish only a marginal living in Britain were
secretly readying them to thrive in resource-abundant America. Moreover,
the case for continuity is weakened because, while celebrating what was
retained, it neglects what was discarded and contains no intrinsic means of
telling which was which. The Scotch-Irish clung to the cramped dimensions of the houses they used to build at home where good building timber
had been scarce. That they persisted with the same dimensions when they
had no need to stint themselves among the tall timber of the backwoods is
taken as evidence of path-dependence: in reality, they modified their ways
enough to copy corner timbering from the Germans in Pennsylvania and
to invent the dog-trot house, which was two houses of the old size under a
single roof. In terms of function, if not of form, this suggests adaptability
rather than continuity. That grin of the Cheshire cat, the retention of old
forms, has too readily been taken to imply the meaningful persistence of
European localisms.

The Scotch-Irish also eventually caused soil erosion by continuing their
old habit of plowing up and down hill instead of along the contours. Yet
they abandoned run-rig (in which the arable strips plowed by individuals
were scattered about separately). The American wilderness may not have
functioned in the diametrically opposite way envisaged by the Frontier
Thesis – as an "environmental grindstone, pulverizing the cultural attributes that Europeans brought over" – but it did winnow them. When the
matter became urgent or when it self-evidently paid, settlers were willing
to change elements that might otherwise be taken as the very core of their
economic and social being. Much later, Americans could still be found

borrowing from England, but they were actually selecting what suited their book – for instance, the liberal ideas of the opposition rather than the conservative notions of government in the lead-up to the War of Independence.

In this way, conscious choices were made from the available, still largely European, menu. The choices were more often unconscious. Americans continued to behave like Europeans because that is what they had been and conceived themselves still to be, especially as defined in opposition to the red man. Laws and institutions creaked within a mainly English frame, which was obliged to adapt to new circumstances, although it often seemed to do no more than create across the Atlantic an array of regions mirroring those of the mother country. These variants were like the syntheses of a playwright, catching the flavor but not the substance of the originals.

The new American regions shared a frontier location. In British terms, they were most like the Border Country. By the standards of lowland England, the Scotch-Irish were indeed to assume a quite disproportionate role in America. Nevertheless, older, economically more complex societies, East Anglian and West Country Puritan communities, Londoners, and southern English gentry were now juxtaposed with the life of the frontier. Contemplate transferring parts of the community from Suffolk, London, or Dorset to Ulster, and one has, perhaps, a little of the flavor of the experiment. The fact that no analogy completely fits acknowledges the element of strangeness in the settlement of America, like dreaming of the old country rather than remembering it.

Many processes contended to perpetuate or modify European forms. Cultural regions have supposedly been identified as representing British or European regions, ethnic enclaves with fossilized old-country systems of farming and ways of life. Here the Amish stand out, although in general the Middle Colonies exemplify another process, the simplification of Europe overseas, and the Amish would be exceptional anywhere. To English eyes, trans-Atlantic cultural regions are sometimes faintly reminiscent of districts at home, but the landscape as a whole is relatively undifferentiated. American regions are typically large; the Pennsylvania Dutch country in Lancaster County is atypically small.

Regions of the United States, especially in the East, can thus appear like parts of Britain or occasionally Europe, synthesized from ancestral tales. In English, British, or European terms, a faint air of unreality must exist, because before the seventeenth century the United States was not trans-

Atlantic Europe at all. Landscapes created at that date may have started with a summary, implicit in their forms, of processes that had taken place in the history of somewhere else. Not even an exile was going to re-create the redundant detail of all past occupancies through which, as R.A. Dodgshon described it in a memorable phrase, the seventeenth-century English landscape had ghosted. American settlements were the Potemkin villages of seventeenth-century England.

The propensity of the first effective settlement to make a durable imprint even when new ethnic stock replaced the first-comers may have produced a patchwork landscape comparable in some respects to that of Europe, though never with Europe's variety. Yet the fact that streams of immigrants came from known districts did not mean that the full richness of Europe was represented. It was not. Many cultural influences collapsed into a handful in the American setting. A classic example was where English, German, and Scotch-Irish influences fused into a Pennsylvanian economic style: the common law and the English language; the long rifle from the Rhineland; the Conestoga wagon and Dutch barn, also both from Germany; and whiskey, the Ulster cabin plan, potatoes, and the infield–outfield method of hill farming from the Scotch-Irish. No single European region could supply all these traits and tools; although this does not guarantee that the mix was optimal, mixing there was.

The extent of mixing reinforces the point that, potentially and actually, malleability underlay the observable British and European features. Choice was possible. The European background mattered because the costs of obtaining information about non-European possibilities would have been enormous. Had they been as cheap, even these alternatives might have been introduced piecemeal, as was the growing of Indian corn. Admittedly, there would have been psychological resistance (which translates as high costs) to introducing complexes of such oddities en bloc.

There were always radicals and black sheep, innovators and entrepreneurs, but community norms and established old-country institutions reinforced conventional behavior. For immigrants to what was largely a cultural void, origins mattered more than they do now; migrants today are entering an established American society whose commercialized mores are hard to resist. In the past, Englishness might wear out for the American-born but was constantly refashioned not simply by the authority of the British crown and the pull of British markets but by the arrival of migrants fresh from "home." Americans thought of themselves as Britons living and working at a distance. Although after the 1760s this self-identification began to disappear from their rhetoric, they remained Anglomorphs – people of whatever descent whose manner is English, or at least English enough to distinguish them from their own ancestors. Modes of running the economy were as much part of this assemblage as any other traits.

The speed and extent of Americanization is a matter of judgment. Various explanations of the nature of the economy exist. One is a nativist view, which claims that the American environment, especially the frontier, created "this new man, the American." Another is that frontier resources created Atlantic capitalism as a whole, tying America to Europe. The next is that Europe was for all practical purposes reestablished and re-created across the ocean. Yet another is that new social forms, latent but suppressed in Europe, flowered from European stock in the new environment.

The nativist school proclaims that the new setting created a novel Euro-American culture. From the nativist position, the frontier reshaped all relationships along lines made famous by Frederick Jackson Turner. In a variant, Ellen Semple urged that, whereas cultural regions directly descended from Europe did emerge up and down the East coast, things changed with the westward movement. Once the pioneers had been siphoned through the bottlenecks of Appalachian passes like the Cumberland Gap, subsequent isolation hindered their access to coastal and of course European markets, halted the establishment of landed estates, and induced a western classlessness. But as Louis Hartz observed, the common thread of the Frontier Thesis is that the land and the same novel society is assumed to have been created by abundant land wherever it was occupied. On the contrary, in his opinion, when we compare all the neo-Europes, or even all the Thirteen Colonies, their common European origin becomes clear. This exposes the inadequacy of the Frontier Thesis to explain the ultimately European nature of America. Land and resources vary but not enough to obscure the common origin, while the Frontier may explain the scale but never the character of American life. Factor proportions models do not account for the social structures that came to dominate in particular frontier regions.

The main alternative to the nativist conception is not so much Hartzian as a market-driven model of the core-periphery type favored long ago by Walter Prescott Webb. In this formulation, interior America was indissolubly linked to Europe by trade. The link was not the creation of an exploitative metropolis, whatever the Western resentment of east-coast merchants. Rather, the primary *cause* of the rise of capitalism throughout the western world was found in a resources boom created by the immensity of cheap land. The Frontier Thesis is here turned on its head. Abundant land ties America economically to Europe and makes the European background matter; it does not free Americans to be more than variants of European, capitalistic man.

The nativist arguments apply best to the period of the frontier movement after 1790. The greater divergence of American life after that date is explicable as a result of a larger, more self-contained market, more immigrants of non-British stock, and greater average distances from any original influence. It is easier to envisage the seaboard economies during the seventeenth and eighteenth centuries as European fragments, although blurring, simplifying, and becoming more exempt from the complexities and archaisms of England and Europe.

Whether one should be more surprised at the persistence of an English essence than at the innovations is a little like asking whether a glass is half-full or half-empty. In any event, the possibility exists that Britain and America to a degree changed in tandem because they responded similarly to similar circumstances. This is explicitly urged by Marxists who see the law, for example, transformed in both countries in the nineteenth century to meet the desires of industrial employers. Empirical work suggests that this was not so, that the legal system as handed down was too tenacious to allow a takeover by class-interest law. Perhaps there was little need. Premodern legal attitudes were scarcely pro-labor. More broadly than just the law, some of the persistent similarity between institutions and techniques on either side of the Atlantic may well have been due to a similar root-stock growing in substantially the same market soil.

"It is too clear to require the support of argument," proclaimed Chief Justice Marshall, "that all contracts and rights, respecting property, remained unchanged by the Revolution." How much more, then, had those contracts and rights been English before Independence, down to the final comma. Matters may have been a fraction different thereafter: "when the people of the United Colonies separated from Great Britain, they changed the form, but not the substance, of their government," said Chief Justice Morrison Waite.

The debate between continuity and discontinuity may be summed up by triaging the phenomena involved. At the first level, cultural phenomena including house types, dialects, and the like often survived evocatively. This need be no more than a "survival of the mediocre," not a tribute to the optimality of British or European attributes.

At a second level, economically important phenomena often give the appearance of surviving, but may do so mainly as labels, without their full original content and meaning. New World forces hollowed them out. Old forms may have acquired a fresh but different content in Britain, since Britain too continued to change. Thus we see that within an undeniably descendant agrarian organization in America, content may have changed with new crops adopted, such as maize (resisted in Britain). But in Britain, in came turnips (resisted in America).

At a third and more fundamental level, deep behaviors were undoubtedly transmitted and did persist: the work ethic, decentralized government, a willingness to take public office, and a preference for independent family forms rather than collectives. In addition to the similarity of commonplace cultural and institutional forms, it was this level that kept the British and Americans as kissing cousins. Many of these attitudes had profound economic significance.

ECONOMIC SYSTEMS

This section is a sketch of major components of the economic system of the host culture of seventeenth- and eighteenth-century Britain. To appreciate its significance in terms of what was and was not carried to North America, it should be read with colonial American economic history in mind. By no means every feature from Britain was transported. Nevertheless, the pieces from which a new jigsaw puzzle was put together in America, recognizably a version of the old one, were the elements of British economic life.

The literature of economic systems is highly stylized. It has been concerned for a generation with contrasting the structures and performances of the United States and the U.S.S.R. To a degree which must disturb any economic historian, exercises of this kind have been made to depend on freezing the frame – on selecting supposed equilibrium states (and dates) from which individual items may be abstracted and compared. The approach relies crucially on the concept of closure – that is to say, on the identification of fully matured economic systems, despite the fact that any system continues to change over time.

When we turn to early modern Britain and Europe, we find that the past generation of economic historians has shifted in the opposite direction, toward depicting the economy as in a nonequilibrium state. Because the literature has sought, consciously or unconsciously, to assimilate the late preindustrial period to the "relevant" period of the Industrial Revolution, it has perhaps gone to extremes in emphasizing change rather than continuity. Compared with the descriptive, institutionalist focus of earlier work, it has played down the substantial elements of custom and what (by the standards of later periods in the same economies) were relatively limited markets.

Much, perhaps everything, depends on the base period from which we choose to view the past. Compared with medieval times, or with the great empires that still dominated organized economic life over much of the rest of populous Eurasia during the "early modern" centuries, the economies of Europe, especially western Europe, and above all those of the United Provinces and Britain, were abnormally mobile. Nevertheless, switching to the vantage point of the end of the twentieth century, the changes were slow enough for the frame to seem frozen.

Due allowance has also to be made for the complexity of regional differences within Britain, as shown for instance by the multiplicity of fine-grained vernacular architectural traditions. The British scene is shot through like patterned silk with variety in everything from geology to linguistics: strata and dialects change almost every ten miles. Past economic life varied in detail from place to place, too. While it is a matter of judgment what breaks we try to impose on its continua, the categories are certain to be more numerous than in most countries. It also has to be remembered that Americans drew items from the stock of other traditions, from the Palatine barn to the Greek revival. The establishment of colonial economies represented a shaking of the European kaleidoscope.

The account of the British background which follows is in four parts, compiled from methods of analyzing economic systems: (1) modes of coordination; (2) factors of production; (3) sectors of the economy; and (4) evaluations of performance.

MODES OF COORDINATION

The mechanisms by which economies are coordinated are typically discussed under the headings of custom, command, and market. The last comes first to the modern mind, but economic systems are not free-floating and neither are markets self-enforcing. They are parts of the larger social and political system, of society as a whole. This was more evident in the past when markets were less free of the influence of customary norms or the dictates of rulers.

In Britain, the systems of control were already more mixed than almost anywhere else in the world. The market was more accentuated than anywhere except in a few trading cities, of which the most prominent was London's competitor, Amsterdam. The United Provinces were ahead of England in developing a prosperous world trade. The difference was that London had as its hinterland a nation-state with a larger population. It manufactured a stronger economy than the Netherlands by integrating the hinterland with its metropolitan market. England, later Britain, thus did not remain a city-state with a rural tail but became the first widely developed country.

Tasks were to some extent allocated, and investment and output were determined, by individual responses to the signals of prices. Nonmarket regulation by custom or the dictate of a government or ruler was not as dominant in England as it had been in most places and periods of history. Moreover, change was in the direction of extending the market, despite the political turmoil of the mid-seventeenth century, which was connected with the unsuccessful attempt of the Crown to turn back the clock.

Elements of routine, "vegetative" custom remained. They represented the self-organization of small communities with limited trade, little contact with anything like a central policy-making government, and a mainly oral tradition. Such communities survive in the villages that still predominate in the Third World. Nonmarket allocations were made above all within the household, allied to which many tasks continued to be determined on a basis of gender. Age was less of a criterion because children in a poorer economy were usually put to work early, and in the absence of regular nonfamily support in old age, the elderly were obliged to stay at work.

The formative period of American colonialism corresponded with a time in English history when the monasteries had already been dissolved and the charitable role of the church had shrunk without a compensating rise in secular welfare. The guilds were already beginning to lose their sway, reducing the charitable protection of urban artisans. Inarticulately, growth was starting to edge out welfare as the main consideration. It could be argued that this was sensible given that risk was declining. Nevertheless, a welfare gap opened.

Agriculture was much the largest industry by any measure. Here major customary elements persisted in the shape of common-field farming, whereby individual families farmed strips of land scattered about large open fields. The most widely acknowledged explanation of this arrangement is that it was a form of insurance. Formal insurance markets had scarcely arisen in any sector; fire insurance, for example, only barely came into bud after the Great Fire of London in 1666 and awaited the early years of the next century to flower.

Whether or not the purpose of farming in common fields really was insurance, it meant that in a wide central belt of the country from Yorkshire to the south coast, community norms of husbandry restricted many farmers from following price trends for profit. These rules reduced the scope for innovativeness by setting village times for many operations. They militated against the sowing of unfamiliar crops, since these could be "fed off" by everybody's livestock in a common herd. The innovative farmer could not hope to keep all the gains of his enterprise. While there were more and more agreements or side-payments to permit the sowing of small private plots in the common fields (and many enclosures had been made from at least the fifteenth century), communal elements were still predominant in this chief of all industries.

Viewed over two centuries or so, the British economy saw a distinct waning of central command elements, disguised though this was by attempted resumptions of power on the part of the Stuart kings and by the long retention of the symbols of royal authority. Although as late as the Civil War a few great lords still rode out at the head of their tenants on private quarrels as well as the king's cause, strict feudalism had effectively died long since. The cash nexus had supplemented and was replacing the social bond. As trade increased and the merchant class grew in influence, the central government showed greater concern with commercial policy. In the shires, landlordism, concerned with rent rolls, was in the saddle, though this does not mean that the energies of landowners or their stewards were single-mindedly devoted to maximizing rents. Land remained vitally important for a number of reasons: it offered the main route to political power, social prestige, and preferred activities like hunting.

Although any starting date will bisect change, a simple way of looking at the reduced role of nonmarket, political decision making is to start in the fifteenth century with the Wars of the Roses. These went some way toward eliminating part of the old Norman aristocracy and establishing the Tudor dynasty in the person of Henry VII. This may seem no more than the sort of succession coup that typified the premodern world. However, coupled with the new men who were his supporters, the particular goals and personality of Henry VII made a difference. He was inclined to punish by fines rather than executions. He pacified the country, being one of those rare monarchs who perceived the value of law and order as well as seeing the role of financial management in attaining them and being prepared to do plenty of the necessary office work himself. His pacification favored merchants and artisans. Violence was externalized – thereafter exported to the Celtic fringes and, eventually, to colonial frontiers.

Although Henry VIII did not sustain the attention to detail needed to keep up the momentum of a commercializing society, he did free resources by abolishing the monasteries. Monastic lands and other assets were sold to bidders who, to recoup, put them to productive use. The economy tended to expand under its own steam with relatively little further encouragement. Merchants rose from subservience to some political power in the course of the sixteenth century. After the convulsions associated with the Eleven Years' Tyranny and the Civil War, which may be looked on as arising out of the attempts of a hard-up crown to raid other people's property, the merchant position became secure.

The Stuarts would have loved to regain absolute power and exert central control over the economy. This was symbolized by Charles II's abortive effort to have Sir Christopher Wren build him a castle like Versailles at Winchester, the historic capital. Lord Torrington in 1782 called this "a miserable deserted intention of Royalty." The Stuarts lost. The Puritans had long since gone to Massachusetts, and although in the 1640s some had sailed back to support the Parliament, waves of other disaffected or persecuted sects, like the Quakers, as well as migrants with openly economic aims, continued to leave. In broad terms, nevertheless, and despite Jacobite invasions and uprisings such as those in 1715 and 1745, the issue had been resolved in favor of limitations on the crown by the Restoration Settlement in 1660 and more particularly by the Glorious Revolution of 1688. Parliaments composed of large, relatively businesslike landowners and big London merchants were able to protect the market economy. By the early eighteenth century, most landed families owned some commercial investments. Political stability and internal pacification were matched by a fall in rates of interest.

Agriculture's large share in the economy declined only slowly, and landed society remained important. A law as late as 1711 required merchants who wished to enter the House of Commons to buy themselves estates. Many sinecures remained in the nineteenth century. But even Charles I's monopolies had never gone as far as the handouts and patronage typical of absolute monarchs in mainland Europe. The British colonists who left for America were leaving an economy that was changing faster than any other, though with many remaining frictions. Ironically, it was often the intrusion of market forces, rather than Absolutist decisions, that dislodged the emigrants.

Externally, the policies of the state remained for a long time broadly mercantilist. Internally, there remained an admixture of nonmarket regulation. Local measures to restrain competition among groups of neighbors in villages and very small towns, as well as to abate nuisances of all kinds, gave the economy an interventionist cast. At no time was the market untrammeled, though many of the interventions were made by local rather than central government.

The decline of royal absolutism was thus not matched by a comparable reduction in nonmarket controls. Early emigrants would not have expected anything else. They were accustomed to a great deal of regulation. In many respects concerning sales and settlements, property rights and policing, nonmarket elements remained. Important customary features of economic life did, however, lose force over the early modern period: examples are the erosion of common-field farming by enclosure, starting with enclosure by agreement; the abandonment of sumptuary laws, which had dictated what might be consumed according to social rank; and the gradual removal of legal protection for guild monopolies.

Individual price-responsive firms had long been evident, although well into the period many businesses did remain subject to guild control over entry, size of firm (regulated in terms of numbers of employees), quality of product, and prices charged. Yet the guilds were already being undermined, not only by legal changes but by the spread of industry into rural cottages, whose occupants escaped guild control and accepted lower pay than artisans in the incorporated towns. Rural domestic industry and workshop trades continued to increase into the period of the classic industrial revolution.

In commerce, much activity remained in the hands of "resident strangers" who lived in particular parts of town and worshiped in their own churches. Insofar as this was a restriction on entry, it was an ascriptive feature that sat oddly with the "capitalist" nature of trade. Commercial expansion nevertheless brought more British subjects into the relevant occupations alongside aliens. These occupations included the transhipping of goods and moving them about by hand, virtual coolie labor on a forgotten scale.

Sluggish, uneven, and resisted though it was, the main theme of the early modern period was the extension of market considerations into areas that had hitherto been ruled by command or more often by custom. This development was not a linear one, and its success in all sectors should not be taken for granted. For all that, it was the dominant trend.

FACTORS OF PRODUCTION

The standard classification of factors of production is land, labor, and capital, though classical economists referred to "capital-in-land," capital, and labor. They thereby acknowledged the large element of investment in usable land which is made up of farmhouses and farm buildings, accommodation roads, hedges, drains, and even the improved tilth of cultivated soil. Although colonization was not an obligatory response to resource scarcity – hence Adam Smith's allusion to American settlement arising through "no necessity" – emigration was partly shaped by relative resource scarcities, especially demand for the cheaper land that was to be found in America.

By modern standards, the density of population in Britain was not high, being in 1600 about nine times less than today, between eleven and twelve times less in England and Wales. This was offset by the much weaker agricultural technology, which meant that more land was needed to produce a given output. Livestock production and some of the feeding of horses was from grass, much of it poor-quality permanent pasture on commons and moors. "Artificial" sources of fodder were still scarce; a high proportion of all land cultivable with existing methods had to be devoted to growing cereal crops for human consumption. Essentially, there was a fertilizer shortage. Greater intensities of cropping began to be possible with the introduction of rotations involving "new" crops like clover. A surge of these changes seems to have begun in the 1650s. The rental price of meadowland began to fall rather quickly.

Common land could be used for the hunting of various species of mammals and birds, an activity that overlapped with pest control. There was ample precedent for the great ring shoots of later Pennsylvania in the communal village hunts for foxes, which preceded the ritualized form of fox-hunting adopted in modern England. Riparian rights were more restricted, some of those which had belonged to the monasteries having passed directly into private hands. The physical existence of resources did not always mean they were accessible.

Most English settlements did possess commons that were used for grazing and sources of fuel in the form of timber or bushes such as gorse, the last being extensively used (to all intents and purposes, cropped) as charcoal in forges and ovens. Although fuel wood was in short supply in London in hard winters, and dramas occurred like the burning of church pews, shortages may have originated as much in poor transport as in inadequate production. The price data do not support the idea of a "timber famine." Clearly there was a trade-off among various uses for land, including supplying timber, but timber is a crop and does not run out once and for all. Coppices produced sticks suitable for firing on rotation every few years. In any case, the price of fuel as a whole fell with the coastal shipping of "sea-coal" from the middle of the seventeenth century, and after that time the canalization of rivers made inland distribution much easier. On the other hand, although the English situation was by no means dire, settlers in America would have found both timber and fuel agreeably cheap by English standards.

While Ireland, the Hebrides, and fringes of the Scottish Highlands were exploited as a kind of internal frontier in the sixteenth and seventeenth centuries, and there were major projects of fen drainage in England, it is not possible to piece these examples together to demonstrate a general pressure of population on land. The introduction of German miners to the Lake District, which is commonly cited to indicate that Britain was a backward area catching up with south-central Europe, ignores the fact that they were not very successful, not involved with many types of minerals, and not responsible for the main developments of English mining.

As to labor as a factor of production, there were signs of underemployment and unemployment. Poverty was a problem, and various attempts to solve it were ineffective. There was not enough economic growth generating new capital to invest in ways that would have created work while, as we will see, some existing sources of capital were slow to be invested in the most productive ways.

Despite prohibitions, people kept moving into the suburbs of London, which were more like Third World barrios than the bland residential areas which the term now implies. Labor was moving out of agriculture without finding a wholly adequate alternative. Undoubtedly, adjustment to structural change lagged. Extruded labor could not readily find work in secondary industry, shifted around looking for it – "hark, hark, the dogs do bark, the beggars are coming to town" – and was absorbed only slowly. Part of the problem may have arisen from rhythms in some types of farming that left labor with little to do at certain seasons. Other trades were also dependent on seasonally available resources and had similar spells when work was not to be had.

This problem of outflow from the land was to some extent cushioned by the rise of rural domestic industry. Cottage work took up labor at slack times and in districts where arable farming was starting to contract, besides employing female and child labor in general. In addition to seasonal fluctuations and short-term ones caused by bad weather, industry was not immune from slack periods arising from downturns in trade. Much has been made of a depression in the cloth trade as the cause of emigration from the West Country in the 1620s. Daniel Boone's father was a weaver who left Bradninch in Devon, a county that experienced a long deindustrialization. Other powerful motives, such as religious disaffection, are not so easy to identify. It would not be possible to predict migrant origins solely from what we know of industrial depression; some depressed regions seem not to have sent out many migrants. After all, emigration was only one available "exit" response to hardship, and there seem to have been other reasons that explain much of it.

As noted, a deeper problem of capital formation may have lain beneath the problems of unemployment and underemployment. Speaking very broadly indeed, the difficulty lay less in the availability of savings than in the weak will to invest. Initially, the bulk of savings was in the hands of landowners. As M. M. Postan pointed out in a celebrated passage, many a baron of the fifteenth century possessed enough resources to have financed the start of a cotton industry on the scale of the eighteenth century. None did. Such holders of capital were wedded to the land, to militarism, to consumption. They were also accustomed to a face-to-face society and were unwilling to lend money to people they did not know, for purposes with which they were not familiar and could not evaluate. When anything other than farming was involved, they seemed to want to keep their money at call.

The enormous returns sometimes achieved by treasure hunting on the Spanish Main began to erode this resistance. Trade, and indeed colonization, played a bigger part. In any case, as the merchant class expanded, especially in the Commercial Revolution after 1660, it showed the way and created the instruments for passive investment. By the early eighteenth century, more and more mercantile families were descended from younger sons who had made their own fortunes in trade before reentering the landed class. There was thus an intermingling of types of enterprise.

The supply of factors of production should not be thought of as fixed. Resources, after all, are a function of the technology available to exploit them, while in the medium or long run, enterprise is engendered by the creation of opportunities to invest. In this respect, as in others, one's impression of the British economy depends very much on which period, and how long a period, one surveys. Viewed over the early modern centuries as a whole, the impression is of an unprecedented freeing of factor supplies. Labor increasingly became detached from the land. To a degree this was because, given the modes of inheritance (which tended to eschew the continental solution of subdivision), the growth of population tended to outstrip the supply of farms.

Land became more of a commodity as a result of political events such as the Dissolution of the Monasteries, already mentioned, and the forced sale of indebted Royalist estates under the Commonwealth. The purchasers wanted to get a return for their money and, despite the Restoration of Charles II, were able to retain the estates they had acquired, to the disappointment of royalists.

Commodity markets had existed throughout history. Free markets for factors of production, enabling them to move to where they could make the highest marginal return or come into the hands of those who sought to do so, are a better touchstone of economic change. The early modern period saw real advances in this respect. None of this means that the transition was smooth. The economy was an increasingly enterprising one, but its state of disequilibrium meant plenty of upsets. In a polity which offered the weak, the unfortunate, and the dissenter few and unreliable occasions to express their political "voice," emigration as an "exit" solution was almost to be expected.

Deviance showed up in other ways. As religious ferment gave way to an uneasy pluralism and a greater secularism disguised by the required rituals of an established church, opportunities for the independently minded remained limited. Energies were deflected into more productive channels. An artisan society emerged in which a good deal of effort went into technological creativity. This was not accompanied by commensurate attention to high science. What it produced was a "tinkering" society with an outlet for talents that might have gone elsewhere – maybe back into disputation and religious wars like those of sixteenth-century Europe. Emigration across the Atlantic may be thought of as one option among many for people caught up in the complexities of slow, irregular economic development and every other kind of societal change.

SECTORS OF THE ECONOMY

The usual sectoral division of the economy is threefold: primary production (agriculture, forestry, fishing, mining, and quarrying), secondary production (manufacturing), and the tertiary sector (services). Economic growth is usually accompanied by a movement of some fraction of the labor supply from primary production into the secondary or even tertiary sectors, where its productivity is higher.

Agriculture was certainly much the largest employer during the early modern period. It was undergoing fundamental change and relatively speaking was slowly shedding labor into the other sectors. As much as any indirect sign can, this suggests that the economy was growing. Among the underlying forces bringing about agricultural change were improvements in communications and the growth of income from other activities, notably trade. Markets for food grew, particularly in London. More regional specialization became possible. There is an apparent circularity here in that part of the rise in London's population was due to agriculture's ability to shed labor. That this labor could eventually earn an income providing services in the financial, commercial, and administrative capital made London a large market for the output of those who remained on the land.

Change thus revealed itself in a regionalization of agriculture, or rather an intensification of the pattern of regions which already existed. As it became unnecessary for each and every parish or farm to grow its own grain, specialization developed. Whole districts did remain as cereal producers, finally integrating this with the production of livestock. These districts tended to be ones with easily tilled soil and reasonable market access. Others, however, found that they could not grow their own bread competitively. They turned to buying it and specializing in the rearing or feeding of store and fatstock – that is to say, growing and fattening cattle – on grass.

Because specialist livestock production does not require as much labor as cereal growing, these districts had workers – or, more precisely, part of the time, some of the workforce – to spare. The villages where this happened were the ones in which rural domestic industry tended to take hold most strongly. An economic geography emerged which differed from the archetypal medieval pattern, which was rather uniformly agricultural with a closer approach to universal self-sufficiency in cereals. But the new geography did not yet approach the industrial pattern in which manufacturing withdrew from the countryside and concentrated in towns on coalfields.

Accompanying the changes was a more marked shift from communal, open-field farming to "several" or independent farms. This had been going on for some time, first voluntarily in the form of enclosures by agreement but in the eighteenth century by Acts of Parliament that gave objectors little or no choice and affected the final one-third of the land of England. While the distribution of open fields and enclosed districts was also highly patterned, the pattern did not closely fit the emergent cropping regions. In other words, technical and organizational change were not fully congruent. English regions were small enough for most emigrants to have been familiar with the concepts of both enclosed and common fields, and after the mid-seventeenth century at the latest, most would also have known about improvements in cropping. In a direct sense, this was not vital to them, since abundant American land reduced the need to concentrate on productivity per acre. What was important was a background of adaptability and change – by historical standards.

Attempts to interpret early American agricultural systems in terms of direct transfers of open fields or enclosed farms do not allow for the fact that both were common knowledge and either could be chosen. Indeed, for a surprisingly long time given the greater availability of land, common fields were reconstituted in Massachusetts.

Later British developments involved more and more complex rotations, closely integrating crop and livestock production. As the eastern seaboard became more densely settled in the eighteenth century, American visitors went to Thomas Coke's famous estate at Holkham in Norfolk to observe the latest systems. There was plenty of other contact whereby intensive British agricultural methods could be transferred or adopted. Archives of correspondence between landowners and natural scientists on either side of the Atlantic have been published. Washington's correspondence with the agriculturist, Sir James Sinclair, is well known. In 1785, when Washington was enlarging the garden at Mount Vernon, the Fairfaxes of Writhlington near Radstock, Somerset, sent him plants, seeds, and even a farmer.

In the absence of countervailing pressures, the methods of laying out settlements and managing farms were certainly likely to remain the ones with which settlers were already familiar. But these things were negotiable. There were choices of crops, as witness the early switch to maize from the small grains of Europe. Where Americans did not find that adopting a new crop was worth the effort, they refrained from using it. There were better sources of fodder than the turnip, for instance, which does not mean that the colonists either did not know about this emblem of eighteenth-century English farming or could not obtain the seed. Middle-colonies estates did experiment with it. Most of the inventory of crops remained European, but this fact does not tell us much about the calculus of choice that really determined the Americanizing of agriculture.

Northwestern Europe was not fundamentally unlike the northeastern seaboard. Climatically it was less rugged. The winters were scarcely harsher than those of the Carolinas; the summers were seldom hotter than those of New England. The trees, plants, birds, and animals of Europe were related to those of America. The colonists did not find it hard to attach familiar names to approximately similar species, nor to discover resources comparable with those to which they were accustomed, such as types of timber. The differences were significant but not overwhelming, nor perhaps numerous. Wheat, barley, and the other grains would grow, even if maize was adopted, a cereal sufficiently unknown to the English for John Locke in the 1670s to note it carefully in southern France as *"bled d'Espagne"* (Spanish wheat).

In comparing productivities it would be hard to subtract the effects of all the "made land" of Europe, the capital-in-land. This resulted from millennia spent clearing forest and hauling rocks from the fields, as well as from millennia spent adapting what were originally often southwest Asian plant species to the moist environment north of the Alps or west of the Channel. By contrast, North American pasture proved to be of less nutritive value for stock, few of the grasses being able to withstand grazing. The winters were severe enough to put great strain on stocks of hay. But Europeans were used to a shortage of hay: the pressure points in their farming were similar in kind, if different in intensity, and they possessed pasture species which they could introduce. The introduction of clover from England to the United States brought down the value of wet meadows by 1800, as it had at home a century earlier.

The English were less familiar with some of the problems of predatory animals. The last wolves had been killed centuries earlier, leaving only traces in Saxon place-names like Wolf Pits or Wolfhall. Fortunately, farmers now had powder and shot, while other techniques like seven-foot deer fences were well enough known. Against this, the adjustment of agriculture to the environment had not been perfected even in England.

Settlers brought the rats and mice, cereal rusts and smuts, and the field weeds incident to farming in Britain and Europe. Crop disease among the small grains made shifting to maize a fortunate opportunity for the New Englanders. In 1672, John Josslyn listed twenty-two weeds as having "sprung up since the English planted and kept Cattle in New England." One was plantain, which the Indians were already calling "white man's foot." In the new environment, shorn of the checks and balances in the ecosystems of the old country, some of the interlopers became runaway pests.

In the wilderness, men had to farm. Yet a proportion of early English (and Dutch) settlers were townsfolk. Admittedly, the towns were tiny, except for London, Bristol, Norwich, and Amsterdam. On the other hand, the cities were still small and meadowed enough for rural life not to be strange in principle. Similarly, most country-dwellers had lived close enough to trade and industry for their ways to be familiar. Industrial plant was small, much of it was located in small towns or even villages, and it worked up agriculturally produced raw materials. In any case, those who crossed the Atlantic usually left from one of the bigger port cities; over time, 10,000 indentured servants emigrated from the port of Bristol alone. They had at least cast their eyes on vastly larger settlements than any they would find in the colonies, besides workshops, docks, and big warehouses. By virtue of the journey itself, they could no longer be completely rustic.

The people who became Americans came from the more developed parts of northwestern Europe, approximately from a broad belt stretching from Bristol or Exeter to Amsterdam or later the Rhineland. Thus, when we turn to industry, we find a heritage of experience of an economy in which many commodities were made for sale, usually in small workshops or the home, and were often traded at a distance. Firm size was perhaps not quite as small on average as the domestic system would suggest, since part of the operation involved control by large "putting out" merchants who disposed of raw materials and sold the finished product. Occasional attempts to achieve economies of scale had already been made by men like Thomas Stumpe of Malmesbury, with his workshop in the abbey after the Dissolution, and John Winchcombe, better known as Jack o' Newbury, with his long weaving shop stretching back a block from Northbrook Street in that borough. But before mechanization, the gains were apparently insufficient to establish this trend.

Most of the goods produced were small consumer items, though the trades making edge tools and other producer goods were to flourish on the basis of the colonial need to import such things. Part of the original trade contact between New England and old England was highly personal. To cite just one case, members of the Wolcott family, originating in 1630 from Wellington, Somerset, were back there as late as 1675 buying goods to carry to the colonies. In the hands of merchants, exporting grew, though it had to be protected by the Enumerated Lists attached to the Navigation Act. The Lists restricted the range of commodities that colonials were permitted to produce for sale. An Act of 1731 (5 Geo.II) captures the flavor: it was "to prevent the Exportation of Hats out of any of His Majesty's Colonies or Plantations in *America*, and to restrain the Number of Apprentices taken by the Hat-makers in the said Colonies or Plantations, and for the better encouraging the making Hats in *Great Britain.*"

Before the Civil War, woolens had been dominant among manufactured goods, especially those for export. Their proportion shrank in the Commercial Revolution, which after 1660 extended the range of British exports, shifted their direction substantially from trade with continental Europe, and greatly increased the receipts. The expansion of secondary industry after the Restoration was part and parcel of the regionalization of the economy. Certain regions became more thickly dotted with works and industrial cottages. Metal goods towns such as Birmingham and Sheffield – but not yet the cotton capital of Manchester – expanded. For the time being, much expansion in most industries was "traditional," accomplished by the replication of existing units and methods of production.

The outstanding development in the tertiary sector was the growth of commerce. The establishment of several companies to engage in foreign trade had followed the founding of the Muscovy Company in 1553, leading to those of the Plymouth Adventurers to New England in 1620 and the Massachusetts Bay Company in 1628. Behind this lay an upsurge in commercial activity along the coasts of northwestern Europe as a whole. It was partly consequent on the loss of centrality by the Italian city-states. Their trade was displaced by the westward extension of the Ottoman empire. Compensating maritime trade between the Mediterranean and Baltic Seas expanded. The shores of the southern North Sea were pivotal in this, hence the long, uneasy competition and conflict between the Low Countries, England, and to some extent France.

Of these, England came out on top. While her methods were often external to the market – sweeping the Dutch from the seas – she succeeded better than her competitors in exploiting the growth area of extra-European trade, the triangular trade between Europe, West Africa, and the West Indies. To this trade, New England was linked as an additional supply base for the West Indies sugar plantations, although England made sure to retain direct links with the northern colonies as well as with the tobacco plantations in Virginia.

After 1660, as a result, Britain began to import as well as re-export new crops among which sugar and tobacco figured most prominently. Her port cities and domestic trade expanded greatly. With this came an increase in the mobilization of capital, the emergence of financial institutions, better communications, and the development of retailing (where shops took market share from fairs, and specialist shops took it from general stores). The successful integration of trade and industry stimulated economic development, including some technical change. In the 1690s, patent activity reached two to three times the level of the previous thirty years, yet thereafter it slumped until the second half of the eighteenth century. Rapid industrialization was deferred, and the economy remained heavily agricultural-cum-commercial for some generations.

ECONOMIC PERFORMANCE

The criteria by which the performance of an economy is judged relate in the main to the efficiency with which resources are allocated and used. Others relate to equity and the ability to meet exogenous shocks. As is well known, the difficulty is to sum up: there is no agreed, unambiguous way to weigh the different criteria in a single balance. When economies do better than one another in some respects but worse in others, the economist qua economist has little to add. Since our present purpose is the more straightforward one of categorizing the British economy as a storehouse of resources available to early Americans, we do not have to concern ourselves much with a consolidated balance sheet. Insofar as a judgment is necessary, or possible, Britain should be compared with other countries from which emigrants might have come.

The first touchstone is how closely resources came to being fully mobilized. They did not come very close. An uneven wealth and income distribution meant that the rich could afford to hold assets out of the marketplace. Private property rights over land retained large areas for hunting and excluded them from cultivation. Far less capital was expended on religious structures than in medieval times, but much of it was still withheld from investment for conspicuous consumption or militarism.

It is with respect to labor that the idea of *full resource mobilization* becomes most unhistorical. The endemic problems of poverty, the systematic undereducation of women and the poor of both genders, and sluggishness in redeploying labor that left the land, all show the limitations of both cultural values and available investment funds. At the higher levels of society, talent (male talent) was drawn heavily into professions like the law and the church, where material productivity was not high. Society was highly structured, and many groups, like the younger sons of the defeated Royalists, felt that the chances of improving their lot were limited. Had that not been so, only ideologues and adventurers might have left.

From this it is all too evident that a second requirement, *static allocative efficiency*, was not met, meaning that all factors were not allocated so as to earn their highest marginal return. Many institutions, customs, and ascriptive features (such as the guilds and the control of particular trades by resident strangers) interfered with such an outcome. Reallocative changes did take place but were hampered by the limited integration of the communications network and poor means of disseminating information. A provincial press did not appear until the start of the eighteenth century.

A further criterion, *dynamic allocative efficiency*, could be met by definition only if capital accumulation took place at an optimal rate, determined by some combination of individual preferences and national priorities. This is a somewhat anachronistic demand of an age that lacked clearly defined policy goals. In any case, capital from higher-earning activities notoriously returned to the land for reasons of prestige and power. This undoubtedly reduced the rate of economic growth below what would have been desirable in a world of such poverty. After 1663, landowner-dominated parliaments protected the farm sector by offering bounties on the export of grain. The emergence of an influential nonlanded bourgeoisie, other than individuals primarily involved in trade, was slow. For instance, it was the end of the eighteenth century before a cluster of resort-town residents supportive of colonization, and including Sir William Grant, attorney-general of Canada after 1776, appeared in Devon as the "Dawleish circle." By then, the opportunity to promote further official British colonization in the land south of Canada had passed.

Nor was there *static technical efficiency*, which requires the economy to operate on the production frontier. Static technical efficiency may be defined as the full use of best-practice technique. That would have been the ideal; the question is, how closely did early modern Britain approach the goal? As always, the position from which this is judged could be historical, with a "base-weight" in the preceding period, or modern, looking back from the present. Another possibility is to compare early-modern Britain with one of its contemporaries, say France or the Netherlands.

Making a bold stab at a conclusion, we should certainly keep in mind the level of technical practice in medieval times and in the neighboring countries. By those standards, Britain performed quite well, despite a great mix of industrial and agricultural methods and plant size. Better methods were spreading in a number of industries and certainly in agriculture. But the great variety of practice means that the best techniques known were very far from universally adopted.

As to *dynamic technical efficiency*, England was one of the more creative societies known by that period. Much of the scientific theory underpinning late eighteenth-century industrialization was actually developed in France, but it was of signal importance that an artisan class had emerged in England capable of giving practical embodiment to the ideas. The continent, France especially, did not do as well in that respect.

Authorities differ with respect to the desirability of an *equal distribution of income*. Some feel that the taxes and regulations needed to approach equality must fatally reduce incentives to produce. But the degree of inequality was very marked, and it is noteworthy that, by the time of Independence, Americans had not only become far less unequal but had achieved higher average incomes, too. While that presumably owed much to abundant resources, the implication may be that British extremes of poverty failed to provide an equivalent spur to effort.

Finally, what may be said about the *speed of adaptation to "exogenous" shocks?* By reasonable historical standards, it was good. As Adam Smith noted, neither wars, nor plagues, nor fires had prevented the accumulation of national wealth. An excellent example of resilience is provided by the speed of rebuilding after fires, and not merely after the Great Fire of 1666 in London, where restrictions on work by nonresident craftsmen were readily lifted. Many other towns experienced severe fires that destroyed much of their housing and capital stock, hundreds of houses at a time (13,200 were razed in the Great Fire). Local resources and informal mutual assistance among towns, together with the issuing of "Briefs" (licensing the collecting of alms for individuals), almost always facilitated rapid rebuilding.

England, even more the whole of Britain, was not an equitable society, not one that mobilized its resources to the full, and not one that allocated its factors of production optimally. However, compared with most and perhaps all economies of the day, it was relatively flexible. Its factor markets were becoming freer, technical change was being generated, and society as a whole was rich and energetic. The colonists of America had the best start then possible.

OTHER EUROPEAN ECONOMIES

The European migrations to North America and Australasia were not the biggest in history, but they were among the biggest that failed to blend significantly with existing cultures. The Native American presence, like that of the Australian aborigines, tended to fade away. There was conflict, contact, and a little borrowing, but on the whole, the Europeans usurped the territory and set about populating it with whites engaging in European-style economic life.

Among the Europeans, the role of the British and especially the English clearly predominated. The question arises, why did other countries even in the western half of Europe play a so much lesser role? As it happens, their role was probably greater than the number of their settlers suggests, at least regarding the introduction of techniques which were then borrowed by migrants from Britain. Nevertheless, their participation was rather small. The colonies that some of them established were taken over by migrants from the British Isles.

Certain European countries were larger in population than Britain, and some of them tapped a richer vein of technical change – for instance, the metallurgy of southern Germany. The fact that most had more rigid social systems and more arthritic factor markets than England (the United Provinces was the main exception) did not necessarily dissuade them from major acts of imperialism: Spain, after all, secured a vast empire in Central and South America. That the Spanish and other colonies did less well in the long run than the British colonies in North America is not quite the point. In any case, British colonies in the Caribbean did not always do very well. The present question is, why was colonizing by other northern Europeans in North America so much feebler than that by the British?

The first and obvious answer is that Britain blocked them. There is something to it. Britain did restrict or usurp the settlements of smaller peoples like the Swedes, Dutch, and Danes. Yet Britain's ability to defeat even a small nation like the Dutch was not certain, and her tussle with the French was neither brief nor one-sided.

For central Europeans, there were alternatives, not merely the eastward movement of earlier centuries but internal colonization like draining marshes and Frederick the Great's settling of 300,000 people in 1,200 new agricultural villages. However, that option might be interpreted by some as a response to the British monopolization of North America.

Other nationals did manage to settle in the British colonies. After 1685, with the Huguenot dispersion, the diversity of origins increased, especially in the Middle Colonies; there were also Sephardic Jews and many Dutchmen, while by the middle of the eighteenth century, one-third of the inhabitants of Pennsylvania were German. The Dutch and German languages long survived, and Benjamin Franklin was not the only one who objected to this and saw in it a threat of Balkanization. On the whole, non-British public institutions were not introduced. The Germans and Swedes tended to settle in distinct communities, often inland in the Middle Colonies. Continental Europeans distrusted the law, since in their own countries it had tended to defend privilege. They kept away from state churches and politics. Bunching together was linguistically easiest. The German language was vital for the intellectual and emotional survival of Lutheranism, and many of the Germans saw themselves as members of "redeeming communities," among which the Amish survives. Their self-sufficient, reclusive behavior was typical of the Palatines, who swarmed in 1709–10 from their Rhenish land, which the French had devastated in 1697. Religious, linguistic, and cultural isolation from British settlers promoted little chain migrations of people from certain regions in continental Europe, reinforcing their particularism in the New World, protecting the retention of their own folkways, and slowing the rate at which their ideas mingled with those of British origin.

Governments in the interior of Europe had few resources and little access to the sea. Among the several hundred principalities, some "not the breadth of a shoe," that made up Germany at the end of the Thirty Years' War, only the Hanseatic cities of Hamburg and Bremen had coastal access west of the Baltic. The others had no fleets and would have been obliged to hire shipping from the Dutch or the English, raising the costs of already expensive ventures. There were some negotiations along these lines, but most of the protagonists were inept. They were more interested in a quick killing in the sugar islands of the West Indies. The seaboard countries offered more competition to Britain, notably France, which had 123 ports along a mere 600 kilometers of its northwest coast.

The rulers of mainland Europe had more personal preoccupations, which came to center on the building of extravagant palaces: Versailles and its many replicas. France had the task of refilling the state coffers after Louis XIV's disastrous wars. Her attempts to establish a profitable export staple in Louisiana or Canada did not succeed. Once a few of them had found colonial adventures did not pay, European rulers turned back to domestic measures designed to increase and attract population to their own states. They often restricted the private emigration of their subjects.

All in all, there was little free capital and less willingness to invest it in colonial ventures. Economies were semideveloped, with a patchy distribution of workshop and rural domestic industry, but with so many political jurisdictions that markets were poorly integrated. Seen in the round, continental agricultures lagged behind the institutional and husbandry developments of seventeenth- and eighteenth-century England. In France, the proportion of land under forage crops was only four percent ca. 1700 and no more than six percent as late as 1789. Matters were a little better in northwest Germany, but everywhere else they were worse. An absence of net investment in the land may have been characteristic of wide areas; the rents extracted from French estates went to enable the nobility "to live *noblement* on the banks of the Seine."

Trade was hampered by frequent tolls. Furthermore, during the mid-seventeenth century, most of Europe was affected by a decrease of population and an economic downturn related to the political disruptions of the so-called "General Crisis." The worst manifestation was the Thirty Years' War (1618–48), which supposedly cost the German states one-third of their population. Thereafter, until the nineteenth century, Germany became the "backyard of Europe" and missed out on the Atlantic expansion.

Conspicuous consumption, a high-liquidity preference, and preoccupation with war typified the rulers and nobility of the mainland European states. The landowners tended to consume their rents and, for fear of social obloquy, most invested covertly, where at all, in trade and industry. Merchants hurried to buy land for its status value.

European elites remained captive to a syndrome of underdevelopment longer than their peers did in England, while their merchant class seldom shared in the early gains of overseas expansion. Historically, there is nothing surprising in this; the rigidities and lack of a growth ethic were greater still among Asian potentates. England and the United Provinces, at base London and Amsterdam, were world exceptions. Their growth, resting on European coastwise trade, plus the outcome of Anglo–Dutch rivalry, is what has first to be accounted for in any explanation of the role played by the English in North American settlement.

BACKWASH EFFECTS

By historical standards, England and Europe were changing fast before and during the period of North American settlement. Most of that change was internal, but some of it was a feedback effect from the act of colonization itself. What forms did this backwash take?

Some of them were small beer. America, Baltimore, Georgia, New England, New York, North Carolina, Pennsylvania, Philadelphia, and South Carolina are all frequent as the names of fields in England. The point is that the names are in the category known as "nicknames of remoteness," and the fields were distant from the farmhouses or away on some parish boundary. England was long settled and had a large, complicated society. American influences were remote in most respects.

The big biological effects that the discovery of America had on Europe do not belong here. Maize, the white potato, and perhaps syphilis were transmitted from farther south. New commodities like tobacco, indigo, and later cotton, together with still others already known to Europe, such as furs, fish, and timber, did flow across the north Atlantic. Taken together, they added to the resource stream that created the Commercial Revolution. The economic and political effects of that were not negligible.

Crops that could be physically produced in Europe, like tobacco, were discouraged in line with the international division of labor dreamt up by the British crown. Ecologically, the settlement of North America was not like the discovery of a new planet, in the way that the opening of the tropics or Australasia has been described. The problems that North America raised for European settlement were unusual only in their scale. The products supplied went to swell and redirect existing branches of the economy rather than to create new industries.

As Sir John Seeley concluded in the nineteenth century, England's success in competing with Spain, Portugal, the Netherlands, and France to control the New World was because she was the least hampered by involvement in struggles on the European mainland. Disraeli urged that England had outgrown Europe.

The Commercial Revolution had helped to change the balance of power.

It made Britain more maritime and extended the theater of European conflict. It made Britain richer and increased the commercialism of its economy, although few from the Thirteen Colonies brought back wealth and stayed in Britain. It increased the size of the market served, although scarcely to an extent commensurate with the geographical reach. The consequences include some responsibility for Britain's rise to foremost power and foremost economy in Europe. Market growth, then, and a reshaping of geopolitics were the outcomes.

Incorporated in this was an increase in the geographical and scientific inventory at the disposal of Europeans, a new faith in a Providence which seemed to offer a new frontier whenever an old one was passed. Ample contact at the official, commercial, and personal levels guaranteed that Europeans could begin to grasp the layout of the globe and what it offered. This sense of a Manifest Destiny for Europe was partly responsible for the later, relatively casual, penetration and colonization of the southern hemisphere.

Some North American settlers returned home permanently. The best-known reverse flow was that which promptly returned from the "errand" to build the City on a Hill in New England, back to fight the good fight for Parliament during the Civil wars or to settle again in a purified Commonwealth.

Finally, beyond the effects on foreign trade and foreign affairs, the outflow to colonial America has been seen as a source of British liberties. Many among the colonists were in their day bigots and ideologues like Puritans, Quakers, cavaliers who left when they lost the war, violent Scotch-Irish from the borders, and convicts and whores transported at state expense. Others, not especially poor, were motivated by restless earthly ambition. The going of all these sorts and conditions left England potentially a less troubled and more tolerant country.

CONCLUSION

What difference did it all make? Origins – or parallels? – for most features of early America can be found in northwestern Europe, Britain, or England. Even the quintessential "American System" of mass-producing interchangeable parts had precursors in the French government arsenals, the Taylors' block-making plant at Wood Mills on the Itchen in Hampshire, and Brunel's machinery in the Royal Naval dockyard at Portsmouth. The details could be spelled out, one by one. We can see in the rapid rise of import-substituting industries during the 1640s and the War of Independence that in the latent structure of their economic life, the colonies were even more like Europe than they were actually permitted to remain.

The colonies and the early Republic were tightly bound to the British trading system. They were a vast, distant, experimental annex of Britain, but not a colony on the moon. Their ability to outdo their origins and escape the Third-World status of other colonies, like those in nineteenth-century Latin America, was outstanding. The precise paths by which they brought British or European ways to the wilderness are matters of record. This potential arose from the unbalanced, decentralized, and energized nature of northwestern European and especially British society, from which vigorous and motley emigration took place.

The North American colonies, then, descended from the fastest-developing economy of the most developed part of the world. They had their birth at the right juncture. Although the British government had strong views on the mix of economic activities proper to its empire, and did not hesitate to impose its views in the Navigation Acts, the colonies were less trammeled than any other home country might have made them. Britain herself was struggling free of Absolutism and *dirigisme (étatisme)*, with its confiscations, monopoly grants, and forced loans.

Moreover, many immigrant groups were radical, originating from the disgruntled sections of society. Although they carried all the obvious equipment and most of any Englishman's "invisible baggage" with them, what they were disinclined to carry was as important: they were impatient with archaic restraints on the individual. The element of choice in what they kept and what they left behind is too easily discounted in the presence of so patently a British and European heritage. European (chiefly English) tastes, technologies, and institutions – the discarding of some restraints, all in a context of resource abundance – brewed a novel, vaster, more prosperous, and more equal trans-Atlantic Europe.

4

THE SETTLEMENT AND GROWTH OF THE COLONIES: POPULATION, LABOR, AND ECONOMIC DEVELOPMENT

DAVID W. GALENSON

INSTITUTIONS OF SETTLEMENT

In the years following its establishment of a settlement at Jamestown in 1607, the Virginia Company set out to build an agricultural colony that would earn profits for investors. Toward this end, beginning in 1609 it raised both capital and labor through the device of a commercial company organized as a joint-stock venture. Shares in the company could be acquired either through a subscription of capital or through the pledge of one's labor in America for a period of seven years. The excitement created in England by earlier explorations in North America, fueled by optimistic reports sent back by early settlers in Jamestown, enabled the Virginia Company to raise one of the largest sums ever invested in an English maritime venture.

An early failure of the settlement at Jamestown, marked by extremely high rates of mortality and shortages of food and fresh water that resulted in debilitating illness among many of those who survived, was met by a response from the company that would not have surprised English employers of the day. The colony's governor attributed the infamous starving time to the idleness of Virginia's labor force, and during the following years the company moved to eliminate this problem with sterner measures. From 1611 to 1618 the colony was ruled with iron discipline, with a detailed plan for all economic operations. All land was to be owned by the company and farmed collectively. The workers, all men, were to be treated as bound servants of the company for their specified terms. They were to be housed in barracks and provided with strict rations. For building fortifications and growing crops they were to be divided into work gangs, in military fashion, each of which was to be supervised by an overseer. The company's officers governed the colony under martial law, and punishments for misdeeds, including execution for serious crimes, were harsh and summary.

Within less than a decade after this plan was devised, however, sweeping changes — so fundamental as to constitute a social revolution — had transformed the economic and social organization of Virginia. By 1620 the company had freed the earlier settlers from their contracts and given them their own land and houses. The company had also brought women to Virginia, so the settlers could marry and have families. Martial law had been abolished. And a General Assembly was convened in 1619, with two representatives from each of Virginia's eleven settlements; the extraordinarily liberal suffrage privilege extended the vote for these representatives to all the adult males in the colony.

All these changes were the result of the company's recognition that greater positive inducements were necessary to permit the recruitment and motivation of a labor force sufficient to reverse the economic decline that had begun during the company's earlier regimen. The company had begun with the intention of contracting to pay the workers little more than the low wage rate that prevailed in the English labor market, and transporting them to America, where the abundant land would greatly increase the value of their labor. The substantial difference between the workers' high productivity in Virginia and their low English wages would reimburse the company for the cost of transportation and leave a handsome surplus that would accrue to the company as profits. Although the workers could have been expected to realize that their own work effort would have little impact on the return they would receive when the company's profits were distributed, the company believed the workers would have no choice but to cooperate because of their total reliance on the company in the hostile American wilderness. What the company failed to anticipate, however, was that its protection was not essential to the workers, who could consequently rebel against their harsh treatment by finding alternative employments, whether by running away to live with the Indians or simply by starting their own small settlements. Faced with this effective competition for the workers' labor, the company had to recognize that it did not enjoy the monopsony position it had anticipated as the only employer in the region's labor market and was forced to respond by offering workers higher wages and better living and working conditions.

So it was that at the very outset of English settlement in North America, employers were introduced to the colonial labor problem. The directors of the Virginia Company were only the first of many who had to adapt to a world completely unlike the one they knew and had assumed to be universal. Seventeenth-century Englishmen lived in an economy in which land had long been scarce and labor abundant, and employers simply took for granted the availability of workers at very low wages. In the course of the settlement of English America, a succession of employers and workers would be surprised at the full social and economic implications of a new world in which factor proportions were radically different. Employers throughout the colonies complained of the scarcity and high cost of labor, and bemoaned the new independence of what had been a docile and subservient laboring class in England. In a typical example of what became a litany of appeals for labor from seventeenth-century colonists, in 1645 a Barbados planter wrote to a relative in Scotland: "Want of servants is my greatest bane and will hinder my designe . . . . So pray if you come neare to any port where shipping comes hither indenture procure and send me [servants] . . . lett them be of any sort . . . what I shall not make use of and are not serviceable for me I can exchange with others." In the same year, Massachusetts' former governor John Winthrop complained that the supply of new servants from England was inadequate, and that in consequence those already in the colony "could not be hired, when their times were out, but upon unreasonable terms." The manager of a Maine estate complained to his English employer in 1639 that "workmen in this Country ar very deare." Reporting the "great wages" required by farm workers, he declared "I cannot Conceave which way their masters can pay yt, but yf yt Continue this rates the servants wilbe masters & the masters servants." From the other side of the employment relation, colonial workers reveled in the increased prosperity and autonomy that the scarcity of their labor conferred on them. A settler in early Virginia remarked with astonishment that "our cowekeeper here of James citty on Sundays goes accowtered all in freshe flaming silke; and a wife of one that in England had professed the black arte, not of a scholler, but of a collier of Croydon, weares her rough bever hatt with a faire perle hatband, and a silken suite thereto correspondent." Later in the colonial period, shortly after his arrival in Pennsylvania a hired farm laborer wrote to his family in Lancashire that "if any of my relations have a mind to come to this country, I think it is a very good country and that they may do well." Three years later the same man, now the proprietor of a weaving shop and owner of 450 acres of land, reiterated his advice more confidently, telling his family that "it is a great deal better living here than in England for working people, poor working people doth live as well here, as landed men doth live with you."[1]

The labor problem in early Virginia was greatly intensified by the beginnings of the commercial cultivation of tobacco in the colony. Europeans had found tobacco in cultivation and use by Indians in the Americas during the sixteenth century, but little tobacco had been brought back to Europe, and in the early seventeenth century it remained an exotic and expensive product in England. In 1612 John Rolfe, who would later marry the Indian princess Pocahontas, began to experiment with tobacco in Virginia. The success of his experiments was so great that Virginians soon began growing tobacco on every cleared patch of ground, even in the streets; in 1616 the colony's governor, fearing that the obsession with tobacco would result in famine, declared that no colonist would be allowed to grow tobacco unless he planted at least two acres of corn for himself and every servant. Yet the profitability of tobacco was so great that this and later attempts at restraining its production had no more effect than King James' vehement denunciation of the crop's evils, and tobacco quickly came to dominate Virginia's economy. In 1619 the colony's secretary reported that one man growing tobacco had cleared £200 sterling by his own labor, while another with six servants had made £1,000 from a single crop; he admitted that these were "indeed rare examples, yet possible to be done by others." Another resident of early Virginia declared in 1622 that "any laborious honest man may in a shorte time become ritche in this Country."[2] During the 1620s Virginia became English America's first boom country, as tobacco production reached levels greater than 500,000 pounds per year.

During the first decade after the initial settlement at Jamestown, the Virginia Company had been severely weakened by the colony's lack of economic success, and the poor returns paid to those who had invested in the enterprise. Although tobacco became a source of great prosperity in the colony's second decade, it did not prove a source of salvation to the

[1] William Hay to Archibald Hay, Barbados, September 10, 1645; Scottish Record Office, Hay of Haystoun Papers, GD 34/945; James Kendall Hosmer, ed., *Winthrop's Journal: "History of New England," 1630–1649*, Vol. 2 (New York: 1908), 228; James Phinney Baxter, ed., *Documentary History of the State of Maine*, Vol. 3 (Portland, ME: 1884), 163–4; Lyon Gardiner Tyler, ed., *Narratives of Early Virginia, 1606–1625* (New York: 1907), 284–5; "Early Letters from Pennsylvania, 1699–1722," *Pennsylvania Magazine of History and Biography*, 37 (1913), 332, 334.
[2] Tyler, ed., *Narratives of Early Virginia*, 284–5; Susan Myra Kingsbury, ed., *Records of the Virginia Company of London*, Vol. 3 (Washington, D.C.: 1933), 589.

company and in fact served to weaken the company even further: while tobacco made fortunes for many individual settlers, including a number of the company's officers, the wealth it conferred on many planters gave them the power to become increasingly independent of the company. Ironically, the extraordinary profitability of tobacco was no more compatible with successful control of the colony by the Virginia Company than economic failure had been. The company had wished for a stable society, where men could earn reasonable profits and live normal lives, but neither the starving time of the first decade nor the boom that followed created conditions that could achieve this end.

For nearly two decades the Virginia Company fought what ultimately proved to be a losing battle. In 1624 its charter was annulled, and Virginia was taken under the direct supervision of the king as the first royal colony in England's history. Although debate continues even today over the relative importance of the causes of the Virginia Company's failure, whatever the precise contribution of the company's own shortcomings, it is clear that many of its greatest problems, including persistent epidemic sickness and occasional Indian massacres, were largely beyond its control. And although its career was brief, the company was responsible for a number of important institutional innovations that were to spread widely and become central to the colonial settlement of English America. One of these was the use of the joint-stock device. Familiar to seventeenth-century Englishmen from mercantile shipping ventures, the Virginia Company adapted this device to colonization and introduced investors to the idea of placing their funds for relatively long periods, fixed at the time of subscription. The company launched a publicity campaign in 1609 that captured not only the imagination of the English public, but of enough wealthy members of London's mercantile community to enable the Virginia Company to raise a sum of capital larger than any other colonizing company of the early seventeenth century, and second among joint-stock companies of its time only to the staid and powerful East India Company. Another innovation of the Virginia Company was indentured servitude, an early solution to the labor problem, which will be discussed later in this chapter. Yet another innovation was the headright system. In one of a series of initiatives aimed at increasing immigration to Virginia, in 1618 the company began a policy of granting fifty acres of land for every person settled in the colony. A man could receive this amount – one headright – not only for himself and each member of his family who came to Virginia but also for each bound laborer he imported. With these grants the

Virginia Company established the principle of using American land to help finance immigration. In the later years of the seventeenth century, long after the demise of the Virginia Company, the headright system remained perhaps the single most powerful device attracting immigrants to Virginia. And with some variations in the amount of land and the form of the transaction, the headright system was later adopted by nearly all the colonies of English America.

Beyond initiating the headright system, the Virginia Company introduced another device intended to speed up settlement within its territory. Groups of shareholders were allowed to combine their landholdings into jointly owned associations, called private plantations or hundreds, and the investors in each of these small communities were given local governmental powers over other settlers. Many of these small settlements were established as investors rushed to expand tobacco production on fertile lands with access to the region's many waterways, which could serve to transport their crops to market. The system of private plantations promoted several tendencies that became characteristic of Virginia later in the colonial period. One was the relatively great degree of local power, political as well as economic, of the country gentlemen who dominated the colony in much the same way that the English gentry dominated many rural counties in the mother country. Another was the widespread dispersion of the region's population along the Chesapeake's waterways, with the consequent absence of towns, which was often noted with disapproval by English visitors.

The Virginia Company made another contribution to the settlement of English America that was less concrete but perhaps even more important than any of these specific innovations. Although the company ultimately failed, it did establish a settlement that persisted, and in tobacco it successfully began to produce a staple crop that could profitably be exported to Europe. These accomplishments may have been the final encouragement necessary for many Englishmen, rich as well as poor, to stop merely considering migration to the New World and to take action. By 1620 a new burst of migration was under way that in the course of the next two decades not only would bring much larger numbers of new settlers to Virginia, but would include concerted and successful attempts to settle in the West Indies, New England, and Maryland. Although this later migration did nothing to save the Virginia Company from economic failure, to the extent that the company's experiences helped to increase the size of the later migration and influenced the behavior of its settlers, the impact of the Virginia Company on the settlement of English America extended far beyond its geographic domain, and continued long after its own demise.

In the years following the dissolution of the Virginia Company, the colony's leading planters struggled to retain the political rights they had gained earlier. After more than a decade of uncertainty, the King recognized the authority of Virginia's representative assembly to make the colony's laws, subject to the governor's veto. Once this privilege was granted, it set a precedent of a significant degree of self-government that would extend to all later royal colonies.

During the middle of the seventeenth century, Virginia came to be dominated politically and economically by a small group of wealthy planters. Many of these were recruited to Virginia by its powerful governor, Sir William Berkeley, who arrived in the colony in 1642 and held office for nearly 30 years. Berkeley attracted many younger sons of eminent English families to Virginia through liberal use of his patronage powers. His appointments to high public offices, which in turn brought great land grants and valuable trading licenses, succeeded in establishing his followers as such a powerful ruling elite that they and their descendants retained substantial political control over Virginia for much of the balance of the colonial period.

As the colonization of English America proceeded, other forms of settlement appeared, as new institutions were devised to fit particular circumstances. As larger numbers of Englishmen became willing to migrate to America, a new form of commercial organization grew increasingly attractive to wealthy and politically powerful English investors. One or more gentlemen might become owners of a new colony and induce migrants to settle on their lands under an essentially manorial plan of government. The wealth and political connections of the promoter would place him in a good position to obtain title to a grant of land from an English government anxious to encourage English settlement of the New World at other than public expense, and the prominence and fortune of the promoter would help to inspire the confidence of settlers in choosing their American destination.

A series of attempts to establish proprietary settlements occurred in the early history of the English West Indies. In 1627, with the authority of a royal patent, Sir William Courteen organized a venture that sponsored the first English settlement in Barbados. Two years later, however, the Earl of Carlisle obtained a royal patent that made him proprietor of both Barbados and the Leeward Islands. After a struggle for power Carlisle prevailed.

Under the plans of these early ventures, Barbados was to be an estate cultivated for the benefit of the proprietors. Land grants of moderate size were to be made to cultivators, who were to pay proprietary dues to the absentee owners of the colony.

During the first two decades of settlement, Barbados and the Leeward Islands – St. Christopher, Nevis, Montserrat, and Antigua – were the sites of small settlements where farmers cultivated a variety of crops for export, including tobacco, cotton, and ginger, without great commercial success. In the early 1640s, however, Dutch settlers from Brazil helped English planters introduce sugar cultivation into Barbados, and the sugar revolution quickly changed every aspect of the economy and society of the English West Indies. The new crop was immediately enormously profitable. Sugar was most efficiently grown on large plantations, and a number of young, ambitious English merchants and gentlemen rushed to the West Indies to buy up small farms and consolidate them into great plantations. When the supply of English workers proved inadequate to grow the labor-intensive export crop, the planters rapidly began to import large numbers of African slaves.

The growing wealth of Barbados' planters emboldened them. In 1643 they ceased paying rents to their absentee proprietor and declared themselves freeholders. A period of political maneuvering followed, and after the English Restoration, at the planters' request Charles II officially annulled Carlisle's proprietary patent and confirmed the validity of all land purchases made in earlier decades. With the formal demise of the proprietorship, Barbados became a royal colony under the direct control of the king, who levied a duty on all exports from the island while leaving the planters largely in control of their own local government. Similar developments occurred in the Leeward Islands, where the great sugar planters grew increasingly powerful both politically and economically. When the Spanish were driven out of Jamaica in 1660, it also became an English royal colony. Although the settlement of Jamaica was for many years disrupted by struggles between planters and English buccaneers who used the island as a base of operations, over time great sugar plantations emerged there too, and wealthy planters imported armies of African slaves to grow their crops. Throughout the English West Indies, economic prosperity gave rise to considerable economic independence, and the enormous wealth created by sugar cultivation led to the great planters being allowed to govern their colonies as oligarchies subject only to the relatively permissive control of the king.

The first major example of the proprietary form of settlement on the North American mainland was the grant of Maryland to Cecilius Calvert, the second Lord Baltimore, in 1632. A royal charter granted Baltimore sole title to more than 10 million acres on upper Chesapeake Bay. The remarkable charter also gave Baltimore virtually complete legal authority over his territory, with the power to establish a government in whatever form he pleased. Baltimore established the colony's first settlement at St. Mary's in 1634 and installed his brother as governor, with detailed instructions on how the colony was to be organized. Religious tolerance was to be one of the colony's fundamental tenets. The first Lord Baltimore, a convert to Catholicism, had envisioned Maryland as an asylum for Catholics, where they would be free to worship without fear of reprisals or discrimination, and his son wished to realize this goal without in any way alienating the more numerous Protestant settlers who would be essential to the successful establishment of a colony. The organization of Maryland's economy was to be familiar to Englishmen, as Baltimore laid out plans for the most complete transplanting of a manorial system that was to be attempted anywhere in English America. The proprietor would grant estates of thousands of acres to manorial lords, who would hold the legal power to operate courts on their lands. The lords would recruit tenants to settle on their estates and pay rent on their lands. The lords would pledge to support the proprietor in return for their grants, and would pay him quitrents in recognition of their economic obligations.

The manorial organization of Baltimore's colony failed to materialize, as Maryland's history during the seventeenth century witnessed the gradual breaking down of rigid proprietary control in spite of the proprietors' concerted efforts to maintain their position in the face of growing popular opposition. As in Virginia, tobacco quickly became the primary cash crop and provided a basis for the colony's economic success. The grants of large estates were initially of little practical political or economic significance because of the shortage of workers to cultivate them as tenants or laborers. The extreme labor shortage early in the colony's history allowed many early settlers to gain their economic independence from the manorial lords, and to establish separate farms where they could work for their own profit, often accumulating sizable estates. Thus just as in Virginia, in Maryland the colonial labor problem undermined the initial plans for a rigid social hierarchy, as Lord Baltimore's blueprints for a manorial society were largely swept away and early Maryland became an open and fluid society, which offered considerable economic and social opportunity for poor settlers from England. In time, the colony's growing population would serve to push up land prices and confer great wealth on Lord Baltimore's original grantees and their heirs, and these men would play a central role in the colony's government as in its economy. But like the economy, the government that emerged was much more broadly based than Baltimore had planned. The colony's bitter political strife came to center around the growing efforts of the elected assembly to gain power and greater autonomy at the expense of the governor and the lords of his appointed council. A long and bitter struggle concluded with the successful attempt of the assembly in 1691 to have Maryland declared a royal province. Although the proprietor retained his rights to the colony's lands, the political power of the proprietor had been removed. This was the culmination of a process that had begun almost at Maryland's first settlement, for the economic realities of the New World meant that the primary importance of the proprietor and his grantees stemmed from their position as wealthy landowners and tobacco planters rather than from the legal privileges granted to them as manorial lords.

A number of similar proprietary settlements followed in later years; these included the founding of Carolina in 1663 by eight proprietors, among them the Duke of Albemarle and Sir Anthony Ashley Cooper, the grant of New York to the Duke of York upon its conquest in 1664, the subsequent grant of Jersey by York to Lord John Berkeley and Sir George Carteret, and the grant of the proprietorship of Pennsylvania to William Penn in 1681. While the specific governmental forms and economic practices varied from one colony to another, all of these ventures shared the characteristic that their proprietors treated their grants as private estates from which they expected to derive personal incomes. They were willing to take advantage of any kind of economic opportunity that appeared promising, but in all cases their most valuable asset was ownership of a vast amount of land. Their profits consequently depended on attracting settlers whose efforts would produce output from the land, which would serve as the basis for tax revenue to the proprietors as well as raising the price at which the remaining lands could be sold to later settlers. Although the establishment of large estates to be worked by tenants and landless laborers was the initial model on which these proprietary colonies were usually based, the greater economic power conferred on settlers by the New World's labor scarcity prevented these English tenures and practices from effectively taking hold, and proprietors were often forced to adapt by simply selling their land outright to settlers.

A dramatic example of this process occurred on the southern mainland coast in the last decades of the seventeenth century. A successful Barbados plantation owner, Sir John Colleton, recognized that the rapid growth of the Barbados economy had created a large group of land-hungry farmers, experienced in colonial settlement, who might easily be enticed to the territory south of Virginia with the promise of abundant land. Colleton assembled a group of wealthy and influential backers and with their support in 1663 obtained a royal charter granting his partnership title to all the land between Virginia and Florida. None of the proprietors intended to settle in Carolina, for Colleton had convinced them that they could simply design and appoint a government, distribute land in the colony, and collect rent from settlers. Few settlers responded to their plan, however, and many of those who did reacted unfavorably to conditions on the swampy Carolina coast. In 1669, with the Carolina settlement close to extinction, one of the proprietors, Sir Anthony Ashley Cooper, set out to provide the basis for a new initiative. With the help of his secretary, the political philosopher John Locke, Ashley designed a new approach to the colony's settlement, including a more active role for the proprietors in directing and funding its development. The two men also wrote the Fundamental Constitutions of Carolina, which outlined an elaborate legal framework for a society that was to be based on land ownership. The constitution provided for a class of wealthy aristocrats, who were to make large investments in the colony and receive great estates, a large class of lesser property-holders who would pay quitrents to the colony's proprietors, and another class of tenants, who would have no political role. The constitution also recognized that blacks would be held as chattel slaves. Political stability was to be gained in the colony by giving the primary political and judiciary positions to the nobility, while creating a limited degree of democracy by allowing all landowners to vote for representatives to a parliament that could accept or reject legislation initiated by a council of the noblemen.

The settlement initiated by Ashley's efforts, centered around the town that would later be named Charleston, grew into the prosperous colony of South Carolina. Yet it developed in a way very different from that envisioned by Ashley and Locke, as a group of experienced and ambitious settlers from the West Indies dominated the early settlement and gave its society a number of features borrowed from the sugar islands. Initially, the displaced Barbadians made South Carolina's economy a complement to that of the West Indies, as they sent beef and pork to feed the islands' populations, and lumber to make the barrels for shipping their sugar. As time went on, their continuing search for a staple crop led to the discovery that the Carolina lowlands were ideally suited for rice cultivation, and during the eighteenth century many colonists established great plantations to grow rice for export. The early recognition that the swampy lowlands posed a great danger to settlers in the form of malaria discouraged English immigrants, so the Carolina planters readily imported large numbers of slaves to do the onerous work of growing rice in the hot Carolina summers. Over time the planters challenged the authority of the proprietors in a variety of ways, and after a number of lesser acts of defiance, in 1719 they formed their own government and announced that they would no longer recognize the proprietary authority. The English government accepted the new government's invitation to take over, and in 1720 South Carolina became a royal colony. The end of proprietary rule did not end the proprietors' ownership of the colony's lands, which was not accomplished until 1729, when the proprietors gave up their land rights in exchange for payments from the English exchequer.

The experience of New York affords another example of the failure of a proprietorship. New Netherland had been founded by the Dutch West Indies Company in 1626 as a base for its North American fur trade. Fearing that agricultural development would be a costly distraction from the colony's main purpose, the company discouraged the establishment of commercial farming. As a consequence the colony grew very slowly, and its small population offered no resistance when a fleet sent by the English government seized New Amsterdam in 1664. The king's subsequent grant of the colony to his younger brother made New York the only proprietary possession in colonial history to be held by a member of the royal family. Fittingly, the charter was unique for its brevity and minimal restrictions. The Duke of York was allowed to rule without popular representation, make all appointments and laws, and determine all judicial matters, with a right of appeal only to the king. He was to have complete power over the colony's trade, and he could fix its customs rates, regulate the assigning of its lands, and provide for the colony's defense.

Although New York's charter was the most extreme expression of proprietary authority to be found anywhere in English America, the Duke of York did not rule despotically, and in practice his rule was more benevolent than those of some other proprietary colonies. He did wish to profit financially from his investment in the colony, and to this end he set customs rates for exports and imports, as well as land rents and manorial payments. These profits failed to materialize, however, as the colony's inhabitants resented their lack of political privileges compared to their neighbors in New England, and objected to the imposition of taxes without popular consent. After resisting the establishment of an assembly for a number of years, the duke relented, and a general assembly was convened in 1683. The assembly passed a series of new laws that provided the basis for a constitution for the colony, but these had not yet taken effect in 1685 when the duke became King of England. James' accession to the throne changed the legal status of New York from a ducal seignory to a royal colony, subordinate not only to the king but also the other branches of the executive government in England. The colony's assembly was dissolved, and New York was again ruled by a governor, under the control of the English government. Conflict between the government and the general population continued, until in 1689 the king called on a new governor to establish a general assembly of the colony's freeholders, as in other colonies. New York then became a normal royal colony, with popular representation in government, but with a history of political contentiousness that had never made it profitable for its proprietor.

A very different example of the defeat of a proprietorship, as a result of a colony's economic success, is afforded by the most famous of proprietary settlements. In 1681 Charles II granted to William Penn title to the last unassigned segment of the North American coast, stretching from New York to Maryland, with boundaries encompassing a territory nearly as large as that of England. Penn received personal title to all the land of the territory, as well as the authority to form a government, to appoint most of its officers, and to enact laws subject only to the agreement of an assembly of settlers and the king. In 1682, Penn issued a Frame of Government, which he considered a constitution for the new colony. Since Penn intended his colony to be a refuge for persecuted Quakers, the Frame provided for complete freedom of religion. Politically, Penn's constitution created an oligarchic structure in which laws were to be initiated by a governor and council, with an assembly, elected only by landowners, able to veto but not to amend legislation. In Penn's scheme, political power was reserved primarily for the wealthy, as he planned to use appointive offices in the colony as an inducement for wealthy Englishmen to purchase large tracts of land.

Penn was an extremely successful recruiter of settlers. Beginning in 1681, he circulated pamphlets throughout Great Britain, the Netherlands, and Germany, and soon made Pennsylvania the most widely advertised American colony. Penn's advertising efforts, together with his liberal policy of land distribution, quickly gained Pennsylvania a reputation as a place where settlers of modest means could prosper. Not only English Quakers but also Europeans from a wide variety of countries responded to the call. Philadelphia soon became a major commercial center, and many more settlers spread out to the west on Pennsylvania's fertile farm lands.

Yet Penn was much less successful in his role as a proprietor than as a recruiter. Almost from the beginning of settlement, the representative assembly challenged the dominant political power held by the governor and his council, and a continuing series of struggles over the form and practice of government left Penn discouraged and disillusioned. The culmination of these struggles came in 1701, when Penn was forced to replace the original Frame of Government with a new charter of liberties. Under the new charter the upper council was eliminated from the legislative process, and the power to initiate legislation was to be held by the assembly, subject to veto by the king, but not by Penn. Except for the appointment of the governor, proprietary rule of Pennsylvania came to an end, as the colony's residents were to have no special allegiance to Penn or his descendants. Although Penn retained rights to all undistributed land in the colony, this did not prove to be of sufficient value to compensate for his past expenses and the damage done by a steward who embezzled from his estate, and Penn was a poor man when he died in 1718. Yet Pennsylvania prospered. Although it never became the peaceful religious utopia Penn had wished for, the colony was a great economic success, with a rapidly growing population of more heterogeneous origins than any other major colony of English America. Pennsylvania's many small farms stood in sharp contrast to the great plantations of South Carolina, but both colonies shared an experience in which the economic prosperity of their settlers empowered them to eliminate the control of proprietary government.

A very different method of settlement appeared in the colonization of New England. In 1628 a group of English Puritans obtained a land patent encompassing most of present-day Massachusetts and New Hampshire. They received a royal charter in 1629 for the Massachusetts Bay Company, a joint-stock organization similar to the Virginia Company. As a result of deteriorating economic conditions in England as well as growing fears of religious repression for critics of the Church of England, in 1630 the Puritan leaders of the Massachusetts Bay Company took the novel step of migrating to America, taking the company and its charter with them. Unlike the other colonizing companies, the New England settlers therefore would not be accountable to an English organization holding title to their land and the profits from its settlement. All the major investors in the Puritan colonies migrated to New England, carrying with them their capital and their title to the company, and leaving further promotional work in England to a network of associations based on religious interest. The system proved an effective one, as the relocation of whole congregations to America in groups resulted in a substantial movement of Englishmen to Massachusetts between 1630 and 1643, when improving prospects for Puritans in England brought an end to the initial migration.

The spread of settlement throughout New England proceeded very differently from the patterns of colonization to the south. Many of the initial plans made by companies for English settlements in America had called for their colonists to create towns and villages like those of England in the new lands, in order to transplant familiar ways of life to the New World. Yet to the dismay of those who planned the settlements, in most of the early colonies the desired compact communities did not develop, as the advantages of large landholdings for commercial agriculture and the need for access to waterways for transporting bulky cash crops to market generally tended to disperse settlers over the countryside in a pattern of isolated plantations and farms very different from that of England. Such was not the case in New England, however. The leaders of the Massachusetts Bay Company had originally intended to distribute land to householders using a headright system, with the amount of land granted to each settler to be determined by the number of family members and servants arriving in the colony. Yet when they reached America, the leaders realized that use of this policy might produce the kind of scattering of the settlers that had occurred in Virginia, and would not guarantee the attainment of their communal goals. The Puritans consequently designed a system for the settlement of their lands based on the strict and centralized control of regimented communities, and unlike in other regions this plan was not undermined by the existence of lucrative agricultural opportunities.

A group that wished to establish a new town in Massachusetts needed the permission of the colony's legislature. When the legislature approved a request, its franchise not only conferred the right to create a government for a new town, and the right to send representatives to the legislature, but also carried title to an allotment of land. This land was legally deeded to a group of leaders, or proprietors, of the planned settlement. These leaders distributed the land, to themselves as well as others, according to a number of criteria, including social status, family size, and extent of

investment in the colony. In each town much of the land was initially not
distributed but was held out for common use and grants to later settlers,
as well as for later division among the original proprietors when the
growth of their families made larger landholdings advantageous. The same
leaders who owned the town's land were among the initial voting membership of the town's political meeting, and made up an important part of the
members of the town's covenanted church.

Although opposition to the tight control of these small groups of
leaders would develop later, in the early colonial period the villages organized in this way remained cohesive, and the settlement of New England
proceeded with the orderly establishment of new towns founded and managed by these procedures. The Massachusetts Bay Company evolved from a
commercial company into the government of a commonwealth, and the
colony's government consequently ceased to have the profit motivation of
the other companies of colonial settlement. As a result, initial land settlement was often done through grants rather than purchases, with the speed
of the expansion of landholding determined by political and social as well
as economic considerations. The ability of the colony's leaders successfully
to impose and maintain their control over economic resources may have
been in large part a consequence of the absence of the extraordinary profit
opportunities that existed in other regions of English America, for potential entrepreneurs in New England lacked the powerful incentive of their
counterparts to the south to establish the large plantations that would
have conflicted with the social goals of the Massachusetts Bay Company's
elite. Conflict was also reduced by the fact that when a number of
nonproprietary residents of an existing town became dissatisfied with their
restricted economic opportunities, they were often able to obtain permission from the legislature to establish a new town and thus become proprietors in their own right. The region in which English ways of life were
most successfully replicated in America was also the region which would
achieve the least economic prosperity.

Another group that shared the Puritans' objection to the Church of
England had also settled in New England. A small group of religious
radicals arrived in Plymouth in 1620. The Pilgrims rejected the pursuit
of wealth and worldly comforts in their attempts to establish a primitive
religious utopia. When they failed to achieve the religious commitment
they had sought, their lack of material success left them with no cohesive
political or social structure, and their small settlement was formally
absorbed into Massachusetts in 1691. Although intellectual historians

have long been fascinated by the Pilgrims' self-abnegating quest for religious purity, their impact on the colonial economy and society was negligible.

A survey of the institutions of settlement of English America quickly reveals not only a variety of ways in which existing English methods of organization were adapted to particular problems involved in settling the wilderness, but also the frustration in most cases of the original goals of those who initiated the ventures. The model of settlement common to most of these ventures — indeed the term normally used by seventeenth-century Englishmen to refer to colonies — was that of the plantation, in which English settlers would transplant their traditional communities and established ways of life to new lands. Yet in most places this failed to happen, and from very early in the colonial period it became commonplace for English visitors to America to remark on the unfamiliarity of the societies they found there. The failure of the original plans of many of the earliest colonizers was in part a consequence of the common economic basis of their efforts in profit-seeking joint-stock companies or proprietorships. The need to produce dividends for shareholders or proprietors placed great pressure on settlers to produce quick profits for their companies, but to their disappointment they found no sources of immediate profits in America. The result was often the financial weakening of the companies, even their bankruptcy, and a growing need for the settlers to assume greater responsibility for the survival of their own communities. The remainder of this chapter will survey some of the main adaptations they made and the consequences that followed from them, but a central element in the history of all the colonies of English America is the early use of new economic and social institutions, as the result of a painful transition to the very different economic realities of a new world. The early colonizers' great plans for enormous profits and utopian social and religious communities were based on the assumption that employers and workmen would stand in much the same relation in America as they had in England. These plans were quickly thwarted, however, by the economic realities of the New World: the radically greater ratio of land to labor in America, and the much greater labor productivity this produced in most of the new regions of settlement, meant that the employment relationship would be very different from that of England. Out of the adjustment by both employers and workers to the new economic realities of America came genuinely new forms of society.

Although the focus of the following section of this chapter will be on labor market institutions, these were obviously not the only important features of the colonial economy and society that were transformed in the process of transfer from the Old World to the New. A few other features of fundamental importance deserve mention. One of these involved land tenure. The ownership and control of land came to be much more closely linked in America than in England. Although the trend in England at the time of colonization had long been toward the increasing importance of land tenure in fee simple, and although tenancy was far from nonexistent in the colonies, the ownership of land by those who worked it was much more common in the colonies than in the mother country. This was not simply the result of the greater abundance of land in America, for the effect of the higher colonial ratio of land to labor was reinforced by the attitudes of many settlers, who had come to America precisely to avoid the tenancy that faced them in England. The combination of this widespread desire for independent ownership and control of land with the ample supply of American land to be cleared and cultivated meant that freehold land ownership became a dominant characteristic of the colonial economy.

Another characteristic of the colonial economy often remarked by contemporaries was that the extent of control exercised by formal community structures – not only government, but also private associations such as guilds – was much less than in England. From a very early date, many governments at the level of both the colony and the local community recognized that the colonial economy was simply not subject to their oversight and control. Guilds and many other private economic associations either never began in the colonies or never developed effective control of markets. Although the actual degree of control over the economy that was exercised by governments and guilds in seventeenth-century England has long been debated by historians, in colonial America many governments and other formal organizations failed to maintain even a pretense of being able to regulate economic activity. While in some regions the dispersion of settlement clearly made government control of most economic activity impractical almost from the beginning of colonization, even in areas where settlement proceeded in more traditionally English fashion, based on central towns, it soon became apparent that decisions concerning production and trade would be largely independent of government intervention, and would be determined almost entirely by the abilities and desires of the individuals and families who populated English America.

LABOR MARKET INSTITUTIONS

The key to economic success in colonial America, for individual planters as well as entire colonies, was to obtain an adequate supply of agricultural labor to grow crops that would satisfy the demands of the large European market or of the expanding markets of the colonies. Stark contrasts appeared among the solutions to this problem that were developed in colonial America. Three major institutions emerged as solutions – indentured servitude, slavery, and hired labor – and the differences among them affected nearly all aspects of life in the societies that produced and sustained them.

The first of the three institutions to emerge on a large scale was indentured servitude. This was a credit system under which labor was leased. In England servants signed contracts, called indentures, promising to work for a recruiting agent or his assigns in a particular colony for a specified period of years. The servant was then transported to the agreed destination, where his contract was sold to a colonial planter who provided the servant with food, lodging, and clothing during the time the servant worked for him. The design and practice of indentured servitude overcame considerable obstacles, in the form of capital market imperfections and principal–agent problems, to make the indenture system a key institution in early English America. A brief account of its development and operation shows how the efficiency of the system was achieved.

Ten years after the initial settlement of Jamestown, Virginia's planters began to export tobacco to England. The introduction of the crop raised the value of labor sharply. In the fall of 1619 the secretary of the colony wrote excitedly of its new prosperity, proclaiming that "all our riches for the present doe consiste in Tobacco," but then corrected himself, explaining that "our principall wealth (I should have said) consisteth in servants."[3] To meet the resulting high demand for labor, late in 1619 the Virginia Company sent one hundred new workers to the colony, each bound to the company for a period of years. Upon their arrival, the company rented out the majority of these servants to private planters on annual contracts. This arrangement proved costly to the company, however, because of the new principal–agent relationship that it created between the company and the private planters. The company quickly recognized that the planters lacked sufficient incentives to protect the company's substantial investment in the

---

[3] Kingsbury, ed., *The Records of the Virginia Company of London*, Vol. 3, 221.

labor of their hired workers, both in providing adequate maintenance and health care in the colony's unhealthy disease environment and in preventing runaways. The following year, the Virginia Company made a new shipment of one hundred servants. Their distribution among the planters became the first large-scale example of the characteristic form of the indenture system, as colonists paid a lump sum of money to the company and in return received title to the services of the worker for a fixed term of years. This transaction solved the agency problem the company had encountered earlier, for now the servant's supervisor was the owner of his labor contract, with appropriate incentives to care for the servant and prevent him from running away.

This transaction provided a systematic means by which a substantial supply of English labor could be connected with colonial demand. A majority of all hired labor in preindustrial England was performed by workers called servants in husbandry — youths of both sexes, usually aged in their teens or early twenties, who lived and worked in the households of their masters on annual contracts. Passage fares to America in the seventeenth century were high relative to the earnings of these servants in husbandry, and few prospective migrants were able to pay the cost of the voyage out of their own savings. The Virginia Company's solution was to provide passage to America to prospective settlers as a loan to the migrants, who contracted to repay their debts with their labor services after their arrival in America.

The large size of the debt for passage meant that repayment would take substantially longer than the single year that normally characterized the employment of farm servants in England, and this potentially raised new problems of work incentives. The migrant typically faced a term of four or more years as a bound laborer after he or she had received the major benefit of the bargain, in the form of passage to America. One historian has recently argued that under these circumstances, with the servant lacking the motivation of either future wages or the desire to be rehired, masters had to rely heavily on physical violence to extract work from indentured servants.[4] Corporal punishment of servants may have been more common in the colonies than in England; although colonial laws protected servants from excessive punishment, masters were permitted considerable latitude in beating their servants. Yet it would be surprising if such physical abuse had been very widespread, for harming their servants would obviously

[4] Edmund Morgan, *American Slavery, American Freedom: The Ordeal of Colonial Virginia* (New York: 1975), 126.

reduce the profits that masters could gain from their work. There is evidence that positive work incentives for servants were created within the operation of the indenture system. Masters appear typically to have exceeded the legally required minimum levels for food and clothing provided to their servants, and freedom dues – the master's payment to the servant at the end of the contract – could also be raised above the legally specified levels. Wages could be paid to servants during their terms, and some masters made bargains with their workers that allowed the servants to be released early from their terms of servitude. The opportunities created by these positive work incentives clearly contributed to the flexibility of the indenture system in practice.

The legal basis of indentured servitude originated in the English statutes and practices that regulated service in husbandry, but over time throughout the colonies the indenture system developed into a distinctive institution in law. In addition to laws that permitted masters to whip their servants for misbehavior, most colonies enacted a system of laws to enforce the servants' contracts. Servants caught in attempts to run away were to be put in jail until they could be returned to their masters; in most colonies the servant was then bound to compensate his master by having his term extended, in some cases by as much as ten days for every day of his absence. Masters were entitled to transfer their rights to their servants' labor, and servants could be – and regularly were – legally sold. Servants were not allowed to marry without their masters' permission; servants who married secretly would have their marriage declared invalid and their terms of servitude extended. In spite of the considerable control their masters enjoyed over them, indentured servants nonetheless retained many basic legal rights and enjoyed important legal protections. Servants' indentures were legal contracts, and their terms were upheld and enforced by colonial courts. A number of servants whose masters tried to hold them beyond their agreed terms were freed by colonial courts upon presentation of their indentures. Servants had the right to sue their masters for mistreatment, and in extreme cases of abuse servants would be released from their contracts. Although instances in which servants were freed by courts were rare, county courts frequently ordered that masters improve the treatment of their servants, often by increasing the food or clothing they provided. Masters who caused the death of a servant were to be tried for murder, in the words of a Maryland act of 1642, "as near as may be to the law of England."

Like servants in husbandry in England, indentured servants bound for the colonies were generally young. Five sets of English registrations of departing servants made between the 1680s and the 1770s show that at least two-thirds of the migrants throughout this period were between the ages of 15 and 25. It was extremely rare for servants to be below the teen ages or above the twenties; the share of servants between 10 and 30 was consistently above 90 percent. Throughout the colonial period, English indentured servants were predominantly males. Surviving registrations from the seventeenth century show that males accounted for 75 percent of the migrants, while their share increased to 90 percent in the eighteenth century. This shift may have been the result of changing demands for skilled and unskilled servants, as discussed later in this essay.

Although the Virginia Company first developed the method by which the indenture system operated, once the practice of outright sale of the contracts had been established a large company no longer had any significant advantage in servant transportation, and the indenture transaction was quickly borrowed by smaller merchants and planters. The trade in servants was a natural one for European merchants who imported sugar, tobacco, rice, or other crops from the colonies, for servants could be exchanged directly for colonial produce. There were no legal barriers to entry into the trade, and economic barriers to entry were small for merchants or captains already involved in trans-Atlantic shipping. As a result, throughout the colonial period in the principal European ports large numbers of recruiters engaged in the trade, and servant transportation was typically carried on in highly competitive markets.

Fare quotations indicate that charges for passage from England to America were constant for all servants at any date: they did not vary with individual characteristics or among colonial destinations. All servants who migrated to America consequently incurred implicit debts of similar value. With recruitment under competitive conditions, the value of all servants' contracts should have been the same at the time they were negotiated. However, since the productivity of the servants differed, the conditions of their indentures had to vary: the higher a servant's expected productivity in America, the faster he could repay the implicit loan made to him, and the shorter the contract he should have received.

Several sizable collections of indentures, which have survived among English legal records, provide detailed evidence about the characteristics of several thousand servants and the conditions on which they migrated to America. Econometric analysis of the length of the servants' contracts confirms the prediction of an inverse relationship between the term of

servitude and individual productivity. The length of indenture was inversely related to age, skill, and education, as older servants, those who
had skilled occupations, and those able to sign their contracts received
shorter terms. Servants bound for the West Indies furthermore received
considerably shorter terms than those bound for the colonies of the North
American mainland. This reduction in term was clearly a compensating
wage differential paid to servants willing to travel to less desirable destinations, because both working conditions for servants and economic opportunities after servitude were known to be much worse in the Caribbean
islands than on the mainland. West Indian planters were well aware of
their disadvantage in recruiting English servants. In 1675, for example,
the Council of Barbados complained in a petition to the King of England
that "In former tymes Wee were plentifully furnished with Christian
servants from England . . . but now Wee can gett few English, haveing
noe Lands to give them at the end of their tyme, which formerly was theire
main allurement."[5] The length of indenture furthermore responded to
changes in the colonial demand for labor. The terms of servants bound for
the West Indies varied inversely with the price of sugar. With the region's
virtual monoculture in sugar, high prices for the staple signaled times of
prosperity in the islands, and the high demand for labor during these
periods improved the conditions on which servants could travel to the
region.

The highly competitive European markets in which servants entered
indentures produced economically efficient outcomes. The lengths of the
contracts were no greater than was necessary to reimburse merchants for
the full cost of transporting the servants to the colonies. Thus the prices
for which servants were sold to colonial planters were only slightly higher
than the fares charged free passengers for the trans-Atlantic voyage; the
difference was a premium received by merchants for bearing the risk of
servant mortality on the crossing. The high degree of competition in the
European markets in which servants signed contracts therefore protected
the servants from economic exploitation by merchants, who might have
wished to bind servants to contracts much longer than necessary to pay for
their passage. The adjustment of contract lengths furthermore was sufficient to equalize the expected sale prices of all contracts at the time the
servants were bound. Thus a number of variables that represented information known by recruiting merchants at the time the servants' bargains

---

[5] "Petition of the Council and Assembly of Barbados to the King," 1675; Public Record Office,
London, C.O. 1/35, f.237v.

were made in Europe, including characteristics both of the servants and of
the contracts they entered, were found to have no systematic effect on the
sale prices of the servants' contracts in America. This implies that more
productive servants were able to capture the rewards from their greater
value in the form of shorter terms, instead of having these benefits accrue
to merchants as higher sale prices for their contracts. Additional evidence
of the efficiency of the market for servants comes from the analysis of
fluctuations in the volume of the servant trade over time. The number of
servants arriving annually in Maryland and Virginia varied positively with
tobacco prices. As for sugar in the West Indies, the central position of
tobacco in the early Chesapeake made the crop's price a good indicator of
the state of the region's economy. That high tobacco prices resulted in
high levels of immigration again attests to the efficiency with which the
trans-Atlantic market for servants transmitted information about the state
of colonial labor demand to Europe.

Indentured servitude was an important early solution to the labor problem in many parts of English America, and it was widely adopted: the
leading historian of the institution estimated that between one-half and
two-thirds of all white immigrants to the colonies between the 1630s and
the Revolution came under indenture.[6] Whereas initially all the servants
came from England, in time migrants from other countries joined the flow
of servants to English America; especially in the eighteenth century, substantial numbers of Scottish, Irish, and German immigrants came to the
colonies under indenture. In particular, the large migration of Germans to
Pennsylvania produced an innovation in the form of a variation on indentured servitude called the redemptioner system. Before sailing from Europe, a passenger signed an agreement to pay his fare on arrival in America. After arrival, a period of two weeks was allowed for the servant to raise
the fare. If he failed to raise the money, he was sold into servitude by the
ship's captain for a length of time just sufficient to repay his debt. The
value of this system to immigrants appears to have stemmed from the fact
that the concentration of the German migration to Philadelphia meant
that many migrants could hope to find family or friends already in Pennsylvania who might give or lend them the funds necessary to cancel their
debts. English criminals also joined the flow of indentured servants; those
convicted of felonies could be sentenced to transportation to the colonies,
where they would be bound to serve terms of from seven to fourteen years.

---

[6] Abbot Emerson Smith, *Colonists in Bondage: White Servitude and Convict Labor in America, 1607–1776*
(Chapel Hill, NC: 1947), 336.

During the eighteenth century a large fraction of England's felons were sent to the Chesapeake Bay colonies under indenture.

Although indentured servitude played a major role in the colonial labor market, in most places its importance declined significantly before the time of the Revolution. Indeed, in precisely those regions that initially depended most heavily on white servants for their labor needs, planters eventually turned to black slaves as their principal source of bound labor. Although these substitutions of slaves for servants occurred at different times in different regions, in each case the functions of indentured labor evolved in similar ways over time.

Indentured servants were quantitatively most important in the early development of those regions that produced staple crops for export. The major need was for workers to clear the land and grow the staple, and initially planters relied on indentured labor to do this work. As time went on there was also a rising demand for skilled craftsmen to do the work of building finer houses, processing and packing the products for export, and catering to the demands of the growing domestic markets, and servants were purchased for these jobs.

A second stage in the evolution of the function of indentured servitude occurred in the West Indies after the introduction of sugar, in the Chesapeake Bay colonies during the last quarter of the seventeenth century, and in South Carolina and Georgia in the eighteenth century, after planters had replaced their European field workers with Africans. In each of these cases, this substitution of slaves for servants caused the majority of the bound labor force to change from white to black. The initial transition from servants to slaves was not complete, however, because the newly arrived Africans lacked many of the craft skills required by colonial planters. Planters generally did not train their adult Africans to do skilled jobs, instead waiting to train either those imported as children or slaves born in America. For a time a racial division of labor by skill therefore existed, as unskilled labor forces were made up of slaves, while indentured servants continued to function as craftsmen and often to act as plantation managers.

As colonial output continued to increase, the demand for both skilled and unskilled labor grew further. The eventual outcome in the plantation economies was widespread investment in the training of slaves to take over the skilled work. By the time of the Revolution the substitution of slaves for servants had been largely completed in all the staple-producing colonies of English America. In the West Indies and the southern mainland colonies there were many plantations based almost exclusively on slave labor, with many slaves employed as skilled artisans in addition to those who did unskilled field work. The adoption and growth of slavery in those regions of English America that were characterized by plantation agriculture did not bring a complete end to the immigration of white servants, but it did produce systematic shifts over time in their occupational composition, and eventually in their principal regions of destination. By the end of the mainland's colonial period, the West Indies had ceased to import white servants in significant numbers, and among the plantation economies only the Chesapeake Bay colonies continued to receive sizable flows of indentured labor. Among the economies not characterized by plantation production of staple crops, only Pennsylvania received large numbers of servants for an extended period, beginning in the late seventeenth century and continuing through the end of the colonial period.

The decline of indentured servitude was thus linked in many colonial regions to the growth of slavery. Unlike the trade in indentured servants, the trans-Atlantic trade in African slaves began long before the English colonization of America. Portuguese merchants began to trade for slaves on the coast of West Africa as early as the middle of the fifteenth century, and a substantial trans-Atlantic trade in slaves arose in the course of the sixteenth century, with Portuguese ships carrying African workers to Spanish America and Brazil. By the end of the sixteenth century the Portuguese were joined in the trade by Spanish and Dutch merchants. More than 100,000 African slaves were brought to the Americas by the end of the sixteenth century, and another half million by the middle of the seventeenth – still before English involvement in the trade began.

When English merchants entered the trans-Atlantic slave trade in the second half of the seventeenth century, they therefore found a highly competitive international industry in the process of rapid expansion. The spread of sugar production from Brazil to the West Indies after 1640 produced a booming demand for labor in English America, which coincided with a general expansion of sugar production in the Americas, so that more African slaves were sold to Europeans in the five decades after 1650 than during the preceding 200 years combined. The desire of English merchants to capture a share of the lucrative trans-Atlantic trade in slaves eventually led to the grant in 1663 by Charles II of a charter to the Company of Royal Adventurers Trading into Africa. The company was badly organized, however, and its operations were interrupted by the outbreak of war between the English and Dutch in 1665. When peace was restored in 1667 the company was beyond saving, and its liquidation began in 1670.

The Company of Royal Adventurers was succeeded by the Royal African Company, which received a charter from Charles II in 1672. The new company was granted a legal monopoly of the slave trade to English America in return for agreeing to establish and maintain fortified settlements on the West African coast. The forts, where company factors would purchase and hold slaves prior to shipment, were desired by the King to prevent the military domination of the region and possible exclusion of the English by another European power.

The expected monopoly of the slave trade to the English colonies failed to materialize. From the beginning of its career the Royal African Company suffered infringements of its monopoly in the form of illegal deliveries of slave cargoes to the English colonies by smaller traders, referred to by the company as interlopers. Surrounded by wealthy planters who favored an open trade in slaves, the company's resident agents in the West Indies fought a losing battle to stop these illegal shipments. The agents could rarely persuade colonial governors to apprehend the interlopers, and when they did, colonial juries made up of planters would rarely give judgments against the smaller traders. As a result, at most times the Royal African Company does not appear to have carried even a majority of the slaves delivered to the English sugar islands. Having failed to produce adequate profits for its investors, and suffering from outstanding debts from West Indian planters that grew steadily over time, the Royal African Company's activity in the slave trade dwindled after the 1680s, it became inactive in that trade after 1730, and the company went out of business in 1752.

The economic history of the Royal African Company's legal monopoly has long been misunderstood. A notable early misinterpretation, which has subsequently been repeated by many historians, was offered by Adam Smith. Part of Smith's famous attack on mercantilism in *The Wealth of Nations* was devoted to a discussion of the unfortunate economic consequences that resulted when legal monopolies were granted to merchants to set up joint-stock companies to carry on England's foreign trade. In summarizing the Royal African Company's career, Smith stated that it had enjoyed a monopoly of the slave trade until 1688, when the flight of James II from England nullified royal monopolies. Exposed to competition, the company was unable to survive, in spite of a parliamentary act of 1698 granting the company the proceeds of a tax levied on its English competitors in the slave trade. In Smith's view the reason for the company's economic failure upon being exposed to competition was not hard to find, for he believed the company to have been twice cursed by inefficiency, with the "negligence and profusion" of both a joint-stock company and a legally protected monopoly.[7]

Smith's explanation of the Royal African Company's failure appears incorrect, because his analysis was based on false premises. The company's failure was not caused by inefficiency spawned by a sheltered monopoly position, but on the contrary by the very competitiveness of the trans-Atlantic slave trade. The company's African forts proved an expensive liability that raised the company's costs relative to those of its competitors, while the compensatory benefits the royal charter was supposed to confer on the company were never realized, as neither Charles II nor his successor James II proved willing to override the resistance of colonial planters and enforce the company's exclusive right to deliver slaves to the English colonies. As a consequence, company employees overseas convincingly reported to the central office in London that the interlopers were able both to outbid the company for slaves in Africa and to undersell it in the West Indies.

A longstanding belief that the Royal African Company held an effective economic monopoly of the slave trade to English America has often served to obscure the fact that the trans-Atlantic slave trade to the colonies was a highly competitive industry. This has resulted in significant misunderstandings of both the conduct of the trade and the economic basis of one of colonial America's major sources of labor supply. Recent investigations have produced evidence of the conduct of the trade that contrasts with many earlier views, by identifying a number of outcomes that suggest careful and efficient approaches to the business of slave trading.

The mortality of slaves on the trans-Atlantic crossing has long been one of the most intensively studied aspects of the slave trade. The debate over mortality dates back to the British parliamentary hearings on the abolition of the slave trade that began in the late eighteenth century. The slaves' passage mortality rates were higher than those suffered by other travelers crossing the Atlantic: although Royal African Company records show a decline in average slave mortality per voyage from 24 percent during the 1680s to 13 percent in the 1720s, and records from later traders indicate a

---

[7] Adam Smith, *An Inquiry into the Nature and Causes of the Wealth of Nations* (New York: 1937 [orig. publ., 1776]), 700–1, 712–13.

further decline to average mortality rates of 8 to 10 percent in the second half of the eighteenth century, even the latter remained far above the mortality rates of under 4 percent estimated for Europeans traveling to America in the eighteenth century.

The earliest explanation for these high mortality rates, first offered by the abolitionists, attributed them to overcrowding of the slaves on the voyages, which resulted in poor sanitation and rampant spread of disease. Yet recent quantitative investigations of the experience of the Royal African Company and other traders have failed to reveal any systematic relationship between the mortality rate of slaves on a voyage and the degree of crowding of the slaves. Another traditional explanation for the slaves' high mortality attributed it to inadequate provisioning of the ships. Yet again quantitative studies have found no evidence of higher average daily or weekly mortality rates on longer voyages, which would have been most severely affected by the inadequate supplies of food and water. In sum, the results obtained to this point suggest that slave traders were not negligent or careless in the ways often charged in the past. Recent studies of the high passage mortality of slaves have suggested epidemiological explanations of the high mortality. The slaving voyages brought together at close quarters large numbers of people from very different geographic disease environments, and inevitably exposed them to many unfamiliar diseases that could be lethal to those who had no immunity developed through previous contact. Outbreaks of small pox, dysentery, and other diseases would spread rapidly throughout the human cargoes of the small slaving ships, often killing many slaves already weakened from conditions on their journeys to the West African coast and during their imprisonment there prior to shipment. Evidence consistent with explanations that stress the role of contagious diseases has been found in the fact that the European captains and other crew members of the slaving ships suffered from mortality rates much higher than those common among sailors on other types of trans-Atlantic voyages, and often as high as those of the slaves. Indirect support for epidemiological explanations of the high mortality rates on the trans-Atlantic crossing is afforded by a different kind of evidence that demonstrates the extraordinary danger of entering unfamiliar disease environments in the colonial period. A study of English employees of the Royal African Company sent to live on the west coast of Africa found that among 460 new arrivals between 1695 and 1721, one in three died within four months of landing, and three in five failed to survive one full year.

Slavery grew very unevenly in English America. Large-scale slavery appeared earliest and most prominently in the West Indies. All the English colonies in the West Indies had black majorities in their total populations by the end of the seventeenth century, and all reached black shares of more than 80 percent of the total population during the eighteenth century. On the North American mainland only South Carolina developed a black majority in its population during the colonial period, although slaves did come to make up more than one-third of the total population in Maryland, Virginia, North Carolina, and Georgia. The Middle Colonies had much lower black shares in total population, ranging from 5 to 10 percent, and New England never had more than 3 percent of its population made up of blacks.

Beyond these differences in the overall numbers of blacks, there were considerable differences among regions in the typical sizes of slave holdings. The great sugar plantations of the West Indies produced by far the greatest concentration of slave ownership. As early as 1680, more than one-third of all slave owners in Barbados owned more than twenty slaves; plantation sizes grew over time, and in Jamaica during the early 1770s a sugar plantation of median value held more than 200 slaves. Among the mainland colonies, the typical size of slave-holdings was greater among the rice planters of South Carolina and Georgia than among the tobacco planters of the Chesapeake. Thus in 1774, nearly half of all slave owners in Maryland and Virginia owned five slaves or less, compared to less than a quarter of the slave owners of South Carolina, while less than 5 percent of Chesapeake slave owners held more than 25 slaves, compared to fully 30 percent of those of South Carolina.

In all the colonies of English America, slavery came to be well defined as a legal status, involving the perpetual servitude of blacks and their progeny. Yet the legal status of slavery was not created simultaneously or uniformly throughout the colonies; it evolved separately within each colony, and its adoption often occurred piecemeal, as legislators responded to specific questions that arose concerning the status of Africans. The speed with which the status developed varied considerably across colonies. One instance of the rapid legal definition of slavery occurred in the West Indies. In 1636, the council of Barbados declared that "Negros and Indians, that came here to be sold, should serve for life, unless a Contract was before made to the contrary," and no doubts concerning the lifetime servitude of blacks appeared there in later years. Similarly, in South Carolina the rights of masters were very early clearly defined; the colony's

Fundamental Constitutions, drafted by Sir Anthony Ashley Cooper and John Locke in 1669, declared that every freeman of the colony would have "absolute power and authority over his Negro Slaves, of what opinion or Religion soever."

In contrast, property rights in blacks remained much more uncertain for an extended period in the Chesapeake Bay region. Although blacks were present in the region by 1619, no legislation concerning slavery appeared until after mid-century; not until 1661 did Virginia's assembly recognize that some blacks were held for lifetime service. In 1664, Maryland's legislature enacted a law that all blacks held in the colony, and all those imported as slaves in future, would serve for life, as would their children. Yet questions nonetheless remained about the absoluteness of Chesapeake planters' property rights in slaves. Thus in 1667 Virginia's legislature noted that concern had arisen that slaves who were baptized might thereby be freed from their servitude, and passed a law declaring that they would not. While the ostensible purpose of this law was to encourage the spread of religion, its more likely cause was revealed in the title of the parallel law enacted in Maryland in 1671, "An Act for Encouraging the Importation of Negroes and Slaves into this Province." The extension of the property rights of Chesapeake masters in their slaves did not end with these laws. In 1669 Virginia's assembly bluntly extended these property rights to their stark limits in "An act about the casuall killing of slaves": a master who killed his slave would not be guilty of a felony, "since it cannot be assumed that prepensed malice . . . should induce any man to destroy his own estate." Thus fully fifty years passed between the first arrival of blacks in the Chesapeake and the full definition of the legal status of slavery.

Both the practice and legal definition of slavery became established in all the colonies of English America in the course of the colonial period, and although the patterns of development varied considerably among the colonies, the form of the institution that eventually emerged was very similar throughout English America. The English government was aware of the development of black slavery in the colonies, and made no concerted effort to regulate or prevent the status, because it recognized the economic value of the institution. Once established, slavery remained in existence in all the colonies of America through the time of the Revolution. An abolitionist movement did begin in Pennsylvania after 1750, and the growing support of the Quaker church for antislavery led increasing numbers of slaveowners voluntarily to manumit their slaves in the following decades. But mandatory abolition by legislation did not occur until after American independence; Pennsylvania passed a first abolition law in 1780, and a number of other northern states followed this lead thereafter.

Free labor existed throughout colonial history. Yet much less is known about free labor in the colonies than about either servitude or slavery, in part because free labor is a less dramatic subject than bound labor, and in part because of a shortage of primary evidence. The smaller amounts of money at stake in the hire of free labor for short periods attracted less interest from the government and the courts than the larger sums involved in the long-term hire or purchase of bound labor, and records of transactions in free labor are consequently scarcer than those in indentured and slave labor.

Hired workers in colonial America faced a very different legal definition of their obligations than do workers today. Colonial laws and the decisions of courts appear initially to have followed English practices concerning labor contracts in most respects. Thus for example an early Virginia law reenacted an English principle by providing that any worker who agreed to perform a piece of work must not depart before completing it, upon penalty of a month in jail and a fine of £5 sterling. In general, colonial courts initially appear to have accepted the premise, which prevailed in English law, that hired artisans and laborers were legally bound to complete the services they had agreed to perform; at least in the seventeenth century the courts did not hesitate to order the specific performance of all labor agreements, and to impose fines on workers who did not fulfill their contracts. Over time, however, practice in the colonies may have changed. During the eighteenth century the legal requirement that hired workers remain at their jobs until they had fulfilled their agreements seems increasingly to have been replaced by simple civil liability for any damages caused by their premature departure.

Hired labor was present in all the colonies, but its importance varied considerably across regions. In one region, however, hired labor existed almost in isolation from the other two labor types. A study of probate inventories from the mainland colonies in 1774 found that only 5 percent of a sample of New England decedents had owned slaves, and that none had owned indentured servants. The absence of bound labor in New England was well known to contemporaries, as for example a seventeenth-century visitor to the colonies remarked that although "Virginia thrives by keeping many Servants . . . New England conceit they and their children can doe enough, and soe have rarely above one Servant."[8]

Because of the virtual absence of bound labor, an interesting point of comparison for New England's labor market is that of England. Preindustrial England had two distinct types of hired labor. One, service in husbandry, was made up of unmarried youths in their teens and early twenties who lived and worked in the households of their employers, typically on annual contracts. The second type was made up of adult men who worked for wages by the day or week. Both these types of labor existed in New England, but underlying economic differences between Old and New England appear to have changed considerably their quantitative importance and functions in America.

In England, service in husbandry was an efficient method of labor allocation, for it allowed workers to move among farms at minimal cost to increase their productivity. Children could move from the smaller farms of their parents to the larger farms of neighbors or wealthier farmers in nearby villages, thus raising the productivity of their labor. The institution's exclusive use of the unmarried eliminated the problem of tied movers: the cost of migration was lower for these individuals than for whole families, and employers could hire the number of workers they wanted, without having to support or house other family members. Historians have found that in preindustrial England wealthier farmers were less likely than poorer farmers or landless laborers to send their children into service. The larger farms of the wealthier parents meant that they could put their children's labor to better use than the poor, thereby not sacrificing income by keeping their children longer at home. The considerably higher value of labor relative to land in New England meant that rather than sending their children into service on larger farms, more colonial parents could potentially behave like wealthier parents in England and expand their landholdings to take advantage of the labor of their children. Service in husbandry should therefore have been less common in New England than in England. Although data have been analyzed from only a small number of communities, the evidence of the studies done to date does support this analysis, for it indicates that servants in husbandry made up smaller shares of the total population in New England's towns than in those of England during the late seven-

---

[8] "Certaine Notes and Informations concerning New England," ca. 1660–4, British Library, Egerton Mss. 2395, f.415v.

teenth and early eighteenth centuries. New England parents clearly kept their children at home longer than English parents, developing the family estate, rather than sending them to work for others. Colonial America's labor scarcity therefore appears to have reduced considerably the importance of this institution that was central to the preindustrial English labor market.

A similar change appears to have occurred with hired day labor. New England had active markets for hired labor from a very early date, but the region's employers frequently complained that hired labor was both expensive and hard to find. As early as 1641 John Winthrop expressed his frustration at the inability of Massachusetts' legislature to prevent "the excessive rates of laborers' and workmens' wages," noting that "being restrained [by statutory limits on wages], they would either remove to other places where they might have more, or else being able to live by planting and other employments of their own, they would not be hired at all."[9] It appears to have been common in New England for smaller farmers to hire out for wages for short periods; a recent study found that almost every man in one seventeenth-century Massachusetts county performed occasional hired labor at some time in his career, most often for his older and wealthier neighbors. Yet the same study found that the typical periods of hire were short, so that few farmers were able to rely on the hired labor of neighbors or strangers. The study concluded that hired workers accounted for a much smaller share of all labor needs in Massachusetts than in England.

The higher level of wages relative to the price of land in New England meant, as Winthrop recognized, that more men could buy farms and work for themselves in New England, and in consequence fewer adults worked as full-time hired laborers there than in England. Recent estimates indicate that whereas in England in the late seventeenth century more than two-fifths of adult males relied primarily on agricultural wage labor for their livelihood, in New England this share was consistently below one-third. In seventeenth-century Essex County, Massachusetts, the employment of hired labor was in fact so irregular that the identifying occupational designation of laborer almost disappeared from county records.

The settlement of the abundant lands of the New World substantially improved the lot of free workers, not only by raising the wages of those who worked for hire, but also by allowing many others to purchase land

[9] Hosmer, ed., *Winthrop's Journal*, Vol. 2, 24.

and become independent farmers. Although in some areas increasing population densities over time resulted in rising shares of landless laborers in the adult male population, throughout the colonial period hired labor appears to have remained quantitatively less important in America than in England.

POPULATION GROWTH AND
THE LABOR FORCE

Colonial America has been known for its rapid population growth since the time of Benjamin Franklin and Thomas Malthus. Examination of the behavior of total population immediately shows why this has been the case. Between 1650 and 1770 the total population of the English colonies of the West Indies and North America increased from just under 100,000 to more than 2.6 million, an average annual rate of growth of 2.8 percent. During the same period the population of England rose from 5.2 million to 6.5 million, or at a much more modest average annual growth rate of less than 0.2 percent. With an average rate of population growth in America more than fifteen times that of England, it is little wonder that the enormous difference impressed observers in both the colonies and the mother country: in the course of 120 years, the colonial population had increased from less than 2 percent to more than 40 percent as large as that of England. This striking American expansion, which Malthus called "a rapidity of increase probably without parallel in history," became the primary piece of empirical evidence cited by Malthus in support of his belief that population would increase geometrically in the presence of benevolent political institutions and abundant fertile land that together held at bay the great checks of misery and vice.[10]

Yet this growth of the overall colonial population was the result of a number of very disparate component patterns. One facet of this diversity appears when total population is disaggregated by region, as shown in Table 4.1. Average annual regional growth rates on the mainland during 1650–1770 ranged from a low of 2.7 percent for New England, through 3.3 percent for the Upper South and 4.2 percent for the Middle Colonies, to a high of 5.5 percent for the Lower South (for 1660–1770). The lowest regional rate, an annual average of 1.8 percent, was found in the West

---

[10] Thomas Robert Malthus, *An Essay on the Principle of Population* (London: 1970 [orig. publ., 1798]), 105–6.

Table 4.1. *Total population of English America, by region (thousands)*

Year	New England	Middle Colonies	Upper South	Lower South	West Indies	Total
1610						
1620			1			1
1630	2		3		2	7
1640	14	2	8		14	38
1650	23	4	13		59	99
1660	33	6	25	1	81	146
1670	52	7	41	4	96	200
1680	69	15	60	7	118	269
1690	87	35	76	12	135	345
1700	92	54	98	16	148	408
1710	115	70	124	25	178	512
1720	171	103	159	40	212	685
1730	217	147	225	60	258	907
1740	290	221	297	108	285	1201
1750	360	297	378	142	330	1507
1760	450	428	502	214	406	2000
1770	581	556	650	345	479	2611

Note: New England includes Maine, New Hampshire, Vermont,
Plymouth, Massachusetts, Rhode Island, and Connecticut. Middle
Colonies include New York, New Jersey, Pennsylvania, and Delaware.
Upper South includes Maryland and Virginia. Lower South includes
Georgia, North Carolina, and South Carolina. West Indies includes
Barbados, Jamaica, Antigua, Montserrat, Nevis, and St. Kitts.
Source: John J. McCusker and Russell R. Menard, *The Economy of British
America, 1607–1789* (Chapel Hill, NC: 1985), 103, 136, 153, 154, 172,
203.

Indies. Thus the total population of the West Indies increased by only a
factor of eight during 1650–1770, compared with factors of 25 for New
England, 50 for the Upper South, and more than 135 for the Middle Colonies in the same period. As these very different long-run growth rates imply, major shifts occurred over time in the composition of colonial population by region. In 1650, 60 percent of all colonial residents lived in the
West Indies, with just over 20 percent in New England, less than 15 percent in the southern mainland colonies, and less than 5 percent in the Middle Colonies. By the close of the colonial period, less than one-fifth of the
total colonial population was in the West Indies; New England's share had

Table 4.2. *White population of English America, by region (thousands)*

Year	New England	Middle Colonies	Upper South	Lower South	West Indies	Total
1610						
1620			1			1
1630	2		2		2	6
1640	14	2	8		14	38
1650	23	4	12		44	83
1660	33	5	24	1	47	110
1670	52	7	39	4	44	146
1680	68	13	56	6	42	185
1690	86	32	68	10	37	233
1700	91	50	85	14	33	273
1710	113	63	101	19	30	326
1720	167	92	128	25	35	447
1730	211	135	171	34	37	588
1740	281	204	213	58	34	658
1750	349	276	227	82	35	969
1760	437	399	312	120	41	1309
1770	566	521	398	189	45	1719

Source: See Table 4.1.

remained almost constant at just over one-fifth, while the southern mainland had risen to nearly two-fifths and the Middle Colonies to one-fifth.

Still greater contrasts appear when total population is disaggregated by
race. Table 4.2 presents evidence on the growth of the white population
by region. Perhaps most striking is the divergence between the experiences of the West Indies and the mainland regions. In 1650, more than
half of all the whites in the English colonies lived in the West Indies. But
the second half of the seventeenth century witnessed a sharp absolute
decline in the islands' white population, with only a gradual recovery in
the eighteenth century. By the end of the colonial period, consequently,
the white population of the West Indies was no greater absolutely than it
had been a century earlier, and in 1770 West Indian residents accounted
for less than 3 percent of all whites in English America. In sharp contrast,
the white populations of the mainland regions all grew rapidly throughout
the colonial period, with average annual growth rates during 1650–1770
ranging from 2.7 percent in New England to 3.0 percent in the Upper
South, 4.1 percent in the Middle Colonies, and 4.9 percent in the Lower

Table 4.3. *Black population of English America, by region (thousands)*

Year	New England	Middle Colonies	Upper South	Lower South	West Indies	Total
1610						
1620						
1630						
1640						
1650		1			15	16
1660	1	1	1		34	37
1670		1	3		52	56
1680	1	2	4		76	83
1690	1	3	7	2	98	111
1700	2	4	13	3	115	137
1710	3	6	22	7	148	186
1720	4	11	31	15	176	237
1730	6	12	53	26	221	318
1740	9	17	84	50	250	410
1750	11	21	151	60	295	538
1760	13	29	190	95	365	692
1770	15	35	251	155	434	890

Source: See Table 4.1.

South (during 1660–1770). From very unequal beginnings in the seventeenth century, the mainland's white population in 1770 was divided almost equally among New England, the Middle Colonies, and the South.

The growth of the black population by region was radically different, as shown in Table 4.3. For most of the seventeenth century, more than 90 percent of all blacks in English America were located in the West Indies. That region's black population increased throughout the colonial period, with an average annual growth rate of 2.8 percent during 1650–1770. From small numbers in the seventeenth century, however, the black population in the southern mainland colonies grew very rapidly in the eighteenth century, with average annual growth of 4.3 percent in the Upper South during 1700–70, and 5.8 percent in the Lower South. As a result, by 1770 just over half of all blacks in English America were on the mainland. These were heavily concentrated in the South, as few blacks lived in the Middle Colonies, and fewer still in New England.

Table 4.4 shows that the share of blacks in the total population of English America rose sharply in the late seventeenth century, from less

Table 4.4. *Blacks as a percentage of total population, by region*

Year	New England	Middle Colonies	Upper South	Lower South	West Indies	Total
1610						
1620						
1630			4			2
1640	1	11	1			1
1650	2	12	2		25	16
1660	2	11	4		42	25
1670	1	11	6	5	54	28
1680	1	10	7	6	64	31
1690	1	7	10	16	73	32
1700	2	7	13	18	78	34
1710	2	9	18	26	83	36
1720	2	10	19	37	83	35
1730	3	8	24	43	86	35
1740	3	7	28	46	88	34
1750	3	7	40	42	89	36
1760	3	7	38	44	90	35
1770	3	6	39	45	91	34

Source: See Table 4.1.

than one-sixth in 1650 to more than one-third by 1700; it then remained virtually constant at that level during the eighteenth century. But the quantitative importance of blacks varied enormously among regions. Blacks never made up more than 3 percent of the total population of New England, while their share in the Middle Colonies peaked at just over one-tenth in the mid-seventeenth century and declined thereafter. In contrast, a steady growth of the share of blacks occurred in the southern mainland colonies, as blacks accounted for about two-fifths of the total population in both the Upper and Lower South by the end of the colonial period. The West Indies had by far the largest share of blacks: the region had an overall black majority by 1670, more than 80 percent of its population was made up of blacks throughout the eighteenth century, and 90 percent of the total population was made up of blacks by the time of the American Revolution.

These regional differences in population growth rates, and in the racial composition of population, reflect enormous differences in disease environments, demographic behavior, and labor market outcomes among the regions. The case of the West Indies lies at one extreme in a number of respects. As witnessed by the changing racial composition of the population, the growth of the island colonies depended entirely on the growth of slavery. This was a direct consequence of the sugar revolution that began in Barbados in the 1640s and later spread to the other islands. Sugar production for export to Europe was immensely profitable, and the introduction of sugar in the West Indies produced an explosive increase in the demand for labor to plant and harvest the cane. Yet sugar cultivation also required very heavy and arduous labor, most efficiently done by groups of workers organized into gangs. West Indian sugar plantations more than any other preindustrial agricultural enterprise became factories set in the fields, and English indentured servants soon learned to avoid the punishing work of sugar cultivation in the tropics. At the same time, the sugar revolution reduced the attractiveness of the islands to English immigrants of modest means for another reason. The technology of sugar cultivation, with very high fixed capital requirements for the machinery and structures needed to grind the cane, boil the juice, and cure and pack the sugar for shipment, resulted in great economies of scale, and in consequence small farms could not compete with the vast plantations that swallowed up the islands' fertile land. The West Indies quickly became known as a region that offered no real economic opportunity for former indentured servants or poor free settlers. In addition, the mixture of Europeans and Africans from a number of very different disease environments soon created a deadly epidemiological environment that rapidly made the West Indies notorious as a place of widespread disease and extraordinarily high mortality, and most Englishmen were reluctant to risk premature death in the islands' harsh demographic regime. With a rising demand for labor and a declining supply of both indentured and free English immigrants able to choose their colonial destinations, West Indian planters readily turned to the use of workers who did not share this ability, and African slaves quickly came to dominate the labor forces of the sugar islands. Throughout the colonial period the black population of the West Indies suffered a substantial excess of deaths over births, and the islands' slave populations grew over time only as a result of massive continuing importations of Africans in every decade.

Among the mainland colonies, the Lower South, particularly South Carolina, most resembled the West Indies in its heavy reliance on slave labor. Also as in the islands, the increase in the black share of the labor force in South Carolina, and later Georgia, coincided with the rise of a single export crop – rice – to a dominant place in the economy. The commercial cultivation of rice in South Carolina began in the 1690s, and within two decades blacks outnumbered whites in the colony. As in the West Indies, the nature of the work involved in production of the staple crop was a key element in the transition from white to black labor in South Carolina, for the oppressive work of growing rice in labor gangs in the heat of the colony's summers deterred English workers from migrating to the colony after rice became its main product. And like the West Indies, South Carolina quickly gained a reputation for unhealthiness that further reduced the colony's potential white labor supply. The black population in South Carolina, as well as in North Carolina and Georgia, expanded in large part because of an importation of Africans that continued throughout the colonial period.

Although the rise of staple export crops was responsible for the growth of slavery in the West Indies and South Carolina, the same was not true of the Chesapeake Bay colonies. Tobacco was introduced into Virginia by 1620 and quickly became the basis of the Chesapeake region's economy, but it was cultivated primarily by white farmers and their English indentured servants for at least the next five decades. Tobacco was a more delicate plant than either sugar or rice, and was not well suited to the routinized labor of work gangs. Furthermore, tobacco production required much less fixed capital than did sugar, and as a result apparently offered no important economies of scale. Throughout the colonial period, tobacco was grown profitably on small farms as well as on large plantations. Although economic opportunities for immigrants diminished somewhat over time, the region never became as inhospitable to those of modest means as did the West Indies, and the Upper South attracted substantial numbers of English migrants during most of the colonial period.

The most dramatic change in the Chesapeake's labor force occurred in the closing decades of the seventeenth century. The region's planters' holdings of bound labor shifted from a ratio of four indentured servants to one slave during the late 1670s to nearly four slaves to one servant in the early 1690s. Major changes in the conditions of supply of both servants and slaves appear to have caused this rapid transformation in the composition of the region's bound labor force. The supply of servants to the region appears to have declined as a result of both improving labor market conditions in England and deteriorating prospects for migrants to the Chesapeake in the late seventeenth century; the former reduced the total numbers of migrants leaving England for America, while at the same time the latter harmed the Chesapeake in competing for migrants with newly settled Pennsylvania, which offered the abundant inexpensive land that the tobacco colonies no longer had. The result of this decline in servant supply was a sharp increase in the price of servants, together with falling numbers of new arrivals in the 1680s and '90s. At the same time the cost of slaves to Chesapeake planters fell. The 1680s marked the lowest point of a secular decline in slave prices in the West Indies, due to falling sugar prices in European markets, and slave traders dissatisfied with the low prices that they were receiving for their cargoes in the West Indies began to bring the mainland tobacco planters a steady supply of Africans at low prices. The Chesapeake's rapid transition in the 1680s from primary reliance on the bound labor of white servants to the large-scale use of black slaves was therefore the result of a substantial decline in the price of slaves relative to that of servants. Once planters had begun to use African slaves in large numbers, they were clearly satisfied with their new bound laborers, as the Chesapeake's black population rose steadily during the eighteenth century.

The labor force of the Middle Colonies was very different from those of the other regions. No colony in the region relied heavily on slave labor, and sizable flows of both free and indentured immigrants came to the region in almost every decade after the initial settlement of Pennsylvania in the 1680s. A much larger proportion of these immigrants came from places other than England, including most notably Germany and Ireland, than was the case for any other region of English America.

Diversified agriculture based on the family farm characterized most of the rural economy of the Middle Colonies. The region produced a variety of grains, vegetables, and livestock. Its mercantile centers, Philadelphia and New York, exported these products to a number of markets, led by the West Indies and southern Europe. The resulting commercial prosperity and continuing availability of fertile land for immigrants gave the region a widespread and lasting reputation as the best poor man's country in the world, and this reputation was clearly a key factor in attracting the large numbers of immigrants that helped to produce the rapid growth of the Middle Colonies' white population throughout the eighteenth century. At the same time, it appears that the substantial continuing immigration of indentured servants as well as free workers generally held the cost of labor below levels that prevailed in the regions to the south of Pennsylvania, and consequently below a level at which the large-scale importation of slaves would have been profitable.

Colonial New England's demographic history was distinctive among the regions of English America in several important ways. Most notably, New England was the only region that had practically no significant immigration after its initial burst of settlement, which ended by the early 1640s; indeed during most of the remainder of the colonial period New England had net outmigration. Slaves never made up more than 3 percent of the region's population, and New England imported few European indentured servants. Unlike the West Indies and the southern mainland colonies, which increased their populations in spite of high mortality rates, through persistently high rates of immigration, New England enjoyed very low mortality rates throughout the colonial period, and its population grew as a result of high rates of natural increase.

As a consequence, New England was unique among the regions of English America during the eighteenth century in having nearly all its work performed by free native-born whites. In most areas small family farms produced a variety of crops for their own consumption and sale in local markets, as well as some exports to the West Indies. Their labor was overwhelmingly that of the family members, supplemented by only occasional hired labor. The region's relatively low effective demand for labor together with the steady expansion of its population through natural increase appear to have held the cost of labor below levels that would have made it profitable to import either servants or slaves.

As these overviews of the population histories of the major regions suggest, the great differences in the experiences of the regions appear to have stemmed from considerable differences in rates of immigration to each of the regions and in the mortality rates of their populations. The differences among regions in the pattern of white immigration over time are highlighted in Table 4.5, which presents estimates of net migration of whites by decade from 1630. New England's only period of sustained white immigration occurred early in the colonial period, with the Puritan migration to Massachusetts, which had ended by 1670. In a majority of the decades thereafter the region was a net exporter of population. The opening of Pennsylvania first made the Middle Colonies a major destination for immigrants during the 1680s. The region remained among the major receiving regions for white immigrants throughout the rest of the colonial period. Pennsylvania received the bulk of the region's immigrants, but New York also received sizable numbers in the decades following the middle of the eighteenth century.

The prosperity of Virginia's tobacco economy made the Upper South an

Table 4.5. *Decennial net migration of whites to English America, by region* (*thousands*)

Decade beginning	New England	Middle Colonies	Upper South	Lower South	West Indies	Total
1630	11		11		41	63
1640	5		14		40	59
1650	3		18		33	54
1660	8		17	3	12	40
1670	1	4	15	3	15	38
1680	−1	13	9	4	11	36
1690	−17	7	0	3	19	12
1700	−4	0	18	7	10	31
1710	20	10	21	1	18	70
1720	−2	15	38	10	16	77
1730	9	27	30	16	6	88
1740	−10	13	−17	16	9	11
1750	−9	40	20	13	11	75
1760	6	9	−2	34	5	52
1770	−23	12	−25	51	11	26

Sources: Henry Gemery, "Emigration from the British Isles to the New World, 1630–1700," *Research in Economic History*, 5 (1980), 215; David Galenson, *White Servitude in Colonial America* (Cambridge: 1981), 216–18.

important destination for immigrants from early in the colonial period. The region suffered a sharp drop in white immigration in the final two decades of the seventeenth century, but immigration quickly revived, and the Upper South was the leading colonial destination for white immigrants in each of the first four decades of the eighteenth century. Declining rates of immigration followed, and the Upper South became a net exporter of white population late in the colonial period. The Lower South began to receive moderate levels of white immigration in the second half of the seventeenth century and the early eighteenth century. These gave way to higher and steadily rising levels after 1720, as the growth not only of South Carolina but also of North Carolina and Georgia made the Lower South the largest destination for white immigrants in the last two decades of the colonial period.

The West Indies were the major destination for white immigrants in the early colonial period, as the islands received more than half of all whites bound for English America during each of the three decades after

1630. A sharp drop in white immigration to the region occurred after 1660, and the West Indies were never again as important a destination for whites, with generally declining levels of immigration over time for the remainder of the colonial period.

The general patterns of white immigration by region thus include a decline by the mid-seventeenth century of two regions – New England and the West Indies – that were important destinations early in the colonial period; a consistent importance of one region – the Upper South – from the early seventeenth century to the middle of the eighteenth; and a rise of two regions – the Middle Colonies and Lower South – to importance during the eighteenth century.

The demographic composition of this immigration differed considerably across regions. The early migrations to the West Indies and the Chesapeake were overwhelmingly made up of young, single men; for example, 94 percent of a group of 985 passengers who left London for Barbados in 1635 were males, and more than 90 percent were between the ages of 10 and 29, while 86 percent of 2,010 passengers from London to Virginia in the same year were males. In contrast, 35 percent of a group of 1,960 migrants from England to Massachusetts prior to 1650 were females. The ages of the immigrants to New England were also more widely distributed than those to the southern regions; more than one-fifth of this early group were below the age of 10, and more than one-quarter were above the age of 30. The great majority of these early immigrants to New England, more than 70 percent, traveled in family groups. These sex ratios clearly indicate why rapid natural increase could begin so early in New England, as well as suggesting that natural increase in the early West Indies and the Chesapeake would not have been possible even if the disease environment had not been so virulent. Over time, the sex ratio of immigrants to the Chesapeake became more balanced, but male migrants continued to outnumber females by a ratio of two or three to one throughout the seventeenth century.

Differences in the demographic composition of immigration by region clearly also existed later in the colonial period. Half of all English and Scottish immigrants to New York during 1773–6 traveled in families, as did more than two-fifths of those bound for New England, whereas less than one-tenth of those bound for Maryland and Virginia traveled with family members. While females accounted for 40 percent of the immigrants to New York, and 30 percent of those to New England, they made up only 12 percent of those bound for Maryland and 8 percent of those bound for Vir-

Table 4.6. *Decennial net migration of blacks to English America, by region*
(thousands)

Decade beginning	New England	Middle Colonies	Upper South	Lower South	West Indies	Total
1650	0		1		39	40
1660	0		2	0	38	40
1670	0	0	2	0	53	55
1680	0	0	7	1	59	67
1690	0	0	8	1	95	104
1700	0	1	11	2	88	102
1710	1	3	7	10	93	114
1720	1	1	6	11	126	145
1730	1	1	29	11	88	130
1740	0	0	47	12	115	174
1750	−1	2	4	17	127	149
1760	−1	−2	8	32	86	123
1770	−5	−2	−19	9	81	64

Source: David Galenson, *White Servitude in Colonial America* (Cambridge: 1981), 216–18.

ginia. In general, these patterns from the beginning and end of the colonial period appear to have held true throughout. New England and part of the Middle Colonies tended to attract settlers traveling in families, with relatively balanced sex ratios and broader age distributions, while the staple-producing regions of the West Indies and the southern mainland attracted more indentured immigrants, primarily males concentrated in their teens and twenties. Several colonies, including Pennsylvania and North Carolina, appear to have been intermediate between these patterns, with continuing flows of both single indentured servants and family groups.

A comparable overview of the net migration of blacks to the colonies is given in Table 4.6. The dominant role of the West Indies is clear. The sugar islands received more than two-thirds of all blacks imported to English America in every decade, and more than four-fifths in ten of the thirteen decades for which estimates are available. Within the region, Barbados imported the largest numbers of slaves in the three decades after 1650 but was surpassed by Jamaica thereafter. Jamaica remained the leading English American importer of blacks for the next ten decades. By 1710, the majority of all blacks bound for the West Indies were destined for Jamaica, and this generally remained true thereafter.

On the mainland, New England and the Middle Colonies never imported large numbers of blacks. The Upper South increased its imports of
blacks steadily from the mid-seventeenth century to the mid-eighteenth,
and at its peak, in the 1740s, received more than one-quarter of the blacks
bound for the English colonies. The Lower South began to import slaves in
significant numbers after 1710, and its demand grew during the mid-
eighteenth century, as North Carolina joined South Carolina as a significant slave importer. During the 1760s the region received more than one-
quarter of all blacks bound for English America.

Slaves were imported strictly for their value as laborers, and the age
distribution of those transported from Africa to the colonies was consequently much narrower than that of European immigrants, who often
traveled in family groups. Although precise age distributions are not
available for slave migrants, it is clear that they were concentrated almost
exclusively in the prime working ages. For example of 74,000 slaves
carried to the West Indies by the Royal African Company, 52 percent were
categorized as men – 16 to 40 years old – 34 percent as women, from
ages 15 to 35, 10 percent as boys aged 10 to 15, and only 4 percent as
girls aged 10 to 14. More than four-fifths of the slaves were therefore in
their late teens, twenties, or thirties, and negligible numbers were either
below the age of 10 or above that of 40. The sex ratio of these slaves might
appear surprisingly even, as females accounted for nearly 40 percent of
those transported. Although some contemporaries argued that the large
share of females arose from a desire of planters to allow their slaves to have
families, in general it seems more likely that it was a result of the high
relative productivity of females in field work. Among these slaves, on
average girls sold in the West Indies for prices 90 percent as high as those
of boys, and women for 80 percent as much as men.

Mortality rates in the colonies were also marked by great regional
variation. The two areas for which colonial mortality rates have been best
documented are New England and the Chesapeake Bay region. Table 4.7
collects results from a number of studies of particular communities or
populations from these regions. Colonial New England was a very healthy
place. In particular, the region's smaller agricultural communities, like
Andover and Plymouth, enjoyed life expectancies in the seventeenth century that were higher not only than other colonial regions but probably
also than those of England at the time. Mortality rates were considerably
higher in New England's port cities, such as Salem. This was presumably
a result of the greater exposure of the urban population to diseases borne

Table 4.7. *Estimates of life expectancy for white men at age 30*

Place and birth cohort	Years
Andover, MA	
1640–99	40.8
1670–99	38.7
1700–29	33.4
1730–59	36.3
Plymouth, MA	
17th century	40.0
Salem, MA	
17th century	29.2
18th century	30.3
Ipswich, MA	
18th century	32.3
Charles County, MD	
1652–99	20.4
Charles Parish, VA	
1665–99	16.4
Maryland legislators	
1618–49	12.6
1650–99	20.9
1700–49	26.0
1750–67	28.2
South Carolina legislators	
1650–99	24.9
1700–49	21.1
1750–1800	27.5
Northeast	
1760–99	36.1
1800–19	36.4
South Atlantic	
1760–99	33.2
1800–19	33.0

Sources: Maris A. Vinovskis, *Fertility in Massachusetts from the Revolution to the Civil War* (New York: 1981), 29; Lorena S. Walsh and Russell R. Menard, "Death in the Chesapeake: Two Life Tables for Men in Early Colonial Maryland," *Maryland Historical Magazine* (1969), 213; Daniel Blake Smith, "Mortality and Family in the Colonial Chesapeake," *Journal of Interdisciplinary History* (1978), 415; Daniel S. Levy, "The Life Expectancies of Colonial Maryland Legislators," *Historical Methods* (1987), 19; Daniel S. Levy, "The Economic Demography of the Colonial South" (Ph.D. dissertation, University of Chicago, 1991), 123; Clayne Pope, "Adult Mortality in America before 1900: A View from Family Histories," in C. Goldin and H. Rockoff, eds., *Strategic Factors in Nineteenth Century American Economic History* (Chicago: 1992), 286.

by sailors and immigrants from other disease environments, as well as generally poorer conditions of sanitation in more crowded communities. It is difficult to determine whether New England's mortality rates changed over the course of the colonial period, but the available evidence suggests that there was no significant trend over time.

The early Chesapeake was a much less healthy place. Men born in Charles County, Maryland, in the second half of the seventeenth century had a life expectation at age 30 of only 21 years, barely half the expectation of 41 years enjoyed by their counterparts in Andover, Massachusetts. And wealth apparently offered no means of protection against the Chesapeake's harsh disease environment, as the generally prosperous members of Maryland's legislature in the late seventeenth century could expect to live on average a mere half year longer than the general population of Charles County. Furthermore, these grim figures fail to take into account the numerous immigrants who failed to survive seasoning, the dangerous period during the first summer of exposure to the new American disease environment when many newcomers died. Many immigrants died before they had been in America long enough to leave any trace in the legal or religious records used for demographic studies, so seasoning mortality rates cannot be estimated with precision, but the testimony of contemporaries indicates that the risk to new arrivals in the southern colonies could be substantial.

Over time, mortality rates fell substantially in the Chesapeake. The life expectancy of Maryland's legislators at age 30 rose more than seven years in the hundred years after 1650. Although this still left them at a disadvantage relative to men in rural New England, it may have closed most of the gap between them and their contemporaries in the urban North. By the end of the colonial period the differential between North and South may have been very small; a broadly based study has estimated that life expectancy at age 30 for men born during 1760–99 was 36.1 years in the Northeast, compared to 33.2 in the Southeast, as shown in Table 4.7.

Less detailed evidence is available for other colonial regions. The West Indies early established a reputation as a dangerous place for immigrants' health and remained an undesirable destination for most Englishmen thereafter. One visitor to Barbados in 1647 reported that "the Inhabitants of the Ilands . . . were so grievously visited with the plague (or as killing a disease), that before a month was expired after our Arivall, the living were hardly able to bury the dead."[11] Malaria, yellow fever, dysentery, and

[11] Richard Ligon, *A True & Exact History of the Island of Barbados* (London: 1657), 21.

other diseases appear to have made the West Indies the most unhealthy region of English America, although early South Carolina shared many of the same diseases and consequently also suffered from a poor reputation among prospective immigrants. In 1684 the colony's proprietors complained that "Charles Town is no healthy situation . . . people that come to the province and landing there and the most falling sick it brings a Disreputation upon the whole Country."[12] Yet conditions may have varied substantially in different parts of the colony, as the western part of South Carolina appears to have been a substantially healthier place than the eastern lowland regions. Over time the shift of population toward the west tended to increase average life expectancies in South Carolina, and as shown in Table 4.7, a study of South Carolina's legislators indicates that they may not have had life expectancies much shorter than their counterparts in Maryland during most of the colonial period.

Fertility rates were generally high in colonial America. Benjamin Franklin attributed this to the abundance of land in the colonies. He wrote in 1751: "Land being thus plenty in America, and so cheap, as that a laboring man, that understands husbandry, can, in a short time, save money enough to purchase a piece of new land, sufficient for a plantation, whereon he may subsist a family." Franklin argued that "such are not afraid to marry," and consequently "marriages in America are more general, and more generally early, than in Europe."[13] Recent studies have tended to confirm Franklin's observations on colonial nuptiality. In colonial New England, marriage appears to have been nearly universal among adults; local studies have found that the proportions never married were well below 10 percent. In contrast, at times during the seventeenth century more than one-quarter of adults in England never married. The unbalanced sex ratio of the early Chesapeake has been found to have resulted in a high rate of bachelorhood, as an estimated quarter of the region's men in the seventeenth century never married, but this rate apparently fell as the sex ratio neared equality in the eighteenth century.

As Franklin argued, colonial Americans also appear to have married earlier than their English contemporaries. Local studies for both New England and the Chesapeake indicate mean ages at first marriage for men that ranged between 24 and 27, without evidence of secular trend during

---

[12] Quoted in Peter H. Wood, *Black Majority: Negroes in Colonial South Carolina from 1670 through the Stono Rebellion* (New York: 1975), 66.

[13] Benjamin Franklin, "Observations concerning the Increase of Mankind, peopling of Countries, etc.," in *The Works of Benjamin Franklin* 4 (Philadelphia: 1809), 185.

the colonial period. This suggests that colonial men typically married somewhat earlier than their English counterparts, for whom the mean age during the American colonial period was generally between 26 and 28. Even more important for fertility, however, is the fact that colonial women married significantly younger than English women. Women in colonial New England first married at mean ages that ranged from 20 to 23, considerably lower than the mean ages for English women of the time that ranged from 25 to 27. In the Chesapeake, women who had been indentured servants married at ages similar to those of women in New England, but native-born white women married considerably younger, at mean ages from 17 to 20. Limited evidence on marriage ages in the Middle Colonies suggests behavior there similar to that of New England for both men and women.

These lower ages at marriage do appear to have resulted in higher fertility in the colonies than in England. Completed family size averaged from five to six children in England throughout the seventeenth and eighteenth centuries. In comparison, studies of a number of communities throughout the mainland colonies have found that total children born to completed families generally averaged at least six, and often reached eight or more. To the extent that the colonial communities studied to date were typical, births per completed family were therefore higher in the colonies than in England.

Regional differences in fertility within the colonies cannot be described with confidence. The tendency for higher southern fertility due to the earlier ages at marriage might have been offset by higher southern mortality rates, which meant that fewer marriages completed their normal fertility in the South than the North. Yet this latter effect declined in importance as southern life expectancies increased in the eighteenth century. As a result, as shown in Table 4.8, national census data for 1800 indicate a clear tendency for fertility rates in the major states to rise from North to South.

Recent studies of black demography in the Chesapeake suggest that early immigrant slaves in the region did not reproduce themselves, as a result of both the unbalanced sex ratios of the slaves imported and the region's high mortality rates. In the course of the early eighteenth century, however, the region's black population began to grow naturally, as native-born black women, like their white counterparts, married younger and bore more children than their immigrant mothers. Natural increase was never achieved among the black population in the colonial West Indies,

Table 4.8. *Number of children under age 10 per thousand white women aged 16–44, by state, 1800*

State	Number of children
Maine	1974
New Hampshire	1704
Vermont	2068
Massachusetts	1477
Rhode Island	1455
Connecticut	1512
New York	1871
New Jersey	1822
Pennsylvania	1881
Delaware	1509
Maryland	1585
Virginia	1954
North Carolina	1920
South Carolina	2030
Georgia	2116

Source: Yasukichi Yasuba, *Birth Rates of the White Population in the United States, 1800–1860* (Baltimore: 1962), 61.

however, because the region's extraordinary mortality rates prevented the growth of a substantial native-born population.

The evidence on immigration, mortality, and fertility taken together clearly reveals enormous contrasts in the ways in which the different colonial regions achieved rapid population growth. Although many evidentiary gaps remain to be filled, it appears likely that the regions formed a spectrum ordered from North to South, with the role of natural increase descending in importance along this spectrum, and that of sustained immigration increasing in importance. Within the southern regions, the areas with the lowest rates of natural increase faced the greatest barriers in attracting voluntary immigrants, and achieved overall population growth through the purchase of involuntary immigrants. The colonial regions with the lowest rates of natural population growth tended to be those which enjoyed the greatest success in the production of staple products for export to the great European markets. In part, the poor demographic performance of these regions was caused by the geography of disease, as malaria and other dangerous illnesses spread more readily in warmer climates. But the demographic problems of these regions were in part a consequence of their economic opportunities, as the availability of lucrative export crops resulted in harsh labor regimes in which profits could be increased by forcing laborers to work at levels of effort and under adverse conditions that damaged their health and reduced their longevity.

Malthus contended "that there is not a truer criterion of the happiness and innocence of a people than the rapidity of their increase."[14] And he had no doubt that the extraordinarily rapid growth of the population of the English North American colonies was due to extraordinarily favorable economic circumstances, as the availability of vast amounts of fertile land was combined with political institutions favorable to the improvement and cultivation of that land.[15] Although quantitative studies of the economic and social progress of the colonial population cannot provide direct measures of their happiness, these studies can tell us how migrants to the colonies fared materially, and therefore provide indirect evidence on how the settlement of English America was perceived by contemporaries.

The best systematic evidence on the economic and social progress of the immigrants comes from several studies that have traced the careers of sizable groups of indentured servants who migrated to Maryland during the seventeenth century. How migrants fare at their destination is of course an important question in the study of any migration. In the case of indentured servants in early America the question seems particularly interesting in view of the great sacrifices they made in order to migrate, giving up much of their freedom of choice over living and working conditions for substantial periods, as well as considerably increasing their risk of premature death both on the ocean voyage and upon arrival in the New World. The question of whether the servants' gains from migrating could have justified these high costs was hotly debated by contemporaries, as well as by many historians in more recent times.

Servants who arrived in Maryland early in the seventeenth century and who escaped the substantial risk of premature death in the early Chesapeake generally prospered: 90 percent of those who arrived in Maryland during the colony's first decade of settlement and who remained in the

---

[14] Malthus, *Essay on Population*, 106.
[15] Malthus, *Essay on Population*, 105. This analysis appears to have been drawn from Smith, *Wealth of Nations*, 538–9.

colony for at least ten years after completing their terms of servitude became landowners, typically on a scale that afforded them a comfortable living. Some accumulated considerable wealth, and a few gained estates that placed them among the wealthiest planters in the colony. Nearly all of these early former servants who remained in Maryland for a decade or more after gaining their freedom held political office or sat on a jury – not major positions in most cases, but nonetheless substantially above what these men could have expected had they remained in England. Several of these early servants became members of the elite group that ruled early Maryland, even joining the colony's governing Council. The accomplishments of many of these freedmen were very impressive from an English perspective; most could not have expected to do nearly as well had they not emigrated, for England was a place that offered little chance of significant economic or social mobility for those born below the gentry.

Opportunities for immigrants to Maryland deteriorated over time, however. Parallel analysis of the careers of a group of servants who arrived in the colony during the 1660s shows less impressive accomplishments. More than half of those who remained in Maryland for at least a decade as freedmen failed to become landowners, and none of these former servants acquired great wealth. A smaller proportion than of the earlier group participated in government, and of these none rose above minor public office. The opportunity for former servants to become prosperous planters in Maryland was therefore much less late in the seventeenth century than it had been earlier. Freedmen increasingly faced a choice between remaining in the colony as hired workers or moving elsewhere, most often to Pennsylvania, in search of their own land.

Several general conclusions might be drawn from these studies of the success of migrants. One is the simple recognition that the time and destination chosen by an immigrant were crucial determinants of his experience. This point, which emerges strongly from the history of seventeenth-century Maryland, becomes even clearer when differences among colonial regions are considered: whereas the availability of good farmland gave Pennsylvania a favorable reputation among immigrants for a century, the high cost of land and undesirable conditions for hired workers caused indentured servants and free immigrants of modest means very early to avoid traveling to the West Indies, and later the Lower South. But as these decisions by immigrants indicate, information about the desirability of the different colonial regions spread widely among Englishmen who were considering moving to America. It was indeed the choices made by white immigrants to avoid the harsh living and working conditions of the sugar islands and the rice colonies that made slavery the economic solution of planters in these regions, for Africans could be forced to work in places where Europeans chose not to.

A second generalization from the studies of Maryland is that although the degree of economic opportunity available to immigrants declined over time in the Chesapeake, even in the final decades of the seventeenth century there was no shortage of employment. Although the rapid expansion of the tobacco economy, which earlier had made the sparsely settled Chesapeake an excellent place for poor settlers, had given way to slower growth in a more densely settled region where the choicest land had become occupied, freedmen could still find abundant work at good wages. This point again seems subject to wider application: although the extent of opportunity for immigrants varied over time and across places, colonial English America appears throughout its history to have remained a genuine land of opportunity where European migrants might considerably improve their condition if they were willing to risk premature death in the trans-Atlantic crossing and the unfamiliar disease environment of the New World. That the colonies continued to attract large numbers of Europeans, skilled as well as unskilled, throughout the seventeenth and eighteenth centuries is testimony to the fact that many Europeans knew this to be true.

ECONOMIC DEVELOPMENT

Our knowledge of the growth of the aggregate colonial economy is poor. Existing data sources have not been adequate to provide the basis for reliable estimates of the total product or income of the colonies, so it is not possible to summarize the colonies' economic growth by presenting time-series evidence on aggregate colonial output or per capita income. The best summary evidence on overall colonial economic performance has been drawn from probate records, as considerable effort has recently been devoted to developing estimates of the per capita wealth of the living from the inventories of the estates of decedents made by colonial probate courts. Although these wealth estimates cannot be converted convincingly into estimates of per capita income because of a lack of evidence on savings rates, the evidence on wealth is of value in its own right for the insights it yields into colonial economic performance both over time and in cross-sectional comparisons among regions.

The most extensive use of the probate inventories for the estimation of wealth was made by a study that estimated the wealth of all the English mainland regions in the single year of 1774. Estimates for earlier years are scarce, and no comparable study of a large number of colonies has been done for any other time. Some indications of change over time can be gained from narrower studies, however. One study recently found that total wealth per wealthholder in six Maryland tidewater counties in 1700 was £205, and estimated that per capita wealth in these counties at the same date at £34.7.[16] In 1774, total wealth per wealthholder in the southern mainland colonies was £395, while per capita southern wealth was £54.7. After adjusting for price-level changes, the estimate of southern real total wealth per wealthholder for 1774 is 49.8 percent higher than that for Maryland in 1700, while estimated real total wealth per capita in 1774 is 22.6 percent above the estimate for 1700.[17] Comparison of these figures over time can be no more than suggestive, because the geographic coverage of the estimates is very different, and the direction of any resulting bias in comparing the estimates is unknown. The changes in level are substantial, however, as the implied annual average of growth of wealth per wealthholder is 0.55 percent between 1700 and 1774, while the annual average increase of per capita wealth is 0.28 percent. Moreover, it is likely that these growth rates continued a process that had begun earlier in the colonial period, for wealth levels were probably considerably higher in 1700 than in the mid-seventeenth century. The more rapid increase of wealth per wealthholder than of per capita wealth between 1700 and 1774 is consistent with the increase during the eighteenth century of the importance of slaves in the southern colonies, because slaves increased the total population without adding to the numbers of wealthholders. Although obviously imprecise, the indication of growth given by these comparisons is clearly consistent with the consensus among most economic and social historians who have studied the colonies, that significant increases occurred during the colonial era in both productivity and the standard of living.

Although comparable estimates of per capita wealth for the seventeenth century are lacking, some studies of the value of probated estates provide suggestive evidence. One of these found that the mean value of estates in

---

[16] All values in this section are given in £ sterling.

[17] Price-level changes are taken from Henry Phelps Brown and Sheila V. Hopkins, *A Perspective of Wages and Prices* (London: 1981), 30. Because the wealth estimates are quoted in English currency, the appropriate price-level adjustments are those of England.

Jamaica rose steadily during the last quarter of the seventeenth century, with the average value in 1700 more than twice that of 1675. A study of four counties on Maryland's lower western shore found that the mean value of estates rose by 40 percent between the 1660s and the beginning of the eighteenth century. Although these increases are impressive, they are not necessarily the result of economic growth, for to some unknown extent — most likely a large extent in Jamaica — they may represent the effects of a growing concentration of wealth as the number of bound laborers increased. Yet it is likely that in some degree they were caused by genuine gains in productivity. Early in the colonial period, English settlers in those regions that differed most from their homeland with respect to climate and other agricultural endowments began to grow staple crops that were generally new to them, on a scale that was also unfamiliar. The potential profits to be made by growing sugar, tobacco, and other crops more efficiently were great, and might be expected to have led colonists to work at improving their methods of production. This does seem to have occurred, as for example in the early Chesapeake planters both learned how to handle more tobacco plants per worker and developed better strains of the plant. The results were impressive, as one study found that tobacco output per worker in Maryland and Virginia more than doubled between 1620 and 1650, and doubled again between 1650 and the end of the seventeenth century, with the net effect that the amount of the crop harvested per worker rose from 400 pounds in the early decades of tobacco cultivation to 1,900 pounds per worker by 1700. This achievement of early productivity gains was by no means inevitable, however, and it is not likely to have occurred equally throughout all the colonial regions. In some regions, particularly those where agricultural conditions differed less from those of England, there may have been less scope for productivity increases due to improvements in agricultural methods. A study of two rural Massachusetts counties, for example, found no increase in mean wealth per estate between 1680 and 1720. Earlier in this essay, it was seen that the greatest departures from the originally intended forms of government and the greatest modifications in transplanted institutions tended to occur in those regions where economic conditions differed most from those of England. Although detailed investigations remain to establish the economic effects of these adaptations, it may be that the more radical changes coincided with, and perhaps served as the basis for, the greatest gains in productive economic efficiency.

The major study of colonial wealth done to date has estimated that nonhuman per capita wealth in the mainland colonies in 1774 was £37.4. Although comparisons with other countries are again difficult, it is possible to give some indication of where this placed the colonies relative to England. Per capita wealth in England rose from approximately £110 in 1760 to £192 in 1800.[18] Per capita wealth therefore appears to have been substantially lower in America than in England, with the colonial level in 1774 probably significantly less than one-third that of England. Although little research has been done to evaluate this sizable difference, the author who produced the colonial estimates cited here suggested that the large size of this gap in wealth might have been due in part to differences in social structure and institutions between the mother country and the colonies, and that the difference in the level of income might consequently have been smaller than that in wealth:

We are left with the possibility that British wealth per capita, which includes the wealth of the barons, lords . . . and of other great landed estates, was considerably higher than that of the colonists, including the slave population. Income may have been higher in relation to wealth in the colonies because of the much lower value of land here, the importance of "free" income (gathered from the countryside), the lesser elegance of the finer private buildings, the as yet relatively fewer "carriages and coaches," the relatively small amounts of fixed industrial capital.[19]

Support for the proposition that colonial income levels might have compared more favorably with that of England than was the case for wealth is provided by several intriguing pieces of indirect evidence about one important component of the material standard of living, nutrition. A recent study of muster rolls for soldiers who fought in the American Revolution produced the striking result that American-born colonial soldiers of the late 1770s were on average more than three inches taller than their English counterparts who served in the Royal Marines at the same time. Since the genetic potential for height in these populations would not have differed, the most likely cause of this remarkable American advantage in height is superior nutrition. This conclusion becomes somewhat less surprising in view of another recent study that examined the diet of colonists in the Chesapeake region, and found that after the very earliest years of settlement it is likely that nearly all migrants from England to the

---

[18] These figures for national wealth per head are from Charles Feinstein, "Capital Formation in Great Britain," in Peter Mathias and M. M. Postan, eds., *Cambridge Economic History of Europe*, Vol. VII (Cambridge: 1978), Table 24, 83; the figures were converted from constant 1851–60 prices to current prices using the price index given in *ibid.*, Table 5, col. 1, 38.

[19] Alice Hanson Jones, *Wealth of a Nation to Be* (New York: 1980), 69.

Chesapeake improved their diets in the process. Although settlers in the Chesapeake had to adapt to a diet different from the one they knew in England, with an American diet based primarily on Indian corn instead of wheat and other grains, most colonists in the Chesapeake received a more nourishing diet than all but the most affluent Englishmen. These studies of nutrition together suggest that the real standard of living of typical colonists might have been higher relative to those of English workers than has generally been believed in the past, and higher than might be inferred from the comparison of American and English wealth levels.

Another indication of high colonial standards of living is afforded by evidence on levels of education. Literacy rates among free adult males in the colonies were high by contemporary English standards. In the mid-seventeenth century, about two-thirds of New England's adult males were literate, compared to only one-third of adult males in England. Although literacy rates were higher in New England than elsewhere in the colonies, literacy rates for free males in seventeenth-century Virginia were near one-half, still above English levels, and literacy rates in Pennsylvania were probably higher than in Virginia. Literacy rates in a number of colonial areas appear to have fallen in the late seventeenth century, perhaps as a result of the increasing geographic dispersion of the population; as new lands on the frontier were settled, more families had no access to existing schools, and many new towns initially lacked the wealth to build and operate schools. Strong evidence of improving education appears in the eighteenth century, however, as literacy rates rose throughout the main-land colonies. By the close of the colonial period regional differences still existed, but they were considerably smaller; adult male literacy in New England was near 90 percent, and free adult males in Pennsylvania and Virginia had literacy rates near 70 percent. As in the seventeenth century, overall literacy rates for free adult males in the colonies in the late eighteenth century were therefore higher than those of England, where adult male literacy was about 65 percent. Evidence on the extent of literacy therefore suggests that by contemporary standards English America was not only initially settled by a well-educated population, but that after an early decline due to the costs of geographic expansion, the colonial population saw considerable improvements in education during the eighteenth century which kept its levels of literacy above those of England.

While comparisons of colonial living standards with those of England are plagued by severe problems of measurement, comparisons of wealth among the colonial regions in 1774 can be made with greater precision.

These reveal a number of interesting contrasts in the levels as well as the nature of the economic development that had occurred in different places over the course of the colonial period. The first column of Table 4.9 compares total wealth per capita for the mainland regions and Jamaica. The level rises from north to south, with New England's wealth at two-thirds that of the South, the Middle Colonies' at three-fourths the southern level, and Jamaica's 50 percent greater than that of the South. This ranking was familiar to contemporaries, whose understanding of the principal economic basis of these geographic differences was succinctly expressed by Adam Smith: "The profits of a sugar-plantation in any of our West Indian colonies are generally much greater than those of any other cultivation that is known either in Europe or America: And the profits of a tobacco plantation, though inferior to those of sugar, are superior to those of corn."[20]

Although at first glance it might appear natural to consider the wealth measure used in the first column of Table 4.9, obtained by dividing a region's total wealth by its total population, in the case of colonial America it is extremely difficult to interpret this measure. For the legal existence of transferable property rights in humans in colonial America, in the form of slavery and servitude, means that bound laborers are here included both in the numerator of this expression, as part of physical wealth, and in its denominator, as part of the total population.

The second column of Table 4.9 eliminates this problem by removing the value of human capital from total wealth. This treatment is comparable to that typically used for measuring per capita wealth in today's economies, in which property rights in humans cannot be sold. This measure can be interpreted as giving one indication of the productive capacity of an economy relative to its population, by estimating the ratio of nonhuman physical capital to total population. The ordering of the regions changes in this measurement, as the Middle Colonies lead the other mainland regions, and New England and the South are both at the same level below it. Jamaica remains above all the mainland regions. Yet what is most striking about the results obtained with this measure is perhaps not the change in ranking, but the very small differences among the regions: the Middle Colonies' nonhuman wealth per capita is only 10 percent greater than that of the other mainland regions, and Jamaica's is less than 10 percent above that of the Middle Colonies.

[20] Adam Smith, *Wealth of Nations*, 366.

Table 4.9. The wealth of the colonies in 1774

Region	(1) Total wealth per capita (£)	(2) Nonhuman wealth per capita (£)	(3) Total wealth per free capita (£)	(4) Nonhuman wealth per free capita (£)
New England	36.6	36.4	38.2	38.0
Middle Colonies	41.9	40.2	45.8	44.1
Southern Mainland	54.7	36.4	92.7	61.6
Jamaica	84.1	43.0	1200.0	754.3

Note: Nonhuman wealth includes land (real estate) and nonhuman portable physical wealth (livestock, producers' durables, crops, consumers' durables, etc.). Total wealth is the sum of nonhuman wealth and the value of indentured servants and slaves.

Sources: Mainland Colonies: Jones, *Wealth of a Nation to Be*, 58, 96. Jamaica: McCusker and Menard, *The Economy of British America*, 61; McCusker, "The Rum Trade and the Balance of Payments of the Thirteen Continental Colonies, 1650–1775" (unpublished dissertation, University of Pittsburgh, 1970), 692; Stanley L. Engerman, "Notes on the Patterns of Economic Growth in the British North American Colonies in the Seventeenth, Eighteenth, and Nineteenth Centuries," in Paul Bairoch and Maurice Lévy-Leboyer, eds., *Disparities in Economic Development Since the Industrial Revolution* (London: 1981), 50.

Comparing columns 1 and 2 of Table 4.9 serves to emphasize both the central importance of bound labor in the southern mainland colonies and the West Indies and the marginality of bound labor in New England and the Middle Colonies. The difference between the entries for a given region in the two columns is the value of transferable human wealth in a region divided by total population, and this ranges from a mere £0.2 in New England and £1.7 in the Middle Colonies to the much larger amount of £18.3 in the southern mainland and the still greater value of £41.1 in Jamaica.

Although informative, the measure presented in the second column of Table 4.9 fails to capture important aspects of the striking differences in wealthholding that existed among colonial regions. Since human capital could be bought and sold under colonial law, servants and slaves represented valuable physical assets to their owners; at the same time, most bound laborers were not potential wealthholders. The measure given in the third column of Table 4.9 recognizes these facts by including the value of bound laborers in physical wealth while excluding bound laborers from the population measured in the denominator. The resulting measure gives an indication of the ratio of the value of total transferable physical wealth to the size of the free population. The effect of the change in the measure is dramatic. The initial ranking obtained for total wealth per capita, rising from north to south, reappears, but what is most striking is again the relative magnitudes. New England and the Middle Colonies both had less than half the total wealth per free capita of the South. Even more remarkably, Jamaica had more than twelve times the average wealth per free resident of the southern mainland colonies, or equivalently more than twenty-five times the mean level of the Middle Colonies or New England.

This third measure corresponds most closely to the perceptions of contemporaries who compared the wealth of the colonial regions, for what impressed them was the enormous wealth represented by the great plantations of the southern mainland colonies and the West Indies, in contrast to the more modest agricultural economies of New England and the Middle Colonies, which were based on the family farm. Contemporaries were also aware of the great wealth gap between the West Indies and the southern mainland, as witnessed for example by Adam Smith's observation that "our tobacco colonies send us home no such wealthy planters as we see frequently arrive from our sugar islands."[21]

21 Smith, *Wealth of Nations*, 158.

The clarity of contemporaries' perceptions of the differences in the wealth of the major colonial regions was due not only to the striking regional differences in the scale and organization of agriculture, but also in part to the highly visible nature of the economic activity that was key to the accumulation of wealth in these colonial settlements, specifically the export of agricultural products. The prosperity of a colonial region depended heavily on its ability to produce agricultural commodities that were demanded in the much larger European markets. Table 4.10 shows the difference among the regions in this respect in two different periods, centered around 1700 and 1770. The ranking of the regions in the value of exports per capita are similar in the two periods, with the southern mainland colonies substantially higher than both New England and the Middle Colonies, and the West Indies substantially higher than all the mainland regions. The ordering of the regions in per capita exports in 1770 is also similar to the ranking of the regions for total wealth per capita shown in Table 4.9. And as in the case of wealth, the relative magnitudes across regions change sharply when the value of exports is divided not by the total population, but by the free population. In both periods, while the values for the two northern mainland regions remain almost unchanged, the values for the southern mainland colonies increase significantly, and those for the West Indies increase enormously. And because of the increasing quantitative importance of blacks in the southern mainland colonies and the West Indies over time, the value of exports per free capita rises more in these areas relative to simple exports per capita at the end of the colonial period than in the middle. This difference reflects the very important fact that the continuing growth of slavery in the Chesapeake, the Carolinas, and above all the West Indies served to increase the commercial power of many of the free residents of these regions over time. With differences in per capita exports as large as those shown in Table 4.10, as well as in the per capita wealth of the white populations, it is little wonder that contemporaries were so clearly aware of the economic hierarchy that existed among the mature colonial regions.

Not surprisingly, the very different levels of export activity among the regions were associated with very different patterns of trade by destination. Table 4.11 presents the percentage distributions of the value of each region's average annual overseas exports during 1768–72 by place of destination. Although these data do not include evidence on the trade among the North American regions, they do provide interesting insights into the contrasting patterns that had developed by the end of the colonial period.

Table 4.10. Average annual value of commodity exports by region, 1697–1705 and 1768–1722 (£ sterling)

Region	1697–1705			1768–1772		
	Total value of exports	Value of exports per capita	Value of exports per free capita	Total value of exports	Value of exports per capita	Value of exports per free capita
New England	31,392	0.34	0.35	439,101	0.76	0.78
Middle Colonies	15,065	0.28	0.30	526,545	0.95	1.01
Upper South	217,062	2.21	2.55	1,046,883	1.61	2.63
Lower South	11,870	0.72	0.87	551,949	1.60	2.91
West Indies	608,279	4.11	18.43	3,910,600	8.16	86.9

Note: Data for 1697–1705 include only exports to Great Britain; data for 1768–72 include exports to all overseas destinations.
Sources: Sir Charles Whitworth, *State of the Trade of Great Britain in Its Imports and Exports, Progressively from the Year 1697* (London: 1776), 1–9; McCusker and Menard, *The Economy of British America*, 103–8, 130–6, 154–60, 172–4, 199–203.

Table 4.11. *Percentage distributions of the value of average annual regional exports by destination, 1768–1772*

Exporting region	Great Britain and Ireland	Southern Europe	West Indies	Africa	North America	Total
New England	18	15	63	4	—	100
Middle Colonies	23	35	42	0	—	100
Upper South	82	9	9	0	—	100
Lower South	72	10	18	0	—	100
West Indies	87	0	0	0	13	100

Note: For North American mainland colonies, exports to other mainland colonies were not measured, and are consequently not included in this tabulation.

Source: McCusker and Menard, *The Economy of British America*, 108, 130, 160, 175, 199.

New England's major overseas trading partner from very early in the colonial period was the West Indies, which received nearly two-thirds of all New England's exports. The economy of early Massachusetts enjoyed substantial continuing flows of immigrants throughout the 1630s, and during this time many of the earliest settlers prospered by selling cattle and other agricultural products to more recent arrivals. When political prospects for Puritans in England improved in the early 1640s, however, the rate of immigration to New England dropped sharply. Deprived of the infusions of capital provided by new settlers, Massachusetts' economy became depressed, and land and cattle prices fell abruptly. The colony's government searched in vain for a new source of prosperity, passing laws aimed at promoting such activities as the fur trade, iron manufacturing, and cloth production, but no successful solution was found until New England merchants became aware of the increasing need for food that had arisen in the West Indies in the wake of that region's sugar revolution. Boston merchants began to trade with the West Indies in the mid-1640s. In 1647 a correspondent from the islands wrote to John Winthrop in Massachusetts that "Men are so intent upon planting sugar that they had rather buy foode at very deare rates than produce it by labour, so infinite is the profit of sugar workes after once accomplished."[22] New England began to send a variety of foods to the West Indies, with fish, meats, and grain the most important, and this trade continued throughout the remainder of the colonial period. Some parts of the region, including the Narragansett Country in southern Rhode Island, prospered by specializing in raising cattle for export to the Caribbean islands. The Middle Colonies later joined New England's farmers and merchants in benefiting from the West Indies' monoculture in sugar. The Middle Colonies' major export, grain, went in approximately equal amounts to the West Indies and southern Europe. The Middle Colonies also sent meat and other food to the West Indies on a smaller scale.

The trade of the Upper South from a very early date was dominated by tobacco, which made up more than 70 percent of the region's total exports even in 1770, and all of which was sent to Britain. The region's much smaller volume of exports to the West Indies and southern Europe consisted almost entirely of grain. Rice made up more than half of all exports from the Lower South; two-thirds of this was sent to Britain, with the

---

[22] Quoted in Harold Innis, *The Cod Fisheries* (Toronto: 1954), 78.

remainder divided equally between the West Indies and southern Europe. The region's other important export, indigo, was all sent to Britain.

Sugar accounted for 80 percent of the West Indies' total exports in 1770, and virtually all was sent to Britain. The region's other important export, rum, was divided among Britain and the mainland regions from which the sugar islands imported the bulk of their food.

Taken together, Tables 4.10 and 4.11 serve to emphasize not only the general importance of trade in generating colonial wealth, but also the particular importance of trade with Great Britain. It was those colonial regions that found staples that could be sent to Britain that were able to prosper most through the production of exports. Those regions that could not export to Britain on a large scale had to resort to exporting within the colonies, or elsewhere in Europe, on a much smaller scale. The clear division of the regions by degree of success in exporting to Britain, with New England and the Middle Colonies the least favored, the southern mainland regions considerably more successful, and the West Indies by far the leader, furthermore suggests that in these preindustrial economies the key to successful trade was overwhelmingly geographic, as those regions whose climates and natural endowments differed most from those of the mother country had the strongest basis for trade with the metropolis. Contemporaries clearly recognized this, as evidenced by the argument of the English mercantilist, Sir Josiah Child, in the late seventeenth century that "New-England is the most prejudicial Plantation to the Kingdom of England," precisely because of the similarity of its natural endowments to those of England: "All our American Plantations, except that of New England, produce Commodities of different Natures from those of this Kingdom. . . . Whereas New-England produces generally the same we have here, viz. Corn and Cattle." New England's products provided the basis for little trade with England, while the region's export of those foodstuffs to the West Indies reduced England's own trade with the sugar islands. In consequence, Child concluded that "Old England suffers diminution by the growth of those Colonies settled in New-England," while in this regard "that Plantation differs from those more Southerly, with respect to the gain or loss of this Kingdom."[23] Child's argument, based on the straightforward use of the value of a colony's trade with England as a measure of the colony's benefit to the mother country, underlines the fact

---

[23] Sir Josiah Child, *A New Discourse of Trade* (London: 1698), 166, 204–6.

that the prosperity of English American colonies depended in large part on their ability to produce goods that could profitably be sent to England.

The differences noted above in wealth levels may have translated into significant regional differences in the material standard of living. Among native-born colonial recruits for both the French and Indian War and the Revolution, men born in the South were significantly taller than their counterparts from the North. During the 1770s, even after allowing for such characteristics as occupation and urban or rural residence, being born in Virginia rather than New England added an average 0.6 inches to a soldier's height, while being born in the Carolinas added an average of 0.8 inches relative to New England; men born in New York were also taller than those from New England. As in the earlier comparison of the heights of colonial soldiers with the English, the most likely source of these regional differences in mean height is variation in levels of nutrition, which in turn may point to differences in real incomes across regions that follow the rankings of the regions by wealth.

The dominance of agriculture in the American economy even at the close of the colonial era is clearly demonstrated in Table 4.12. Land accounted for 68.4 percent of all nonhuman wealth in the mainland colonies in 1774, while livestock made up another 11.5 percent, and inventories of crops an additional 3.5 percent. Thus agriculture accounted for more than four-fifths of all nonhuman wealth. Nonfarm capital goods accounted for only 0.5 percent of nonhuman wealth in the colonies overall, and nonfarm business inventories only 1.9 percent. Some regional variation does appear in the importance of nonfarm enterprise, as New England and the Middle Colonies, which were more oriented toward mercantile activity than the South, had combined nonfarm equipment and inventories worth 3.8 percent and 4.5 percent of wealth, respectively, compared to only 0.8 percent in the South, but in no region did agricultural capital make up less than three-quarters of nonhuman wealth.

There were also considerable regional differences in the distribution of wealth. Although systematic estimates of wealth distribution in the West Indies are not available, the enormous value of the land, capital, and bound labor of the great plantations must certainly have made wealth inequality much greater in the sugar islands than on the mainland. Comparisons of the mainland regions are shown in Table 4.13, which presents evidence on the distribution of wealth among free adults. New England and the South had somewhat greater concentration of wealthholding than the Middle Colonies, measured by the share of total wealth held by the

Table 4.12. *Composition of nonhuman wealth, 1774*

Category	Thirteen Colonies		New England		Middle Colonies		South	
	£ per capita	%	£ per capita	%	£ per capita	%	£ per capita	%
Total	37.4	100.0	36.4	100.0	40.2	100.0	36.4	100.0
Land	25.6	68.4	26.1	71.1	25.9	64.4	25.1	69.0
Producers' capital:								
Livestock	4.3	11.5	2.8	7.7	4.8	11.9	4.8	13.2
Nonfarm business equipment	0.2	0.5	0.4	1.1	0.3	0.7	0.1	0.3
Crops	1.3	3.5	0.2	0.5	2.1	5.2	1.5	4.1
Nonfarm business inventory	0.7	1.9	1.0	2.7	1.5	3.7	0.2	0.5
Other	1.6	4.3	1.7	4.7	1.7	4.2	1.5	4.1
Consumers' goods	3.7	9.9	4.4	12.1	4.0	10.0	3.1	8.5

Source: Jones, *Wealth of a Nation to Be*, Table 4.2, 96.

Table 4.13. *Distribution of total wealth by region, 1774*

Percentage of total wealth held by richest	Thirteen Colonies	New England	Middle Colonies	South
1 percent	12.9	11.6	12.0	10.4
2 percent	19.6	18.8	16.0	16.9
10 percent	50.7	46.8	35.1	46.9
20 percent	67.9	65.9	52.7	69.6
50 percent	93.3	92.4	88.8	94.2
Gini coefficient	0.66	0.64	0.54	0.67
Mean (£)	252.0	161.2	189.2	394.7
Median (£)	108.7	74.4	152.5	144.5

Note: The population included in this tabulation is those eligible to hold wealth; for definition of this group, see Jones, *Wealth of a Nation to Be*, 33–7. For the definition of the Gini coefficient, see *ibid.*, 164–5.
Source: Jones, *Wealth of a Nation to Be,* Table 6.2, 164–5.

richest 10, 20, or 50 percent of wealthholders, or by the Gini coefficient. New England and the South also had values of mean wealth per free adult more than twice as high as their respective medians, compared with a mean less than 25 percent greater than the median in the Middle Colonies. Yet the South was rich with considerable inequality: the region's mean total wealth per free adult was more than twice as high as those of the other two regions. In sharp contrast, New England was relatively poor, as it had both the lowest mean and the lowest median wealth per free adult among the regions. That wealth inequality should be great in the South is perhaps not surprising, because the region had many large plantations that dwarfed the much more numerous small farms. The considerable concentration of wealth in New England may have been a result of the contrast between the region's large and relatively poor agricultural sector and its small but prosperous mercantile sector. The lesser degree of inequality in the Middle Colonies, together with mean wealth somewhat higher than New England but well below the South, may have been a result of the prosperity of the Middle Colonies' agriculture relative to that of New England, but without the considerable variation in agricultural scale made possible by the large plantations that appeared in the South.

Notwithstanding these regional differences within the colonies in wealth inequality, it is likely that overall economic inequality was considerably less in the mainland colonies than in England at the time. Visiting contemporaries almost unanimously described colonial America, particularly the northern mainland regions, as a remarkably egalitarian society, and regularly commented on both the greater incidence of property ownership and the more limited extent of extreme poverty in the colonies than in Europe. When a visitor to Pennsylvania in 1775 remarked that "it was the best country in the world for people of small fortunes, or in other words, the best poor man's country," he was echoing the words of many earlier immigrants who had contrasted their new homeland with the old in letters to relatives and friends who remained behind.[24] Although careful quantitative comparisons have yet to be carried out, contemporaries' perceptions were probably correct, and modern historians generally believe that wealthholding was considerably less concentrated in colonial America than in England.

Another important question on which little systematic research has been done concerns possible trends in the extent of economic inequality that occurred during the course of the colonial period. No studies of overall wealth inequality throughout the colonies are available for dates prior to 1774. Yet a number of investigations have measured changes in the distribution of wealth over time within particular communities. On the basis of studies that found rising wealth concentration in specific communities, including several large cities and prosperous rural counties settled early in the colonial period, a number of scholars have argued that wealth inequality probably rose throughout the mainland colonies during much of the colonial period. Recently, however, this hypothesis of rising overall colonial inequality has been challenged by an analysis that argues that this generalization from the local studies is flawed by a fallacy of composition. The new analysis recognizes that inequality was rising in cities and in older agrarian regions along the Atlantic coast. Equally significant for overall inequality, however, was the fact that new frontier communities were being settled at very rapid rates during most of the colonial period. The settlers in these new communities were drawn by the economic opportunities offered by the frontier. Per capita wealth grew

[24] Quoted in Jackson Turner Main, *The Social Structure of Revolutionary America* (Princeton, NJ: 1965), 222. For an earlier example of this description, see Susan E. Klepp and Billy G. Smith, eds., *The Infortunate: The Voyage and Adventures of William Moraley, an Indentured Servant* (University Park, PA: 1992), 88–9.

more rapidly in the new frontier communities than in the older coastal settlements, and because the settlers in the newer communities were initially poorer on average than the residents of older cities and towns, the effect of this rapid growth in wealth on the frontier was to reduce overall colonial inequality. The geographic redistribution of the colonial population away from the Atlantic seacoast therefore served to reduce economic inequality by offering younger, poorer, and more ambitious migrants from older communities the opportunity to achieve greater economic success by developing the frontier. Quantitatively, the impact of this redistribution of population may have been large enough to counterbalance the rising economic inequality that has been observed within some older communities, and the net effect may have been to produce relatively little change in overall wealth inequality in the mainland colonies throughout most of the colonial period.

The economic development of the colonies of English America was surely rapid by preindustrial standards, and as in the case of population growth this was clearly recognized by contemporaries. Adam Smith began his general analysis of the economic growth of colonial regions with the proposition that "the colony of a civilized nation which takes possession of a waste country, or of one so thinly inhabited, that the natives easily give place to the settlers, advances more rapidly to wealth and greatness than any other human society."[25] And Smith left no doubt as to the principal evidence on which he based this generalization, stating that "there are no colonies of which the progress has been more rapid than that of the English in North America."[26] From a series of small settlements fighting for their survival in the early seventeenth century, the English colonies both in the West Indies and on the North American mainland reached levels of economic development that afforded not only great riches for the economic elite, but widespread levels of more modest but nonetheless significant economic prosperity for many European settlers and their descendants. Yet it is clear that the differences in the process of development, and in the nature of the economies and societies that emerged, were enormous among the regions that have been treated here. At one end of a spectrum lay New England, which had the least wealth, the least foreign trade, and the least bound labor among all the regions. At the opposite end lay the West Indies, where the greatest volume of trade produced the greatest physical wealth, and the greatest amount of the harshest form of

[25] Smith, *Wealth of Nations*, 531–2.
[26] Smith, *Wealth of Nations*, 538.

bound labor. In intermediate positions along this spectrum in all these respects were the three regions located geographically between New England and the West Indies, with greater trade and wealth and more slavery in the Upper and Lower South, compared to lower levels of trade and wealth and much less reliance on slave labor in the Middle Colonies. In these respects, the characteristics of each of these five major regions of English America were firmly in place by the time of the American Revolution, and they would not change significantly in the coming decades as a result of the operation of purely economic forces. Thus by 1776 the early growth and maturation of the colonial economy, and the operation of the colonial labor market, had clearly laid down the geographic lines along which later rhetorical, political, and military battles would be waged over the abolition of slavery.

While this essay has documented the substantial variations in economic conditions that emerged among the regions of colonial America, and considered the responses of immigrants to these regional differences, it remains apparent that the most substantial economic deprivation in English America was a result not of a lack of economic success of free colonists, but was rather a result of the extremely circumscribed opportunities for the unfree. For the free, opportunities were impressive. Although our view of the growth of the aggregate economy remains clouded, cautious estimates have suggested that the real product per capita of the mainland colonies rose at average annual rates of 0.3–0.5 percent during the eighteenth century. Although modest by the standards of the rapid modern economic growth that would occur in the nineteenth century, these rates were considerable by the standards of Europe in the centuries preceding the colonization of the New World. The achievement of this intensive growth in a preindustrial economy is even more impressive in view of colonial rates of population growth that averaged more than 3 percent per year. It is clear that the colonial period left an auspicious economic legacy to the new republic, and placed it in a most advantaged position from which to begin more rapid economic development. Although more research is needed to chart the economic development of the colonies over time more precisely, there is little doubt that the economic and demographic accomplishments of the colonies of English America together make up one of the most dramatic success stories of the preindustrial world.

5

THE NORTHERN COLONIES:
ECONOMY AND SOCIETY, 1600–1775

DANIEL VICKERS

For most of the sixteenth century, the landholding and trading classes of northwestern Europe imagined the New World, based on the example set by the Spanish and Portuguese empires, as a field for conquest, plunder, and dominion. When English, French, or Dutch adventurers trained their minds on the Atlantic and its western shores, they dreamt of precious metals seized from Spanish galleons and conquered Indian peoples, rich estates worked by Indian or European subjects and supervised by transplanted gentlemen, or lucrative trading posts where willing and naive Indians would trade away their high-valued wares for next to nothing. Such projects would reward their promoters, less in the hard-won profit margins of competitive trade than in booty, rents, swindle, royal favor, and sometimes in the sense of having done one's duty for king, country, or the true faith. With a few magnificent exceptions, however, most of these adventures came to nought. They did not repay their investors, nor did they establish any of the north European countries as a significant colonial power. By the turn of the century, therefore, a new generation of adventurers – first in England and then more gradually on the continent – began to consider a change in strategy. Listening to the arguments of men such as Richard Hakluyt, they planned and promoted overseas settlements where Europeans would support themselves by raising staple commodities for sale in the Atlantic marketplace. This principle – that colonies could be sustained and investors rewarded from the profits of trade – remained the common denominator within all the successful overseas undertakings in the decades to come.

For the settlers who actually founded the seventeenth-century colonies, however, the commercial impulse was not a goal in itself. Having grown up in Europe, they understood the ways of the marketplace, but few of them would have termed themselves professional traders when they embarked for America. Wheeling and dealing was for the great majority only a means to an end. Some, who already possessed money and connections, wished to enrich themselves and quit the drudgery of physical labor for the life of a gentleman. A great many more of plainer backgrounds and more modest ambitions hoped that commercial success would enable them to settle themselves and their families in comfortable circumstances with the power to govern their own working lives – to achieve what Englishmen of the day would have termed a "competency."[1]

For those bent on great fortunes, the northeastern corner of the New World had limited appeal. By 1600, it was clear that if there was gold or silver in the ground, the Indians had not discovered it. With the exception of fur-bearing animals, little of the natural flora and fauna seemed exotic enough in extracted form to command much of a market at home. And since the temperate climate of the Northeast was similar in seasonal outline to most of northern Europe, no bonanza in tropical agriculture, of the sort that was developing around the Caribbean and Portuguese Brazil, was likely to be had there either. For working people interested in achieving a competent living in familiar surroundings, however, the very qualities that drove away the fortune-hunters seemed positive advantages. Those emigrants who sought in the New World a *home* – not just a profitable appendage but an improved replication of the society they had left behind – chose this country precisely for its familiarity. Francis Higginson delighted upon his arrival at Salem in 1629 to discover the apparent ease with which New Englanders were managing to transplant European crops. Not only had the colonists at New Plymouth "tryed . . . all our severall Graines" with some success in what had proved to be "a fitting Soyle for their nature" but even the Governor of Massachusetts after less than a year in residence had "greene Pease growing in his Garden as good as ever I eat in *England.*"[2] The Scottish proprietors of East Jersey attracted the attention of prospective emigrants with reports that the colony could support all of the fundamental elements of Scottish agriculture – perhaps even better than Scotland itself. Similarly, William Penn reassured potential migrants in a promotional pamphlet of 1681 that farmers in Pennsylvania would soon be able to "follow the *English husbandry* as they do in *New*

---

[1] See Daniel Vickers, "Competency and Competition: Economic Culture in Early America," *William and Mary Quarterly*, 3d ser., 47 (1990), 3–29.

[2] Francis Higginson, *New-Englands Plantation* (London: 1630).

England, and *New York.*"[3] These were brave words that reality sometimes belied, but they were rooted in a vision of colonization that was particular to the American Northeast.

In large part, that vision was an article of faith. Although the northern colonies were launched as commercial enterprises that had to provide a return for their investors, they recruited a high proportion of their initial colonists from a variety of reformed Protestant groups that saw in the New World a refuge where true believers could worship free from persecution, from the moral decay around them, and from the temptations into which their own material impoverishment might lead them to fall. Integral to this vision – and in spite of other differences, this was something that Puritans, Quakers, Presbyterians, and German sectarians shared in common – was finding a part of the world that could sustain the household economy. "Nothing sorts better with Piety than compte[n]cy," announced John White, a Puritan divine, on the eve of the Great Migration to New England. In this he was giving voice to the sentiment, shared amongst a great many oppositional sects, that insofar as godliness prospered in well-ordered families, those families needed the proper material support. Since the American Northeast seemed to offer plenty of land in a climate suited to the diversified production of a sort that competent households practiced in Europe, it seemed fit for the purpose. Women could employ their skills in processing the produce that men brought in from the forests and fields. With the prospect of transplanting this basic productive relationship onto untilled soil, therefore, the dissident emigrants of the seventeenth century shipped themselves for New England, the Jerseys, and Pennsylvania in family units. In Massachusetts, where in the Great Migration of the 1630s nine out of ten colonists came with families or near relatives, this was truest. Among the Presbyterian settlers of East Jersey and the Quakers in West Jersey and Pennsylvania, a clear majority did the same. Together all of these groups established household production as the fundamental economic principle of the region.

This dedication to the ideal of competency for families bore fruit in the northern colonies in a number of ways. First, it meant that from the very beginning the settled population included an unusually equal balance between the sexes. The mere presence of women, hence families and the social institutions that growing families demanded, prompted a settle-

3 William Penn to Robert Turner, Mar. 5, 1681; and Penn, *Some Account of the Province of Pennsylvania in America* (London, 1681), in Jean R. Soderlund, ed., *William Penn and the Founding of Pennsylvania, 1680–1684* (Philadelphia: 1983), 64–65.

ment pattern that was expansive enough yet more immediately stable, centralized, and urban than in the plantation colonies. Furthermore, since labor was to be divided by gender, a system of mixed farming that employed women efficiently by generating a variety of raw materials to process made good economic sense. Diversified agriculture demanded in turn a range of supporting services by artisans, and the complex network of regional exchange among these farming and craft manufacturing households created an obvious field of profitable operation for a resident merchant class. The merchant capital, expertise, and enterprise that were natural byproducts of colonization everywhere accumulated in the case of the northern colonies not in London, Glasgow, or Bristol but in Boston, New York, and Philadelphia. In short, the emphasis on families pushed dissident settlers to a land that seemed familiar or potentially so, caused them to replicate the socioeconomic ways of the Old World, and enabled them and the merchant interests that accompanied them to capture business that in the plantation colonies flowed elsewhere. It is no accident that *New* Plymouth, *New* Hampshire, *New* Jersey, *New* England, *New* York, and *Nova* Scotia all sat in a part of the New World that was in the course of time most successful at joining in the process of capitalist development, and it was in the interplay between geography and the devotion to family competency that the roots of economic development lay.

THE FRONTIER ECONOMY

The pursuit of competency might seem on the surface to be a modest enough aspiration, and, from the perspective of the individual family, it was. When entire societies adopted it, however, it lost its benign character and became a force for both military conquest and commercial development. Its imperial consequences were relatively straightforward. The thirst for independent landholdings that had driven families in western Europe to stretch the boundaries of their home countries to the bursting point during the sixteenth century now launched them across the sea in search of new territory — lands that were invariably in the possession of others and had to be conquered. Foremost in this invasion were the English. First in Ireland, then in Virginia and New England, they invaded the country, swept it with musket-fire and infectious diseases, and claimed it for themselves. Although cloaked in a variety of rationalizations — the duty to civilize and carry the gospel to the heathen, or the divine call to subdue a continent that appeared to "lie waste without any improvement" – settlement was initially a military operation.[4] The commercial implications of competency, however, were equally significant. As a social ethic, it included a sense of decent comfort that pushed colonists to furnish their homes with more than crude necessities and involved their finding something – either the surplus or the by-product of domestic economy – to market abroad and pay the expense. Furthermore, even the barest impulse to reproduce one's family in competent circumstances, especially in a healthy country where many children lived to maturity, required some investment in capital goods. New households needed guns, axeheads, plough irons, lumber, hearth equipment, cloth, kitchenware, seed, stock – most of which could be obtained only or most easily through commercial exchange. For all of these reasons, the frontier of settlement possessed by its nature an economy of conquest and commerce.

In the northern colonies, as everywhere, the frontier should be understood not as a line dividing cultures from one another but as an amorphous and shifting zone of interpenetration between a set of intrusive European cultures and their Native American counterparts.[5] It could be broad or narrow, depending on whether the societies in question were at peace or war. It could be advancing or retreating, according to the fortunes of military conflict or the ravages of disease. Where intersocietal trade was important, the frontier was a region of activity and cooperation; but where the appropriation and settlement of land were the main European interests, it could become a no-man's land racked with war and raiding. In general, however, frontier zones had a number of common characteristics. Above all, since neither Indians nor Europeans were effectively dominant there, trade and production always contained a powerful diplomatic and military dimension. Assumptions regarding the propriety of bargaining, the media of exchange, the nature of credit, the rules of property – almost anything that fell under the category of economic culture – were not necessarily shared by members of the different groups who worked and dealt on "the middle ground" of the frontier, and they needed continual redefinition.[6] Consequently, it was a region of some opportunity, at the price of considerable risk, for those short on wealth and power.

[4] John Winthrop, *Reasons to Be Considered . . . for the Intended Plantation in New England* (1629), in Alan Heimert and Andrew Delbanco, eds., *The Puritans in America: A Narrative Anthology* (Cambridge, MA: 1985), 72.

[5] Leonard Thompson and Howard Lamar, "Comparative Frontier History," in Lamar and Thompson, eds., *The Frontier in History: North America and Southern Africa Compared* (New Haven, CT: 1981), 7–11.

[6] Richard White, *The Middle Ground: Indians, Empires, and Republics in the Great Lakes Region, 1650–1815* (Cambridge: 1991), 50.

The fur trade did not create the frontier in the American or maritime Northeast as it did in New France, but it accounted for a great deal of the business transacted within it throughout the colonial period, especially in the Middle Colonies. In Newfoundland, where beaver was relatively scarce and where the native Beothuks acquired most of their metal goods by pilfering from seasonally abandoned European waterfront premises, furring was always distinctly subordinate to fishing. From Nova Scotia southward to Connecticut, the trade only flourished along a few river systems and during the first half of the seventeenth century. About 1650, when the geographic reality that the regions sat astride no major route to the West began to dawn, and when the supply of local beaver began to run out, New England's fur trade dipped into insignificance. In New Netherland and New York, by contrast, the commerce in beaver pelts dominated the frontier economy until well into the eighteenth century. This was partly a consequence of geography; without the Hudson–Mohawk river system that linked the Atlantic coastline with the Great Lakes basin, the trade would never have developed at all. That it flourished, however, resulted from the combined astuteness of European colonists and Iroquois Indians who succeeded in channeling a fairly constant flow of furs from the West (and sometimes through Montreal) into Albany and off to England right up to the American Revolution. After 1730, aggressive traders operating out of Philadelphia, collecting deerskins as well as beaver over a network of overland trails from the Ohio Valley, added still further to the London-bound supply of peltry.

Unlike most early modern commerce, this was not a business in which diversification paid. Although the import of cloth, rum, and other goods for the Indian trade, as well as the export of furs to Europe, usually lay in the hands of the larger merchants of New York City and Philadelphia, who possessed a range of commercial interests, most of the trade on the frontier fell to specialists. Some general merchants – like William Pynchon of Springfield, Massachusetts, and the firm of Baynton, Wharton, and Morgan from Philadelphia – organized the trade directly by sending employees into the interior, but even more preferred to deal through intermediaries who possessed the vast fund of particular knowledge that this far-flung intersocietal commerce required. Through the mechanism of credit, the responsibilities, risks, and rewards of the trade were delegated in large part to a crowd of tough, knowledgeable, and often cutthroat traders who paddled canoes, poled batteaus, and drove pack horses through the frontier zone to contact the Indians in their villages or at remote posts.

Sometimes on straight barter and sometimes on carefully measured terms of credit, trade goods and furs changed hands at fixed prices supplemented by variable gifts in a complex combination, geared at once to the Indians' dislike for open haggling and to the realities of supply and demand. Much could go wrong in this trade. With no polity that was dominant within the frontier zone, Native Americans and Europeans alike could cheat, rob, or murder both partners and competitors and escape the punishment that would have been a probable fate at home. Long lines of communication could lead to confusion and misinformation that at times landed traders in the midst of the forest with trade goods but no customers. Along the attenuated chain by which furs made their way eastward, disease and tribal warfare also could bring this commerce to a halt. And even when trading parties had met up with each other and begun to deal, novice Europeans could, by paying insufficient attention to the diplomatic rituals of trade, so offend the Native American sense of propriety as to cause the business relationship to break down altogether. Since the subtleties of the fur trade were foreign to the experience of most colonists, it usually became the province of specialized frontiersmen.

The main force for order within the trade was the collective self-interest of the tribal units on the one hand and the colonial governments with their merchant supporters on the other. From the Indian standpoint, furs not only paid for the European goods upon which they depended but also served as one of the underpinnings of intercultural diplomacy. The shipments of peltry that the Iroquois could deliver to Albany were in a sense chips that could be played in the negotiation of treaties to protect tribal lands and their other interests. From the perspective of some colonial governors, such as Thomas Dongan of New York, a healthy fur trade was not only a source of customs revenue, personal profit, and patronage but also a fair guarantee of the frontier peace that needed a minimum of policing. Unfortunately for the cause of order, however, furs mattered less to most colonial administrators than did the acquisition of land for settlement. James Logan of Pennsylvania may have made a great deal of money exporting deerskins from Philadelphia while serving as William Penn's colonial secretary at the beginning of the eighteenth century – a business that gave him a clear interest in the survival of his Indian suppliers and customers. But the same Logan took an active role in engineering the seizure of Conestoga and Shawnee lands in the Susquehanna Valley and the settlement of German and English families on property he had acquired there. This was a particularly flagrant version of a contradiction that plagued commerce throughout the frontier: if there was good money to be made in dealing with Indians, there were fortunes to be won in supplanting them.

More than the trade in furs, therefore, the activity of land seizure, speculation, and homesteading dominated the economy of the frontier zone. What many historians have politely termed *migration* or *geographic mobility* was in reality the ceaseless, aggressive, and fundamentally political expansion inherent in the pursuit of family competency. During the first decades of settlement when the frontier itself clung to the coast, most of this movement took place within a small region, and a great deal could be accommodated inside town boundaries. This sort of mobility has often been overlooked by historians who conclude from the absence of migration across town or county boundaries that these were stable times. In reality, scattering was from the very earliest decades of settlement a truth of colonial life – even in New England, where the founders possessed an unusual sensitivity to what John Winthrop called "our . . . community in the work."[7] Thus, as early as 1635 when some of his fellow colonists decamped for Connecticut, even Winthrop could excuse their "strong bent" to move on, for in Massachusetts they were already "much straitened by their own nearness to one another, and their cattle . . . [was] much increased."[8]

The number of different paths that this process of conquest and settlement could take was nearly beyond counting. Sometimes, as in the case of the Puritan migration to Massachusetts Bay, epidemic disease preceded the settlers' arrival and left broad stretches of abandoned land for the Europeans to occupy. On occasion, as in Plymouth Colony's encroachment on the lands of the Wampanoag Indians in the early 1670s (which helped to provoke King Philip's War), the country was cleared of opposition by force of arms. In other cases, as in the westward expansion of Pennsylvania after Penn's departure in 1701, native groups beat a long, negotiated, strategic retreat before the relentless pressure of land speculators, their often ruthless back country agents, and the farm-hungry homesteaders who had risked much to move to the frontier and were not to be disappointed. A great many variables entered into the respective histories of these different frontiers: geography, the relative importance of the fur

---

[7] John Winthrop, "A Model of Christian Charity" (1630), in Heimert and Delbanco, eds., *The Puritans in America*, 91.

[8] James K. Hosmer, ed., *Winthrop's Journal: "History of New England,"* 2 vols., Original Narratives of Early American History (New York: 1908), vol. 1, 142, 151.

trade, and tribal and colonial diplomacy, not to mention the cultural peculiarities of the particular groups that contested the land. Invariably, however, homesteading took place on what was politically contested ground, where settler power eventually prevailed.

This was especially true in the farther reaches of the back country. Trouble commonly resulted when settlers encroached upon territory that Indians had not actually ceded, squatted on proprietorial lands without paying for the privilege, moved into a stretch of country over which there was a dispute between proprietors, or simply set out claims that over-lapped their neighbors'. Thus, Thomas Penn ran into difficulty with squatters who had invaded unsurveyed lands in Lancaster County during the 1730s and organized "claims clubs" when he attempted to coerce them into signing warrants. Along the Pennsylvania–Maryland border, in East Jersey, throughout the Green Mountains, and on the Maine frontier, the indistinct claims of distant proprietors led to chronic conflict not only between landlords and squatters but, in cases where proprietorial jurisdiction was in dispute, between the occupiers themselves. Ultimately, the trouble arose because there was no consensus over what created property rights in conquered land. Was it defined in the terms of an Indian deed, royal charter, or proprietary grant? Or, as one German tenant in Pennsylvania argued before the Privy Council, was "the best Title a man can have" in "new-settled Colonies" one defined by "Possession and Improvement"?[9] Even on a local scale, the founding of towns, manors, and townships, and the assignment of undivided land within them was an intensely political process, in which dozens of potential proprietors or landholders – great and petty – attempted to lever the provincial governments or local authorities into grants that they could either occupy and develop or hold for speculative purposes. Although wildly complex and subject to all sorts of local variation, the struggle that ensued over the establishment of private property in frontier land generally resulted in a qualified victory for those with connections within the colonial administration. As long as it lasted, however, such conflict contributed to the risks and uncertainties of the homesteading economy.

All of this mattered, of course, because on the homesteading frontier the pace of development was so rapid. Even if families could convert no more than a few acres of forest a year to European-style husbandry, it was only a period of decades before towns acquired a settled appearance and

---

[9] Quoted in James T. Lemon, *The Best Poor Man's Country: A Geographical Study of Southeastern Pennsylvania* (Baltimore, MD: 1972), 57.

property values rose. Such development was purchased at the cost of considerable initial poverty. Travelers into frontier regions were often appalled at the meager diet, squalid housing, and near-absence of creature comforts to which homesteaders subjected themselves while they sank most of their own time and resources, plus whatever credit they could obtain from relatives, neighbors, or merchant connections, into the business of farm development. The levels of indebtedness that frontier families assumed were high in relation to the productive capacity of their farms, and this involved diverting considerable effort into making returns. One obvious marketable commodity was timber and cordwood from the forest they felled, and there was almost no region where new settlement did not generate a flourishing, if not always long-lived, export trade in wood products. Even agricultural produce was often pared from domestic consumption and shipped downriver or carted into town very soon after the first fields were cleared in an effort to sustain the vital injections of credit. With an enthusiasm, then, not for commerce in and of itself but for the comfortable independence that was impossible to achieve without an eye to commercial opportunity, homesteading farmers brought one range of frontier land after another into the domain of rural economies on the model of the Old World.

THE RURAL ECONOMY

Had the families of immigrants who sailed for the American and Canadian Northeast in the seventeenth and eighteenth centuries landed in the tropics, the lure of plunder and plantation profits would undoubtedly have proved irresistible, and their commitment to the household economy employing male and female skills in combination would have been silently shelved. That is what happened off the Nicaraguan coast at Providence Island, where Puritan settlers of the 1630s abandoned the attempt to reconstruct the economic institutions of home almost immediately and turned their energies to privateering and the operation of slave-driven cotton and tobacco farms. This also happened in the exotically *cold* climate of the far northern colonies, where the few permanent residents shied away from mixed husbandry and concentrated instead on fur and fish. Newfoundland in particular possessed too short a growing season to plant and harvest grains or to raise enough fodder to see more than a handful of animals through the winter. A small number of families persisted on its cool, infertile shores throughout the seventeenth century, but since there was little productive employment to be had outside of the fishery, female skills were not an economic necessity, and the household economy never flourished.

Newfoundland was in this sense, however, the exception that proved the rule. All the way from the modestly more temperate country of Nova Scotia southward to Pennsylvania, geography confirmed the early immigrants in their intention to transplant the household basis of production. Although farmers adjusted the balance between pasture and tillage land and in different regions gave preference to different animals and crops, virtually all remained wedded in large measure to the principle of agricultural diversity through the end of the colonial period. The Acadian settlers around the Bay of Fundy raised small surpluses of cattle, peas, and wheat, which they sold to Boston and to fishermen on Cape Breton, but the general orientation of their husbandry was toward local self-sufficiency and reflected the same mix of husbandry that prevailed in the west of France, whence most of them hailed. New Englanders had to adjust their agricultural expectations to the reality that neither wheat nor barley prospered there, so they grew rye and Indian corn instead, and eventually they came to depend more on animal husbandry than their English forebears. In a few favored regions, certain specialties arose – sheep raising and cheese making on the shores of Narragansett Bay, horse breeding in the Connecticut valley and growing flax for seed by the Merrimack River in southern New Hampshire – but rarely in New England did farmers stray far from the principle of diversity. In the Hudson River Valley, and throughout New Jersey and Pennsylvania, fertile soil allowed wheat to grow into an important staple export very soon after settlement. Yet the men and women who operated even the most commercial grain farms in the Middle Colonies were hardly specialists, for they pastured cattle and sheep, cut timber, boiled potash, ran dairies, and barreled meat on a scale no less impressive than their counterparts in Connecticut or Massachusetts.

If mixed farming was nearly universal in the northern colonies, so was the division by gender of the labor that powered it. By 1700, every agricultural region north of Maryland (save possibly Pennsylvania, whose population was still dominated by large numbers of young and indentured male immigrants) possessed a sex ratio that was close to equal. Within the gender-balanced households that composed this rural population, the west European tradition by which most men labored in the fields and forests producing raw materials, while women normally worked around the house and barn processing those materials into consumable items, survived the trans-Atlantic passage reasonably intact. There was considerable elasticity in these arrangements, of course, especially at busy seasons and in households where one sex outnumbered the other. Because of the complex mix of German, Welsh, and Scots-Irish ethnicity that prevailed in the Middle Colonies, the division of tasks between men and women there displayed particular variety. As a general rule, however, the skills of domestic production fell mainly within the female province, and with these the economies of the northeastern colonies were peculiarly blessed. In 1788, Brissot de Warville remarked that a bachelor farmer he had met north of Philadelphia could not, without a family, keep poultry or pigeons, make cheese, or "have any spinning done or collect goose feathers." It was, he added, "a great disadvantage for him not to be able to profit from these domestic farm industries, which can be carried on well only by farm women."[10] No factor was more decisive in the northern colonies' long-term success in diversification and import substitution than the roughly equal sex ratio that prevailed there almost from their foundation.

The final element in the economic culture that migrated to the householding colonies was the habit of exchange. To what extent was the rural economy of the Northeast market-driven? Obviously, all farmers and their wives dealt with others on a commercial basis from time to time. Most farmers who kept diaries recorded several trips overland or downriver to the market towns along the coast every year, and the accounts of shopkeepers record the purchase of produce, at least in small quantities, from people at all levels of rural society. Even the dealings that farmers concluded in their own towns and villages were often competitive enough to convince John Winthrop at times that it was "the common rule that most men walked by in all their commerce, to buy as cheap as they could, and to sell as dear."[11] At the same time, however, most rural production was consumed at home and never entered the market at all. Even the highest estimates of the agricultural surplus in typical farm households only place it at between 25 and 40 percent of total output. Families did arrive at decisions about the management of their farms — choosing whether or not to replant a worn-out corn field in apple trees, or when to slaughter a hog — with some awareness of the price at which these products could also be bought or sold. But custom and a sense that family requirements came

---

[10] Brissot de Warville, *New Travels in the United States of America, 1788,* in Joan M. Jensen, *Loosening the Bonds: Mid-Atlantic Farm Women, 1750–1850* (New Haven, CT: 1986), 53.

[11] Hosmer, ed., *Winthrop's Journal,* vol. 2, 20.

first dampened their response; thus market forces impinged on farm management mainly in the broader considerations of long-run strategy. Much of what men and women obtained around their neighborhoods to meet their immediate needs changed hands in a system governed less by haggling over terms than by unspoken reciprocity. The numerous petty debts and credits that farmers built up with one another were rarely settled in the commercial manner by payment in cash or in bookkeeping shuffles; rather, they had to be repaid personally – sometimes in labor but more often in equipment or produce. No farm family could prosper in utter autonomy, or only with neighborly assistance, or simply through market transactions. In their drive to preserve a modicum of competency and confer it upon subsequent generations, men and women moved easily in and out of all three tactical alternatives and, indeed, found the borders between them to be rather indistinct.

None of these features set the northern colonies apart in any absolute sense, for a numerical balance between the sexes and some economic diversification came eventually to most of the New World, and a degree of commercial production was common everywhere. The colonies north of Maryland, however, were *born* with these characteristics and possessed in their economic diversity a potential for constructive regional integration that the southern colonies developed only hesitantly later on. Settlers in the tobacco, rice, and sugar colonies did more business with consumers and suppliers overseas than did their northern counterparts, but they did less, particularly in the early years, with one another. For one thing, most regions of the Northeast were involved, however indirectly, in the provisioning of seaports. As early as 1648, Edward Johnson observed that the inhabitants of Ipswich on Massachusetts' North Shore had "many hundred quarters" of beef to spare and "feed, at the latter end of summer, the Towne of Boston with good Beefe." Some of this was for export and some for consumption, but a significant proportion went into victualing, "both for their owne and Forreiners-ships, who resort hither for that end."[12] Not only in Boston but later in Philadelphia and New York, the rapid settlement of a highly diversified service and manufacturing population hinged on the ability of farm families in the country round to provision them. Although some of the produce that farmers brought into the seaport towns was simply grain and livestock to be warehoused and exported directly, even more produce either had been processed in the countryside (like

[12] J. Franklin Jameson, ed., *Johnson's Wonder-Working Providence, 1629–1651*, Original Narratives of Early American History (New York: 1910), 71, 96.

butter, smoked and salted meat, malt, flour, and boards) or would be
processed by specialists in town (like bread, clothing, furniture, and
leather products). With remarkable speed, a network of regional exchange, connecting mariners to outfitters, bakers, farmers, millers, mill-
wrights, and so forth – in a primitive but recognizable reflection of the
mother country – was reestablished in the northern seaports and their
hinterland. Marketing the mixed surplus of domestic farm production was
not a likely path to fortune, but in a thousand little ways it employed the
talents of housewives, and artisans in town and country, capturing business that would otherwise have fallen to Europeans.

In spite of these trans-Atlantic similarities and the long-term advantages that derived from them, the northern colonies did not instantly nor
entirely replicate the rural economies of their metropolitan parents, owing
mostly to the ease with which the unimproved land and natural resources
of the New World could be appropriated. This reorganized northern agriculture in part by pushing farming households to be extensive in their
exploitation of the natural environment and sparing in their use of labor.
The dominant method of forest clearance – stripping the trees of bark and
waiting till they toppled, while cultivating the ground around them and
planting it with crops – spoke clearly to the way in which other chores
placed competing demands upon people's time. Swine were the favored
livestock in the initial stages of settlement for the same reason: since they
could grub for themselves on unimproved land and defend themselves
against natural predators, they put minimal demands upon human assistance. European travelers across the Northeast remarked on what they
perceived to be sloppy farming: the absence of crop rotation, an inadequate attention to manuring and fodder crops, insufficient housing for
animals, poor selection and quality of implements, unselective breeding,
and so forth. Farmers in New York were said to clear out tracts of forest
and then "crop their fields with corn, till they are absolutely exhausted;
then they leave them, what they call fallow, that is, to run weeds for
several years, till they think the soil has recovered somewhat of its fertility, when they begin again with corn."[13] In an agricultural regime where
so much of the land was periodically abandoned, fencing was sensibly
impermanent and consisted mainly of stumps and logs, then posts and
rails, and sometimes stones, assembled along field boundaries in such

---

[13] Anon.,*American Husbandry* (1775), quoted in Percy Wells Bidwell and John I. Falconer, *History of
Agriculture in the Northern United States, 1620–1860* (Washington: 1925), 86.

haste that complaints about strayed animals became chronic everywhere. Although the agricultural critics of the day attributed most of this to sloth and ignorance, the simple truth was that, where the supply of land was too vast to be exhausted in a future that any colonist could imagine, it seemed foolish to squander scarce labor and capital on conservation or cosmetic tidiness.

Another significant consequence of the easy access to land and resources was that European immigrants found it possible to realize on the western shores of the Atlantic a degree of independence that would have been inconceivable at home. In a rural economy without a highly profitable export staple, this had a number of peculiar consequences. First, it meant that relative to the availability of unimproved land and resources, productive equipment and labor time were in limited supply. Within individual households, tools and livestock were usually inadequate to the opportunities that one's holdings afforded; those holdings themselves were less than fully developed; and the time needed to make the necessary improvements was chronically short. Between households, it meant that there was on the one hand relatively little labor available for hire and on the other hand comparatively little capital to set laborers to work. Although the demand for labor was high in the northern colonies, it was chiefly a demand for help in farm formation, which provided no immediate paying returns sufficient to meet the cost of a large wage bill. Where hands could be obtained and well-to-do colonists could afford the cost, the scarcity of labor drove the wages of common laborers on northern farms up to a level that ranged from 1s. 6d. to 2s. (in British currency) per day – half again as high as those that prevailed in England. Since large employers were relatively scarce, however, the quantity of labor marketed at these handsome wages remained by the standards of the old country comparatively small. Ordinary farm families could not depend on the free market for the help and equipment they needed (at ploughing and harvest times, especially) if they were to raise the surpluses on which the achievement of household competency depended. The very opportunities created by the proximity of the frontier simultaneously saddled farming as a business with an unusual potential for risk.

Accordingly, as elsewhere in the New World, the productive systems inherited from Europe were inadequate to the altered balance in factors of production, and they had to be adjusted. The adoption of slavery was a possibility that some considered. Emmanuel Downing of Massachusetts understood plainly that successive generations would "hardly see this great

Continent filled with people" and that servants would "still desire free-
dome to plant for themselves, and not staye but for verie great wages." By
procuring "a stock of slaves suffitient to do all our busines," he speculated,
the colony might resolve the problem.[14] Yet bound labor was costly, and
most northern farmers did not produce valuable enough surpluses to justify the expense. The adjustments they undertook, therefore, were geared
toward accepting the scarcity of outside help and coping with it by intensifying the burden on their own families. For one thing, rural households
continually sought for ways in which work could be spread across the year.
This reinforced the existing commitment to diversification by encouraging the planting of orchards that could be picked after the grain harvest,
the woodworking and other handicrafts that could be pursued in the
winter months, and the hunting and fishing that could fit into the odd
day spared from agriculture. Another way in which families adapted to the
scarcity of labor was by extending the dependency of their own children.
Living and working at home until marriage had not been universal or even
normal among the rural youth of western Europe in the early modern age.
Most young men and many young women spent a good proportion of their
teen-age and early adult years away from home in service or apprenticeship
to other households needing help. This tradition – a central element in
the regional labor markets of the Old World – did not survive transplanta-
tion to America in anything like its original shape. Here, the interdepen-
dence between parents and children was prolonged until marriage and
even beyond.

In New England, where soils were generally thinner, the climate cooler,
and commercial agriculture seldom capable of supporting the cost of
indentured servants or slaves, family labor was especially important. Virginia might thrive "by keeping many servants" wrote one seventeenth-
century observer, but New Englanders "conceit that they and their Children can doe enough, and soe have rarely above one Servant."[15] Although
all young people took part in the local exchange of favors, very few
actually left home to labor for others, and those who did rarely spent more
than a few months away. By far the greatest portion of their young
adulthood was invested in improving the farms that their parents operated
and developing the property that would one day form the basis of their

---

[14] Emmanuel Downing to John Winthrop, ca. August 1645, *Winthrop Papers, 1498–1649*, 5 vols.
(Boston: 1929–1947), vol. 5, 38.
[15] Anon., Egerton MSS, British Museum, quoted in Abbot Emerson Smith, *Colonists in Bondage:
White Servitude and Convict Labor in America, 1607–1776* (Chapel Hill, NC, 1947), 29.

inheritance. Even when they had grown up, married, and begun to work a corner of parental lands themselves, young men found their fathers reluctant – especially during the first century of settlement – to deed them control over the property they used. The formal marriage portions that had been normal in the mother country were exceptional in colonial New England. This system of household reproduction was very effective for the initial tasks of farm formation and allowed that process to fan outward swiftly from the initial point of settlement around Plymouth and Massachusetts Bay. True, there were local exceptions to this pattern. Where the agricultural potential of the land allowed, wealthier farmers did purchase slaves and indentured servants and did hire common laborers. With an eye to the provisioning market in the West Indies, John Pynchon of Springfield raised wheat, barley, pigs, and cattle on the fertile bottom lands of the Connecticut valley, using immigrant servants and the paid labor of his dependent clients. On the western shores of Narragansett Bay, where dairy and sheep farming proceeded on a large scale, many planters kept Indian and African slaves. Still, in most of the New England countryside, where commercial production was less important, farmers could not afford this sort of help and relied on the more intensive exploitation of family labor instead.

In the milder and more fertile Middle Colonies, where farms generated more for export, especially in the way of cereal crops, household production still dominated though not in quite the same form. For one thing, the commercial potential of the Hudson Valley, the New Jersey lowlands, and the rolling hills of eastern Pennsylvania attracted the attention of many more wealthy developers, anxious to secure large tracts of land and profit thereby. Much of this territory was carved up into proprietorships, manors, and patents during the last quarter of the seventeenth century, and these were then peopled with tenants. Although the leases that tenants assumed ate into the income and independence they could enjoy, the combination of modest annual rents (generally well below 4 percent of farm value) and long credit on arrears (allowed by proprietors often more interested in the speculative profits of having their uncleared land developed for future sale) permitted them to operate much like freeholders. Whether leased or not, farms were larger in the Middle Colonies than in New England – usually a hundred acres or more – and their operators could afford more nonfamilial help. Some of them purchased indentured servants, but in an agricultural system where the commercial crop was wheat, the demand for hired help was highly seasonal, and most farmers preferred to employ laborers by the day. In Pennsylvania, hundreds of young men and women who had come to Philadelphia on indenture served out their time in a craft or domestic workplace and then wandered into the rural labor market. Although some moved in with farming households, even more became "inmates" or "freemen," renting cottages with garden plots on their employer's lands and selling their labor on a casual basis. Many of those who moved to the Middle Colonies in family groups (and disembarked for the most part in New York) would have been needy enough in their earliest years to seek out similar arrangements. In this way, the more productive economy of the Middle Colonies attracted the flow of immigrants who, as free laborers, fueled farm development on a larger and more commercial scale than was possible farther north. Yet the difference is easy to overstate. Even on the best lands of eastern Pennsylvania and the Hudson River Valley, farm production was sufficiently diversified and reliable farm labor sufficiently costly to cause agriculture to remain distinctively a family business.

Although the structural features of the rural economy in the Northeast remained fairly stable across the colonial period, there were shifts and developments within that structure that are equally part of the region's history. Preeminent among these, of course, was the pattern of rapid, extensive growth. Immigration and natural increase, in a balance that shifted decisively toward the latter over time – especially in New England, which received few new immigrants after 1645 – caused the population of most regions to double, as Thomas Malthus observed, about every twenty-five years. With a few local exceptions, demographic growth combined with the favorable geography of the country and with the colonists' military superiority and immunological advantages over the Native Americans to allow settlement to spread and the economy to experience more or less continuous extensive growth. Peculiar difficulties in certain regions restricted colonial expansion. The severe climate and thin soils of Newfoundland and the eastern shore of Nova Scotia caused most potential colonists to think twice before taking up permanent residence there before the middle of the eighteenth century. French–English conflict along the Atlantic Canadian coastline and in the Hudson and Mohawk River valleys slowed settlement there until after the conquest of New France in 1759. Certain Indian peoples – the Iroquois west of Albany and the Abenaki in Maine, for instance – were politically powerful enough to slow European infestation of their lands. Yet the general picture of swift, extensive growth is undeniable; indeed, most of the economic growth that the northern colonies measured before 1775 can be accounted for by the mushrooming reproduction of rural households.

Much less economic growth, by comparison, stemmed from gains in economic productivity. The northern colonists had a model for agricultural improvement in the rural economy of England, which marked steady progress from the late seventeenth century onward, but with land so abundant, it made much more sense to invest time and resources into the development of new land than into any attempt to work previously cleared acreage more intensively. Even on the best soils of eastern Pennsylvania, where the commercial incentive to raise productivity was strongest, interest in proper rotation patterns, nutrient-fixing crops, protein-rich grasses, fertilizers, and selective breeding remained limited to a tiny minority of farmers until after the Revolution. Accordingly, insofar as changes in per capita wealthholdings give some indication of changes in the level of economic activity, it seems that rural people planted European husbandry in American soil and raised its productivity up to European levels within the first generation of settlement but did not improve upon their yields and herds before the end of the colonial period. The livestock holdings of most farmers in Pennsylvania and Massachusetts compared favorably with those of their English counterparts within a quarter-century of settlement but did not grow further before 1775. Grain and hay yields were high on newer lands, but they did not rise (and in New England may, indeed, have fallen) toward the end of the colonial period. The value of land and land improvements climbed over time – most rapidly in the earliest decades of settlement (when much of it was being cleared) and during the third quarter of the eighteenth century (when the demand for foodstuffs overseas was increasing) – but the degree to which this reflected growth in the productivity of farm labor itself is unclear.

A more likely arena for rising productivity in the rural economy was in craft manufacture. During the seventeenth century, when there was, in William Bradford's words, so much "labour and servise to be done aboute building and planting," and when opportunity to hunt and fish was as close as the untamed forest, the craft skills that immigrants had brought with them were largely laid aside.[16] With the development of regional markets and the growth of population in older towns beyond the employment opportunities in agriculture, farm families began to spend more of their time on domestic manufacture, craft services, and wage labor. Al-

[16] William Bradford, *Of Plymouth Plantation, 1620–1647*, ed. Samuel Eliot Morison (New York: 1952), 28.

ways the principal workers in manufacture throughout the early modern world, women participated in this development but probably experienced it as less of a change. Spinning probably came to occupy more of their time in the eighteenth century (or so it seems from the slowly rising incidence of woolen and linen wheels in farm inventories), but textile work had always lain within the female province even at the beginning of settlement. The same was true with tailoring and the running of dairies; although more of this production may have been commercially directed in the later colonial period, the shift was slight. For men, the growing interest in by-employments (craft manufacture and wage work pursued on a part-time basis) marked more of a transformation — or at least a resumption of Old World habits after the frontier interlude. Although a few artisans such as smiths, millers, and carpenters normally moved into newer settlements and stuck to their trades, the great majority of founders, regardless of their training, styled themselves only as planters or farmers and retained little in the way of specialized craft equipment. As communities matured, the outdoor tasks of land clearance, fencing, construction, and hunting — all of which framed the growing season — diminished in importance, and men had to find ways of otherwise improving the idle days between harvest and ploughing times. In the second and third generation, therefore, rural youths began learning trades to support themselves until they came into land of their own and later to supplement the income from their farms. In Acadia, although virtually all the planters worked the land, a census taken as early as 1671 styled many inhabitants by specialized occupational titles that included: surgeon, weaver, cooper, farrier, gunsmith, joiner, mason, carpenter, tailor, and toolmaker. Shoemaking, seafaring, and ironworking, as well as shipbuilding and other forms of carpentry, were especially popular from New England southward to Pennsylvania; but the full range of by-employments, which these young colonists adopted to fortify themselves against the threat of underemployment, was very broad. Although it is impossible to measure the contribution that the combined labors of women and men in such by-employments made to the rural economy, it provided the beginnings of import substitution. In the short run, it produced no industrial transformation of the sort that was gathering force in western Europe after 1750, but it did set the stage for something similar following Independence.

The density of economic integration within rural communities and across the regions of which they formed a part did not distinguish the northern colonies absolutely from their plantation counterparts. Still, the history of that integration – rooted in the diversified household labors of both sexes and patterned on the European example – was already well established in the Northeast when it began to spread across the South. And it was this degree of regional integration that gave the northern colonies a further distinctive quality: their dynamic maritime economy.

THE SEAPORT ECONOMY

Much of the money that financed the original settlement of the New World came from merchants and gentry who planned to win their investment back from profits earned in the transoceanic business of supplying the settlers and shipping their produce to market. Rarely did they anticipate moving to the New World, and rarely was it necessary. Although there were many problems in the organization of production that had to be sorted out on the western shores of the Atlantic, the business of provisioning plantations and assembling staple crops for export was relatively straightforward, and the colonial end could often be handled either by agents or by the planters themselves. The real complexities of the trade lay in the old country, where the problems of recruiting capital, assembling dry goods for shipment to the colonies, distributing the colonial produce to consumers across Europe, and dealing with the imperial administrators and their regulations demanded that the major players be present. For plain business reasons, the great merchant houses that organized the colonial trades remained resident in Seville, Amsterdam, Genoa, Lisbon, London, Bordeaux, and a host of smaller ports, and they rarely migrated to the Americas.

In the northern colonies, trans-Atlantic trade started with vessels from ports like Bristol, Plymouth, Le Havre, La Rochelle, and San Sebastian, which conducted the early migratory fishery and carried dried cod to Southern Europe. The commercial needs of New Englanders – in both the import of dry goods and the export of fish and timber – were first handled chiefly by their Puritan connections within the merchant community of London. The Dutch West India Company held a monopoly on trade in New Netherland until 1639, and a small coterie of Amsterdam merchant families dominated the colony's commerce thereafter. Philadelphia was the last-founded of the major northern colonial ports and launched into overseas trade faster than any other; yet in the first half-century, it too depended on British or New England capital and shipping for most of its

trans-Atlantic business. Throughout the Northeast, even the earliest permanent settlements possessed wholesale merchants, who assembled cargoes of fish and farm produce and placed sizable orders for European
goods, but almost never were these individuals "traders by sea," who
ventured their wealth abroad and assumed the full risk of commerce.[17]

What distinguished the seaboard communities north of the Chesapeake
from their counterparts to the south was the rapidity with which northern
colonial traders evolved into merchants in the full sense of the word:
owning and managing ships, providing banking and insurance services for
other dealers, financing local industries, and buying and selling in a
multitude of different markets. Except for the local underwriting of insurance, most of these functions had developed in Boston before 1675 and
were common to Newport, New York, and Philadelphia by the early
eighteenth century. It is true that through to the end of the colonial
period, even the wealthiest of American merchants remained dependent in
much of their business on European capital. During the commercial boom
that followed the Seven Years' War, for example, British merchants
flooded the colonial ports with dry goods sent on their own accounts to be
sold on commission. By the outbreak of the Revolution, however, the four
port towns mentioned above had become general *entrepôts* (centers of warehousing and distribution), on at least the scale of such secondary European
ports as Bristol, Nantes, or Cadiz.

For many years, historians have rightly celebrated the role of merchants
in the development of these seaport economies. One should not overesti-
mate the merchant contribution, however, since a great many of the
decisions taken in their name – constructing vessels, operating them,
negotiating in foreign ports, managing small manufactories, and so on –
were delegated to the master mariners and craftsmen who were the specialists in their respective fields. Where merchants did play a central role was
in the coordination of these separate activities through the manipulation of
capital. Thomas Doerflinger has argued that the economic dynamism of
the northern colonies depended upon the peculiarly "vigorous spirit of
enterprise" of the business class, which stemmed in turn from the special
challenge of trying to wring profits from a newly developing region that
exported little that could not be obtained within Europe itself.[18] The more

---

[17] Jacob M. Price, "Economic Function and the Growth of American Port Towns in the Eighteenth
Century," *Perspectives in American History* 8 (1974), 138.
[18] Thomas M. Doerflinger, *A Vigorous Spirit of Enterprise: Merchants and Economic Development in Revolutionary Philadelphia* (Chapel Hill, NC: 1986).

fundamental question, however, is why merchants were there in such numbers to begin with. This is an important problem, because the local residency of merchants was not a necessary consequence of settlement itself, even in prosperous colonies, yet it was invariably a factor of considerable economic advantage. The most probable explanation is that in order to profit from coordinating and financing such complex economies – complex because diversified, and diversified because settled in families – successful entrepreneurs had to be on the spot. Relatively simple colonial economies based on one or two staple exports could be serviced from a distance; witness the rapid growth of the Newfoundland fisheries and of the Chesapeake and West Indian plantations – financed and often owned overseas. The same was not true where colonies were more locally integrated. The creative development of the carrying trades and the fisheries was largely a merchant achievement therefore, but it was an achievement that can be understood only within the context of the diversified regional economies that demanded a merchant presence.

In New England, the first local merchants began by acquiring dry goods imported on the accounts of London dealers and retailing them to immigrant planters who paid for their purchases in the coin they had brought with them. The calling of the Long Parliament in 1640 and the subsequent outbreak of the English Civil War, however, brought an end to the Puritan Migration and choked off this inflow of immigrant specie. Merchants in Boston and Salem had to begin casting about immediately for other ways of raising payment to cover their obligations overseas. This they managed in remarkably short order by assembling cargoes of farm produce, timber, and fish for delivery to English vessels and shipment to the Wine Islands and Southern Europe. This was no simple business; it involved coordinating a complex network of independent small producers. In essence, the diversity of Massachusetts' population, even at this early stage in its history, created both a demand for merchant services and an opportunity for merchant profit. Fishermen had settled on the maritime periphery of the Bay Colony because they could obtain there the land, provisions, and equipment they required. Planters had carved farms from the wilderness knowing that they could service precisely the sort of urban market that fishermen provided. And craftsmen had scattered across the region on the understanding that they might supply the specialized needs of seamen and landsmen alike. There was money to be made in facilitating the myriad small transactions that connected these families, and it was in this activity – complicated enough to demand the sort of intricate local knowledge that residence made possible – that the first generation of New England merchants found their niche.

Building on their strategic position within this regional market, traders in Boston (during the 1640s) and then in Salem and Newport (after 1660) began to experiment in launching overseas ventures of their own. With skilled shipwrights in towns like Newbury and Scituate to furnish them with hulls, blacksmiths and riggers in the larger ports to ready these vessels for sea, fishermen outfitted on credit to provide them with cargoes, and farmers with cartloads of produce sufficient to provision voyages, local merchants were in a position to compete effectively with their counterparts in the Old World: first in the coasting trades to Newfoundland, Long Island, and the Chesapeake; then in the West Indian market; and sometimes in voyages to certain portions of Europe itself. The objects of this commerce included not only fish, meat, horses, flour, and barrel staves, but also reexported English manufactures and Caribbean sugar, and even the vessels themselves, which European shipowners appreciated for their reasonable quality and low cost. The volume of trade was not enormous, and into the early eighteenth century, New England commerce retained a speculative flavor. The risks in trading across war-torn waters into relatively thin colonial markets led to a rapid turnover in personal fortunes, the continual reorganization of merchant groupings, and a preference for operations on a fairly small scale. Yet the complexity of this business was considerable, and Boston in particular evolved into a general entrepôt of surprising maturity within a half-century of its foundation.

The maritime economy of New England continued to grow in extent and productivity, though at a diminishing rate, through the end of the colonial period. Although the tonnage of shipping that cleared Boston harbor annually for foreign ports only doubled, from 20,927 in 1714–7 to 42,506 in 1772, the volume of trade out of secondary ports like Newburyport, Salem, and Marblehead picked up much of the pace. Shipbuilding in Massachusetts rose by 150 percent between 1697–1704 and 1769–71, and New Hampshire yards were also launching many more vessels toward the end of the period. Annual exports of codfish from the Bay Colony rose from 120,000 quintals in 1716 to average 350,000 during the period 1765–75, and the yearly product of the whaling industry (launched on Cape Cod and Nantucket at the beginning of the eighteenth century) climbed from 600 barrels in 1715 to 30,000 barrels during 1772–5. During the fifty years leading up to the Revolution, productivity in the various seafaring industries, as reflected (imperfectly) in declining ocean freight rates and rising per capita output of codfish and whale oil, probably climbed at an annual rate of between 0.5 and 1.0 percent. Some of these gains were organizational – mainly economies of scale made possible by the growing safety, regularity, and volume of trade within the developing imperial market. Thus, by the end of the colonial period, merchants could profitably employ larger ships with smaller man/tonnage ratios, turn them around more swiftly in port, and pay less in insurance than they had at the beginning of the eighteenth century. Other advances had more to do with developments in technology. In the fishery, the adoption of schooners untied crews from the coastline and freed them both to follow the seasonal migrations of the cod from one offshore bank to another and to remain in their ocean-bound workplace without interruption when the fish were biting. The whaling industry also moved to larger vessels not only to extend its range but later to accommodate the installation of tryworks, used to render the whale oil on board the ship.

The pace of growth in New England's maritime industries declined in the latter half of the colonial period for a number of reasons. For one thing, as population began to press against the supply of productive land throughout the region, shipowning merchants had to search farther afield for cargoes. New England ports in general, and Boston in particular, had also to bear the progressively sharper competition from their rivals in New York and Philadelphia, and the deep-water transport that Yankees commonly performed for merchants in the Middle Colonies before the mid-eighteenth century gradually dried up. In terms of productivity, moreover, it is almost certain that the greatest gains were captured in the seventeenth century, when merchants, seamen, shipbuilders, and the like were first mastering the task of applying the knowledge of organization and technology developed in the mature economy of the Old World to the resource-abundant but practically undeveloped environment of the New. The whaling industry is a case in point. Initially, the colonists on Long Island and Nantucket prospered at an extraordinary rate simply by first employing an inexpensive and traditional Basque and Dutch boat-based technology on the herds of right whales migrating past their shores and then selling the oil at a world price determined mostly by the far more costly and capital-intensive whale fishery pursued by European whalers in Arctic waters. As the eighteenth century wore on, the adoption of larger ships and the launching of longer voyages allowed output to continue rising but at a progressively slower pace. Thus the quantity of oil landed at Nantucket rose at an annual rate of 12 percent between 1715 and 1730, 6 percent between 1730 and 1748; and only 4 percent between 1748 and 1772. In most branches of this preindustrial northern economy, economic growth was most dynamic in the early days, when there was most to be learned about this rich and lightly exploited environment. In New England – the first-settled of the northern colonies – this slowdown, if mild, was nonetheless measurable from the depression following Queen Anne's War through the Revolutionary War.

New York was the oldest of the major American ports but also the slowest to develop. Founded in the 1620s by the powerful Dutch West India Company as a fort to protect the entry to the New Netherland colony, it served next to no commercial function at first beyond the warehousing of furs and trade goods. After the Company relinquished its trade monopoly in 1639, most local commerce was captured by a handful of Amsterdam firms, but a few colonists – among them, such ex-company officials as Frederick Philipse and Oloff Van Cortlandt – joined in the export trade on their own account. After New Netherlands passed into English hands in the 1660s, merchants based in the colony and experienced in the trade took advantage of the exclusion of Dutch shipping under the Navigation Acts and began shipping furs abroad themselves. Because peltry was high in value relative to its bulk, New Yorkers developed an early interest in searching out complementary cargoes – Virginia tobacco, whale oil from Long Island, or logwood from the Yucatan – to obtain the fullest possible lading for their vessels. Furs arrived in the colonists' hands fully processed and did not become the object of further manufacturing until delivered to the shops of European hatters and furriers, hence they did not provide a particularly strong staple base for diversification and development. Furthermore, since the Dutch West India Company showed little interest in peopling its colony (and there was not much else to persuade prospective emigrants to leave the prosperous, tolerant Netherlands to face the difficulties of homesteading on a frontier contested by English, French, and Iroquois), the growth of an agricultural hinterland and the business of servicing it was also slow to develop.

Beginning in the last quarter of the seventeenth century, however, family farming on the model of the Old World began to develop in New York – owing partly to natural increase amongst earlier inhabitants and partly to the new inflow of German, English, Scottish, and French Huguenot families. With the spread of the household economy that they practiced (mainly as tenants in East Jersey and up the Hudson) arose in tandem the commercial importance of New York as a port. The surplus of home produce found its way into the hands of Manhattan merchants, either through dealings within the regional market or in the form of rents paid directly in wheat (since most of the great landlords lived in town and were also the colony's principal exporters); this fueled the growth of a sizable export trade to the West Indies, southern Europe, and Britain from the 1670s onward. Some items were sent abroad in relatively unprocessed form, but others like potash, whale oil, bread, and barrel staves were products that passed through several hands in their local manufacture and enriched those local traders who facilitated the necessary interregional exchange. The considerable crops of wheat that were harvested in Albany County, for example, kept local millers busy enough in 1769 to fill "31 sloops . . . which carry from 400 to 500 barrels of Flour each, trading constantly from thence to [New] York & . . . make Eleven or 12 Trips a year each."[19] A good many New York merchants had interests in the numerous little mines and iron foundries across the Hudson in New Jersey that they furnished with capital, specie for wage payment, provisions obtained upriver, and shipping both locally and abroad. On the one hand, it was the presence of a sizable merchant community on Manhattan that spurred this sort of productive, linked development; on the other hand, it was the rising activity of settled and diversified rural households from the end of the seventeenth century onward that sustained the growth of a resident trading community and profitable maritime sector in the first place.

Although Philadelphia's history as a port began in 1682, a good half-century after the foundings of Boston and New York, it had passed its colonial competitors in population, cleared tonnage, and value of exports by the middle of the eighteenth century. The city on the Delaware was born with a combination of advantages that, in a preindustrial world, no other North American urban center could match. The first was its large and fertile hinterland – productive enough to allow Philadelphia merchants to have begun a regular provisioning trade to the West Indies that already numbered ten vessels annually in 1689. By 1700, wheat had established itself as the colony's prime commodity and one that local farmers could raise efficiently enough to penetrate even European markets, where it had to compete with local produce. In 1711, Isaac Norris could write that "the country has within 10 or 12 years Encrease to near Ten times its . . . produce of Corne [,] wheat Especially[,] and the Markett of

---

[19] Richard Smith, Journal (1769), quoted in Bidwell and Falconer, *History of Agriculture in the Northern United States*, 140.

Lisbon hath been of great advantage to us."[20] This latter business could be enormously profitable, especially during the years – not uncommon in the eighteenth century – when European harvests failed, prices soared, and the wheat trade commanded at healthy freighting charges every idle ship in the harbor.

Philadelphia's second edge stemmed from the character of Pennsylvania's original migrant population. Like the Massachusetts Bay Company but unlike the Dutch West India Company, William Penn had taken real pains to encourage settlement in family units. Penn realized that although single people might be willing to emigrate to parts of the New World that lacked the diversity of services that Europe afforded, families in general were not. From the beginning, therefore, he consciously recruited a wide variety of skilled tradesmen and a fair community of merchants to coordinate and exploit the complex of local talent, so that they themselves might prosper as they facilitated the reproduction of households about them. Samuel Carpenter, a Quaker merchant from Barbados, came to Pennsylvania in 1683 and launched a collection of enterprises that seized upon this plethora of human capital – organizing the construction of the town's first wharf, financing several grain mills, founding a lime-burning business, and trading to the West Indies – all with such success that by the 1690s, he was the wealthiest trader in the province. Shipowning was an important part of his business, and again he was well-situated in Philadelphia, where local craftsmen had been launching vessels since the year he arrived. By 1692, Isaac Norris could report that already "we are Rarely without ten or twelve Vessels on ye Stocks."[21] The "laborious handicrafts[men]" and "industrious husbandmen" that flocked to Pennsylvania generated enough business in their desire to establish their own ships and farms and in their demand for English imports to support Carpenter and dozens of other dealers.[22]

More than any of the other northern mainland colonies, Pennsylvanians concentrated on the production of a single export crop – wheat. By itself, as the example of the plantation colonies proved, no staple product however valuable could guarantee the parallel development of port facilities, merchant exporters, or a thriving maritime sector. Considered strictly as

[20] Isaac Norris to Joseph Pike [?], June 1711, quoted in Frederick B. Tolles, *Meeting House and Counting House: The Quaker Merchants of Colonial Philadelphia, 1682–1763* (Chapel Hill: 1948), 87n.
[21] Quoted in Joseph A. Goldenberg, *Shipbuilding in Colonial America* (Charlottesville, VA: 1976), 50.
[22] Penn, "Some Account of the Province of Pennsylvania," in Soderlund, ed., *William Penn and the Founding of Pennsylvania*, 63.

an entrepôt, Philadelphia remained the least sophisticated of the major colonial seaports down to the middle of the eighteenth century. Prior to 1750, shipowning exporters confined themselves largely to coastal and West Indian routes, and they purchased most of their European wares through Boston. As a center for the processing of rural produce – milling, tanning, hatmaking, shoemaking, weaving, butchering, and the like – Philadelphia was second to none, but the welter of petty dealings that scores of small producers served to generate broadened the base of the resident merchant community without involving it in much trans-Atlantic commerce. During the Seven Years' War, however, the British government spent heavily in Pennsylvania, and this unprecedented volume of cash business prompted many of the more successful military contractors to step up the scale of their operations. By the 1770s, Philadelphians supplied almost all of their own shipping and had shed their dependence on Boston. The larger firms like Willing and Morris pulled out of direct dealings with individual producers and delegated this business to specialist grocers, flour dealers, and lumber merchants. Now they concentrated on overseas business: multiplying the routes their vessels worked, acquiring correspondents in dozens of different European ports, and drawing heavily on European houses to finance ambitious and speculative grain-bearing voyages abroad. Philadelphia had become such a magnet for American provisions and a market for English dry goods that farmers from New Jersey to the Virginia backcountry now employed it as their market town of choice. At the outbreak of the Revolution, the Quaker seaport was the busiest in America.

The most thoroughly maritime economy in the Northeast, the history of which set the experience of the mainland colonies in powerful relief, was that of Newfoundland. This rugged and windswept island, scraped of topsoil by glaciation and enveloped by the frigid Labrador current, had served as an extended fishing camp for thousands of migrant French, English, and Iberian fishermen since the sixteenth century. Every spring, vessels packed with men – several dozen to more than a hundred – sailed across from a number of ports on Europe's western coast to fish for cod either in Newfoundland's inshore waters or on the Grand Banks themselves. At least in England, projects for settlement had been in the air since 1578, and the advantages of residence in Newfoundland encouraged hundreds of West Countrymen to move there more or less permanently during the seventeenth century. Yet, chiefly because the scope for farming and the female skills that farming required were so limited in Newfound-

land, family householding in the English manner was slow to develop.
The naval raids that became common during the French–English conflicts
of the eighteenth century often dislodged these fragile settlements completely. Since there was limited scope for a diversity of business activities
on the island, and since the fishery itself was more sensibly organized in
England, very few merchants ever settled in Newfoundland prior to the
American Revolution. St. John's, the largest town on the island, counted
only 300 souls permanently resident in 1728 and never more than a
thousand before 1775. Even with its superb harbor and proximity to
fishing grounds, it always remained through this period more of a fishing
than a shipping port, let alone a genuine entrepôt. Marblehead in Massachusetts possessed an inferior harbor and a worse location, hundreds of
miles from the banks, but with a population of 5,000 and a locally owned
fleet of 150 fishing schooners (many of which traded to the West Indies
and Bilbao in winter), it was a far more sophisticated port. The cod fishery
at Newfoundland enriched a small number of entrepreneurs and sustained
a great many more common families, but few of them took up residence
there before 1775.

The economic development of the colonial Northeast is not effectively
characterized as an export-led phenomenon. Many New World colonies
cleared more ships with larger cargoes of far greater value than did any of
the northern seaports without generating markedly more overall prosperity or building the type of economic structure that would facilitate industrial development in the nineteenth century. Although mercantile activity
mattered enormously, of course, to local welfare and economic growth,
what mattered even more was the economic diversity that created enough
local business to sustain a resident trading community in the first place.
Merchants played a vital role within the colonial economy but only in
concert with the commercial interests of farm and craft families whose
petty but complex dealings – in regional and overseas markets – they
coordinated. Where that complexity was lacking, mercantile and maritime communities, along with all of the business they captured, never
took up residence.

PUBLIC INSTITUTIONS AND THE ECONOMY

The northern colonists, like their southern neighbors, were anxious to
transplant British institutions into American soil. All of them developed

forms of government, land tenure, common law, poor relief, ecclesiastical organization, and so forth that were recognizably part of a common inheritance. At the same time, however, there were significant local variations that stemmed both from the original intentions of the settlers and from the nature of the land they encountered. What distinguished the institutional life of the colonial Northeast was, first, the way in which locally developed institutions served to support the social reproduction of competent households, and second, the manner in which these householding colonies were able to capitalize on the mother country's imperial presence. Since it was from the surplus of family production – used in numerous ways – that wealth and power flowed in the colonial Northeast, the creation of social and economic institutions that could attract immigrant families and nourish their mercantile interests was vital to the region's economic development.

Like most British possessions in the New World, but quite unlike those of Spain and France, the northern colonies enjoyed considerable freedom to direct their internal affairs, especially at the outset. New York, owned by the Dutch West India Company until 1664 and a personal possession of James Stuart until 1689, constituted a partial exception to this rule. Nova Scotia, founded in 1749 as a royal colony and ruled by a governor and council with no assembly until 1758, was a bastion of imperial authority until after the American Revolution. Newfoundland was governed from Britain and administered by the Navy and its appointees until 1832. Yet in Pennsylvania and all of the New England colonies, founded in a spirit of religious dissent with their local privileges protected by royal charter, the tradition of local self-government was central to the settlers' purpose. During the Stuart Restoration (1660–89), these charters came under attack, and only those of Pennsylvania, Connecticut, and Rhode Island survived to the Revolution. Overall, however, even in royal colonies, a sense of self-government activated assemblies throughout the Northeast to defend local interests, assert their control over salaries and appointments, and thus shape the practical administration especially of justice and finance. Indeed, in most of these colonies, the commitment to localism extended even further, down to the level of the county or town. This was especially so in New England, where land division, common pasture management, harbor regulation, and the construction of roads and bridges lay in the hands of town authorities. Although this sense of autonomy was not unique within the English possessions, it was probably stronger in the northern colonies than elsewhere, especially in the seven-

teenth century, and it was part of what attracted family units there from
the beginning.

The attachment to local control in political matters was part of a broader
enthusiasm for local institutions in general. Most churches in both New
England and the Middle Colonies were founded in dissent and were quite
independent of metropolitan influences. Colleges primarily for the training
of ministers began in 1636 with the founding of Harvard in Massachusetts;
by the end of the colonial period, there were nearly a dozen similar institutions north of the Chesapeake. Primary schools were particularly widespread in New England, but northern communities in general were better
provided with educational facilities than were their southern counterparts.
The Bay Colony possessed printing facilities within a decade of settlement;
in Pennsylvania, the same was achieved in less than five years; and by 1700,
there were presses in New York, too. By comparison, there were no printing
houses in the southern colonies before 1726. Public marketplaces made
swift appearances in Boston (1634), New York (1648), and Philadelphia
(1685), and each one of them possessed a substantial covered building by
the early eighteenth century. The jails, almshouses, sewers, wharfs, and
bridges that were soon common to all of these towns indicate still further
the institutional depth that most northern colonies managed to achieve in
the first century of their existence. Compared to the influence of the Jesuits
in Portuguese Brazil or that of the Spanish mint in Peru, the direct economic impact of these institutions was minimal. Furthermore, as the example of the British plantation colonies illustrates, a panoply of institutions
was not an essential element of regional prosperity. Yet churches, schools,
and marketplaces did matter in one fundamental way: as a necessary part of
the process by which households might expect to reproduce themselves,
they reinforced the pattern of family immigration.

Although provincial and town governments were obviously concerned
about the course of local development, there is some debate over the
character of their intervention. Were the institutional structures that the
colonists imported from England and then reshaped to fit local preferences
vehicles of capitalist development or mechanisms of social control? In
effect, they served both purposes, but in intention, they were aimed at
something different. Although local and colonial authorities in the Northeast were deeply interested in husbanding the local economy, they understood their goal as *not* to maximize the productivity of capital and labor
but rather to advance the welfare of individual households. When it was
felt that families could protect and advance their interests independently

in a free marketplace, governments did what they could to facilitate
exchange among them. When it seemed, by contrast, that certain well-
connected individuals possessed the power to manipulate transactions in
such a way that fair bargaining was impossible, the authorities felt it
entirely proper to intervene. Thus the price of foodstuffs went almost
unregulated in the colonial countryside, where independence was relatively widespread and monopolies almost impossible to establish. In the
larger seaports, however, wholly dependent on the provisioning trade and
prey to the machinations of speculators, the price of certain necessities
(especially bread) was often subject to public control. This is not to say
that town selectmen, members of colonial legislatures, and local magistrates decided on these policies because they had a direct self-interest in
household production; many depended far more on rents, fees, and the
profits of trade to support themselves. Ultimately, however, those in
power did recognize that the welfare of regions they lived in (and the
profits they could wring from the local economy) depended on the success
with which families in general pursued the goal of comfortable independence. And it was family competency, with the diversified production that
it hung upon, that public economic policy successfully served to promote.

Sometimes public economic policy took the form of direct intervention.
Both chartered companies and proprietors took pains to people their colonies with skilled tradesmen by actively recruiting them. To induce
shipwrights, millers, shoemakers, fishermen, and ironworkers to aid in
the reconstruction of a new England in America, the Massachusetts Bay
Company offered them attractive deals with guaranteed wages and promises of company business. Fifty years later, William Penn used his personal
connections to enlist "*carpenters, masons, smiths, weavers, tailors, shoemakers,
shipwrights, etc.*" for the colony on the Delaware.[23] Colonial assemblies
tailored their economic policies to maintaining an economic environment
in which householders could transact business with efficiency and security.
Thus, recognizing the role that credit would play in the regional economic
development, Massachusetts forbade the seizure of domestic capital or
perishable goods as surety against payment of debts or the imprisonment
of debtors after their trial.

Because the quality of locally finished goods was a real problem in a part
of the world where working people were chronically short of time, governments took a particular interest in promoting the reputation of those

---

[23] Penn, "Some Account of the Province of Pennsylvania," in Soderlund, ed., *William Penn and the
Founding of Pennsylvania*, 63.

goods abroad. New York – in an act of direct intervention – began the compulsory inspection of exported flour in 1665, and Pennsylvania adopted similar regulations in 1722. The General Court in Massachusetts took note of the "damage . . . to merchants trading hence by bade making of fish, and the . . . prejudice of our commerce with other nations," and ordered the institution of fish cullers to grade the product in 1652. In an effort to regularize business, all of the assemblies concerned themselves with enforcing standardized weights and measures, appointing specific market days, licensing ferries, and so forth. Local governments occasionally played the same role on a smaller stage. Towns needing millers and smiths or wishing to establish specialized local industries were quite prepared to offer land and other privileges to prospective settlers with the right skills. It was with an understanding of the difficulties in adapting the household economy to frontier conditions, and the opportunities to draw profit from householding operations, that local and provincial authorities were ready to employ government's hand.

Still, the greatest service that public institutions provided to householders was simply assuring them the means of acquiring propertied independence, and nothing mattered more in this sphere than the security of land tenure. Property rights varied from region to region throughout the Northeast, but insofar as land everywhere was held almost entirely under free and common socage – that is, with full rights to exploit surface and subsurface resources, as well as to sell or lease them and pass them along in inheritance – landowners had considerable latitude to employ their property as they saw fit. Some limitations did exist in certain colonies. Landholders in Pennsylvania were expected to pay quitrents to the Penn family, from whom they had purchased farms, and manorial tenants in New York occupied their lands on terms that carried certain feudal overtones (including light labor services) to the end of the colonial period. In no portion of British America, however, did customary limitations on tenure seriously hamper the development of a commercial market in land. Even on manors in the Hudson Valley, where freehold was unknown, leased farms changed hands in practice with a minimum of fuss. The only important charges on land throughout the colonies were taxes – low enough not to burden improved property, but high enough to encourage the owners of undeveloped land to arrange for its development by working farmers as quickly as possible. Free and common socage provided, therefore, not only the liberty to carve up and employ land in the most profitable manner, but also a penalty through rising taxes on those who did not. So, although it did not necessarily foster family production (slave-operated plantations were also held under the same form of tenure), it was an element of English tradition suited to the pursuit of household competency.

Sometimes colonists in the Northeast went beyond English tradition to encourage the development of land into family-sized parcels by creating institutions of their own. In New England, town governments served at their inception primarily as a means of carving wilderness land into independent freeholds. For three or four decades after their founding – indeed, as long as they possessed common lands at their disposal – town governments devoted the majority of their meetings to the granting and division of land to applicant settlers and settled proprietors. Between 1723 and 1755, Pennsylvania successfully operated a General Loan Office, permitted to issue paper currency to householders on the security of their lands and houses. Only property owners could qualify, and the loans had to be repaid in annual installments, but a maximum limit of £100 per loan ensured their wide distribution and allowed many householders to pursue the small-scale developmental plans that liquid capital afforded.

The primary function of the Pennsylvania Land Office, however, was to found and sustain a local currency. Although the shortage of sterling was common to all of the British colonies, it was north of Maryland, where internal markets were more highly developed, that the scarcity was especially acute and the demand for paper money most insistent. Still, the bills of credit that provincial governments did authorize were not originally intended as vehicles of long-term economic policy. With few exceptions, assemblies issued them only in order to finance immediate expenditures, especially in times of war. Massachusetts became the first to employ paper currency in 1690 after the failure of Sir William Phips' attack on Quebec. As Thomas Hutchinson, later governor of the colony, put it: "The government was utterly unprepared for the return of the forces. They seem to have presumed, not only upon success, but upon the enemy's treasure to bear the charge of the expedition."[24] Since the returning soldiers were on the verge of mutiny for want of pay, the General Court passed an act providing for the issuance of £7,000 in bills of credit that the colony would accept in payment of taxes. Throughout most of the colonial Northeast, the problem of meeting extraordinary expenditures, *not* long-range economic policy, lay at the origin of monetary innovation. Apart from Pennsylvania, all of the mainland colonies north of Maryland that adopted

[24] Thomas Hutchinson, *The History of the Colony and Province of Massachusetts-Bay*, ed. Lawrence Shaw Mayo, 3 vols. (Cambridge, MA: 1936), 1, 340.

paper currency resorted to the expedient for the first time between 1690
and 1711 to pay off their military contributions to the wars with France
and Spain.

In time, however, the economic function that these bills performed
grew apparent to everybody, and the argument for keeping them in circulation (and even augmenting them with new issues) acquired an economic
rationale. Not everyone agreed as to how exactly these currencies should
be managed: how much to issue, whether the issuing institution should be
public or private, how the bills were to be backed, or when they should be
retired. But over the need for some medium of local exchange – "to carry
on our domestick Affairs and Commerce," as the Pennsylvania House of
Representatives explained to the Penn family in 1725 – the vast majority
of colonists, especially in the countryside, concurred.[25] Port merchants
who ran a considerable credit business with primary producers in the
hinterland and landlords whose tenants were in arrears feared the inflation
that resulted when some farmer-dominated legislatures, especially in New
England, began to issue bills in sufficient quantities to provoke their
depreciation. But even wealthy creditors supported more moderate issues
as necessary to the health of the regional markets in which they dealt and
won their profits.

An interesting counterexample to the patterns of institutional development on the colonial mainland was the experience of Newfoundland.
Conceived of from the beginning – by English colonial officials, the
Navy, most merchants, and the great majority of fishermen – as possess-
ing value only as a summer fishing station, the island never developed
before 1775 even the rudiments of church and state. Occasional Anglican
missionaries had been serving the island since the seventeenth century;
Roman Catholic priests defied the law from time to time by ministering to
planters and servants of Irish descent; and by 1770 a few Methodists and
Moravians were preaching to fishermen and Innuit along the coast. Here
and there, many of these missionaries operated churches and schools for a
time, but on the whole, there was nothing established about any of the
Christian denominations in Newfoundland before the 1780s. Nor did the
island possess any recognizably English forms of government. Towns did
not exist; no legislature sat there in the eighteenth century; and property

---

[25] Address of the House of Representatives of the Province of Pennsylvania to the Descendants of the
late Honourable Proprietor, William Penn, Esq., Dec. 7, 1725, quoted in Leslie V. Brock, *The
Currency of the American Colonies, 1700–1764: A Study in Colonial Finance and Imperial Relations* (New
York: 1975), 65.

in land beyond that required for the fishery had no standing at law. Not until 1729 were there governors or magistrates in Newfoundland. In the outports, the most effective justice remained, until late in the century, that administered locally by West Country shipmasters or "fishing admirals." Of the precise relationship between institutional weakness on the one hand and lack of permanent settlement or economic diversification on the other – which was cause and which effect – we cannot know. The correlation between the two, however, was undeniable and its exceptionality confirmed the general truth about the colonial Northeast that family settlement, economic diversification, and institutional richness were inextricably linked.

As householding societies with a resident merchant class, most of the British American possessions were admirably placed to benefit from their membership in the Empire. The Navigation Acts, passed after 1651 and in force throughout British possessions until 1849, may have been costly to the plantation colonies, but from Pennsylvania northward, they served a function that was broadly developmental. True, the provisions that restricted or even prohibited direct trade outside the Empire caused the northern colonists to pay more for manufactures of European origin and some tropical products such as sugar and molasses. But since the important northern exports of timber products, barreled meat, fish, oil, and grain were exempted from these regulations and could be exported directly to any North Atlantic market – British or otherwise – the Navigation Acts weighed easier on the northern colonists than on their southern counterparts. Even the restrictions that existed on paper were often difficult to enforce in practice, and the smuggling of European luxury wares and French colonial sugar into New England and the Middle Colonies continued down to the Revolution. Some of the Acts' provisions actually spurred economic development in the Northeast. Those that forbade colonial ports from employing European carriers created a protected market in shipping, insulated from Dutch competition, that Americans exploited to the hilt. By confining the colonial trades to vessels constructed within the Empire, moreover, the Acts discriminated against European shipbuilders and presented New Englanders in particular with a significant manufacturing opportunity. Although the Navigation Acts were designed to benefit Britain alone, colonies that had successfully replicated the socioeconomic structure of the mother country, and built some mercantile muscle of their own, reaped many of the same rewards.

In its military dimension, the Empire was equally important to the economy of the Northeast, though the balance of its benefits is harder to assess. Over the short run, war brought large injections of British currency into all of the colonies – especially to those north of the Chesapeake and closest to the important theaters of action, and especially during the 1740s and 1750s, when the imperial struggle between France and England intensified. After the Peace of Paris in 1763, Britain decided to maintain a standing North American garrison, which probably generated close to £150,000 of colonial business annually.[26] Military conflict was not an unmitigated economic blessing everywhere, of course, and the struggle for supremacy in North America disrupted farm settlement, provincial finance, shipping, and the fisheries. In Massachusetts, where the colonists themselves bore a real burden of military expenses in the form of higher taxes and runaway inflation, the business of war rarely occasioned any unmitigated local boom. Nova Scotia's tardy development in the seventeenth and eighteenth centuries – owing largely to the ravages of raiding and the disaster of the Acadian expulsion – well illustrates how massive injections of military spending could fail to balance the destruction that the imperial struggle wrought. Yet in colonies that were free of involvement in fighting there was plenty of local business without the drawback of serious fiscal cost or material destruction, and there wartime usually brought prosperity. During King William's War (1689–97), for example, New York served as a major supply base for the British Navy in its Caribbean operations, opened a provisioning trade with the Spanish West Indies, and profited by dealings with pirates and privateers – all with such success that the local fleet grew from 35 vessels just before the outbreak of hostilities to 124 in 1700. Again in King George's War (1740–8), the profits from privateering and illegal trade with the French and Spanish islands (at the extraordinary prices that British naval superiority in the Caribbean had generated) resulted in New York's ship registrations rising from 53 to 157. The immediate impact of war plainly varied according to local circumstances, and it is difficult to tell if military conflict primed the economy of the region as a whole.

The general strategic benefits that the presence of British power brought to the region, however, are impossible to dispute. First, by driving the French out of Nova Scotia, Cape Breton, and Newfoundland, the mother country decisively reinforced New England's commercial perch in the maritime Northeast, multiplied the fishing grounds in which Yan-

---

[26] Robert Paul Thomas, "A Quantitative Approach to the Study of British Imperial Policy upon Colonial Welfare: Some Preliminary Findings," *Journal of Economic History* 25 (1965), 634.

kee schooners could safely operate, and provided New England settlers with both security on their northern frontiers and a windfall of previously cleared Acadian farmland to occupy. Then, by conquering Canada and damaging thereby the bargaining position of the Iroquois, British military might opened the western territories of New York and Pennsylvania to colonial agricultural development. Most important of all was the British Navy's long and successful campaign to achieve dominance over the North Atlantic. Simply put, it helped to be on the winning side; the disruption of foreign fleets and the privilege of operating under the protective wing of the British Navy often enabled American traders and privateers to reap windfalls from war they would otherwise have missed. By countering French privateers, driving pirates from the seas, and paying an annual tribute to the Barbary powers that persuaded the latter to leave British and colonial shipping alone, the Crown and its navy made the North Atlantic of the eighteenth century a protected arena for northern merchant trade.

Britain's struggle against France, Spain, and the Netherlands in the seventeenth and eighteenth centuries was a program of commercial aggression, conceived with little attention to the interests of her colonial possessions. Yet it was inevitable that colonial societies driven by the pursuit of competency and possessed of commercial institutions similar to those of the mother country would have profited too from the imperial triumph.

CONCLUSION

The northern provinces were by no means the most prosperous of Britain's American possessions. By most measures, either in the performance of their own economies or in their significance within the transoceanic economy, they suffered by comparison to the plantation colonies of the South. The significance of their developments up to the outbreak of the Revolutionary War, however, lay not in the quantity of growth they had achieved but in the character of the economy they had acquired. Complex, mercantile, and diversified, the colonies of the Northeast had not yet begun to industrialize, but by 1775, they did possess social structures replete with farmers, traders, seamen, craftsmen, and a matching contingent of skilled housewives and daughters, all of whom would later be mobilized into domestic outwork, petty manufacturing concerns, and factory production. Truthfully, some of the plantation colonies were also moving in the direction of diversification in the eighteenth century. But they started late, and the lead that their northern counterparts had gained early on in craft production, shipping, and merchant services enabled the North to capture much of the business that southern growth eventually did generate. In essence, northeastern North America led the New World into the industrial age, because it had come closest over its colonial history to imitating successfully the first industrial nation of all: Great Britain. And paradoxically, it had done so for reasons that had in the beginning as much to do with matters of faith and self-determination as they had with profit.

6

ECONOMIC AND SOCIAL DEVELOPMENT OF THE SOUTH

RUSSELL R. MENARD

THE SOUTH ON THE EVE OF INDEPENDENCE

At the eve of the American independence movement, the idea of the South is an anachronism, a concept whose time is yet to come. If by the colonial South one means the area bounded on the north by (roughly) the Ohio and Susquehanna rivers, at the west by the Mississippi, and at the east and south by the Atlantic Ocean and the Gulf of Mexico, there is little to tie the region together. Even under more restricted definitions confined to territory long-claimed by the British (excluding, that is, the newly acquired Floridas and the French settlement at Louisiana) or the more limited region actually colonized by the British (excluding the trans-Appalachian west), the area has little unity. In 1775, there was no "South" with a single, integrated economy, a unifying culture, or a cohesive ruling class with a shared vision of the future. We are best served by recognizing diversity from the start and rejecting the notion of a "South" in favor of a concept of "Souths," four proximate but separate regions with distinctive characteristics: the tobacco colonies around Chesapeake Bay; the rice and indigo districts of the Carolina–Georgia lowcountry; an area of mixed farming or "common husbandry" in the backcountry and around the periphery of the plantation districts; and a frontier zone dominated by cross-cultural trade. However, if the South was not yet a region, the factors that would give it greater unity and define its character during the early nineteenth century were firmly in place: an expansive plantation agriculture, African slavery, and an emerging planter class with a sense of purpose.

Table 6.1. *Estimated population of the South in 1775 (000 omitted)*

Region	Red	White	Black	Total
Tobacco Coast				
Maryland	0.2	127.5	69.9	197.6
Virginia	0.3	234.3	181.2	415.8
NC coastal plain	0.2	76.8	44.0	121.0
Total	0.7	438.6	295.1	734.4
Lowcountry				
Cape Fear, NC	0.1	7.0	7.8	14.9
South Carolina	0.1	21.5	71.7	93.3
Georgia	0.1	5.0	12.0	17.1
East Florida	1.5	1.8	1.0	4.3
Total	1.8	35.3	92.5	129.6
Area of "common husbandry"/backcountry				
Western Maryland	0.1	24.3	2.3	26.7
Valley of Virginia	0.1	45.2	5.2	50.5
NC Piedmont	0.2	88.7	22.2	111.1
South Carolina	0.4	50.4	11.8	62.6
Georgia	0.5	9.0	1.0	10.5
Total	1.3	217.6	42.5	261.4
Frontier				
West Florida	5.0	4.0	1.5	10.5
Southern Interior	33.2	2.1	0.7	36.0
Northern Interior	2.0	0.3	0.0	2.3
Louisiana	3.7	10.9	9.6	24.2
Total	43.9	17.3	11.8	73.0
Total	47.7	708.8	441.9	1,198.4

Sources: Estimated by the author from a variety of sources, principally: U.S. Bureau of the Census, *Historical Statistics of the United States, Colonial Times to 1970* (Washington, DC: 1975), II, 1168 (Ser. Z, 1–19); John J. McCusker and Russell R. Menard, *The Economy of British America, 1607–1789* (Chapel Hill, NC, 1985), 136, 172; Evarts B. Greene and Virginia D. Harrington, *American Population before the Federal Census of 1790* (New York, 1937); Stella H. Sutherland, *Population Distribution in Colonial America* (New York, 1936); Peter H. Wood, "The Changing Population of the Colonial South: An Overview by Race and Region, 1685–1790," in Peter H. Wood, Gregory A. Waselkov, and M. Thomas Hartley, eds., *Powhatan's Mantle: Indians in the Colonial Southeast* (Lincoln, NE, 1989), 35–103.

As a point of entry to the "South" and its several regions, Table 6.1 offers some population estimates for 1775. These numbers are at best approximate. The regions do not conform to the boundaries of colonies, for which we have reliable (or at least widely accepted) figures, while the inclusion of Indians requires estimating the size of groups seldom counted, let alone counted carefully. Although rough, the figures are accurate enough to capture major differences between the regions and to establish some important points about the South. The area was home to about 1.2 million people in 1775. A substantial majority (slightly less than 60 percent) were whites, immigrants from Europe and their descendants, who had begun to settle ("invade" is perhaps the more accurate term) the region early in the seventeenth century. A bit more than a third were Africans and their descendants brought as slaves to work for European masters. Only a small proportion – just under 50,000, about 4 percent of the total – were Indians, descendants of the region's aboriginal inhabitants.

From a British perspective, the oldest South was the tobacco coast, the regions around Chesapeake Bay that, in some degree at least, had an economy built around tobacco. The area includes all of Maryland and Virginia east of the Blue Ridge as well as North Carolina's coastal plain above Cape Fear. The oldest region was also the most populous, its 700,000-plus inhabitants accounting for more than 60 percent of the South's people. European Americans were the majority in the region, but Africans at 40 percent of the total were a substantial presence and in some areas outnumbered whites. Tobacco production had thoroughly dominated the regional economy in the seventeenth century, but as the colonial era progressed, a gradual diversification ended the relative homogeneity. By the eve of the Revolution, the region resembled a horseshoe with a plantation district raising tobacco for European markets at the center and a farming area producing grains and forest products around the periphery.

The lowcountry, a narrow coastal strip stretching from Cape Fear in North Carolina to the Altamaha River in Georgia and including the newly acquired British colony of East Florida, was home to roughly 130,000 people, just over 10 percent of the population of the South. In contrast to the Chesapeake, blacks were a majority in the lowcountry, accounting for over 70 percent of the total, even higher in the great plantation district around Charlestown. The regional economy was dominated by rice and indigo, produced by slaves on big plantations for export to Europe, crops which made the great planters rich and lowcountry prosperity legendary.

The backcountry, a region of "common husbandry" stretching from Western Maryland down the great Valley of Virginia to include North Carolina's piedmont and the small farming areas of South Carolina and Georgia, grew rapidly during the eighteenth century. By 1775, it had some 260,000 inhabitants, just over 20 percent of the South's population.[1] In contrast to the longer-settled regions nearer the coast, slaves were a minor part of the population, only 15 percent of the total. The region was dominated by small, family-operated farms producing livestock and grains for home consumption, although some of that output was shipped to the coast. Families often made small quantities of tobacco, hemp and flax, and forest products for export. As a region, the backcountry exhibited less unity than either the lowcountry or the tobacco coast, in part because its various segments were loosely integrated into the Atlantic world through ties to the tidewater, but also because it was a shifting, transitional area gradually acquiring plantation characteristics.

The frontier, a vast but sparsely settled area stretching from the backcountry to the Ohio and Mississippi rivers and the Gulf of Mexico, was inhabited by some 73,000 people in 1775, only 6 percent of the South's population. The region exhibited considerable diversity, with a rapidly developing plantation district in the Mississippi delta and some areas of small farms where the frontier receded and became backcountry. The region's distinguishing characteristic was the large native presence. More than 90 percent of the South's native peoples lived in this section, principally Creeks, Cherokees, Choctaws, and Chickasaws but including numerous smaller groups, and they accounted for more than 60 percent of the population of the frontier. Despite the growing plantation district and the pressure of European settlers, the frontier was "Indian country" in 1775, a place where native peoples shaped the rules of exchange and where their behavior and aspirations continued to structure the economy.

The South was overwhelmingly rural in 1775. If we use a modest threshold of 2,000, perhaps 4 percent of the "colonial" (persons of European and African descent) population lived in towns; a lower threshold of 1,000 increases the proportion only to about 5 percent. While all of the subregions were largely rural, there were notable differences. Oddly, the frontier region, where the European presence was recent and still tenuous, was the most urbanized. New Orleans, whose population approached 5,000 in 1775, was home to nearly 20 percent of the area's colonial inhabitants. The tobacco coast, the oldest colonial region, may have been the least urbanized with perhaps 3 percent of its residents living in substantial towns. The backcountry displayed a level of urbanization similar to that along the tobacco coast, but the rapid growth of Frederick and Winchester as well as the proliferation of small towns along the Great

---

[1] The phrase "common husbandry" is from Harry J. Carman, ed., *American Husbandry* (New York: 1939 [orig. publ. 1775]), 240.

Wagon Road suggests a great potential for town development. Roughly 12 percent of the lowcountry's colonial population lived in towns, in large part because of Charlestown's rise as a market center but also because of its role as the seat of government and as a consumer city where rich planters gathered to socialize and spend. With 12,000 inhabitants in 1775, Charlestown was by far the South's largest city. It was also the richest, reflecting its place as the capital of British North America's wealthiest agricultural region.

The economic history of the South usually is told as a story of growth, what Adam Smith described as an "advance . . . to wealth and greatness."[2] For the most part, this essay follows convention. While that growth was bought at an enormous cost to the region's aboriginal inhabitants and to African slaves, Smith identified from a European perspective the central theme in the economic history of the South during the colonial era. The evidence describes a remarkable and broadly shared prosperity among European Americans on the eve of the Revolution. Colonists were well fed by the standards of the time, hardly surprising given the abundance of land and an economy in which perhaps 85 percent of the labor force worked on farms and plantations. The quality of diet is revealed in the stature of the population: by the time of the Revolution, southern-born men of European ancestry were, on average, just over 5′8″ tall, about 3.5 inches taller than their English counterparts, slightly taller than northerners, and about the same height as Americans who served in the military during World War II.

White southerners were also well clothed, in part because their lively export economies and membership in the British Empire during the early states of industrialization gave them easy access to English textiles. Even families with modest incomes were able to acquire amenities that made life more comfortable: good bedding, tableware and ceramics, sugar, tea, spices, and the like. Such high levels of comfort were not always the case. Food was ample from the beginning, at least after the terrible "starving times" that afflicted several early settlements were overcome, but the standard of life remained crude for several decades after the initial English invasion. By the mid-eighteenth century, however, there had been a considerable improvement.

Improvements were less marked in housing, and by this measure, most colonists did not live as well as their peers in the parent country. The great

---

[2] *An Inquiry into the Nature and Causes of the Wealth of Nations*, ed. R. H. Campbell, A. S. Skinner, and W. B. Todd (Oxford: 1976 [orig. pub., 1776]), II, 564.

planters of the South built in the grand style, especially in the years after 1725, but the majority of European settlers lagged behind. Their houses were generally small and had few rooms, lacked foundations or wood floors, and were often of wood construction. By the eve of the Revolution, perhaps only 15 percent of the housing stock in the South consisted of substantial two-story stone structures with stairways, differentiated rooms, brick chimneys, and glass windows. In the backcountry and, indeed, among most small planters nearer the coast, the typical house was a 20' by 16' box frame structure sided with clapboards and roofed with shingles, with a wattle and daub chimney and a floor of beaten earth. Such houses had a single room or at most two and a loft; glassless, curtainless windows with shutters to keep out the cold; and unadorned, unpainted walls chinked with clay against the elements. The inferiority of southern dwellings reflects the rapid growth of population, which put great pressure on the housing stock, the scarcity of skilled craftsmen, and the high price of labor generally, all of which made substantial homes relatively expensive. Despite their prosperity, southerners put up with houses that were crowded, poorly insulated, dark, unsafe, and unattractive by the standards of the English-speaking world.

Perhaps the most compelling evidence of southern economic performance is found in the growth of population, which increased at a rate "without parallel in history."[3] The "colonial" segment of the population grew from less than 15,000 in 1650 to nearly 120,000 by 1700, more than half a million by 1750, and to well over a million by 1775 (Figure 6.1). The contrast with Europe is striking. From 1700 to 1750, when the South's population rose more than fourfold, England's increased by 14 percent from 5.1 million to 5.8 million, while that of Europe as a whole grew by 17 percent from 125 million to 146 million.

Reflection on the sources of population growth clarifies the relationship between demographic performance and southern prosperity. Immigration made an important contribution. Thousands of Europeans crossed the Atlantic to pursue colonial opportunities; thousands of Africans were wrenched to the South to make some European dreams a reality. But much of the high southern growth rate was a product of natural increase. This was not because of lower mortality; death rates were higher in the South than in England. Rather, the rapid increases stemmed from colonial marriage patterns. Women in the South — white or black, rich or poor, tidewater or backcountry — married earlier and in higher proportions than in

[3] Thomas Robert Malthus, *An Essay on the Principle of Population, as It Affects the Future Improvement of Mankind* (London: 1798), 105.

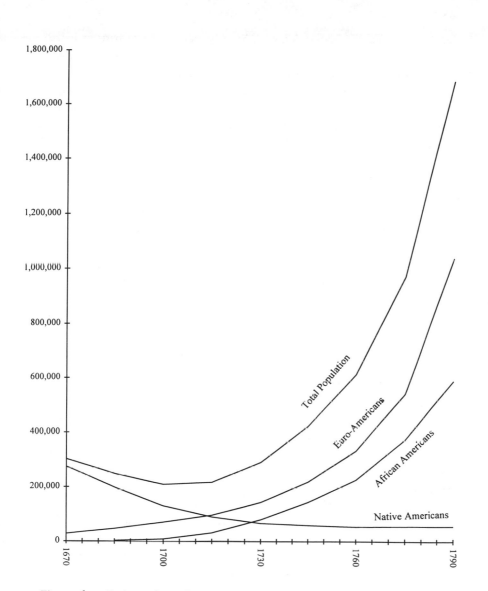

Figure 6.1. Estimated southern population. (Source: See source note to Table 6.1.)

England or the northern colonies. This distinct marriage pattern led to larger numbers of children and played the main role in the high southern growth rates. As contemporaries often explained, these "more general, and more generally early" marriages were rooted in colonial prosperity, especially in the "liberal reward of labour," the abundance of land, and the consequent "Ease and Convenience of supporting a Family."[4]

By combining data on population size with estimates of per capita income, it is possible to chart the size of the economy in that part of the South that joined the American independence movement. Based on a careful analysis of probate records, Alice Hanson Jones concluded that per capita income in the South in 1774 ranged between £10.4 and £12.1 sterling, or $1,145 to $1,332 in 1990 dollars. Given a population of 1.12 million and using the midpoint of Jones' range yields a gross product for the South in 1775 of $1,387 billion (1990 dollars). With an assumption about rates of productivity gain, it is possible to chart the growth of the southern economy from the mid-seventeenth century to the end of the colonial era. Table 6.2 performs such a calculation, assuming that per capita incomes rose at 0.5 percent annually over the 125 years following 1650, a rate near the midpoint of the range for that period suggested by recent scholarship. Under that assumption, per capita income in the South was roughly $660 in 1650 and $935 in 1720. In the aggregate, the economy expanded at a rate of 4.2 percent annually over the entire period, 3.7 percent in the years following 1720. That is an impressive performance by any standard. For the early modern era, when stagnation and decline were more common than growth and when even the highly successful English economy grew at only 0.5 percent per year, it is remarkable.

To a large extent, southern prosperity rested on the performance of the export sector, especially of the major plantation crops – tobacco, rice, and indigo. Together, those three crops accounted for about three-quarters of the value of all exports from the South on the eve of the Revolution and roughly 40 percent of the value of exports from all of Britain's continental colonies. In per capita terms, southern exports averaged about £1.8 sterling per year at the end of the colonial period, roughly twice the level achieved by New England and the Middle Colonies. If attention is confined to the free population, which, after all, controlled the resulting

[4] Benjamin Franklin, "Observations Concerning the Increase of Mankind, Peopling of Countries, etc." (1751), in Leonard W. Labaree et al., eds., *The Papers of Benjamin Franklin* (New Haven, CT: 1959–), IV, 228; Smith, *Wealth of Nations*, II, 565.

Table 6.2. *Estimated income in the southern colonies, 1650–1774 (1990 dollars)*

Year	Per capita regional product	Aggregate regional product (millions)
1650	$660	$8.4
1720	$935	$185.3
1774	$1,238	$1,387.9

Note: The calculation begins with the midpoint of Alice Hanson Jones's estimate of per capita GNP in 1774. *Wealth of a Nation to Be: The American Colonies on the Eve of the Revolution* (New York, 1980), 63. Figures for 1650 and 1720 were then derived assuming an annual growth rate of 0.5 percent. Aggregate GNP was derived by multiplying the per capita figure by the population estimate in Table 6.1. Figures were converted to 1990 dollars by the price index in John J. McCusker, "How Much Is That in Real Money? A Historical Price Index for Use as a Deflator of Money Values in the Economy of the United States," American Antiquarian Society, *Proceedings*, 101 (Oct. 1991), 323–32. Compare John J. McCusker and Russell R. Menard, *The Economy of British America, 1607–1789* (Chapel Hill, NC: 1985), 57.

income, exports averaged more than £3 sterling per head, triple that for the northern colonies.

While exports were critical, production for home consumption and for local exchange accounted for the bulk of the output in the southern economy, even in the plantation districts. Given per capita incomes in the neighborhood of £10 sterling, export earnings made up some 15 to 20 percent of the total. For example, on the Cole estate, a small plantation in southern Maryland, exports accounted for just over one-third of total revenues during the 1660s, production for home use a bit less than one-half, and local exchanges just under one-fifth. In the late eighteenth century, when dependency ratios were higher and local markets larger, the export sector must have contributed even a smaller share of the whole. European American women, it is important to note, although restricted by the conventions of a patriarchal society to only limited participation in the export sector, played a central role in production for home use and in managing local exchange, especially at the neighborhood level. Such activities are poorly documented and are only now finding their historians, but we should not let their obscurity conceal their contribution to colonial living standards.

The benefits of southern economic growth were not evenly distributed. For one thing, there were substantial regional differences. The extent of those differences is illustrated in Table 6.3, which summarizes data from probate inventories taken in 1774 for three places: Anne Arundel County, Maryland, along the tobacco coast; Orange County, North Carolina, in the backcountry; and the Charlestown district of South Carolina, at the heart of the lowcountry. The lowcountry was by far the richest of the three regions: probated decedents in the Charlestown area were worth nearly four times their counterparts along the Chesapeake and nearly ten times those in Orange County. The data reveal other notable differences in the structure of wealth between the three regions. The most striking is the importance of slavery, which clearly was more central to the economies of the tidewater plantation districts than to the backcountry. Real estate accounted for a smaller share of wealth in the backcountry than in the other two regions, reflecting differences in the availability of land as well as the limited improvements in a region still in the farm-building state. Differences in product mix are also evident: livestock was relatively more important in the backcountry than along the coast, crops less so, a function of distance from markets and of participation in the great export trades of the Atlantic economy. While the differences are striking, there are some important similarities. Residents of Orange County invested the same share of their assets in consumer goods as did their coastal counterparts, and as their financial assets and liabilities show, they were equally engaged in the world of credit and debt. Living standards in the backcountry may have been crude, but settlers did not abandon their aspirations for the good life or turn their backs to the market when they moved to the interior.

There were striking differences in wealth by region in the South by the end of the colonial era, but it is unclear whether inequality among free whites increased during the eighteenth century. While abundant resources and scarce labor kept inequality among free colonists low by comparison to Europe, many historians now argue that the poor were on the rise and that a growing share of regional income was captured by a few big merchants and great planters. That position finds support in studies of long-settled

Table 6.3. *Property owned by probate-type wealthholders in selected counties, 1774 (in pounds sterling)*

	Anne Arundel Co., MD	Orange Co., NC	Charlestown District, SC
Total worth	711.7	274.6	2690.3
Servants and slaves	169.2	89.6 (32.6%)	1325.0 (49.3%)
Estates (%) with servants or slaves	66.7%	37.5%	83.3%
Servants and slaves[a]	7.1	2.2	27.9
Nonhuman wealth[a]	540.8	193.9	1359.6
Real estate[a]	352.1 (65.1%)	60.7 (31.3%)	734.9 (54.1%)
Livestock[a]	43.4 (8.0%)	52.3 (27.0%)	65.2 (4.8%)
Crops[a]	25.7 (4.8%)	1.9 (1.0%)	68.9 (5.1%)
Consumers' goods[a]	42.9 (7.9%)	16.7 (8.6%)	99.1 (3.7%)
Financial assets[a]	53.3 (9.9%)	38.2 (19.7%)	352.6 (26.3%)
Financial liabilities[a]	51.3 (9.5%)	47.1 (24.2%)	352.6 (25.9%)
Net worth[a]	660.4	227.5	2337.7
N inventories	27	32	84

[a]Per estate.

Source: Alice Hanson Jones, *Wealth of a Nation to Be: The American Colonies on the Eve of the Revolution* (New York, 1976), 379; Jones, *American Colonial Wealth: Documents and Methods* (New York, 1977), II, 1239–94, 1443–71; III, 1473–1619.

communities in the tidewater where overcrowding led to higher rents, lower wages, and rising inequality. On the other hand, limited opportunities on the coast encouraged migration to the interior, where prospects were better and wealth more evenly distributed. Whether movement to areas of low inequality fully offset coastal trends is uncertain, but it is clear that inequality remained low by comparison to England or to later periods in southern history and that the benefits of growth were widely shared among free colonists.[5]

The issue has a different look if we consider slaves and slavery. The African American population of the South grew rapidly over the period (Figure 6.1) from roughly 900 blacks (3 percent of the total) in 1730 to over 400,000 (41 percent) in 1770. Slaves played a critical role in the southern economy and made a major contribution to the living standards of the free population. Their presence tempers romantic notions of a region marked by equality, opportunity, and a widely shared prosperity. This is not to say that slaves were without income or even that those incomes failed to rise over the colonial period. Slaves had to be fed, housed, and clothed, and there is evidence that their material conditions improved over time. The best evidence of such improvement is demographic. Beginning in the 1720s in the Chesapeake region and in the 1750s in the lowcountry, the African American population grew rapidly through reproduction, a rare achievement among New World slave societies. But they paid a frightful price for those modest gains.

The economy of the South grew impressively in the 125 years following 1650, and it distributed the benefits of growth widely among those of European ancestry. Given the sharp differences in the South, the dynamics of growth are best approached through analysis of the several subregions. Before narrowing the focus, however, it is useful to think about the South more broadly, to incorporate a Native American perspective. Although Adam Smith's notion of an "advance . . . to wealth and greatness" aptly summarizes southern economic history from a European point of view, colonization brought disaster to native peoples. We do not know how many people lived in the South on the eve of Europe's invasion, nor is it likely that we ever will. In 1670, however, by which time the evidence will support an informed guess, there were roughly 250,000 to 300,000 Indians in the region. While this already represented a substantial reduction since the beginning of the century, their numbers fell further, reach-

---

[5] Peter H. Lindert and Jeffery G. Williamson, "Three Centuries of American Inequality," in *Research in Economic History* I (1976), 69–123.

ing 100,000 in 1700 and 50,000 in 1750. By now, of course, this is a familiar pattern, well-known from all parts of Americas. What is less-often recognized is the impact of that decline on the population as a whole. As Figure 6.1 shows, the total population of the South actually fell until 1700 and it was only in the 1720s that it surpassed its level of 1670, and doubtless much later when it regained the size attained on the eve of the invasion. "Advances to wealth and greatness," it would seem, depend on the beholder's breadth of vision.

TOBACCO AND THE RISE OF THE CHESAPEAKE ECONOMY

"Tobacco is the only solid Staple Commodity" of the Chesapeake colonies, George Alsop reported in 1666, a crop "generally made by all the Inhabitants. . . . " "Tobacco as our Staple is our All," Governor Benedict Leonard Calvert added in 1729, "and indeed leaves no room for anything else."[6] Both men exaggerated – not everyone grew tobacco, and there were other products – but they did not exaggerate by much. Tobacco was "king" in the region, as dominant as sugar in the islands, rice in the lowcountry, and cotton in the antebellum South. It was not king from the start, however, and Virginia floundered before planters discovered that they could build prosperity on smoke. As late as 1616 – nearly a decade following the arrival at Jamestown, after an investment of more than £50,000 sterling and the migration of over 1,700 settlers – there were only 351 Europeans in the colony, many of them hungry, most of them disgruntled and disappointed. In that year, John Rolfe shipped off the first crop of Virginia leaf to London. The Chesapeake boom was on.

An overview of price and production trends in the Chesapeake tobacco industry suggests three stages – two lengthy eras of expansion that surrounded a shorter period of little or no growth. During the first growth phase, lasting into the 1680s, tobacco output rose at a rapid but decelerating pace while prices fell. Output grew more rapidly than prices dropped, however, and the farm value of the crop climbed, from £20,000 sterling at mid-century to more than £100,000 by the 1680s. During the second

---

[6] George Alsop, "A Character of the Province of Maryland" (1666), in Clayton Colman Hall, ed., *Narratives of Early Maryland, 1633–1684* (New York, 1910), 363; Benedict Leonard Calvert to the Lord Proprietary, October 26, 1729, in W. H. Browne et al., eds., *Archives of Maryland* (Baltimore, 1883–), XXV, 602.

expansion, which began about 1720 and lasted until the Revolution,
output and prices rose in tandem, pushing the value of the crop to more
than £750,000 by the 1770s. These two periods of expansion sandwiched
a generation of stagnation, stretching from the 1680s to the 1710s, when
both prices and production showed little change over the long run. Cutting across all three periods was a recurring pattern of boom and bust in
which prices and output rose and fell in the short term and earnings from
the staple fluctuated dramatically.

The seventeenth-century expansion of the tobacco industry has puzzled
historians because it was accompanied by sharply falling prices. Falling
prices, it is often argued, reflected: a restrictive mercantilist policy that
kept the Dutch out of the trade and channeled tobacco through England
no matter where its final market; parasitic governments, which laid high
taxes on the leaf and thus restricted its market; and overproduction by
hard-pressed planters struggling to make ends meet. And low prices
brought hard times, leading some scholars to characterize the second half
of the seventeenth century as a period of prolonged depression around the
Bay. While not entirely wrong, that argument misses the main point.
Prices fell because planters and merchants improved productivity and
lowered costs. Lower costs meant lower prices, and lower prices meant
more people could afford the Chesapeake leaf. More customers meant
larger markets, and larger markets fueled the expansion of the tobacco
industry. It was not until the 1680s, when the long-term decline in prices
stopped in the face of rising production costs (a function of higher prices
for land and labor), that the industry stagnated. Planters then weathered
thirty years of "hard times."

One reason for the confusion among historians is that planters often
complained of depressed tobacco prices, and they blamed their difficulties
on mercantilist policies, taxes, and overproduction. Such complaints were
not constant but rather followed a recurring pattern rooted in the instability of the Atlantic economy. The long-term movements of price and
production were not smooth but occurred in a series of sharp, short swings
as the tobacco industry moved quickly from buoyant prosperity to deep
depression in a largely self-contained price and production cycle. Short-
term increases in European demand led to a flurry of activity along the Bay
as planters bought new workers and put new land into cultivation to raise
output and capture the profits that higher prices promised. The response
was usually too robust, however, and markets were quickly glutted. Prices
fell, and planters reduced investments in new workers and new land.
Lower prices made Chesapeake leaf more competitive with tobacco grown

elsewhere and permitted the penetration of new markets. Demand rose, boom followed bust, and the cycle repeated itself.

While planters muttered about "mysterys in Trade . . . as great as those in Religion" that alternately swelled and shrank their incomes, they acted vigorously to control the economy, especially during the downturns.[7] Their efforts were both public and private. Depression encouraged legislation to raise tobacco prices by limiting production and controlling quality, to diversify the economy by promoting towns and local manufactures, to develop new markets, and to promote other exports. Individually, planters tried to lower costs and increase productivity in tobacco and to create more self-sufficient and diverse operations so they would be better able to ride out the hard times. Eventually those efforts, especially the private efforts, erected a hedge, but the hedge proved low, and it grew slowly. The problem persisted in large part because boom regularly followed bust, and when tobacco prices improved, planters again concentrated on the staple.

The productivity gains that fueled the expansion of the tobacco industry in the seventeenth century had several sources. There were, for one thing, major savings in distribution costs as the industry was transformed from a high-risk venture "accompanied both by Sea and land with . . . many hazards" into "a certaine and orderly kind of trade."[8] In particular, freight charges on shipping the crop to London fell from 3d per pound in the mid-1620s to less than a penny by the 1680s, largely because of better packaging, while the commission that English merchants charged for selling tobacco on consignment tumbled from 10 percent to 2.5 percent. Also, prices for English manufactured goods fell as trade risks declined and higher settlement densities permitted some scale economies in marketing, while food became cheaper as planters built working farms. Most important, the amount of tobacco produced per worker more than doubled across the seventeenth century, from about 700 pounds in the 1620s to more than 1800 by the 1680s.

The development of what has been called "the Chesapeake system of husbandry" played the key role in improving agricultural productivity around the Bay.[9] The system blended European and Native American farming techniques with new methods worked out locally through experimentation. As planters "learned by doing," they created a long-fallow

[7] William Byrd to Mr. C. Smith, August 23, 1735, *Virginia Magazine of History and Biography* IX (1901–2), 118.

[8] S. Kingsbury, ed., *The Records of the Virginia Company of London* (Washington: 1906–35), IV, 264.

[9] The phrase is from Lois Green Carr, Russell R. Menard, and Lorena S. Walsh, *Robert Cole's World: Agriculture and Society in Early Maryland* (Chapel Hill: 1991).

agriculture with a twenty-year field rotation system using simple tools (hoes and axes were sufficient) to grow tobacco and corn, and they raised cattle and hogs that were allowed to range freely in the still sparsely populated colonies. Contemporaries were sharply critical, even contemptuous, of the system — an "exceeding Ill-Husbandry" Robert Beverley called it — but they underestimated its suitability to local circumstances.[10] The Chesapeake system of husbandry yielded export income to purchase manufactured goods and servants while producing food for the family. It both saved labor, the scarce resource in the seventeenth century, and preserved the long-term fertility of the soil. Critics also failed to appreciate the creativity of the achievement. As planters worked out the details of the system — discovered, for example, the optimum distance between hills for setting plants, the best methods for curing the leaf, how to bring new land into cultivation without plowing or pulling stumps, how to manage work schedules to maximize output, and how to raise livestock without fencing it in — they greatly improved both the productivity of their agriculture and their standard of living. The precise particulars of the process of development are now lost, but their obscurity should not undermine appreciation of their significance.

The Chesapeake system of husbandry also helped to shape the structure of society along the tobacco coast in the seventeenth century. One needed only a few simple tools, a few head of cattle, and about fifty acres of land to set up as an independent planter, all within reach of newly freed servants or free immigrants of modest means, especially while a rapidly expanding tobacco industry generated easy credit. Further, the system offered few returns to scale, and it placed substantial barriers in the way of large plantations. Given the land requirements of tobacco and corn, most planters could manage only four or five workers efficiently. Going beyond that required the establishment of a separate operation, called a "quarter," which was hard to do incrementally but instead required a plunge — the purchase of several workers who had to be provided with tools, livestock, food, and clothing while the new plantation was put into working order. As a result, small owner-operated farms worked by a family with the help of a few servants and hired hands dominated the economy, while small planters played a major role in government, often dominating the local level. The seventeenth century was "the age of the yeoman planter" in the Chesapeake region.

---

[10] Robert Beverley, *The History and Present State of Virginia* (Chapel Hill: 1947 [orig. publ. 1705]), 291.

This open, relatively undifferentiated society of small planters was transformed in the decades surrounding 1700. For one thing, the long expansion of the tobacco industry slowly ground to a halt in the 1680s, and output stagnated at just under 30 million pounds before beginning another sustained rise around 1720. The inability of planters to achieve further cost reductions was chiefly responsible for the slowdown and eventual stagnation. The major efficiencies in the Chesapeake system of husbandry had been achieved by the 1680s, and planters faced increasing prices for land and labor. Merchants did reduce transport and marketing costs after 1680, but the savings had to be passed on to the planter to offset rising production costs. The tobacco industry could no longer expand by lowering consumer prices. Further expansion would require increased demand, unlikely while the Atlantic economy was disrupted by war and Europe's population was in decline. As a result, the Chesapeake region suffered three decades of hard times, interrupted only by a brief boom around 1700, and a sharp contraction in opportunities for poor families to climb the agricultural ladder.

The turn of the century also witnessed major changes in demography. The growth of slavery was the most striking change. Indentured servants, who often shared a common social origin with the planters they served and who hoped to become masters in their own right once they completed their indenture, dominated the unfree work force before 1680. As the century progressed, planters faced difficulties in recruiting enough servants. A declining population, depression, and slowly rising real wages in England joined with constricting opportunities in the Chesapeake and growing American demand for workers to produce a shortage of indentured labor on the tobacco coast and a change in the composition of the work force as planters purchased slaves to replace servants. In 1680, servants outnumbered slaves along the Bay by about three to one, and blacks were only 7 percent of the region's population. By 1720, slaves greatly outnumbered servants, and blacks were nearly 20 percent of the population, while in some areas their proportion approached one-third.

Changes in the composition of the white population reflected the gradual rise of a native-born majority in the colonies. The Chesapeake demographic regime of the seventeenth century was harsh and peculiar. Immigrants were predominantly male, with sex ratios ranging from over 600 men per 100 women in the 1630s to about 250 by the 1670s, and they encountered a destructive disease environment that kept more than half of both men and women from reaching age 40, nearly three-quarters from age 50. The few women who did immigrate, furthermore, married late, in their middle twenties on average, as most had to finish indenture terms before they could find a husband, set up a household, and begin having children. As a result, deaths exceeded births until near the end of the seventeenth century, and the region long retained the male surplus and low dependency ratios characteristic of frontier populations. Those immigrants did have some children, however, and they gradually transformed the demographic regime. The native-born lived longer than their immigrant forebears, the sex ratio among them was balanced, and they married much earlier. By the early eighteenth century, native-born adults were a majority in the region, rapid growth through reproduction had begun, and the age structure and sex ratio acquired a more settled character.

The decades around 1700 also witnessed the first, tentative steps toward a gradual diversification of the Chesapeake Planters in coastal North Carolina, the lower James River basin in Virginia, and on the lower eastern shore, where soils yielded only low-grade leaf. They abandoned tobacco almost entirely during periods of low prices after 1680. They concentrated instead on naval stores, wood products, grains, livestock, and subsistence farming, and they looked more to markets in the Caribbean than in England. Although planters made some tobacco when prices were especially high, the region did not again become a major participant in the tobacco trade. The pace of diversification increased in the eighteenth century, especially after 1750, when rising food prices persuaded planters in northern Maryland to abandon tobacco for wheat and planters elsewhere to supplement their income from the traditional staple with grains. Table 6.4, which describes exports from Maryland, Virginia, and North Carolina on the eve of independence, understates the extent of diversification because it does not include the growing coastal trade to other regions in British North America nor the substantial overland business with Philadelphia. Nevertheless, it suggests the extent and limits of change. Tobacco remained the dominant export, accounting for about two-thirds of the total value; Great Britain was still the dominant trading partner, taking more than three-quarters of all exports. However, those shares had dropped considerably, from perhaps 95 percent of the total in 1700, in large part due to the rise of the grain trade to the sugar islands and southern Europe.

The Chesapeake tobacco industry entered a period of renewed expansion around 1720. At first, growth brought only slight encouragement. Tobacco prices rose slowly (if at all) over the long term, and there were severe

Table 6.4. *Average annual value of exports from Maryland, Virginia, and North Carolina, 1768–72, by destination (in thousands of pounds sterling)*

Commodity	Great Britain	Ireland	Southern Europe	West Indies	Total
Tobacco	763.8				763.8
Grains, grain products	10.6	23.5	98.6	75.5	208.1
Naval stores	35.4				35.4
Wood products	7.0	2.3	2.4	23.2	34.9
Iron	28.3	0.4		0.5	29.2
Other	20.9	3.9	0.9	16.7	42.4
Total	866.0	30.1	101.9	115.9	1,113.8

Source: James F. Shepherd and Gary M. Walton, *Shipping, Maritime Trade, and the Economic Development of Colonial North America* (Cambridge, 1972), 213–25.

depressions in the industry during the late 1720s to early 1730s and again in the mid-1740s. Prices rose fairly steadily after 1750, although there were periods of contraction in the later stages of the Seven Years' War and in the aftermath of the British credit crisis of 1772. Rising prices joined with growing output to push up incomes, bringing an era of unprecedented prosperity to the tobacco coast while extending cultivation of the crop and tidewater social institutions into Virginia's southside and piedmont regions.

The eighteenth-century expansion of the export sector led to some modest urbanization in the area. The region had been almost entirely rural before 1720. The extensive river system permitted decentralized trade, while tobacco needed little processing and did not require elaborate storage facilities or a highly developed internal transport network. Further, the trade was controlled by metropolitan rather than colonial merchants, which meant that transport and finance remained in English hands. Changes in the organization of the tobacco trade led to a proliferation of small towns in the plantation district after 1720 as the colonial legislatures set up inspection and warehouse systems to control quality, and British merchants centralized collection of the crop to reduce port times for the fleet. The most important developments occurred on the periphery of the plantation sector and reflected the diversification of exports. Grains required more processing, storage, and transport facilities than tobacco, and the grain trade was dominated by local rather than metropolitan merchants. Baltimore and Norfolk, each with about 6,000 inhabitants in 1775, were the two largest cities in the region by far. Each owed its success more to the relatively modest business of supplying grains and wood products to the Caribbean and southern Europe than to the much larger tobacco trade with Great Britain.

The expansion of the export sector first stretched and then transformed the Chesapeake system of husbandry. To take advantage of eighteenth-century opportunities in grains, planters had to find ways around the land and labor constraints that made it impossible to raise large surpluses of corn or wheat without cutting back on tobacco. Some labor time was freed up by the introduction of plows, a possibility once the region was deforested and fields slowly cleared of stumps and roots. The change in the work force also provided additional time since planters could push slaves harder than indentured servants, making them work more intensely for more hours in the day and more days in the year. Some of the new labor time was used to pen and feed livestock, which meant that manure was made available to fertilize fields, permitting shorter fallow periods and higher yields per acre. These changes were related in what has been called "the plow–corn–livestock–manure complex."[11] The use of plows during planting season released labor that could be used to grow more corn; the corn was fed to animals, now penned, fed, and trained to the plow; and the animals produced fertilizer, which permitted planters to add workers without adding new land. While the new complex eventually exhausted and eroded the soil, it allowed planters to respond to the rising prices for food and tobacco and made an important contribution to Chesapeake prosperity.

A remarkable set of probate records permit estimates of wealth per capita on Maryland's lower western shore from the mid-seventeenth century to the Revolution. These show a rapid increase at a rate of about 2.5 percent annually from 1660 to the early 1680s followed by a slight decline to the beginning of the eighteenth century. Per capita wealth then leveled out or perhaps fell gently until about 1750 before growing rapidly, again at a yearly rate of roughly 2.5 percent, in the quarter-century preceding independence. The pattern seems consistent with an export-led growth process. The seventeenth-century expansion of the tobacco industry apparently led to real gains in income and wealth, while the period of stagnation around 1700 produced decline. The renewed expansion of tobacco exports after 1720 ended or at least slowed the decline, but this growth was achieved without major productivity gains and through the geographic extension of cultivation. It was not of the sort to produce rising wealth per head. Beginning in 1750, however, rising prices for grains and tobacco created new opportunities and drove per capita wealth to new highs. Apparently, incomes along the tobacco coast were driven by the foreign sector.

Or so it would seem. However, there are difficulties with the argument, at least for the seventeenth century. For one thing, income per head from tobacco declined sharply until 1640 and then fell slowly. The staple placed a floor under incomes, but it was an unstable floor with a gently falling slope. For another, when wealth levels for the lower western shore are disaggregated, it becomes clear that each neighborhood went through a period of initially rapid increase lasting about 20 years followed by a leveling out, with the timing of change related not to the behavior of

[11] The phrase is from Lois Green Carr and Russell R. Menard, "Land, Labor, and Economies of Scale in Early Maryland: Some Limits to Growth in Chesapeake System of Husbandry," *Journal of Economic History* 49 (1989), 417.

tobacco exports but to the date of settlement and to rising dependency ratios as the population shed its early, frontier characteristics.

The increase in wealth during the seventeenth century occurred despite falling income per head from exports and in the face of demographic changes that reduced the share of the population in the work force. The gains were a result of farm building. New settlements were poor and living standards crude, but carving out farms provided opportunities for saving, investment, and accumulation and pushed wealth levels up. Families worked hard to clear land, erect buildings and fences, build up their livestock herds, plant orchards and gardens, construct and improve their homes. While these activities drove per capita wealth higher, there were limits to the process. Once it had a farm in full operation, there was little a family could do to further increase wealth. The early growth spurt was followed by a long period of stability, perhaps by slight decline as dependency ratios continued to rise, lasting until the mid-eighteenth century. World food shortages, rising prices for tobacco, and shifts in the terms of trade toward agriculture then pushed Chesapeake wealth levels up.

The wealth of the region was not evenly shared by colonists of European ancestry. The early settlements at Jamestown and St. Mary's were marked by high levels of inequality as both colonies were at first dominated by ambitious, grasping men who used family fortunes and English connections to control development. Early inequalities diminished, however, as rapid expansion under the constraints imposed by the Chesapeake system of husbandry ushered in the small planter's age. Thereafter, inequality rose in response to four largely sequential processes. First, farm building created opportunities for accumulation and permitted some men to pull ahead of their neighbors. Second, the rise of a native-born population contributed to inequalities as inherited fortunes became a major source of wealth and power. Third, slavery furthered the progress of inequality by allowing some planters to command much larger work forces than had been possible in the seventeenth century. Finally, while the diversification of the export sector created new opportunities along the Bay, many small planters lacked the resources to adopt the new methods and found themselves trapped in the old style of husbandry, unable to participate in the wave of prosperity that followed 1750. The cumulative effect of these processes was substantial. In the middle of the seventeenth century, at the height of the small planter's age, the richest 10 percent of the families in the tidewater owned roughly 40 percent of the wealth, a figure that was to approach 70 percent by the eve of independence.

To some extent, the progress of inequality in the tidewater was countered by the extension of the Chesapeake frontier. From the middle decades of the seventeenth century to the Revolutionary era, the area of the colonial occupation increased steadily in response to a recurring process. Frontier opportunities – cheap land, the possibilities of farm making, and credit supplied by land developers and merchants – attracted migrants, especially newly freed servants and the children of poor families, to the edge of colonial settlement. Migrants both relieved the pressures produced by growing population in the tidewater and re-created the social structures of the yeoman planter's age. Initially, the prospects that poor planters could establish households and acquire land were good and levels of inequality low. However, rapid population growth, differential success in farm building and inheritance, and the arrival of planters of means, who moved in with substantial slave work forces as the region's potential for development became clear, transformed the new settlement in ways that made it increasingly like the old tidewater. As population densities grew, land prices and inequalities rose, tenancy became more common, and young adults left the region with growing frequency to find better prospects, thereby further extending the Chesapeake frontier.

While this process operated as a brake on inequality and preserved some measure of opportunity in the Chesapeake region throughout the colonial era, there is evidence of strain as the eighteenth century progressed. By the 1750s, more than half the households in many tidewater counties were established on rented lands, often with short-term leases that offered little chance to build equity and slowly climb the agricultural ladder. Tenancy was less common and prospects somewhat brighter in the piedmont and on the Virginia southside, but even those regions were filling up, with little unimproved land remaining and that too expensive for poor men to purchase. By the 1780s, there was no longer any place in the Chesapeake region that could be described as "good poor man's country." Poor men and women now had to leave the area altogether, strike out for the raw frontiers of the southern backcountry, Kentucky and Tennessee, or the Northwest to find land and opportunity.

Any discussion of inequality must consider the rise of slavery and the lives of African Americans. Blacks were only 2 percent of the region's population in 1650, but their share grew steadily over the next century, reaching 13 percent by 1700, 25 percent by 1730s, and 40 percent by 1750, where it hovered into the nineteenth century. The rise of slavery contributed to the growth of inequality among whites by permitting the

accumulation of great estates while clearly separating planters who worked
their fields from gentlemen who supervised others. Evidence from Prince
George's County, Maryland, a prime tobacco region on the Potomac,
documents the emerging structure. During the initial decade of the eighteenth century, when slaves were first brought into the county in large
numbers, roughly one-quarter of the households owned slaves. The majority held only three or fewer blacks, and there were only a handful of great
planters; perhaps 5 percent of the masters (less than 2 percent of the
household heads) owned 20 or more slaves. Although tenancy was on the
rise, small, owner-operated farms without slaves remained the typical unit
of production in the county. By the 1770s, conditions had changed. More
than half the households owned slaves, the average size of slaveholdings
more than doubled (although it remained small by lowcountry standards),
and the number and wealth of great planters rose sharply. Perhaps the
most striking development was the near disappearance of small landowners without slaves, who by then accounted for fewer than 10 percent of the
households. Slavery brought sharp distinctions to Euro-American society
in the Chesapeake, dividing it into masters who owned both land and
slaves and those who owned neither, while at the same time permitting a
few great planters to pull far ahead of their neighbors.

More important was the impact of slavery on African Americans themselves. Uncertainties surrounding the status of blacks in the middle decades of the seventeenth century permitted a few to acquire freedom and
modest estates, but as their numbers grew, racial lines hardened into a
rigid class system, and opportunities disappeared. By the late 1670s,
when Africans began to arrive in large numbers, their fate was sealed: they
would be slaves in a harsh regime. Like white immigrants, they faced a
severe disease environment and a skewed sex ratio that limited reproduction. But their situation was worsened by isolation on small plantations,
restrictions on mobility, more rigorous work demands, the degradations of
slavery, and masters harsh enough to use dismemberment as a regular
method of discipline, as with Robert Carter who boasted of having "cured
many a negro of running away" by cutting off their toes.[12]

Despite these brutal circumstances, blacks experienced a demographic
transition similar to that among whites as the gradual growth of an
American-born slave population led to the beginnings of reproductive
increase in the 1720s. By the eve of the Revolution, most blacks had been

[12] Robert Carter to Robert Jones, 10 October 1727, *Virginia Magazine of History and Biography* 101
(1993), 280.

born in the region, and the rate of natural population growth was high enough to push the slave trade into sharp decline. Slavery remained harsh and oppressive, but reproductive growth, rising population densities, and increasing plantation sizes helped slaves to build ties of affection, family, and friendship while permitting the articulation of a distinct African American culture that shaped black identities and undermined the cultural homogeneity of Chesapeake colonial society.

The growing inequalities in Chesapeake society are perhaps most evident at the top, in the rise of the gentry. A disruptive demographic regime, high rates of immigration, rapid upward mobility, and constraints on wealth accumulation had forestalled the development of a cohesive ruling class during the seventeenth century. Things began to change around 1700, however, as demographic conditions permitted longer lives, more stable families, and dense kin networks, as immigration fell off and opportunities contracted, and as slavery allowed some to build great plantations. The Chesapeake gentry slowly emerged as a cohesive ruling class in the early decades of the eighteenth century. Its wealth was based on land and slaves, its solidarity rested on shared interests nurtured by family ties and a common culture that set them apart from the majority of planters, its world view informed by an ideology that mixed racism, republicanism, and patriarchalism, and its cohesiveness reinforced by the need to control blacks and retain the cooperation of poor whites. By the 1730s, a powerful class of great planters was established in the tidewater and was slowly extending its reach onto the Chesapeake frontier. Despite occasional challenges to its authority – for example, the riots against tobacco regulation in the 1730s, and the evangelical revolt of the 1760s – the great planters were confident of their abilities and secure in their position, sufficiently so to lead the region into rebellion and to play the major role in the construction of the new nation that followed in the rebellion's wake.

RICE AND THE RISE OF THE LOWCOUNTRY

By the beginning of the American independence movement, the rapid growth of the lowcountry economy and the opportunities it provided had assumed legendary dimensions. The lowcountry was "the most opulent and flourishing" region in British North America, even "the most thriving Country perhaps on this Globe." It was a place where a "frugal and industrious" white man was promised "a sure road to competency and independence," where planters could "all get rich," and where merchants rose "from humble and moderate Fortunes to great affluence." Contemporaries were amazed by lowcountry achievements, by "the rapid ascendency of families which in less than ten years have risen from the lowest rank, have acquired upward of £100,000, and have moreover, gained this wealth in a simple and easy manner." Josiah Quincy's notes on Joseph Allston, a Winyah Bay planter, are typical. Allston started just "a few years ago" at 40 years of age "with only five negroes" but now had "an immense income all of his own acquisition" resting on five plantations and more than 500 slaves, which yielded a net income of £5,000 to £6,000 a year. And, Quincy added, as if the story were not yet up to the legend, "he is reputed much richer."[13]

Lowcountry wealth rested on the remarkable growth of its leading exports, rice and indigo. Success was not immediate, however, at least by the standards of the early colonists, many of whom measured their performance against the incomes earned by sugar planters. Such expectations were come by honestly, for the first English settlements in the lowcountry were rooted in the Barbadian sugar revolution of the mid-seventeenth century. By 1660, Barbados was overcrowded by American colonial standards: its population density had reached 250 persons per square mile, most of the arable land was occupied and cultivated, and entry costs into sugar production were high enough to keep all but those with substantial resources out of the planter class. Indentured servants who finished their terms found few opportunities, and many simply left, sometimes signing new indentures to finance the move – stark comment on island prospects. By one estimate, roughly 10,000 Barbadians, most of them recently freed servants, left the colony for other parts of British America during the seventeenth century. An expanding market for provisions and timber accompanied this outmigration as planters concentrated on sugar and denuded the island of trees, creating opportunities for colonists elsewhere to grow food for the large and increasing slave population and to supply Barbados with wood for building, fuel, and cask making. By 1660, entrepreneurs realized that by tapping the Barbadian migrant stream, the North American coastline between the Chesapeake and Spanish Florida, as

---

[13] For the sources of the quotations, see Russell R. Menard, "Slavery, Economic Growth, and Revolutionary Ideology in the South Carolina Lowcountry," in Ronald Hoffman, John J. McCusker, Russell R. Menard, and Peter J. Albert, eds., *The Economy of Early America: The Revolutionary Period, 1763–1790* (Charlottesville, VA: 1988), 256, 268–9.

yet unoccupied by Europeans, could be colonized, the imperial designs of competing nations preempted, and the needs of the sugar islands for wood and food met.

After several false starts, a permanent settlement was established on the Ashley River in 1670, near the site of Charlestown. Although troubled by food shortages and disease, the colony grew steadily: by 1700, it was home to roughly 3,300 Europeans and about 2,600 African and Native American slaves. The first several decades were years of experimentation during which Carolinians explored the local resource base and tested overseas demand. In the process, they built a diverse economy by colonial standards. Self-sufficient agriculture and farm building were the major activities, but settlers also produced exports that could be exchanged for manufactured goods, servants, and slaves. The early export trade centered on the supply of provisions and wood products to Barbados (making early Carolina a colony's colony) supplemented by a trade in furs to England. The economy did not generate great fortunes, but it provided local merchants and planters a variety of opportunities for small-scale production and exchange.

The experimentation ended with the emergence of rice as the major commercial product of the lowcountry early in the eighteenth century. The industry grew rapidly at first, as exports of a mere 10,000 pounds in 1698 reached 6.5 million by 1720, and peaked at more than 43 million in 1740 before entering a decade of stagnation and decline. A reliable price series is not available before the 1720s, but scattered observations suggest a steady fall, indicating that productivity gains helped to fuel the initial expansion. Exports rose more rapidly than prices fell, and the value of the crop increased, from roughly £20,000 sterling around 1720 to about £100,000 around 1740. By then, rice was one of the major exports of British America and the dominant crop in the lowcountry, "the chief support" of the region and "its great source of opulence," as much the "staple Commodity" of the area "as Sugar is to Barbados or Jamaica, or Tobacco to Virginia and Maryland."[14]

While rice became *the* lowcountry staple in the early decades of the eighteenth century, initially the growth of that industry was part of a more general expansion, an export boom that began around 1700. Some of that boom reflected continued growth in trades established during the

---

[14] Alexander Hewatt, *An Historical Account of the Rise and Progress of the Colonies of South Carolina and Georgia*, 2 vols. (London: 1779), I, 119; [James Glen], *A Description of South Carolina . . .* (London: 1761), 87.

seventeenth century, especially the production of food stuffs and timber for the sugar islands and the shipment of deerskins to England. Much of the boom turned on naval stores, a new set of products of little importance before 1700. The English government, reacting to wartime disruption of its supply from the Baltic, provided the incentive for the industry in 1705 in the form of bounties for products made in the colonies. The incentives worked: Charlestown exports of pitch and tar exceeded 6,500 barrels in 1712, 50,000 in 1718, and peaked at nearly 60,000 in 1725.

The export boom continued until about 1740, but in its latter stages, its character changed as planters concentrated on rice. Corn exports, for example, reached nearly 95,000 bushels in 1735 before falling to only 15,000 in 1739. Exports of barrel staves fell by half over the same period, while leather exports, a byproduct of meat production, fell by about two-thirds from 1734 to 1739. The most important change, however, was in the naval stores industry. Exports of pitch, tar, and turpentine peaked at about 60,000 barrels worth perhaps £25,000 sterling in the mid-1720s. By 1732, exports were at roughly 25,000 barrels worth £7,000; by 1739, 11,000 barrels worth less than £3,000.

The decline of the lowcountry naval stores industry is usually attributed to shifts in British policy. In 1724, the government insisted that quality standards be met before bounties were paid, and in 1729, it reduced the premiums substantially. While it is true that high labor costs in the colonies led producers to use methods that sacrificed quality for quantity, and that bounties were important to the beginnings of the industry, the decline had other sources. Naval stores were crowded out of the lowcountry, along with foodstuffs and wood products for the sugar industry, being pushed to the periphery of the plantation district, to the South Carolina backcountry, to Georgia, and, especially, to the Cape Fear River Valley of North Carolina. Lowcountry planters concentrated on rice, their most profitable staple, and had little time for anything else. The consequences of that focus are apparent in the increased specialization of the lowcountry economy revealed in the growth of rice exports per capita, which rose from about 70 pounds in 1700 to 380 in 1720 and to nearly 1,000 in 1740.

The lowcountry export boom transformed coastal South Carolina, making it into a plantation society more similar to the British Caribbean than to the other mainland colonies. The extent of that transformation is evident in the population of the region, especially in the growth of slavery. The export boom led to a sharp increase in demand for labor, an increase met largely by African slaves. Charlestown slave imports averaged 275 a year in the 1710s, almost 900 in the 1720s, and more than 2,000 in the 1730s. Slaves were a majority in colonial Carolina by 1708 and accounted for 72 percent of the population by 1740, making the region seem "more like a negro country than like a country settled by white people."[15] The change is also evident in the difficulties both whites and blacks had achieving reproduction, as the export boom and the articulation of a plantation complex brought the destructive demographic regime of the sugar islands to the lowcountry. The impact on slaves was especially harsh, because rise production (like sugar) consumed workers. "The cultivation of it is dreadful," the author of *American Husbandry* noted, a "horrible employment, . . . not far short of digging in Potosi."[16]

Demographic changes tell only part of the story. Other aspects of the export-led transformation of the lowcountry are reflected in the probate inventories summarized in Table 6.5. Perhaps the most striking change was in the scale of operations and in wealth levels, especially among the rich. Average estate values (exclusive of real property) rose from just over £200 sterling in the seventeenth century to more than £350 in the 1720s and nearly £540 in the 1740s, just following the end of the export boom. Those increases reflected a substantial growth in scale as large plantations "swallowed up" small farms: the average number of slaves per estate rose from less than 3 in the seventeenth century to 10 in the 1720s and 17 in the 1740s. Change was especially impressive at the top of the wealth distribution, as the mean estate value for the richest 10 percent doubled during the early stages of the export boom and then increased by half again from the 1720s to the 1740s, while the number of slaves in those estates grew even faster. The data reflect the centrality of slavery in the transformation of the lowcountry. Slaves accounted for only 20 percent of inventoried wealth in the seventeenth century, before the start of the export boom, but nearly 60 percent by the 1720s and 65 percent in the 1740s. Indeed, the net wealth exclusive of slaves in the region actually fell before the 1720s and then rose only modestly until the 1740s.

In the sharp increase in wealth and in scale as well as in the growing centrality of slavery, the export-led transformation of the lowcountry resembled the earlier, sugar-induced changes in the West Indies. There were limits to the resemblance, however, due to ways in which the lowcountry

---

[15] Letter of Samuel Syssli, Dec. 3, 1737, *South Carolina Historical and Genealogical Magazine* 23 (1922), 90.
[16] Carman, ed., *American Husbandry*, 277.

Table 6.5. *Some characteristics of lowcountry South Carolina probate inventories, 1678–1764*

	1678–98	1722–6	1743–5	1764
N inventories	50	158	154	142
Mean movables (in sterling)	204	357	539	1,145
% wealth in slaves	21	58	65	54
Slaves per estate	2.6	9.6	16.7	17.9
% estates with slaves	62	78	81	88
% planters with slaves	69	93	94	96
% estates with land	—	73	70	68
% planters with land	—	90	93	92
Share wealth, top 10%	41	46	44	60
Share slaves, top 10%	48	49	43	51
Mean wealth, top 10%	£835	1,636	2,422	7,018
Mean slaves, top 10%	12.6	46.8	74.5	92
Mean nonhuman movable wealth	£161	150	189	527

Sources: Records of the Secretary of the Province, 1675–95, 1692–1700, 1700–10, 1722–6; Wills, Inventories & Miscellaneous Records, 1722–4, 1724–5; Inventories, 1739–44, 1744–6, 1763–7. South Carolina Department of Archives and History, Columbia. All values converted to sterling following the exchange rates in John J. McCusker, *Money and Exchange in Europe and America, 1600–1775: A Handbook* (Chapel Hill, NC: 1978), 222–4. For the period before 1699, when McCusker reports no exchange rates, I assumed that £1 sterling equaled £1.1 in South Carolina currency. Readers should note that these figures have not been adjusted for changes in age structure among inventoried decedents or for changes in the proportion of wealthowning decedents whose estates were inventoried.

developed its own distinctive plantation complex. Some of the differences are apparent in the probate inventories. Remarkably, the export boom was accompanied by little increase in inequality among wealthowners and by widespread access to the basic factors of production among whites. In the 1740s, following half a century of rapid growth, the share of wealth owned by the richest 10 percent barely differed from seventeenth-century levels, while the great majority of decedents (and nearly all planters) owned both land and slaves. The export boom had made the lowcountry a republic of slaveowners.

Other developments further distinguished the lowcountry from the sugar islands. For one thing, in Charlestown, British America's fourth largest city for most of the eighteenth century, the lowcountry had a commercial, political, and social center that provided a focus not found in the West Indies. For another, the region developed a merchant class much larger and wealthier and with more independence than in the sugar islands, where traders remained thoroughly subordinate to metropolitan interests. Thirdly, a region of "common husbandry" developed around the edges of the plantation district, providing planters food for their slaves and Charlestown merchants a flow of diversified products for export and a lively market for manufactured goods and commercial services. Perhaps most important were differences in scale. Rice plantations were large by mainland standards but much smaller than sugar estates; lowcountry planters were not as rich as sugar magnates. As a result, absenteeism was more limited in the lowcountry than on the islands, planters more often managed their plantations, and they spent a larger share of their income at home. The limits on planter absenteeism had important political consequences, for it permitted the growth of an indigenous ruling class, a powerful, self-conscious group capable of shaping the region's future.

The lowcountry's transformation was bought at a frightful price, particularly in the lives of Indian and African slaves, chief victims of the planter's vicious scramble to capture the fruits of the export boom. It was also expensive: over the course of the boom, planters spent roughly a million sterling on slaves alone, to which must be added expenditures on land, buildings, tools, and livestock needed to start plantations. Given the costs, it is worth asking how the export boom was financed. There are several possibilities. Planters could have borrowed from English investors or on a local credit market, acquired short-term commercial credit from English merchants, brought substantial capital with them when they immigrated, or paid for slaves out of current income. All of these methods were used in all of the colonies, but their importance differed between regions. Outside capital was apparently a greater source of credit during the Barbadian sugar boom than at other times or places. In the Chesapeake, the slow pace of Africanization suggests that savings and current income played the central role. In coastal Carolina, a local mortgage market that was developed early in the eighteenth century was especially important. Planters were able to borrow funds to pay for agricultural development, particularly for the purchase of Africans, in the local capital market where Charlestown merchants loaned money earned in trade on mortgages secured by land and, especially, slaves. The local mortgage market played a key role in the growth of the Carolina economy. It quickened the pace of development beyond what would have been possible had planters been forced to rely on savings, while providing local lenders the opportunity to make secure investments in a rapidly expanding export sector. And it permitted small and middling planters with modest incomes but high aspirations, who perhaps seemed poor risks in other credit markets, access to capital to acquire labor and build estates. If there was any truth to the claims of Revolutionary ideologues that the lowcountry was both a slaveholder's republic and a good poor man's country, the local mortgage market deserves some credit for making their perverse vision a reality.

The great lowcountry export boom ground to a halt around 1740 in a series of events sufficiently disruptive and threatening to shake planter confidence and make them wonder about the choices they had made and the society they had built. The first shock was a yellow fever epidemic that struck Charlestown in late August 1739, bringing with it a "great Sickness & Mortality the like whereof has never been known in the Province."[17] Coming on the heels of a major outbreak of smallpox the previous year, the epidemic was terrifying. And it was only the beginning. On September 9, with the fever still raging in the city, a small band of slaves from the western branch of Stono River, hoping to reach the Spanish settlement at St. Augustine, rose in insurrection. Although most of the rebels were quickly "taken or Cut to Peices[sic]," the group grew to some 60 to 100 blacks on the march south, and they "murthered in their way there between Twenty & Thirty white People & Burnt Severall houses."[18] Stono was the culmination of a decade of mounting African protest, a resistance more frightening because of the supposed refuge at St. Augustine and persistent rumors of an imminent Spanish invasion of the lowcountry. And Stono was followed by continued unrest among slaves, by a failed English invasion of St. Augustine, by a major fire in Charlestown in September 1740 (attributed by some to black arsonists, feared by others as likely opportunity for another insurrection), by the landing of a large Spanish force at St. Simon's off the Georgia coast, and by a gradual slide into a long depression as the lowcountry economy felt the impact of King George's War. "This province," Robert Pringle lamented, "Seems to be Subject to Series of Accidents & Missfortunes."[19]

The 1740s depression marked a turning point in the history of the lowcountry. King George's War (1739–48) hit the region hard, especially

---

[17] Robert Pringle to Thomas Burrill, Oct. 10, 1739, Walter B. Edgar, ed., *The Letterbook of Robert Pringle*, 2 vols. (Columbia, SC, 1972), I, 139.
[18] Pringle to John Richards, Sept. 26, 1739, ibid., I, 135.
[19] Pringle to Andrew Pringle, July 10, 1742, ibid., I, 388.

once France joined the fray and fighting intensified in the Atlantic in 1744. War pushed shipping costs up, and rice profitability declined, since rice was a bulky commodity that soon lost its competitive edge in European markets when burdened with heavy freight and insurance charges. Prices, which had fallen gently as productivity gains were passed on to consumers, plummeted from as much as 9 shillings per hundredweight in the late 1730s to just over 2 shillings in the mid-1740s. Exports, too, fell sharply, from an average approaching 40 million pounds a year around 1740 to less than 30 million in the last half of the decade. Lower prices and declining exports pushed the value of the crop down dramatically, from a peak of nearly £150,000 sterling in 1740 to less than £30,000 in 1746, at the bottom of the depression. Since rice was "king" in the lowcountry, its troubles affected everything. The land boom of the 1730s came to a halt, planters stopped importing Africans (in part because of a high tax on imports imposed in Stono's wake), European goods became scarce and expensive, the local credit market tightened, and overextended planters were forced into bankruptcy. Other trades did better than rice, but those had long since become too small to carry planters through a long period of hard times. The great lowcountry export boom had clearly run its course as King George's War brought the region "to the Brink of Ruin."[20]

Although severely shaken by events of the 1740s, planters quickly regained confidence in the lowcountry economy after mid-century. For one thing, planters emerged from the depression with more diverse operations, as they trained slaves in crafts, organized workers to grow their own food, and began to make some of the shoes and clothing needed by slaves. More important than the development of plantation self-sufficiency was experimentation with new crops in an effort to find additional exports that would provide alternatives or supplements to rice. With indigo they had a great success. The war gave lowcountry planters an opening by cutting off supplies of the dye from the French Caribbean, while the British government boosted the infant industry with a bounty. Early efforts produced a poor quality dye, however, and exports collapsed when peace restored trade with the French islands. The Seven Years' War brought a rapid recovery, and the crop entered what contemporaries called its "golden days" when indigo planters were "full of money."[21] The value of exports

[20] James Glen to Robert Dinwiddie, Mar. 3, 1754, in William L. McDowell, Jr., ed., *Colonial Records of South Carolina: Documents Relating to Indian Affairs, May 21, 1750 – August 7, 1754* (Columbia, SC, 1958), 478.

[21] Quoted in Robert M. Weir, *Colonial South Carolina: A History* (Millwood, NY: 1983), 146.

grew enormously, from an annual average of less than £10,000 in the early 1750s to nearly £150,000 in the early 1770s, when it approached 40 percent of the value of the lowcountry rice crop. The rise of indigo let planters and merchants face the possibility of war with optimism, with the hope that "a new War will learn us how to propogate [*sic*] other useful Articles."[22]

It was also critical to growing planter confidence that the slave population seemed less threatening after mid-century. That is not to say that *all* planters slept easily *all* the time, but Stono was the last major scare of the eighteenth century. The reasons for growing planter confidence in their abilities to control slaves are complex. Stono left masters determined to discipline slaves more effectively; the Spanish threat gradually receded and was finally eliminated when Florida passed to the British in 1763; and the settlement of the backcountry left lowcountry whites, although still outnumbered, confident of help should an emergency arise. Also important were changes in the composition of the population and the organization of plantation work. Many slaves, Gov. James Glen explained in 1751, "are natives of Carolina" who "have been brought up among white people." The conclusion Glen drew from this observation – that they had "no notion of liberty, nor no longing after any other country," that slaves were "pleased with their masters, contented with their condition, reconciled to servitude" – is stunning in its complacency, but he did isolate an important truth.[23] The growth of a creole majority, a process quickened when African imports stopped in the 1740s, transformed the slave population in ways that made them less terrifying to their owners. That transformation also permitted slaves to form families, make firm and lasting friendships, and build communities on the large lowcountry plantations. The slaves also utilized the development of a task system to gain some control over their working lives; this provided opportunities to work on their own account and accumulate small amounts of property. Lowcountry slavery remained harsh and oppressive, but the changes that occurred around mid-century left blacks less willing to risk all in open rebellion.

The renewed success of the lowcountry rice industry provided a further source of growing planter confidence. The value of the crop grew more than threefold in the quarter-century following King George's War, from roughly £115,000 sterling around 1750 to £380,000 in the early 1770s.

[22] Henry Laurens to Sarah Nickelson, Aug. 1, 1755, *Laurens Papers* I, 309.
[23] Glen to the Lords Commissioners for Trade and Plantations, March 1751, in H. Roy Merrens, ed., *The Colonial South Carolina Scene: Contemporary Views, 1697–1774* (Columbia, SC: 1977), 183.

It was not simply that the rice industry grew; planters achieved major improvements in productivity, evident both in technical changes in rice production and in the ability to hold prices stable in the face of rising costs. "The culture of rice" in the region, David Ramsay noted, "was in a state of constant improvement" as production shifted first from the moist uplands to inland swamps and later to the tidewater, as complex irrigation systems were developed, as new varieties were discovered better suited to local conditions, and as the cleaning process was improved.[24] It is possible that this creativity rested on the skills of slaves. Indeed, it has been suggested that Africans introduced the technology of rice cultivation to the lowcountry and that rice planters sought (and paid premium prices for) slaves from ethnic groups familiar with the crop. While the notion that technological restraints were removed only with the arrival of skilled Africans after having been a major barrier to the commercial cultivation of rice seems insufficiently attentive to the key role played by rising European demand, Africans did bring important technical skills across the Atlantic, and the abilities and accumulated knowledge of slaves was crucial to the success of plantation economies. This may have been particularly true with rice. The crop was widely grown in West Africa under a variety of conditions and by different techniques, while the lowcountry tasking system placed major responsibilities for the organization of work in the hands of slaves and offered them incentives to work efficiently. It would not be surprising if some of the productivity gains rested on innovations by slaves. Planters took the credit, however, reading into the renewed expansion of the rice industry, the growing diversity of their plantations, the rise of indigo, and the general success of lowcountry agriculture clear evidence of their creativity and inventiveness, their ability to manage slaves and deal with adversity, and their competence to shape the future.

The growing expansiveness of lowcountry planters was reflected in the geographic expansion of the lowcountry plantation complex. Georgia was the focus of that expansion and its greatest success. Georgia's founders had not intended that the colony become a "new Carolina." The Georgia Trustees designed the colony as an area of "common husbandry," a settlement of farms rather than plantations where a society of sturdy white yeomen would work for their own account without slaves, forming both a buffer against Spanish and French ambitions and a refuge for England's dispossessed. By the early 1750s, only 20 years after the colony's found-

---

[24] David Ramsey, *The History of South Carolina, from Its First Settlement in 1670, to the Year 1808*, 2 vols. (Charleston, SC, 1809), II, 206.

ing, the vision had collapsed, victim of the Trustee's incompetence, the ambitions of Georgia settlers, and the demands of Carolina planters for fresh rice lands. The prohibition against slavery was lifted, planters and slaves poured in, and Georgia became both a royal colony and "a province to South Carolina" as the lowcountry plantation complex took root on the coastal strip and along the southern bank of the Savannah River.[25] By 1770, blacks were 45 percent of the colony's population (70 percent in the coastal strip), its rice and indigo crops worth more than £40,000 sterling.

The years before the Revolution also witnessed the spread of the lowcountry plantation complex to the lower Cape Fear region of North Carolina as well as efforts to establish it below the Altamaha River and in the newly acquired colony of East Florida. The Cape Fear district had become a South Carolina satellite much earlier, in the 1730s, as the naval stores industry displaced by the expansion of rice moved north. By the 1760s, the process that had earlier transformed coastal South Carolina reached the lower Cape Fear when large plantations, rice, indigo, and slaves pushed small farmers and naval stores producers into the interior. The other efforts proved less successful. The Altamaha project collapsed almost before it started, as royal authorities first prohibited settlement while the region was claimed by Spain and then, after 1763 when the Spanish claim was removed, proved unable to settle complex land title disputes that had to be unraveled before investment could proceed. East Florida at least got off the ground when British investors went "Florida mad" and lowcountry planters moved in to build a new Carolina. A few large plantations were established and small crops of indigo produced by the early 1770s, but that effort too proved a failure as investors fell victim to the strange environment and (again) British administrative incompetence.

The success of rice and indigo and the geographic expansion of the plantation complex suggest that the lowcountry export sector witnessed extraordinary growth in the quarter-century before the American Revolution. Comprehensive trade statistics specific to the region are not available, but data for South Carolina and Georgia capture the pattern. In 1748, when Georgia's exports were minimal, a contemporary valued exports from South Carolina at £160,000 sterling. Between 1768 and 1772, exports from South Carolina and Georgia were worth an average of £511,000, a more than threefold increase in only 20 years (Table 6.6). If we exclude all commodities but rice and indigo as likely to have been

---

[25] James Habersham to Benjamin Martyn, March 15, 1756, Habersham Papers, Library of Congress.

Table 6.6. *Average annual value of exports from South Carolina and Georgia, 1768–72, by destination (in thousands of pounds sterling)*

Commodity	Great Britain	Southern Europe	West Indies	Mainland Colonies	Total
Rice	198.2	51.0	55.7	21.3	326.2
Indigo	111.8				111.8
Deerskins	28.1				28.1
Naval stores	6.0			0.7	6.7
Wood products	0.5	0.2	8.8	0.2	9.7
Grains	0.2	0.3	5.0	5.0	10.5
Livestock, beef, and pork	0.1	0.1	6.8		7.0
Other	2.7	0.4	2.1	5.7	10.9
Total	347.6	52.0	78.4	32.9	510.9

Source: James F. Shepherd and Gary M. Walton, *Shipping, Maritime Trade, and the Economic Development of Colonial North America* (Cambridge, 1972), 215–27; Shepherd and Samuel H. Williamson, "The Coastal Trade of the British North American Colonies, 1768–1772," *Journal of Economic History* 32 (1972), 809.

produced in the interior, these data suggest that lowcountry exports per capita approached £4, roughly three times the figure for the rest of the mainland. For the lowcountry whites, exports per head approached £17, perhaps half again as large as total income per capita for the colonies as a whole.

The successes of the export sector were accomplished by a substantial increase in lowcountry wealth — it emerged as the richest area in British North America. Estate inventories show that mean wealth among probated decedents nearly doubled from the 1740s to the 1760s and continued to grow impressively into the next decade. By the eve of the Revolution, wealthholders in the Charlestown district at the center of the lowcountry held assets valued at more than seven times those owned by their counterparts in the thirteen continental colonies as a whole. In contrast to the process during the initial export boom, this later growth was accompanied by a fall in the share of all wealth represented by slaves and by a sharp increase in inequality as the great planters and big merchants built substantial estates and pulled far ahead of their neighbors.

Despite the rise of inequality, there is evidence of an impressive solidarity — "harmony" was how contemporaries described it — among European Americans in the region, especially among the very rich. It was, for one, a small population of only 35,000 people, perhaps 6,000 families, in

1775, a group bound together by frequent face-to-face contact, high rates of intermarriage, and a gradual blurring of the distinction between merchant and planter. It was also a population bound together by its isolation: the substantial black majority within the region and the restive backcountry farmers encircling it to the west combined to curb disagreements and foster group consciousness. In the end, however, that solidarity was rooted less in fear and isolation than in an optimism and expansiveness that grew out of a defining characteristic of the lowcountry plantation regime: an impressive prosperity that provided most white men access to land and labor, made a favored few very rich indeed, and took the region into the revolutionary era as a slaveowner's republic.

BACKCOUNTRY AND FRONTIER

In contrast to the coastal districts, where the regional constructs of lowcountry and tobacco coast have a certain integrity and firmness, backcountry and frontier are problematic concepts. Despite the still-looming presence of Frederick Jackson Turner's Frontier Thesis, this reflects the force of historiographic tradition. At least among colonialists, the interior has received much less attention than the seaboard. It also reflects reality. True, there is some fuzziness about the edges of the coastal regions, especially the Chesapeake, where high rates of migration led to rapid expansion and the sometimes problematic integration of new territory, and where diversification had removed some older settlements from the tobacco economy by the revolutionary era. However, lowcountry and tobacco coast were held together by a shared commitment to common exports, plantation agriculture, and African slavery as well as by emerging planter classes gradually consolidating power, growing in solidarity, and developing a vision for the future. Backcountry and frontier lacked the stability and cohesiveness produced by such integrating institutions. They were places in the process of transformation as the aspirations of settlers joined with the aggressive expansion of tidewater society to first turn frontier into backcountry and then build a plantation regime in the backcountry settlements.

The characteristic economic institution of the southern frontier was the trade in animal pelts, especially deerskins, much in demand in Europe where they were turned into gloves and bookbindings. Unfortunately, it is impossible to describe the volume of that trade precisely. Deerskins were shipped out of several colonial ports and to various European nations; since volume and prices fluctuated dramatically with changing conditions in the interior, no one has yet compiled a consistent series. However, evidence from Charlestown and New Orleans, the dominant export centers, suggests a slow expansion from a total of roughly £30,000 sterling around 1710 to perhaps £50,000 in 1750, and £80,000 in 1770. The trade made an important contribution to southern export earnings, although its share declined as plantation agriculture expanded. Still, at mid-century, deerskins accounted for about a third of the value of exports through New Orleans, and 18 percent for Charlestown, figures that fell to about 20 percent and 6 percent, respectively, by the 1770s.

For a time, a trade in Native American slaves was also an important part of the frontier economy. The evidence will not support a precise description of the volume of that trade, but it is possible to sketch its outline. The Spanish had raided the Southeast for slaves since the sixteenth century, while the English in Virginia and the French in Louisiana acquired Indian slaves when opportunities appeared. The trade, however, centered on Charlestown and the lowcountry. Although Indian slaves appeared in South Carolina as early as 1683, the trade was initially a secondary activity, subordinate to the trade in deerskins and the political aims of the English and their Native allies. Indian slaves were captured almost incidentally, as a byproduct of other processes, and most were exported to earn foreign exchange. After 1700, however, the lowcountry export boom led to a sharp increase in demand for labor, which transformed relationships between the English and Native peoples. The slave trade gained in importance and was no longer subordinated to the deerskin trade or to political concerns. More Indians were captured and more were kept in the lowcountry to make rice, grow provisions, and produce naval stores. During the first decade of the eighteenth century, Indian slaves were the fastest growing group in South Carolina, rising from 200 (3 percent of the total population) in 1700 to 1500 (15 percent) by 1710. Their numbers continued to grow in the next decade, but less rapidly. In 1720, there were roughly 2,000 Indian slaves, but they made up only 11 percent of the population. Thereafter, both their numbers and their share fell sharply, to fewer than 500 and less than 1 percent of the inhabitants by 1740.

The intensification of the slave trade proved devastating to the Indians. It was a bloody, violent business, impossible to institutionalize, that demanded increased warfare and ever more raiding. It produced sharp population decline and the total destruction of several smaller groups. And it led to major political changes as Indians struggled to protect themselves by forming larger and more effective federations and by elaborating a "play-off" system in which rivalries between the English, French, and Spanish were exploited in efforts to control the worst excesses of the European invasion. Population decline and political restructuring quickly lowered the supply of Indian slaves, reducing it to a mere trickle by the 1720s.

It has been argued that planter preferences played the key role in the decline of Native slavery, that they found Indians unsatisfactory as workers and replaced them with Africans as soon as possible. However, prices for Indian slaves rose rather than fell as their numbers declined, by 50 to 100 percent from the 1720s to the 1730s, suggesting that planters would have purchased more had they been available. But if the preferences of the individual planter purchasers did not produce the collapse of the native slave trade, their political concerns as members of an emerging ruling class proved critical. Beginning in 1716, the Carolina Assembly began to assert control over the Indian trade, enacting over the next 15 years legislation that, among other things, restricted dealing in slaves. The legislation was a reaction to the dangers that trade posed, dangers clearly revealed in the Yamasee War of 1715–17. While the origins of the conflict are complex, it is clear that Indian grievances against the slave trade helped to initiate it and that slave traders welcomed it as a way of increasing supplies. The war devastated the colony. Some 400 colonists were killed, more than £100,000 in property was destroyed, half the cultivated land was abandoned, starvation threatened, trade was disrupted, and taxes rose sharply to pay for defense. And it was nearly worse, with only luck and skillful diplomacy preventing the alliance of Creeks, Choctaws, and Yamasees from overwhelming Carolina and destroying the colony. In the midst of a rapid expansion produced by the export boom, Carolina planters had too much at stake to tolerate such risks.

While the consequences of the Indian slave trade were clearly disastrous for Native peoples, the impact of the trade in deerskins is less certain. On the one hand, it led to increases in income as commercial hunting raised productivity and as access to guns, metal tools and utensils, and manufactured textiles improved material living standards. On the other hand, it led to dependency and decline over the long term. When pelt supplies fell, Indians were left with heavy debts and dependent on European manufactures, but with much smaller incomes from deerskin production and a territory so reduced in size that return to precontact forms of economic organization was no longer an option. There is evidence that for some Native peoples on the southern frontier, the gains outweighed the costs during the middle to late decades of the eighteenth century. Although there were periods of ferocious conflict when Indian groups fought each other over territory, resisted European expansion, or were caught up in imperial wars, the level of violence declined with the collapse of the slave trade. Further, some groups were able to use the play-off system to maintain or even increase autonomy as the French (and later Spanish) presence in the lower Mississippi valley grew. The slow expansion of the deerskin trade apparently did not deplete supplies, and many Indian groups were able to integrate commercial hunting with agriculture, fishing, and gathering in ways that enhanced income. Moreover, the activity generated by the trade offered some additional employment opportunities, especially in transport, while the growing European presence provided a market for food and handicrafts. The best evidence of relative prosperity is demographic. The rapid decline that reduced Indian numbers began to slow in the 1720s and was actually replaced by a modest increase starting in the 1750s (see Figure 6.1). Decline continued among natives along the coast, but in the southern interior, in what was still "Indian country," some groups registered remarkable gains. The Choctaws and Chickasaws, for example, grew from a low of about 14,000 in 1730 to nearly 18,000 in 1790, while the Creeks increased from 10,000 in 1715 to 15,000 in 1790.

This relatively prosperous interlude between the demographic collapse of the early stages of contact and the nineteenth-century era of removal was threatened and ultimately destroyed by European expansion. One threat came from the French settlements along the Gulf Coast and in the lower Mississippi valley, a region usefully thought of as "greater Louisiana." Although they established a permanent presence in 1699, the French were slow to gain a firm foothold: as late as 1715, the colonial population amounted to only 400 people, most of them soldiers, officials, or clerics scattered among several small administrative outposts. The region experienced a minor population boom in the 1720s, shortly after the French government turned the colony over to John Law's *Compagnie des Indes* in 1717. Over the next 15 years, the Company shipped some 7,000 Europeans and an equal number of Africans to the colony. Conditions were terrible, however, "and the country was emptied as rapidly as it had filled."[26]

---

[26] Pierre Francois Xavier de Charlevoix, *History and General Description of New France*, 6 vols., trans. John Gilmary Shea (New York, 1866–72), VI, 69.

By 1730, the colonial population numbered only 5,300, about two-thirds of them African slaves. Disappointment with the Company's effort was compounded by a deterioration in relations with neighboring Indians, culminating in the destructive Natchez War of 1729–31. In the aftermath, the French government resumed control of the colony but showed little interest in its development. In 1760, the colonial population of greater Louisiana amounted to just over 9,000, including perhaps 5,300 slaves.

Colonial development quickened when the region was partitioned in the aftermath of the Seven Years' War. France ceded its territory east of the Mississippi above Lake Pontchartrain to Great Britain, which reorganized the region as West Florida. New Orleans, the lower delta, and the west bank became Spanish Louisiana. Both colonial powers worked to promote trade and plantation agriculture, attract immigrants, and encourage investment. Population boomed, more than doubling between 1760 and 1775, doubling again by 1790, when the colonial inhabitants surpassed 42,000, including some 23,000 slaves. By then, the entire region was under Spanish control, albeit temporarily, as a result of Spain's conquest of West Florida in 1783.

Economic developments mirrored the growth of population. Until the end of the French period, the economy was dominated by the Indian trade. A small plantation sector began to emerge during the 1720s around New Orleans and upriver at Point Coupee, where planters used slaves to make modest quantities of tobacco, indigo, and timber products for export as well as foodstuffs for the local market. That sector grew slowly for the next 40 years, but it was not until the era of partition that greater Louisiana emerged as a plantation colony. By 1775, annual exports of indigo and tobacco from New Orleans were worth more than six times the value of deerskin exports. Plantation development was less rapid in British West Florida, and peltries remained the dominant export there for a longer time. However, that colony also produced significant amounts of indigo, tobacco, and forest products by 1775.

While the expansion of great Louisiana intruded on "Indian country" during the middle decades of the eighteenth century, the greater threat came from the east and the invasion of the southern backcountry. Although there is a sense in which the South had a backcountry from the last decades of the seventeenth century as relentless expansion extended the area of colonial occupation steadily inland from the Chesapeake Bay, it was not until the 1730s when settlers crossed the Fall Line (the line east of the

Appalachians marking the end of the coastal plains and the beginning of the Piedmont Plateau) in substantial numbers that phrases such as "Back Parts," "Back Settlements," and "Back Country" entered contemporary usage. The concept was clearly Eurocentric: from the perspective of Native peoples, a phrase such as "front country" appears more apt. And it served to contrast the orderly, hierarchical, "civilized" coast with the violent, leveling, "primitive" interior. Historians, following Turner, have stripped the notion of its pejorative implications but retained the contrast and its underlying assumption that a fundamental social, economic, and cultural unity bound the backcountry into a coherent region with an integrity of its own.

There is evidence to support the assumption. The regions' population was chiefly European in background, without the substantial African presence so critical to coastal societies. The backcountry was dominated by farms rather than plantations, shipped less of its output abroad than did the tidewater, and exhibited lower wealth levels and less inequality. Backcountry settlers also had grievances against coastal-dominated governments, grievances which sometimes brought large numbers of them together to advance a common political agenda. Nevertheless, the assumption that the backcountry formed a coherent, unified social, economic, and cultural region is misleading, on several counts.

For one thing, the region grew explosively in the half-century before the American Revolution, at rates more than twice the mainland average. Still "Indian country" in 1730, by 1775 the backcountry was home to more than a quarter of a million colonials, more than 20 percent of the South's population and nearly a third of the whites. Such rapid growth would test the coherence and unity of any society, but the migrant streams which fed that rapid increase were especially diverse. Immigrants from the north of England, Scotland, Ireland, and Germany, most of whom entered the region by way of Philadelphia (leading Turner to call the region a "new Pennsylvania"[27]), were joined by migrants from the East, many of them third- or fourth-generation Americans seeking the opportunity no longer found in the tidewater. Many of the men who moved to the backcountry shared aspirations, especially a determination to maintain their "independence" — meaning that they and their dependents could live comfortably and securely without relying on the good will of others — and to achieve "improvement" by acquiring the capital and labor to develop their farms and by transform-

---

[27] Frederick Jackson Turner, *The Frontier in American History* (New York: 1947), 68.

ing the backcountry in ways that would make it more like the societies of
the seaboard.[28] However, broadly shared aspirations did not mean an absence of conflict or the general acceptance of the rule of those in power, and
political authority remained fragile at the eve of the Revolution.

Further, sharp regional differences quickly appeared in the structure of
backcountry society, differences in large part related to the date of European settlement and the degree of integration to the coast. New settlements in the backcountry went through a process similar to that along the
tobacco coast. Opportunities attracted migrants who at first built a relatively egalitarian (if poor) society that later witnessed rising wealth levels,
growing inequality, a contraction of opportunities as the region filled up,
and high rates of outmigration as residents, unable to achieve independence, struck out for better prospects. These developments were often
accompanied by a noticeable economic reorientation as farmers, who had
initially concentrated on food production for home use and the local
market, gradually increased their wealth through the farm-making process, acquired slaves, and began to ship livestock and livestock products,
tobacco, indigo, hemp, and grains overland and downriver to tidewater
ports for sale abroad. Coastal planters and merchants often encouraged
such reorientation as they invested in land, sent out their younger sons
with slaves to develop estates, extended credit, and built stores both to
purchase backcountry produce for export and to supply settlers tools,
clothing, and amenities. These processes led to considerable differentia-
tion within the region as the oldest parts of the backcountry were "improved" and became more like the coast. In South Carolina on the eve of
the Revolution, for example, the inventories of decedents who lived near
the Fall Line were appraised at slightly more than about £300 sterling and
reported an average of six slaves; those who lived farther inland were worth
£150, with only two slaves per estate. Eventually, contemporaries acknowledged the process by using the terms *middlecountry* and *upcountry* to
distinguish the two areas.[29]

Perhaps the strongest evidence that the backcountry was a coherent
region comes from the *regulator movements,* the outbreaks of insurrectionary
violence that shook North and South Carolina in the 1760s and 1770s. In

---

[28] See Jack P. Greene, "Independence, Improvement, and Authority: Towards a Framework for
Understanding the Histories of the Southern Backcountry during the Era of the American Revolu-
tion," in Ronald Hoffman, Thad W. Tate, and Peter J. Albert, eds., *An Uncivil War: The Southern
Backcountry during the American Revolution* (Charlottesville, VA, 1985), 3–36.

[29] For the terminology, see Rachel N. Klein, *Unification of a Slave State: The Rise of the Planter Class in
the South Carolina Backcountry, 1760–1808* (Chapel Hill, 1990), 7.

part, the violence aimed to redress grievances against governments dominated by tidewater planters and unresponsive to backcountry interests. Complaints included inadequate representation, corruption in land policy and local government, tax policies that favored the tidewater, and a lack of concern with defense of the frontier, control of local criminals, and public improvements, especially in transport. While the regulator movements built solidarity and distinguished backcountry from tidewater, they also served the interests of some settlers to "improve" the region, to hasten its transformation by creating conditions important to the development of plantation agriculture. Most regulator violence was directed not against the coast but internally, against "vagrants" who were "little more than white Indians," "back inhabitants who choose to live by the wandering indolence of hunting than by the more honest and domestic employment of planting."[30] It was not simply that such people offended the sensibilities of improving farmers. They also threatened security by stealing property, taking livestock, and, especially, offering refuge to escaped slaves. While the region remained frontier, such "vagrants" were of slight concern, but as settlers flooded in, built farms, and aspired to plantation agriculture, the "vagrants" had to be forced out so that the process of "improvement" could proceed apace.

CONCLUSION

The economy of the several Souths grew impressively during the century and a half of British colonial rule. While growth came at a high price to Indians and Africans, its benefits were shared widely among white southerners, and a few big planters and merchants grew rich. Growth and the prosperity it brought rested not simply on American resources but on the ability to exploit opportunities within the framework provided by the Old Empire, to take advantage of its markets, cheap manufactured goods, protection, commercial services, and credit. Given the apparent material benefits of membership in the Empire, why did colonists mount a resistance to Great Britain after 1760 and then fight a long, costly war for independence? The puzzle deepens when it is recalled that growth was especially rapid in the quarter-century leading up to the Revolution, and it deepens yet further when the short-term costs of independence are

[30] For the quotations, see ibid., 51.

assessed. For the colonies as a whole, incomes fell sharply during the war and recovery was slow: it was not until the first decade of the nineteenth century that per capita incomes in the United States again reached the level achieved in the colonies in 1774. The costs of independence were especially high in the South. Southern per capita incomes, at or above the "national" average in 1774, were perhaps one-third below that average in 1798, while the southern share of "national" exports fell from 63 percent in ca. 1770 to 40–45 percent in the early 1790s. Colonists, and especially the southern gentry, seem to have committed "econocide." Why?

One answer is that southerners were heavily indebted to British merchants and saw the Revolution as an opportunity to escape those obligations. This line of reasoning implies that colonial prosperity was false and achieved by mortgaging the future. While British credit helped to finance the purchase of manufactures and slaves, and while some planters were overextended and burdened by chronic indebtedness, for the South as a whole, the size of the debt owed to foreign creditors was not excessive. The average annual value of southern exports seems to have been larger than that debt. Most planters were good risks, and the debt they carried was modest given their incomes. Nor were southerners overly dependent on Britain for investment capital: by the 1770s, the internal debt (loans between southerners) dwarfed the external one, suggesting that the South could finance continued growth out of its own resources. Southern prosperity did not rest on mortgaged futures and planters who lived beyond their means but on the productivity of its farms and plantations and especially on its ability to produce crops much in demand elsewhere in the Atlantic world.

Another answer is that economic concerns were unimportant to the Revolutionary leadership, that the conflict turned on politics, especially questions of liberty, representation, and self-government. That is a narrow view of the movement, however. Economic developments provided the means for independence and shaped the aspirations that gave colonists the nerve to take the risks. Independence was thinkable in the 1770s because growth in the colonial era had created an economy that could stand alone and support a government able to hold its own against the great powers of the day. Perhaps more important, economic progress filled colonists with pride in their accomplishments and nurtured visions of a bountiful future. Southerners were surrounded by evidence of their rise to "wealth and greatness" in the form of prosperous farms and big plantations, impressive fortunes held by the gentry, great crops of tobacco, rice, and indigo, and the growth of population and of colonized territory. That evidence was pro-jected into the future by southern gentlemen, eager for their "turn to figure on the face of the earth, and in the annals of the world," whose aspirations were shaped by visions of an American empire that would extend the accomplishments of the colonial economy and the key institutions of an emerging South – plantation agriculture, African slavery, and the develop-ing planter class – into the next century and across the continent.[31]

[31] David Ramsey, *The History of the American Revolution*, 2 vols. (Trenton, NJ: 1811), II, 452.

7

ECONOMIC AND SOCIAL DEVELOPMENT OF THE BRITISH WEST INDIES, FROM SETTLEMENT TO ca. 1850

B. W. HIGMAN

In 1775, it was an open question whether Britain's colonies in the Caribbean would follow the thirteen continental colonies into independence. The tropical colonies were integral elements in an economic system that linked them with the North American mainland; to a large extent, they shared common cultural and political traditions. As McCusker and Menard comment, "The economies of the mainland and the islands were so tightly intertwined that full understanding of development in one is impossible without an appreciation of developments in the other."[1] At the same time, the Caribbean colonies possessed characteristics that distinguished them from the English settlements to the north; it was these features that determined their unique political and economic future.

The principal distinguishing characteristics of the British West Indian colonial economy were its monocultural focus and dependence on external trade, the dominance of large-scale plantations and involuntary labor systems, the drain of wealth associated with a high ratio of absentee proprietorship, and the role of the servile population in the internal market. Why these features occurred in exaggerated form in the Caribbean rather than in other regions of the Atlantic system is an important question for debate. The British colonies in the Caribbean were subject to an imperial policy common to all of that state's territories, and the colonizing stock of "settlers" was essentially the same for all of the regions occupied by the British before the middle of the seventeenth century, the formative stage of settlement. Thus, the role of (imperial) cultural and political factors in

[1] John J. McCusker and Russell R. Menard, *The Economy of British America, 1607–1789* (Chapel Hill: 1985), p. 145.

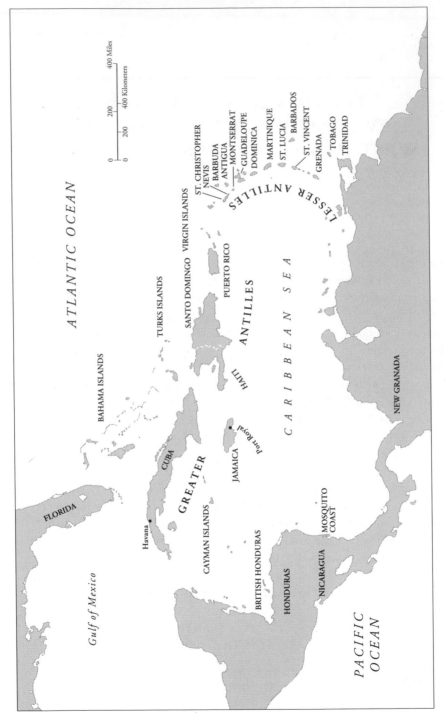

The West Indies

engendering British West Indian distinctiveness is likely to have been insignificant.

Two aspects of the physical environment were crucial: the fact that almost all of the British colonies in the Caribbean were *islands,* and the *tropical climate* which permitted the growth of certain crops. Islands were particularly suited to development as export-oriented plantation economies because, with the available technologies of the early seventeenth century, they presented great opportunities for occupation and territorial control, and they minimized transportation costs by offering easy or direct access to the sea. Thus, as Richard Sheridan has observed, the system was articulated first on the small islands of the eastern Caribbean and later applied to larger islands and mainland coastal and riverine areas.[2] Not only were these small islands closer to Europe and Africa, reducing costs of transportation and defense, but they also possessed high ratios of coastline to land area, which enabled plantations to have direct or cheap access to ocean-going ships. Thus, the early settled British sugar island of St. Kitts had a ratio of 8.8 miles of coastline to every 10 square miles of area, Nevis 6.9, and Barbados 3.5. In St. Kitts and Nevis, the elongated plantations were simply strung around the islands, each holding having a piece of the coast and a slice of every possible ecological zone proceeding into the interior. Jamaica, the largest of the British island-colonies, had only 1.1 miles of coastline per 10 square miles of area, but even this ratio was high compared to any mainland area other than the Chesapeake.

The second critical environmental factor was the tropical climate of the Caribbean. This made possible the efficient cultivation of tropical crops, for which there was a significant demand on the European market. Sugar was the most important of these crops and quickly came to dominate the landscape. The choice was important, because the technological requirements of sugar making brought in their train a whole series of consequences.

The emphasis placed on these physical factors in the development of the British West Indian economy is not meant to echo any crude form of environmental determinism. Arguments of this type – purporting to explain the dependence on African slave labor by reference to the inability of Europeans to perform manual work in the tropics – were popular elements of the *climatic theory of the plantation* until about 1940. The more recent historiography rightly has no place for such interpretations, but the fact that the tropical Caribbean region was made up of fragmented, insular

---

[2] Richard B. Sheridan, *Sugar and Slavery: An Economic History of the British West Indies, 1623–1775* (Barbados, 1974), p. 104.

units rather than presenting a solid land mass to the European colonizing class was surely significant. It permitted the development of a plantation system in which the planter could operate in a highly independent fashion, relying on long-distance trade rather than local markets and inputs, creating a landscape in which the colonial town and merchant had only a marginal place.

Although the analysis that follows in this essay is not intended as a review of the historiography, emphasis will be placed on questions of interpretation that have concerned historians of the British West Indian economy. Most if not all of these questions have significance beyond the region, so that the development of a Caribbean perspective must not be seen as an indication of a creeping parochialism. In terms of theory, the most influential has been the *plantation economy* model, designed to explain the role of the plantation system in the Atlantic economy and the implications of that system for economic growth within the Caribbean. This model draws on staple theory and, more particularly, ideas advanced by Eric Williams in his seminal work, *Capitalism and Slavery,* first published in 1944. Particular questions that can be linked with this set of concepts concern the sources of capital for the plantation system, the "profitability" of the colonies for the British Empire, the drain of wealth from the colonies to Great Britain and the role of that capital in the Industrial Revolution, the failure of industrialization in the colonies themselves, and the causes of slavery and abolition.

Questions more obviously internal to the history of the region, many of which have emerged from discussion of the larger issues, include the reasons for the negative rate of natural increase in the West Indian slave population (often compared to the rapid natural growth experienced in North America); the structure and significance of the domestic economy; the extent of internal economic diversification and of regional variations; the role of trade with non-British imperial territories within the Caribbean; the chronology of plantation profitability and the decline of the British West Indies; the significance of absentee proprietorship for social and economic development; the variety of systems of labor domination after emancipation; and the relationship between the free peasantry and the protopeasantry of the slave period. It is issues such as these that have in recent times provoked substantial debate within the historiography of the British West Indies, emphasizing as they do the equal significance of local perspectives and events with those broader structures and external events that made the region an integral part of the Atlantic world economy.

SUGAR AND SLAVERY

TERRITORIAL EXPANSION

Spanish colonization of the Americas had its beginnings in the Caribbean, but the focus of settlement was the larger western islands that provided springboards to the mainland and the treasure of Mexico and Peru (see map on page 298). The streams of precious metals passed through the islands on their way to the coffers of the King of Spain, placing immense temptation in the way of his European rivals. Contact with the Spanish reduced the indigenous populations of the Greater Antilles to a mere remnant by the middle of the sixteenth century through deliberate genocide, disease, and hard labor. The French and later the English took advantage of the hundreds of islands and thousands of miles of sparsely occupied coastline to engage in illicit trade with the Spanish settlements and to raid and plunder these and the precious metals fleets themselves. English ventures to the Caribbean began with John Hawkins in the 1560s, but it was not until the outbreak of war between England and Spain in 1585 that privateers entered the region in numbers. Privateering, which gave way to piracy in the seventeenth century, was an important source of the capital required for initial settlement and the source of the swashbuckling, risky image of the tropical plantation economies that was to stick fast very much longer.

When the English moved from plunder to settlement in the 1620s, they established themselves in the eastern Caribbean islands of St. Kitts, Nevis, and Barbados, far from the securely fortified western bases of the Spanish. By that time, English as well as French and Dutch marauders had demonstrated the vulnerability of the outlying possessions, and the Spanish had shown themselves unwilling to commit resources to the retention of islands that appeared both unproductive and costly to control. For the private colonizing parties of the English, the first settled islands held the attractions of fertile soils suited to tobacco cultivation, safe harbors, and small Amerindian populations. Antigua and Montserrat were soon added (Table 7.1). Small-scale agricultural economies were created, based largely on tobacco cultivation and the labor of indentured white servants and Amerindian and African slaves. Such fragile settlements were naturally the subject of European rivalry

The Sugar Revolution, felt first in Barbados in the 1640s, transformed the settlers' expectations of profit and led to the addition of the relatively

Table 7.1. *Populations of the British West Indian colonies, 1750 and 1830*

Colony	Year of British Colonization	Area (square miles)	Population 1750				Population 1830			
			Slaves	Whites	Free colored	Total	Slaves	Whites	Free colored	Total
Barbados	1627	166	63,410	16,772	235	80,417	82,026	14,812	5,312	102,150
St. Kitts	1625	65	21,782	2,783	109	24,674	19,094	1,498	2,808	23,400
Nevis	1628	36	8,299	1,118	81	9,498	9,194	453	1,403	11,050
Antigua	1632	108	31,123	3,435	305	34,863	29,600	1,887	5,513	37,000
Montserrat	1632	39	8,767	1,430	86	10,283	6,300	353	847	7,500
Virgin Islands	1672	59	6,062	1,184	59	7,305	5,148	603	1,699	7,450
Jamaica	1655	4,411	127,881	12,000	2,119	142,000	319,074	18,903	40,073	378,050
Dominica	1763	305	5,769	1,718	300	7,787	14,706	703	3,591	19,000
St. Lucia	1803	233	9,764	2,524	506	12,794	13,395	1,012	3,993	18,400
St. Vincent	1763	150	7,184	2,104	230	9,518	23,100	1,400	3,500	28,000
Grenada	1763	133	12,000	1,285	455	13,740	23,884	710	3,806	28,400
Tobago	1763	114	3,082	238	82	3,402	12,551	453	1,146	14,150
Trinidad	1797	1,864	310	126	295	731	22,757	3,323	15,985	42,065
British Guiana	1803	83,000	7,987	726	65	8,778	88,665	3,701	8,234	100,600
British Honduras	1670	8,867	114	50	6	170	1,898	302	2,000	4,200
Cayman Islands	1734	100	100	70	—	170	1,000	350	150	1,500
Bahamas	1648	5,548	1,145	1,268	76	2,489	9,503	5,007	2,520	17,030
Anguilla	1650	35	1,962	350	38	2,350	2,600	300	400	3,300
Barbuda	1685	62	150	40	—	190	500	3	—	503
			316,891	49,221	5,047	371,159	684,995	55,773	102,980	843,748

Sources: B. W. Higman, *Slave Populations of the British Caribbean, 1807–1834* (Baltimore, 1984), 41; Stanley L. Engerman and B. W. Higman, "The Demographic Structure of the Caribbean Slave Societies in the Eighteenth and Nineteenth Centuries," in Franklin W. Knight, ed., *UNESCO General History of the Caribbean*, Vol. III (in press).

large island of Jamaica to the English colonies in 1655. Throughout the seventeenth century, however, the wealth to be gained by piracy and plunder rivaled that offered by sugar planting, and Jamaica moved only gradually from a mercantile to a plantation economy. The capture of Jamaica from the Spanish was unusual in being a state venture, an unintended result of Oliver Cromwell's "Western Design," which was really meant to take Cuba or Hispaniola and to displace the Dutch.

In the second phase of British settlement, during the 1760s, the state became the instigator. All of the Caribbean islands added to the Empire in that decade were "conquered" colonies, acquired through European treaties rather than being taken directly from indigenous peoples. Dominica, St. Vincent, Tobago, Grenada, and the Grenadines were ceded to Britain under the Peace of Paris, concluded in 1763, but did not remain secure as British territory. Tobago was occupied by the French between 1780 and 1803, and Dominica between 1778 and 1784. All of the islands in this group were relatively small, adding only 700 square miles to the British Empire, compared to the 10,000 square miles acquired in the seventeenth century.

This second phase of British expansion occurred during what Richard Pares termed the *silver age* of sugar (in contrast to the short-lived *golden age* of the 1640s). During this "era of West Indian prosperity," stretching from 1750 to 1775, according to Richard Sheridan, metropolitan sugar prices remained high, and British settlement quickly changed the diversified agricultural economies of the ceded islands into sugar monocultures.[3] The minor export staples – cacao, coffee, and cotton – were not completely abandoned, however, because the wet and mountainous environments of the islands prevented a transformation as total as that seen in Barbados and the Leeward Islands.

The third and final phase of British expansion in the Caribbean saw Trinidad taken from the Spanish in 1797, St. Lucia from the French in 1803, and Demerara, Essequibo, and Berbice (which came to be called collectively British Guiana and, later, Guyana) taken from the Dutch in the same year. Trinidad and St. Lucia were, like the ceded islands, latecomers to the Sugar Revolution. The British continued the trend toward sugar cultivation, but once again the physical environments of the islands prevented the emergence of full-scale monocultures. The mainland colonies of Guyana became a focus for planters in the long-settled British islands, many of

---

[3] Richard Pares, *Merchants and Planters,* Economic History Review Supplement 4 (Cambridge, 1960), p. 40; Richard Sheridan, *An Era of West Indian Prosperity, 1750–1775* (Barbados, 1970).

whom moved their slaves to plantations on the rich coastal soils. For a brief period, these colonies became the largest producers of cotton and coffee in the British Empire, but they were forced to retreat as sugar was promoted and United States cotton came to dominate the market. The total land area added to the Empire in this final phase was large (Table 7.1), but the effective area of settlement was limited to the coastal and riverine zones of Guyana, making the gross amount misleading.

In terms of territorial extent, the British Empire in the Caribbean was a constantly expanding entity with regular increments to its resource base and potential for production. Thus, there was always the possibility of increasing output by bringing new lands into cultivation as well as by improving factor productivity. This potential was closed off only in the early nineteenth century, and even then several of the newly acquired colonies contained within them a significant open frontier.

Another important feature of the pattern of British territorial expansion in the Caribbean is that it reflected the fragmented, insular character of the region as a whole. Spain's colonies came to be confined to the larger islands of the western Caribbean, but for the British as well as the French and Dutch, there was a dispersion and interdigitation of colonial possessions that served to exaggerate the insular nature of the settlements and their separate political and economic relations, and, simultaneously, to facilitate trade and communication with the colonies of other empires whether or not this was permitted by law. These aspects of colonization were particularly important for the British, because their colonies were the most widely scattered within the Caribbean.

Of great significance for the British West Indian economy was the diversity of land types and resource bases contained within the Empire's possessions. Not only did the colonies differ in size, shape, and location; they also varied in topography, soils, and climate. Some were flat, never rising above 200 feet. This was true of the Bahamas, Anguilla, Barbuda, and the Cayman Islands, none of which produced sugar or depended on the plantation system. It was also true of the coastal settlements of British Honduras (Belize) and Guyana, the latter supporting one of the most complete plantation regimes. The low-lying islands were made up of shallow limestone banks and coral reefs, with thin soils, light rainfall, and frequent droughts. The other island colonies belonged to partially submerged mountain systems and tended to be relatively rugged, while Barbados was composed of coral terraces resting on a submarine ridge and hence displayed a more gentle topography. Especially in the larger islands, such as Jamaica, the internal variety of topography, soil, and climate was great.

POPULATION AND LABOR

The population history of the British West Indies until 1850 was a product of the plantation system's demand for labor. In the initial stages of settlement, before the Sugar Revolution, it seemed the islands might follow the same course as the mainland colonies. The Sugar Revolution dramatically altered that trajectory, creating a population dominated by African slaves, in which the white component declined persistently and the mixed or "coloured" sector grew. Both the African and the white populations depended on immigration to sustain their numbers – forced migration through the Atlantic slave trade in the case of the Africans, and a mixture of voluntary and involuntary movements in the case of the whites.

Only in the later phases of British expansion in the Caribbean did colonization begin with a substantial existing population. The small Amerindian communities of the Leeward Islands were sometimes enslaved but were more often the subject of genocide. One reason why Barbados was so attractive to the English was that it was uninhabited at the time of settlement. The Amerindian population of Jamaica had been almost completely destroyed as a result of the encounter with the Spanish, and the smallness of the slave and free population facilitated the island's capture by the English. Amerindians made up larger proportions of the populations found in the Windward Islands, Trinidad, and Guyana, but in no case did they have a significant impact on the overall pattern of growth. On the other hand, the established French, Dutch, and Spanish settler populations of the colonies acquired late by the British, and more importantly their slave populations, provided a substantial base and tended to be more influential culturally.

British territorial expansion in the Caribbean did not mean an increasing share of the region's population or of that of the British Empire in the Americas. Rather, the British West Indian population reached an early peak on these indicators and experienced a steady relative decline from about 1700. The islands did have a larger population than the mainland colonies until the 1660s but then quickly slipped behind; by 1775, the colonies that joined the Revolution had more than four times as many people (2,204,500 according to Robert Wells) as the British West Indies

(483,000).[4] This disparity is not surprising in view of the difference in the available land area; it is the initial dominance of the tropical island colonies that requires explanation.

Further contrasts of significance appear when the components of the populations are considered. The most obvious, something very apparent to contemporary observers, was the relative importance of blacks and whites. In 1670, when the mainland settlements first outstripped the islands, already had twice as many whites yet the islands had more than ten times the number of blacks, almost all of them slaves. It was not until the time of the American Revolution that the slave population of the mainland (460,000 according to John McCusker) exceeded that of the islands (434,000).[5] Thereafter, the gap widened dramatically. The slave population of the British West Indies failed to achieve a positive natural increase and depended for continued growth on the Atlantic slave trade, which was closed by the British in 1808. The slave population of the mainland, on the other hand, grew rapidly through natural increase and relied relatively little on imports. Once again, this contrast struck contemporaries forcibly and demands analysis.

In both the island and mainland colonies, the ratio of blacks to whites increased steadily between 1620 and 1770, but the ratio on the mainland in 1770 (0.27) was barely above that found on the islands as early as 1640. In the sugar colonies, however, the ratio jumped to 1.2 by 1670, 5.0 in 1720, 10.2 in 1780, and 12.5 in 1830 immediately before emancipation.[6] Even within the Caribbean, the British colonies exhibited a relatively high black:white ratio; only the French settlements approached similar levels.

Why did black slavery become such a dominant feature of the British West Indian labor force? Contemporary whites explained this development in simple racial terms, referring to the inability of the white man to perform manual labor in a tropical climate and, on the other hand, the natural place of the black in such an environment. The English in the West Indies, much more than the Spanish and even the French, saw the islands as sites of production rather than colonies of settlement. In consequence, they became absentee proprietors as soon as their plantation profits could support them at home, thus escaping the debilitating diseases of the tropics and fulfilling ambitions of elevated status in English society.

[4] Robert V. Wells, *The Population of the British Colonies in America before 1776: A Survey of Census Data* (Princeton, 1975), p. 284.

[5] John J. McCusker, *Rum and the American Revolution: The Rum Trade and the Balance of Payments of the Thirteen Continental Colonies* (New York, 1989), 584, 712.

[6] B. W. Higman, *Slave Populations of the British Caribbean, 1807–1834* (Baltimore, 1984), 77, 112.

They played for high stakes, hoping to make their fortunes quicker than death could catch them in this high-risk disease environment. By concentrating on the production of sugar, the crop with the greatest returns to investment, and employing large gangs of black slave labor working under a small corps of white supervisors, a high proportion of planters in the British West Indies managed to achieve their long-term goals and become absentees within a generation or so.

Absentee proprietorship tended to be most common in colonies with the heaviest focus on sugar. The exception was Barbados, which retained a significant residential planter class throughout the period of slavery. In 1830, for example, whites still made up 14.5 percent of the population of Barbados, compared to less than 5.0 percent in almost all of the other British sugar colonies. This pattern reflected the relatively small scale of the sugar plantations of Barbados. Wherever sugar was produced on really large units (of more than 1,000 acres or 250 slaves), absentee ownership had become the norm by the late eighteenth century. At the time of emancipation, more than half of the slaves of Jamaica belonged to absentees. Only in the marginal, nonsugar colonies, such as the Bahamas and the Cayman Islands, did whites amount to more than 20 percent of the population, and these islands contained no more than a minute proportion of the total British West Indian population.

Modern explanations for the dominance of black slavery in the British West Indies generally draw on large-scale theories applicable to all regions of the Americas. An argument particularly associated with Evsey Domar in its modern version contends that slavery and other forms of involuntary labor tend to occur in areas with low population densities or "open resources."[7] In places such as Barbados, according to this model, entrepreneurs wishing to produce a high-value product like sugar needed to make a large investment in land and processing plant and, therefore, had to secure large labor forces in order to ensure continuity of output and profits. Free persons were too easily able to obtain land of their own in Barbados, or in other parts of the seventeenth-century Caribbean and North American mainland, to supply dependable and productive wage labor on sugar plantations.

Barbados and most of the other Caribbean territories colonized by the British in the seventeenth and eighteenth centuries had no significant indigenous populations by that time; hence, population density was indeed low, and all labor had to be imported. It is clear, however, that

---

[7] Evsey D. Domar, "The Causes of Slavery or Serfdom: A Hypothesis," *Journal of Economic History* 30 (1970), 18–32.

population density by itself cannot account for the central role of involuntary labor in the British West Indies. The existence of a capitalist entrepreneurial class, determined to make fortunes without themselves performing manual labor, was equally essential. The *population-density theory* in its simple form may also be challenged on the grounds that it cannot say why slaves came to be preferred over indentured servants – a transition that occurred in Barbados as a consequence of the sugar revolution of the 1640s – or why blacks were enslaved while whites were indentured. Once the system had been firmly established, these questions could be answered with a sense of inevitability, and the system could easily spread to new areas which lacked the originating variables. But it was in the Caribbean and, most fundamentally for the British, in Barbados that the decisions were first made. There was nothing inevitable about that genesis. Models existed in Brazil and the Atlantic Islands, but the association of sugar and slavery was cemented in Barbados and the other British West Indian colonies. The planters or protoplanters of Barbados have been conceived as rational profit maximizers, who shifted from white indentured servants to black slaves because the marginal revenues derivable from slave labor came to be larger.[8] This shift had to do with changes on the supply side, in Great Britain and Africa, and the advantages to the planter of having a slave's labor for life as well as the labor of his/her children, contrasted to the limited labor periods of indenture. As long as the white servants remained under indenture, it has been argued, their conditions of labor and standards of living were very similar to those experienced by black slaves, and their labor time had a capital value that was equally transferable. At the same time, all of the decisions underlying these conditions and transitions were taken within the context of a deep-seated racism that, at the very least, provided ideological rationalizations for behavior that appeared to conform with economic rationality on the planter's part.

Once established, the slave system of the British West Indies proved a voracious consumer of black people. If the planters saw profit in the offspring of the slaves, they also saw disadvantages in having pregnant and nursing women in their field gangs, and they chose to "buy rather than

---

[8] Hilary McD. Beckles and Andrew Downes, "An Economic Formalisation of the Origins of Black Slavery in the British West Indies, 1624–1645," *Social and Economic Studies* 34 (1985), 1–24; Hilary McD. Beckles, *White Servitude and Black Slavery in Barbados, 1627–1715* (Knoxville, 1989); David W. Galenson, *White Servitude in Colonial America: An Economic Analysis* (Cambridge, 1981); and Russell R. Menard, "From Servants to Slaves: The Transformation of the Chesapeake Labor Force," *Southern Studies* 16 (1973), 355–90.

breed." There is debate among scholars regarding the relative importance of fertility and mortality in this general failure of the West Indian slave population to grow by natural increase. What is certain is that there was a very strong association between sugar production on large-scale plantations and the decline of the slave population. Only in the case of Barbados did a positive natural increase occur, before the abolition of the British Atlantic slave trade in 1808. Where crops other than sugar were grown, particularly in the nonplantation colonies, there was, however, quite rapid growth through natural increase. This contrast seems to have little to do with differences in the natural environment or the disease environment in which the slaves lived. Nutritional deficiencies played a part, as can be seen in the relatively short stature of the slaves in the sugar colonies, but it was the environment of labor in gangs, under brutal management, together with unusually long hours of work in factory as well as field, that best explains the demographic crisis.[9]

The failure of natural increase was accompanied by very large imports of Africans into the British West Indian colonies. Over the whole history of the Atlantic slave trade, according to the estimates of Philip Curtin, the British West Indies (excluding Guyana) imported 1,657,000 slaves, or 17.3 percent of the total inflow into the Americas. By comparison, the territories of the United States received only 4.5 percent of the total, reflecting a very different demand and experience of growth by natural increase. Of the British West Indian colonies, the largest receiver was Jamaica, with 748,000 slaves imported, and a slave population of just 354,000 in 1808 at the end of the Atlantic trade. Barbados took 387,000, and the Leeward Islands 346,000. Territories settled by the British at the end of the eighteenth century saw high levels of imports in the short-term but did not experience the sustained inflows typical of the older colonies.[10] Some of the British territories, especially Jamaica, engaged in a reexport trade, sending slaves to nearby Spanish Caribbean colonies.

Whites in the British West Indies also experienced relatively high mortality rates, so high that Richard Dunn has called the region a demographic disaster area.[11] This experience was a spur to absentee proprietorship, and it also contributed to the emigration and resettlement of some

[9] Higman, *Slave Populations*, 280–378.
[10] Philip D. Curtin, *The Atlantic Slave Trade: A Census* (Madison, 1969), 88–9; Stanley L. Engerman and B. W. Higman, "The Demographic Structure of the Caribbean Slave Societies in the Eighteenth and Nineteenth Centuries," in Franklin W. Knight, ed., *UNESCO General History of the Caribbean*, Vol. III (forthcoming).
[11] Richard S. Dunn, *Sugar and Slaves: The Rise of the Planter Class in the English West Indies, 1624–1713* (Chapel Hill, 1972), 334.

English colonizers and time-expired indentured servants. Most of the latter moved to the mainland colonies of North America, remaining within the British imperial system. Occasionally, planters forced their slaves and servants to move with them, as in the well-known migration from Barbados to South Carolina in the second half of the seventeenth century. There was also a steady stream of movement from the older sugar colonies and the nonplantation colonies to the newly settled British territories within the Caribbean, continuing to the time of emancipation. Very often this meant removal from relatively healthy locations to sites of intense plantation production and high mortality. For the white population, migration within the Atlantic world led to a complex network of kinship and communication that contributed to the development of interregional trade and placed the tropical and temperate colonies of the British in reciprocal economic dependence within the larger framework of mercantilism. In many respects, this was an experience denied the black slave population, tied as they were to their owners' plantations.

Settlement patterns within the British West Indian colonies during slavery were fairly simple. More than 90 percent of the population was rural; the majority lived in large plantation units, each with its own community identity and clearly defined boundaries. The slaves typically lived in "villages" of 30 to 70 huts or houses (hardly ever in barracks) located close to the sugar factory and the "great house" of the owner or overseer. These plantation domains dominated the landscape. Interspersed were smallholders' farms with their own minor population nucleations. In the larger territories, such as Jamaica and Guyana, Maroons lived in separate, isolated communities in the interior, on lands granted by treaty following successful guerrilla warfare by slave bands. Almost all of the true towns of the colonies were also ports, strung along the coastlines of the islands. The largest of these towns, Kingston in Jamaica, had a total population of about 35,000 in 1810, and the concentration of slaves in towns was in fact significantly greater in the West Indies than in the United States at that time.[12]

PLANTATION ECONOMY

Just as there was nothing inevitable about the centrality of black slavery in the labor force of the British West Indian colonies, so the commanding role of sugar and the plantation was by no means foreordained. Arguments

[12] Higman, *Slave Populations*, 93–4.

advanced to account for these patterns of economic organization often see sugar, slavery, and the plantation as a trinity, indivisible and essentially determined by the production function of sugar associated with a particular stage of technological development. This can be regarded as a variety of crop determinism, more sophisticated than earlier determinist models based on climate or race but still reductionist in effect if not in intent.

Sugar cane requires intensive cultivation. In the seventeenth century, this meant hand hoeing and digging of cane holes in preparation for planting; regular weeding during the growing phase; and heavy labor in the cutting of canes during a harvest or "crop" season, often extending over half the year. More important than these requirements was the fact that the milling (grinding) of sugar cane should take place within 48 hours of harvest in order to obtain satisfactory returns of juice. The milling machinery used in the West Indies in the seventeenth and eighteenth centuries was relatively advanced; it used animal, wind, or water power, dependent on expensive aqueducts, mill towers, or herds of livestock. The boiling and curing processes also required heavy capital investment in buildings and machinery, and additional resources were needed if rum was to be distilled as a part of the enterprise.

Cane could be grown by smallholders, using their own labor, and it is indeed grown this way to some extent in many parts of the tropical world today. As long as sugar mills remained small-scale, however, the cane farmer could sell to competing mills in a region, merely having to weigh the cost of cartage. No miller could dominate an entire region in the way that modern central sugar mills can do. Further, the smallholder could in turn choose to produce alternate crops, such as tobacco or cotton, in response to short-term changes in market conditions. Thus, the seventeenth-century sugar miller, having invested in expensive capital equipment, was determined to maximize returns by ensuring a constant supply of cane and, in order to achieve this goal, sought to monopolize ownership of land immediately surrounding the mill site to an extent sufficient to cultivate cane equal to the annual capacity of the mill. The outcome was that millers came also to be planters, controlling large estates. The demands of intensive cultivation and harvest operations meant, in turn, the need for a large labor force, committed to labor on the planter's property. The planter's solution was black slavery, which involved the most total control of people as workers. The high demand for sugar in Europe, and the consequent high price for the commodity, created large profits and confirmed for the planter-miller the correctness of his choice.

The 1640s, the primary decade of the Sugar Revolution, saw a great deal of experimentation. Different types of labor arrangements were tried, as were different methods of relating cane cultivation to sugar processing, and different technologies in field and factory. There was also experimentation with alternative crops. Sugar emerged as champion because of the high returns it offered to investment; once this choice had been made by the potential nonlaboring, protocapitalist class, the plantation economy emerged as the most profitable solution within the constraints of contemporary technology and allowable systems of exploiting the labor of specified groups of human beings. All of these decisions were embedded in seventeenth-century European economic ideology and moral philosophy. It must be emphasized also that the English were not required to be the original creators of this system. They manipulated models of plantation economy and technology that had been already established in Brazil and carried to the West Indies by Dutch traders, who also provided slaves and credit to enable the English planters to establish plantations on a grand scale.[13]

Once the sugar-slavery-plantation system had been firmly established in Barbados and the Leeward Islands, it was rapidly diffused to other English West Indian colonies and replicated in detail. Some scholars have argued that the technology remained fixed until the time of emancipation and that slavery was incompatible with invention and innovation. It is also argued by some that absenteeism made the planters poorly informed managers of their properties and reluctant innovators. Recent research has largely rejected this view. In fact, there is evidence of significant innovation in cultivation techniques during the eighteenth century and a willingness to accept new high-yield cane varieties. Numerous inventions were patented in the islands for improved milling and processing machinery, and Jamaica was the site of the first industrial application of steam power to any manufacturing process, in 1768. Boulton and Watt found a substantial market for their steam engines, particularly in Jamaica and the new sugar colonies of the British Caribbean.[14]

[13] Robert Carlyle Batie, "Why Sugar? Economic Cycles and the Changing of Staples on the English and French Antilles, 1624–54," *Journal of Caribbean History* 8 (1976), 1–41; Jonathan I. Israel, *Dutch Primacy in World Trade, 1585–1740* (Oxford, 1989), 236–7; P. C. Emmer, "The Dutch and the Making of the Second Atlantic System," in Barbara L. Solow, ed., *Slavery and the Rise of the Atlantic System* (Cambridge, 1991), 75–96.

[14] J. H. Galloway, *The Sugar Cane Industry: An Historical Geography from Its Origins to 1914* (Cambridge, 1989), 134–42; Noel Deerr and Alexander Brooks, "The Early Use of Steam Power in the Cane Sugar Industry," *Transactions of the Newcomen Society* 21 (1940–1), 11–21; B. W. Higman, *Jamaica Surveyed: Plantation Maps and Plans of the Eighteenth and Nineteenth Centuries* (Kingston, 1988), 111–58; Veront M. Satchell, *Technological Change and the Jamaican Sugar Industry, 1750–1830* (unpublished Ph.D. dissertation, University of the West Indies, Mona, 1994).

The plantation itself was only the most fundamental unit in a much larger system, called by some the *plantation complex,* which was in turn an essential element in the Atlantic world economy.[15] The distinguishing characteristics of the *plantation economy model* were export-orientation, monoculture, and large-scale production units. This model, articulated by West Indian political economists in the 1960s, has since come to be seen as too rigid to represent accurately the historical experience of the region.[16] In the first place, there were breaches in the system resulting from slave resistance and accommodation, from diversity in the resource base, and from changes in the political and commercial regulation of the colonies. To some extent, it may be argued that the significance of these breaches depends on the perspective taken. From a metropolitan point of view, they did not always appear to upset seriously the system as a whole. From the vantage point of the Caribbean, and particularly from the perspective of the slave community, the breaches were important in indicating the creation of a "dual" or "creole economy," which challenged the basic assumptions of the planter class about the distribution of power and affirmed the cultural creativity and economic productivity of the Africans and the "lesser whites."[17]

Plantation land-use patterns varied according to topography. Where the whole of a plantation's land area consisted of soils suited to cane cultivation — as was commonly the case in, for example, Barbados — other crops were given little space. Some land was used for pasture, to feed the animals used in traction, and food crops for consumption by the slaves were intercropped with cane. Overall, plantations of this type fitted very closely the plantation economy model of monoculture and export-orientation, depending heavily on external sources for many of their inputs — food, livestock, and timber, in particular. Elsewhere, and most obviously in the case of Jamaica, the plantations were normally much larger (1,000 acres compared to 200 in Barbados) and contained within their boundaries a variety of

---

[15] Philip D. Curtin, *The Rise and Fall of the Plantation Complex: Essays in Atlantic History* (Cambridge, 1990).

[16] Lloyd Best, "Outlines of a Model of Pure Plantation Economy," *Social and Economic Studies* 17 (1968), 283–326; George L. Beckford, *Persistent Poverty: Underdevelopment in Plantation Economies of the Third World* (New York, 1972); Hilary McD. Beckles, " 'The Williams Effect': Eric Williams's *Capitalism and Slavery* and the Growth of West Indian Political Economy," in Barbara L. Solow and Stanley L. Engerman, eds., *British Capitalism and Caribbean Slavery: The Legacy of Eric Williams* (Cambridge, 1987); Alex Dupuy, "Slavery and Underdevelopment in the Caribbean: A Critique of the 'Plantation Economy' Perspective," *Dialectical Anthropology,* 7 (1983), 237–51.

[17] Richard B. Sheridan, "From Chattel to Wage Slavery in Jamaica, 1740–1860," *Slavery and Abolition* 14 (1993), 13; Edward Brathwaite, *The Development of Creole Society in Jamaica, 1770–1820* (Oxford, 1971), 80–95.

soils and topographic zones. This variety meant that even where, say, 300 acres were planted in cane, a large proportion of the space could be retained in woodland (to supply fuel, lumber for building and furniture, and staves for the sugar casks, for example), pasture (to raise and maintain livestock), and most importantly "provision grounds" (for the slaves' cultivation of food crops for their own use). The diversity of land types in Jamaica also meant that plantations could combine other export staples (such as coffee, cotton, indigo, and pimento) with sugar production, and that plantations specializing in different crops could be found in different regions of the island, creating the potential for an internal trade between plantation units. Extensive areas of Jamaica were devoted to livestock raising on properties known as *pens,* and these played a vital role in the internal trade of the island.[18] Between the extremes of Jamaica and Barbados, the other British West Indian sugar colonies showed a range of variety in their mix of crops, while the nonsugar colonies concentrated on items such as logwood, mahogany, cotton, and salt, all for export, and food crops for local consumption.

It was the *provision-ground system* that did most to transform the character of plantation economy, since it provided a strictly domestic orientation and must be seen as the joint creation of the slave and slaveowning classes. This system emerged early in Jamaica and came to be common in many other colonies where the resource base was conducive. Its ultimate origin can be found in the planters' desire to reduce expenditure both on imported food supplies for their slaves and on the alternative method of producing food by the slave mode of supervised gang labor. Where lands existed that were unsuited to sugar cultivation, or in excess of the factory's ability to process, the planters allocated plots to the slaves and forced them to cultivate their own food crops. The planters also allocated small areas around the slaves' huts to be used as gardens. Although this provision-ground system meant that the slaves had to work longer hours than where rationed allowances were provided, the system had attractions that made most slaves willing participants. Above all, it provided the potential for choice. The slaves could decide what to plant and when, how to cultivate, when and what to harvest, whether to consume or market the produce, with whom to share, and how to use the proceeds of sales and exchange. The system also provided a temporary escape from the regimentation of gang labor, the whip of the driver, and the routine of the factory. It offered

[18] B. W. Higman, *Slave Population and Economy in Jamaica, 1807–1834* (Cambridge, 1976); Verene A. Shepherd, "Livestock and Sugar: Aspects of Jamaica's Agricultural Development from the Late Seventeenth to the Early Nineteenth Century," *Historical Journal* 34 (1991), 627–43.

opportunities for marketing, accumulation, and the acquisition of consumption goods, including imported items.[19] It is less certain that the system served to improve nutrition, and the reverse may be true. But there is no doubt that the provision-ground system, together with the diversity of plantation production, created an economic landscape which from many points of view was not composed of an unbroken blanket of sugar cane.

PRODUCTION AND TRADE

Throughout the period of slavery, British West Indian production was measured by the planters and imperial government almost exclusively in terms of the quantities of sugar shipped by the colonies. The profitability of plantation enterprise and of empire were measured in the same way. From the colonial perspective, however, the slave community must have thought more of variations in the productivity of their provision grounds, their most immediate source of sustenance, and the prices which their produce could command in the local markets. Drought and hunger walked hand in hand, and the price of sugar in the London market meant relatively little for the everyday living standard of the slave. The free colored people and the lesser whites often shared this domestic orientation, though the markets for their goods and services tended to depend more directly on what was happening in the sugar sector.

Attempts to quantify the output and productivity of the different sectors of the British West Indian economy are constrained by the state's limited conception of the kinds of data that should be collected. Even in the case of sugar, statistics are available for exports but not for total production, because data were collected only where goods entered the net of the customs house. The same applied to rum, coffee, the other export staples, and all perishable products which were not exportable with existing technology. Thus, the extent to which an accurate picture of total output can be constructed depends on the ratio of exports to production for each item.

West Indian slaves were surrounded by vast storehouses of energy, the cane fields, yet they were permitted to consume only a small proportion of that bounty. In general, less than 2 percent of the sugar produced was sold within the colonies, to local merchants and planters, and an even

---

[19] Sidney W. Mintz and Douglas Hall, "The Origins of the Jamaican Internal Marketing System," *Yale University Publications in Anthropology*, No. 57 (1960); Sidney W. Mintz, "Caribbean Marketplaces and Caribbean History," *Nova Americana* 1 (1978), 333–44; Higman, *Slave Populations*, 204–18.

smaller proportion was consumed by the producers. The byproduct molasses was also largely directed toward the export market. Rum, on the other hand, was consumed heavily by the colonial population.[20] It was used to lubricate the internal market, covering local costs wherever possible. The other export staples — coffee, cotton, indigo, pimento, cacao, logwood, mahogany — all had very high export:output ratios, so it is only for rum that the external trade data provide a truly inadequate measure of production. For the products directed entirely at the local market, the data are uniformly problematic.

From the 1640s to the time of emancipation, sugar steadily increased its share of output and trade. The minor staples were driven out, surviving successfully only in the late-settled colonies, such as Dominica and Grenada, and in ecological zones unsuited to sugar, such as the Blue Mountain coffee region of Jamaica. By 1830, sugar and its byproducts molasses and rum accounted for 97 to 98 percent of the value of exports from Barbados and the Leeward Islands, and 90 percent for Trinidad. For Jamaica, they composed only 72 percent of total exports, and for most of the late-settled colonies an even smaller proportion.

Seventeenth-century trade data for the British West Indies are fragmentary. Sugar exports from Barbados increased rapidly from about 3,750 tons in 1651 to 9,525 tons in 1669, in which year the Leeward Islands exported only 1,679 tons and Jamaica 500 tons. From 1698 to 1834, the data are much more complete.[21] Trends for a sample of colonies are shown in Figure 7.1. Barbados had by 1698 already increased its exports to more than 13,000 tons, but this proved to be a peak followed by stagnation and absolute decline into the 1770s. Minor troughs in the graph indicate short-term difficulties, such as droughts and hurricanes, but the longer-term decline is generally attributed to soil exhaustion and a failure to innovate. Barbados experienced something of a revival in the late eighteenth century, however, characterized by improved methods of cultivation, adoption of new cane varieties, and better factory technologies. By 1834, exports reached almost 20,000 tons. Jamaica, on the other hand, showed steady and almost uninterrupted growth in the eighteenth century. It had surpassed Barbados by 1730 and the Leeward Islands group by

[20] B. W. Higman, "Jamaican Port Towns in the Early Nineteenth Century," in Franklin W. Knight and Peggy K. Liss, eds., *Atlantic Port Cities: Economy, Culture, and Society in the Atlantic World, 1650–1850* (Knoxville, 1991), 117–48; Higman, *Slave Populations*, 52–66; Higman, *Slave Population and Economy*, 21.

[21] Noel Deerr, *The History of Sugar* (London, 1949–50); Galloway, *Sugar Cane Industry*, 86; Hilary McD. Beckles, *A History of Barbados: From Amerindian Settlement to Nation-state* (Cambridge, 1990), 22.

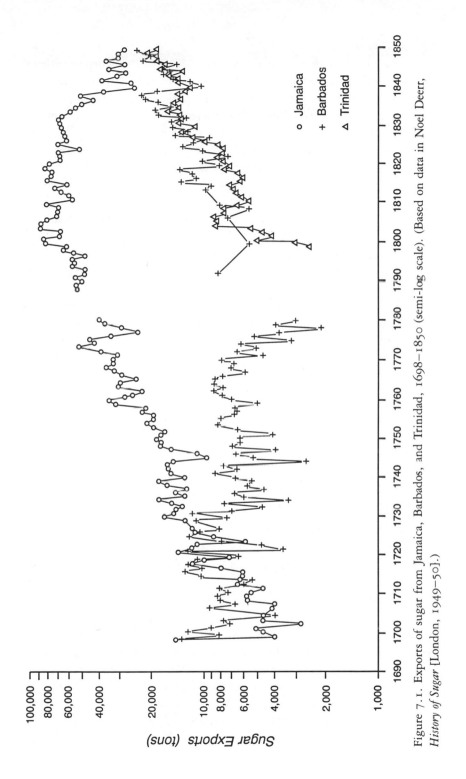

Figure 7.1. Exports of sugar from Jamaica, Barbados, and Trinidad, 1698–1850 (semi-log scale). (Based on data in Noel Deerr, *History of Sugar* [London, 1949–50].)

1740, reaching a peak of almost 100,000 tons in 1805, when the island was the world's largest exporter. Jamaica then declined and stagnated through the same period that saw growth in Barbados, until the time of emancipation. By then, Guyana had increased its output to become a serious rival. Jamaica had already been overtaken by Cuba, in 1829. The dominance of the British West Indies as a group in the early nineteenth century owed much to the collapse of the sugar industry in St. Domingue/ Haiti following the great slave revolution of the 1790s. St. Domingue's exports had exceeded those of Jamaica by the 1750s and did so regularly until 1792. But the segmentation of international/imperial markets, which persisted until 1834, meant that the sugar of the British West Indies did not have to compete on equal terms with the products of the French and Spanish colonies, and competition tended more often to be between the individual British colonies.

Long-term trends in the production and export of other crops are harder to establish. Rum production tended to move in tandem with sugar but became relatively more important during the eighteenth century as markets developed and expanded in North America. Jamaica's export of rum peaked at 6.8 million gallons in 1806, the year following peak sugar exports. Molasses, the base ingredient of rum, naturally became somewhat less important as an export commodity. North American distillers took the most. By about 1770, according to McCusker and Menard, the British West Indies exported molasses to the value of £9,648 sterling to North America and only £222 to Great Britain. Rum exports, however, valued £380,943 to Great Britain and £333,337 to North America, and sugar exports valued £3,002,750 to Great Britain and £183,700 to North America.[22]

Coffee came late to the Caribbean but exhibited rapid growth for a brief period. The case of Jamaica was most spectacular. Exports increased sharply from just 1 million pounds in 1789 to peak at 34 million in 1814, falling off to 17 million in 1834. This boom and bust pattern followed deforestation of the Jamaican mountains and disastrous erosion in storms. In the new sugar colonies of the eastern Caribbean, coffee exports fell sharply after 1800 but as a consequence of crop replacement rather than environmental disaster. Cotton exports declined in the long term, sometimes being replaced by sugar and sometimes as a result of the depletion of the soil, as in the Bahamas. Cacao boomed in Trinidad,

---

[22] McCusker and Menard, *Economy of British America*, 160.

in the early nineteenth century, and various other crops experienced brief periods of significance in some colonies. Occasionally, minor crops produced by slaves in their own time entered the export markets – as, for example, arrowroot in St. Vincent and Barbados[23] – but the lion's share of British West Indian external trade consisted of plantation-produced sugar and rum.

National income estimates are rare for the British West Indies in the period before 1850. Accounts have, however, been prepared for Jamaica in 1832 and 1850, and Guyana in 1832 and 1852, calculated by Gisela Eisner and Michael Moohr, respectively.[24] Unfortunately, these data are not easily compared because Moohr's estimates are expressed only in 1913 prices, whereas Eisner offers estimates at both current and 1910 prices. The difference is significant, particularly due to the substantial decline in metropolitan sugar prices over the long term. In spite of these deficiencies, the accounts provide the best approach to an understanding of the components of the total economies.

According to Eisner, exports accounted for 41.4 percent of the Gross Domestic Product of Jamaica in 1832, at current prices, or 31.7 percent at 1910 prices, compared to 43.3 percent for Guyana at 1913 prices. Recalculating Moohr's data gives roughly 56 percent at 1832 prices. These gross contrasts show at least that the internal economy of Jamaica was relatively very important, since comparison with the "pure" plantation economies of Barbados and the Leeward Islands would certainly reveal an even greater disparity than Guyana. Eisner estimated "food production for local consumption" at 17.8 percent of Gross Domestic Product in Jamaica in 1832 at current prices (or 28.6 percent at 1910 prices), a proportion very similar to Moohr's estimate for Guyana. Eisner attributed the vast majority of this food production to "Ground Provisions," meaning the basic tuber and tree crops cultivated by the slaves on their provision grounds. Other items that contributed significantly to Jamaica's Gross Domestic Product in 1832 were ownership of houses (11.0 percent at current prices), public administration (6.4 percent), manufacturing for local consumption (6.3 percent), and distribution (5.7 percent).

Of particular interest in this national-income accounting exercise is the categorization of Gross Domestic Product, in which the models of both

[23] J. S. Handler, "The History of Arrowroot and the Origin of Peasantries in the British West Indies," *Journal of Caribbean History* 2 (1971), 46–93.

[24] Gisela Eisner, *Jamaica, 1830–1930: A Study in Economic Growth* (Manchester, 1961), 118–9; Michael Moohr, "The Economic Impact of Slave Emancipation in British Guiana, 1832–1852," *Economic History Review* 25 (1972), 589.

Eisner and Moohr distinguish "exports" from "manufacturing for local consumption" but make no attempt to separate the product of agriculture and manufacturing generally. The category "manufacturing for local consumption" was made up entirely of sugar and rum consumed within the colony, and it is acceptable to assume that other manufacturing for the domestic market was indeed on a small scale. On the other hand, the category "exports" includes the majority of the rum and most of the sugar produced by the plantations. The question is, should this not be divided into agricultural and manufacturing components? Eisner explicitly argues that manufacturing in Jamaica "was limited to the processing necessary to ensure good condition for overseas markets." The fact that sugar cane and its juice could not be exported efficiently because of the bulk and rapid rate of deterioration did not make the sugar factory a mere site for "processing" rather than manufacturing. These processes were quite elaborate and the technology complex. Eisner's bald statement that "rum distillation has to be done locally" is not supportable and is actually denied by the vibrant trade in molasses from the British and French colonies of the eastern Caribbean to the distilleries of New England. Planters could choose to make different proportions of sugar, molasses, and rum from a fixed quantity of sugar cane. It is equally misleading to say that "manufacturing industry in Jamaica lacked the natural stimulus of raw materials and cheap fuel."[25] The raw material was the cane, and the cheap fuel was, above all, water power, just as it was in the "first" Industrial Revolution in Great Britain.

The sugar factory and distillery had a volume of output and labor force on a scale rarely matched in European or North American factories before the end of the eighteenth century, and it had a management regime with many "modern" industrial features. It is true that the linkages of this system were largely external to the region and that the development of the factory did not lead to an industrial revolution within the Caribbean. But the "exports" category in the Gross Domestic Product estimates for both Jamaica and Guyana needs to be disaggregated to indicate a substantial contribution from manufacturing alongside agriculture. The result is a reduction in (1) the apparent gap between pre-industrial Europe, colonial North America, and the sugar plantation economies of the British West Indies in terms of their relative stages of development as indicated by the quantity and composition of their output, and (2) the gap between core

[25] Eisner, *Jamaica*, 172–3.

and periphery that gives the plantation a much more central and innovative role, while recognizing the growing divergence in systems of labor domination.

WEALTH AND INCOME

The significance of the British West Indies in the Atlantic world economy of the seventeenth and eighteenth centuries is strikingly revealed by the wealth of the colonies. Slavery created gross disparities, the slave being defined by European law and ideology as chattel, as property, and incapable of being the possessor of property. Such definition, depriving the mass of the population of the right to become wealthholders, did not in itself prevent the creation of a large capital wealth stock. Indeed, the definition of the slave as property meant that capital which might have been used to pay wages, or the transaction costs of alternate systems of labor domination, was allocated to slaveownership and thus entered the concept of wealth and its measurement. From a more theoretical point of view, it may be asked how far inequality in the distribution of wealth was an inescapable partner of economic growth.

Interest in the capacity of the plantation colonies to generate wealth and income for the British Empire has been a source of controversy since the time of Adam Smith and the American Revolution, at least, and a definitive answer to the question of whether the colonies were a source of profit or loss remains elusive. For the British West Indies, the most systematic attempt to provide a quantitative measure of wealth is that of Richard Sheridan published in 1965. Using the probate inventories for Jamaica in the years immediately preceding the American Revolution, Sheridan found a total capital wealth stock of £18 million sterling. Application of the income-capitalization formula produced a similar result. He extended his estimate to cover the entire British West Indies, on the assumption that Jamaica accounted for 60 percent of the total, for an aggregate wealth of about £30 million.

Sheridan has also offered measures of income. He found £1.5 million "a close approximation of the annual net income of the Jamaicans and the British merchants and absentees who were closely identified with that island." Multiplying the Jamaican figure to find the total for the colonies, Sheridan concludes that "it may be conservatively estimated that from 8 to 10 percent of the income of the mother country came from the West Indies in the closing years of the eighteenth century, and probably a larger percentage in the period preceding the American War of Independence."[26] In arguing that the tropical colonies were vital contributors to British economic growth, Sheridan rejects the opinion of Smith and lends support to the model advanced by Eric Williams in *Capitalism and Slavery,* in which the Atlantic system based on sugar and slavery in the British West Indies is seen as fundamental to the capitalization of the British Industrial Revolution.

Sheridan's wealth and income estimates have been criticized by Robert Paul Thomas. Using the same database, Thomas recalculated the measures to find higher figures than Sheridan for the wealth stock, at about £22 million for Jamaica and £37 for the British West Indies as a whole. On the other hand, Thomas reduces Sheridan's estimate of annual income by almost one-half, to £870,450 for Jamaica and £1,450,750 for the British West Indies, calling this "an optimistic measure of the profits received by the merchants and planters engaged in the West Indies."[27] In order to move beyond this estimate of private profit, Thomas argues that the social profit or loss to Great Britain at large must take account of the costs of Empire, particularly in terms of (1) the mercantilist tariff preferences granted to the sugar planters, and (2) the administration and defense of the colonies. Sugar imported to Great Britain from its colonies paid duties one-third to one-half less than sugars imported from foreign colonies, the duty varying according to the quality of the sugar. Thomas contends that the tariff cost British consumers at least £383,250 per annum between 1771 and 1775. Adding the costs of defense and administration, Thomas finds a total social return of £660,750, or less than 2 percent on invested capital. Thus, the British would have been better off investing their capital at home and buying their sugar from more efficient foreign producers, notably the French.

Sheridan's rejoinder to this argument of Thomas raises many methodological issues but no significantly different wealth estimates. Sheridan concludes that for Britain's Atlantic Empire of the seventeenth and eighteenth centuries, in its informal as well as its formal aspects, it is "a misreading of economic history to deny the contribution of the West Indian colonies."[28] The literature surrounding this debate has grown sub-

[26] R. B. Sheridan, "The Wealth of Jamaica in the Eighteenth Century," *Economic History Review* 18 (1965), 306.

[27] Robert Paul Thomas, "The Sugar Colonies of the Old Empire: Profit or Loss for Great Britain?" *Economic History Review* 21 (1968), 36.

[28] R. B. Sheridan, "The Wealth of Jamaica in the Eighteenth Century: A Rejoinder," *Economic History Review* 21 (1968), 61.

stantially since the exchange between Sheridan and Thomas, but definitive answers to the central questions remain elusive. It appears, however, that there is a growing acknowledgment of (1) the significance of slavery in the development of the Atlantic system, and (2) the fundamental role of commodities produced by slaves within that system in the genesis of industrial capitalism.[29] That Great Britain was the "first industrial nation" necessarily implies a strong link with the British West Indies, where sugar and slavery created the most specialized subregion of the Atlantic economy, a booming sector that not only produced investment capital but perhaps also offered a paradoxical model of the factory complex, with its mix of modern technologies and ancient mode of labor domination.

The importance of the British West Indies can also be seen by comparison with wealth estimates for the North American colonies. In 1774, the British West Indies had a total population only one-fifth that of the thirteen colonies but, according to the estimates of Alice Hanson Jones, a total private physical wealth one-third as large as the mainland.[30] Jamaica's wealth was almost exactly equivalent to that of the New England colonies, but the composition of this wealth was quite different. In the thirteen colonies, slaves and servants accounted for only 19.6 percent of private physical wealth, whereas in the dominant sugar sector of Jamaica, slaves made up 81.6 percent of total inventory valuation in 1771–5 (increasing from 55 percent in 1741–5). Even in the South, slaves and servants accounted for just 33.6 percent.

These data demonstrate clearly the significance of slavery for the British West Indian economy and society and, at the same time, indicate the concentration of wealth in the hands of the planter class. They also highlight the problems of definition and categorization that challenge attempts to measure wealth. Jones, Sheridan, and Thomas all accept contemporary legal and customary definitions of wealthholders, generally including only the free white and black adult male population, and some free women.[31] The picture changes substantially if slaves are excluded from the accounting or if, on the other hand, the undoubtedly meager possessions of the slaves are included in the calculation. In the British West Indies, custom came to acknowledge the rights of the slaves to inherit and otherwise transmit goods and chattels and even access to particular plots of land. The planters rapidly

[29] Barbara L. Solow, ed., *Slavery and the Rise of the Atlantic System* (Cambridge, 1991); Joseph E. Inikori, *Slavery and the Rise of Capitalism* (Mona, 1993).
[30] Alice Hanson Jones, *Wealth of a Nation to Be: The American Colonies on the Eve of the Revolution* (New York, 1980), 51.
[31] McCusker and Menard, *Economy of British America*, 262–5.

recognized the advantages of actively encouraging the slaves' marketing and other income-generating activities. Writing in 1751, an anonymous author commented on the current shortage of coin in Jamaica and warned that any attempt to withdraw the slaves' access to money and markets would only create discontent and rebellion. Couching the argument in explicit social control terms, the writer argued,

It is plain that they do not subsist only by the allowance given them by their owners; what renders their slavery tolerable to them, is, that little shadow of property and freedom which they seem to enjoy, in having their own little parcels of ground to occupy and improve; and a great part of its produce they bring to market, there to dispose of it; which, besides supplying the white inhabitants with a great plenty of wholesome provisions, enables the Negroes to purchase little comforts and conveniences for themselves and their little ones; these sweets they have tasted for some years successively.[32]

SLAVE SOCIETY OR CREOLE SOCIETY?

British West Indian society before emancipation has been interpreted by modern scholars according to two competing models. One side of the debate, represented particularly by Elsa Goveia, argues that the term *slave society* best characterizes the structure that emerged in the seventeenth and eighteenth centuries. The opposing view, advocated most strongly by Kamau Brathwaite, prefers to conceive the situation as a *creole society*. Both sides of the debate recognize slavery as the fundamental element of the society. The difference lies in the extent and quality of interaction between slave and free, and the outcome of that process.

Goveia defined slave society as "the whole community based on slavery, including masters and freedmen as well as slaves," and stated that her work sought "to identify the basic principles which held the white masters, coloured freedmen, and Negro slaves together as a community, and to trace the influence of these principles on the relations between the Negro slave and his white master, which largely determined the form and content of the society."[33] In this model, the ultimate sanctions rested in physical coercion — the superior power of the white/slaveowning class being expressed in force and law. But habit and opinion also served to

---

[32] *An Inquiry concerning the trade, commerce, and policy of Jamaica, relative to the scarcity of money, and the causes and bad effects of such scarcity, peculiar to that island* (London: 1759), 32–3.
[33] Elsa V. Goveia, *Slave Society in the British Leeward Islands at the End of the Eighteenth Century* (New Haven, 1965), vii.

ingrain the system through adoption of norms and personality traits that suggested acceptance of caste distinctions between slave, free colored, free black, and white groups. Thus, the slave society of the British West Indies can be seen as fitting very closely the plural society model developed to explain hegemonic relations in tightly structured communities, generally organized on caste lines.

Brathwaite, protagonist of the creole society interpretation, sees the plural society model, with its prognosis of tension and violent conflict, as excessively negative and pessimistic. He is more hopeful for modern West Indian society and argues that such hope can be founded even on the experience of slavery. In characterizing the society as *creole,* he contends that the process of creolization was just as important as the slavery that provided the socioeconomic framework for its development. Creolization emphasizes interculturation rather than a one-way acculturation with its assumption of superior and inferior power relations. Creolization thus gives greater credit to the contributions of Africa and the slaves while reducing the apparent social and cultural dominance of Europe.[34] Evidence of creolization can be found in language, customs, and folkways, as well as in economic organization, most obviously in the internal marketing system with its amalgam of West African and European forms.

Brathwaite's reading of creolization makes it a process comprehending a region much wider than the British West Indian colonies, extending throughout the Americas with variations along a continuum of interactive relations. Recent studies of North America in the eighteenth century have done much to introduce this conception to understanding of those colonial societies, though generally without reference to the West Indian experience or scholarship.[35] Refinement of the concept of creolization is likely, however, to see distinctions emerging from comparative studies, along the lines of Brathwaite's continuum, having to do with differences in economic structures and demographic composition.

British West Indian society before, and after, emancipation recognized a fine gradation of color groups. *Mulatto* was used exclusively to refer to children of black and white parents. On the side approaching white and free, persons could be *quadroon, mustee, musteephino,* while the children of black and mulatto parents were *sambo.* These distinctions were made significant in terms of occupational allocation on the plantations and,

[34] Brathwaite, *Development of Creole Society,* vii, 306–11.
[35] For example, Mechal Sobel, *The World They Made Together: Black and White Values in Eighteenth-Century Virginia* (Princeton, 1987).

hence, affected the ability of slaves to earn and accumulate. It was a general rule that on sugar and other plantations, the females "of color" were put to domestic tasks and the males to skilled trades. These occupations carried a relatively high status compared to field labor, and slaves with these occupations received rations and other material benefits from the masters superior in quantity and quality to that provided to other slaves. The males, and to a lesser extent the females, had marketable skills. Slaves of color thus came to be concentrated in the towns, where they entered a variety of arrangements with their owners for "self-hire" and relatively independent economic activity.

Slaves of color were more likely to be manumitted (freed) than black slaves, partly because of their superior economic resources and, more importantly, because their fathers were most often whites or freedmen. Thus, the freed population tended to have a high proportion of colored people in its ranks; again there developed an urban concentration. Black slaves had a much harder road to freedom through emancipation.

Escape from slavery was achieved not only through manumission. Marronage, or physical escape from slaveowners, similarly resulted in effective freedom for some, within both the urban context and the recognized Maroon communities such as emerged in Jamaica in the eighteenth century. In the eastern Caribbean archipelago, some slaves became *maritime maroons*, taking boats from one island to another, moving out of British imperial territory completely, or leaving the Caribbean for external destinations including the North American mainland. This movement was facilitated by the network of trade and communication that linked the region and created a creole Atlantic world.

THE WEST INDIES AND THE AMERICAN REVOLUTION

The failure of the British West Indies to follow the continental colonies into independence cannot be explained by political passivity on the part of the white colonists or by economic insignificance. Massachusetts and Virginia, leaders of the revolt against British imperial rule, were far less important economically than the sugar colonies, and the representative assemblies of Jamaica and Barbados had long histories of constitutional struggle with the crown. Why, then, did the island colonies not revolt?

One interpretation is that the fundamental division of West Indian society, and the high ratio of slave to free, made the whites fearful for their security and continued prosperity if disconnected from the mother country. Survival without the British navy and army was unthinkable. Thus, when the legislatures of Jamaica, Barbados, Grenada, and Tobago passed resolutions in support of the American colonies during the Stamp Duties crisis, they attacked parliamentary tyranny rather than self-confidently claiming local autonomy. They merely sought to preserve their powers to govern internal affairs, notably the slave system. Brathwaite has expanded this interpretation to contend that, in the case of Jamaica, the creoles who possessed political power remained essentially colonial in their attitudes, that they were not sufficiently creolized to surrender their dependence on the metropolis.[36]

An alternative interpretation has been advanced by T. R. Clayton, who rejects the security issues and puts sociopolitical factors at the center. The Jamaican political system, Clayton argues, bestowed hegemony on the gentry and, in contrast to the mainland colonies, provided "ample opportunities for ambitious young members of the provincial elite." At the same time, the period between the Seven Years' War and the American Revolution was one of prosperity for the British West Indian plantocracy, whereas for the continental colonies it was "a period of increasing social, economic, and political crisis."[37]

The British West Indian legislatures' decision to align with the mother country rather than with the continental colonies had major economic implications in both the short term and the long run. The naval war resulted in (1) heavy loss of shipping in trade between the West Indies and Europe, and (2) a consequent rise in freight rates and insurance. Increases in the prices of American commodities were less immediate, since most colonies had large stocks on hand at the beginning of 1776. Indeed, it can be argued that these stocks and the relatively low prices charged for American commodities were an important cause of the Revolution in that they resulted from a mercantilist imbalance within the British Empire. The removal of this imbalance was perhaps the most important aspect of the Revolution from the Caribbean point of view.

The embargo placed on trade between the British West Indies and the rebel colonies during the War of Independence broke the close commerce that had linked the temperate zone producers of fish, flour, corn, and lumber with the tropical sugar islands. Efforts by the West Indian planters and merchants to reorganize their resources took several forms. The imme-

---

[36] Brathwaite, *Development of Creole Society*, 100.
[37] T. R. Clayton, "Sophistry, Security, and Socio-political Structures in the American Revolution; or, Why did Jamaica not Rebel?" *Historical Journal* 29 (1986), 344.

diate problem of short supplies was avoided to some extent by putting more emphasis on the provision-ground system, using available back lands, or taking land out of cane and planting food crops. Great Britain relaxed the Corn Laws to permit exportation of wheat, and some islands were able to import provisions and lumber from French and Spanish colonies. New sources of supply were provided by the opening of trade with Ireland in 1778. Contraband trade with the Americans flourished. The Dutch colony of St. Eustatius, for example, became an entrepôt (distribution center), selling manufactured goods and military supplies to the Americans, on the one hand, and mainland lumber and provisions to the British islands, on the other. Some historians argue that these adjustments enabled the planters and their slaves to obtain ample and cheap supplies of food. Others, however, have contended that the consequences of trade restrictions were disastrous. Sheridan holds that the Revolution created a crisis of slave subsistence, in which "hunger stalked the islands and thousands of slaves died from causes either directly or indirectly related to the war."[38] The crisis was exacerbated by severe hurricanes that hit the islands six times between 1780 and 1786.

Another immediate effect of the Revolution was that in order to pay for the war, the British increased customs duties on imports of sugar. It was at this point that the duties first came to be seen as a source of revenue rather than simply the means of regulating trade. The duty was doubled between 1776 and 1782, and doubled again by 1830. Sugar prices (exclusive of duty) increased significantly during the American war, however, and those planters who managed to find shipping to get their product to market reaped large profits. Prices fell after 1783 but remained fairly stable at levels a little above prewar averages until 1820.

The Revolution also had a minor demographic impact on the British West Indies. Although most of the North American colonists who chose to remain loyal to the crown went to Canada, significant numbers settled in the Bahamas, Jamaica, and Dominica. Their slaves were forced to follow. As a result, the population of the Bahamas tripled between 1783 and 1789. Many of these Loyalists had been cotton planters, and the introduction of the crop to the Bahamas resulted in a minor plantation revolution. In Jamaica, on the other hand, areas granted by the Assembly were swamplands, and many Loyalists chose to locate in the towns.

With the Peace of Versailles in 1783, the Americans looked forward to a

[38] Richard B. Sheridan, "The Crisis of Slave Subsistence in the British West Indies during and after the American Revolution," *William and Mary Quarterly* 3d ser., 33 (1976), 641.

reopening of their previously profitable trade with the British West Indies. Similarly, the sugar planters called for reestablishment of the trade on a liberal footing. But British reluctance to enter into a commercial treaty with the United States meant that from 1783 to 1822, provisions and supplies could enter the islands only if carried in British ships. In turn, the colonies could export their staples to the United States only under restrictive tariff regulations. Illicit trading became common. Canada, Nova Scotia, and Newfoundland increased their trade in fish and lumber, but the United States retained the trade in flour. Thus, trade between the tropical and temperate zones continued along established lines, though indirectly and at greatly increased prices. Most of the restrictions were removed in 1822, but it was not until 1830 that the trade was truly reopened. By that time, the Atlantic slave trade of the British had been abolished, and the price of sugar had collapsed.

ECONOMIC DECLINE AND THE ABOLITION OF SLAVERY

The identification of "economic decline" has an important place in the historiography of the British West Indies. This importance may be traced in part to a fundamental cyclic metaphor. Something that went so high, as in the superprofits of the golden and silver ages of sugar, must inevitably suffer a mighty fall. The concept of economic decline also has a central role in the history of the region, because it undermines the traditional British humanitarian interpretation, in which the slave trade and slavery were abolished for righteous rather than material motives. The significance of this last debate is also rooted in a long continued focus on movements toward abolition rather than on the experience of slavery or even adjustments to freedom after emancipation.

Modern historiographic interests have shifted away from these preoccupations; this, in turn, demands a rethinking of the notion of economic decline. Most historians have measured decline in terms of the plantation economy: the output of sugar, metropolitan prices for export commodities, and the profitability of the system to the planter class and the larger British imperial economy. There is little place here for a colonial or creole perspective, and none at all for measures that mattered to the slave population: the output of grounds and gardens, opportunities for accumulation through self-hire, marronage and the internal marketing system, and changes in nutrition and levels of living. Trends in these indexes did not follow in any simple fashion the patterns observed in the plantation export sector, and the income of the planter had little immediate impact on the life of the slave. For the long term, it can, however, be argued that the planter-slaveowner was the key to the system and that changes in the plantation sector's profitability determined imperial policy, including the legality of different forms of labor domination. If this argument is accepted, then the debate over "economic decline" remains important.

Questions of chronology are basic to the interpretation. The British Parliament passed a bill for the abolition of the Atlantic slave trade in 1807, with effect from 1808. In 1833, the Emancipation Act was passed. Slaves in some islands, such as Antigua, were freed from 1834, but the majority entered a period of compulsory "Apprenticeship" to their former masters, which did not end until 1838. The British provided £20 million for the compensation of slaveowners throughout the Empire for the loss of their slave property, nothing for the slaves themselves. In terms of this chronology, the question is, did the plantation economy based on the slave system enter decline before 1833 or 1807 and so bring about abolition and emancipation, or were abolition and emancipation responsible for that decline?

There is general agreement that sugar prices declined significantly during the 1820s, undercutting the profits of the planters. Thus, it is easily conceded that economic decline was a contributory factor in the passing of the Emancipation Act. Other important factors, only tenuously linked to decline, were the Jamaican slave rebellion of 1831–2, the mobilization of public opinion in Great Britain, and Reform of the British Parliament in 1832. By 1833, the political power of the West Indian "interest," or lobby, was reduced to a shadow, and many absentee planters expressed a willingness to accept emancipation with compensation.

Debate centers on the abolition of the slave trade and the state of the plantation economy between 1750 and 1820. Some argue that the seeds of destruction were planted in 1763, when the Peace of Paris added new territories to the British tropical Empire, removing the effective protection formerly enjoyed by the old sugar colonies and leading to overproduction.[39] According to this interpretation, the failure of the planter class to adopt technological innovations in field and factory, as well as the exhaustion of the soil, and the inefficiencies of absentee management, led inevitably to the bankruptcy of the planters and the collapse of the system. Other interpretations date the decline of the system to the American Revolution,

[39] Lowell Joseph Ragatz, *The Fall of the Planter Class in the British Caribbean, 1763–1833* (New York, 1928), 111–3.

placing particular emphasis on the dislocation of trade between the tropical and temperate colonies, the consequent increase in costs of production, and the British government's desire to extract revenue from the sugar trade.[40] The revolution in St. Domingue, on the other hand, provided an artificial respite for the British West Indies, removing its major competitor from the European market and pushing up metropolitan prices.

Interpretations that deny the importance of 1763 and the American Revolution generally identify continued planter prosperity until about 1815, after which sugar prices fell consistently until 1830, when they were only one-third the level of 1815.[41] Sugar production declined in some British West Indian colonies after 1800, but overall they showed substantial growth until emancipation. It can be argued, therefore, that (1) the British abolition of the Atlantic slave trade in 1807 occurred at a point when the system of sugar and slavery was flourishing rather than in decline, and (2) the abolition was itself an important factor in the reduction of planter profits after 1815. The demographic structure of the slave labor force was also changed by the abolition of the slave trade, creating tensions that worked to undermine the system indirectly, and made it increasingly creole in composition and outlook. These transformations, in turn, affected the expectations of slaves and planters, within both creole/slave society and the coming world of freedom.

POSTEMANCIPATION ADJUSTMENTS

DEMOGRAPHIC AND SOCIAL CHANGE

Political power remained in the hands of the colonial planter and merchant classes until 1850, with the exception of the Crown Colonies (Trinidad, St. Lucia, and Guyana), which were ruled directly from London. Regardless of the locus of authority, the state sought to maintain the export-oriented plantation system as the basis of the British West Indian economy. The capitalist classes believed that (1) the plantation was the best possible mode of organizing land and labor for the extraction of profit, and

---

[40] Eric Williams, *Capitalism and Slavery* (Chapel Hill, 1944), 108–25; Sheridan, "Crisis of Slave Subsistence," 641; Selwyn H. H. Carrington, *The British West Indies during the American Revolution* (Dordrecht, 1988), 180–1.

[41] Seymour Drescher, *Econocide: British Slavery in the Era of Abolition* (Pittsburgh, 1977), 15–37; J. R. Ward, "The Profitability of Sugar Planting in the British West Indies, 1650–1834," *Economic History Review* 31 (1978), 197–213.

(2) saw it as an institution with a civilizing force capable of defending colonial society from the barbarism of Africa and the more insidious features of creolization. Thus, government was deployed in the service of the planter class, seeking to control labor and restrict access to land.

The politically marginalized ex-slave population of the British West Indies, on the other hand, saw in freedom not only the right to bargain for wages and the right to mobility within the labor market but also rights to the houses and gardens that they and their ancestors had occupied for generations and to the grounds that they had cultivated in their own time. They were the true inheritors of the land and believed that the Crown intended them to have access to this resource as well as freeing their labor from their former masters.

The consequence of these conflicting readings of the meaning of freedom was competition for land and labor that, by 1850, resulted in new forms of labor domination, the establishment of an independent peasantry, and population moves within the Caribbean region. But the pattern of adjustment was by no means uniform throughout the British West Indies, and historians continue to debate the causes of these variations. One particularly resilient theory is tied to population density and the existence of open or closed resources.[42] This theory is, of course, the counterpart to the population-density interpretation of the *emergence* of involuntary labor systems. Where the population was dense, as in Barbados and the Leeward Islands, the ex-slaves had no real alternatives to remaining on the plantations and working as tied wage laborers at low rates of remuneration. For this reason, the planters of Antigua decided to dispense completely with the Apprenticeship. In such situations, the plantation system survived intact, and a peasantry emerged only painfully on the margins of the estates. Where population was sparse, as in Jamaica and the Windward Islands, the planters were unable to hold the ex-slaves to wage labor because of the attractions of free or cheap land, which permitted the establishment of a thriving peasantry, with its roots in the protopeasantry spawned by the provision-ground and internal marketing systems during slavery. In these colonies, many sugar plantations were abandoned, with the white population migrating out of the region, and attempts were

[42] William A. Green, *British Slave Emancipation: The Sugar Colonies and the Great Experiment 1830–1865* (Oxford, 1976), 192–3; Stanley L. Engerman, "Economic Adjustments to Emancipation in the United States and the British West Indies," *Journal of Interdisciplinary History* 13 (1982), 191–220; Stanley L. Engerman, "Economic Change and Contract Labor in the British Caribbean: The End of Slavery and the Adjustment to Emancipation," *Explorations in Economic History* 21 (1984), 133–50.

made to introduce assisted immigrants and contract labor. In colonies with sparse populations and new, vibrant sugar economies, such as Trinidad and Guyana, the planters brought in large numbers of indentured immigrants to meet the demand for labor and ensure continuance of the plantation system.

In general terms, the population-density model appears to fit the British West Indian case quite well. It has, however, been subjected to criticism in recent times, particularly by Nigel Bolland, who argues that population density is too simple a ratio to capture fully the experience of the colonies.[43] Bolland introduces the case of Belize, a colony with low population density but little peasant development or immigration, to show that the structure of planter hegemony was equally important. To understand the pattern in all its ramifications, contends Bolland, it is necessary to see the struggle for labor domination in dialectical terms. This argument links directly with other current issues in postemancipation historiography. Until recently, it was widely believed that the ex-slave population left the plantations behind as quickly as possible, wherever free land was available, in order to escape the scene of their enslavement. It has been shown, however, that the ex-slaves' attachment to their community, as expressed in houses, gardens, grounds, kinship, and burial sites, was well developed and embodied an alternative reading of the plantation landscape. Rather than a "flight from the estates," it is argued, the ex-slaves were pushed off by a planter class that adopted a crude interpretation of freehold property rights, charging rents for houses and yards occupied by generations and requiring plantation labor as a precondition of continued residence.[44] Here the dialectic was played out in the politics of plantation economy, in competition for resources within the separate niches of planter and ex-slave.

In this struggle, the planters used state funds to assist immigration to the British West Indies in order to put both moral and numerical pressure on the ex-slave population to offer its labor to the plantation sector. British and German settlers were brought to Jamaica, and Portuguese to Trinidad and Guyana, beginning in 1834.[45] Efforts were also made during the Apprenticeship period to recruit contract labor from the marginal islands of the Bahamas and the Leeward Islands to Trinidad and Guyana,

---

[43] O. Nigel Bolland, "Systems of Domination after Slavery: The Control of Land and Labour in the British West Indies after 1838," *Comparative Studies in Society and History* 23 (1981), 591–619.

[44] Douglas Hall, "The Flight from the Estates Reconsidered: The British West Indies, 1838–42," *Journal of Caribbean History* 10/11 (1978), 7–24; Woodville K. Marshall, *The Post-Slavery Problem Revisited* (Mona, Department of History, University of the West Indies, 1991).

[45] K. O. Laurence, *Immigration into the West Indies in the 19th Century* (Barbados, 1971), 9–23.

but this practice was prohibited by the Colonial Office. The Barbados legislature did everything possible to prevent labor recruiters from entering that island. Indentured Indians arrived first in Guyana in May 1838 and thus inaugurated the major flow of contract labor into the region, which was to continue until 1917, substantially augmenting the population of Guyana and Trinidad and, to a lesser extent, Jamaica. Bountied and "liberated" Africans also added to the numbers. Thus, the 1840s saw considerable experimentation with immigrant labor, under a variety of styles of contract and from a variety of origins, but the financial crisis of 1847 and the equalization of the sugar duties resulted in bankruptcy for many sugar planters. Large-scale immigration based on long-term contracts was not commenced until the 1850s.

Immigration created an increasingly plural society in the British West Indies, separating the older sugar colonies and marginal colonies, with their large African and small white (essentially British) populations, from the new sugar colonies with their growing Asian and varied European components. It is in the postemancipation period that the plural society model comes to prove most convincing as an explanation of social segmentation and its relation to political power.[46] The increasing complexity of the populations of Guyana and Trinidad also resulted from a relatively slow growth of the ex-slave population by natural increase. Elsewhere in the British West Indies, emancipation was followed by a quite rapid shift from decline to positive natural increase, and the high black:white ratios of the period of slavery became even higher.

PRODUCTION AND TRADE

The period between 1834 and 1850 witnessed a significant overall decline in the export of sugar from the British West Indies in consequence of the abandonment of plantations and the reduced output of the surviving estates (Figure 7.1). In Jamaica, the leading producer, exports were halved: Jamaica exported 62,812 tons of sugar in 1834 but only 28,750 tons in 1850, and output did not return to preemancipation levels until the 1930s. The next most important producer, Guyana, experienced a similar decline in the short term but saw recovery by the late 1840s and exceeded its preemancipation peak by 1863. Trinidad reached a peak position by 1845, demonstrating the importance of contract labor in

---

[46] Brian L. Moore, *Race, Power and Social Segmentation in Colonial Society: Guyana after Slavery, 1838–1891* (New York, 1987).

maintaining output in the new sugar colonies. Guyana and Trinidad also led the way in introducing new factory technologies derived from steam power – productivity gains were not simply a matter of altered labor inputs.

In the old sugar colonies, where the population was dense and the state held tight control of the community, exports increased in many cases without resort to contract labor or technological innovations. Barbados, for example, peaked in 1838 when 23,679 tons of sugar were exported, and it peaked again in 1849 and 1850 by exporting more than 24,000 tons. St. Kitts, Nevis, and Antigua followed a similar trajectory, but Montserrat's production fell off dramatically to recover only in the 1860s, and the British Virgin Islands stopped exporting sugar completely soon after 1850. Marginal, small-scale producers were forced from the market. The Windward Islands experienced reduced production but stayed in the market until the end of the nineteenth century.

Decline in the export sector was not balanced by growth in the domestic sector. In Jamaica, exports contributed 41.4 percent of Gross Domestic Product in 1832 (at current prices) but only 23.4 percent in 1850, according to the calculations of Eisner.[47] Food production for local consumption, on the other hand, moved from 17.8 percent to 28.1 percent, indicating the growth of the independent peasantry and its role in perpetuating the productivity of the provision-ground system in new and old settings. In absolute terms, Eisner's calculations show an increase of only 16.2 percent in the local food sector, yet this was the major growth area. Jamaica's Gross Domestic Product overall fell by 26.1 percent between 1832 and 1850.

Guyana, the other British West Indian colony for which national income estimates have been prepared, experienced a somewhat different pattern.[48] Between 1832 and 1852, Guyana's Gross Domestic Product increased by 8.2 percent absolutely (at 1913 prices), while the export sector's share fell from 43.3 to 22.8 percent. Food production for local consumption moved from 27.3 to 31.6 percent, but the real gains were in manufacturing for local consumption, public administration, and professional services. As in Jamaica, the immediate postemancipation period saw growth in building and construction, largely in response to the demand for improved housing among the peasantry and free villagers.

The external trade of the British West Indies was until the 1840s gov-

[47] Eisner, *Jamaica 1830–1930*, 118.
[48] Moohr, "Economic Impact of Slave Emancipation," 589.

erned by the Navigation Laws, which tied the colonies to Great Britain. But the relaxation of restrictions on trade with the United States, beginning in 1830, initiated significant changes in the geographical pattern of markets for exports and sources of imports. By 1850, Jamaica, for example, took 20.4 percent of its imports from the United States and another 10.2 percent from Canada. The United States received 6.0 percent of Jamaica's exports and South America 11.7 percent. Great Britain remained overwhelming in the pattern of trade, however, supplying 64.6 percent of imports to Jamaica in 1850, and taking 77.9 percent of its exports.[49] By the early 1830s, the British West Indies already imported most of its lumber, flour, meal, and corn from the United States, largely restoring the pre-1776 pattern; by 1850, hardly any food supplies came from Europe.

Growth of the peasantry and expansion of food production for local consumption went together, in at least some of the major British West Indian colonies, with further articulation of the internal marketing system. The establishment of interior market towns moved rapidly, as plantation villages were deserted following planter pressure or actual clearances, and church-founded free villages emerged. The profitability of such marketing continued to depend, however, on cash flow among the wage-earning plantation labor force. Abandonment of estates and planters' attempts to reduce wages, by the later 1840s, undercut the growth of the peasant and distributive sectors to some extent.

The second half of the nineteenth century was thus marked by a prolonged process of readjustment. In some of the British West Indian colonies, such as Jamaica and the Windward Islands, the economies became increasingly inward-looking until the 1870s, when new technologies created external consumer markets and investment opportunities for trade in crops such as bananas, formerly the food of the poor. The consequence was a growing penetration by United States capital; in 1890, the United States came to replace Great Britain as Jamaica's major trading partner. In other British West Indian colonies, such as Barbados and the Leeward Islands, the sugar plantation economy survived relatively intact throughout this period, and trade patterns changed less dramatically, though the American connection expanded everywhere. The British West Indies gradually became less important elements in the Caribbean region at the same time as American influences and interests became increasingly pervasive.

[49] Eisner, *Jamaica 1830–1930*, 269–70.

8

BRITISH MERCANTILIST POLICIES
AND THE AMERICAN COLONIES

JOHN J. McCUSKER

Mercantilism was the guiding doctrine behind the attempts of regimes and peoples of the early modern Atlantic World to organize their economic existence. The aim of mercantilism was to structure the financial foundation of the nation-state — the emerging postmedieval governmental mode that rapidly replaced feudal localism in northern and western Europe after the mid-fifteenth century — so that the state could survive and prosper. Nationalism held the promise of political stability and a better life for all, a considerable improvement over the chaos of an earlier era. Mercantilist policies were thus meant to be the economic means to larger political and social ends.

Like similar economic belief systems — socialism and capitalism, for instance — mercantilism had its faithful few and its querulous many. Nevertheless, all of early modern Europe recognized and conformed, in various degrees, to the doctrines of mercantilism.[1] It became "the unchallenged assumption that . . . government had the right and responsibility to regulate economic activities in the interest of the common good."[2] Mercantilism attracted a following because it seemed to work. Relative to the earlier era, there was more peace and greater prosperity. Yet the success of the nation-states of early modern Atlantic Europe encouraged dissenters as well as the faithful. Inherent in a system that promised all a greater good — and more goods — was the potential that, in its success or in its failure, it might encourage the expression of alternative voices and other doctrines.

---

[1] See John J. McCusker, "Mercantilism," in Jacob E. Cooke, ed., *The Encyclopedia of the North American Colonies,* 3 vols. (New York, 1993), I, 459–65.

[2] Joyce Oldham Appleby, *Economic Thought and Ideology in Seventeenth-Century England* (Princeton, NJ, 1978), 99.

337

Mercantilist thinkers argued that a strong central government was so important that the Crown had to have the power to turn every element of the state to achieving that purpose, including the economy. Mercantilism recognized broadly the needs and concerns of both of the other components of the economy – businesses and workers. Mercantilism argued just that the organizers of production and those who did the work could attain satisfaction only within the protective embrace of a strong nation-state. Thus, business and labor must be prepared not only to accept the sacrifices necessary to establish and support that state but also to acquiesce in its guidance. The national interest was paramount; the Crown knew best. (Capitalism and socialism, the competing successors to mercantilism, aspire to the same grand objective – general human happiness – and appreciate that the same three elements are in play. Capitalism argues that the organizers of production are the people best equipped to make the necessary decisions. Socialism says that it is the workers who know best.[3] After two hundred years of struggle, the world of the twenty-first century seems headed toward socially managed capitalism as the dominant doctrine.)

What the nation-state needed most from the economy was money: regular revenues to meet the continuing demands of government and dependable sources of support to meet emergencies. The traditional ways in which these needs had been met were no longer satisfactory, either because they did not yield enough money or because they ran counter to the larger goals of the mercantilist state. Taxes on land created internal dissent; taxes on internal trade fragmented the national economy; the monarch's borrowing abroad limited the independence of the state. New ways had to be found to fund the monarch's diplomats in peace and armies in war. International trade provided the mechanism. Duties on foreign trade, funneled directly to the monarch's treasury, were seen as both more reliable and less divisive than land taxes. Loans from the nation's large-scale merchants, exacted or merely solicited, tapped into a group of people

---

[3] Or, put another way: "Mercantilism called upon government to develop the economy in the best interests of the state. Capitalism called upon government to develop the economy in the best interests of business. Socialism called upon government to develop the economy in the best interests of the workers. None of these three doctrines necessarily denied the need for attention to the concerns of the other partners in the enterprise. All three recognized the symbiotic relationship of the state, business, and workers. The focus of each was simply a matter of emphasis, of subordination" (McCusker, "Mercantilism," in Cooke, ed., *Encyclopedia of the North American Colonies*, I, 459).

Compare, among many others, the depiction of the latter stage in this progression in the essays by Joseph A. Schumpeter, *Capitalism, Socialism, and Democracy* (New York, 1942).

It should not be necessary to remind readers that the origin and even the widespread acceptance of a doctrine and the enthronement of that doctrine as public policy do not necessarily follow one another either quickly or surely.

whose allegiance could be assured by the nation's encouragement and protection of their overseas enterprises.[4] According to Benjamin Worsley, the author of the Ordinance of 1651 and other English statutes that enacted mercantilism into law, "it is by Trade, and the due ordering and governing of it, and by no other means, that Wealth and Shipping can either bee encreased, or upheld; and consequently by . . . no other, that the power or any Nation can bee susteined."[5]

Mercantilism's infatuation with expanding overseas trade was reinforced by an important corollary. The promotion of one's own merchants diminished the power of foreign merchants. The increase of one's own overseas trade came at a cost to the overseas trade of other, competing nation-states. The gold in our own monarch's treasury and the gold in our own merchants' money chests was gold denied others. That, at least, is what mercantilists believed. The world of the mercantilist was a "zero-sum" world, a world in which trade and bullion were fixed in amount. It was a predatory world. Our gains were our enemies' losses. In the words of Thomas Mun, writing in the mid-1620s: "Onely so much will remain and abide with us as is gained and incorporated into the estate of the Kingdom by the overballance of the trade."[6] All the better, then, that we follow the

---

[4] One is reminded in this context of the remark about the role of Jewish businessmen during the years before the reign of Edward I when they alone in England were allowed to lend money at interest and became rich doing so. Joseph Bridges Matthews, *The Law of Money-Lending, Past and Present: Being a Short History of the Usury Laws in England* . . . (London, 1906), 3, recalls that. "Under the Norman and early Angevin kings the Jews were employed as a sponge to suck up the wealth of their subjects, and be periodically squeezed to supply the wants of the Crown." See Thomas Madox, *The History and Antiquities of the Exchequer of the Kings of England* . . . , 2d ed., 2 vols. (London, 1769), I, 221–61. Compare Alfred Marshall, *Industry and Trade: A Study of Industrial Technique and Business Organization; and of Their Influences on the Conditions of Various Classes and Nations* (London, 1919), 171: ". . . but gradually even powerful rulers began to lean for financial support on the shoulders of those who had reaped the harvests of large mercantile business."

[5] Benjamin Worsley, *The Advocate* (London, 1651), 12. In 1651 Worsley was secretary to the Commonwealth Council of Trade. He was continuously active thereafter as a paid expert advisor to government on matters of trade and the colonies, "in all probability [he] had . . . some part in drafting the navigation act of 1660," he sat on other, later committees similar to the first one, and he ended his career as secretary to the Council for Trade and Plantations set up in 1672. For more on Worsley, see Charles M. Andrews, *England's Commercial and Colonial Policy*, Vol. IV of *The Colonial Period of American History* (New Haven, CT, 1938), 41, n. 1, 58–60, and elsewhere (quotation, p. 58); Robert Brenner, *Merchants and Revolution: Commercial Change, Political Conflict, and London's Overseas Traders, 1550–1653* (Princeton, NJ, 1993), 588–90, 605–7, 626–7.

Another useful definition thus sees "mercantilism as an inclusive system of economic regulation, which was designed to provide revenues for the nation-state and monopoly rents for successful 'projectors' of monopoly and cartel schemes." Robert B. Ekelund, Jr., and Robert D. Tollison, *Mercantilism as a Rent-Seeking Society: Economic Regulation in Historical Perspective* (College Station, TX, 1981), xi–xii.

[6] Thomas Mun, *England's Treasure by Forraign Trade* (London, 1664), 84, as quoted in Appleby, *Economic Thought and Ideology in Seventeenth-Century England*, 39. See also Lynn Muchmore, "A Note on Thomas Mun's 'England's Treasure by Forraign Trade,' " *Economic History Review*, 2d Ser., 23 (1970), 498–503.

dictates of mercantilist doctrine. Our nation will prosper and prevail over its enemies. Victory for us will ensure *our* peace and prosperity.

One suggested mechanism for expanding overseas trade in the highly competitive world of sixteenth-century Europe was by adding to the territory over which the monarch wielded power. The success of Portugal and Spain provided an extraordinary incentive. In the space of a few decades, Spain had proceeded from a patchwork of principalities on the Iberian Peninsula to the premier nation-state of Europe, the possessor of a worldwide empire. Its overseas trade grew from negligible to enormous; Spanish ships and Spanish merchants dominated Atlantic Europe; and the Spanish monarchy became the richest and most powerful in the world. The secret of its success was no secret at all. Spanish colonies in the Far East and the Far West tremendously increased the overseas trade of the nation. Taxes on that trade swelled the Crown's coffers. And Spain, which, like most of pre–sixteenth-century Europe, had bowed to the merchant bankers of the Italian city states when it needed to borrow, no longer had the need. The new capital of trade and finance in Atlantic Europe was Antwerp in the Spanish Netherlands. Spain was the best possible example for the apostles of mercantilism.

The lesson of the Spanish and Portuguese empires was not lost upon the rest of Europe. Englishmen, in particular, appreciated and envied the effect on their own country of English consumption of Portuguese sugars from Brazil imported into London from the sugar refineries of Antwerp, and of Spanish tobacco from the Spanish colonies in the New World imported from Iberian ports. Every English silver penny spent on such commodities paid some profit to a Spanish merchant, paid some duty to the Spanish Crown, enhanced and empowered the nation-state of Spain, which, not incidentally, threatened ever more the much weaker nation, England. It is in no way coincidental that the reign of Queen Elizabeth I (1558–1603) experienced the nearly successful invasion by the Spanish Armada and the first if feeble attempts to gain control of and expand the overseas trade of the country. Expanding that trade meant among other things the creation of joint-stock companies to establish an English commercial presence in both East and West. The English East India Company was formed in 1600; the London Company of Virginia was set up in 1606; and there were others. In encouraging all of this activity, the government of Queen Elizabeth I was acting upon the dictates of mercantilism and appealing for her subjects' support using mercantilist mantras. It was in tribute to their mercantilist queen, the greatest of Great Britain's monarchs, that the first successful colony was named in her honor, Virginia.

Just as mercantilist thinking provoked and justified the establishment of British colonies in the New World, so also did mercantilist imperatives dictate the expectations that Great Britain had for those colonies. As the nation-state and its empire grew, the formalization of the relationship between the parts of that interrelated whole became more structured. The structure was a mercantilist one, in theory, at the start. The policies of the Old Empire, the First British Empire, toward the entirety of that empire, at home and abroad, had their roots in mercantilist theory just as the nation-state Great Britain did. Nevertheless, as the Empire developed, so did the thinking of those who were its citizens, its administrators, its beneficiaries, at home and abroad. The tensions between the older, mercantilist ideas and the newer realities resolved themselves in many different ways. Ultimately, of course, inspired by the likes of Adam Smith, Great Britain shook itself loose of mercantilist doctrines altogether. By then, it had become *the* nation-state of Europe, the Atlantic World, indeed the entire world. The seat of power need no longer be the monarchy; it could shift. Under capitalism, it could shift to those who controlled production; or, alternatively, under socialism to those who spoke for the working classes; or, perhaps, under a managed capitalism, to those who claimed to speak for both management and labor. We who are the witnesses of the latest stage in that progression may understand our current condition better by knowing something more about it origins.

In the same way that Great Britain eventually threw off the mantle of mercantilism, so did some of its colonies throw down the bonds of Empire, at much the same time and for closely related reasons. Those imperial links, fashioned of regulation and statute, mercantilist in origin, were forged in the interests of the rising nation-state. Such policies were successful. They helped to establish the nation Great Britain, to create, at home, the desired era of peace and prosperity, and, not incidentally, to enrich the European inhabitants who settled in the colonies that constituted the outlying regions of that same empire. Among the latter were some people who eventually used a fair portion of their economic prosperity to acquire political independence and become a successful, and rival, nation-state. Those colonies – and, most particularly, one of the nations that hived off the British Empire, the United States – are the focus of this volume. The policies that the British Empire – better, the Old Empire – developed and introduced over time are the subject of this essay.

Even though there were significant temporal variations, the policies of

Great Britain toward its New World colonies – as we will see – were essentially mercantilistic almost to the very end. They were all fashioned solely with the interests of the nation-state at heart. The nation-state may well have included all the parts, including the colonies, but first among the parts was always England itself. The successful establishment of the nation-state England required that everything possible be done to secure and increase royal revenues – both the regular revenues of peacetime and the reserve revenues to be tapped in emergencies. Mercantilist colonial policies always pursued those purposes. Many of the seeming disagreements and contradictions during the history of British colonial administration can be clarified when viewed in this light. The nation Great Britain was the end; controlling every aspect of the economy of the Empire to the nation's benefit was one means toward that end.

Government policies changed over time, nevertheless, as the times changed. The initial period, up to the Restoration of King Charles II in 1660, is the first of three periods in the development of British colonial policy. The changes wrought in the first years of King Charles II's reign established the essential framework of mercantilist policy in the Old Empire and set the tone for about a century, the second period in that progress. The reforms initiated in the middle of the eighteenth century and installed by the end of the Seven Years' War were the beginning of a third phase – but one much less mercantilistic than earlier, in the end marked more by a rejection of what had gone before, a period of transition. In all three periods there was much variety, a certain confusion, sometimes a weakness in purpose, and certainly differences among regions in the Empire, but the essential goals stayed constant. The central government and its need for financial strength were matters of first priority; central government domination of everything – including the economy – was required to attain that objective. Only after the end of the Old Empire, indeed only after the final defeat of Napoleon and victory in the Second Hundred Years' War (1689–1815), did "free trade" replace the Acts of Trade, did capitalism replace mercantilism as the doctrine that dictated public policy.

For the mercantilist, getting full benefit out of colonies involved the development, implementation, and enforcement of policies designed to attain three interrelated objectives. One can recite them, as in a catechism. England (later, after 1707, Great Britain) was to be the exclusive beneficiary of the trade in the products of its colonies. England (later Great Britain) was to be the exclusive beneficiary of the trade in the supply of goods to its colonies. England (later Great Britain) was to be the exclusive beneficiary of the carrying trade of the colonies. The emphasis in all these matters was on the trade itself. Other things to do with the colonies, even the general economy, mattered much less. Maintaining as far as possible a monopoly on the movement of goods and ships into and out of the colonies ensured both that the revenue from the duties would be maximized and that the profits to English merchants would be maximized. Effecting all of this, reconciling some inherent contradictions, and enforcing the policies all became a major part of the story of English colonial administration.

One overarching element in this story needs to be clear from the beginning. England viewed the colonies as a simple extension of itself; the colonies were, for the most part, merely English counties somewhere to the south and west of Cornwall. England considered the colonists as English citizens living at a distance. The colonists thought likewise; thus they, as much as Lancashire or Yorkshire men and women, were to be both the subjects of those mercantilistic policies and the people who benefited from them. Merchants resident in colonial ports were English merchants. Ships built and owned in the colonies qualified in every way as English ships. It followed, then, in theory, at least at first, that no distinctions of a mercantilistic nature were ever to exist between colonists and residents of the metropolis. Other ideas, other expectations might emerge. The government was to sort out conflicts, claims of preferment from different groups from different parts of the realm, Boston as well as Bristol, but the colonists were at no necessary disadvantage, from the mercantilistic perspective. The law of the realm applied for all, to all, everywhere – at least at first, certainly in theory.

The failure of the colonists to conform in practice to mercantilist doctrines became a major problem during the first of the three periods into which we divide the colonial experience (1600–60). England did not help matters by being vague in its expectations and inconsistent, nearly invisible, when it came to encouraging or enforcing behavior consistent with mercantilist maxims. The first six decades of the seventeenth century were a painful period of learning for all parties.

Prior to 1660, there was considerable confusion as to how best to turn the colonies to mercantilist ends. Thus, it is not surprising that, by the middle of the seventeenth century, each of the several colonies had gone its own way. We can feel some sympathy with all of a mercantilistic bent in England who expressed concern about what was happening. Not only were the nation's colonies not benefiting the nation but, in fact, they were enriching England's chief rival, The Netherlands. These well-based perceptions and fears, sounding as they did a profoundly dissonant chord in a mercantilistic world, became the call to arms that finally established in statute law the colonial policy of the Old Empire.

The situation that developed over the first half of the seventeenth century is completely understandable. The English men and women who had migrated to the New World pursued their own self-interest there, just as they had done at home, with little regard for the mercantilistic expectations of a remote government. They sold their produce to the highest bidder, increasingly often a Dutch merchant. Many of the colonists, especially in the West Indies, had earlier borrowed from a Dutch merchant house the capital to set up their enterprises. While this was especially true of the sugar planters of Barbados, the frequency with which the names of Dutch traders turn up in the county records of Virginia argues their importance there, too. The colonists found it efficient — and cheaper — to buy what they needed from the same company. The company's representative, the supercargo of the Dutch vessel that had brought out the European goods which the colonists had just purchased, offered to buy and ship to market the products that the colonists had for sale. The price that he offered was higher and the freight rates and insurance costs that he offered were lower than any English vessel could offer. The Dutch were the masters of the carrying trades and commerce generally during the first two-thirds of the seventeenth century. It was the "Golden Age of The Netherlands." On a level playing field, the wholesale merchants based in London or Bristol could not hope to compete.

Worse still, during much of this time, the field of play was tipped against the English side. As the Puritan Revolution turned into the Civil War during the second half of this early period, whatever hope the English had to better the Dutch evaporated. By the late 1630s, all modes of economic life in England, but especially trade and transportation, were suffering increasingly. With Cavalier and Roundhead more interested in destroying each other than carrying on business, concern about the colonies became lost in a haze of musket-fire. Nor were the Dutch shy about pursuing their competitive advantage. Sailing from their trading posts in the Caribbean, on Curaçao and St. Eustatius, and in North America, at New Amsterdam, they became a regular presence in the ports of Boston and Bridgetown and the estuaries of the Chesapeake that served as ports for Maryland and Virginia.

What had begun for the English colonists as a passive acceptance of the opportunities offered by the Dutch presence, quickly became an absolute necessity to be promoted and protected. Even had the Virginians preferred to deal with other Englishmen, events soon denied them that opportunity. Prior to the Virginia Company's dissolution in 1624, the company had insisted upon its monopoly right to all the planters' trade; after the company's demise, the English monarchs issued orders-in-council that sought fitfully to secure the colony's trade in English hands and English ships. But, in the absence of English ships during the Civil War, Virginia's tobacco planters faced ruin if they did not accept the Dutch offer – and at a good profit, too. In the 1640s, several colonies, from Massachusetts south, passed legislation to ease the way for Dutch merchants and Dutch vessels. It was a matter of survival.

Consider, nevertheless, the implications of these actions for the English mercantilist. The English nation suffered in several ways from this turn of events. Lost were any profits to the English wholesale merchant from the sale of the Chesapeake tobacco; lost, too, were the profits on the foregone sale of any goods shipped from England to the colonies. Lost to the English shipowners were the profits from the freighting of goods in both directions. Additionally, the loss of income to the English – almost exclusively London – merchant elite diminished the very group upon which the government relied, increasingly, for material support. Most significantly, lost to the central government were the import and export duties that would have been paid had the goods passed through metropolitan ports. Worse still, all those losses to the English went, guilder for pound, into the treasury of the Dutch government and the purses of Dutch merchants. The fat burghers of Amsterdam prospered; fair England languished.

Not mentioned among the list of losses was the diminished employment for English seamen or the damage to English industry from the lost sale of English manufactured goods. England's chief industry during this era was her woolen industry. To the extent that the colonists bought woolen cloth, it was ultimately English woolen goods no matter from whom they bought it. English wool and English cloth made from English wool had long dominated the cloth trade of northern Europe. A good deal of the finishing of English cloth still took place on the Continent, much of it in The Netherlands, north and south; thus, it passed through England's ports and paid the duties.[7]

---

[7] English clothiers were ardent supporters of mercantilism, because they believed that it would result in heightened exports of wool. See Appleby, *Economic Thought and Ideology in Seventeenth-Century England,* 158–98 and elsewhere.

In the seventeenth century, however much the stimulation of English industry may have been the text of English mercantilist tracts, it was considerably less significant as a matter of public policy. During this period and after, mercantilist legislation and regulation was more concerned with promoting English trade than with promoting English industry. In 1641, Lewes Roberts, the well-connected merchant and writer on commercial matters, indicated a willingness to accept government promotion of manufacturing provided it offered English wholesale merchants compensation for the lost trade.[8] Even later attempts at limiting colonial manufacturing give evidence of this same ambivalence. Manufacturing of whatever in the colonies was not so much outlawed as was the export of colonial manufactured goods prohibited. It was the trade that mattered, because it was the trade that was taxed.[9] British manufacturers benefited the Crown much less, because their business yielded no direct tax revenues. Only after the middle of the eighteenth century, when more broadly based British business interests began to assume more power, did the attitude of central government change — and for reasons that had nothing to do with mercantilism but that looked to a newer doctrine for guidance and justification.

Similarly, the argument that the Empire helped the nation by encouraging the merchant marine was never consistently pursued. There were strategic benefits, of course, in having a trained corps of seamen readily accessible during time of war. Yet that realization did not turn into a pursuit of commercial policy, per se. The benefit was frequently mentioned; such statements reoccurred as part of the rhetoric of debate when acts were deliberated. But laws and regulations in pursuit of this end exist nowhere by themselves. For instance, the provisions in both the major navigation acts of the post-Restoration period that stipulated that colonial trade had to take place in vessels having crews at least three-quarters English had nothing to do with promoting English sailors. "The predominant, if not the only reason for the requirement was to identify vessels more easily," to guarantee that they were English bottoms, owned by English owners.[10] The benefit as pursued in policy was a subsidiary bene-

---

[8] Lewes Roberts, *The Treasure of Traffike. Or a Discourse of Forraign Trade* (London, 1641). See Valerie Pearl, *London and the Outbreak of the Puritan Revolution: City Government and National Politics, 1625–43* (Oxford, 1961), 283.

[9] "The injurious effects of the Wool Act of 1699, the Hat Act of 1732 [and] the Iron Act of 1750 . . . have been greatly overstated." Andrews, *England's Commercial and Colonial Policy,* 349, n. 4. He referred, respectively, to 10 William III, c. 16; 5 George II, c. 22; and 23 George II, c. 29.

[10] Lawrence A. Harper, *The English Navigation Laws: A Seventeenth-Century Experiment in Social Engineering* (New York, 1939), 55.

fit.[11] When a conflict arose between what may have resulted in the promotion of seamen and the multiplication of the duties, the latter won. If it came to it, money could – and did – buy fighting men, just as it bought ships. Money was all-important to the mercantilist nation state.

And so it came to pass that, when King Charles I was dead and the Parliament needed money to put England back together again, the shambles of the Empire cried out for reform. The "Navigation Act" of 1651, the Act of 8 October 1651, "the first parliamentary statute that in any comprehensive way defined England's commercial policy" proved itself quintessentially mercantilistic by seeking money, first, and the reform of trade within the Empire hardly at all.[12] The primary concern of its several sections was to enhance the role that the London merchant elite played in the vital trades into and out of England's own ports by restricting the role of Dutch merchants. With certain exceptions, only English ships – including the English in the colonies – could carry goods *into* English ports from Asia, Africa, the Americas, or Europe. A key exception was the trade with Europe, in that a merchant of any other European nation could bring goods produced in that nation directly to England. The purpose of the act was twofold: to deny the Dutch their carrying trade, insofar as it involved England, and to encourage English businesses to take over the carrying trade that had previously been Dutch. The English merchants, especially the largest London merchant houses, upon which the Puritan Commonwealth depended for its financial support, were the beneficiaries – and backers – of this act.[13] As Charles M. Andrews put it: "The ordinance of 1651 was the work of the great commercial companies concerned in the 'rich trades,' as over against the lesser merchants of London and the outports . . . ."[14] One particularly well-informed contemporary observer, Daniel O'Neill, wrote that the "act was procured by some few men for their interest."[15]

Consider – as many did during the 1650s – what the Act of 1651 did

---

[11] In the exception that proves my rule, the promotion of the fisheries as "the nursery of seamen" was pursued. Thus, there evolved the policy of discouraging permanent settlements on the island of Newfoundland. See C[lifford] Grant Head, *Eighteenth Century Newfoundland: A Geographer's Perspective* (Toronto, 1976), 38–41 and elsewhere.

[12] Andrews, *England's Commercial and Colonial Policy*, 36.

[13] Brenner, *Merchants and Revolution*, 577–632 and elsewhere.

[14] Andrews, *England's Commercial and Colonial Policy*, 42.

[15] "A brief relation of the affares of England, March 1653," as quoted in C[harles] H. Firth, "Cromwell and the Expulsion of the Long Parliament in 1653," *English Historical Review*, VIII (July 1893), 531. Compare G[eorge] N. Clark, "The English Navigation Act of 1651," *History: The Journal of the Historical Association*, New Series, VII (Jan. 1923), 285–6.

not address, at least as far as the colonies were concerned. While the act barred Dutch ships from carrying anything but Dutch goods into colonial ports, it did not outlaw them from being there. That omission alone left the gate swinging wide. Moreover, any English vessel could bring goods from anywhere into colonial ports. And every one of those ships, Dutch as well as English, could do what they had always been doing and carry the produce of the colonies anywhere at all. Chesapeake tobacco and Barbados sugar could, and was, quite legitimately, carried by English and Dutch vessels to any port, London or Amsterdam. Indeed, some recognized in the free trade in Barbadian sugar a major opportunity to promote the English sugar industry and to squelch both the established industry of Brazil (then in the hands of the Dutch) and the new sugar industry being set up in the French West Indies. Yet the Act of 1651, by taking a first step in the control of England's trade, made a second step that much easier. More English trade was in the hands of London's mercantile magnates. Secured and enhanced, thereby, were the nation's financial resources for emergencies, such as Oliver Cromwell's Anglo–Dutch War (1652–4) and his "Western Design" (1654–5). King Charles II would secure an increase in the regular revenues.

The Restoration of King Charles II, and the Restoration Compromise that eased his way, ushered in a new era, the second of the three periods into which we can break English trade policies prior to the American Revolution. The Restoration also swept the Act of 1651 into a constitutional waste bin. While the lawmakers and the wholesale merchants had to begin again, they had now both theory and some practice to draw upon as they confronted the needs of the nation England. Their appetites whetted by their success under the protection of the first navigation act, English merchant princes sought the restoration of that coverage and more. Having successfully excluded the merchants of The Netherlands from some of the trade at English metropolitan ports, they argued to exclude them from more ports, elsewhere in the Old Empire. The appetites of the merchant elite for greater profits was more than matched by the appetite of the monarchy – King Charles II, Nell Gwynn, and company – for more money. The revenues from the customs duties, usually easier to increase than the land taxes and the excise taxes, seemed especially attractive in this regard. The trade of the colonies and the trade in colonial commodities combined to offer an easy opportunity to achieve both Crown and company purposes. The first years of the new regime witnessed the passage of the famed Act of 1660 (12 Charles II, c. 18) and

Act of 1663 (15 Charles II, c.7), which accomplished the immediate needs of a mercantilistic empire and established a colonial system under which that empire existed for over a century.

The navigation acts of 1660 and 1663 – the Acts of Trade – must be understood for both what they did and what they did not do. While we are here concerned most particularly with their impact on those of England's colonies that later became the United States of America, the acts had as their target not just those colonies but all of England's then and future overseas colonies, not only its colonies but the entirety of the Empire, including England itself, and its trade with the rest of the world – especially, again, The Netherlands. These two acts were designed, directly and specifically, to guide the trade of the Empire into directions that benefited the rising nation-state of England and, very particularly, the central government of that state, most especially, the monarch. The benefit to government came in the ways already recounted: a reliable and increasing flow of revenue from the customs duties, and an increasing pool of wealthy businessmen whose fortunes were tied to trade – and, thus, to government – and who could be counted on to lend funds to government when the need arose. Both regular revenues and emergency support served to buttress the government, which, in turn, used its strength to support and expand the Empire and its trade. From a mercantilistic perspective, colonies were important only insofar as they enhanced the trade and, thus, the power of the English nation-state.

The Act of 1660 and Act of 1663 addressed colonial trade from the perspective of the mercantilist. These two acts and other later acts supplemental to them (1662, 1670, 1671, 1673, and 1696), strove to direct more trade through English ports and to establish more of that trade in the hands of the major English companies.[16] The Act of 1660 in its first section set the tone for all that were to follow. No trade into or out of any English colony could take place in anything but an English ship. An English ship was defined, once again, as one built in England, owned by Englishmen, captained by an English master, and sailed by a crew three-quarters of which was English. Note that in this instance as in others, the English colonies and English colonists are English for all the purposes of the act. Excluded from English colonial trade of every sort were all foreign ships, sailors, masters, and merchants. The clear beneficiary of

[16] The supplemental pieces of legislation referred to are: 14 Charles II, c. 11 (the "Act of Frauds"); 22 and 23 Charles II, c. 11; 22 and 23 Charles II, c. 26; 25 Charles II, c. 7; 7 and 8 William III, c. 22.

the act was the important English merchant to whom was handed, exclusively, the lucrative and expanding trade of the colonies.

The next several paragraphs of the Act of 1660 dealt with the same issues as had the Act of 1651. In a highly convoluted way, the Act of 1651 had sought to enhance the trade of English wholesale merchants by limiting the carrying trade of the Dutch in English ports. It attempted to do so by stipulating that commodities produced in any particular place could be shipped to England only by merchants of that place in their own ships or by English merchants in English ships. For instance, wine from Bordeaux could be carried to London by either French merchants in French ships or English merchants in English ships. The Act of 1651, by its inclusiveness, had become a burden on trade. The Act of 1660 pursued essentially the same purposes but by precisely the opposite means. Instead of saying that all such goods should be traded in such fashion, it specified only those products that were of most importance. The act included two lists, one of European products – including such vital commodities as salt, grain ("corn" in the English usage), wine, timber, and all Turkish goods – and one of the produce of the English colonies. What these goods had in common was their value in the carrying trade and their worth to the royal revenue.

The enumeration or listing of colonial commodities did not echo the Act of 1651. While it did hearken back to an earlier era, much more importantly, it sounded a significant advance, signaled a different tack. In ways reminiscent of attempts under King James I and King Charles I to circumscribe the market for tobacco, not only were the listed commodities to be carried only in English ships, but they were also to be brought only to English ports.[17] Included in the original list and the subsequent additions to it were all those colonial commodities that earned the wholesale merchants good profits and brought the revenue considerable custom duties. They were the major staple commodities produced in English colonies, profit makers for English merchants and revenue earners for the Royal customs. They included goods in demand among England's consumers – ginger, sugar, and tobacco – and goods in demand by England's producers – cotton and dye stuffs, such as indigo. Later legislation (1705) added rice to that first group and added molasses, for distillation, and a variety of products vital in the building of ships ("naval stores") to the second group. Copper and the pelts of fur-bearing animals such as the

---

[17] Harper, *English Navigation Laws*, 35–6; George Louis Beer, *The Origins of the British Colonial System, 1578–1660* (New York, 1908), 89–240.

beaver were designated enumerated commodities in 1721; and in 1763, the list grew again when numerous other commodities were appended to the benefit of English manufacturing interests. By then, however, a century after the Act of 1660, the fundamental nature of English legislation had changed, as we will see. The additions of 1763 reflect that change more than they do the intention of those who drafted the Act of 1660.[18]

The Act of 1660 erected the first of the two mercantilist pillars designed to support the nation-state England; the Act of 1663 erected the second. Just as the first law sought to direct the export trade of the colonies into channels that would benefit England exclusively, so did the second law seek to accomplish the same objective with the import trade of the colonies. As in 1660, the Act of 1663 dealt with numerous issues besides the colonial import trade, but its central thrust was significant. No goods were to be imported into the colonies from Europe other than by way of England. (Reasonable exceptions made the rules more bearable.) In coming by way of England, such goods had, of course, to pay English customs duties. They all had to travel on English ships. English merchant houses earned the money from the carrying of the goods and from the profits in their sale. The government of England earned the revenues from the duties.

Two later seventeenth-century pieces of legislation supplemented the Act of 1660 and the Act of 1663. The Act of 1673 and the Act of 1696 added nothing of substance to the earlier acts. They were almost exclusively administrative in character. Even the Act of 1673, popularly known as the Revenue Act (or "Plantation Duty" Act) of that year, was not designed to raise any revenue. The purpose of that and the later acts was to hone the administration of the earlier acts, the better to effect their enforcement and assure their observance. Of all the provisions of the two acts, the one that went furthest toward that goal was a section of the earlier law. The Act of 1673 installed royal appointees as customs collectors in every port in the colonies. From that time forward, the royal revenues and the monopoly of the commercial magnates was ensured. One of the most powerful and strident contemporary critics of the navigation acts of the 1660s recognized them for just what they were. The effect of the acts was to fatten the coffers of the Crown and the treasure chests of rich merchants. Roger Coke lamented the result – "the Kings Customs, and particular men may grow rich by a trade" – but many more, then and

---

[18] Andrews, *England's Commercial and Colonial Policy,* 106–7. The acts mentioned are 3 & 4 Anne, c. 5; 3 & 4 Anne, c. 9; 8 George I, c. 15; 4 George III, c. 15.

later, had no such complaint.[19] That is what mercantilism was all about. Mercantilism was a star, rising.

The century of Great Britain's ascendancy after the passage of these early acts was a powerful confirmation of their successful implementation. The century also witnessed great changes in the nation, the Empire, and the way people thought about the economics of building and sustaining a nation-state. The success that mercantilism created for the British nation also encouraged among many a dissatisfaction with the way in which that success was shared. As with other successful ideas, mercantilism in England sowed and nurtured the seeds of its own destruction. While many prospered within the realm, the extreme prosperity of a very few motivated others to claim more for themselves. Businessmen generally decided that the state should no longer be the chief beneficiary of the growing economy. After all, they, the producers of goods and services, were central to its functioning. By the middle of the eighteenth century, mercantilistic thinking had begun to give way to the ideas of David Hume and Adam Smith. They preached to a choir of converts the "good news" of free trade. The gospel of mercantilism was about to be replaced by a new doctrine, capitalism.

Over the century between 1660 and 1760, England and its Empire epitomized the power of the mercantilist nation-state. The Acts of Trade were enforced, and they were obeyed. Englishmen and Englishwomen, at home and abroad, were far better off at the end of that hundred years than their ancestors had been four and five generations earlier. The European settlers in England's colonies, nearly one-third the population of the realm, had attained, on average, higher levels of income and wealth than any other group of people in the world.[20] (That their African American slave laborers

---

[19] Coke, *A Discourse of Trade, In Two Parts. The First Treats of the Reason of the Decay of the Strength, Wealth, and Trade of England. The Latter, of the Growth and Increase of the Dutch Trade above the English* (London, 1670), 40. See Andrews, *England's Commercial and Colonial Policy,* 132–3. Compare the writings of Francis Brewster, John Cary, Josiah Child, Joshua Gee, and others, as Andrews suggests (*England's Commercial and Colonial Policy,* 134). See, particularly, John Cary's *An Essay on the State of England in Relation to Its Trade . . .* (Bristol, 1695), which Andrews calls, "the most uncompromising defense of orthodox mercantilism in the seventeenth century" (ibid., 134).

[20] So claimed in John J. McCusker and Russell R. Menard, *The Economy of British America, 1607–1789,* 2nd ed. (Chapel Hill, 1991), 55, based on Alice Hanson Jones, "Wealth Estimates for the American Middle Colonies, 1774," *Economic Development and Cultural Change,* XVIII (1970). Revised calculations suggest an even higher figure for average per capita gross national product, roughly £13 sterling (1774). Compare Peter Mathias and Patrick [K.] O'Brien, "Taxation in Britain and France, 1715–1810: A Comparison of the Social and Economic Incidence of Taxes Collected for the Central Governments," *The Journal of European Economic History,* V (1976), 601–50, who presented data (611, 613) that indicate per capita commodity output figures of £7 for Great Britain and £6 for France (1775).

were denied a share in this abundance mattered not in the European settlers' accounting, however much the descendants of both groups have lived to bear the cost of such blind greed.) The colonists correctly perceived threats to that good life in Parliament's late-mercantilist revision of the Acts of Trade to accommodate, first one interest group and then another. The decision to resist and then rebel rent the Old Empire. Yet England, the nation-state built on mercantilism, showed how powerful it really had become by emerging from that defeat to fight again. The ultimate victory over its ancient rival France in the final phase of the Second Hundred Years' War was the consummate tribute to a nation-state that could and did draw on its revenues from trade to maintain itself in peacetime and to fund its needs in war.[21] Central to the success of the English nation-state in its long contest with France was its ability to create and service a national debt to meet such national emergencies. That, after all, was what mercantilism was about.[22]

The English colonists, at once both subject to and nurtured by the Empire and the Acts of Trade, quickly fitted into the laws and regulations promulgated from Westminster and Whitehall. They had to; they had no other choice. The Act of 1660 and Act of 1663 contained provisions to enforce compliance. Alternatives evaporated. The lessons taught to the Dutch in the three Anglo–Dutch wars (1652–4, 1665–7, 1672–4) were reinforced for that nation by the increasingly predatory armies and navies of France. It was surely better for The Netherlands to accept a limited economic defeat at the hands of Protestant England than a total annihilation by the cannons of Catholic France. With the Dutch absent from their ports and their markets, the English colonists rapidly realized the new reality. Colonial staple commodities, neatly enumerated by the acts, traveled to the proper markets along the proper paths. Colonial purchases of European goods came by way of English ports in English ships. Bonding procedures,

---

[21] The lessons that John Brewer draws most powerfully for the first five phases of that war apply even more forcefully for the sixth and last phase. See Brewer, *The Sinews of Power: War, Money and the English State, 1688–1783* (London, 1988).

[22] That France, the larger and grander of the two powers, lost this contest may with equal justice be laid to the difficulty it had in creating and servicing a national debt. The failure of the French government to overcome institutional obstacles to the regular funding of its indebtedness irreparably inhibited its ability to borrow in emergencies. See François J. Velde and David R. Weir, "The Financial Market and Government Debt Policy in France, 1746–1793," *Journal of Economic History*, LII (1992), 1–39, and the many works which they cite there, including, most especially, the pathbreaking studies by James C. Riley, *International Government Finance and the Amsterdam Capital Market, 1740–1815* (Cambridge, 1980); and *The Seven Years War and the Old Regime in France: The Economic and Financial Toll* (Princeton, NJ, 1986).

customs officers, admiralty courts, and the Royal Navy were marshaled to encourage colonial compliance with the Acts of Trade. The governments of the colonies themselves were enlisted to ensure their enforcement. All served together to limit the ability of the colonists to do other than obey.

Such a formulation might suggest colonial resistance to the Acts of Trade when, in fact, there was little.[23] The colonists, just as did everyone else affected by these laws, debated and petitioned for and against processes they liked and disliked. The history of the passage of each of the laws that constitute the corpus of statutory mercantilism is rich with the exchanges that are part of the legislative processes of Parliament. We would be very wrong to read these debates as anything precursory to the American Revolution. We would be very wrong to sense in any of the debaters a precursor to the likes of Patrick Henry, Sam Adams, or Thomas Paine.

What smuggling occurred hardly mattered over the long haul in the large scope of things. Again, seeing in any smuggling during the pre-1763 period some kind of "patriotic resistance" to English oppression before the fact is to distort greatly both in intention and scale what was simply the pursuit of immediate self-interest. And doing so badly distorts what the American Revolution was really about. Considerable anecdotal evidence of the existence of smugglers and their activities does little more than lend a flavor to the history of the period – on both sides of the Atlantic. Such evidence contributes not at all to any discussion of either the importance of such activity to the overall trade or the attitudes of smugglers or the motives of their supporters. The fallacy of composition should be a significant caution in such matters. The economic historian who worked hardest on this subject, Lawrence A. Harper, settled the issue: "illicit trade constituted only a small fraction of the legitimate commerce of the colonies."[24] Full stop; end of discussion.

This is not to suggest for one moment that in 1660 every colonist from Newfoundland to Barbados fell instantly into lock step, marching to the beat of Parliament's drum. There were loud and continuing protests against the restraints on trade, more vocal from some groups, more persistent from others. The tobacco planters of the Chesapeake and the sugar planters of the West Indies felt the constraints most and argued strongly against the Acts of Trade. Yet the number of their petitions fell off rapidly

---

[23] The case for this position is powerfully made by Oliver M. Dickerson, *The Navigation Acts and the American Revolution* (Philadelphia, PA, 1951).
[24] Harper, *English Navigation Laws*, 263.

in the 1660s; after the passage of the Act of 1673 (the "Plantation Duty" Act), their objections were heard little more. Later on, they and others in the Empire petitioned in favor or against some new measure within the compass of Acts of Trade. But such actions evince rather more their acceptance of the Old Colonial System than they do resistance to it.

The New England merchants, sustained by a government that recognized no Parliamentary limitation on the rights granted by the charter given the Massachusetts Bay Company in 1629, maintained their rather more belligerent arguments and actions into the 1680s. In 1677, John Hull, merchant of Boston, lamented that the Acts of Trade hurt New England's trade greatly: it "is as the cutting off o[u]r hands & feet . . . we must neither doe nor walke any more . . . . This orphant Plantation will be Crushed."[25] All they accomplished was to attract the attention of a new government agency, a "Lord Committee of Trade and Plantations" – the first Board of Trade – that put in suit their sacred charter. In 1684, the English government won the suit, abrogated the charter, dissolved the colony's government, and installed a new royal government of a new colony, the Dominion of New England. The merchant community in New England quickly had a change of heart, even the good merchants of Boston.[26] The Act of 1696 crowned the government's successes. Even Charles M. Andrews, even if unenthusiastically, did allow that by the end of the seventeenth century, Britain's leaders "had been able to win the day."[27]

Part of that change of heart occurred because the merchants of Boston had come to appreciate that the new order allowed them considerable advantages over the older scheme of things. Much more significant than what English colonists in the New World were forbidden to do by the Acts of Trade was what they could now profitably do. The most important opportunity opened to the colonists was the expanded role for merchants engaged in the carrying trade. Colonial merchants seized this chance and turned it to their best advantage. Consider, first, that within the Acts of Trade, the colonists were English in every sense. Colonial ships were English ships; colonial captains were English captains; and colonial sailors were English sailors. Every trade newly protected within the Empire by the Act of 1660 and the Act of 1663 was just as open to the merchants of Boston as it was to the merchants of Bristol.

---

[25] John Hull, at Boston, to [William] Stoughton and Peter Bulkeley, at London, Boston, 22 Dec. 1677, John Hull Letter Book, 1670–1685, [section 15], John Hull Papers, American Antiquarian Society, Worcester, MA.

[26] Bernard Bailyn, *The New England Merchants in the Seventeenth Century* (Cambridge, MA, 1955).

[27] Andrews, *England's Commercial and Colonial Policy*, 177.

There was more. Colonial merchants had an even better opportunity in the intercolonial trade of the Western Hemisphere than did merchants based in London or "the outports" (the other ports of England). Colonial merchants were closer at hand, had better sources of information, and ran smaller vessels that could operate more efficiently in the colonial trades and navigate more easily in coastal waterways.[28] Before 1664, the Dutch merchants based at Curaçao, St. Eustatius, and New Amsterdam had nearly monopolized trade along the eastern seaboard of the Americas. The colonists quickly and smartly took over their role and even one of their bases. New Amsterdam became New York with unseemly ease. By the 1690s, Londoners could well complain that the New Englanders were fast becoming the Dutch of the Empire, but no one moved to limit that role, at least not until much later.

There was still more. Nothing in the Acts of Trade prevented the English colonial merchant from trading with the colonists of other powers in the New World. The governments that owned such colonies might object, but the English government passed no law against it. As long as colonial merchants did not import into the English colonies any goods of European origin, and as long as colonial merchants did not export from the English colonies any enumerated commodities, the colonial merchant who traded anywhere in the Western Hemisphere was never in breach of the navigation acts. The "Molasses Act" of 1733 (6 George III, c.13) in effect confirmed the legality of these trades by levying a tax on certain of the imports from the foreign West Indies (sugar, molasses, and rum). The trade with the French, the Dutch, the Danes, and the Spanish was perfectly legal from the perspective of Parliament.

So were many other trades legal for the colonists under the Acts of Trade. Most notably, colonial merchants and colonial ships could carry enumerated commodities to England itself, could carry nonenumerated commodities from the colonies to some European ports, and could carry European goods to English ports, pay the duties, and bring them back to the colonies.[29] Colonial ships could engage in the African trade on the same footing as other English merchants, once the monopoly of the Royal African Company had been ended. Some did, even if the number was insignificant. While the East India Company maintained its monopoly of

---

[28] See Ian K. Steele, *The English Atlantic, 1675–1740: An Exploration of Communication and Continuity* (New York, 1986), on the increasingly facile flow of information within the Old Empire over the century after the Restoration.

[29] Andrews, *England's Commercial and Colonial Policy*, 62 and after; Harper, *English Navigation Laws*, 248.

English trade beyond the Cape of Good Hope, any trade within the Atlantic World that was open to the merchants of the metropolis was also open to merchants resident in any of the colonial ports.

Nor should that surprise us. The mercantilist minds that moved the Restoration Parliament of Charles II were more concerned about promoting English trade than in accomplishing anything else. Although few thought it through in quite this fashion, from the mercantilistic perspective ships owned by colonial merchants that freighted goods which paid the custom duties were no different from ships owned by merchants who lived in metropolitan ports. The legislation itself, by never drawing any such distinction, carries that point. It was the duties that mattered. Moreover, at least insofar as these trades profited the larger London merchant houses who traded in the staple commodities and who supplied the colonists with European goods, colonial traders served the second purpose that mercantilism sought to attain — enriching a class of wealthy supporters of government. Eventually, some colonial planters and some colonial merchants grew rich enough themselves to buy English government bonds, to lend the English government money in the emergencies of the Second Hundred Years' War. Mercantilists could hardly complain.

Some colonists did indeed become rich. Richest of all were the sugar planters of the West Indies. The planters of South Carolina and the Chesapeake were not far behind their Caribbean counterparts. Many of the merchants in the ports of Boston and New York, Philadelphia and Charleston also earned considerable fortunes. Their wealth was founded on the opportunities encompassed and encouraged by a British Empire bounded and bonded by the Acts of Trade. The effect was, sooner rather than later, to weld the concerns of all to the rising nation-state Great Britain.

Nevertheless, some did complain. The Old Empire, run by the very few for the well-being of a very few more, had left little scope for influence by any but the largest trading companies, which had been, in effect, extensions of the central government. The Glorious Revolution of 1688–9 and the profound political changes that had followed from it inaugurated a new mode of government that found it wise and proper to draw support more broadly. After the end of the seventeenth century, the older metropolitan mercantile elite, based in London, came to be supplanted by the more numerous middling and smaller businesses of London and elsewhere who were organized not through the once great chartered companies but

into interest groups that lobbied from a different perspective.[30] Some
among them grumbled that they should not have to face competition from
colonial enterprises. Such objections and the greater merit accorded them
were part of a changing climate of opinion which contended, essentially,
that the financial concerns of central government should no longer be
given exclusive priority. British businessmen, the producers of goods and
services, needed to have their concerns addressed, also. When, in the
middle of the eighteenth century, some of these new ideas and new interest
groups moved Parliament to a different track that threatened significantly
the basis of the prosperity of the Continental Colonies, only then did the
bonds of the Old Empire begin to weaken.

The beginning of the end, "the close of the great creative period of
mercantilism," as Charles Wilson has noted, can be marked to 1721–42,
the "Age of Walpole."[31] In 1721, in the speech from the throne opening
the new Parliamentary session that Robert Walpole wrote as Prime Minis-
ter and that King George I delivered, the government announced its
intention to restructure the existing mercantile law. The emphasis would
shift away from the purely fiscal to a new encouragement of manufacturing. Duties on the import of raw materials used by British manufactures
would be lowered or dropped. Export duties on British manufactures
would also be lowered, while duties on imported foreign manufactured
goods would be raised. Walpole won thereby the support of both the
rising manufacturing interest and the more broadly based business interests. In playing to the interests of the era, he ushered in a change of
profound significance. While the full course of that change would not be
run out for another hundred years, well begun was truly half done.

The North American colonists felt the results of this shift in emphasis
almost immediately. The Molasses Act of 1733 signaled that change,
although, given the lack of its enforcement, nothing much really happened. The "Age of Walpole" had, obviously, opened up the corridors of
power to a wider range of interests. Among them was the West Indian

---

[30] See, among others, Michael Kammen, *Empire and Interest: The American Colonies and the Politics of Mercantilism* (Philadelphia, 1970). "The two decades separating 1763 and 1783 may properly be called an age of interests, for . . . [the interests] so dominated [British] politics that men observed that mercantilism had changed from the control of trade in the interest of national policy to the control of national policy in the interest of trade" (ibid., 95).

[31] C[harles] H. Wilson, "Trade, Society and the State," in E[dwin] E. Rich and C[harles] H. Wilson, eds., *The Economy of Expanding Europe in the Sixteenth and Seventeenth Centuries,* Volume IV of *The Cambridge Economic History of Europe* (Cambridge, 1967), 516. For the address, given 19 October 1721, see [Great Britain, Parliament, House of Commons], *The Journals of the House of Commons,* in progress ([London]: [House of Commons], 1742 to date), XIX, 645–66.

lobby. In the late 1720s and the early 1730s, the supporters of the British West Indians worked to gain advantage for them by having Parliament pass a law designed effectively to enthrall British North America. What the West Indian interest wanted was a ban on any trade between the North Americans and the foreign West Indian colonies. What Parliament passed was a set of taxes designed to inhibit that trade. What applied in practice was much less than that. The North Americans, nevertheless, got quite a scare — and a pointed message.

The message for the North Americans in the passage of the Molasses Act was that some of the older imperatives dictated by mercantilist theory were not quite as powerful as they had been. The nation-state, much more secure financially, was now prepared to diminish some trades — notably those of the North Americans — and thereby to sacrifice some immediate revenue on the altar of political expediency. The West Indian business lobby, much more a political power in Westminster than the North Americans, could expect to have its desires attended to by a government that increasingly recognized such distinctions and deferred to such differences. Other interest groups would avail themselves of a similar hearing. The era of the nation-state was giving way to an era of the interests. It is for these reasons that Charles M. Andrews could call the passage of the Molasses Act a mercantilist defeat.[32]

The primacy of the nation-state — ever so securely installed — would yield to the primacy of the managers of business. Reality and theory would coincide in the eventual replacement of mercantilist doctrine by capitalist doctrine: government must be organized to the benefit of business. The monarchy, the epitome of the earlier mode, had already succumbed to Parliament, increasingly the instrument of the rising business interest. For the North American colonists, who had grown up under the former arrangements, this new situation was becoming uncomfortable because their economic concerns — whatever the financial contribution of their trade to the nation-state — were less valued. Indeed, with almost no voice at all in Parliament, the economic agenda of the Continental Colonies came increasingly to be ignored. When the colonists were recognized, it was as competitors to those who did have a say in Parliament.[33]

All of this came to a head beginning at midcentury. The reconstituted

---

[32] Andrews, *England's Commercial and Colonial Policy*, 89, n. 2.

[33] The careers of some of those who had such a say, members of the new order of British businessmen, is the subject of the work of David J. Hancock, now a thesis, soon to be a series of books: " 'Citizen of the World': Commercial Success, Social Development and the Experience of Eighteenth-Century British Merchants Who Traded with America" (Ph.D. dissertation, Harvard University, 1990).

Board of Trade of 1748 and after, enjoined by government partially to reform "the problems" with the colonies, was just a start. The subsequent acts of a Parliament increasingly at odds with reluctant, recalcitrant, eventually rebellious colonists are well known. These acts were not "acts of trade"; they do not concern us here. These new statutes of the 1760s and 1770s were designed to manage better an empire in order to obtain full compliance from its component parts with the needs of the central government, but these were new needs. They were needs as perceived by a Parliament increasingly controlled by or at least willing to accede to the demands of the most powerful economic groups among its constituencies, now, increasingly, the middling merchants and manufacturers of the nation.

As an example, the British financial community that had funded British success in the Seven Years' War with France demanded that government fully and immediately service that indebtedness. Failure to do so raised the threat that future borrowing could not be guaranteed. The contrast has to be drawn with the actions of that grand mercantilist monarch, King Charles II. When, early in 1672, he was told that future borrowing was in some doubt because of concerns about sums already owed, he simply stopped payment on the national debt; he put a "Stop to the Exchequer."[34] By declaring national bankruptcy, the government effectively collected a massive tax on the same businessmen that its Acts of Trade had enriched. They could and did do nothing. Existing tax revenues, now unencumbered by earlier loans, became available to service new debts. New loans were soon forthcoming.

A century later, the British government behaved very differently toward its business community. There would be no "Stop to the Exchequer"; indeed, there would be no new taxes either. After a review of revenue sources and an intense debate within Parliament, the government effectively negated any resort to further increases in domestic taxes. British business could not tolerate it.[35] In 1767, the House of Commons absolutely refused to vote higher land taxes. All recognized an easier solution of the problem, a shift of the tax burden away from the metropolis and to the colonies. For instance, the imposition of a transactions tax on business conducted within the colonies, to be collected as in England by charges for

---

[34] J. Keith Horsefield, "The 'Stop of the Exchequer' Revisited," *Economic History Review*, 2d. Ser., XXXV (1982), 511–28.

[35] By the end of the war, it was feared that taxes were already high enough to "be detremental to many branches of the manufactures, produce, and trade of This Kingdom." [Thomas Whately], *Considerations on the Trade and Finances of this Kingdom, and on the Measures of Administration, with Respect to Those Great National Objects since the Conclusion of the Peace* (London, 1766), 11.

affixing a seal or a stamp on documents, had every potential for raising considerable revenue.[36] Its novelty to the colonists – operational, financial, and constitutional – mattered not at all. It was certainly no act of trade. The objections registered against the "Stamp Act" of 1765 (5 George III, c.12), fiercer in the West Indies even than in North America, were seen in London only as the self-serving rationalizations of colonial tax-dodgers. "We need more revenue; we will tax them one way or another; they will pay" was the government's response. It was all just an administrative matter. The Old Empire had changed. The Acts of Trade, crafted, successfully, to empower the nation-state in a mercantilist mode, had been superseded a century later by revenue acts designed to spread out the burden of direct taxes in a powerful nation-state. While central government revenues were a continuing issue, significant differences separated the generations. The former strove merely to maximize them; the latter, to diminish the burden borne by business. A set of ideas – mercantilism – that sought to mold trade into patterns that had the design of underpinning central government had achieved their purpose. Trade to be taxed directly and wealthy merchants to be taxed indirectly had been the means to that essentially political end. A newer set of ideas – capitalism – that sought to order the economy to the best interests of business were just coming into play on the eve of the American Revolution. Using government to deflect the burden of taxation away from trade toward consumption and the colonies – the better to guarantee profits to producers – became the new objective. Great Britain had become, in the disparaging words of Adam Smith, "a nation that is governed by shopkeepers."[37] Just as Jean-Baptiste Colbert was a student of Thomas Mun, so also does Napoleon seem to have read his Adam Smith.

Colonies fit one way into a nation governed by the grander, national goals of the King in Council and quite a different way into a nation governed by a Parliament ruled by the narrower, more immediate con-

---

[36] John L. Bullion, *A Great and Necessary Measure: George Grenville and the Genesis of the Stamp Act, 1763–1765* (Columbia, MO, 1982).

[37] Adam Smith, *An Inquiry into the Nature and Causes of the Wealth of Nations* (1776), edited by R[oy] H. Campbell, A[ndrew] S. Skinner, and W[illiam] B. Todd, 2 vols. (Oxford, 1976), II, 613. Smith actually argued that this was the case at the time of the passage of the Acts of Trade. He stretched his point anachronistically in order to make it. Worsley, Roberts, and company were hardly shopkeepers. Compare Andrews' description of the people whose interests were served by the passage of the Act of 1651 quoted above. Smith was much more accurate in describing what England had become.

In his revisions for the second edition of *Wealth of Nations*, Smith altered the passage to read "a nation whose government is influenced by shopkeepers."

cerns of businessmen. Central to that difference, as far as the North Americans were concerned, was the government's attitude toward the colonists' own economic behavior. As long as what the colonists did increased the taxable trade of the Empire, mercantilists were content. When what the colonists were doing somehow competed with metropolitan businessmen, capitalists were not happy.[38] English business groups, increasingly adept at pulling the levers of political power, pushed Parliament to deal harshly with tax-dodgers in the colonies.[39] They brushed aside colonial constitutional objections as mere words. So far from mercantilist doctrine had Westminster and Whitehall strayed by the 1760s and 1770s that plans were even discussed in government circles to circumscribe the commercial activity of the colonists, perhaps to restrict them each to the carrying trade of their own colonies.[40] The potential for a colonial empire more strictly divided into colonial providers of raw materials and metropolitan producers of finished manufactures, whatever the immediate implications for central government finance, seemed altogether appropriate to those who shared such thinking. Thence came a rebellion, a rebellion that, just like such thinking, had nothing to do with the Acts of Trade and nothing to do with mercantilism.

[38] See, in this regard, Bernard Donoughue's explanation as to why the merchants of Great Britain withdrew their support of the colonists' cause on the eve of the American Revolution (*British Politics and the American Revolution: The Path to War, 1773–75* [London, 1964], 150–6).

[39] Should one be at all tempted to think that the Stamp Act of 1765 was solely a revenue measure, he or she should read about the fiercely repressive way in which the British government applied essentially the same law in Ireland, Great Britain's oldest colony. For the law, see the Act of 13 and 14 George III, c. 6, in [Ireland (Eire), Laws and Statutes], *The Statutes at Large, Passed in the Parliaments Held in Ireland from . . . 1310 . . . to 1800*, 20 vols. (Dublin, 1786–1801), X, 366–79. For its execution, see M[ary] Pollard, *Dublin's Trade in Books, 1550–1800* (Oxford, 1989), 22–30.

[40] Precisely these restrictions were imposed as part of the punitive measures that Parliament passed in the spring of 1775 (15 George III, c. 10; 15 George III, c. 18). They were said to be temporary and coercive in nature, but that did not prevent John Montagu, the Earl of Sandwich, First Lord of the Admiralty, from arguing during the debate over the second bill's passage that it should be made "a perpetual law of commercial regulation, operating to extend our trade, to increase our seamen, and to strengthen our naval power." [Great Britain, Parliament], *The Parliamentary History of England from the Earliest Period to the Year 1803*, edited by William Cobbett, 36 vols. (London, 1806–20), XVIII, 448. The "our" in Lord Sandwich's pronouncement had none of the inclusive sense common to the Acts of Trade.

Compare the nearly contemporary comment by Charles Whitworth, *State of the Trade of Great Britain in Its Imports and Exports Progressively from the Year 1697 {to 1773}* . . . . (London, 1776), lv, on the reason for the establishment of the colony of Georgia: ". . . to turn the industry of this new people from the timber and provision trade, which the other colonies had prosecuted too largely, into channels more advantageous to the public." The "other colonies," had been engaging in trade "too largely," which he deemed was not "advantageous to the public"!

Dickerson, *The Navigation Acts and the American Revolution*, x, calls all the post-1764 laws and regulations an "anti-trade policy" – and they were.

9

THE REVOLUTION, THE CONSTITUTION, AND THE NEW NATION

CATHY MATSON

THE REVOLUTION

Although a fundamental economic transformation took place in America only after the Revolutionary and Constitutional periods, many colonists expressed heightened expectations for rapid international and internal development even in the 1750s. Their expectations derived largely from the accelerated pace of economic change in the late colonial years, as well as from the visible signs of material improvement. Although predominantly a rural people, the revolutionary generation experienced aspects of a trans-Atlantic "consumer revolution" affecting the colonial cities and coastal villages before the Imperial Crisis. The aggressive market behavior of importing dry goods merchants connected colonists to British sources of textiles, sewing notions, agricultural implements, glassware, pottery, and other finished goods. By the 1740s, tea, coffee, citrus fruits, sugar and candy, snuff, and smaller quantities of exotic foodstuffs were common in coastal cities. More diverse consumption was made possible by the positive benefits of imperial membership, including naval protection, easy and long credit from British firms, inexpensive British manufactures, and the many unregulated export commodities that could be marketed competitively and without duties. Expanding consumption among "middling" colonists was also made possible by greater agricultural productivity in the mid-Atlantic and Chesapeake regions, as well as by increased staples exportation from southern colonies.

Economic successes over the late colonial period were in turn nurtured by republican ideology, which offered a language about the common good and a polity in virtuous control of its own economic destiny. As fears and frustrations peaked in response to imperial political relations after 1763, colonists referred more often to their own achievements and the potential of their commerce. Modestly successful experiments with reorganized production under the aegis of the nonimportation movements of 1765 to 1774, as well as the Continental Congress's Association Agreement of 1774, linked political liberty with autonomous international commerce; their sponsors also promised Americans that temporary sacrifices of self-interest for the common welfare would lay the groundwork for a bounteous economic future. When English government tried to keep colonial economic interests subordinate to mercantile goals with new legislation, colonial merchants redoubled their efforts to create colonial economic autonomy. The Sugar Act of 1764, which taxed and regulated trade centered at the West Indies, and the Currency Act of 1764, which curtailed the emission of independent currencies that colonists believed they needed to expand trade, were especially irksome to commercial interests.

In reality, these hopes were delayed, for the Revolutionary War both disrupted and redirected a significant portion of the colonial foreign market economy, and the war absorbed domestic economic energies in trying to sustain basic military and civilian needs. The nonimportation, nonexportation, and nonconsumption policies outlined in the Continental Congress's Association Agreement of 1774 eliminated all direct legal trade between the colonies and other portions of the British Empire. By mid-1775, there were acute shortages of war materiel such as muskets, gunpowder, salt, shoes, and clothing. Merchants made myriad complaints about losing British credit and British buyers for American-made vessels, as well as paying higher freight rates for bulky exports. To satisfy some of the country's military need, Congress entertained resolutions presented by Benjamin Franklin to create "free trade" for American merchants; Congress's partial acceptance of the resolutions resulted in limited trade in late 1775 to the non-British West Indies. On April 6, 1776, Congress passed a more extensive "free trade" decree to permit trade with any foreign nation or colony.[1] Until mid-1778, France, Spain, and the Netherlands – and in particular, their island colonies – became important sources of necessary commodities.

However, Congress's policy of creating free ports proved difficult to

---

[1] For proposals and the final resolution of "free trade," see [Feb. 26?], Apr. 6, 1776, *Journals of the Continental Congress*, ed. Worthington Ford, 34 vols. (Washington, DC, 1904–39), II:200, IV:257–9; and *Letters of Members of the Continental Congress*, ed. Edmund Cody Burnett, 8 vols. (Washington, DC, 1921–36), I:402–3.

sustain. As the war progressed, delegates at Philadelphia voiced strong objections. Moreover, British blockades at various American ports, British depredations against American ships in the West Indies, and long-term British occupation of New York City dampened efforts by both American and foreign merchants to enter and clear goods along the coastline. As a consequence, Congress resorted to negotiating specific treaties of commerce with individual nations. France was the most important trading partner to agree, in early 1778; thereafter, Spain and the Netherlands joined the American side of the war and continued to carry Chesapeake tobacco and mid-Atlantic naval stores and grain to European markets. In addition, Dutch St. Eustatius (until 1781) and Spanish Cuba continued to receive small amounts of American surpluses. Although a few merchants were able to accumulate modest fortunes from commissions earned in supplying troops, their more common preference was to enter the venerable traffic in privateering against the enemy; the capture and sale of over 2,000 British vessels and their cargoes added a great quantity of consumer goods to American markets, gave the satisfaction of significant fortunes to a few merchants, employed hundreds of American seamen, and bolstered the American fleet. By the last year of the war, however, all commerce diminished due to stepped-up British blockade activity.

Indeed, wartime American commerce was significantly lower from 1779 to 1781 than during the 1750s or mid-1770s. Blockades increased the risks and costs of trans-Atlantic trade – including higher freight and insurance rates – with the result that lower quantities of imports of manufactured goods marked the war years. As British demand for southern tobacco declined, production of that commodity fell to about one-third of its prewar level. Americans lost British bounties on indigo and naval stores, and shipbuilding suffered because of the loss of cordage, sail cloth, and specialized hardware that was essential to the enterprise. British blockades curtailed the transport of sugar (which would have been refined), molasses (which would have been distilled), and cotton (which would have been spun and woven) from West Indies ports to the new northern states. Everywhere there were shortages of containers and molds for snuff, eggs, cheese, medicines, and other perishables. Troop movements disrupted settled areas of commercial farming in the mid-Atlantic area, and long-established trade linkages were suspended – especially those northern ones related to grain shipments and shipbuilding. Many wholesale exporters who hoped for economic success turned from international trade to Congress's private contract system and internal business by 1779. Working through the commissary and paymaster departments, dozens of the most eminent former merchants proposed to construct barracks, start ironworks, hire wagons, transport rations and supplies, raise sheep for wool, or distill substitutes for rum.

The discontinuities of international commerce were the most consequential economic difficulty that Americans faced during the war; but it was the domestic economy that captured the attention of Congress as it faced the ongoing exigencies of sustaining an army. Overall, the role of government in economic activity, regulation, and public welfare was not clarified in these years. Weakened by Revolutionary ideology that opposed centralized political authority, Congress turned to the new state legislatures for help in harnessing private energies at all levels of society to the service of army and country. Together, Congress and the states pursued policies intended to meet the most pressing demands of the war. In the most important cases, these policies drew upon experiences associated with their former condition as colonists. But the ability of the new states to respond more directly and effectively to diverse local circumstances strengthened their authority, at the expense of Congress's, by the later years of the war.

One legacy of colonial policies was "currency finance," by which Congress followed an inflationary policy of issuing paper bills of credit – *continentals* – in increasing quantities and delaying their retirement from circulation. From 1777 through 1779, Congress issued $191 million in bills of credit, and from 1776 to 1778, it issued approximately $67 million in loan certificates to private creditors at 3 percent and 6 percent interest. Together, these paper obligations were used to purchase supplies from farmers and artisans, on the pledge of their future redemption in either silver or gold specie or canceled tax obligations. In addition, Congress received over $12 million as loans from France, Holland, and Spain, which bolstered the confidence of the new government's private creditors and war contractors. Despite these infusions of specie, however, Congress continued to issue larger amounts of bills of credit than the foreign loans covered, and the country experienced a steeply rising rate of inflation. Farmers and local businessmen across the states who accepted the currency complained bitterly about its declining value.

The states separately emitted their own supplies of paper money, which often were connected to sounder funding schemes. Virginia, North Carolina, and South Carolina emitted the largest sums; together, all the states emitted over $200 million between 1777 and 1781. In some northern states, merchants began to place their faith in state regimes and make their loans to local authorities rather than to Congress; many states in turn began to issue great quantities of IOUs to these merchants in anticipation of tax revenues to pay the state debts. In numerous rural areas, taxes rose to two to six times higher than prewar levels. As states like Connecticut, New Jersey, and New York tried to supply nearby armies and hold down the rate of inflation, local groups of farmers and shopkeepers resisted paying the taxes that would help to retire outstanding currency emissions and, simultaneously, demanded more paper money. Other regional interests argued that the vast tracts of unsettled land in their former colonial domains could provide the sinking fund for land banks as well as for militia veterans' pay. Georgia, North Carolina, New York, Pennsylvania, and Virginia were especially well endowed with western tracts, and all of the states had large contingents of advocates for state control over their currency and debts. Although colonial governments that found themselves in serious deficit-spending spirals typically resorted to hard currency policies, many of the new states responded favorably after 1777 to myriad local interests clamoring for more paper money, legal tender laws, and higher agricultural prices.

Meanwhile, Congress's monetary system slowly collapsed. By 1777, it took 3 dollars in Congressional bills to buy goods that cost 1 dollar in gold or silver. By 1778, the ratio increased to 7:1; by 1779, it was 42:1; by 1780, it was 100:1; and by April 1781, it took about $147 of Congressional bills to purchase what one dollar in silver specie obtained. Congress received a loan of $6 million in specie from France in 1778, which it set aside as security for a Continental Loan Office that dispersed $27 million in government certificates to domestic investors who expected to earn interest at over prewar market rates (normally 4 percent to 5 percent in northern cities in 1774). Military need, however, prevented timely repayment of this government debt and diminished the credibility of Congress when it sought further loans during the later months of the war.

By March 1780, there was still $200 million of Congressional currency and certificates in circulation, and delegates requested the states to tax some of the national currency out of circulation at the rate of one silver dollar for every forty paper continentals. Devaluation at such a steep ratio increased speculative activities throughout the states; over 1781 and 1782, Americans in all walks of life with even small amounts of specie accumulated Congressional bills of credit, at the rates of 80, 100, and even 120 to 1. Those who accumulated the bills cashed them in at state locations for double or triple their investment. This plan redeemed $120 million in continental currency at a cost of about \$3 million in specie. A small number of speculators held most of the remaining \$71 million of Congressional issues in the hope that political independence would pave the way for policies supportive of their full redemption at face value.

The second legacy of colonial-era policies appeared beginning in early 1777, as Congress recognized the difficulties of uniting the new states in order to conduct the war; given the enduring localism of the states, Congress urged them to assume neomercantile responsibilities for regulation, promotion, and production of wartime necessities. Some states responded to this mandate enthusiastically by creating new enterprises, channeling domestic resources into import substitutes, and promoting greater wartime production in traditional economic areas. Furnaces, forges, and rolling mills that dotted the countryside of New Jersey, Pennsylvania, Maryland, Delaware, and Virginia since the 1750s increased the size of their operations during the war, and some produced higher-quality pig and bar iron and higher-quality finished goods. Greater quantities of bar iron were "put out" to independent craftsmen for finishing into pails, nails, and horseshoes. Ambitious farmers responded to state government appeals to open up new tracts of land for grazing sheep for wool, which did not require as much labor in clearing and tilling as grain and vegetable crops. States aided farmers in getting sheep and cattle closer to armies and urban markets by offering commissions to appointed drivers. They also offered state payments for (1) wool to convert into army blankets and clothing, and (2) the services of butchers, coopers, carters, and weavers. Further, the states promoted increased use of cereals in making beer and whiskey, which lessened dependence on imported wines and West Indies rum. In addition, states hired skilled workmen to make and repair thousands of barges, bridges, barracks, and wagons.

Various states also resorted to wage- and price-fixing schemes. "Unworthy" as these laws might be in "infant republics," noted Congressional delegates, they had "become necessary to supply the defect of public virtue" unleashed by the Revolution.[2] Delegates from the New England states had met in late 1776 to set prices for goods produced and traded domestically. The following year, a meeting took place in Hartford for similar reasons but added wage guidelines for farm laborers and artisans as well. New Englanders were asked to limit prices for both agricultural products and finished crafts to 75 percent over 1774 specie prices, al-

[2] Feb. 15, Nov. 22, Dec. 20, 1777, *Journals of the Continental Congress*, VII:124, IX:953–7, 1043–7, quote at 1046.

though certain urban trades were limited to a mere 25 percent increase. By early 1779, regional conventions had discussed, and individual state legislatures had enacted, an impressive array of import and export duties; wage and price ceilings, laws against forestalling; limits on profits of 25 percent to 40 percent; embargoes on foodstuffs; and, in some northern states, requisitions of wagons, horses, and forage.

Not all urban and rural inhabitants believed that wage and price fixing was wise. Rather, the issue helped draw lines of economic interest between, as well as within, groups of commercial farmers and urban producers more sharply, preparing the way for post-Revolutionary discussions about the role of state governments in the economy. Current research suggests that inhabitants who provided needed services and scarce supplies to the state militias and Continental Army were sometimes in a position to inflate prices for their labor and commodities far beyond what state legislation permitted. Sterling prices of grain, for example, rose 200 to 600 percent in the first 2 years of the war around at least Hartford, Providence, and Philadelphia. Despite state price-fixing legislation, Maryland salt appreciated in value 3,900 percent between 1777 and 1780; wheat appreciated 5,000 percent in the same period. Despite state embargoes of exports from the major ports, exports of flour continued, and the price of flour rose 100 to 300 percent in Philadelphia and Wilmington by 1779. Merchants trading on their own credit, local producers, appointed wagonmasters, rations masters, deputy quartermasters, and overland hunters and herders were among the growing number of creditors of military suppliers.

Few rural inhabitants became prosperous from these activities, and nowhere did the countryside experience uniform benefits from wartime opportunities. Indeed, beyond the ribbon of settlement along the northern coastline, rural Americans may have experienced significant short-term hardship. Military recruitment took away a significant proportion of farm laborers and livestock. Worn-down equipment was virtually impossible to replace as long as the war effort absorbed new production of wood crafts, earthenware, and metalware. Many farmers claimed that prices of farm commodities did not keep up with urban black-market prices of shoes and clothing for their families. Farmers who suffered economic distress through the war often complained that state financing schemes were reckless, that embargoes deprived them of markets, and that army officials seized their grain and paid for it well below market prices. State officials compounded their fears by fixing farm prices at unacceptably low prices, while peddlers and domestic retailers charged them steeply rising prices for necessities produced in coastal towns. Rural seasonal and day laborers joined commercial farmers in protesting state policies because their own fixed wages diminished in purchasing power as prices rose for basic needs that they had to obtain from towns.

Urban craftsmen and small retailers were more supportive of price-fixing measures in Massachusetts, New York, New Jersey, Rhode Island, Connecticut, and Pennsylvania, where local populations at times resorted to "taxation populaire," or the community's efforts to enforce customary pricing and marketing. In 1779, for example, a crowd in Philadelphia seized a merchant suspected of exporting flour that was needed at home. After forcing him to sell the flour to them at prices they were willing to pay, a public meeting proceeded to post prices – both wholesale and retail – for over thirty commodities that civilians and soldiers required. Boston and New York experienced similar actions, and fishermen's wives in small ports periodically forced local merchants to lower their markups on imports as well.

Conflicts in the states over currency finance and myriad economic regulations should not obscure the significant degree to which the new sovereign states met pressing war needs. Moreover, certain kinds of local production received an impetus from wartime need to expand and mature. Home manufacturing provides an important example of widespread productive energies that were applauded by state governments and that flourished in the absence of any concerted efforts by the states to foster new technology or a new division of labor. As they flourished, home manufactures promoted new connections between city and country, merchants and rural villagers. In some regions, Americans responded to military demands by simply producing greater quantities of agricultural commodities, such as hemp, linen, and woolens, with traditional household methods. Independent rural artisans owned their own tools and raw materials, worked largely for a local market with relatively stable demand, did not require complex merchandising or credit operations, and may have weathered the vagaries of markets with informal and often noncash arrangements. This form of protoindustrialization, the most traditional and slowest to change, often involved females of a household between adolescence and old age spinning – and weaving, once the Revolution skimmed off itinerant skilled males – for local storekeepers, who provided the linkage to customers. Farmers in near-western Massachusetts, and skilled slaves and free whites in Virginia and Maryland, produced large quantities of yarn and somewhat less cloth for local markets. Although New York and Massachusetts made periodic experiments with "factories" that clustered large numbers of spinners and weavers under one roof, the more prevalent form of production was the single independent craftsman who responded to local demand.

In other areas, more mature commercial agriculture and nearby commercial ports combined in ways that promoted some reorganization of textiles production before the advent of factories. At Philadelphia, Wilmington, Newport, Salem, and other northern coastal cities, merchant-manufacturers who were dependent on foreign or major urban markets and sources of credit assumed responsibility for putting out raw and semi-finished materials to *cotters*, who lived in the countryside or small villages and usually owned spinning wheels and sometimes their own looms, but relied on the merchant for raw materials, collection of the cloth, and its subsequent marketing. In addition to market and credit needs, merchants involved in this system required fairly large numbers of local rural laborers to be successful. Sudden outmigration, or dramatic changes in crop prices that demanded more intensive farming and less attention to by-employments in textiles, adversely affected the merchant's labor supply. However, where textiles production expanded during the Revolution, it linked women who performed a traditional household activity to the far-flung requirements of the Revolutionary war and challenged extant values associated with female domestic labor. New patterns of production and distribution based on household manufacturing prepared a way for more capital-intensive investments and factories in later years.

Many wartime economic experiments taught Revolutionary leaders that governmental regulation and protection of the domestic economy were essential for Americans' success – their critique of mercantilism notwithstanding – and that international commerce could be forsaken only at the peril of the new union. They believed that the new rural enterprises could not be accomplished by self-interested economic agents in self-regulating markets. They further charged that new state legislatures vied among themselves for scarce resources and funds, and failed to provide the states with sufficient revenue from taxation. However, even when these critics articulated the necessity for greater central government control over the domestic economy, they expressed the hope that international commerce would be *less* encumbered with regulations in the future. Revolutionaries like John Jay predicted that political independence would make "the whole world open to us, and we shall be at liberty to purchase from those who will sell on the best terms" and perhaps make possible "a prohibition of all laws in restraint of trade" only in the context of restored international commerce.[3] By 1781, disgruntled army officers, frustrated Congressional and state leaders, and many urban residents who had not yet recovered from wartime dislocations all began to identify with a group known as the *Nationalists*, who called for familiar remedies to economic dislocation: healthy international commerce, sound credit based on the reputation of a commercial elite, and specie-based currency.

THE CRITICAL PERIOD

Nationalists did not represent a majority of Americans between 1781 and 1784, but their numbers grew. Many urban inhabitants joined merchants in celebrating a great flurry of commercial importation in response to pent-up consumer demand, from the end of active war in 1781 to the beginning of 1784. Eager to replenish depleted inventories and make quick profits, American merchants placed orders with former correspondents in British ports. As before, British imports were cheaper, of higher quality, and of greater variety than those of any other foreign country. Despite increased domestic productivity during the war, Americans could not supply enough of the woolens, Irish linens, and hardwares and housewares to satisfy demand after 1781, which further underscored their reliance on international commerce. The bitterness of war did not completely overwhelm Americans' long-standing cultural ties to Britain. Commercial correspondence with British firms resumed; prices and terms of sales were communicated easily in familiar channels.

Outside the ranks of Nationalists, many observers insisted that postwar commerce would flourish best if it was linked to the expanding domestic economy and independent of European connections. Optimism about mutual interest in commerce and the internal economy often arose in the ranks of state leaders, of merchants and overland traders who prospered during the Revolution, and of commercial farmers who looked forward to internal improvements and rising demand for their surpluses. In a wide-ranging public discussion of America's prospects, they described how commerce aided initiatives in state banking and brokerage, as well as

---

[3] John Jay to Robert R. Livingston, Paris, Nov. 17, 1782, in Francis Wharton, ed., *The Revolutionary Diplomatic Correspondence of the United States*, 6 vols. (Washington, DC, 1889), VI:11–49, quote at 31.

recovery of shipbuilding and shipping services, on which urban growth depended. Rapid resettlement of farms and rising land values throughout the western reaches of the new states were portrayed as the natural concomitant of successful commerce. The same optimists noted that commercial policies ought to be linked to the "civilizing tendencies" of small farmers and planters, who hoped to earn additional income from by-employments related to the production and transport of exportable surpluses. Higher incomes would make consumption of more imported goods within reach of most Americans in the near future, argued these writers. They also noted natural interregional dependencies: commercial centers would be most successful in their manufacturing when they could draw on sources of both rural surplus foodstuffs and necessary raw materials like lumber, hides, wool, and stone. By the end of the war, they reminded readers, small producers could provide great quantities of necessary commodities and move them over long distances to markets. What was not consumed in coastal settlements could be exported, in turn attracting foreign coin and correcting the persistent shortages of specie. Some state leaders added that public education, promotional societies, and widespread experimentation in agriculture and technology would prepare the ground for interclass and interregional cooperation and teach Americans to avoid the dangers of expensive luxury imports. Internal migration to western lands and immigration to coastal towns and cities would provide a necessary pool of labor. Recent estimates of what observers in the 1780s only roughly beheld show that the total American population grew from 1.2 million in 1750 to 2.3 million in 1776; it increased to 3.9 million by 1790.

Two sets of circumstances dampened this postwar enthusiasm and reoriented public and private views toward the Nationalists. The first was troubled international commerce. After 1783, governments in England and other nations enacted laws that interfered with Americans' ability to compete freely for foreign markets, thereby worsening the effects of a mid-decade depression in American port cities. The second set of circumstances was the centrifugal, contentious economic interests rising among the states. Together, international and domestic economic crises underscored that American hopes for rapid recovery and new development after the Revolution might be misplaced; many Americans who were initially optimistic about political and economic arrangements in the new state governments began to turn to Nationalists for different solutions after 1785.

Aggressive British actions against American trade were initiated beginning on July 2, 1783, despite the policy of open British ports negotiated at the time of the peace treaty that same year. British Orders in Council decreed that England would no longer tolerate the presence of American-built ships in trade to the British West Indies, a measure that sharply curtailed business for American shipbuilders and their artisans and halted West Indies exports of rum, molasses, sugar, cocoa-nuts, ginger, coffee, and pimento to northern ports. By mid-1785, additional legislation banned American meat and salted fish from British Caribbean possessions and placed heavy duties on American whale oil, rice, tobacco, naval stores, pig and bar iron, and certain kinds of peltry going to Britain. By 1784, Britain cut off the Newfoundland and Nova Scotia whale and fishing traffic to American vessels and prohibited American fish, whale oil, and salted meats from entering England. The combined losses of ship sales and services, declining commerce in fish and dressed meats, and steep duties on American whale oil and naval stores traded directly to Britain hit New England hardest. But southern exporters also faced the longer-term prospects of stagnating markets for tobacco and rice due to high duties. Even without legislation, however, New York and Pennsylvania merchants encountered obstacles to grain exporting to England and British West Indies possessions because of fluctuating price levels and periodic foreign gluts between mid-1784 and early 1787.

American observers noted uniformly that the Orders seriously damaged American economic interests; as John Adams wrote, "They [the West Indies] can neither do without us, nor we without them."[4] In fact, Americans sold one-third fewer finished vessels to West Indies buyers from 1784 to 1787 than in the final colonial years; they also experienced dramatically reduced demand from West Indians for American shipping services over these years. At first, American merchants were able to shift some trade toward the French West Indies, building on experiences during the Revolution. However, France and Spain also passed mercantile restrictions against American trading of fish and beef with their West Indies possessions. In July 1784, Spain also closed the lower Mississippi River to American traffic, which raised serious concerns among southerners about their access to the transmontane hinterland.

Trade with other areas of the world was not sufficient to offset the losses in traditional American exports or in the valuable benefits that Americans had enjoyed as members of the British Empire. In fact, increased imports of

---

[4] John Adams to Robert R. Livingston, July 14, 1783, in ibid., VI:540–2.

European and far eastern goods called forth renewed fears of exotic luxuries and their corrupting effect on the American consumer. Until American policy makers sanctioned the invasion of Tripoli in 1805, the Mediterranean trade was threatened by Barbary pirates. The wine, olive oil, slave, and spice trades with Madeira and the Canary Islands revived slowly after the Revolution, reaching prewar levels only about 1800. Commerce with the Low Countries and France revived in part very quickly – especially under the auspices of the mid-Atlantic states' merchants who were active in the war years – but did not reach prewar levels until the Napoleonic Wars. New arenas of commerce after 1784, especially the East Indies and China trades, replaced many of England's reexport items, such as spices, textiles, dried fruits, and medicinal herbs. But their value as a portion of all American imports was small before the 1840s, and the extent of their consumption by the American population is still uncertain.

Commercial instability reached its heights during the mid-1780s depression. It began as a serious credit crisis, not unlike the one Americans had experienced as recently as 1772. Everywhere, consumer spending had risen precipitously in 1783–4, prompted by generous long-term credit from English firms that permitted Americans to assuage pent-up demand. But by late 1784, many state governments lowered private purchasing power by raising taxes, making further purchases and repayment of current debts problematic. Americans imported goods valued at about 2.75 million pounds sterling from England per year in 1784 and 1785, compared to the 2.5 million pounds sterling of American imports from England per year over 1772 to 1774. In 1784, New England merchants purchased British goods valued at £600,000 sterling, which was approximately the annual amount they imported over the mid-1760s to mid-1770s.

Even if merchants and shopkeepers had not imported so heavily immediately after the Revolution, the declining and temporarily dislocated export trades would have accounted for many mid-decade hardships. Exports to Great Britain and British West Indies possessions over 1771 to 1773 averaged $7.5 million per year. While Americans exported a total value of about $10.7 million in 1775, they exported only about $5.8 million per year over 1785 to 1787, and the export total recovered to only $11.6 million in 1787. From 1781 to 1783, northern farm prices began to recover, only to fall below prewar levels by mid-1784. Between mid-1784 and mid-1789, wholesale commodity prices at Philadelphia and Charleston declined about 25 percent and 12 percent, respectively. This decline was perhaps clearest in near-coastal areas, especially for semiprocessed farm goods that were exported to the West Indies. Export prices for flour, timber products, cheese, and shoes fell faster than the prices of European imports. In addition, there were increased domestic land and property taxes. Moreover, lower prices for rural and village consumers' agricultural surpluses resulted in delays in repaying debts and lower levels of consumption until the depression abated after 1786 (1787 in areas of western New York and frontier New England). Most urban craftsmen fared better during these years, because prices of necessary commodities remained stable at relatively high levels, as did consumer demand for their goods.

By mid-1784, it was clear that foreign firms remained reluctant to extend enough credit to American merchants to satisfy pent-up wartime demand for their imports; nor did merchants in the northern states have sufficient specie to pay debts to foreign creditors. Observers in Massachusetts estimated only £150,000 in specie in circulation there, and the chain of unpaid debts stretched far into the countryside, into the regional courthouses and homes of western Massachusetts farmers, until the outbreak of violence associated with Daniel Shays in September 1786. But the pattern of crisis and reaction was similar in most states that had both active commercial ports and populated hinterlands. Debts connected to land usage and improvements increased everywhere. Three new commercial banks, in Philadelphia, New York, and Boston – which issued IOUs, held deposits, made loans, and discounted foreign currencies – served the merchant populations of those cities. Few middling and lower-class Americans shared the benefits of these new institutions. Moreover, through the 1780s, bank note issues were greatly surpassed by the traditional forms of mercantile business, primarily the use of bills of exchange drawn on a merchant's private reputation. Larger-scale enterprises that required more capital outlay than commercial ventures, such as sugar refining and candy making, distilling, paper making, tobacco refining, or glass and pottery working, were hit hard with bankruptcies by 1785, as were most peltry and lumber exporters. Plans to initiate new manufactures were discussed only rarely between 1785 and 1787.

The South may have suffered postwar setbacks in international commerce even more than New England, and these persisted long after northern agricultural recovery began. Tobacco, the staple export of greatest value before the war, would never reach prewar levels again. Although the volume of southern tobacco exports to England and Europe steadily rose until 1786, it declined thereafter. Even more important, British duties on tobacco imports, higher warehousing fees in England, and lower consumer prices there reduced dramatically the value of American exports by the mid-1780s. And after 1792, the direct trade of tobacco to Holland and France entered permanent decline. Southern rice and naval stores exports also declined in value during the 1780s because of British restrictions, and only during the years of high demand for these commodities during the Napoleonic Wars did values and volume increase temporarily. Finally, although northern states were steadily gaining over England in the ability to carry southern exports in northern vessels, England still transported about 50 percent of southern exports in 1789.

Some commercial decline was doubtless a result of the reorganization and restructuring in the domestic economy in the wake of the Revolution. The growing domestic population was most likely consuming much of the rise in production of agricultural and small craft commodities, until western farm output rose faster than demand. It may also be true that a growing population in settled areas absorbed farm surpluses that might otherwise have been exported. Small retailers, grocers, merchant-manufacturers with little capital, ambitious peddlers, and "mechanicks" all created demand for food and rural byproducts. Although immigrants often brought investment capital with them and the sons of American merchants diverted investments toward coastal trade and some "infant manufactures," many of these new efforts involved minimal amounts of capital and little or no changes in the organization of production and labor. Unstable international commercial conditions prevailed. Although the various regions of the country experienced great differences in their productive capacities and in their pace of economic recovery following the Revolution, current estimates of per capita exports, as well as of per capita wealth, suggest that there was little or no growth nationwide over the period 1781 to 1793. Some evidence suggests years of declining incomes in many locales.

The commercial troubles of the 1780s derived not only from the downturn in international markets and from British policies but also from the limitations of Congressional power under the Articles of Confederation. The various states stepped into this vacuum, much as they had during the Revolutionary years, and responded to particular immediate interests with bold and timely measures that at first drew praise for state leaders. By the mid-1780s, however, it was becoming clear to Americans concerned about international and interstate developments that distinct state policies often pitted some groups of Americans against others. Different state taxation policies, or discriminatory legislation against the commerce of neighboring states, said Nationalists, weakened the economies of all states. "State particularism" heightened the critical character of the decade.

In a retreat from reliance on the now-worthless continental paper money, leading Nationalists helped to convince Congress to appoint Robert Morris as Superintendent of Finance and to give him significant powers over the conduct of the war in the first years of Congress's existence under the new Articles of Confederation. In February 1781, Congress chartered the first note and specie bank of national proportions, the Bank of North America, and located it near Congress in Philadelphia. In his capacity as Superintendent from May 1781 to December 1784, Morris issued notes redeemable in specie and covered by the credit and reputation of Congress and Morris' own fortune; its function was to discharge the great public war debt. His bank might have functioned well during the 1780s except that both potential sources for providing a fund for the BNA failed to materialize: foreign loans of specie, and the grant from the states to Congress of the power to levy a uniform national impost. Congress's February 1781 proposal for a permanent uniform national duty of 5 percent on the value of all goods imported – which was dependent on the united consent of all the states – was defeated by some northern state legislatures, as were similar proposals in 1783 and 1785.

Instead, the states continued to experiment with their own means of raising revenues and defraying financial obligations, thereby undermining further Congress's minimal authority. In the North, varied interests threw their support behind state attempts to (1) raise revenue from commerce, (2) repay private and public debts, (3) create temporary monopolies to foster the development of inland navigation routes, (4) promote new inventions to advance commercial agriculture, and (5) support shipbuilding and immigration of skilled labor. Although some degree of state promotion and regulation continued over the 1780s, state efforts to provide a circulating currency and to retire Revolutionary debts were more consequential during depression years. Some states also reverted to the colonial experiments in *land banks* – a practice whereby individual subscribers put up personal real estate as collateral against a loan of paper money for conducting long-distance exchange. But even these measures were insufficient, and only seven states were issuing paper money by 1785, when the depression hit. By declaring this paper money legal tender, and by fixing the periods of its circulation, these states were somewhat successful in their efforts to ease the burden of Revolutionary war debts. Moreover, although the Nationalists made familiar warnings against inflationary panaceas, there was widespread sentiment that the states were providing a circulating medium to which urban artisans, lesser merchants, and itinerant craftsmen all could subscribe. State issues of paper currency, they argued, were superior to federal notes such as Robert Morris's because they were locally controlled and more conveniently obtained. Pennsylvania, New Jersey, and New York could point to a relatively smooth system of state finance; Georgia, South Carolina, and North Carolina also emitted their own monies. New York, Connecticut, and Pennsylvania fostered alliances between agricultural and commercial interests by effectively balancing solicitude for creditors with a popular commitment to paper currency. Their assumption plans neither repudiated Revolutionary debts nor depreciated them into oblivion, nor did they repay state debts with specie. But just as often these Confederation-era currencies depreciated in value in relation to specie – Rhode Island's abuses were the most serious – and caused endless quarrels about whether they should be accepted at face or depreciated value. Massachusetts legislators compounded the problem of using paper money by requiring that all taxes and private debts be paid in specie, which in effect scoffed at individual efforts to use paper money at all.

In addition, six states enacted their own imposts rather than approve a uniform Congressional form of revenue. Nine states interpreted the 1783 British Orders in Council as a cue to pass steeper duties against British imports than other foreign imports after 1784. Duties ranged from 5 percent to 25 percent; Rhode Island placed a treble duty on British goods. Pennsylvania passed an act in 1785 that became a model for the first national tariff in 1789. Seven of the states passed duties on British ship entrances and commodities, varying from 5 percent to 8 percent ad valorem. A few states also passed duties against other foreign trade, although in nominal amounts ranging from 2 percent to 4.5 percent. Three New England states even prohibited British vessels from exporting American products, thus forcing the ships to unload their British and European goods and then retreat to another port with an empty hold.

Although state commercial discrimination seemed to combine the best contemporary wisdom about protecting "infant manufactures" at home and providing "free trade" for American ships and agricultural surpluses, results were mixed. At first, state protective tariffs on luxuries and new American manufactures seemed to abet initiatives for "useful manufactures." New York, Pennsylvania, Massachusetts, New Hampshire, Maryland, and Virginia passed legislation to prohibit imports of certain finished commodities; the list grew to fifty-eight items in Massachusetts by 1786. By 1785–6, some states passed additional tonnage and ad valorem duties on foreign commerce.

Many northern wholesale importers objected that duties were a burdensome additional cost to them. Some wholesalers went so far as to assert that the costs of commercial taxation prevented them from seeking supplemental investment opportunities in processing imported goods. Nor did state paper-currency emissions offer consolation to retailers and wholesalers, who required specie for international remittances. Their long-term credit had been stretched to the breaking point by late 1785, as commercial farmers and "country buyers" proved unable to pay dry goods importers their debts. Particularly where state duties on the imports of sugar, molasses, and tobacco were high, distilling, refining, and snuff manufacturing became costly enough to drive even established concerns into bankruptcy and their workers into unemployment. Only five New York distilleries were in business in 1786, compared to twelve in 1774; in Boston, sugar, barreled salted meat, and snuff manufactories frequently suffered until at least 1788. Nominal prices of iron goods and textiles fluctuated until the time of the ratification controversy, when they finally began to increase.

States with major port cities, especially New York and Massachusetts, took advantage of their superior position in international commerce and in regional markets to pass discriminatory duties against neighboring states' traffic at their ports, while weaker states tried to divert trade to themselves by abolishing duties altogether, thus setting parameters for intense interstate rivalries by mid-1785. In early 1785, the New York legislature imposed an additional 5 percent tax on all commodities imported from other states for sale to New Yorkers. New York pursued interstate discrimination with respect to exports, too, when it continued a long-term policy of embargoing exports of its own wheat and flour – thereby encouraging bolters and bakers to lower prices to consumers as supplies accumulated – while raising prices of wheat and flour from Connecticut and New Jersey. Since 1784, New York had extended the double duty on British imports to reexports destined for out-of-state customers.

But these policies did not necessarily establish a preeminent place for large ports in New York, Pennsylvania, and Massachusetts; weaker states could counter with distinct policies. New Jersey and Delaware, states without dominant ports, established free-floating grain prices and free exporting, while they simultaneously discouraged the flow of raw materials to manufacturers in states which assessed heavy taxes on "foreign" –

that is, other states' — commodities. These initiatives enjoyed some success, at least in the region around Wilmington where numerous flour mills and a vigorous shipping industry flourished. But merchants in Providence, Rhode Island, believed that they were virtually barred from trade by 1785 because of the high state duties at Massachusetts and New York ports. Moreover, it is unclear whether "free ports" in Rhode Island, Connecticut, and New Jersey alienated portions of the agrarian farmers and middling artisans in those states; until we know who benefited from untaxed wholesale prices and who paid the burdensome transport fees and export duties at some ports, we will not be able to say how such "free trade" satisfied specific interests. It can be said with a degree of certainty, however, that Connecticut's free ports policy did not succeed in attracting British carriers to New Haven and New London; Connecticut's commercial farmers continued to gather agricultural surpluses from the countryside for transshipment to New York. Most of Connecticut's foreign goods also came through New York between 1783 and 1786. Other state laws were not especially helpful to aspiring manufacturers and artisans, because the effects of protective legislation were undercut by the high duties placed on raw materials and farm goods imported from nearby states. The consequences were that (1) artisans and exporters could not compete with their British counterparts for the trade of the southern states, and (2) the mutual dependencies of country and city could not be developed to their fullest potential. And, as noted by many contemporaries, state duties promoted smuggling across state borders in the interiors.

The crises of international commercial recovery and interstate rivalries made it impossible for Congress to attend to the most pressing issues threatening the stability of the republic. From the vantage point of Nationalists in the mid-1780s, one issue was the enormous sum of Revolutionary debts still outstanding. From 1776 to 1780, Congress emitted certificates with a face value of $241.6 million; the specie value of this debt was approximately $3.7 million by 1782. From 1776 to 1782, Congress also borrowed $63.6 million from private American sources. The specie value of the foreign debt was about $7.8 million by 1783. Although state requisitions of money and state assumption of some war debts reduced Congress's debts in the first months of peace, the total federal debt by 1784 came to $39.3 million owed to domestic and foreign creditors. In 1785 and 1786, only $1,110,000 was remitted by states to help defray a small portion of the interest due to foreign governments and private American creditors. By January 1790, Congress reported the federal Revo-

lutionary war debt at $52,788,000. The total of individual state debts
came to about $13.5 million in 1787, even after commendable efforts by
some of the states to repay large portions of it. North Carolina owed
private creditors over $1.7 million; Virginia owed about $2.7 million. By
January 1790, the combined state debt was well over $18 million.

Although the remaining debts of the states tended to concentrate in
fewer hands over the early 1780s, it was the concentration of the federal
debt at tremendously discounted prices that drew most public attention.
Small war suppliers, commercial farmers, and veterans tended to sell their
Congressional warrants and notes quickly. Some were in desperate need of
ready cash to meet postwar needs. Others feared that because Congress had
no authority to tax the states – and thus no means to create a revenue
which might serve as a fund to convert its note obligations to citizens into
cash – it was prudent to dispense with the notes quickly. Buyers, on the
other hand, were willing to accumulate large quantities of these notes at
low prices, because they anticipated that Congress would redeem the debt
at face value.

But, argued Nationalists, redemption could proceed only if Congress
secured a reliable source of revenue. It had failed to secure impost duties
and tariffs on foreign goods and ships, and the states enjoyed the benefits
of commercial revenues from their own imposts. Taxes on land, most
policy makers admitted, would be difficult to secure; a national domain
created by the land cessions of states with vast western reserves would not
produce significant revenue from the anticipated numbers of small farmers
moving west, while such a policy might see land passed into the hands of
speculators. And manufacturing for markets accounted for a minuscule
part of American productive energies as yet; although some rising small
entrepreneurs began to insist on protective tariffs, they were forced to rely
on the rather piecemeal efforts of states trying to serve myriad distinct
interests. The specter of mutually annihilating special interests – a common lament of Nationalists by 1785 – seemed to endanger the continued
existence of the new republic.

FEDERALISTS AND ANTIFEDERALISTS

By early 1786, the core of Nationalists had broadened to incorporate
interests suffering from the decline in international commerce and from
thwarted expectations in manufactures, as well as state leaders who grew

disgruntled with fragmented responses to conflicting interstate – and intrastate – demands. By mid-1786, a vocal group of Americans in each region, occupation, and socioeconomic standing expressed opposition to state particularism. Nationalists who met at Annapolis in September 1786 to promote a "uniform system in their commercial intercourse and regulations" articulated an increasingly representative sentiment for a more authoritative central government. Expansionists, developers, and "projectors" joined Nationalists in Congress and state governments to call for the creation of a national domain that might be surveyed and sold to citizens who sponsored commercialization of the frontier with new enterprises and settlement; proceeds from land sales might also help to defray the national debt. Westward migration held out the prospect for new agricultural bounty only if the "drain" of population into "savage" country could be given sufficient economic and social order, and if distinct state jurisdictional quarrels could be halted. Squatters and speculators who spread onto the frontier in advance of surveys or with little regard for developmental transformation of the frontier thwarted hopes of national leaders to create a national domain that would provide revenue from, and give coherence to, settlement west of the Appalachian ridge.

Following the Revolutionary peace settlement, the old Northwest Territory comprised the claims of many former colonies to lands granted in original charters or acquired from Indians. Virginia's claims overlapped all of the others. Complicating the issue for Nationalists was Maryland's insistence that, as a "landless" state without western claims, it would not ratify the Articles of Confederation until other states made cessions to a national domain that settled overlapping and extensive western claims. New York did so in 1781–2, establishing agreements with the Iroquois and also setting a western boundary; Virginia made its momentous contribution to the national domain in 1784. Following these cessions, Congress passed the Land Ordinance of May 20, 1785, a plan for creating an extensive national domain that would be surveyed, sold, and deeded in regular portions and governed much as extant states were. Following the venerable New England township tradition, surveys were to be of 6-mile-square tracts, each with 36 sections of 640 acres. The Northwest Ordinance of 1787 furthered these plans by creating one large territory that included three to five potential new states; further, it prohibited the extension of slavery into this new domain.

But ambiguities remained. For one, the Ordinance itself could not ensure the integration of new states into the national political economy without a centralized enforcement of its provisions. For another, the insecurities of frontier life required that an external authority be created with the power to negotiate ongoing disputes as the region was integrated into the union. Conflicting claims of migrants showed repeatedly the need for resources and planning for newly settled areas. New roads and canals built by the states inspired even grander interstate projects that would promote production in the budding local markets along internal waterways, except when continuous disruption in the countryside – exemplified by the turmoil in western Massachusetts starting in September 1786 under Captain Daniel Shays – could not be tamed by state authorities.

Nationalists were also joined by failing distillers and sugar refiners who decried the West Indies British Orders in Council, and by shipbuilders and whalers who wanted their Newfoundland and general Atlantic trading rights returned but found the states incapable of securing their interests. Real estate brokers, retailers, and ambitious tradesmen joined in the attack against state sovereignty by arguing that banks and other urban institutions would boost commodities exchange, money transactions, invention, education, and a host of services; but contemporary state experiments along these lines were inadequate to the magnitude of these tasks and deprived creditors of essential confidence in their dealings with debtors. Aspiring urban entrepreneurs, some of them craftsmen and some of them former merchants, began to promote regulations for the uniform quality and transport of agricultural goods, uniform tender laws, and a uniform currency in order to correct discriminatory interstate laws.

Delegates at the Constitutional Convention made important strides toward creating the political authority necessary for establishing America's commercial reputation among nations and its own internal economic development. On some issues, especially the creation of a federal revenue through a uniform 5 percent impost, there was considerable agreement among delegates. Such a measure recognized that international commerce was (1) a primary source of revenue from which to repay outstanding foreign and domestic debts, and (2) the basis for national accountability in seeking future international loans for internal development. A uniform tax on imports, they continued, would curb the most damaging contentions among the states, because its burdens would be shared relatively equally among importers.

More consequential in the long run, but less easy to glimpse in 1787, was delegates' agreement to eliminate barriers against competitive trade among the states: they began to create an arena of what Hamilton would call in *Federalist* Nos. 11 and 12 the "natural reciprocity" among various interest *within* America. What has come to be called the *interstate commerce clause* of the Constitution embodied a grant of authority to Congress that created the conditions for the free movement of people, transport of products and capital, and uniform institutions that, together, proved crucial to establishing a national market. A similar grant of power to Congress to settle the conditions under which (1) new territory would be developed, (2) new states admitted to the union, and (3) boundaries set was also integral to creating this national market over time.

Many delegates at the Convention anticipated a market economy of great dimensions when they established the theoretical and institutional safeguards for contracts and the rights of private property against customary rights or popular agitation — Shaysites and Rhode Island debtors were fresh on the minds of the founders. The national government would regulate the commerce of Americans as citizens of the same country, with the same obligations and immunities, irrespective of state of residence — thus setting the stage for standardization of business practices, weights and measures, patenting, and dissemination of information and invention across the states and national sections. Finally, America's international reputation would be fostered by the federal government's power over foreign affairs, especially those on the high seas. The Constitution also granted the federal government power over unorganized territory and over admitting new states to the union, steps that would bolster central control over the creation of a national market. Further, Congress alone would coin money, regulate its value, and establish uniform rules about bankruptcy and naturalization, thereby overcoming additional state particularisms.

However, despite Nationalist expectations for a more authoritative central government that would dispense with divisive forms of state sovereignty, they neither destroyed all state economic powers nor extended federal economic powers as far as their avowed hopes during the 1780s. The federal system created in 1787 permitted a dual governmental authority over economic affairs; with respect to the powers granted to the proposed national government, only a few of the far-reaching possible grants of power were adopted by the delegates. The most plausible explanation for their self-limiting tendencies lay in delegates' acute awareness of the distinct interests they represented, and the likelihood that those interests had even more varied representation in the several states. If they made more than a few significant alterations in the structure of the political economy, they might invite opposition that could collectively defeat the whole plan.

Unlike the impost discussion, controversy over export taxes most clearly revealed delegates' broadly divergent and apparently contradictory assessments of local and regional interests represented at the Convention. Since the early years of the Revolution, such divisions over commerce had been apparent.[5] During the 1780s, in the face of British discrimination, southerners called even more loudly for open, competitive trade with all foreign nations, thereby keeping freight rates down and prices for staples up. Southerners were afraid that the northern states would exploit their temporary advantage in Congress to impoverish the South; southern staple exporters were convinced that export duties would burden their region with a disproportionate share of the national taxes and that resulting higher transport costs would undermine its prosperity. For their part, northern merchants believed that export duties were generally less harmful than import duties; while exports usually bore lower rates, Americans' "taste for refinements" created demand for luxuries and foreign imports that were taxed steeply. Many importers argued that higher import duties would be passed along to consumers in the form of higher prices. However, they argued, lower import duties would encourage greater consumption and promote American shipping and commercial interests, while a tolerable rise in export duties would support American manufactures by discouraging the exportation of valuable raw materials.

The Convention delegates proposed to compromise such differences by circumscribing national power over exports, but they were aware of the sectionalism that would be made manifest with the discussion over slavery after July 13. Although many Convention delegates from northern states opposed slavery on moral grounds, almost all the delegates were willing to make important concessions to the South's continued reliance on the institution in order to gain approval for northern navigation rights. In the famous Convention compromise of August 16–24, delegates guaranteed the interests of slaveholding staple producers by denying Congress the right to prohibit the importation of slaves before 1800; at the same time, however, Congress would have the power to pass, by a simple majority vote, navigation acts that affected shipping and commodities at American ports – a concession to northern commercial interests. The next day, delegates easily passed a motion to extend the limit on congressional interfer-

[5] See early examples of admitted sectionalism in Speech of William Henry Drayton to the South Carolina Assembly, Jan. 1778, repr. in Hezekiah Niles, *Principles and Acts of the Revolution in America* (Baltimore, MD, 1822), 357–64, esp. 363; and *Journals of the Continental Congress*, Jan. 20, 1778.

ence in the slave trade to 1808; on August 28, they agreed not to permit export duties by the states, although on September 13, they settled on the principle that a state might levy "incidental duties necessary for the inspection & safekeeping" of exports. In effect, delegates had created a written structure that recognized the rift between North and South that had developed over the colonial and Revolutionary periods.[6]

With respect to internal improvements and manufacturing, Convention committees charged with considering these issues never reported back to the whole delegation, probably out of fear that specific proposals for development would jeopardize intersectional harmony. Some delegates privately admitted that different parts of the country would benefit unequally from improved transportation links among frontier settlements. Others worried about the interregional conflicts resulting from measures fostering manufactures. The idea that the new union might serve these diverse, sometimes conflicting interests was crucial to its appeal. Equally crucial was its ability to avoid express commitments that showed a regional bias. Along the same lines, the Convention delegates hesitated to give Congress specific authority to issue paper currency, even as they prevented state emissions in the future. The prospects of assuming state debts and eradicating the dilemma of depreciating paper currencies came up only briefly. Delegates also explicitly excluded sumptuary legislation from the powers of the federal government, and they limited monopoly rights to patents and copyrights.

As Nationalists – identified after 1787 as Federalists – sought ratification of the Constitution, their opponents rallied. Antifederalists were not convinced that the Constitution was a truly representative or federal proposal, and they opposed its economic provisions in every major particular. Especially when contemplating whether the new settlements of the West would favor economic and cultural exchange with the North or South, they feared deepening sectional divisions. Other opponents challenged the right of delegates to destroy the sovereign powers of the states and give them to the new Federal government. Tax powers would be shared between federal and state authorities in the future, and uniform import duties threatened to eradicate the states' control over their commerce. They feared Federalists would resort to excise taxes – a fear proved correct in 1791 – and they predicted that a federal Congress would sooner or later

---

[6] James Madison Notes, and George Mason Speech, Sept. 13, Sept. 15, 1787, *The Records of the Federal Convention of 1787*, ed. Max Farrand, 4 vols. (New Haven, CT, 1911; repr. 1966), 2:605, 631.

levy export taxes. Finally, Antifederalists also expressed opposition to the
distinct class interests served by Constitutional provisions. Melancthon
Smith spoke for the "respectable yeomanry," or "middling classes," who
were "the best possible security to liberty" in the republic; by creating a
consolidated regime, the new national government would reduce the economic rights of an emerging middle class that had pinned its hopes on
state governments, thereby subverting the liberty of the nation.

Antifederalists were not economic naysayers. They welcomed self-
interest, entrepreneurship, and legislation agreeable to protection and
promotion of new business and internal improvements controlled locally.
They chided Federalists for blaming the mid-1780s depression on state
economic policies, and they correctly identified deeper causes for the
trauma. Finally, it was the local economy, Antifederalists believed, that
would remain most responsive to the plural economic interests of citizens,
especially the "men of middling property." A national economy was a
chimera, a ruse to satisfy the interests of a few "commercial aristocrats."
Many critics of the Constitution had internalized this outspoken antipathy
to consolidation of the political economy. Others hoped to imitate
neomercantilist policies in the various states; these rising entrepreneurs
and commercial agriculturalists hoped to channel revenues into commercial banks and internal improvements that would remain under state
control. Ironically, although Federalists appropriated the language and
demands of spokesmen for territorial expansion, internal improvements,
and institutional reforms as they moved ahead to create a nationally coordinated economy, some of the most vital, ongoing economic activism would
originate in the states for decades to come.

THE EARLY NATIONAL PERIOD

Temporarily at least, a majority of Americans approved of the expansive,
developmental, international vision of Federalists. Their enthusiasm for
the potential of America's political economy that accompanied ratification
of the Constitution was bolstered in May and June 1789 as the first
Congress set immediately to the task of creating a revenue for conducting
government and servicing portions of the war debts. Delegates quickly
approved the principles of an impost, a measure maligned by various states
during the Revolutionary and Confederation years. These tariffs – and
their increases until 1816 – would provide roughly 90 percent of the

income of the national government, the remainder coming from periodic public land sales. Federalist efforts to use this income for the assumption of state debts and the funding of the public debt also contributed to the international reputation as well as to the power of central government.

The second Congressional measure in 1789 was a Tonnage Act, which was intended to raise revenue by levying duties on ships entering American ports according to a scale: highest taxes − 50 cents a ton − on foreign-owned and foreign-built ships, less taxation on foreign-owned, American-built ships, and virtually no duties on American-built, American-owned vessels. The twofold effect of this act was to give American shippers a distinct advantage over foreign shippers and to eliminate almost all competition from the coastal trade and northern fisheries. Indeed, Congressional delegates made arguments that were strikingly similar to those made by British policymakers who passed the Orders in Council against American commerce in 1783.

The Tonnage Act raised few serious objections in Congress, since its purpose was primarily to protect American shipping. Even the committed "agrarian" Thomas Jefferson assented to the wisdom of legislation that would "render the use of [the sea] as great as possible" and "preserve an equality of right to [exporters] in the transportation of commodities," with the goal of more reciprocal trade with foreign nations in the future.[7] But while most of the delegates had supported the 1789 Tariff Act as a modest attempt at protectionism and a valuable source of government revenue, opposition to the act arose outside of Congress. The tariff and tonnage measures underscored to contemporaries that "southern and northern will often be the division of Congress − The thought is disagreeable; but the distinction is founded in nature, and will last as long as the Union."[8] And there were more than sectional tensions; some artisan groups were dissatisfied with the particular commodities being taxed, while some others protested that the level of protection was too low to be an effective deterrent for importation of foreign goods.

This opposition did not grow significantly until the "consolidationists," or Hamiltonians, brought forward additional proposals that intensified

[7] Jefferson indicated his support for temporary commercial discrimination many times. See, e.g., Thomas Jefferson to John Jay, Paris, Aug. 23, 1785, *The Papers of Thomas Jefferson*, eds. Julian Boyd, et al., 24 vols. to date (Princeton, NJ, 1950 −), 8:426−8; Jefferson, *Notes on the State of Virginia*, written 1781−3, first publ. Paris, 1784, ed. William Peden (Chapel Hill, NC, 1955), chap. 19, 22; and Jefferson to Madison, 27 April 1785, and to Monroe, 16 June 1785, *Papers*, 8:110−1, 216.

[8] Edward Bangs to George Thatcher, [1791], Thatcher Papers, Boston Public Library.

Congressional and public debates. One thing was clear to all Congressional delegates, as well as to the many Americans watching carefully to see whether the government would endure: those who controlled the funding and repayment of war-era debts held enormous potential power. In 1790, it was still not clear if the debts would be repaid and, if so, whether by the states or federal government, and under what conditions. Sensitive to the pressures of prominent public creditors outside Congress, Robert Morris asked fellow Congressmen to create a permanent national debt with a funding system to service portions of the public obligations left over from the Revolutionary years. He called for exchanging the securities issued over the course of the Revolution for new securities, without discriminating among original holders and their subsequent purchasers. Moreover, only the interest on the debt should be paid, from revenue created by the impost, while the principal would remain in a central fund administered by Congress. Such a fund would give tangible, material form to the federal government, thereby enhancing its reputation at home and abroad.

It was not a new argument; the same reasoning lay behind the Bank of England in the late seventeenth century and was revived by Morris and others in the early years of the Revolutionary War to support the Continental Army and Congress's suppliers. Now Hamilton was asked to prepare a report embodying Morris's argument, which he offered to the House of Representatives in January 1790 in the Report on Public Credit. The national debt, he wrote, amounted to more than $54 million, of which nearly $12 million was owed to foreign nations. The total state debts he estimated at about $25 million. Moreover, these many financial obligations were dispersed widely: in other countries, to war veterans, to former suppliers, to urban merchant creditors. Hamilton proposed to tie significant amounts of federal revenues to a fund for making long-term payments of the interest on the debt, in order to consolidate the various kinds of certificates and warrants issued during the Revolution into a more uniform system of federal certificates — without discriminating between original and subsequent holders — to assume the outstanding state debts, and to pass an excise on certain "luxuries" to generate additional revenue. Overarching the entire proposal, Hamilton asked Congress to establish a national bank.

James Madison was an early and strong opponent of Hamilton's report. He countered with arguments (1) to discriminate between original holders — soldiers and small suppliers, for the most part — and the speculators who currently held most of the debt, and (2) to leave the individual states' Revolutionary War debt in the states. Madison and a minority of supporters in Congress pointed out that securities speculation had become a major business in America, especially in the northern states, over the 1780s; more recently, scholars have shown that by 1790, almost 80 percent of all federal securities issued to citizens of Massachusetts were sold to a few inhabitants who had sufficient specie to purchase them. Investors in the Low Countries held nearly $3 million of Congress's certificates.

On February 11, Madison proposed (1) that current holders of public securities who were not original holders should receive no more than the highest market value they could acquire on their sale, and (2) that the balance due from the public – presumably the national government's fund – be paid to the original holders. However much justice Congressmen saw in this proposal, it would have been an accounting nightmare, since original holders, as well as intervening holders, amounted to thousands of citizens dispersed throughout a shifting and growing population. Some Hamiltonians argued that Madison's plan was not just at all, since it represented a violation of contracts implicitly made among exchangers of securities in their capacities as buyers and sellers of property. Congress defeated Madison's proposal, 36 to 13, on February 22.

Madison led Congressional opposition again when discussion turned to assumption of state debts. More than the other measures, assumption bore the marks of sectional interests, since many of the northern states remained heavily indebted to public creditors, and most southern states – South Carolina was the main exception – had repaid large portions. Moreover, northern speculators had bought much of the outstanding southern debt; forty-seven northerners owned $3.2 million of the Virginia, North Carolina, and South Carolina securities, a figure representing 40 percent of those states' unpaid debts. Of the $3.2 million, thirteen or fourteen persons in New York and New Jersey owned about 63 percent. Thus, southern Congressmen tended to see northern interests conspiring to annihilate the powers of the states with a consolidated debt. Although the House defeated assumption in early April, in a vote of 31 to 29, the Senate overrode the House in late July with a one-vote margin and combined assumption with a funding bill as well as an agreement to place the capital along the Potomac.

Until the end of 1790, opponents of the Hamiltonian proposals only hinted at their class and sectional disagreements; when the Report on a National Bank and a bill for an excise tax to raise federal revenues were introduced officially in January 1791, the thorny issues of institutional ethics and the moral virtue of a citizenry were brought to the fore. The Bank, argued its opponents, would tie disreputable interests to the reputation of the national government; it would also create an overweening structure at great distance from the watchful eyes of the electorate. Some even argued that public banks of any kind stretched the virtues of a people, since they created artificial sources of credit, development, and circulating currency.

These same opponents believed that the excise tax also was an excessive use of federal power over the market relationships of ordinary Americans of the interior. Albert Gallatin argued that it was proper to tax foreign commerce but impermissible to tax the internal traffic of citizens in the nation. Bolstering this opposition were myriad public appeals in newspapers and pamphlets to defeat internal taxing schemes; Hamiltonians seemed to be treating the American people as British policymakers had in the 1760s, when the latter insisted on their absolute authority to tax.

Objections notwithstanding, Hamilton's bank bill passed with a significant Congressional margin. Operations of the Bank of the United States (BUS), begun in 1791, were a joint venture between private and federal government capital. The BUS was chartered for 20 years, with one-fifth of its stock held by the U.S. Treasury and the rest by private persons. The central bank in Philadelphia soon spawned branches in Boston, New York, Charleston, Norfolk, Washington, Baltimore, Savannah, and New Orleans. It was a fully commercial bank, issuing notes that circulated, holding deposits of investors, and making loans. Moreover, it held deposits of the federal government's revenue, and it lent the government money upon its reputation. Further, the BUS was a conservative brake on the lending policies of state banks; since it received large quantities of state bank notes as part of its reserves, it could present the former for redemption at any time, thus forcing the state banks to moderate the quantities of notes they issued. In 1792, the Mint Act provided for a mint in Philadelphia and set the United States on a bimetallic course of 15 ounces of silver to 1 ounce of gold and a plan to circulate specie coins instead of paper money in common business transactions.

This financial and taxing infrastructure shaped crucial aspects of America's economy for decades to come. But 2 years after Hamilton's first report, his December 1791 Report on Manufactures failed to pass Congress. On the surface of it, the Report was modeled upon the current wisdom about the compatibility of commerce, agriculture, and manufactures; it called for creating bounties, premiums, and awards for contributions to economic development and recommended twenty-one tariff increases on finished imports and five tariff reductions on raw materials. Increased productivity, Hamilton argued, would spur increases of revenue and consumption while promoting further investment, new inventions, and the immigration of skilled labor. Manufacturers and their laborers would absorb agricultural surpluses; the new institutions would provide extensive employment for women and children. But when critics began to connect the Report to Hamilton's ill-fated Society for Establishing Useful Manufactures (SEUM) in Paterson, New Jersey, these broader goals dissolved into fears that a few securities holders in northern cities would be the sole beneficiaries of manufacturing incentives. Hamilton's Report also opened the door for bickering among individual promoters or inventors who would compete for the benefits of government bounties he proposed – far better, argued critics of the Report, to create general protective duties that would affect myriad artisans and lesser merchants. Southerners and commercial farmers producing for export predicted that the excise taxes recommended by Hamilton would fall disproportionately on their staple products; these anxieties flourished among western Pennsylvanians involved in the Whiskey Rebellion of 1792–4.

Objections to the first federal administration's programs grew stronger over the 1790s, culminating in the Democratic-Republican victory of 1800 and a greatly weakened Federalist party. Democratic-Republican strength derived not only from the as-yet unproved capacity of Federalists to aid many economic interests and growing impatience among Americans for rapid change. It also derived from the continuing importance of state assistance to small entrepreneurs and rising artisans after 1790. Although the Bank of the United States continued to place checks on the note issues of state banks, the latter grew in number. In 1795, there were about twenty state banks; by 1812, there were ninety, and their combined circulating loans and bills of credit were far greater than the BUS's. Northern and southern state legislatures also assisted commercial farmers with canals and turnpikes in the 1790s. New York, Pennsylvania, Virginia, and Massachusetts extended loans to private enterprises such as potteries, iron furnaces, tanneries, and textile spinning factories. Even in the absence of funds, state governments promoted conditions for innovative private economic endeavors. Some commercial firms, for example, began to specialize in the commodities they traded with the help of beneficial commercial codes. Some even curtailed their commodities exchanges in order to begin functioning as brokers, as in the case of Alexander Brown and Sons of Baltimore, when the firm shifted from wheat exports and textiles imports toward negotiating "paper" obligations and acting as brokers for other commercial firms. A portion of this company's commissions typically went toward speculation in foreign securities. Other firms in Philadelphia and Boston organized lotteries that drew on the small savings of myriad local inhabitants to fund state-backed projects in education and manufacturing.

From 1789 to 1819, state legislatures issued over 2,500 special charters to new businesses, over 300 of which were state-chartered banks. Although the BUS was huge compared to these experimental, and fragile, operations, it was not indispensable; when the BUS was not rechartered in 1811, the gap was filled with almost 200 new state and local banks by 1816. Most charters defined businesses' privileges in borrowing private capital and their immunities from tax or right-of-way legislation. Increasingly, these charters gave monopoly rights over routes or roadways and stipulated the private collection of toll monies. But many charters remained "mixed enterprises" of combined state and private revenues. The governments in Connecticut and Maryland acknowledged that the typical weaver could produce about 5 yards of cloth per day; with state aid to private merchant establishments that set up ten to twenty looms, however, it was easy to produce 100 yards of linen or woolen cloth per day. The Erie Canal project also received state aid in the form of tax revenues and government-issued "Erie bonds." The latter attracted British financial investment; firms and individuals looking for secure investments by the end of the Napoleonic Wars purchased over one-half of the debt of "Clinton's Ditch" during the 1820s.

Efforts to shape federal economic policy and stretch innovatively the resources of state governments must be set within a larger context of American economic development. Statesmen and publicists recognized two clusters of circumstances that shaped the greater contours of America's economy: (1) wars and famine in European nations between 1792 and 1814, and (2) major demographic realignment within America that would subtly, but decisively, prepare the country for regional conflicts and interdependencies influencing generations to come.

Recovery and development of the national economy was most consequentially affected by events of the Napoleonic war years, when European demand for foodstuffs and shipping services soared, and when American carriers filled the positions formerly held by Europeans in trans-Atlantic trade. Reveling in the neutral position of the United States, farmers, planters, and merchants channeled exports toward the belligerent nations. Already large numbers of mid-Atlantic and Chesapeake farmers had shifted from tobacco production toward grain. Following the recent disruption of American warfare, European conflicts offered unprecedented opportunities to expand their exports. Although prices varied sharply from month to month, those for traditional commodities, such as grain, flour, prepared meat, lumber, and fish, rose steadily from 1792 to 1818, with the exception of the embargo years 1807 and 1808. Over the 1790s, the value of domestic exports from New York, New Jersey, and portions of New England rose rapidly. The value of reexports from northern ports of southern cotton, and of foreign and British West Indies sugar and dyewoods, rose even more rapidly. Overall, all American exports rose, albeit unevenly, from about $20 million in 1790 to more than $108 million in 1807. Over the same period, earnings from the carrying trade rose steeply as well. Only the end of 1802 and beginning of 1803 saw a partial decline in European demand. Thereafter, not only the war but continuous poor harvests in France and Eastern Europe drew as much surplus grain and flour as Americans could export. Both England and France were forced to suspend their mercantile regulations against American trade in order to take advantage of American merchants' services in transporting Caribbean and East Indies goods to trans-Atlantic ports. Pepper, salt, tea, coffee, and sugar were among American merchants' reexports to England and France; however, the same commodities also figured more significantly in the northern states' patterns of consumption as well.

Earnings from American exports and reexports allowed Americans to import large quantities of finished goods without increasing their debt to foreign nations. Although the value of exports increased rapidly during the 1790s, freight earnings of merchant vessels also accounted for Americans' ability to consume more imports. The latter averaged more than $20 million a year between 1793 and 1802, compared to about $6.3 million in 1792. From 1803 to 1812, they rose to an annual average of $31 million, despite the embargo in the middle of that decade. Added to freight earnings are those from shipbuilding and ship sales. Tonnage owned by American merchants increased from 355,000 tons in 1790 to 1,089,000 tons in 1808. In 1790, 59 percent of the entrances and clearances in American ports involved domestically owned vessels; in 1807, it was 92 percent. Records indicate that American shippers were also increasing the size of the cargoes and the fees that they charged foreign nations for services; they were also decreasing turnaround time during the war. Until 1807–8, sales of vessels to warring European countries also rose steadily. Incomplete information also suggests that the coastal trade, especially that between the southern cotton states and the northeastern corridor, provided lucrative opportunities for lesser merchants and new, aggressive interests in shipping services. Together, these circumstances enhanced the vitality of seaport towns and reemployed great numbers of local young men. New jobs and relatively stable employment existed for artisans of all sorts, as well as insurance and notes brokers, warehouse and port facilities personnel, millers, and internal transport workers.

Coinciding with trans-Atlantic events was the equally important redistribution of America's population, and the distinctive characteristics that southern, western, and northeastern regions began to develop as a result. In 1790, America's total population stood at 3.9 million, of whom 3.7 million were rural and fewer than 62,000 lived in the two largest cities. Since about 1770, the white population had grown about 80 percent; the high birth rate pressed down the median age of the white male population to 15.9 years in 1790. By 1820, the total number of inhabitants reached about 9.6 million; it continued to grow at a rate that doubled the country's inhabitants every 23 years, as it had in pre-Revolutionary decades.

Population growth was accompanied by territorial expansion west of the Alleghenies, especially in the first three states carved out of the former Northwest Territory. Kentucky grew from 73,677 in 1790 to 220,955 in 1800 and to 406,511 in 1810; Tennessee grew from 35,691 in 1790 to 105,602 in 1800 and to 261,727 in 1810; and Ohio rose even more rapidly, from 45,365 in 1800 to 230,760 in 1810. In the entire area west and north of the Revolutionary generation's settlement in 1770, to the Mississippi River, there were nearly 1.5 million new residents by 1810; by 1820, there were nearly 2.5 million. To the west of the Mississippi River, the Louisiana Purchase of 1803 offered opportunities not only to small farmers but for expanding cotton production and slavery as well, The peace of 1783 yielded Americans 889,000 square miles of territory; the 1803 purchase from Napoleon for $15 million netted another 827,000 square miles.

Although scholars of the early "transportation revolution" have shown the steady momentum toward integrated, long-distance routes of exchange, until the 1820s, the predominant organization of the Midwest involved little urbanization, little labor specialization, and – for the majority of new settlers – integration of markets mainly on only a local scale. The truly interregional economic contact between this first post-Revolutionary frontier and the settled southern, mid-Atlantic, and northeastern sectors awaited subsequent generations.

Still, developments in older areas were consequential for the pace of westward movement. Southerners were in the envious position of having ready markets for cotton exports beginning during the Napoleonic war years, especially with respect to bundled cotton for Britain's textile industry. Cotton exports from the southern states accounted for nearly one-half the growth of American exports from 1793 to 1807. Although the main story of a booming cotton economy is to be told after 1815, Eli Whitney's introduction of the cotton gin, and its immediate adoption, permitted a far greater amount of cotton to be processed for export. Moreover, cultivation of short staple cotton (a variety that adapted well to dry inland areas) and the creation of plantations in the future states of Alabama, Mississippi, Louisiana, and Tennessee was well underway by 1815. Slavery grew and expanded with the cotton economy. In 1790, there were about 700,000 slaves, largely in the settled plantation states producing tobacco, rice, and indigo. By 1820, the number of slaves grew to 1.8 million, nearly 20 percent of the American population, and had shifted to a very great degree into the lucrative cotton lands of Alabama, Mississippi, Louisiana, and west Tennessee. Annual cotton production rose from 3 million pounds in 1793 to 93 million pounds in 1815. Although southerners exported almost no cotton over the 1780s, by 1800, American exports amounted to 18 million pounds.

The East Coast also showed significant amounts of interregional reorganization between 1790 and 1815, before eastern urban and industrializing inhabitants were ready to absorb the commodities that would eventually flow to them from the West. Already large numbers of mid-Atlantic and Chesapeake farmers had shifted toward grain production, spurred by the disruptions of the Revolution and the unprecedented opportunities to export to other nations following it. Other eastern farmers began to specialize in those perishable goods that could be marketed locally – cheese, milk, fruits, and vegetables. Some farmers gave up grain cultivation and turned to grazing sheep for wool for the textile industry that was emerging near them; others turned to raising cattle and pigs for both meat and hides. Some eastern rural peoples migrated out of their villages in these early national decades, but probably an equal number combined traditional farming with home production for small amounts of cash, day labor in the community, or apprenticeships to acquire skills. Thus, while some eastern farmers specialized, others diversified their forms of labor. Until at least the 1820s, no particular trend characterized the majority of eastern rural people from Maine to Maryland.

The Erie Canal, completed in 1825, epitomized the transition from traditional agriculture to interregional capitalist markets that was occurring in certain eastern areas. The steamboat, invented in 1807, made the trip from New Orleans to Louisville against the river current regularly by 1820, making another contribution to cheaper transportation costs and more rapid conveyance of manufactured imports and urban crafts. The return trip brought perishable goods to the southern states and eastern coastal cities. In other ways, too, the local markets of the Northeast began to expand, especially when one accounts for the proliferation of turnpike companies and licenses for peddlers and tavern owners who doubled as shopkeepers. But the majority of farmers were probably utilizing the same tools and techniques, methods of fertilization, crop rotation, deep furrowing, soil banking, and cross-breeding of crops that were known from at least 1700 to at least the 1820s. Those farmers who exploited new opportunities for exporting surpluses to long-distance markets often cultivated fields without using fertilizers or permitting periods of fallow, thereby maximizing short-term productivity but exhausting soil in the long run.

Although many contemporary political economists recognized that America's future prosperity lay as much with manufactures as with agriculture, it was when the Napoleonic war years spurred commerce to new heights that entrepreneurs could undertake the creation and operation of many new manufactures. After a period of indirect protection by European and American wars that curtailed importation from roughly 1792 to 1815, cotton textiles manufacturers appealed to Congress to legislate protective tariffs for their "infant industries." Moreover, by 1800, numerous iron furnaces dotted major eastern waterways, most of them representing a proliferating of traditional-style establishments that produced only pig iron. Within the next decade, many foundries in New England and Pennsylvania began to produce simple cooking or agricultural implements, a portion of which found their way to Europe. Whitney got a government contract in 1799 to produce 10,000 muskets, in the making of which he claimed he would use stamping and cutting machines to create interchangeable parts. After 1802, the Du Pont family produced gunpowder on the Brandywine River with large work forces and extensive real estate and capital investments. Although inventors like Oliver Evans of Philadelphia improved flour milling techniques as early as the 1780s, only after 1810 did rapidly rising export demand provide the impetus for many commercial firms to adopt those innovations. The organization of textiles production begun by Samuel Slater in Pawtucket, Rhode Island, in the 1790s was replicated in at least thirteen other locations where the correct combination of labor supply, numbers of spinning machines, and entrepreneurial impetus existed.

But if it was foreign war that enhanced demand for some "infant manufactures," the Embargo of December 1807 to March 1809 affected small producers and wealthy capitalists in uneven ways. The effect of the Embargo was drastic for shippers and shipbuilders. It also brought down the prices of farm goods and threw many urban artisans into unemployment by mid-1808. Although the Embargo was repealed in March 1809 and replaced with a Non-Intercourse Act, which permitted trade with all nations except Britain and France, prosperity did not return. In 1810, France agreed to repeal its decrees against American trade in return for American refusal to trade with Britain. From that time until late 1813, American shipping declined once again, especially once Britain declared war and blockaded American traffic.

Although some small manufacturers suffered bankruptcy during the embargo years, others were able to grow, especially those that were related to the still predominantly agricultural economy. New textile mills were appearing wherever there was a sufficient water supply; there were over eighty such mills by 1809. In 1813, the largest establishment to that date – the Boston Manufacturing Company in Waltham, Massachusetts – was created with the capital of wealthy Lowell and Cabot family members. Waltham was the first mill of its kind to integrate weaving and spinning in one factory; it was also one of the few genuine factories to survive the postwar depression and economic panic of 1819, perhaps because it drew on an available labor pool of young women and minors.

The rate of growth in textiles, shoes, construction, furniture making, and iron goods production should not be overestimated. In 1809, six textile factories in Philadelphia produced 65,000 yards of material, but nearby cottage spinners and weavers produced 230,000 yards. More and more, women were setting up looms and undertaking the tasks that were traditionally left to itinerant males; some villages had their own fulling mills as well, where cloth, especially wool, was shrunk or thickened with moisture, heat, and pressure. First spurred by the Revolution, and then reinforced during the Embargo years, urban promoters encouraged rural inhabitants to keep sheep for meat and wool and to build fulling and

spinning mills along waterways. Still, there was little technological innovation or business reorganization required to produce these home manufactures; indeed, treatise writers called them an ideal occupation for a rural
people.

Urban craftsmen often resisted the new market arrangements, especially
when they involved replacing the small craft shop with large establishments controlled by merchant-manufacturers. Artisans who had earlier
attempted to exclude lower-priced foreign imports of comparable commodities now also struggled to establish uniform wage rates to be paid by
masters who owned shops or by merchants who marketed their finished
goods. Also, within crafts such as cordwainers (leatherworkers) and tailors, the increasing separation of traditional roles of master and journey-
man, brought on by a transition toward wage labor, led to frequent labor
quarrels. Nevertheless, by the 1820s, many artisans were being eliminated from traditional sectors of the economy; some became self-employed
property owners, while many gravitated toward factories or became unskilled laborers.

The Panic of 1819, precipitated by the revival of European farming and
a sharp drop in world agricultural prices, marked the end of almost three
decades of commercial recovery. Peace was far less prosperous than war, as
many colonists in the eighteenth century would have agreed. The market
for American cotton fell quickly, as did those for grain and flour, thus
reducing incomes in both northern and southern states. The drop in farm
prices caused widespread default on loans from local and state banks –
especially in the Ohio River Valley – and defaults on credit from coastal
merchants. By the end of 1819, the credit system linking commercial
agriculture and banking had collapsed. As it recovered in the 1820s, the
export-centered economy would experience more orientation toward internal economic development.

Was there economic growth between 1790 and 1820? Evidence to date
suggests that although there was commercial recovery at particular mo-
ments, and although farm prices and artisans' regular employment may
have been satisfactory at certain times over these decades, per capita
incomes probably rose more slowly in these years than for the 1760s, and
long-term recovery was uncertain in all regions. Among mariners and
laborers, real wages fell dramatically in the 1780s and rose to prewar levels
during the late 1790s; for almost two decades after 1800, weekly wages of
semiskilled artisans barely kept up with the rising cost of living. Farmers'

and large planters' prices rose and fell erratically within short cycles. Even with significant activity in scientific societies, entrepreneurial investment, and promotional government legislation, very few infant manufactures survived the War of 1812. Although population continued to grow rapidly between 1790 and 1820, the rate of increase was slower than for the 1780s. America's economy was not yet fully integrated; regions and even small locales continued to show distinct patterns of development for some time to come. Moreover, within regions, the rapid changes in social relations of poor and middling urban residents, farm laborers, and commercial exporters were not yet accompanied by the more sophisticated credit, consumption, and wage labor arrangements that integrated Americans to a higher degree during industrialization.

Still, important transformations were beginning. Although export values per capita declined after 1815, this probably signaled a reallocation of human and material resources into domestic channels. Ultimately, these changes would lead to industrialization. Moreover, despite the setbacks and slow-growth years of the Revolution and 1780s, Americans sustained the highest standard of living known in the world during the 1790s. Thus, if they had not yet realized the economic promise of political independence – the intensive economic growth that would raise their standard of living – neither had they experienced the ravages of war and agricultural famine that so many European nations had in the same years.

BIBLIOGRAPHICAL ESSAYS

CHAPTER 1 (SALISBURY)

The coming generation of basic reference works on Native American history is in the process of publication. When complete, the twenty volumes of *Handbook of North American Indians*, gen. ed. William C. Sturtevant (9 vols. to date, Washington, DC, 1978–), will provide exhaustive coverage by region and topic. Especially relevant for economic history are many of the essays in Vol. 4: *History of Indian–White Relations*, ed. Wilcomb E. Washburn (1988). The *Cambridge History of the Native Peoples of the Americas*, Vol. 1: *North America*, ed. Bruce G. Trigger and Wilcomb E. Washburn (Cambridge, England, in preparation), will consist of chapters covering the entire span of Native American history, from the earliest arrivals via the Bering land bridge to the present. Two valuable historical atlases are: R. Cole Harris, ed., *Historical Atlas of Canada*, Vol. 1: *From the Beginning to 1800* (Toronto, 1987); and Helen Hornbeck Tanner, ed., *Atlas of Great Lakes Indian History* (Norman, 1987). The best overviews of precontact archaeology are Brian M. Fagan, *Ancient North America: The Archaeology of a Continent* (London, 1991) and Stuart J. Fiedel, *Prehistory of the Americas*, 2nd ed. (Cambridge, England, 1992). See also Michael Coe et al., eds., *Atlas of Ancient America* (New York, 1986), and Lynda Norene Shaffer, *Native Americans Before 1492: The Moundbuilding Centers of the Eastern Woodlands* (Armonk, NY, 1992). For a brief but illuminating discussion of exchange in pre-Columbian North American, see William A. Turnbaugh, "Wide-Area Connections in Native North America," *American Indian Culture and Research Journal* 1:4 (1976), 22–8.

General considerations of Indian–European interactions have been undertaken from a number of perspectives. On epidemiology and ecology, see two works by Alfred W. Crosby: *The Columbian Exchange: Biological and Cultural Consequences of 1492* Westport, CT, 1972), and *Ecological Imperialism: The Biological Expansion of Europe, 900–1900* (Cambridge, England, 1986). On demography, the survey by Russell Thornton, *American Indian Holocaust and Survival: A Population History Since 1492* (Norman, 1987), should be supplemented by Sheila Ryan Johansson, "The Demographic History of the Native Peoples of North America: A Selective Bibliography," *Yearbook of Physical Anthropology* 25 (1982), 133–52, and John D. Daniels, "The Indian Population of North American in 1492," *William and Mary Quarterly*, 3d ser., 49 (1992), 298–320. On economic relations, see Eric R. Wolf, *Europe and the People without History* (Berkeley, 1982), ch. 6, and Ronald L. Trosper, "That Other Discipline: Economics and American Indian History," in Colin G. Calloway, ed., *New Directions in American Indian History* (Norman, 1988). See also Ian K. Steele, *Warpaths: Invasions of North America* (New York, 1994); the relevant chapters of Howard Lamar and Leonard Thompson, eds., *The Frontier in History: North America and Southern Africa Compared* (New Haven, 1981); and James Axtell, *The European and the Indian: Essays in the Ethnohistory of Colonial North America* (New York, 1981), chs. 9–10.

The very first contacts between Indians and Europeans remain the least understood. Carl Ortwin Sauer, *Sixteenth Century North America* (Berkeley, 1971), is still useful. Charles Hudson and Carmen Chaves Tesser, eds., *The Forgotten Centuries: Indians and Europeans in the American South, 1521–1704* (Atlanta, GA, 1994) greatly advances understanding of that region. On the Atlantic coast and northeastern interior, see William W. Fitzhugh, ed., *Cultures in Contact: The Impact of European Contacts on Native American Cultural Institutions, A.D. 1000–1800* (Washington, 1985), and James Axtell, "At the Water's Edge: Trading in the Sixteenth Century," in his *After Columbus: Essays in the Ethnohistory of Colonial North America* (New York, 1988). On the multifaceted debate as to Indians' motives in their earliest interactions with Europeans, see Calvin Martin, *Keepers of the Game: Indian–Animal Relationships and the Fur Trade* (Berkeley, 1978); Shepard Krech III, ed., *Indians, Animals, and the Fur Trade: A Critique of Keepers of the Game* (Athens, GA, 1981); Christopher L. Miller and George R. Hammell, "A New Perspective on Indian–White Contact: Cultural Symbols and Colonial Trade, " *Journal of American History* 73 (1986), 311–28; Bruce G. Trigger, "Early Native North American responses to European Contact: Romantic versus Rationalistic Interpretations," *Journal of American History* 78 (1991), 1195–1215.

Seventeenth-century contacts between natives and colonizers in the Northeast are treated in Francis Jennings, *The Invasion of America: Indians, Colonialism, and the Cant of Conquest* (Chapel Hill, 1975); Neal Salisbury, *Manitou and Providence: Indians, Europeans, and the Making of New England, 1500–1643* (New York, 1982); William Cronon, *Changes in the Land: Indians, Colonists, and the Ecology of New England* (New York, 1983); Bruce G. Trigger, *Natives and Newcomers: Canada's "Heroic Age" Reconsidered* (Montreal, 1985); Daniel K. Richter, *The Ordeal of the Longhouse: The Peoples of the Iroquois League in the Era of European Colonization* (Chapel Hill, 1992). On the Southeast, see J. Leitch Wright, Jr., *The Only Land They Knew: The Tragic Story of the Indians of the Old South* (New York, 1983). On the Southwest, see Elizabeth A. H. John, *Storms Brewed in Other Men's Worlds: The Confrontation of Indians, Spanish, and French in the Southwest, 1540–1795* (Lincoln, NE, 1975); Edward H. Spicer, *Cycles of Conquest: the Impact of Spain, Mexico, and the United States on the Indians of the Southwest, 1533–1960* (Tucson, 1962); Allen H. Anderson, "The Encomienda in New Mexico, 1598–1680," *New Mexico Historical Review* 60 (1985), 353–77; John L. Kessell, *Kiva, Cross, and Crown: The Pecos Indians and New Mexico, 1540–1840* (Washington, 1979), and Ramón A. Gutiérrez, *When Jesus Came, the Corn Mothers Went Away: Marriage, Sexuality, and Power in New Mexico, 1500–1846* (Stanford, 1991).

During the eighteenth century, Indians east of the Mississippi went from positions of relative autonomy to dependency and subjugation. Among the highlights of the vast literature on this era, see especially Richard White, *The Middle Ground: Indians, Empires, and Republics in the Great Lakes Region, 1650–1815* (Cambridge, England, 1991); Francis Jennings, *The Ambiguous Iroquois Empire: The Covenant Chain Confederation of Indian Tribes with English Colonies from its Beginnings to the Lancaster Treaty of 1744* (New York, 1984), and *Empire of Fortune: Crowns, Colonies, and Tribes in the Seven Years War in America* (New York, 1988); Anthony F. C. Wallace, *The Death and Rebirth of the Seneca* (New York, 1969); Michael N. McConnell, *A Country Between: The Upper Ohio Valley and Its Peoples 1724–1774* (Lincoln, NE, 1992); and Randolph C. Downes, *Council Fires on the Upper Ohio: A Narrative of Indian Affairs in the Upper Ohio valley until 1795* (Pittsburgh, 1940) on the Northeast. On the Southeast, see Wright, *Only Land They Knew* (cited above); Verner W. Crane, *The Southern Frontier, 1670–1732* (Ann Arbor, 1956); Peter H. Wood et al., eds., *Powhatan's Mantle: Indians in the Colonial Southeast* (Lincoln, NE, 1989); Timothy Silver, *A New Face on the Countryside: Indians, Colonists, and Slaves in South Atlantic Forests, 1500–1800* (Cambridge, England, 1990); James H. Merrell, *The Indians' New World: Catawbas and Their Neighbors from European Contact through the Era of Removal* (Chapel Hill, 1989); Daniel H. Usner, Jr., *Indians, Settlers, and Slaves in a Frontier Exchange Economy: The Lower Mississippi Valley before 1783* (Chapel Hill, 1992); Richard White, *Roots of Dependency: Subsistence, Environment, and Social Change among the Choctaws, Pawnees, and Navajos* (Lincoln, NE, 1983), chs. 1–5; and James H. O'Donnell, III, *Southern Indians in the American Revolution* (Knoxville, 1973).

Eastern Indians and their relations with the United States are treated in Francis Paul Prucha, *The Great Father: The United States Government and the American Indian*, 2 vols. (Lincoln, NE, 1984); Reginald Horsman, *Expansion and American Indian Policy, 1783-1812* (Lansing, MI, 1967); R. David Edmunds, *The Shawnee Prophet* (Lincoln, NE, 1983); William G. McLoughlin, *Cherokee Renascence: 1794–1833* (Princeton, 1987); Theda Perdue, *Slavery and the Evolution of Cherokee Society, 1540–1866* (Knoxville, 1979); Michael D. Green, *The Politics of Indian Removal: Creek Government and Society in Crisis* (Lincoln, NE, 1985); Mary E. Young, *Redskins, Ruffleshirts, and Rednecks: Indian Allotments in Alabama and Mississippi, 1830–1860* (Norman, 1961); and Anthony F. C. Wallace, *Prelude to Disaster: The Course of Indian–White Relations Which Led to the Black Hawk War of 1832* (Springfield, IL, 1970).

The fur trade in eastern and central Canada during the eighteenth and nineteenth centuries has been studied from several perspectives. See, especially, W. J. Eccles, "The Fur Trade and Eighteenth Century Imperialism," *William and Mary Quarterly*, 3d ser., 40 (1983), 341–62; E. E. Rich, *The Fur Trade and the Northwest to 1857* (Toronto, 1967); Arthur J. Ray, *Indians in the Fur Trade: Their Role as Hunters, Trappers, and Middlemen in the Lands Southwest of Hudson Bay, 1660–1870* (Toronto, 1974); Ray and Donald Freeman, *"Give Us Good Measure": An Economic Analysis of Relations between the Indians and the Hudson's Bay Company before 1763* (Toronto, 1978); Daniel Francis and Toby Morantz, *Partners in Furs: A History of the Fur Trade in Eastern James Bay, 1600–1870* (Montreal, 1983); Shepard Krech, III, *The Subarctic Fur Trade* (Vancouver, 1984); Jenifer S. H. Brown, *Strangers in Blood: Fur Trade Company Families in Indian Country* (Vancouver, 1980); Sylvia Van Kirk, *Many Tender Ties: Women in Fur Trade Society, 1670–1870* (Norman, 1980). On Canadian government policy, see Robert J. Surtees, "The Development of an Indian Reserve Policy in Canada," *Ontario History* 61 (1979), 87–98; and John L. Tobias, "Protection, Civilization, Assimilation: an Outline History of Canada's Indian Policy," *Western Canadian Journal of Anthropology* 6 (1976), 13–30.

On the economic and cultural transformations overtaking peoples of the Plains and Rocky Mountains, see Robert M. Utley, *The Indian Frontier of the American West, 1846–1890* (Albuquerque, NM, 1984), chs. 1–3; Richard White, "The Winning of the West: The Expansion of the Western Sioux in the Eighteenth and Nineteenth Centuries," *Journal of American History* 65 (1978), 319–43; White, *Roots of Dependency* (cited above), chs. 6–9; John C. Ewers, *The Blackfeet: Raiders on the Northwestern Plains* (Norman, 1958), and *Indian Life on the Upper Missouri* (Norman, 1968); Preston Holder, *The Hoe and the Horse on the Plains: A Study of Cultural Development among North American Indians* (Lincoln, NE, 1970); Joseph Jablow, *The Cheyenne in Plains Indian Trade Relations, 1795–1840* (New York, 1950); Paul C. Phillips, *The Fur Trade*, 2 vols. (Norman, 1961); Richard E. Ogelsby, *Manuel Lisa and the Opening of the Missouri Fur Trade* (Norman, 1963); David J. Wishart, *The Fur Trade of the American West: A Geographical Synthesis* (Lincoln, NE, 1979). On the Southwest during the same period, see John, *Storms Brewed in Other Men's Worlds*, and Spicer, *Cycles of Conquest* (both cited above); David J. Weber, *The Taos Trappers: The Fur Trade in the Far Southwest, 1540–1846* (Norman, 1971); Oakah L. Jones, Jr., *Pueblo Warriors and Spanish Conquest* (Norman, 1966); Dolores A. Gunnerson, *The Jicarilla Apaches: A Study in Survival* (DeKalb, IL, 1974); Charles L. Kenner, *A History of New Mexican–Plains Indian Relations* (Norman, 1969). For California, see Sherburne F. Cook, *The Conflict between the California Indian and White Civilization* (Berkeley, 1943; reprinted 1976); George H. Phillips, Jr., *Chiefs and Challengers: Indian Resistance and Cooperation in Southern California* (Berkeley, 1975); and Albert Hurtado, *Indian Survival on the California Borderland Frontier, 1819–1860* (New Haven, 1988). On the Northwest, see Robin Fisher, *Contact and Conflict: Indian–European Relations in British Columbia, 1774–1890* (Vancouver, 1977); and James R. Gibson, *Otter Skins, Boston Ships and China Goods: The Maritime Fur Trade of the Northwest Coast, 1785–1841* (Seattle, 1992).

CHAPTER 2 (THORNTON)

The primary sources for Atlantic Africa in the seventeenth through nineteenth centuries are chiefly written documents of African writers, where there was literacy, and European visitors and residents. Oral traditions collected in more recent times are sometimes valuable for dynastic history and military chronicles; they are much less helpful for social and economic history. Archaeology has occasionally provided insights, although most archaeological work has focused on somewhat earlier periods.

Written documents vary widely in quality and regional distribution. For a discussion of their problems and case studies, see Adam Jones and Beatrix Heintze, eds., *European Sources for Sub-Saharan Africa before 1900: Use and Abuse*, special issue of *Paideuma* 33 (1987). John Fage, *A Guide to Original Sources for Precoloonial Western Africa Published in European Languages* (rev. ed., Madison, 1994), provides an annotated survey of sources published up to that date. Writing is of the best quality where there were long-lasting on-shore European bases (Senegambia, the Gold Coast, Slave Coast, and Angola) or where there were literate African societies (Senegambia and Angola). Areas that were visited only for trade, such as the Ivory Coast, Niger Delta, and Gabon Coast, are very poorly documented.

Written material is in many languages; most western European languages are represented, but Portuguese, English, French, Dutch, and Danish are the most important. In addition, useful material is in Arabic. African language texts from the period exist, but their value is largely for cultural and religious issues rather than for social and economic ones. Publication and translation of manuscript documentation has just begun, and many of the texts published in earlier times still need modern or accessible editions and translations. An evaluation of the quality of modern editions and translations is found in Adam Jones, *Raw, Medium, and Well Done: A Critical Review of Editorial and Quasi-Editorial Work on Pre-1885 European Sources for Sub-Saharan Africa, 1960–1986* (Madison, 1986). For the earliest periods, up to 1700, a large body of archival materials has been published in António Brásio, *Monumenta Missionaria Africana* (First series, 15 volumes, Lisbonn, 1952–88), in original languages for Angola, and for the Upper Guinea Coast (Second series, 5 volumes, Lisbon, 1958–79). The Linschoten Vereeniging (Hague) has published many Dutch and German documents in the original languages, while the Haklyut Society (London) has published English texts and English translations of many other primarily pre-1700 texts. P.E.H. Hair has translated many of the Upper Guinea Coast documents for the seventeenth century in "Sources for Early Sierra Leone," *African Research Bulletin* (Freetown) 4–13 (1974–84). The Centro da Cartografia Antiga (Lisbon) has also produced editions and translations (into various languages) of additional material.

For the later periods much less has been published, and thousands of valuable documents remain in archives. The most valuable archival collections are the records of the English, French, Dutch, and Danish African companies. The Vatican archives are also extremely valuable. Albert Van Dantzig, *The Dutch on the Guinea Coast 1674–1742: A Collection of Documents from the General State Archives at the Hague* (Accra, 1978), represents an initial attempt to publish English translations of selected documents from Dutch archives for the Gold Coast. English documents for the Slave Coast have been published by Robin Law, *Correspondence from the Royal African Company's Factories at Offra and Whydah* (Edinburgh, 1990) and *Further Correspondence of the Royal African Company Relating to the 'Slave Coast,' 1681–1699* (Madison, 1991). For Senegambia, a good number of useful documents have been published in the *Bulletin* of the *Institut Fondamental de l'Afrique noire*. Those not in French have been translated into French. Many eighteenth-century books on Africa have been reprinted in recent years, although critical editions are more rare.

Secondary literature on Africa in this period has grown immensely since 1960. Earlier work tended to focus almost entirely on the lives and work of Europeans in Africa. The earliest scholars focused on political history and relations between Africans and Europeans; social and economic history has grown much more slowly. Comprehensive surveys of the results of this first thrust can be found in *The Cambridge History of Africa*, especially volume 4 (Cambridge, 1975), which covers 1600–1790; a different but more recent survey is in *UNESCO General History of Africa*, especially volume 5 (Berkeley, 1992). Another important survey for this period is found in J.F.A. Ajayi and Michael Crowder, eds., *History of West Africa* (2 vols., 3rd edition, London, 1985), volume 1, which focuses on west Africa. An interpretation of the relation of African social and economic history to the slave trade and African American history in the period before 1680 is in John Thorton, *African and Africans in the Making of the Atlantic World, 1400–1680* (Cambridge, 1992). Writing on the history of the African economy in this period was stimulated by A.G. Hopkins, *An Economic History of West Africa* (London, 1973) for west Africa; Philip D. Curtin, *Economic Change in Precolonial Africa: Senegambia in the Era of the Slave Trade* (2 vols., Madison, 1975) for Senegambia; and Ralph Austen, *African Economic History* (London, 1987) for Africa as a whole. Valuable background information on the environment and its impact on the history of the region can be found in Thornton, *Africa and Africans*; George Brooks, *Landlords and Strangers: Ecology, Society, and Trade in Western Africa,*

1000–1630 (Boulder, 1993) for Senegambia; and Joseph C. Miller, *Way of Death: Merchant Capitalism and the Angolan Slave Trade, 1730–1830* (Madison, 1986), and "The Significance of drought, disease and famine in the agriculturally marginal zone of west-central Africa," *Journal of African History* 22 (1982): 17–61, for Angola.

I. A. Akinjogbin, *Dahomey and Its Neighbours, 1708–1818* (Cambridge, 1967); A.F.C. Ryder, *Benin and the Europeans, 1485–1897* (London, 1969); Daaku, *Trade and Politics on the Gold Coast, 1600–1700* (Oxford, 1970); Walter Rodney, *A History of the Upper Guinea Coast* (Oxford, 1970); and Boubacar Barry, *Le royaume du Waalo: Sénégal avant la conquête* (Paris, 1972), and *La Sénégambie du XVe au XIXe Siècle: Traite Négrière, Islam et Conquêt Coloniale* (Paris, 1988), pioneered a number of issues in the social and economic history of west Africa; their focus was particularly the impact of European commerce. A later generation of work focusing on Senegambia has continued many of these themes in greater detail, among them Abdulaye Bathily, *Les Portes de l'Or: Le royaume de Galam (Sénégal) de l'ère musulmane au temps des négriers (VIIIe-XVIiie siècles)* (Paris, 1989); Sékéné-Mody Cissoko, *Contribution à l'histoire politique de Khasso dans le Haut-Sénégal, Des origines à 1854* (Paris, 1986); James Searing, *West African Slavery and Atlantic Commerce: The Senegal River Valley, 1700–1860* (Cambridge, 1993); and Michael Gomez, *Pragmatism in the Age of Jihad: The Precolonial State of Bundu* (Cambridge, 1991). R. A. Kea's history of the seventeenth-century Gold Coast, *Settlements, Trade and Politics on the Seventeenth Century Gold Coast* (Baltimore, 1982), is important for the systematic detail it gives to internal dynamics of an African society, as is the more detailed work of Yann Deffontaine, *Guerre et Société au royaume de Fetu, Ghana, 1471–1720* (Paris, 1993). Similar work has been published by Robin Law, *The Slave Coast of West Africa, 1550–1750: The Impact of the Atlantic Slave Trade on an African Society* (Oxford, 1991), building on earlier work, *The Oyo Empire, c. 1500–1836* (Oxford, 1977). The discussion of Dahomey as a slave-trading kingdom has been particularly developed, beginning with Karl Polanyi, *Dahomey and the Slave Trade: An Analysis of an Archaic Economy* (Seattle, 1966), and including discussion by Werner Peukert, *Der Atlantische Sklavenhandel von Dahomey, 1749–1797* (Wiesbaden, 1978); Patrick Manning, *Slavery, Colonialism, and Economic Growth in Dahomey, 1640–1960* (Cambridge, 1982); and Law, *The Slave Coast*. In central Africa, an important early survey of the whole region by Jan Vansina, *Kingdoms of the Savanna* (Madison, 1966), set the tone for further work. The Kingdom of Kongo, especially the period before 1700, has attracted considerable attention. Anthropological interpretation goes back to Georges Balandieri, *Daily Life in the Kingdom of the Kongo, Sixteenth to Eighteenth Centuries* (New York, 1968); and W.G.L. Randles, *L'ancien royaume du Congo des origines à la fin du XIXe siècle* (Paris, 1968). Historians working on these lines include John Thornton, *The Kingdom of Kongo: Civil War and Transition, 1641–1718* (Madison, 1983); and Anne Hilton, *The Kingdom of Kongo* (Oxford, 1985). Angolan history was pioneered by David Birmingham, *Trade and Conquest in Angola: The Mbundu and Their Neighbours under the Influence of the Portuguese, 1483–1790* (Oxford, 1966), and continued by Joseph C. Miller, *Kings and Kinsmen: Early Mbundu States in Angola* (Oxford, 1976); and *Way of Death*. Jean-Luc Vellut, "Notes sur le Lunda at la frontière luso-africaine, 1700–1900," *Études d'histoire africaines* 3 (1972): 61–166, produced an additional important study of Lunda in the eighteenth century.

The study of slavery in Africa has been developed as a part of a general investigation of social history and the impact of the slave trade. Important early work was done by Claude Meillassoux, ed., *L'esclavage en afrique précoloniale* (Paris, 1976); Suzanne Miers and Igor Kopytoff, eds., *Slavery in Africa: Historical and Anthropological Perspectives* (Madison, 1977); J. E. Inikori, ed., *Forced Migration* (London, 1982); and Claire Robertson and Martin Klein, eds., *Women and Slavery in Africa* (Madison, 1983).

A considerable amount of work has been done on quantifying the slave trade since Philip Curtin, *The Atlantic Slave Trade: A Census* (Madison, 1969), a pioneering study. More recent work, such as that of Paul Lovejoy, *Transformations in Slavery: A History of Slavery in Africa* (Cambridge, 1983), and Patrick Manning, *Slavery and African Life: Occidental, Oriental, and African Slavery* (Cambridge, 1990), has shifted from quantification of exports to examining impacts on Africa. Work on African demography, both in its own terms and in response to the slave trade, includes Christopher Fyfe and David McMaster, eds., *African Historical Demography* (2 vols., Edinburgh, 1977, 1981); Thornton, "Demography and History in the Kingsom of Kongo, 1660–1750," *Journal of African History* 18 (1977):507–30, and "The slave trade in eighteenth century Angola: effects oon demographic structure," *Canadian Journal of African Studies* 14 (1981):417–27. Modeling exercises, beginning with John Fage, *A History of West Africa* (London, 1969), and continuing with Thornton, "The Demographic Effect of the Slave Trade on Western Africa, 1500–1800" (in Fyfe and McMaster, eds., *African Historical Demography*), 2:691–720, and Manning, *Slavery and African Life*, have sought to explore the demographic impact of the slave trade beyond the direct evidence of documentation.

CHAPTER 3 (JONES)

Works that trace detailed similarities between Europe and North America include J. R. T. Hughes, *Social Control in the Colonial Economy* (Charlottesville, VA: 1976) and his "Transference and Development of Institutional Constraints Upon Economic Activity," *Research in Economic History* I (1976), 45–68; and Terry G. Jordan and Matti Kaups, *The American Backwoods Frontier: An Ethnic and Ecological Interpretation* (Baltimore: 1989). Terry G. Jordan, "Readaptation and European Colonization in Rural North America," *Annals* of the Association of American Geographers 79 (1989), 489–500, states the preadaptationist case as well as reviewing other explanations. Another statement of the continuity and readaptation hypotheses is Forrest McDonald, "Cultural Continuity and the Shaping of the American South," in Eugene D. Genovese and Leonard Hochberg, eds., *Geographical Perspectives in History* (Oxford: 1989). A different interpretation can be derived from R. Cole Harris, "The Simplification of Europe Overseas," *Annals* of the Association of American Geographers 67 (1977), 469–83.

David H. Fischer, *Albion's Seed: Four British Folkways in America* (Oxford: 1989), is the major exposition of regional continuity by an historian. See also the "Forum" on this book in *The William and Mary Quarterly*, 3rd ser., XLVIII (1991), 223–308, especially Fischer's conceptual remarks, pp. 303–7.

C. M. White, *Russia and America: The Roots of Economic Divergence* (London: 1987), thoughtfully treats the economic implications of colonizing North America, in the Russian mirror. W. A. Knittle, *Early Eighteenth-century Palatine Emigration* (Philadelphia, PA: 1937), and John A. Hostetler, *Amish Society* (Baltimore: 1963), are useful on European groups in America. An interesting account of one regional group that emigrated to early Massachusetts is Frank Thistlewaite, *Dorset Pilgrims: the Story of West Country Pilgrims who went to New England in the 17th Century* (London: 1989). Material on what was transmitted is to be found in W. C. MacLeod, "Celt and Indian: Britain's old world frontier in relation to the new," in Paul Bohannon and Fred Plog, eds., *Beyond the Frontier: Social*

Process and Cultural Change (Garden City, NY: 1967), 25–41, and K. R. Andrews, ed., *The Westward Enterprise* (Liverpool: 1978).

The isolationist literature on the American frontier in the tradition of Frederick Jackson Turner is usually unhelpful. Related but different explanations of the relationship between the old and new worlds include Walter Prescott Webb, *The Great Frontier* (Boston, MA: 1952) and Louis Hartz et al., *The Founding of New Societies* (New York: 1964). Whether both sides of the Atlantic changed in response to common stimuli is addressed by Peter Karsten, "'Bottomed on Justice': A Reappraisal of Critical Legal Studies Scholarship Concerning Breaches of Labor Contracts by Quitting or Firing in Britain and the U.S., 1630–1889," *American Journal of Legal History* 34 (1990), 213–61.

On the British and European side, two useful bibliographies are Charles Wilson and Geoffrey Parker, eds., *An Introduction to the Sources of European Economic History 1500–1800* (London 1980), and W. H. Chaloner and R. C. Richardson, eds., *British Economic and Social History: A Bibliographical Guide* (Manchester, 1976). For European background, see E. L. Jones, *The European Miracle: Environments, Economies and Geopolitics in the History of Europe and Asia*, second ed. (Cambridge 1987), R. A. Dodgshon, *The European Past: Social Evolution and Spatial Order* (Basingstoke, 1987) (on process) and N. J. G. Pounds, *An Historical Geography of Europe 1500–1840* (Cambridge, 1979) (for description, though excluding Britain and Russia).

On rural life in continental Europe, see Jerome Blum, *The End of the Old Order in Rural Europe* (Princeton, 1978). Dudley Dillard, *Economic Development of the North Atlantic Community: Historical Introduction to Modern Economics* (Englewood Cliffs, NJ, 1967), covers economic change on both sides of the Atlantic fully. See also Ralph Davis, *The Rise of the Atlantic Economies* (London, 1973).

Jan de Vries, *The Economy of Europe in an Age of Crisis, 1600–1750* (Cambridge: 1976), is an accessible economic history of early modern Europe. Among economic histories of England, see D. C. Coleman, *The Economy of England 1450–1750* (Oxford: 1977); B. A. Holderness, *Pre-industrial England: Economy and Society, 1500–1750* (Totowa, NJ: 1976); and Brian Murphy, *A History of the British Economy 1086–1740* (London: 1973).

The classic study of English society by an American is Carl Bridenbaugh, *Vexed and Troubled Englishmen 1590–1642* (New York: 1968). For the American side, see Carl N. Degler, *Out of Our Past: The Forces That Shaped Modern America*, second ed. (New York: 1970); from the European, see Edward P. Cheyney, *European Background of American History 1300–1600* (New York: 1961).

On agriculture and ecology, see Carl O. Sauer, *Selected Essays 1963–1975* (Berkeley, CA: 1981) especially "The Settlement of the Humid East" and "European Backgrounds of American Agricultural Settlement." See also Homer L. Kerr, "Introduction of Forage Plants Into Ante-Bellum United States," *Agricultural History* 38 (1964), 87–9 and E. L. Jones, "Creative Disruptions in American Agriculture, 1620–1820," *Agricultural History* 48 (1974), 510–28.

Ann Kussmaul, *A General View of the Rural Economy of England, 1538–1840* (Cambridge: 1989), is analytically excellent on English agricultural history in the period. A fuller descriptive coverage is Joan Thirsk, ed., *The Agrarian History of England and Wales, Vol. IV, 1500–1640* (Cambridge: 1967). From the American side, Sumner Chilton Powell, *Puritan Village: The Formation of a New England Town* (Garden City, NY: 1965), emphasizes English agrarian origins.

CHAPTER 4 (GALENSON)

INSTITUTIONS OF SETTLEMENT

The most authoritative and detailed survey of the history of English colonization in North America and the West Indies is Charles M. Andrews, *The Colonial Period of American History*, 4 vols. (New Haven, 1934–8). Good brief introductions are given by W. Frank Craven, "The Early Settlements: A European Investment of Capital and Labor," in Harold F. Williamson, ed., *The Growth of the American Economy*, second ed. (New York, 1951), 19–43, and Bernard Bailyn, "Shaping the Republic," in Bailyn et. al., *The Great Republic*, Vol. 1 (Lexington, MA, 1977), 1–225. Other general accounts of the early development of the colonies include William B. Weeden, *Economic and Social History of New England, 1620–1789*, 2 vols. (Boston, 1891); George Louis Beer, *The Origins of the British Colonial System, 1578–1660* (New York, 1908); Lewis Cecil Gray, *History of Agriculture in the Southern United States to 1860*, 2 vols. (Washington, D.C., 1933); W. F. Craven, *The Southern Colonies in the Seventeenth Century, 1607–1689* (Baton Rouge, LA, 1949); Richard Pares, *Merchants and Planters* (Cambridge, 1960); W. F. Craven, *The Colonies in Transition, 1660–1713* (New York, 1968); John E. Pomfret, *Founding the American Colonies,*

1583–1660 (New York, 1970); and K. G. Davies, *The North Atlantic World in the Seventeenth Century* (Minneapolis, 1974), which also compares the English colonization experience to those of other European nations.

The classic study of the Virginia Company is W. F. Craven, *Dissolution of the Virginia Company* (New York, 1932); a more recent account is included in Edmund S. Morgan, *American Slavery, American Freedom: The Ordeal of Colonial Virginia* (New York, 1975). On investment in English joint-stock companies at the time, see Theodore Rabb, *Enterprise and Empire* (Cambridge, MA, 1967). On the labor problem and the social revolution in early Virginia, see Sigmund Diamond, "From Organization to Society: Virginia in the Seventeenth Century," *American Journal of Sociology* 63 (1958), 457–75; and Diamond, "Values as an Obstacle to Economic Growth: The American Colonies," *Journal of Economic History* 27 (1967), 561–75. A recent account of the early settlement of New England is given by John Frederick Martin, *Profits in the Wilderness: Entrepreneurship and the Founding of New England Towns in the Seventeenth Century* (Chapel Hill, 1991). On the evolution of the colonial economy and society, see E. A. J. Johnson, *American Economic Thought in the Seventeenth Century* (London, 1932); J. R. T. Hughes, *Social Control in the Colonial Economy* (Charlottesville, VA, 1976); David W. Galenson and Russell R. Menard, "Approaches to the Analysis of Economic Growth in Colonial British America," *Historical Methods* 13 (1980), 3–18; James T. Lemon, "Spatial Order: Households in Local Communities and Regions," in Jack P. Greene and J. R. Pole, *Colonial British America* (Baltimore, 1984); John J. McCusker and Russell R. Menard, *The Economy of British America, 1607–1789* (Chapel Hill, 1985); and Barbara L. Solow, "Slavery and Colonization," in Solow, ed., *Slavery and the Rise of the Atlantic System* (Cambridge, 1991), 21–42.

LABOR MARKET INSTITUTIONS

The authoritative history of indentured servitude is Abbot Emerson Smith, *Colonists in Bondage: White Servitude and Convict Labor in America, 1607–1776* (Chapel Hill, 1947); a more recent treatment is David W. Galenson, *White Servitude in Colonial America: An Economic Analysis* (Cambridge, 1981). On the English background of indentured servitude, see Peter Laslett, *The World We Have Lost*, second ed. (London, 1971); Laslett, *Family Life and Illicit Love in Earlier Generations* (Cambridge, 1977); Alan Macfarlane, *The Origins of English Individualism* (Oxford, 1978); David Souden, " 'Rogues, Whores and Vagabonds'? Indentured Servant

Emigrants to North America, and the Case of Mid-Seventeenth-Century Bristol," *Social History* 3 (1978), 23–41; Ann Kussmaul, *Servants in Husbandry in Early Modern England* (Cambridge, 1981); and David W. Galenson, "The Rise of Free Labor: Economic Change and the Enforcement of Service Contracts in England, 1351–1875," in John James and Mark Thomas, eds., *Capitalism in Context: Essays on Economic Development and Cultural Change in Honor of R. M. Hartwell* (Chicago, 1994). Additional information on indentured servitude is contained in J. C. Ballagh, *White Servitude in the Colony of Virginia* (Baltimore, 1895); Karl Frederick Geiser, *Redemptioners and Indentured Servants in the Colony and Commonwealth of Pennsylvania* (New Haven, 1901); Eugene I. McCormac, *White Servitude in Maryland, 1634–1820* (Baltimore, 1904); Philip Alexander Bruce, *Economic History of Virginia in the Seventeenth Century*, 2 vols. (New York, 1907); Cheesman A. Herrick, *White Servitude in Pennsylvania* (Philadelphia, 1926); Richard B. Morris, *Government and Labor in Early America* (New York, 1946); Wesley Frank Craven, *White, Red and Black: The Seventeenth-Century Virginian* (Charlottesville, VA, 1971); A. Roger Ekirch, *Bound for America: The Transportation of British Convicts to the Colonies* (Oxford, 1987); and Hilary Beckles, *White Servitude and Black Slavery in Barbados, 1627–1715* (Knoxville, TN, 1989). On the trans-Atlantic trade in servants, see David Souden, "English Indentured Servants and the Transatlantic Colonial Economy," in Shula Marks and Peter Richardson, eds., *International Labour Migration: Historical Perspectives* (London, 1984), 19–33; Farley Grubb, "The Market for Indentured Immigrants: Evidence on the Efficiency of Forward-Labor Contracting in Philadelphia, 1745–1773," *Journal of Economic History* 45 (1985), 855–68; and Russell R. Menard, "British Migration to the Chesapeake Colonies in the Seventeenth Century," in Lois Green Carr, Philip D. Morgan, and Jean B. Russo, eds., *Colonial Chesapeake Society* (Chapel Hill, 1988), 99–132. On the legal basis of indentured servitude, see Robert J. Steinfeld, *The Invention of Free Labor: The Employment Relation in English and American Law and Culture, 1350–1870* (Chapel Hill, 1991). The evolution of servitude is treated in David W. Galenson, "The Rise and Fall of Indentured Servitude in the Americas: An Economic Analysis," *Journal of Economic History* 44 (1984), 1–26.

Basic studies of the volume and routes of the slave trade include Philip D. Curtin, *The Atlantic Slave Trade: A Census* (Madison, WI, 1969); Paul Lovejoy, "The Volume of the Atlantic Slave Trade: A Synthesis," *Journal of African History* 23 (1982), 473–501; and Lovejoy, *Transformations in Slav-*

ery: A History of Slavery in Africa (Cambridge, 1983). On slavery within Africa, see also Philip D. Curtin, *Economic Change in Precolonial Africa: Senegambia in the Era of the Slave Trade*, 2 vols. (Madison, WI, 1975); Suzanne Miers and Igor Kopytoff, eds., *Slavery in Africa* (Madison, WI, 1977); John Thornton, "The Slave Trade in Eighteenth Century Angola: Effects on Demographic Structures," *Canadian Journal of African Studies* 14 (1980), 417–27; Philip D. Curtin, "The Abolition of the Slave Trade from Senegambia," in David Eltis and James Walvin, eds., *The Abolition of the Atlantic Slave Trade* (Madison, WI, 1981), 83–98; Claire C. Robertson and Martin A. Klein, eds., *Women and Slavery in Africa* (Madison, WI, 1983); and Martin A. Klein, "The Impact of the Atlantic Slave Trade on the Societies of the Western Sudan," *Social Science History* 14 (1990), 231–53. Primary evidence on the slave trade is presented in Elizabeth Donnan, ed., *Documents Illustrative of the Slave Trade to America*, 4 vols. (Washington, D.C., 1930–5).

Recent studies of the operation of the trans-Atlantic slave trade include Herbert S. Klein, *The Middle Passage: Comparative Studies in the Atlantic Slave Trade* (Princeton, NJ, 1978); Henry Gemery and Jan Hogendorn, eds., *The Uncommon Market: Essays on the Economic History of the Atlantic Slave Trade* (New York, 1978); Colin Palmer, *Human Cargoes: The British Slave Trade to Spanish America* (Urbana, IL, 1981); James A. Rawley, *The Transatlantic Slave Trade* (New York, 1981); and Barbara L. Solow, ed., *Slavery and the Rise of the Atlantic System* (Cambridge, 1991). On the economics of the trade, also see Henry A. Gemery and Jan S. Hogendorn, "The Atlantic Slave Trade: A Tentative Economic Model," *Journal of African History* 15 (1974), 223–46; Richard N. Bean, *The British Trans-Atlantic Slave Trade, 1650–1775* (New York, 1975); and Richard N. Bean and Robert P. Thomas, "The Adoption of Slave Labor in British America," in Gemery and Hogendorn, eds., *The Uncommon Market*, 377–98. For the history of the English slave-trading companies, see George Frederick Zook, *The Company of Royal Adventurers Trading into Africa* (Lancaster, PA, 1919); K. G. Davies, *The Royal African Company* (London, 1957); and David W. Galenson, *Traders, Planters, and Slaves: Market Behavior in Early English America* (Cambridge, 1986). On the demographic composition of the trade, see David Eltis and Stanley L. Engerman, "Fluctuations in Sex and Age Ratios in the Transatlantic Slave Trade, 1663–1864," *Economic History Review*, 2d. Ser. 46 (1993), 308–23. On the finance of the slave trade, see Jacob M. Price, "Credit in the Slave Trade and the Plantation Economies," in Solow, ed., *Slavery and the Rise of the Atlantic System*, 293–

339. On mortality in the slave trade, among many studies see Philip D. Curtin, "Epidemiology and the Slave Trade," *Political Science Quarterly* 83 (1968), 190–216; Roger T. Anstey, *The Atlantic Slave Trade and British Abolition, 1760–1810* (London, 1975); Joseph C. Miller, "Mortality in the Atlantic Slave Trade: Statistical Evidence on Casuality," *Journal of Interdisciplinary History* 11 (1981), 385–423; and Richard B. Sheridan, *Doctors and Slaves: a Medical and Demographic History of Slavery in the British West Indies, 1680–1834* (Cambridge, 1985). For comparative evidence on the mortality of whites on trans-Atlantic voyages, see Kenneth Morgan, "The Organization of the Convict Trade to Maryland: Stevenson, Randolph & Cheston, 1768–1775," *William and Mary Quarterly*, 3d. Ser., 42 (1985); and Farley Grubb, "Morbidity and Mortality on the North Atlantic Passage: Eighteenth-Century German Immigration," *Journal of Interdisciplinary History* 17 (1987), 565–85. The mortality in Africa of English employees of the Royal African Company is treated by K. G. Davies, "The Living and the Dead: White Mortality in West Africa, 1684–1732," in Stanley Engerman and Eugene Genovese, eds., *Race and Slavery in the Western Hemisphere: Quantitative Studies* (Princeton, 1975).

For evidence on slavery in particular colonial regions, see Lorenzo Johnston Greene, *The Negro in Colonial New England* (New York, 1942); Richard S. Dunn, *Sugar and Slaves: The Rise of the Planter Class in the English West Indies, 1624–1713* (Chapel Hill, 1972); Carl Bridenbaugh and Roberta Bridenbaugh, *No Peace Beyond the Line: The English in the Caribbean, 1624–1690* (New York, 1972); Gerald W. Mullin, *Flight and Rebellion: Slave Resistance in Eighteenth-Century Virginia* (London, 1972); Richard B. Sheridan, *Sugar and Slavery: An Economic History of the British West Indies, 1623–1775* (Barbados, 1974); Peter H. Wood, *Black Majority: Negroes in Colonial South Carolina from 1670 through the Stono Rebellion* (New York, 1975); Betty Wood, *Slavery in Colonial Georgia, 1730–1775* (Athens, GA, 1984); Jean R. Soderlund, *Quakers and Slavery* (Princeton, NJ, 1985); and Allan Kulikoff, *Tobacco and Slaves: the Development of Southern Cultures in the Chesapeake, 1680–1800* (Chapel Hill, 1986). For treatments of many particular aspects of slavery, see Randall M. Miller and John David Smith, eds., *Dictionary of Afro-American Slavery* (New York, 1988). On the legal development of slavery, see Winthrop D. Jordan, *White Over Black: American Attitudes Toward the Negro, 1550–1812* (Chapel Hill, 1968); and A. Leon Higginbotham, *In the Matter of Color: Race and the American Legal Process, The Colonial Period* (New York, 1978). The economics of the growth of slavery in the Chesapeake is analyzed by Russell R. Menard, "From Servants to Slaves:

The Transformation of the Chesapeake Labor System," *Southern Studies* 16 (1977), 355–90; and David W. Galenson, "Economic Aspects of the Growth of Slavery in the Seventeenth-Century Chesapeake," in Solow, ed., *Slavery and the Rise of the Atlantic System*, 265–92.

On hired labor in the English colonies, see Percy Wells Bidwell and John I. Falconer, *History of Agriculture in the Northern United States to 1860*, (Washington, D.C., 1925); Edmund S. Morgan, *The Puritan Family: Religion and Domestic Relations in Seventeenth-Century New England* (Boston, 1944); Charles S. Grant, *Democracy in the Connecticut Frontier Town of Kent* (New York, 1961); John Demos, "Families in Colonial Bristol, Rhode Island: An Exercise in Historical Demography," *William and Mary Quarterly*, 3d. Ser., 25 (1968), 40–57; Philip J. Greven, *Four Generations: Population, Land, and Family in Colonial Andover, Massachusetts* (Ithaca, NY, 1970); John Demos, *A Little Commonwealth: Family Life in Plymouth Colony* (London, 1970); Kenneth A. Lockridge, *A New England Town: The First Hundred Years* (New York, 1970); Stephen Innes, *Labor in a New Land: Economy and Society in Seventeenth-Century Springfield* (Princeton, NJ, 1983); Jackson Turner Main, *Society and Economy in Colonial Connecticut* (Princeton, NJ, 1985); Daniel Vickers, "Working the Fields in a Developing Economy: Essex County, Massachusetts, 1630–1675," in Stephen Innes, ed., *Work and Labor in Early America* (Chapel Hill, 1988), 49–69; Vickers, "Merchant Credit and Labour Strategies in the Cod Fishery of Colonial Massachusetts," in Rosemary E. Ommer, ed., *Merchant Credit and Labour Strategies in Historical Perspective* (Fredericton, New Brunswick, 1990), 36–48; and Winifred B. Rothenberg, *From Market-Places to a Market Economy: The Transformation of Rural Massachusetts, 1750–1850* (Chicago, 1992). On the evolving legal basis of hired labor, see Christopher Tomlins, *Law, Labor and Ideology in the Early Republic* (Cambridge, 1993).

For overviews of the colonial labor market, see Richard S. Dunn, "Servants and Slaves: The Recruitment and Employment of Labor," in Greene and Pole, eds., *Colonial British America*, 157–94; and David W. Galenson, "Labor Market Behavior in Colonial America: Servitude, Slavery, and Free Labor," in Galenson, ed., *Markets in History: Economic Studies of the Past* (Cambridge, 1989), 52–96.

POPULATION GROWTH AND THE LABOR FORCE

Population estimates by region are presented and discussed in McCusker and Menard, *The Economy of British America, 1607–1789*; these were constructed from earlier works including Evarts B. Greene and Virginia D. Harrington, *American Population Before the Federal Census of 1790* (New York, 1932); Stella H. Sutherland, *Population Distribution in Colonial America* (New York, 1936); and Robert V. Wells, *The Population of the British Colonies in America before 1776* (Princeton, NJ, 1975). For estimates of white immigration, see Henry Gemery, "Emigration from the British Isles to the New World, 1630–1700: Inferences from Colonial Populations," *Research in Economic History* 5 (1980), 170–231; and Gemery, "European Emigration to North America, 1700–1820," *Perspectives in American History* (1984), 283–342.

Studies of migration to the colonies include Mildred Campbell, "English Emigration on the Eve of the American Revolution," *American Historical Review* 61 (1955), 1–20; David Hackett Fischer, *Albion's Seed: Four British Folkways to America* (New York, 1989); Bernard Bailyn, *The Peopling of British North America* (New York, 1986); Bailyn, *Voyagers to the West: A Passage in the Peopling of America on the Eve of the Revolution* (New York, 1986); David Cressy, *Coming Over: Migration and Communication between England and New England in the Seventeenth Century* (Cambridge, 1987); Richard Archer, "New England Mosaic: A Demographic Analysis for the Seventeenth Century," *William and Mary Quarterly*, 3d. Ser., 47 (1990), 477–502; and Ida Altman and James Horn, eds., *"To Make America": European Emigration in the Early Modern Period* (Berkeley, 1991).

The determinants of the population growth in the colonies are analyzed by J. Potter, "The Growth of Population in America, 1700–1860," in D. Glass and D. Eversley, eds., *Population in History* (London, 1965), 631–88; Daniel Scott Smith, "The Demographic History of Colonial New England," *Journal of Economic History* 32 (1972), 165–83; Lorena S. Walsh and Russell R. Menard, "Death in the Chesapeake: Two Life Tables for Men in Early Colonial Maryland," *Maryland Historical Magazine* 69 (1974), 211–27; Russell R. Menard, "The Maryland Slave Population, 1658 to 1730: A Demographic Profile of Blacks in Four Counties," *William and Mary Quarterly*, 3d. Ser., 32 (1975), 29–54; Russell R. Menard, "Immigrants and Their Increase: The Process of Population Growth in Early Colonial Maryland," in Aubrey Land, Lois Carr, and Edward Papenfuse, eds., *Law, Society, and Politics in Early Maryland* (Baltimore, 1977), 88–110; Maris Vinovskis, ed., *Studies in American Historical Demography* (New York, 1979); Vinovskis, *Fertility in Massachusetts from the Revolution to the Civil War* (New York, 1981); Darrett B. Rutman and Anita H. Rutman, *A Place in Time: Middlesex County, Virginia, 1650–1750*, 2 vols.

(New York, 1984); Jim Potter, "Demographic Development and Family Structure," in Greene and Pole, eds., *Colonial British America*, 123–56; Daniel S. Levy, "The Life Expectancies of Colonial Maryland Legislators," *Historical Methods* 20 (1987), 17–28; Levy, "The Economic Demography of the Colonial South" (unpublished dissertation, University of Chicago, 1991); and Robert V. Wells, "The Population of England's Colonies in America: Old English or New Americans?," *Population Studies* 46 (1992), 85–102. For comparative evidence on population growth in England, see E. A. Wrigley and R. S. Schofield, *The Population History of England, 1541–1871* (Cambridge, MA, 1981).

The economic progress of immigrants to the colonies is studied by Russell R. Menard, "From Servant to Freeholder: Status Mobility and Property Accumulation in Seventeenth-Century Maryland," *William and Mary Quarterly*, 3d. Ser., 30 (1973), 37–64; and Lois Green Carr and Menard, "Immigration and Opportunity: The Freedman in Early Colonial Maryland," in Thad Tate and David Ammerman, eds., *The Chesapeake in the Seventeenth Century* (New York, 1979), 206–42.

ECONOMIC DEVELOPMENT

The authoritative study of wealth in the late colonial period is Alice Hanson Jones, *Wealth of a Nation To Be: The American Colonies on the Eve of the Revolution* (New York, 1980); supporting evidence is provided in Jones, *American Colonial Wealth: Documents and Methods*, 3 vols., rev. ed. (New York, 1978). Wealth in Maryland in 1700 is estimated by Gloria L. Main, *Tobacco Colony: Life in Early Maryland, 1650–1720* (Princeton, NJ, 1982). For additional colonial wealth estimates, see Dunn, *Sugar and Slaves*; Russell R. Menard, P. M. G. Harris, and Lois Green Carr, "Opportunity and Inequality: The Distribution of Wealth on the Lower Western Shore of Maryland, 1638–1705," *Maryland Historical Magazine* 69 (1974), 169–184; and Gloria Main, "Personal Wealth in Colonial America: Explorations in the Use of Probate Records from Maryland and Massachusetts, 1650–1720," (unpublished dissertation, Columbia University, 1972). Comparative estimates for England can be found in C. H. Feinstein, "Capital Formation in Great Britain," in Peter Mathias and M. M. Postan, eds., *Cambridge Economic History of Europe*, vol. 7 (Cambridge, 1978), 28–96.

For discussions of agricultural productivity change in the early Chesapeake, see Lorena S. Walsh, "Plantation Management in the Chesapeake,

1620–1820," *Journal of Economic History* 49 (1989), 393–406; Lois Green Carr and Russell R. Menard, "Land, Labor and Economies of Scale in Early Maryland: Some Limits to Growth in the Chesapeake System of Husbandry," *Journal of Economic History*, 49 (1989), 407–18; and Lois Green Carr, Russell R. Menard, and Lorena S. Walsh, *Robert Cole's World: Agriculture and Society in Early Maryland* (Chapel Hill, 1991).

On the heights of colonial soldiers and implications for the standard of living, see Kenneth Sokoloff and Georgia Villaflor, "The Early Achievement of Modern Stature in America," *Social Science History* 6 (1982), 453–81; for English comparisons, see Roderick Floud, Kenneth Wachter, and Annabel Gregory, *Height, Health and History: Nutritional Status in the United Kingdom, 1750–1980* (Cambridge, 1990). On the material standard of living in the early Chesapeake, see Lois Green Carr, "Emigration and the Standard of Living: the Seventeenth Century Chesapeake," *Journal of Economic History*, 52 (1992), 271–91.

Studies of literacy rates in England and the colonies include R. S. Schofield, "Dimensions of Illiteracy, 1750–1850," *Explorations in Economic History* 10 (1973), 437–54; Kenneth A. Lockridge, *Literacy in Colonial New England* (New York, 1974); David W. Galenson, "Literacy and the Social Origins of Some Early Americans," *Historical Journal* 22 (1979), 75–91; David Cressy, *Literacy and the Social Order: Reading and Writing in Tudor and Stuart England* (Cambridge, 1980); David W. Galenson, "Literacy and Age in Preindustrial England: Quantitative Evidence and Implications," *Economic Development and Cultural Change* 29 (1981), 813–29; Lee Soltow and Edward Stevens, *The Rise of Literacy and the Common School in the United States* (Chicago, 1981); Robert E. Gallman, "Two Problems in the Measurement of American Colonial Signature-Mark Literacy," *Historical Methods* 20 (1987), 137–41; and Gallman, "Changes in the Level of Literacy in a New Community of Early America," *Journal of Economic History* 48 (1988), 567–82.

For comparisons of wealth across colonies and discussion, see Jackson Turner Main, *The Social Structure of Revolutionary America* (Princeton, NJ, 1965); S. L. Engerman, "Notes on the Patterns of Economic Growth in the British North American Colonies in the Seventeenth, Eighteenth, and Nineteenth Centuries," in Paul Bairoch and Maurice Lévy-Leboyer, eds., *Disparities in Economic Development Since the Industrial Revolution* (London, 1981), 46–57; Jacob M. Price, "The Transatlantic Economy," in Greene and Pole, eds., *Colonial British America*, 18–42; Richard B. Sheridan, "The Domestic Economy," in ibid., 43–85; and Jackson Turner Main, *Society and Economy in Colonial Connecticut* (Princeton, NJ, 1985). On the measurement and analysis of economic inequality in the mainland colonies over time, see Jeffrey G. Williamson and Peter H. Lindert, "Long-Term Trends in American Wealth Inequality," in James D. Smith, ed., *Modeling the Distribution and Intergenerational Transmission of Wealth* (Chicago, 1980), 9–93.

On colonial trade, see Elizabeth Boody Schumpeter, *English Overseas Trade Statistics, 1697–1808* (Oxford, 1960); Bernard Bailyn, *The New England Merchants in the Seventeenth Century* (Cambridge, MA, 1955); Ralph Davis, *The Rise of the English Shipping Industry in the Seventeenth and Eighteenth Centuries* (London, 1962); James F. Shepherd and Gary M. Walton, *Shipping, Maritime Trade, and the Economic Development of Colonial North America* (Cambridge, 1972); Jacob M. Price, *Capital and Credit in British Overseas Trade: The View from the Chesapeake, 1700–1776* (Cambridge, MA, 1980); and Price, *Perry of London: A Family and a Firm on the Seaborne Frontier, 1615–1753* (Cambridge, MA, 1992). For colonial exchange rates, see John J. McCusker, *Money and Exchange in Europe and America, 1600–1775: A Handbook* (Chapel Hill, 1978).

CHAPTER 5 (VICKERS)

The social and economic history of the northern colonies is best approached through the appropriate chapters in two comprehensive and superbly referenced studies: John J. McCusker and Russell R. Menard, *The Economy of British America, 1607–1789* (Chapel Hill, 1985); and Jack P. Greene, *Pursuits of Happiness: The Social Development of Early Modern British Colonies and the Formation of American Culture* (Chapel Hill, 1988). The former contains an excellent bibliography that is particularly strong in older studies and published primary sources. These two studies may be supplemented by Frank Freidel, ed., *Harvard Guide to American History*, 2 vols. (Cambridge, MA, 1974), which is extensive although dated. The core periodical in the field is the *William and Mary Quarterly*, 3d Ser. (1944–   ), which contains many seminal articles and which reviews virtually all of the important published work on the American colonies – North and South. Much useful material also appears in regional historical journals, especially *Acadiensis*, the *New England Quarterly, Pennsylvania Magazine of History and Biography*, Essex Institute, *Historical Collections*, and *New York History*.

The history of settlement and the transfer of European culture to New

England and the middle colonies is the subject of David Hackett Fischer, *Albion's Seed: Four British Folkways in America* (New York, 1989), a comprehensive and stimulating, if sometimes eccentric, overview. The regional literature is strongest on New England: see especially David G. Allen, *In English Ways: The Movement of Societies and the Transfer of English Local Law and Custom to Massachusetts Bay in the Seventeenth Century* (Chapel Hill, 1981); and Virginia DeJohn Anderson, *New England's Generation: The Great Migration and the Formation of Society and Culture in the Seventeenth Century* (Cambridge, 1991). The middle colonies are less well-served, but see the excellent studies by Ned Landsman, *Scotland and its First American Colony, 1683–1765* (Princeton, NJ, 1985) on East Jersey; Barry Levy, *Quakers and the American Family: Settlement in the Delaware Valley* (New York, 1988) on the Welsh Tract in Pennsylvania; and Oliver A. Rink, *Holland on the Hudson: An Economic and Social History of Dutch New York* (Ithaca, NY, 1986) on the Hudson Valley. The settlement of the colonial North is best followed into the eighteenth century in Bernard Bailyn, *The Peopling of British North America: An Introduction* (New York, 1986); and *Voyagers to the West: A Passage in the Peopling of America on the Eve of the Revolution* (New York, 1986).

Studies of the northern frontier do not usefully fall into discrete fields of history, and this probably constitutes their advantage. Since shared assumptions amongst the many Indian and European groups that dealt with one another along the frontier were few in number, culture there had to be the product of continuous negotiation; this has forced those who study the frontier into treatments that cross the borders between economic, social, political, and military history. The most sophisticated treatment of this theme is Richard White, *The Middle Ground: Indians, Empires, and Republics in the Great Lakes Region, 1650–1815* (Cambridge, 1991). In the Atlantic Canadian context, one can still begin with Alfred G. Bailey, *The Conflict of European and Eastern Algonkian Cultures* (St. John, N.B., 1937); the controversial study by Calvin Martin, *Keepers of the Game: Indian–Animal Relationships and the Fur Trade* (Berkeley, CA, 1978); Shepard Krech III, *Indians, Animals and the Fur Trade: A Critique of Keepers of the Game* (Athens, GA, 1981); and a review of subsequent literature by Ralph T. Pastore, "Native History in the Atlantic Region During the Colonial Period," *Acadiensis* XX (1990), 200–25. For New England, there are some older studies: Francis X. Moloney, *The Fur Trade in New England, 1620–1676* (Cambridge, MA, 1931); Douglas Edward Leach, *The Northern Colonial Frontier, 1607–1763* (New York, 1966); and Alden T.

Vaughan, *The New England Frontier: Puritans and Indians, 1620–1675* (Boston, MA, 1965). But these have largely been supplanted by Francis Jennings, *The Invasion of America: Indians, Colonists, and the Cant of Conquest* (Chapel Hill, 1975); William Cronon, *Changes in the Land: Indians, Colonists, and the Ecology of New England* (New York, 1983); and Peter A. Thomas, "Cultural Change on the Southern New England Frontier, 1630–1665," in William W. Fitzhugh, ed., *Cultures in Conflict: the European Impact on Native Cultural Institutions in Eastern North America, 1000–1800* (Washington, D.C., 1985), 131–62. On the Middle Colonies, see Thomas Eliot Norton, *The Fur Trade in Colonial New York, 1686–1776* (Madison, WI, 1974); and especially two works by Francis Jennings: *The Ambiguous Iroquois Empire: The Covenant Chain Confederation of Indian Tribes with English Colonists from its beginnings to the Lancaster Treaty of 1744* (New York, 1984); and *Empire of Fortune: Crowns, Colonies, and the Seven Years War in America* (New York, 1988). For the way in which Europeans operated within the frontier zone, there is much suggestive material in George W. Franz, *Paxton: A Study of Community Structure and Mobility in the Colonial Pennsylvania Backcountry* (New York, 1989); Bailyn's *Voyagers to the West*, especially the chapters on Nova Scotia and New York; and the early chapters of both Thomas P. Slaughter, *The Whiskey Rebellion: Frontier Epilogue to the American Revolution* (New York, 1986); and Alan Taylor, *Liberty Men and Great Proprietors: The Revolutionary Settlement on the Maine Frontier, 1760–1820* (Chapel Hill, 1990).

The best single overview of rural economy in the northern colonies remains Percy Wells Bidwell and John I. Falconer, *History of Agriculture in the Northern United States, 1620–1860* (Washington, D.C., 1925), although New England has more recently received two rather different synthetic treatments in Howard S. Russell, *A Long, Deep Furrow: Three Centuries of Farming in New England* (Hanover, NH, 1976), parts 1 and 2; and Carolyn Merchant, *Ecological Revolutions: Nature, Gender, and Science in New England* (Chapel Hill, 1989). Beyond these, the reader is best advised to investigate the immense regional and local literature produced by the "new social" and "new economic" historians of the past 30 years.

On Pennsylvania, see James T. Lemon, *The Best Poor Man's Country: A Geographical Study of Early Southeastern Pennsylvania* (Baltimore, MD, 1972); Duane E. Ball and Gary M. Walton, "Agricultural Productivity Change in Eighteenth-Century Pennsylvania," *Journal of Economic History* 36 (1976), 102–17; and "Discussion" by Russell M. Menard in ibid., 118–25; Lucy Simler, "Tenancy in Colonial Pennsylvania: The Case of

Chester County," *William and Mary Quarterly*, 3d Ser., XLIII (1986), 542–69; Paul G. E. Clemens and Lucy Simler, "Rural Labor and the Farm Household in Chester County, Pennsylvania, 1750–1820," in Stephen Innes, ed., *Work and Labor in Early America* (Chapel Hill, 1988), 106–43; Joan M. Jensen, *Loosening the Bonds: Mid-Atlantic Farm Women, 1750–1850* (New Haven, CT, 1986); as well as Levy, *Quakers and the American Family*. Historians have tended to ignore New Jersey, but see John E. Pomfret, *The New Jersey Proprietors and their Lands, 1664–1776* (Princeton, NJ, 1964); Peter O. Wacker, *Land and People: A Cultural Geography of Preindustrial New Jersey: Origins and Settlement Patterns* (New Brunswick, NJ, 1975); as well as Landsman, *Scotland in America*. The rural history of colonial New York is dominated by discussions of its manorial system, and on this topic, Sung Bok Kim, *Landlord and Tenant in Colonial New York: Manorial Society, 1664–1775* (Chapel Hill, 1978), is now authoritative.

The literature on the New England town used to slight questions of political economy, but this is no longer the case. John Frederick Martin, *Profits in the Wilderness: Entrepreneurship and the Founding of New England Towns in the Seventeenth Century* (Chapel Hill, 1991), is one fine recent study that reflects this recent trend to reconceptualize the New England experience in precisely these terms. Some important regional studies that focus on the question of growth are Terry L. Anderson, "Economic Growth in Colonial New England: "Statistical Renaissance," *Journal of Economic History*, 39 (1979), 243–57; Bruce C. Daniels, "Economic Development in Colonial and Revolutionary Connecticut: An Overview" *William and Mary Quarterly*, 3d Ser., 37 (1980), 429–50; and Gloria L. Main and Jackson T. Main, "Economic Growth and the Standard of Living in Southern New England, 1640–1774," *Journal of Economic History*, 48 (1988), 27–46. On social structure, Jackson Turner Main, *Society and Economy in Colonial Connecticut* (Princeton, NJ, 1985), contains much useful information; and on geographic mobility, see Fred Anderson, "A People's Army: Provincial Military Service in Massachusetts During the Seven Years' War," *William and Mary Quarterly*, 3d Ser., 40 (1983), 499–527; and Douglas Lamar Jones, "The Strolling Poor: Transiency in Eighteenth-Century Massachusetts," *Journal of Social History*, 8 (1975), 28–54. The role of women and of gender relations within the rural economy needs further study, but for two contrasting perspectives, see Laurel Thatcher Ulrich, *Good Wives: Image and Reality in the Lives of Women in Northern New England, 1650–1750* (New York, 1980), especially part 1; and Carol Karlsen, *The Devil in the Shape of a Woman: Witchcraft in Colonial New England* (New York, 1987). The importance of market relationships within the rural economy of the colonial North (and especially New England) has been the subject of lively debate among many historians, including Michael Merrill, "Cash Is Good to Eat: Self-Sufficiency and Exchange in the Rural Economy of the United States," *Radical History Review*, 3 (1977), 42–71; James A. Henretta, "Families and Farms: *Mentalité* in Pre-Industrial America," *William and Mary Quarterly*, 3d Ser., 35 (1978), 3–32; Bettye Hobbs Pruitt, "Self-Sufficiency and the Agricultural Economy of Eighteenth-Century Massachusetts," ibid., 3d Ser., 41 (1984), 333–64; Winifred Barr Rothenberg, *From Market-Places to a Market Economy: the Transformation of Rural Massachusetts, 1750–1850*. (Chicago, IL, 1992). The issues within this debate are well summarized in Allan Kulikoff, *The Agrarian Origins of American Capitalism* (Charlottesville, VA, 1992).

There are dozens of useful studies that deal with these and other subjects in the context of a single New England town or county but space here to mention only the most significant. Philip J. Greven, *Four Generations: Population, Land, and Family in Colonial Andover, Massachusetts* (Ithaca, NY, 1970); Kenneth A. Lockridge, *A New England Town: The First Hundred Years: Dedham, Massachusetts, 1636–1736* (New York, 1970); and Robert A. Gross, *The Minutemen and Their World* (New York, 1976) offer a Malthusian interpretation of initial abundance followed by mounting population and social crisis. This has been challenged from different perspectives by Christopher M. Jedrey, *The World of John Cleaveland: Family and Community in Eighteenth-Century New England* (New York, 1979); Stephen Innes, *Labor in a New Land: Economy and Society in Seventeenth-Century Springfield* (Princeton, NJ, 1983); Toby L. Ditz, *Property and Kinship: Inheritance in Early Connecticut, 1750–1820* (Princeton, NJ, 1986); John L. Brooke, *The Heart of the Commonwealth: Society and Political Culture in Worcester County, Massachusetts, 1713–1861* (Cambridge, 1989); and Daniel Vickers, *Farmers and Fishermen: Two Centuries of Work in Essex County, Massachusetts, 1630–1850* (Chapel Hill, 1994).

North of Massachusetts, the countryside thinned out, as does the historical literature. The development of rural New Hampshire and Maine are covered in Charles E. Clarke, *The Eastern Frontier: The Settlement of Northern New England, 1610–1763* (New York, 1970); and David E. Van Deventer, *The Emergence of Provincial New Hampshire, 1623–1741* (Baltimore, MD, 1976). Andrew Hill Clark, *Acadia: The Geography of Early Nova Scotia to 1760* (Madison, WI, 1968), does a very thorough job on the early history of Nova Scotia.

The maritime industries of the northern colonies possess even less in the way of synthetic treatment than does the rural economy. K. R. Andrews, *Trade, Plunder, and Settlement: Maritime Enterprise and the Genesis of the British Empire, 1480–1630* (Cambridge, 1984) covers the subject well but only in its earliest and essentially pre-colonial years. For later periods, even the broadest treatments focus in on specific subjects. On trade and shipping, Ralph Davis, *The Rise of the English Shipping Industry* (London, 1962), is still fundamental; it can be supplemented with James F. Shepherd and Gary M. Walton, *Shipping, Maritime Trade, and the Economic Development of Colonial America* (Cambridge, 1972). James F. Shepherd, "Commodity Exports from the British North American Colonies to Overseas Areas, 1768–1772: Magnitudes and Patterns of Trade," *Explorations in Economic History*, 2d Ser., 8 (1970–71), 5–76, is especially useful for the trade statistics it presents. One way to study trade is through the men who organized it, and colonial American history is very rich in merchant studies. There are several excellent biographies including William T. Baxter, *The House of Hancock: Business in Boston, 1724–1775* (Cambridge, MA, 1945); and James B. Hedges, *The Browns of Providence Plantations: The Colonial Years* (Cambridge, MA, 1952). Virginia D. Harrington, *The New York Merchant on the Eve of the Revolution* (New York, 1935); Frederick B. Tolles, *Meeting House and Counting House: The Quaker Merchants of Colonial Philadelphia, 1682–1763* (Chapel Hill, 1948); Bernard Bailyn, *The New England Merchants in the Seventeenth Century* (Cambridge, MA, 1955); and most recently, Thomas M. Doerflinger, *A Vigorous Spirit of Enterprise: Merchants and Economic Development in Revolutionary Philadelphia* (Chapel Hill, 1986) are all excellent collective portraits of the merchant class and indispensable to an understanding of colonial trade. Since the urban history of the northern colonies is also port history, there is much about trade in such works as Carl Bridenbaugh, *Cities in the Wilderness: The First Century of Urban Life in America, 1625–1742* (New York, 1938); and *Cities in Revolt: Urban Life in American, 1743–1776* (New York, 1955); Gary B. Nash, *The Urban Crucible: Social Change, Political Consciousness, and the Origins of the American Revolution* (Cambridge, MA, 1979), Lynne Withey, *Urban Growth in Colonial Rhode Island: Newport and Providence in the Eighteenth Century* (Albany, NY, 1983); Jacob Price, "Economic Function and the Growth of American Port towns in the Eighteenth Century," *Perspectives in American History*, 8 (1974), 121–86. Other useful studies on the social and economic life of colonial ports include Billy G. Smith, *The "Lower Sort": Philadelphia's Laboring People, 1750–1800* (Ithaca, NY,

1990); and Sharon V. Salinger, *"To serve well and faithfully": Labor and Indentured Servants in Pennsylvania, 1682–1800* (New York, 1987).

Other branches of the maritime economy deserve more attention than they have previously received. The trans-Atlantic fisheries are reasonably well covered by Harold A. Innis, *The Cod Fisheries: The History of an International Economy* (Toronto, 1940); Gillian T. Cell, *English Enterprise in Newfoundland, 1577–1660* (Toronto, 1969); Keith Matthews "A History of the West of England–Newfoundland Fishery" (Ph.D. diss., Oxford University, 1968); and the superb Plates 21–28 in R. Cole Harris, ed., *Historical Atlas of Canada*, Vol. I, *From the Beginning to 1800* (Toronto, 1987). Two recent works on the resident cod fishery in Massachusetts are Christine Heyrman, *Commerce and Culture: The Maritime Communities of Colonial Massachusetts, 1690–1760* (New York, 1983) and Daniel Vickers, *Farmers and Fishermen* (cited above). The colonial whaling industry has received less attention, but the best introduction is contained in Edward Byers, *The Nation of Nantucket: Society and Politics in an Early American Commercial Center, 1660–1820* (Boston, MA, 1987). The history of shipbuilding and, indeed, all waterfront crafts is practically nonexistent, but see Joseph A. Goldenberg's cautious *Shipbuilding in Colonial America* (Charlottesville, VA, 1976); and Bernard Bailyn and Lotte Bailyn, *Massachusetts Shipping, 1697–1714: A Statistical Study* (Cambridge, MA, 1959).

On the role of government in the public economy of the northern colonies, the literature is daunting in quantity; one can begin at the top with some classic imperial overviews, including Charles M. Andrews, *The Colonial Period of American History*, 4 vols. (New Haven, CT, 1934–8), especially Vol. IV, *England's Commercial and Colonial Policy*; Lawrence A. Harper, *The English Navigation Laws: A Seventeenth-Century Experiment in Social Engineering* (New York, 1939); Wesley Frank Craven, *The Colonies in Transition, 1660–1713* (New York, 1968); Michael Kammen, *Empire and Interest: the American Colonies and the Politics of Mercantilism* (Philadelphia, PA, 1970); Jack P. Greene, "An Uneasy Connection: An Analysis of the Preconditions of the American Revolution," in Stephen G. Kurtz and James H. Hutson, eds., *Essays on the American Revolution* (Chapel Hill, 1973), 32–80; and Robert Paul Thomas, "A Quantitative Approach to the Study of the Effects of British Imperial Policy upon Colonial Welfare: Some Preliminary Findings," *Journal of Economic History*, 25 (1965), 615–38; with Jacob Price, "Discussion," in ibid., 656–69. Some useful studies that deal specifically with imperial policy in the colonial Northeast include G. M. Waller, *Samuel Vetch: Colonial Enterpriser* (Chapel Hill, 1960);

George A. Rawlyk, *Nova Scotia's Massachusetts: A Study of Massachusetts–Nova Scotia Relations, 1630–1784* (Montreal, 1973); Michael G. Hall, *Edward Randolph and the American Colonies, 1676–1703* (Chapel Hill, 1960); J. A. Schutz, *William Shirley, King's Governor of Massachusetts* (Chapel Hill, NC, 1961); Stanley N. Katz, *Newcastle's New York: Anglo–American Politics, 1732–1753* (Cambridge, MA, 1968); and James H. Hutson, *Pennsylvania Politics, 1746–1770: The Movement for Royal Government and its Consequences* (Princeton, NJ, 1972).

On the social policies of colonial governments as well as the connections between law and the economy, see such overviews as J. R. T. Hughes, *Social Control in the Colonial Economy* (Charlottesville, VA, 1976); Richard B. Morris, *Government and Labor in Early America* (New York, 1946); and Leslie V. Brock, *The Currency of the American Colonies, 1700–1764: A Study in Colonial Finance and Imperial Relations* (New York, 1975). Studies that deal effectively with individual colonies include George Lee Haskins, *Law and Authority in Early Massachusetts: A Study in Tradition and Design* (New York, 1960); Bruce H. Mann, *Neighbors and Strangers: Law and Community in Early Connecticut* (Chapel Hill, 1987); and Mary Schweitzer, *Custom and Contract: Household, Government, and the Economy in Colonial Pennsylvania* (New York, 1987).

CHAPTER 6 (MENARD)

Given the uncertain nature of the South as a concept in the eighteenth century, it should come as no surprise that there is little literature focused on the region as a whole, and that interested scholars have to turn to more general works on the colonies as a whole or on more focused studies of particular regions. Having laid down those rules, let me begin with an exception to them; what in my view remains the best book on the economic history of the colonial South, and a good starting point for nearly any research in early southern economic history, Lewis C. Gray, *History of Agriculture in the Southern United States to 1860*, 2 vols. 430 (Washington, D.C., 1933). Especially useful colonial-wide studies include, for wealth and welfare issues, Alice Hanson Jones, *The Wealth of a Nation to Be: The American Colonies on the Eve of the Revolution* (New York, 1980); for the labor force, David Galenson, *White Servitude in Colonial America* (New York, 1981); for external trade, James F. Shepherd and Gary M. Walton, *Shipping, Maritime Trade and the Economic Development of Colonial North America*

(Cambridge, 1972). John J. McCusker and Russell R. Menard, *The Economy of British America, 1607–1789* (Chapel Hill, 1985), touches on the major issues and has a fairly comprehensive bibliography. Peter Wood's, "The Changing Population of the Colonial South: An Overview by Race and Region, 1685–1790," in Peter Wood, Gregory A. Waselkov, and M. Thomas Hatley, eds., *Powhatan's Mantle: Indians in the Colonial Southeast* (Lincoln, NE, 1991) 35–127, offers a comprehensive set of population estimates that seem to me more reliable than earlier estimates.

The past 25 years or so have witnessed a major boom in scholarship on the tobacco coast. A good starting point is Edmund S. Morgan's magnificent overview: *American Slavery, American Freedom: The Ordeal of Colonial Virginia* (New York, 1975). Three collections of essays introduce the new scholarships: Thad W. Tate and David L. Ammerman, eds., *The Chesapeake in the Seventeenth Century: Essays on Anglo-American Society & Politics* (Chapel Hill, 1979); Aubrey C. Land, Lois Green Carr, and Edward C. Papenfuse eds., *Law, Society and Politics in Early Maryland* (Baltimore, 1977); and Lois Green Carr, Philip D. Morgan, and Jean B. Russo, eds., *Colonial Chesapeake Society* (Chapel Hill, 1988). There are also several recent books that are essential reading. Lois Green Carr, Russell R. Menard, and Lorena S. Walsh, *Robert Cole's World: Agriculture and Society in Early Maryland* (Chapel Hill, 1991), is a detailed study of the farm-building process. Gloria L. Main, *Tobacco Colony: Life in Early Maryland, 1650–1720* (Princeton, NJ, 1982), is especially good on wealth and welfare issues. On the process of diversification, see Paul G. E. Clemens, *The Atlantic Economy and Colonial Maryland's Eastern Shore: From Tobacco to Slaves* (Ithaca, NY, 1980). Allan Kulikoff, *Tobacco and Slaves: The Development of Southern Cultures in the Chesapeake, 1680–1800* (Chapel Hill, 1986), is an extraordinarily well-executed local history. Jacob M. Price is the premier historian of the tobacco trade. Students of the industry should read his numerous essays and his books, particularly: *Capital and Credit in British Overseas Trade: The View from the Chesapeake, 1700–1776* (Cambridge, MA, 1980); *France and the Chesapeake: A History of the French Tobacco Monopoly, 1674–1791, and of its Relationship to the British American Tobacco Trade*, 2 vols., (Ann Arbor, MI, 1973); *Perry of London: A Family and a Firm on the Seaborne Frontier, 1615–1753* (Cambridge, MA, 1992).

While the recent scholarship on the lower South remains slim by Chesapeake standards, there have been some impressive recent works. Peter H. Wood's *Black Majority: Negroes in Colonial South Carolina from 1670 through the Stono Rebellion* (New York, 1974) has already earned itself a secure place in the canon of early American historiography. Joyce Chaplin, *An Anxious Pursuit: Agricultural Innovation and Modernity in the Lower South* (Chapel Hill, 1993), is a stunning combination of intellectual and economic history. Peter Coclanis, *The Shadow of a Dream: Economic Life and Death in the South Carolina Low Country, 1670–1920* (New York, 1989) is a useful overview. Russell R. Menard, "Financing the Lowcountry Export Boom: Capital and Credit in Early South Carolina," *William and Mary Quarterly*, 3d. Ser., 51 (1994), 659–76, examines how plantation development was financed.

There are signs that a major boom in backcountry studies is about to begin. Especially impressive recent work includes books by: Rachel Klein, *Unification of a Slave State: The Rise of the Planter Class in the South Carolina Backcountry, 1760–1800* (Chapel Hill, 1990); Robert D. Mitchell, *Commercialism and Frontier: Perspectives on the Early Shenandoah Valley* (Charlottesville, VA, 1977); and Richard Beeman, *Evolution of the Southern Backcountry: A Case Study of Lunenburg County, Virginia, 1746–1832* (Philadelphia, PA, 1984). Gregory Nobles, "Breaking into the Backcountry: New Approaches to the Early American Frontier," in *William and Mary Quarterly*, 3d Ser., 46 (1989) 641–70, is a helpful survey of the literature and the major issues. Unfortunately, much of the scholarship on backcountry agriculture is being conducted in the "moral economy tradition" and within the "transition to capitalism debate." For the tradition and debate, see Winifred B. Rothenberg, *From Market-Places to a Market Economy: The Transformation of Rural Massachusetts, 1750–1850* (Chicago, IL, 1992), and Allan Kulikoff, *The Agrarian Origins of American Capitalism* (Charlottesville, VA, 1992). That tradition and debate seems to me to have confounded capitalism and commercialism. Whereas, if I understand Drew McCoy's *The Elusive Republic*, many contemporaries saw commercial farming as a way of avoiding capitalism, or at least of avoiding some of its worst consequences.

CHAPTER 7 (HIGMAN)

In the historiography of the British West Indies, emphasis has shifted from seeing the tropical colonies as elements of an imperial system, in which the colonies had no real, internal history of their own, to interpretations based on local, Caribbean perspectives. The first historians of the colonies, writing before the American Revolution, had no doubt of the importance of the tropical units and focused on their contributions to the imperial economy. In the nineteenth century, however, the relative decline of the British West Indies was paralleled by a failing in the historiography. The emergence of a vibrant school of American colonial history in the early twentieth century, associated with the establishment of "professional" history in the universities of the United States, was not matched by the British West Indies before the middle of the twentieth century. It was not until the achievement of political independence, beginning with Jamaica in 1962, that a truly Caribbean vision of history made its appearance.

By comparison with the United States, the historiography of the British West Indies for the period before 1850 remains incomplete. Many features of the economic history of the region remain to be studied. It is symptomatic of this state of historiographical underdevelopment that there is still no general economic history text for the region as a whole or indeed for any large part of the region. If this inability to reach synthesis is unfortunate, it is not proof of an absence of sophisticated work on certain topics, nor is it evidence of a lack of debate on central issues of interpretation.

The most recent general work covering the history of the region as a whole is Franklin W. Knight, *The Caribbean: The Genesis of a Fragmented Nationalism*, second ed. (New York, 1990). Valuable for its broad environmental perspective is *The West Indies: Patterns of Development, Culture and Environmental Change since 1492* by David Watts (Cambridge, 1987). There are several useful works with a strong focus on the economic history of the British West Indies, covering long periods of time. From the economist's point of view, the most important of these is Richard B. Sheridan, *Sugar and Slavery: An Economic History of the British West Indies, 1623–1775* (Barbados, 1974). Richard S. Dunn, *Sugar and Slaves: The Rise of the Planter Class in the English West Indies, 1624–1713* (Chapel Hill, 1972), covers the Sugar Revolution, while J. R. Ward, *British West Indian Slavery, 1750–1834: The Process of Amelioration* (Oxford, 1988), carries the account from the middle of the eighteenth century to the abolition of slavery; the postemancipation period is surveyed in William A. Green, *British Slave Emancipation: The Sugar Colonies and the Great Experiment 1830–1865* (Oxford, 1976). Useful collections of papers from journals are found in *Caribbean Slave Society and Economy: A Student Reader* (Kingston, 1991) and *Caribbean Freedom: Economy and Society from Emancipation to the Present* (Kingston, 1993), edited by Hilary Beckles and Verene Shepherd. Still important in the historiography is Lowell Joseph Ragatz, *The Fall of the Planter Class in the British Caribbean, 1763–1833* (New York, 1928).

For the larger context, placing the British West Indies within the

Atlantic world, useful studies include John J. McCusker and Russell R. Menard, *The Economy of British America, 1607–1789* (Chapel Hill, 1985); Barbara L. Solow, ed., *Slavery and the Rise of the Atlantic System* (Cambridge, 1991); Philip D. Curtin, *The Rise and Fall of the Plantation Complex: Essays in Atlantic History* (Cambridge, 1990); Ralph Davis, *The Rise of the Atlantic Economies* (Ithaca, 1973); Ian K. Steele, *The English Atlantic 1675–1740: An Exploration of Communication and Community* (New York, 1986); Peggy K. Liss, *Atlantic Empires: The Network of Trade and Revolution, 1713–1826* (Baltimore, 1983); and D. W. Meinig, *The Shaping of America: A Geographical Perspective of 500 Years of History:* vol. I, *Atlantic America, 1492–1800* (New Haven, 1986).

Demographic studies covering the British West Indies as a whole are Robert V. Wells, *The Population of the British Colonies in America before 1776: A Survey of Census Data* (Princeton, 1975); Richard B. Sheridan, *Doctors and Slaves: A Medical and Demographic History of Slavery in the British West Indies, 1680–1834* (Cambridge, 1985); Kenneth F. Kiple, *The Caribbean Slave: A Biological History* (Cambridge, 1984); B. W. Higman, *Slave Populations of the British Caribbean, 1807–1834* (Baltimore, 1984); and Stanley L. Engerman and B. W. Higman, "The Demographic Structure of the Caribbean Slave Societies in the Eighteenth and Nineteenth Centuries," *UNESCO General History of the Caribbean*, Vol. III, edited by Franklin W. Knight (in press). Much useful population data is included in John J. McCusker, *Rum and the American Revolution: The Rum Trade and the Balance of Payments of the Thirteen Continental Colonies* (New York, 1989).

The transition from indentured to slave labor is covered by Hilary McD. Beckles, *White Servitude and Black Slavery in Barbados, 1627–1715* (Knoxville, 1989), and David W. Galenson, *White Servitude in Colonial America: An Economic Analysis* (Cambridge, 1981). For the Atlantic slave trade, the classic study is Philip D. Curtin, *The Atlantic Slave Trade: A Census* (Madison, 1969). Other useful works on the slave trade include Johannes Menne Postma, *The Dutch in the Atlantic Slave Trade 1600–1815* (Cambridge, 1990), and David W. Galenson, *Traders, Planters, and Slaves: Market Behaviour in Early English America* (Cambridge, 1986).

Studies of slave labor and plantation economy in particular colonies include A. Meredith John, *The Plantation Slaves of Trinidad, 1783–1816: A Mathematical and Demographic Enquiry* (Cambridge, 1988); Michael Craton, *Searching for the Invisible Man: Slaves and Plantation Life in Jamaica* (Cambridge, MA, 1978); B. W. Higman, *Slave Population and Economy in*

Jamaica, 1807–1834 (Cambridge, 1976); and Richard Pares, *A West-India Fortune* (London, 1950).

The general history of the sugar industry has been studied by Noel Deerr in *The History of Sugar* (London, 1949–50), and more recently by J. H. Galloway, *The Sugar Cane Industry: An Historical Geography from Its Origins to 1914* (Cambridge, 1989). Deerr remains the best source for production and price statistics, although he is not always reliable. The most important work on rum is McCusker's *Rum and the American Revolution*. Coffee and the other export staples await their students.

For the structure and organization of plantation space see B. W. Higman, *Jamaica Surveyed: Plantation Maps and Plans of the Eighteenth and Nineteenth Centuries* (Kingston, 1988). An important study, combining historical and archaeological materials to reveal the inner economy, is *Plantation Slavery in Barbados* by Jerome S. Handler and Frederick W. Lange (Cambridge, MA, 1978). The most recent works on the provision-ground system and the internal marketing system are Roderick A. Mc-Donald, *The Economy and Material Culture of Slaves: Goods and Chattels on the Sugar Plantations of Jamaica and Louisiana* (Baton Rouge, 1993), and Robert Dirks, *The Black Saturnalia: Conflict and its Ritual Expression on British West Indian Slave Plantations* (Gainesville, 1987). Still useful is the classic paper by Sidney W. Mintz and Douglas Hall, "The Origins of the Jamaican Internal Marketing System," *Yale University Publications in Anthropology*, No. 57 (1960). Interesting studies of the white population within slave plantation society include Douglas Hall, *In Miserable Slavery: Thomas Thistlewood in Jamaica, 1750–86* (London, 1989), and Alan L. Karras, *Sojourners in the Sun: Scottish Migrants in Jamaica and the Chesapeake, 1740–1800* (Ithaca, NY, 1992).

External trade is analyzed in Richard Pares, *Merchants and Planters* (Cambridge, 1960); Thomas M. Truxes, *Irish-American Trade, 1660–1783* (Cambridge 1988); Frances Armytage, *The Free Port System in the British West Indies: A Study in Commercial Policy, 1766–1822* (London, 1953); and Richard Pares' still useful *War and Trade in the West Indies, 1739–1763* (London, 1936).

Economic relations between the British West Indies and the continental colonies are covered by Richard Pares, *Yankees and Creoles: The Trade between North America and the West Indies before the American Revolution* (London, 1956); James F. Shepherd and Gary M. Walton, *Shipping, Maritime Trade and the Economic Development of Colonial North America* (Cambridge, 1972);

and Thomas M. Doerflinger, *A Vigorous Spirit of Enterprise: Merchants and Economic Development in Revolutionary Philadelphia* (New York, 1986). The most important modern work dealing particularly with the impact of the American Revolution is Selwyn H. H. Carrington, *The British West Indies during the American Revolution* (Dordrecht, 1988).

Discussions of the role of slavery and the slave trade in the rise of capitalism in Great Britain, and of the decline and fall of the slave system, must begin with Eric Williams' *Capitalism and Slavery* (Chapel Hill, 1944). Later contributions to the debate include Seymour Drescher, *Econocide: British Slavery in the Era of Abolition* (Pittsburgh, 1977); Seymour Drescher, *Capitalism and Antislavery: British Mobilization in Comparative Perspective* (New York, 1987); Barbara L. Solow and Stanley L. Engerman, eds., *British Capitalism and Caribbean Slavery: The Legacy of Eric Williams* (Cambridge, 1987); Robin Blackburn, *The Overthrow of Colonial Slavery 1776–1848* (London, 1988); and Joseph E. Inikori, *Slavery and the Rise of Capitalism* (Mona, 1993).

Social structure and cultural interaction are central to Elsa V. Goveia, *Slave Society in the British Leeward Islands at the End of the Eighteenth Century* (New Haven, 1965); Orlando Patterson, *The Sociology of Slavery: An Analysis of the Origins, Development and Structure of Negro Slave Society in Jamaica* (London, 1967); and Edward Brathwaite, *The Development of Creole Society in Jamaica 1770–1820* (Oxford, 1971). Gender issues are addressed in Marietta Morrissey, *Slave Women in the New World: Gender Stratification in the Caribbean* (Lawrence, 1989); Hilary McD. Beckles, *Natural Rebels: A Social History of Enslaved Black Women in Barbados* (New Brunswick, 1989); and Barbara Bush, *Slave Women in Caribbean Society, 1650–1838* (Kingston, 1990). Works on the free colored and free black population include Jerome S. Handler, *The Unappropriated People: Freedmen in the Slave Society of Barbados* (Baltimore, 1974); Gad J. Heuman, *Between Black and White: Race, Politics, and the Free Coloreds in Jamaica, 1792–1865* (Westport, 1981); Edward L. Cox, *Free Coloreds in the Slave Societies of St. Kitts and Grenada, 1763–1833* (Knoxville, 1984); and Carl C. Campbell, *Cedulants and Capitulants: The Politics of the Coloured Opposition in the Slave Society of Trinidad 1783–1838* (Port of Spain, 1992). Resistance struggles are taken up in Michael Craton, *Testing the Chains: Resistance to Slavery in the British West Indies* (Ithaca, NY, 1982); Mavis C. Campbell, *The Maroons of Jamaica 1655–1796: A History of Resistance, Collaboration and Betrayal* (Granby, MA, 1988); Hilary Beckles, *Black Rebellion in Barbados: The Struggle Against Slavery, 1627–1838* (Bridgetown, 1984); and David Barry Gaspar, *Bondmen and Rebels: A Study of Master–Slave Relations in Antigua* (Baltimore, 1985).

For the postemancipation period, the most important studies of particular colonies or groups of colonies include Douglas Hall, *Free Jamaica, 1838–1865* (New Haven, CT, 1959); Gisela Eisner, *Jamaica, 1830–1930: A Study in Economic Growth* (Manchester, 1961); Thomas C. Holt, *The Problem of Freedom: Race, Labor, and Politics in Jamaica and Britain, 1832–1938* (Baltimore, 1992); Douglas Hall, *Five of the Leewards: The Major Problems of the Post-Emancipation Period in Antigua, Barbuda, Montserrat, Nevis and St. Kitts* (Barbados, 1971); Donald Wood, *Trinidad in Transition: The Years after Slavery* (London, 1968); Alan H. Adamson, *Sugar Without Slaves: The Political Economy of British Guiana, 1838–1904* (New Haven, 1972); Brian L. Moore, *Race, Power and Social Segmentation in Colonial Society: Guyana after Slavery, 1838–1891* (New York, 1987).

Valuable works on the nonsugar, marginal colonies include Narda Dobson, *A History of Belize* (London, 1973); O. Nigel Bolland, *The Formation of a Colonial Society: Belize, from Conquest to Crown Colony* (Baltimore, 1977); Michael Craton and Gail Saunders, *Islanders in the Stream: A History of the Bahamian People:* vol. 1, *From Aboriginal Times to the End of Slavery* (Athens, GA, 1992); and Howard Johnson, *The Bahamas in Slavery and Freedom* (Kingston, 1991).

CHAPTER 8 (McCUSKER)

The basic modern interpretative works on mercantilism – Von Schmoller, Heckscher, and the rest – are all referenced in three very valuable encyclopedic essays: William R. Allen, "Mercantilism," in John Eatwell, Murray Milgate, and Peter Newman, eds., *The New Palgrave: A Dictionary of Economics*, 4 vols. (London, 1987), III, 445–9; Raymond [A.] DeRoover, "Ancient and Medieval [Economic] Thought," in David L. Sills, ed., *International Encyclopedia of the Social Sciences*, 17 vols. ([New York:] [1968]), IV, 430–5; and Jacob Viner, "Mercantilist [Economic] Thought," in ibid., IV, 435–43. There is no point in repeating the contents of their bibliographies here.

What is better done is to explicate the items referred to in the text and notes of this chapter. At the same level as all the usual "standard treatments" mentioned above, if not of greater importance, is the discussion of mercantilism in Joseph A. Schumpeter, *History of Economic Analysis*, edited by [Romaine] Elizabeth Boody Schumpeter (New York: [1954]). It is not always cited in such company but should be. See also Joseph A. Schumpeter, *Capitalism, Socialism, and Democracy* (New York: 1942). These essays were published in two subsequent editions and a German translation during Schumpeter's lifetime and in several later editions. Contrast the reception given them, on the one hand, in Arnold Heertje, ed., *Schumpeter's Vision: Capitalism, Socialism, and Democracy after 40 Years* (New York: 1981), and, on the other hand, by F[rederic] M. Scherer, "Schumpeter and Plausible Capitalism," *Journal of Economic Literature*, 30 (1992), 1416–33.

For a wider view of economic thought in the early modern era and one of a more recent vintage, see the quite learned analysis of Terence [W.] Hutchison, *Before Adam Smith: The Emergence of Political Economy, 1662–1776* (Oxford: 1988). Other, more general treatments of mercantilism cited herein are Joyce Oldham Appleby, *Economic Thought and Ideology in Seventeenth-Century England* (Princeton, NJ: 1978); Alfred Marshall, *Industry and Trade: A Study of Industrial Technique and Business Organization; and of Their Influences on the Conditions of Various Classes and Nations* (London: 1919); Robert B. Ekelund, Jr., and Robert D. Tollison, *Mercantilism as a Rent-Seeking Society: Economic Regulation in Historical Perspective* (College Station, TX: [1981]); and C[harles] H. Wilson, "Trade, Society and the State," in *The Economy of Expanding Europe in the Sixteenth and Seventeenth Centuries*, edited by E[dwin] E. Rich and C[harles] H. Wilson, Vol. IV of *The Cambridge Economic History of Europe* (Cambridge: 1967), 487–575.

Most of the works mentioned so far pay only the most peripheral attention to early British America, but they are fundamental to any appreciation that the colonies were central to mercantilism. Some articles and books that focus more precisely on that point are: Charles M. Andrews, "The Acts of Trade," in *The Old Empire: From the Beginnings to 1783*, Vol. I of *The Cambridge History of the British Empire*, edited by J[ohn] Holland Rose, A[rthur] P. Newton, and E[rnest] A. Benians (Cambridge: 1929), 268–99; Andrews, *England's Commercial and Colonial Policy*, Vol. IV of *The Colonial Period of American History* (New Haven, CT: 1938); Andrews, "The Government of the Empire, 1660–1763," in *The Old Empire*, edited by Rose, Newton, and Benians, 405–36; George Louis Beer, *The Origins of the British Colonial System, 1578–1660* (New York: 1908); G[eorge] N. Clark, "The English Navigation Act of 1651," *History: The Journal of the Historical Association*, New Series, 7 (1923), 282–6; Oliver M. Dickerson, *The Navigation Acts and the American Revolution* (Philadelphia, PA: University of Pennsylvania Press, 1951); Albert Arthur Giesecke, *American Commercial Legislation before 1789* (New York: D. Appleton, 1910); Lawrence A. Harper, *The English Navigation Laws: A Seventeenth-Century Experiment in Social Engineering* (New York: 1939); Michael Kammen, *Empire and Interest: The American Colonies and the Politics of Mercantilism* (Philadelphia: [1970]); John J. McCusker, "Mercantilism," in Jacob E. Cooke, ed., *The Encyclopedia of the North American Colonies*, 3 vols. (New York: Charles Scribner's Sons, 1993), I, 459–65; McCusker and Russell R. Menard, *The Economy of British America, 1607–1789*, 2nd ed. (Chapel Hill, 1991); and J[ames] F. Rees, "Mercantilism and the Colonies," in Rose, Newton, and Benians, eds., *The Old Empire*, 561–602. There are relevant bibliographies in all of these works. See especially the bibliography in McCusker, "Mercantilism," 464–5; and the notes and bibliography in McCusker and Menard, *Economy of British America*, 35–50, 381–487.

Other works that treat one or more aspects of the British colonial story are, as cited herein, Bernard Bailyn, *The New England Merchants in the Seventeenth Century* (Cambridge, MA: 1955); Robert Brenner, *Merchants and Revolution: Commercial Change, Political Conflict, and London's Overseas Traders, 1550–1653* (Princeton, NJ: 1993); John Brewer, *The Sinews of Power: War, Money and the English State, 1688–1783* (London: 1988); John L. Bullion, *A Great and Necessary Measure: George Grenville and the Genesis of the Stamp Act, 1763–1765* (Columbia, MO: 1982); Bernard Donoughue, *British Politics and the American Revolution: The Path to War, 1773–75* (London: 1964); C[harles] H. Firth, "Cromwell and the Expulsion of the Long Parliament in 1653," *English Historical Review* 8 (1893), 526–34; David J. Hancock, " 'Citizen of the World': Commercial Success, Social Development and the Experience of Eighteenth-Century British Merchants Who Traded with America" (Ph.D. dissertation, Harvard University, 1990); C[lifford] Grant Head, *Eighteenth Century Newfoundland: A Geographer's Perspective* (Toronto: 1976); J. Keith Horsefield, "The 'Stop of the Exchequer' Revisited." *Economic History Review*, 2d Ser., 35 (1982), 511–28; Alice Hanson Jones, "Wealth Estimates for the American Middle Colonies, 1774," *Economic Development and Cultural Change*, 18, (1970); Valerie Pearl, *London and the Outbreak of the Puritan Revolution: City Government and National Politics, 1625–43* (Oxford: 1961); M[ary] Pollard, *Dublin's Trade in Books, 1550–1800* (Oxford: 1989); John Reeves, *A History of the Law of Shipping and Navigation* (London: 1792); and Ian K. Steele, *The English Atlantic, 1675–1740: An Exploration of Communication and Continuity* (New York: 1986).

Some of the wider, comparative dimensions of the discussion are dealt with in Peter Mathias and Patrick [K.] O'Brien "Taxation in Britain and France, 1715–1810: A Comparison of the Social and Economic Incidence of Taxes Collected for the Central Governments," *The Journal of European Economic History*, 5 (1976), 601–50; James C. Riley, *International Government Finance and the Amsterdam Capital Market, 1740–1815* (Cambridge: [1980]); Riley, *The Seven Years War and the Old Regime in France: The Economic and Financial Toll* (Princeton, NJ: 1986); and François J. Velde and David R. Weir, "The Financial Market and Government Debt Policy in France, 1746–1793" *Journal of Economic History*, 52 (1992), 1–39.

Some important contemporary tracts are: Francis Brewster, *New Essays on Trade* (London: 1702); John Cary, *An Essay on the State of England in Relation to Its Trade* . . . (Bristol: 1695); [Josiah Child], *A Discourse about Trade* ([London]: 1690); Roger Coke, *A Discourse of Trade. In Two Parts. The First Treats of the Reason of the Decay of Strength, Wealth, and Trade of England. The Latter, of the Growth and Increase of the Dutch Trade above the English* (London: 1670); [Joshua Gee] *The Trade and Navigation of Great-Britain Considered*, [1st ed.] (London: 1729); Thomas Mun, *England's Treasure by Forraign Trade* (London: 1664); Lewes Roberts, *The Treasure of Traffike. Or a Discourse of Forraign Trade* (London: 1641); Adam Smith, *An Inquiry into the Nature and Causes of the Wealth of Nations* (1776), edited by R[oy] H. Campbell, A[ndrew] S. Skinner, and W[illiam] B. Todd, 2 vols. (Oxford: 1976); [Thomas Whately], *Considerations on the Trade and Finances of this Kingdom, and on the Measures of Administration, with Respect to Those Great National Objects since the Conclusion of the Peace*, (London: 1766); and Charles Whitworth, *State of the Trade of Great Britain in Its Imports and Exports Progressively from the Year 1697 {to 1773}* . . . (London, 1776). See especially [Benjamin Worsley], *The Advocate* (London: [Nicholas Bourne (?)], 1651). There was a second, corrected version of his pamphlet published in 1652. See also the other of the two anonymously issued pamphlets that we now know Worsley wrote: *Free Ports: The Nature and Necessitie of Them Stated* (London: 1652). It, too, had been published in a slightly different version, in 1651. Worsley issued *The Advocate* under the pseudonym Φιλοπατρισ. Compare similar ideas expressed later by an author (although not Sir Josiah Child) who used the same pseudonym: *A Treatise Wherein is Demonstrated* . . . *That the East-India Trade is the Most National of all Foreign Trades* . . . (London: 1681). Concerning Mun, see Lynn Muchmore, "A Note on Thomas Mun's 'England's Treasure by Forraign Trade' " *Economic History Review*, 2d Ser., 23 (1970), 498–503.

See also Joseph Bridges Matthews, *The Law of Money-Lending, Past and Present: Being a Short History of the Usury Laws in England* . . . (London, 1906); and Thomas Madox, *The History and Antiquities of the Exchequer of the Kings of England* . . . 2d ed., 2 vols. (London, 1769).

The text of all English and British statute laws mentioned herein can be found in more than one collection. See, for instance, [Great Britain, Laws and Statutes], *The Statutes at Large . . . of Great Britain*, edited by Danby Pickering, 46 vols. (Cambridge: 1762–1807). The acts passed during the Commonwealth are in [Great Britain, Laws and Statutes, 1649–1660 (Commonwealth)], *Acts and Ordinances of the Interregnum, 1642–1660*, edited by C[harles] H. Firth and R[obert] S. Raith, 3 vols. (London: 1911). At the Restoration, all such acts were expunged from the regular statute books. For the limited record of the activities of Parliament, see [Great Britain, Parliament], *The Parliamentary History of England from the Earliest Period to the Year 1803*, edited by William Cobbett, 36 vols. (London: 1806–20); [Great Britain, Parliament, House of Commons], *The Journals of the House of Commons*, in progress ([London]: [House of Commons], 1742 to date). For acts passed by the Irish Parliament in Dublin, see [Ireland (Eire), Laws and Statutes], *The Statutes at Large, Passed in the Parliaments Held in Ireland from . . . 1310 . . . to 1800*, 20 vols. (Dublin: 1786–1801).

CHAPTER 9 (MATSON)

Primary sources for the period 1776 to 1815 are abundant, and only a few of the major collections that incorporate observations about many states or interregional perspectives are noted here. For research into specific states, or particular issues, see the bibliographies of secondary sources that follow. The most extensive collection of revolutionary records is in William Sumner Jenkins, ed., *Records of the States of the United States* (Washington, D.C., 1950, 1951), on reels of microfilm, available through the Library of Congress; and the manuscripts, "Papers of the Continental Congress," at the National Archives. For the Revolution and Critical Period, consult Paul H. Smith, ed., *Letters of Delegates to Congress, 1774–1789*, 25 vols. when complete, (Washington, D.C.: 1976–   ); and Merrill Jensen, John P. Kaminski, Gaspare P. Saladino, and Richard Leffler, eds., *The Documentary History of the Ratification of the Constitution*, 10 vols. to date, (Madison: State Historical Society of Wisconsin, 1976–   ). Few of the myriad manuscript collections of merchants' accounts and general shipping records spanning this period have been edited and published; two exceptions include Philip L. White, ed., *The Beekman Mercantile Papers, 1746–1799*, 3 vols. (New York: 1956); and Arthur H. Cole, ed., *Industrial and Commercial Correspondence of Alexander Hamilton, Anticipating his Report on Manufactures*, (New York: 1968; orig. publ. 1928). Scholars who wish to pursue contemporary views of economic circumstances should consult the papers of prominent statesmen such as Washington, Hamilton, Jefferson, and Franklin, as well as the editorial columns of extant newspapers. This latter source contains a wealth of information about the ideological debates of this era, as well as useful data about shipping, prices, internal improvements, and new manufactures; for Pennsylvania, consult Anne Bezanson, *Wholesale Prices in Philadelphia, 1784–1861* (Philadelphia: 1936).

Contemporary essays and pamphlets tended to present polemical views of certain aspects of the political economy rather than systematic appreciations of economic activities. Nevertheless, they illustrate economic visions that went along with concrete economic possibilities and limitations. It is useful to start with some of the following tracts. See Matthew Carey, ed., *Debates and Proceedings of the General Assembly of Pennsylvania, on the . . . Charter of the Bank*, (Philadelphia, 1786); Tench Coxe, *A View of the United States of America* (Philadelphia, 1784); Timothy Davis, *Thoughts on Taxation in a Letter to a Friend* (New York, 1784); Timothy Pitkin, *Statistical View of the Commerce of the United States of America*, 2nd ed. (Hartford, 1817); Samuel Wells, *The Dangers of our National Prosperity* (Hartford, 1785); Noah Webster, *Sketches of American Policy* (Hartford, 1785); Peletiah Webster, *Political Essays on the Nature and Operations of Money, Public Finance and Other Subjects* (Philadelphia, 1791); [St. George Tucker], *Reflections on the Policy and Necessity of Encouraging the Commerce . . . of the United States*, (New York, 1786); and John Witherspoon, *Essay on Money as a Medium of Commerce*, (Philadelphia, 1786).

For general secondary treatments of the entire era, 1776 to 1815, scholars must start with John J. McCusker and Russell R. Menard, *The Economy of British America, 1607–1789* (Chapel Hill: 1985), Chap. 17; the essays in Ronald Hoffman, John J. McCusker, Russell R. Menard, and Peter J. Albert eds., *The Economy of Early America: The Revolutionary Period, 1763–1789* (Charlottesville, VA, 1988) – especially those by James Henretta, James Shepherd, Thomas Doerflinger, and Jacob Price; and C. P. Nettels, *The Emergence of a National Economy, 1775–1815* (New York: 1962), especially his bibliography.

For the Revolutionary war as a transforming economic experience, see Jackson Turner Main, *The Sovereign States in the New Nation, 1775–1783* (New York, 1973); Allan Nevins, *The American States During and After the Revolution, 1775–1789* (New York, 1924); Gary M. Walton and James F. Shepherd, *The Economic Rise of Early America* (Cambridge, 1979), chap. 7, 8, 9; Thomas Doerflinger, *A Vigorous Spirit of Enterprise: Merchants and Economic Development in Revolutionary Philadelphia* (Chapel Hill: 1986); Ronald Hoffman, *A Spirit of Dissention: Economics, Politics, and the Revolution in Maryland* (Baltimore, 1973); Robert A. East, *Business Enterprise in the American Revolutionary War Era* (Gloucester, MA, 1964); Edward Papenfuse, *In Pursuit of Profit: The Annapolis Merchants in the Era of the American Revolution* (Baltimore, 1975); and Marc Egnal and Joseph A. Ernst, "An Economic Interpretation of the American Revolution," *William and Mary Quarterly*, 3rd Ser., 29 (1972), 3–32.

For the economic circumstances of the 1780s see Merrill Jensen, *The New Nation: A History of the United States during the Confederation, 1781–1789* (New York, 1950), for the view that there was not much critical about the decade. Contrast his work with that of Nettels, *Emergence*; Gordon C. Bjork, "The Weaning of the American Economy: Independence, Market Changes, and Economic Development," *Journal of Economic History* 24 (Dec. 1964), 541–60; Ronald Hoffman and Peter J. Albert, eds., *The Sovereign States in an Age of Uncertainty* (Charlottesville, VA: 1981); John E. Crowley, "Neo-Mercantilism and *The Wealth of Nations*: British Commercial Policy after the American Revolution," *Historical Journal* 33 (1990), 339–60; James F. Shepherd and Gary M. Walton, "Economic Change after the American Revolution: Pre- and Post-War Comparisons of Maritime Shipping and Trade," *Explorations in Economic History* 13 (1976); Vernon G. Setser, *The Commercial Reciprocity Policy of the United States* (Philadelphia, 1937); Albert Giesecke, *American Commercial Legislation Before 1789* (Philadelphia, 1910); W. A. Low, "Merchant and Planter Relations in Post-Revolutionary Virginia, 1783–1789," *Virginia Magazine of History and Biography* 61 (1953), 314–24; and Cathy Matson, "American Political Economy in the Constitutional Decade," R. C. Simmons and A. E. Dick Howard, eds., *The United States Constitution: The First 200 Years* (Manchester, UK, 1988), 16–35. McCusker and Menard itemize the numerous dissertations and articles on individual states during the 1780s on p. 367, n. 27, of *Economy of British America*. For the credit, debt, and currency crisis of the 1780s, the best source is still E. James Ferguson, *The Power of the Purse: A History of American Public Finance,*

1776–1790 (Chapel Hill, 1961). See also, idem., "State Assumption of the Federal Debt During the Confederation," *Mississippi Valley Historical Review* 38 (1951), 403–24; Joseph S. Davis, *Essays in the Earlier History of American Corporations*, 2 vols. (Cambridge, MA, 1917); and Janet Riesman, "Money, Credit, and Federalist Political Economy," in Richard Beeman et al., eds., *Beyond Confederation: Origins of the Constitution and American National Identity* (Chapel Hill, 1987), 128–61.

For the vision of political economists in the 1780s–90s and the glimmerings of manufactures, see Samuel Rezneck, "The Rise and Early Development of Industrial Consciousness in the United States, 1760–1830," *Journal of Economic and Business History* 4 (1932), 784–811; Drew McCoy, *The Elusive Republic: Political Economy in Jeffersonian America* (Chapel Hill, 1980); and Cathy D. Matson and Peter S. Onuf, *A Union of Interests: Economy and Politics in the Revolutionary Era* (Lawrence, KS, 1990).

Other valuable works on the 1790s include Merrill D. Peterson, "Thomas Jefferson and Commercial Policy, 1783–1793," *William and Mary Quarterly*, 3rd ser., 21 (1965), 584–610; John R. Nelson, Jr., "Alexander Hamilton and American Manufacturing: A Reexamination," *Journal of American History* 65 (1979), 971–95; and Douglass C. North, *The Economic Growth of the United States, 1790–1860* (Englewood Cliffs, NJ, 1961), chaps. 1 and 2. A recent influential view is found in Joyce Appleby, *Capitalism and a New Social Order: The Republican Vision of the 1790's* (New York, 1984).

Until relatively recently, only a few scholars studied the economic developments that affected early farmers, westward migrants, rural shopkeepers, and protomanufacturers. But see older works by Percy Bidwell and John Falconer, *History of Agriculture in the Northern United States, 1620–1860* (Washington, D.C., 1925); Victor S. Clark, *A History of Manufactures in the United States*, Vol. 1: *1607–1860*, (Washington, D.C., 1929); and their citations. New research about this majority of Americans, including their economic roles as both producers and consumers, promises to increase our knowledge of the era significantly. See, for example, Carole Shammas, "How Self-Sufficient Was Early America?" *Journal of Interdisciplinary History* 13 (1982), 247–72; Billy G. Smith, "The Material Lives of Laboring Philadelphians, 1750–1800," *William and Mary Quarterly*, 3d. Ser., 38 (1981), 163–202; Joan Jensen, "Cloth, Butter, and Boarders: Women's Household Production for the Market," *Reviews in Radical Political Economy* 12 (1980), 14–24; and Lois Green Carr and Lorena S. Walsh, "Economic Diversification and Labor Organization in the Chesapeake, 1650–1820," in Stephen Innes, ed., *Work and Labor in Early American* (Chapel Hill, 1988), 144–88.

For the period 1800–15, scholars will want to consult Paul A. David, "The Growth of Real Product in the United States Before 1840," *Journal of Economic History*, 27 (1967); George Rogers Taylor, *The Transportation Revolution, 1815–1860* (New York, 1968); Rolla M. Tryon, *Household Manufactures in the United States: 1640–1860* (New York [orig. publ., 1917]); Jonathan Prude, *The Coming of the Industrial Order: Town and Factory Life in Rural Massachusetts, 1810–1860* (New York, 1983), chap. 1; John R. Nelson, Jr., *Liberty and Property: Political Economy and Policymaking in the New Nation, 1789–1812* (Baltimore, 1987); and Allan Pred, "Manufacturing in the Mercantile City, 1800–1840," *Annals* of the Association of American Geographers 56 (1966), 307–25

INDEX